Literary Voice

Literary Voice

JOSHUA DICKINSON

SUNY OER SERVICES

Published by SUNY OER Services

State University of New York Office of Library and Information Services
10 N Pearl
Albany, NY 12207

Distributed by State University of New York Press

This book was produced using Pressbooks.com, and PDF rendering was done by PrinceXML.

ISBN: 978-1-64176-073-7

Contents

4. Fiction

5. Drama

6. Poetry

7. Literary Nonfiction

About The Literary Voice

The Literary Voice is an introduction to literature text created through the SUNY OER Initiative. This is my tenth OER work. More titles can be viewed at: https://sunyjefferson.libguides.com/JCCOERtextbooks

With few exceptions (noted in the credits for each page), the mini-lectures are self-created. *The Literary Voice* has a genre-based focus, with the readings being listed within each genre's chapter in rough chronology. Many of the works are linked. (In any cases where the link breaks, the work could be located using an author or title search or by adding *PDF* to the query.)

The text contains five plays and a lengthy literary nonfiction chapter in addition to the fiction and poetry chapters. *Siddhartha*, Hermann Hesse's modernist novel of India, is included in its entirety. I intentionally include more readings than any one course would get through in case instructors wish to tailor the content. Just as easily, they could organize the course either chronologically or thematically. Several chapters discuss academic writing, specifically as it applies to literary analysis. Several of the readings are personal favorites that adapt well to an introduction to literature survey.

Feel free to contact me at joshdickinson15@gmail.com if you have any questions. Enjoy the text!

1. EXPERIENCING LITERATURE: THE BASICS

Defining Literature

Defining literature is always difficult. There are several overlapping definitions. Some concentrate of where the words are—as our discussion is when it questions whether something can be literature if it's oral. This gets at only part of the question. Other definitions get at what literature feels like to the audience/reader. Other definitions focus on the *differences* between literature and everyday use of language. By using a combination of approaches (being flexible) we can arrive at a definition.

I'm including a long quote from Jonathan Culler's wonderful little book *Literary Theory: A Very Short Introduction*. Culler teaches at Cornell. If any of you are serious about English as a major, you should probably read this book. The reason I mention this is that Culler makes literary theory understandable and he cuts through a lot of the current trends in criticism—that's saying a lot, if you've seen some of the strange things to come out of our field of study lately. I wish I had read a book like this before tackling those English classes! Anyway, I'm not going to say much else about this—he goes from pages 18-41 trying to define this strange thing we call literature.

See what you can say about Culler's take on defining literature. You could respond to it for some discussion postings.

Remember that epic poems like *The Odyssey* and *The Iliad* were initially oral—they were only written down much later. They are in our canon. The origins of poetry are oral rather than written.

Note that Culler's book is published by Oxford UP, so it's going to have single quotes where there should be double—and other British usages like single – instead of the– for quick shifts in thought. You should continue using Standard American English and MLA format.

The Definition of Literature

What sort of question?

We find ourselves back at the key question, 'What is literature?', which will not go away. But what sort of question is it? If a 5-year-old is asking, it's easy. 'Literature', you answer, 'is stories, poems, and plays.' But if the questioner is a literary theorist, it's harder to know how to take the query. It might be a question about the general nature of this object, literature, which both of you already know well. What sort of object or activity is it? What does it do? What purposes does it serve? Thus understood, 'What is literature?' asks not for a definition but for an analysis, even an argument about why one might concern oneself with literature at all.

But 'What is literature?' might also be a question about distinguishing characteristics of the works known as literature: what distinguishes them from non-literary works? What differentiates literature from other human activities or pastimes? Now people might ask this question because they were wondering how to decide which books are literature and which are not, but it is more likely that they already have an idea what counts as literature and want to know something else: are there any essential, distinguishing features that literary works share?

This is a difficult question. Theorists have wrestled with it, but without notable success. The reasons are not far to seek: works of literature come in all shapes and sizes and most of them seem to have more in common with works that aren't usually called literature than they do with some other works recognized as literature. Charlotte Bronte's *Jane Eyre,* for instance, more closely resembles an autobiography than it does a sonnet, and a poem by Robert Burns – 'My love is like a red, red rose' -resembles a folk-song more than it does Shakespeare's *Hamlet.* Are there qualities shared by poems, plays, and novels that distinguish them from, say, songs, transcriptions of conversations, and autobiographies?

Historical Variations

Even a bit of historical perspective makes this question more complex. For twenty-five centuries people have written works that we call literature today, but the modern sense of *literature* is scarcely two centuries old. Prior to 1800 *literature* and analogous terms in other European languages meant writings' or "book knowledge." Even today, a scientist who says 'the literature on evolution is immense' means not that many poems and novels treat the topic but that much has been written about it. And works that today are studied as literature in English or Latin classes in schools and universities were once treated not as a special kind of writing but as fine examples of the use of language and rhetoric. They were instances of a larger category of exemplary practices of writing and thinking, which included speeches, sermons, history, and philosophy. Students were not asked to interpret them, as we now interpret literary works, seeking to explain what they are 'really about'. On the contrary, students memorized them, studied their grammar, identified their rhetorical figures and their structures or procedures of argument. A work such as Virgil's *Aeneid,* which today g is studied as literature, was treated very differently in schools prior to 1850.

The modern Western sense of literature as imaginative writing can be traced to the German Romantic theorists of the late eighteenth century and, if we want a particular source, to a book published in 1800 by a French Baroness, Madame de Staël's On *Literature Considered in its Relations with Social Institutions.* But even if we restrict ourselves to the last two centuries, the category of literature becomes slippery:

would works which today count as literature—say poems that seem snippets of ordinary conversation, without rhyme or discernible metre -have qualified as literature for Madame de Staël? And once we begin to think about non-European cultures, the question of what counts as literature becomes increasingly difficult. It is tempting to give it up and conclude that literature is whatever a given society treats as literature—a set of texts that arbiters [tastemakers, critics] recognize as belonging to literature.

I hope this helps!

Experiencing Literature

Terms and Concepts

Students of literature read and notice things. They also need a working vocabulary of literary terms. Luckily (for me), you already know a few dozen literary terms. I'll expect you to use these. In addition, I want to introduce you to a few less- familiar topics (e.g., subversion, irony, and stereotyping). You can find out about these terms—and more—in the following lectures.

As we go on, you'll become more familiar with how different authors use irony, subversion, etc., in order to achieve certain effects.

Paradox

No, it's not a pair of ducks! Paradox is a seeming contradiction. It is an intricate device that gets readers to think. Paradox is often linked with irony.

Native American authors often deal with the paradoxes of white treatment of Indians. There's a lot of history there. What I want you to do is to notice when paradoxes appear, and alert us to them. We can interpret them after the class notices them. Check out the list below for just some of the paradoxical issues in Native American writers treat:

Binaries

Binaries are pairs of choices, like the "ones" and "zeros" making up the information on cds. They offer a way of reducing things. Think about the either/or choices consumers are faced with. Authors can't leave these binaries alone. . . they like to play with easy choices, showing how artificial they are. As I'll say elsewhere, we don't live in a simple world. It's not all "Pepsi or Coke," and authors like to challenge binaries.

Think about other examples of paradox you encounter. Be willing to share these.

General Stuff

If you get stuck interpreting, look for setting and conflict. You can always talk about those, and then get into more complex areas of the piece from these.

Binaries (otherwise known as polar oppositions or polar opposites) can be found in Native American literature. Here are some that I thought of quickly. What ones can you find?

	vs.
Past	Present
Victimization	Triumph
Richness (spiritual, physical)	Poverty
Being "a Mohawk," "a Paiute," "a Lakota," etc.	"Indian" in general

Paradoxical Binaries Treated by Native American Authors

Now look at what some Native authors do with seemingly simple binaries. You might find stories in which characters are:

- living in two cultural worlds simultaneously

- both rich and poor—ways of seeing wealth are confused, downplayed, or overwhelming
- Native Americans who act as "super patriots"

or in which

- past, present and future are seamlessly intermixed
- Christianity and Native roots get mixed without one winning out over the other
- Victimization and triumph exist simultaneously, defining the same character
- tradition vs. modernity never gets solved or resolved for a character
- personal identity and communal identity cannot be separated
- Native identity exists—independent of white culture
- mixed blood identity is the most important aspect of life for a character

This list probably makes little sense to you right now. It's meant to get you thinking about the many "moves" you will see Indian writers make. Be active as a reader, and as a questioner! Let me know what sorts of things you see happening in our readings. Critical thinking is just that: critical. I am curious to see what you'll find in this semester's literature.

Six Tips for Being a Better Literature Student

Literature courses can be handled inappropriately and there is often not enough time to figure that out in a fifteen-week session. I have a few tips that should help us avoid recurring errors. Each of these tips relates to critical thinking and writing:

1. The audience knows the play, poem, or story. Summaries that just fill space are useless, so avoid writing a review or a running account of the plot. It would be like telling someone the directions to their own home when you were supposed to be arguing about the best spots along the way.

2. Apply the literary terms such as verbal irony, symbolism, theme, and metaphor. Do more than just point them out. Yes, they exist. (Skeptical readers like the ones you'll have in the course would just say "Okay. . . so what?") What is a metaphor doing in a given paragraph or stanza, though? You can always argue about functions or effects.

3. Everything we do is thesis-driven, meaning that it's argument. A thesis is not just a statement of what you'll do. It's an arguable, provable claim that should have some substance. It's not a question. It's not a fact. It is an opinion—though you need not use *I*.

4. Anticipate what the audience thinks about a piece of literature. It's important to realize that you're writing in a public way about works which may have been valued and argued over for hundreds of years. Value that and take yourself seriously as a critic.

5. Plagiarism is easy to catch and will be dealt with harshly. If you are in doubt, cite the material. Remember that MLA is exacting, so be sure you're using the correct style models. There is not much time to get used to this, so look at the Unit 1 mini-lectures and links on citing. The expectation is that you can look at a model and "get it right" in your writing. Ask questions and pay attention to the style, since how something looks is often as important as what it says.

6. Lastly, really work to avoid lateness. Be on the correct side of any due dates, as it's really tough to make up work.

Not Taking Sides is Like the Beetlejuice Waiting Room Scene. . .

It is important that we recognize the benefits and limitations of methodology. Likely, you know your major discipline's approaches well. There are ways of being recognized or not. For instance, in *Jeopardy* contests, one has to phrase the answer in the form of a question. In discussion postings, many instructors require the post subject to be in sentence form. In *Fast Times at Ridgemont High*, Jeff Spicoli, the surfer doesn't recognize his little brother: "Curtis, you know I don't hear you unless you knock. . ." (Heckerling). In science, hypotheses have to be provable. In academic writing, thesis claims must be both provable and arguable.

I'm reminded of the notion of Purgatory, an invention of Dante in his *La Divina Commedia* (*Divine Comedy*). This gets played up famously in *Beetlejuice* and its waiting room scene:

What's interesting is that this echoes Dante, who puts people who failed to distinguish themselves into Hell. For Dante's Italians, not choosing was worse than choosing an opposite side to one's preferred side. Strangely enough, we are often more knowledgeable of our opponents—more tolerant of them, even—than of those who never choose. He even puts the neutral angels into Hell. In that era (1300 Florence), he even put living people into Hell, claiming that these people were so bad that demons inhabited their bodies and they were already in hell.

So these ideas can receive dogmatic answers. They get recognized or not, but over time they accrete meaning, slow down, and become concrete. (No *Dogma* references necessary. . .)

What I find interesting is that we're often struggling with the miniscule rules of MLA style in the same way.

> As with science, though, we can essentialize this a bit: We are always already entering ongoing conversations. We do have to be for or against something. Likely ways of being against something are going to lead to tone issues and assumptions about audience agreement.

As the *Beetlejuice* move states, "Take a number!" and "It's showtime!" (Burton).

Literary Terms: A Guide

Metre

Metre refers to the rhythmic structure of lines of verse. The majority of English verse since Chaucer is in **accentual-syllabic metre**, which consists of alternating stressed and unstressed syllables within a fixed total number of syllables in each line. The metrical rhythm is thus the pattern of stressed and unstressed syllables in each line. Groups of syllables are known as metrical **feet**; each line of verse is made up of a set number of feet. Thus:

Monometer: one foot per line
Dimeter: two feet per line
Trimeter: three feet per line
Tetrameter: four feet per line
Pentameter: five feet per line
Hexameter: six feet per line
Heptameter: seven feet per line
Octameter: eight feet per line

Each foot usually consists of a single stressed syllable—though there are some important variations—therefore these patterns correspond to the number of stressed syllables in a line; thus tetrameter has four, pentameter five, etc.

There are two types of metrical feet in English accentual-syllabic metre: **duple metre**, consisting of disyllabic (2-syllable) feet, in which stressed syllables (**x**) and unstressed syllables (**o**) alternate in pairs; and **triple metre**, consisting of trisyllabic (3-syllable) feet, in which single stressed syllables are grouped with a pair of unstressed syllables. Duple metre is the metre most commonly found in English verse.

The following metrical feet make up the most common rhythmical patterns:

> **Duple metre**:
>
> **Iamb** (iambic foot): **o x**
> **Trochee** (trochaic foot): **x o**
> **Spondee** (spondaic foot): **x x**
> **Pyrrhus** / dibrach (pyrrhic foot): **o o**
>
> **Triple metre**:
>
> **Dactyl** (dactylic foot): **x o o**
> **Anapaest** (anapaestic foot): **o o x**
> **Amphibrach**: **o x o**
> **Molossus**: **x x x**

Note that the spondee, pyrrhus and molossus do not usually form the basis for whole lines of verse, but are considered forms of **substitution**: that is, when a foot required by the metrical pattern being used is replaced by a different sort of foot. A frequently-found example of substitution is the replacement of the initial iamb in an iambic line by a trochee, e.g. (underlined syllables represent stressed syllables):

> In <u>me</u> thou seest the <u>twi</u>light <u>of</u> such <u>day</u>
> As <u>after sunset fadeth in</u> the <u>west</u>,
> Which <u>by</u> and <u>by</u> black <u>night</u> doth <u>take away</u>,
> <u>Death's</u> second <u>self</u>, that <u>seals</u> up <u>all</u> in <u>rest</u>.

—Shakespeare, Sonnet 73

(The first three lines of this quatrain are perfectly iambic; the initial foot of the fourth line is an example of trochaic substitution, also known as **inversion**.)

Other variations in metrical rhythm include **acephalexis**, in which the first syllable of a line that would be expected according to the regular metre of the line, is lacking; and **catalexis**, in which a line lacks the final syllable expected by its metrical pattern. **A masculine ending** is a line that ends on a stressed syllable, while a **feminine ending** is a line that ends on an unstressed syllable.

Freeverse is poetry that does not conform to any regular metre.

Examples of different meters and metrical substitutions:

Iambic pentameter:

> We <u>few</u>, we <u>happy</u> <u>few</u>, we <u>band</u> of <u>bro</u>thers.
> For <u>he</u> to<u>day</u> that <u>sheds</u> his <u>blood</u> with <u>me</u>
> Shall <u>be</u> my <u>brother</u>; <u>be</u> he <u>ne'er</u> so <u>vile</u>,
> This <u>day</u> shall <u>gentle</u> <u>his</u> con<u>di</u>tion.
> Shall <u>think</u> them<u>selves</u> ac<u>cursed</u> they <u>were</u> not <u>here</u>,
> And hold their manhoods cheap whiles any speaks
> That <u>fought</u> with <u>us</u> up<u>on</u> Saint <u>Crispin's</u> <u>day</u>.
>
> —Shakespeare, *Henry V*, IV.iii

An example of perfect iambic pentameter. Note the feminine ending in l.1 (in iambic metre a feminine ending adds an extra syllable to the line), and how the stresses follow the sense of the lines.

Trochaic tetrameter:

> <u>In</u> what <u>distant</u> <u>deeps</u> or <u>skies</u>
> <u>Burnt</u> the <u>fire</u> <u>of</u> thine <u>eyes</u>?
> <u>On</u> what <u>wings</u> dare <u>he</u> as<u>pire</u>?
> <u>What</u> the <u>hand</u> dare <u>seize</u> the <u>fire</u>?
>
> —Blake, "The Tyger"

The first two lines exhibit masculine endings, and thus are catalectic according to the regular pattern of trochaic metre; that is, they lack their final syllable. Arguably, the second foot in l.4 could be read as a spondaic substitution (if *dare* is stressed).

Spondaic substitution in iambic pentameter (l.3):

> Or <u>if</u> thy <u>mistress</u> <u>some</u> rich <u>anger</u> <u>shows</u>,
> Em <u>prison</u> <u>her</u> soft <u>hand</u>, and <u>let</u> her <u>rave</u>,
> And <u>feed</u> <u>deep</u>, <u>deep</u> up<u>on</u> her <u>peer</u>less <u>eyes</u>.
>
> —Keats, "Ode on Melancholy"

Pyrrhic substitution in iambic tetrameter (l.2):

The <u>woo</u>ds are <u>love</u>ly, <u>dark</u> and <u>deep</u>.
But <u>I</u> have <u>pro</u>mises to <u>keep</u>,
And <u>miles</u> to <u>go</u> be<u>fore</u> I <u>sleep</u>,
And <u>miles</u> to <u>go</u> be<u>fore</u> I <u>sleep</u>.

 —Frost, "Stopping by Woods on a Snowy Evening"

Dactylic dimeter:

<u>Theirs</u> not to <u>make</u> reply,
<u>Theirs</u> not to <u>reason</u> why,
<u>Theirs</u> but to <u>do</u> and die

 —Tennyson, "The Charge of the Light Brigade"

Anapaestic metre:

There <u>was</u> an Old <u>La</u>dy of <u>Chert</u>sey,
Who <u>made</u> a re<u>mar</u>kable <u>curt</u>sey;
She <u>twirled</u> round and <u>round</u>,
Till she <u>sunk</u> under<u>ground</u>,
Which di<u>stressed</u> all the people of <u>Chert</u>sey.

 —Edward Lear, "There Was an Old Lady of Chertsey"

As is common in limericks, this example includes multiple iambic substitutions, here in the initial syllables of lines 1-3.

Amphibrach:

And <u>now</u> comes an <u>act</u> of e<u>norm</u>ous e<u>norm</u>ance!
No <u>form</u>er per<u>form</u>er's per<u>formed</u> this per<u>form</u>ance!

 —Dr. Seuss, *If I Ran the Circus*

Molossus:

<u>Break</u>, <u>break</u>, <u>break</u>,
On thy <u>coldgraystones</u>, O <u>Sea</u>!
And I <u>would</u> that my <u>tongue</u> could <u>utter</u>
The <u>thoughts</u> that a<u>rise</u> in <u>me</u>.

 —Tennyson, "Break, Break, Break"

The first line is an example of a molossus; it is also an example of epizeuxis (see below).

Stanzas

When a poem is divided into sections, each section is known as a stanza. Stanzas usually share the same structure as the other stanzas within the poem.

> **Tercet**: a unit or stanza of three verse lines
> **Quatrain**: a unit or stanza of four verse lines
> **Quintain**: a stanza of five verse lines

Sestet: a unit or stanza of six verse lines

Septet or **heptastich**: a stanza of seven lines

Octave: a unit or stanza of eight verse lines

Decastich: a stanza or poem of ten lines

Note that many of these terms refer to a unit of this number of lines within a larger stanza or within a poem not divided into stanzas (e.g. a Shakespearean sonnet, which consists of three quatrains followed by a couplet).

Refrain: a line or lines regularly repeated throughout a poem, traditionally at the end of each stanza. Very often found in ballads; it was also used to great effect by Yeats (see for example 'The Withering of the Boughs' or 'The Black Tower'). Usually nowadays printed in *italic* to distinguish it from the main body of the poem.

Enjambment: when the sense of a verse line runs over into the next line with no punctuated pause. The opposite is known as an **end-stopped** line. An example of enjambment in iambic pentameter:

A dungeon horrible, on all sides round

As one great furnace flamed, yet from those flames

No light, but rather darkness visible

Served only to discover sights of woe

—Milton, *Paradise Lost*, I

Rhyme

End rhyme: rhyme occurring on stressed syllables at the ends of verse lines. The most common form of rhyme. Couplet: a pair of end-rhyming verse lines, usually of the same length. E.g.:

Had we but World enough, and Time,

This coyness Lady were no crime.

We would sit down, and think which way

To walk, and pass our long Loves Day.

—Marvell, "To his Coy Mistress"

Internal rhyme: rhyme occurring within a single verse line.

Crossed rhyme: the rhyming of one word in the middle of a verse line with a word in the middle of the following line.

Half rhyme: also known as **slant rhyme**; an incomplete form of rhyme in which final consonants match but vowel sounds do not. E.g.:

I have heard that hysterical women say

They are sick of the palette and fiddle-bow.

Of poets that are always gay,

For everybody knows or else should know

That if nothing drastic is done

Aeroplane and Zeppelin will come out.

Pitch like King Billy bomb-balls in

Until the town lie beaten flat.

—Yeats, "Lapis Lazuli"

The first quatrain is an example of full end rhyme; the second quatrain an example of half rhyme.

Para-rhyme: a form of half rhymel; when all the consonants of the relevant words match, not just the final consonants. E.g.:

It seemed that out of battle I escaped
Down some profound dull tunnel, long since scooped
Through granites which titanic wars had groined.
Yet also there encumbered sleepers groaned,
Too fast in thought or death to be bestirred.
Then, as I probed them, one sprang up, and stared
With piteous recognition in fixed eyes,
Lifting distressful hands, as if to bless.
And by his smile, I knew that sullen hall, –
By his dead smile I knew we stood in Hell.

—Wilfred Owen, "Strange Meeting"

Eye rhyme: a visual-only rhyme; i.e. when spellings match but in pronunciation there is no rhyme, e.g. want/pant, five/give.

Double rhyme: a rhyme on two syllables, the first stressed, the second unstressed. E.g.

I want a hero: —an uncommon want,

When every year and month sends forth a new one,

Till, after cloying the gazettes with can't,

The age discovers he is not the true one

—Byron, *Don Juan*, I.i

The second and fourth lines are double rhymes; the first and third lines are examples of half rhyme/eye rhyme.

Assonance: the recurrence of similar vowel sounds in neighbouring words where the consonants do not match. E.g.:

For the rare and radiant maiden whom the angels name Lenore—
Nameless here for evermore.

—Poe, "The Raven"

Consonance: the recurrence of similar consonants in neighbouring words where the vowel sounds do not match. The most commonly found forms of consonance, other than half rhyme and para-rhyme, are alliteration and sibilance.

Alliteration: the repetition of initial consonants in a sequence of neighbouring words. E.g.:

Hear the loud alarum bells—

Brazen **B**ells!

What a **t**ale of **t**error, now, their **t**urbulency **t**ells!

—Poe, "The Bells"

Sibilance: the repetition of sibilants, i.e. consonants producing a hissing sound. E.g.:

Ships that pass in the night, and speak each other in passing;

Only a signal shown and a distant voice in the darkness

—Longfellow, *Tales of a Wayside Inn*

Blank verse: metrical verse that does not rhyme. Milton's *Paradise Lost* is an example; the majority of Shakespeare is also in blank verse.

Figurative, rhetorical, and structural devices

Metaphor: when one thing is said to be another thing, or is described in terms normally connected to another thing, in order to suggest a quality shared by both. E.g.:

Love, fame, ambition, avarice—'tis the same,

Each idle, and all ill, and none the worst—

For all are meteors with a different name,

And Death the sable smoke where vanishes the flame.

—Byron, *Childe Harold's Pilgrimage*, IV

Simile: when one thing is directly compared with another thing; indicated by use of the words "as" or "like." E.g.:

I wandered lonely as a cloud

—Wordsworth, "Daffodils"

Metonymy: when something is referred to by an aspect or attribute of it, or by something associated with it. E.g.:

Now is the winter of our discontent

Made glorious summer by this son of York . . .

—Shakespeare, *Richard III*, I.i

Here "winter" and "summer" are examples of metaphor; "son of York" is an example of metonymy, being an attribute of Richard's brother, Edward IV, here the person being referred to.

Synecdoche: a form of metonymy in which something is referred to by a specific part of its whole. "All hands on deck" is an example, in which the crew are being referred to by one specific part—their hands. E.g.:

Take thy face hence.

—Shakespeare, *Macbeth*, V.iii

Personification or **prosopopoeia**: when inanimate objects, animals or ideas are referred to as if they were human. Similar terms are anthropomorphism, when human form is ascribed to something not human, e.g., a deity; and the pathetic fallacy, when natural phenomena are described as if they could feel as humans do. Shelley's 'Invocation to Misery' is an example.

Onomatopoeia: a word that imitates the sound to which it refers. E.g. "clang," "crackle," "bang," etc.

Synaesthesia: the application of terms relating to one sense to a different one, e.g., "a warm sound." For example:

> Odours there are . . . green as meadow grass
>
> —Baudelaire, "Correspondences"

Oxymoron: the combination of two contradictory terms. E.g.:

> Feather of lead, bright smoke, cold fire, sick health,
>
> Still-waking sleep that is not what it is!
>
> —Shakespeare, *Romeo and Juliet*, I.i

Hendiadys: when a single idea is expressed by two nouns, used in conjunction. E.g. "house and home" or Hamlet's "Angels and ministers of grace" (*Hamlet*, I.iv).

Anaphora: the repetition of the same word or group of words at the beginnings of successive lines or clauses. E.g.:

> Is **this** the region, **this** the soil, the clime,
>
> Said then the lost archangel, **this** the seat
>
> That we must change for heaven . . .
>
> —Milton, *Paradise Lost*, I

Epistrophe: the repetition of the same word or group of words at the ends of successive lines or clauses. E.g.:

> I know **thee**, I have found **thee**, & I will not let **thee** go
>
> —Blake, "America—a Prophecy"

Epizeuxis: the repetition of a word with no intervening words. E.g., Tennyson's "Break, break, break," quoted above.

Polysyndeton: use of more than the required amount of conjunctions. E.g.:

> Havoc and spoil and ruin are my gain.
>
> —Milton, *Paradise Lost*, II

The opposite of asyndeton, which refers to the deliberate omission of conjunctions.

Anachronism: when an object, custom or idea is misplaced outside of its proper historical time. A famous example is the clock in Shakespeare's *Julius Caesar*.

Apostrophe: an address to an inanimate object, abstraction, or a dead or absent person. E.g.:

> Busie old foole, unruly Sunne,
>
> Why dost thou thus,

Through windowes, and through curtaines call on us?

—Donne, "The Sunne Rising"

Hyperbole: extreme exaggeration, not intended literally. E.g.:

Since Hero's time hath half the world been black.

—Marlowe, *Hero and Leander*

Adynaton: a form of hyperbole—a figure of speech that stresses the inexpressibility of something, usually by stating that words cannot describe it. H. P. Lovecraft's short story "The Unnamable" is essentially a riff on this figure of speech, satirizing Lovecraft's own regular use of it in his work.

Meiosis: an intentional understatement in which something is described as less significant than it really is. A well-known example is found in *Romeo and Juliet* when Mercutio describes his death-wound as 'a scratch' (III.iii).

Litotes: a form of meiosis; the affirmation of something by the denial of its opposite, e.g. "not uncommon," "not bad." Erotesis (rhetorical question): asking a question without requiring an answer, in order to assert or deny a statement. E.g.:

What though the field be lost? All is not lost . . .

—*Paradise Lost*, I

In medias res: the technique of beginning a narrative in the middle of the action, before relating preceding events at a later point. *Paradise Lost* is an example (following the convention of epic poetry).

Leitmotif: a phrase, image or situation frequently repeated throughout a work, supporting a central theme. An example is the personification of the mine shaft lift as a devouring creature in Zola's
Germinal, repeated throughout the novel. Remember! Simply being able to identify the devices and knowing the terms is not enough. They are only a means to an end. You must always consider: why they are being used, what effect they have, and how they affect meaning(s).

Further reading

Baldick, C., *Oxford Dictionary of Literary Terms*, Oxford: Oxford University Press, 2008.

Preminger, A., Brogan, T. and Warnke, F. (eds), *The New Princeton Encyclopedia of Poetry and Poetics*, Princeton, NJ: Princeton University Press, 1993.

Hollander, J., *Rhyme's Reason: A Guide to English Verse*, New Haven, CT: Yale University Press, 2001.

Attridge, D., *Poetic Rhythm: An Introduction*, Cambridge: Cambridge University Press, 1995.

Strand, M., *The Making of a Poem: A Norton Anthology of Poetic Forms*, New York: W. W. Norton & Co., 2001.

Narrative Point of View

Point of view gets a section all its own. It's that important!

Identifying a piece of literature's point of view is crucial. We need to know the direction from which the narrative is being told. If a narrator plays a role, their perspective alters our experience of the events being told, right? Here are the basic narrative points of view:

Omniscient (all seeing): This narrative perspective gets into any characters' thoughts. Readers are given details that no one person could know or see. Works with this point of view allow readers an "all access pass" to events.

First person: This narration adopts the point of view of one character. Usually, we identify with that character. You can tell firstperson narration by looking for "I" and "you" in the story. Readers often lump in the author and the narrator of first person pieces; avoid conflating (confusing) the author and the narrator. For example, readers of Edgar Poe all too often assume that he is speaking when the bizarre narratives occur. Or readers of Native American literature assume that the author is the speaker.

*Third person: According to *Merriam Webster's Reader's Handbook: Your Complete Guide to Literary Terms*, third person:

> [. . .] is the voice in which a story is presented when the narrator is not a character in the story. The term actually refers to either of two narrative voices. A story told in the third person singular is one in which the narrator writes from the point of view of a single character, describing and noticing only what that character has the opportunity to see and hear and know, but not in the voice of that character, as in Henry James' What Maisie Knew. A third person omniscient narrator is not limited in viewpoint to any one character and thus can comment on every aspect of that story. (4001)

Think of third person narration as a third option, then.
Each of the narrative perspectives allows authors to depict lived reality. This is an impossible task, though, using only language. Just think of the many times you were unable to convey exactly what you meant through words. Words let us down, however brilliant their descriptive capabilities.
Please Note
*There are only fine distinctions between third person narration styles.

This quote is from my old lit text, *Literature: An Introduction to Fiction, Poetry and Drama* (8th ed.), by Kennedy and Gioia:

"Third person: A type of narration in which the narrator is a nonparticipant. In a third-person narrative the characters are referred to as 'he', 'she', or 'they'. Third-person narrators are most commonly omniscient, but the level of their knowledge may vary from total omniscience (the narrator knows everything about the characters and their lives) to limited omniscience (the narrator is limited to the perceptions of a single character" (G31).

Connecting Reading & Writing: The Voice You Hear Response

Too often, reading is viewed as a passive act where the information is poured into static readers' minds. To succeed at the college level, a reworking of the way one reads may be necessary. Read the following passage from reading researcher Katherine McCormick and jot down your interpretation of its meaning:

Tony slowly got up from the mat, planning his escape. He hesitated a moment and thought. Things were not going well. What bothered him the most was being held, especially since the charge against him had been weak. He considered his present situation. The lock that held him was strong but he thought he could break it . . . . He was being ridden unmercifully . . . . He felt that he was ready to make his move.

From the two possible interpretations here, it seems clear that 1) readers use their previous experiences to make meaning out of a text, and 2) context influences meaning. After all, if we knew we were reading a short story on wrestling, our understanding of the passage would differ. Reading needs to be recognized as an active process. **Read the following poem by Thomas Lux and answer all of the questions below in complete sentences. The questions appear after the poem.**

The Voice You Hear When You Read Silently

is not silent, it is a speaking-out-loud voice in your head;

it is *spoken*, a voice is *saying* it as you read.

It's the writer's words, of course, in a literary sense his or her "voice"

but the sound of that voice is the sound of *your* voice.

Not the sound your friends know or the sound of a tape played back

but your voice

caught in the dark cathedral of your skull, your voice heard by an internal

ear informed by internal abstracts

and what you know by feeling, having felt.

It is your voice saying, for example, the word "barn" that the writer wrote

but the "barn" you say is a barn you know or knew.

The voice in your head, speaking as you read, never says anything

neutrally—some people hated the barn they knew,

some people love the barn they know

so you hear the word loaded and a sensory constellation is lit:

horse-gnawed stalls, hayloft, black heat tape wrapping a water pipe,

a slippery spilled *chirr* of oats from a split sack,

the bony, filthy haunches of cows . . .

And "barn" is only a noun—no verb or subject has entered into the sentence yet!

The voice you hear when you read to yourself is the clearest voice: you speak its speaking to you.

1. When you hear the word *barn*, what barn or barns from your own life do you first see? What feelings and associations do you have with this word? How do you think the barn in your head is different from the barns in your classmates' heads?

2. When you hear the word *cathedral*, what images and associations from your own life come into your head? Once again, how might your classmates' internal images and associations with the word *cathedral* differ from yours?

3. Now reread the poem and consider the lines "Not the sound your friends know or the sound of a tape played back / but your voice / caught in the dark cathedral of your skull." What do you think Lux means by the metaphor "dark cathedral of your skull"? What seems important about his choice of the word *cathedral* (rather than, say, *house* or *cave* or *gymnasium* or *mansion*)? How does *skull* work (rather than *mind* or *brain* or *head*)? Freewriting for several minutes, create your interpretation of "dark cathedral of the skull."

4. Finally, reflect for a moment about your thinking processes in trying to interpret "cathedral of the skull." Did you go back and reread the poem, looking for how this line fits other lines of the poem? Did you explore further your own ideas about cathedrals and skull? See if you can catch yourself in the act of interacting with the text—or actively constructing meaning.

Tragedy and Comedy

Tragedy isn't Accidental

"That was such a tragic accident." Huh?

Tragedy is a balloon word, like "culture" or "freedom." It has been used in so many ways that its exact meaning is lost. I'll expect you to be more precise with it. Know its roots. Tragedy and comedy are complementary forms. Stemming from early drama (with its rituals), a tragic protagonist makes a choice which leads to their eventual, inevitable destruction. Conversely, comedy's choices are about marriage and sex. There is usually a marriage at the end of a comedy—they are life-affirming in a positive way.

Typically, tragic protagonists fall from on high and we enjoy watching this inevitable, choice-driven event while noticing the characteristic within them that led to it. In this way, tragedy is much like blues music, where we might feel joy at hearing that someone is "diggin' my potatoes" (cheating on the singer with "his" woman). The Greeks called this *catharsis*, a ritual purging (out both ends, grossly enough, but we politely think of the upper one).

What Tragedies Accomplish

Tragedies are life-affirming in a negative sense. The "body count" at the end usually evokes "pity" and "terror." Aristotle used these terms, and we still do today. And why do we feel good after a tragedy? Why, it didn't happen to us! That's one reason. Another is that we shared in someone's suffering, and this causes us to reflect on things. Are there many ways in which Americans communally share anything? How much more individualized are we now than we were 100 years ago?

Genres and categories like tragedy and comedy are artificially applied to much modern literature, and to all NA literature. When a Mohawk writer is intentionally using tragedy, they are also using their Mohawk culture and mixing in elements from white culture, too. How are readers going to separate these threads? Is it even possible? Do you see what an interesting mess this provides for us as readers? It's not necessarily a bad thing that we can't get easy answers.

Problems Using Terms like Tragedy

Not only is tragedy a misused term, then, but when applied to another world literature—like Native American literature—it becomes problematic. If we can test some of these, we won't have to rely on problem terms like "tragedy" that much.

I'd like you to leave this lecture as a seeker for the tragic and the non-tragic in their properly literary senses, and not merely the pop culture idea of good/bad, which is oversimplified.

What of Comedy, Then?

Well, comedy is easy. . . it's about union, with most comedies featuring sexual union occurring offstage while the wedding guests joke about how long it will take till the wife starts cheating on the husband. It's a strange genre, really, with old people trying to create matches for the young, often involving their older friends marrying to maintain wealth and control. Critic Northrop Frye on comedy: "A comedy is not a play which ends happily: it is a play in which a certain structure is present and works through to its own logical end [. . .]"

Frye's Use of Mythical Cycles—and I'm not talking Harleys!

Frye continues, connecting comedy and tragedy with the workings of the four seasons.

The mythical backbone of all literature is the cycle of nature, which rolls from birth to death and back again to rebirth. The first half of this cycle, the movement from birth to death, spring to winter, dawn to dark, is the basis of the great alliance of nature and reason, the sense of nature as a rational order in which all movement is toward the increasingly predictable . . . [T]ragedy [and] the history play (always very close to tragedy) . . . are always close to this first half. There may be surprises in the last act of a Shakespearean tragedy, but the pervading feeling is of something inevitable working itself out . . . Comedy, however, is based on the second half of the great cycle, moving from death to rebirth, decadence to renewal, winter to spring, darkness to a new dawn . . . This movement from sterility to renewed life is as natural as the tragic movement, because it happens. But though natural it is somehow irrational: the sense of the alliance of nature with reason and predictable order is no longer present. We can see that death is the inevitable result of birth, but new life is not the inevitable result of death. It is hoped for, even expected, but at its core is something unpredictable and mysterious, something that belongs to the imaginative equivalents of faith, hope, and love, not to the rational virtues (119-22).

So we're often partly correct about these genres while perhaps missing the key workings of each. There! You are cursed to correct any newscaster who utters "That was a tragic accident!"

And if all this isn't strangely contingent enough, do some web searches to see how the original festivals of Dionysus worked out (with their Maenads) prior to the Greeks settling down and merely watching plays! See the connections?

"Dionysus Mosaic" by miriam.mollerus is licensed under CC BY 2.0

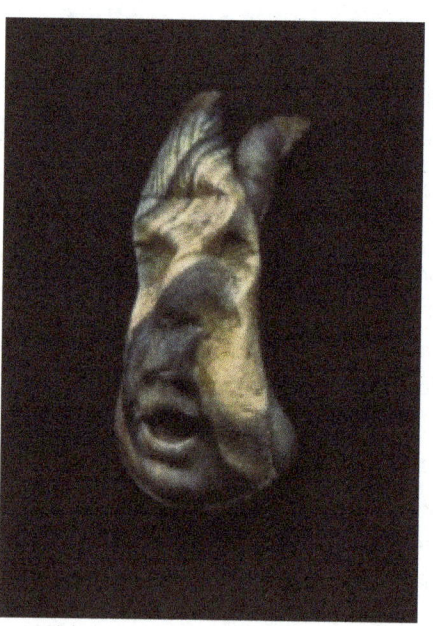

"Dionysus" by TheoJunior is licensed under CC BY 2.0

Analysis is the Breaking Down of a Whole into its Parts

Part-to-whole relationships and breaking those down into their functions is what we do when we analyze. We argue about how the parts function.

For practice, look at the following image. It is Edward Hicks's *The Cornell Farm*. The image has a fascinating composition, so watch the way one's eyes are directed from area to area in the painting. Are there any symbols? Signs? (Do you know the difference between a sign and a symbol?)

When we write, we analyze most of the time. Whether we are reading a student post or model essay, we look over each text and think about how we are looking. It's a composition, so some of the vocabulary we use in its analysis is shared with other humanities courses like art appreciation or music appreciation.

Consider how the whole is broken down. If its artful, then there's a guiding of one's eyes as well as a frustration of easy expectations. See what you see and share that! Again, italicize the artworks' titles.

Edward Hicks, The Cornell Farm (1848).

Clearly, we can argue the parts and how they function. Analysis is all about functions in the structure and effects upon the viewer/reader. It's worth remembering that the act is destructive (*lysis* meaning just that), sort of like taking apart a watch and seeing if it will function without this or that gear. And, no, don't use the creationist blind watchmaker argument here just because I mentioned watches. Their idea that something as sophisticated as an eye could not have evolved is easily-enough refuted.

With Analysis, Focus Upon Functions or Effects

At the college level, putting in the right-sounding quotes in the right-looking spots of a body paragraph is insufficient. Writers are expected to use the quotes as excuses to argue their points. Close reading is a crucial skill which helps the writer make sense of how something makes sense. Humanities courses largely aim to enhance or bring about readers' abilities to handle complex, indirect texts that demand multiple responses.

Close reading is an analytical activity where the writer picks parts of larger whole and discusses how they function. This can be done while annotating or deciding what to say about an annotated chunk of text. Because your audience often knows the text and has ideas about how it works, it is up to you to do more than simply point out the existence of an important line, phrase, or word. Within the line, the critic must move from pointing out an idea to arguing how it functions. What effect is created by that phrase? How does this word affect readers? These questions get proved after careful setup and cited quotation work.

Once you have dissected a speech, description, or dialogue, remember that you have committed a fairly aggressive, destructive act. You yanked a part from the whole. Remember to use the late portions of paragraphs to put the pieces back together. ("Pick up your toys when you are done with them!")

What You Might Look for in a Text

Focus on an author's use of complexity by discussing the effects of any of the following:

word choice (diction) word order (syntax)

connotation denotation

irony (dramatic, situational, verbal) symbolism

mood tone

paradox (seeming contradiction) how words fit/bring about character

rhetorical appeals (logos, ethos, pathos) logical patterns (valid or not)

Rhetorical modes (description, narration, definition, process, illustration, comparison/contrast, classification/division, cause/effect, argument)

Basically, looking for moves of any sort is a good starting point with analysis.

Annotation: Why Mark Up Your Texts?

Marking up your book properly is a survival skill in college literature classes. Most instructors expect you to develop your own system for noting "significant stuff" when reading. Marking up your book will allow you to locate information while testing.

Even if you are renting a text or reading it on a Kindle or other device, there are annotation tools. In fact, some of the electronic tools can allow you collection your annotations.

How to Mark Up Your Book

There is no set way to mark up a text, but active readers tend to do several of the following things:

- Underline important passages. As an alternative, you could put vertical lines in the margin next to important areas.
- Put ?, ! or questions of your own in the margins next to confusing or surprising passages. This way, you won't have to stop your reading for too long in order to look up words, phrases, etc.
- Draw lines and arrows between connected ideas. Try and find your own level of connections so that these become more meaningful.
- List concepts, themes, or the names of other authors in the margins. These indicate connections.
- List the page number or beginning of a quote similar to the one you're annotating. Connect one quote with another. Quotes can be linked based on similarity, difference, emphasis, subtlety, etc. It's up to you.
- Doubt the author. Be skeptical this in the margins! Insults work, too. . .
- Use literary terms like irony, ambiguity, symbolism, tone to indicate where the author is making these moves.
- Create your own shorthand for marking the book. This could be as simple as using the triangle (delta), the mathematical symbol for change. I have a bunch of these. Seriously, this works.

American Literature Sites

I recommend the following sites and have found them useful in contextualizing different readings for students.

Perspectives in American Literature: An Ongoing Research and Reference Guide: http://www.paulreuben.website/pal

The Melville Society: http://melvillesociety.org/

Book Graphics: Rockwell Kent's Illustrations for *Moby-Dick*: http://book-graphics.blogspot.com/2013/08/moby-dick-or-whale-illustrated-by.html

The Sublime: http://www.webpages.uidaho.edu/engl_258/Lecture%20Notes/sublime.htm

The Gothic in Literature

Definition

Note this definition by Claire Kahane from *The Mother Tongue: Essays in Psychoanalytic Interpretation* from our talks about the Gothic:

"Leatherstocking's Rescue" by John Quidor (1801–1881) via The Metropolitan Museum of Art is licensed under CC0 1.0

Within an imprisoning structure, a protagonist, typically a young woman whose mother has died, is compelled to seek out the center of a mystery, while vague and usually sexual threats to her person from some powerful male figure hover on the periphery of her consciousness. Following clues that pull her onward and inward—bloodstains, mysterious sounds—she penetrates the obscure recesses of a vast labyrinthean space and discovers a secret room sealed off by its association with death. (334)

At first glance, you might not think that this novella is Gothic. It's not literally filled with death, there are no graveyards, and the boat isn't literally a ghost ship! Looking further at how this narrative includes Gothic elements, though, we can see it fits the structure aptly.

Well, is Melville doing that "Gothic thing" in her story? Kinda? Sorta? Let's look at how he uses the pattern and innovates upon it. Remember, when did we say that the Gothic got started? Oh, that's right, around 1790. This is much later, but then again the Gothic is incredibly popular even today.

Tip: Look up the works of an artist such as John Quidor to gauge how closely they fit the Gothic. Do the same with artists or even movies and television programs you enjoy.

Introduction to Romantic Literature

All things must change to something new, to something strange. – Henry Wadsworth Longfellow

Learning Outcomes

- Describe the major historical and cultural developments of the Romantic period; explain key concepts and terms (e.g., the sentimental)
- Describe the major conventions, tropes, and themes of Romantic literature; identify and discuss those features with regard to individual authors/works
- Describe the major conventions, tropes, and themes of Gothic literature; identify and discuss those features with regard to individual authors/works
- Describe the major conventions, tropes, and themes of transcendental literature; identify and discuss those features with regard to individual authors/works
- Describe the major conventions, tropes, and themes of abolitionist literature and slave narratives; identify and discuss those features with regard to individual authors/works

"Kindred Spirits" oil painting by Asher Durand, 1849

The Romantic Period, 1820–1860: Essayists and Poets -- American Literature I

Fresh New Vision Electrified Artistic and Intellectual Circles

The Romantic movement, which originated in Germany but quickly spread to England, France, and beyond, reached America around the year 1820, some twenty years after William Wordsworth and Samuel Taylor Coleridge had revolutionized English poetry by publishing *Lyrical Ballads*. In America as in Europe, fresh new vision electrified artistic and intellectual circles. Yet there was an important difference: Romanticism in America coincided with the period of national expansion and the discovery of a distinctive American voice. The solidification of a national identity and the surging idealism and passion of Romanticism nurtured the masterpieces of "the American Renaissance."

Romantic ideas centered around art as inspiration, the spiritual and aesthetic dimension of nature, and metaphors of organic growth. Art, rather than science, Romantics argued, could best express universal truth. The Romantics underscored the importance of expressive art for the individual and society. In his essay "The Poet" (1844), Ralph Waldo Emerson, perhaps the most influential writer of the Romantic era, asserts:

> For all men live by truth, and stand in need of expression. In love, in art, in avarice, in politics, in labor, in games, we study to utter our painful secret. The man is only half himself, the other half is his expression.

The development of the self became a major theme; self-awareness a primary method. If, according to Romantic theory, self and nature were one, self-awareness was not a selfish dead end but a mode of knowledge opening up the universe. If one's self were one with all humanity, then the individual had a moral duty to reform social inequalities and relieve human suffering. The idea of "self"—which suggested selfishness to earlier generations—was redefined. New compound words with positive meanings emerged: "self-realization," "self-expression," "self-reliance."

As the unique, subjective self became important, so did the realm of psychology. Exceptional artistic effects and techniques were developed to evoke heightened psychological states. The "sublime"—an effect of beauty in grandeur (for example, a view from a mountaintop)—produced feelings of awe, reverence, vastness, and a power beyond human comprehension.

Romanticism was affirmative and appropriate for most American poets and creative essayists. America's vast mountains, deserts, and tropics embodied the sublime. The Romantic spirit seemed particularly suited to American democracy: It stressed individualism, affirmed the value of the common person, and looked to the inspired imagination for its aesthetic and ethical values. Certainly the New England Transcendentalists—Ralph Waldo Emerson, Henry David Thoreau, and their associates—were inspired to a new optimistic affirmation by the Romantic movement. In New England, Romanticism fell upon fertile soil.

Transcendentalism

The Transcendentalist movement was a reaction against 18th century rationalism and a manifestation of the general humanitarian trend of nineteenth century thought. The movement was based on a fundamental belief in the unity of the world and God. The soul of each individual was thought to be identical with the world—a microcosm of the world itself. The doctrine of self-reliance and individualism developed through the belief in the identification of the individual soul with God.

Transcendentalism was intimately connected with Concord, a small New England village thirty-two kilometers west of Boston. Concord was the first inland settlement of the original Massachusetts Bay Colony. Surrounded by forest, it was and remains a peaceful town close enough to Boston's lectures, bookstores, and colleges to be intensely cultivated, but far enough away to be serene. Concord was the site of the first battle of the American Revolution, and Ralph Waldo Emerson's poem commemorating the battle, "Concord Hymn," has one of the most famous opening stanzas in American literature:

> By the rude bridge that arched the flood
> Their flag to April's breeze unfurled,
> Here once the embattled farmers stood
> And fired the shot heard round the world.

Concord was the first rural artist's colony, and the first place to offer a spiritual and cultural alternative to American materialism. It was a place of high-minded conversation and simple living (Emerson and Henry David Thoreau both had vegetable gardens). Emerson, who moved to Concord in 1834, and Thoreau are most closely associated with the town, but the locale also attracted the novelist Nathaniel Hawthorne, the feminist writer Margaret Fuller, the educator (and father of novelist Louisa May Alcott) Bronson Alcott, and the poet William Ellery Channing. The Transcendental Club was loosely organized in 1836 and included, at various times, Emerson, Thoreau, Fuller, Channing, Bronson Alcott, Orestes Brownson (a leading minister), Theodore Parker (abolitionist and minister), and others.

The Transcendentalists published a quarterly magazine, *The Dial*, which lasted four years and was first edited by Margaret Fuller and later by Emerson. Reform efforts engaged them as well as literature. A number of Transcendentalists were abolitionists, and some were involved in experimental utopian communities such as nearby Brook Farm (described in Hawthorne's *The Blithedale Romance*) and Fruitlands.

Unlike many European groups, the Transcendentalists never issued a manifesto. They insisted on individual differences — on the unique viewpoint of the individual. American Transcendental Romantics pushed radical individualism to the extreme. American writers often saw themselves as lonely explorers outside society and convention. The American hero—like Herman Melville's Captain Ahab, or Mark Twain's Huck Finn, or Edgar Allan Poe's Arthur Gordon Pym—typically faced risk, or even certain destruction, in the pursuit of metaphysical self-discovery. For the Romantic American writer, nothing was a given. Literary and social conventions, far from being helpful, were dangerous. There was tremendous pressure to discover an authentic literary form, content, and voice — all at the same time. It is clear from the many masterpieces produced in the three decades before the U.S. Civil War (1861–65) that American writers rose to the challenge.

Ralph Waldo Emerson (1803–1882)

Ralph Waldo Emerson, the towering figure of his era, had a religious sense of mission. Although many accused him of subverting Christianity, he explained that, for him "to be a good minister, it was necessary to leave the church." The address he delivered in 1838 at his alma mater, the Harvard Divinity School, made him unwelcome at Harvard for thirty years. In it, Emerson accused the church of acting "as if God were dead" and of emphasizing dogma while stifling the spirit.

Emerson's philosophy has been called contradictory, and it is true that he consciously avoided building a logical intellectual system because such a rational system would have negated his Romantic belief in intuition and flexibility. In his essay "Self-Reliance," Emerson remarks: "A foolish consistency is the hobgoblin of little minds." Yet he is remarkably consistent in his call for the birth of American individualism inspired by nature. Most of his major ideas—the need for a new national vision, the use of personal experience, the notion of the cosmic Over-Soul, and the doctrine of compensation—are suggested in his first publication,
Nature (1836). This essay opens:

> Our age is retrospective. It builds the sepulchres of the fathers. It writes biographies, histories, criticism. The foregoing generations beheld God and nature face to face; we, through their eyes. Why should not we also enjoy an original relation to the universe? Why should not we have a poetry of insight and not of tradition, and a religion by revelation to us, and not the history of theirs. Embosomed for a season in nature, whose floods of life stream around and through us, and invite us by the powers they supply, to action proportioned to nature, why should we grope among the dry bones of the past...? The sun shines today also. There is more wool and flax in the fields. There are new lands, new men, new thoughts. Let us demand our own works and laws and worship.

Emerson loved the aphoristic genius of the sixteenth-century French essayist Montaigne, and he once told Bronson Alcott that he wanted to write a book like Montaigne's, "full of fun, poetry, business, divinity, philosophy, anecdotes, smut." He complained that Alcott's abstract style omitted "the light that shines on a man's hat, in a child's spoon."

Spiritual vision and practical, aphoristic expression make Emerson exhilarating; one of the Concord Transcendentalists aptly compared listening to him with "going to heaven in a swing." Much of his spiritual insight comes from his readings in Eastern religion, especially Hinduism, Confucianism, and Islamic Sufism. For example, his poem "Brahma" relies on Hindu sources to assert a cosmic order beyond the limited perception of mortals:

> If the red slayer think he slay Or the slain think he is slain, They know not well the subtle ways I keep, and pass, and turn again.
> Far or forgot to me is near Shadow and sunlight are the same; The vanished gods to me appear; And one to me are shame and fame.

They reckon ill who leave me out; When me they fly, I am the wings; I am the doubter and the doubt, And I the hymn the Brahmin sings

The strong gods pine for my abode, And pine in vain the sacred Seven, But thou, meek lover of the good! Find me, and turn thy back on heaven.

This poem, published in the first number of the *Atlantic Monthly* magazine (1857), confused readers unfamiliar with Brahma, the highest Hindu god, the eternal and infinite soul of the universe. Emerson had this advice for his readers: "Tell them to say Jehovah instead of Brahma."

The British critic Matthew Arnold said the most important writings in English in the nineteenth century had been Wordsworth's poems and Emerson's essays. A great prose-poet, Emerson influenced a long line of American poets, including Walt Whitman, Emily Dickinson, Edwin Arlington Robinson, Wallace Stevens, Hart Crane, and Robert Frost. He is also credited with influencing the philosophies of John Dewey, George Santayana, Friedrich Nietzsche, and William James.

Henry David Thoreau (1817–1862)

Henry David Thoreau, of French and Scottish descent, was born in Concord and made it his permanent home. From a poor family, like Emerson, he worked his way through Harvard. Throughout his life, he reduced his needs to the simplest level and managed to live on very little money, thus maintaining his independence. In essence, he made living his career. A nonconformist, he attempted to live his life at all times according to his rigorous principles. This attempt was the subject of many of his writings.

Thoreau's masterpiece, *Walden, or Life in the Woods* (1854), is the result of two years, two months, and two days (from 1845 to 1847) he spent living in a cabin he built at Walden Pond on property owned by Emerson. In *Walden*, Thoreau consciously shapes this time into one year, and the book is carefully constructed so the seasons are subtly evoked in order. The book also is organized so that the simplest earthly concerns come first (in the section called "Economy," he describes the expenses of building a cabin); by the ending, the book has progressed to meditations on the stars.

In *Walden*, Thoreau, a lover of travel books and the author of several, gives us an anti-travel book that paradoxically opens the inner frontier of self-discovery as no American book had up to this time. As deceptively modest as Thoreau's ascetic life, it is no less than a guide to living the classical ideal of the good life. Both poetry and philosophy, this long poetic essay challenges the reader to examine his or her life and live it authentically. The building of the cabin, described in great detail, is a concrete metaphor for the careful building of a soul. In his journal for January 30, 1852, Thoreau explains his preference for living rooted in one place: "I am afraid to travel much or to famous places, lest it might completely dissipate the mind."

Thoreau's method of retreat and concentration resembles Asian meditation techniques. The resemblance is not accidental: like Emerson and Whitman, he was influenced by Hindu and Buddhist philosophy. His most treasured possession was his library of Asian classics, which he shared with Emerson. His eclectic style draws on Greek and Latin classics and is crystalline, punning, and as richly metaphorical as the English metaphysical writers of the late Renaissance.

In *Walden*, Thoreau not only tests the theories of Transcendentalism, he reenacts the collective American experience of the nineteenth century: living on the frontier. Thoreau felt that his contribution would be to renew a sense of the wilderness in language. His journal has an undated entry from 1851:

English literature from the days of the minstrels to the Lake Poets, Chaucer and Spenser and Shakespeare and Milton included, breathes no quite fresh and in this sense, wild strain. It is an essentially tame and civilized literature, reflecting Greece and Rome. Her wilderness is a greenwood, her wildman a Robin Hood. There is plenty of genial love of nature in her poets, but not so much of nature herself. Her chronicles inform us when her wild animals, but not the wildman in her, became extinct. There was need of America.

Walden inspired William Butler Yeats, a passionate Irish nationalist, to write "The Lake Isle of Innisfree," while Thoreau's essay "Civil Disobedience," with its theory of passive resistance based on the moral necessity for the just individual to disobey unjust laws, was an inspiration for Mahatma Gandhi's Indian independence movement and Martin Luther King's struggle for black Americans' civil rights in the twentieth century.

Thoreau is the most attractive of the Transcendentalists today because of his ecological consciousness, do-it-yourself independence, ethical commitment to abolitionism, and political theory of civil disobedience and peaceful resistance. His ideas are still fresh, and his incisive poetic style and habit of close observation are still modern.

Walt Whitman (1819–1892)

Born on Long Island, New York, Walt Whitman was a part-time carpenter and man of the people, whose brilliant, innovative work expressed the country's democratic spirit. Whitman was largely self-taught; he left school at the age of 11 to go to work, missing the sort of traditional education that made most American authors respectful imitators of the English. His *Leaves of Grass* (1855), which he rewrote and revised throughout his life, contains "Song of Myself," the most stunningly original poem ever written by an American. The enthusiastic praise that Emerson and a few others heaped on this daring volume confirmed Whitman in his poetic vocation, although the book was not a popular success.

A visionary book celebrating all creation, *Leaves of Grass* was inspired largely by Emerson's writings, especially his essay "The Poet," which predicted a robust, open-hearted, universal kind of poet uncannily like Whitman himself. The poem's innovative, unrhymed, free-verse form, open celebration of sexuality, vibrant democratic sensibility, and extreme Romantic assertion that the poet's self was one with the poem, the universe, and the reader permanently altered the course of American poetry.

Leaves of Grass is as vast, energetic, and natural as the American continent; it was the epic generations of American critics had been calling for, although they did not recognize it. Movement ripples through "Song of Myself" like restless music:

My ties and ballasts leave me . . . I skirt sierras, my palms cover continents I am afoot with my vision.

The poem bulges with myriad concrete sights and sounds. Whitman's birds are not the conventional "winged spirits" of poetry. His "yellow-crown'd heron comes to the edge of the marsh at night and feeds upon small crabs." Whitman seems to project himself into everything that he sees or imagines. He is mass man, "Voyaging to every port to dicker and adventure, / Hurrying with the modern crowd as eager and fickle as any." But he is equally the suffering individual, "The mother of old, condemn'd for a witch, burnt with dry wood, her children gazing on....I am the hounded slave, I wince at the bite of the dogs....I am the mash'd fireman with breast-bone broken...."

More than any other writer, Whitman invented the myth of democratic America. "The Americans of all nations at any time upon the earth have probably the fullest poetical nature. The United States is essentially the greatest poem." When Whitman wrote this, he daringly turned upside down the general opinion that America was too brash and new to be poetic. He invented a timeless America of the free imagination, peopled with pioneering spirits of all nations. D.H. Lawrence, the British novelist and poet, accurately called him the poet of the "open road."

Whitman's greatness is visible in many of his poems, among them "Crossing Brooklyn Ferry," "Out of the Cradle Endlessly Rocking," and "When Lilacs Last in the Dooryard Bloom'd," a moving elegy on the death of Abraham Lincoln. Another important work is his long essay "Democratic Vistas" (1871), written during the unrestrained materialism of industrialism's "Gilded Age." In this essay, Whitman justly criticizes America for its "mighty, many-threaded wealth and industry" that mask an underlying "dry and flat Sahara" of soul. He calls for a new kind of literature to revive the American population ("Not the book needs so much to be the complete thing, but the reader of the book does"). Yet ultimately, Whitman's main claim to immortality lies in "Song of Myself." Here he places the Romantic self at the center of the consciousness of the poem:

I celebrate myself, and sing myself, And what I assume you shall assume, For every atom belonging to me as good belongs to you.

Whitman's voice electrifies even modern readers with his proclamation of the unity and vital force of all creation. He was enormously innovative. From him spring the poem as autobiography, the American Everyman as bard, the reader as creator, and the still-contemporary discovery of "experimental," or organic, form.

The Brahmin Poets

In their time, the Boston Brahmins (as the patrician, Harvard-educated class came to be called) supplied the most respected and genuinely cultivated literary arbiters of the United States. Their lives fitted a pleasant pattern of wealth and leisure directed by the strong New England work ethic and respect for learning.

In an earlier Puritan age, the Boston Brahmins would have been ministers; in the nineteenth century, they became professors, often at Harvard. Late in life they sometimes became ambassadors or received honorary degrees from European institutions. Most of them travelled or were educated in Europe: They were familiar with the ideas and books of Britain, Germany, and France, and often Italy and Spain. Upper class in background but democratic in sympathy, the Brahmin poets carried their genteel, European-oriented views to every section of the United States, through public lectures at the three thousand lyceums (centers for public lectures) and in the pages of two influential Boston magazines, the *North American Review* and the *Atlantic Monthly*.

The writings of the Brahmin poets fused American and European traditions and sought to create a continuity of shared Atlantic experience. These scholar-poets attempted to educate and elevate the general populace by introducing a European dimension to American literature. Ironically, their overall effect was conservative. By insisting on European things and forms, they retarded the growth of a distinctive American consciousness. Well-meaning men, their conservative backgrounds blinded them to the daring innovativeness of Thoreau, Whitman (whom they refused to meet socially), and Edgar Allan Poe (whom even Emerson regarded as the "jingle man"). They were pillars of what was called the "genteel tradition" that three generations of American realists had to battle. Partly because of their benign but bland influence, it was almost one hundred years before the distinctive American genius of Whitman, Melville, Thoreau, and Poe was generally recognized in the United States.

Margaret Fuller (1810–1850)

Margaret Fuller, an outstanding essayist, was born and raised in Cambridge, Massachusetts. From a modest financial background, she was educated at home by her father (women were not allowed to attend Harvard) and became a child prodigy in the classics and modern literatures. Her special passion was German Romantic literature, especially Goethe, whom she translated.

The first professional woman journalist of note in America, Fuller wrote influential book reviews and reports on social issues such as the treatment of women prisoners and the insane. Some of these essays were published in her book *Papers on Literature and Art* (1846). A year earlier, she had her most significant book, *Woman in the Nineteenth Century*. It originally had appeared in the Transcendentalist magazine, *The Dial*, which she edited from 1840 to 1842.

Fuller's *Woman in the Nineteenth Century* is the earliest and most American exploration of women's role in society. Often applying democratic and Transcendental principles, Fuller thoughtfully analyzes the numerous subtle causes and evil consequences of sexual discrimination and suggests positive steps to be taken. Many of her ideas are strikingly modern. She stresses the importance of "self-dependence," which women lack because "they are taught to learn their rule from without, not to unfold it from within."

Fuller is finally not a feminist so much as an activist and reformer dedicated to the cause of creative human freedom and dignity for all:

> . . . Let us be wise and not impede the soul. . . . Let us have one creative energy. . . .Let it take what form it will, and let us not bind it by the past to man or woman, black or white.

Emily Dickinson (1830–1886)

Emily Dickinson is, in a sense, a link between her era and the literary sensitivies of the turn of the century. A radical individualist, she was born and spent her life in Amherst, Massachusetts, a small Calvinist village. She never married, and she led an unconventional life that was outwardly uneventful but was full of inner intensity. She loved nature and found deep inspiration in the birds, animals, plants, and changing seasons of the New England countryside.

Dickinson spent the latter part of her life as a recluse, due to an extremely sensitive psyche and possibly to make time for writing (for stretches of time she wrote about one poem a day). Her day also included homemaking for her attorney father, a prominent figure in Amherst who became a member of Congress.

Dickinson was not widely read, but knew the Bible, the works of William Shakespeare, and works of classical mythology in great depth. These were her true teachers, for Dickinson was certainly the most solitary literary figure of her time. That this shy, withdrawn, village woman, almost unpublished and unknown, created some of the greatest American poetry of the nineteenth century has fascinated the public since the 1950s, when her poetry was rediscovered.

Dickinson's terse, frequently imagistic style is even more modern and innovative than Whitman's. She never uses two words when one will do, and combines concrete things with abstract ideas in an almost proverbial, compressed style. Her best poems have no fat; many mock current sentimentality, and some are even heretical. She sometimes shows a terrifying existential awareness. Like Poe, she explores the dark and hidden part of the mind, dramatizing death and the grave. Yet she also celebrated simple objects – a flower, a bee. Her poetry exhibits great intelligence and often evokes the agonizing paradox of the limits of the human consciousness trapped in time. She had an excellent sense of humor, and her range of subjects and treatment is amazingly wide. Her poems are generally known by the numbers assigned them in Thomas H. Johnson's standard edition of 1955. They bristle with odd capitalizations and dashes.

A nonconformist, like Thoreau she often reversed meanings of words and phrases and used paradox to great effect. From 435:

Much Madness is divinest sense – To a discerning Eye – Much Sense – the starkest Madness – 'Tis the Majority In this, as All, prevail – Assent – and you are sane – Demur – you're straightway dangerous And handled with a chain –

Her wit shines in the following poem (288), which ridicules ambition and public life:

I'm Nobody! Who are you? Are you – Nobody – Too? Then there's a pair of us? Don't tell! they'd advertise – you know!
How dreary – to be – Somebody! How public – like a Frog – To tell one's name – the livelong June – To an admiring Bog!

Dickinson's 1,775 poems continue to intrigue critics, who often disagree about them. Some stress her mystical side, some her sensitivity to nature; many note her odd, exotic appeal. One modern critic, R. P. Blackmur, comments that Dickinson's poetry sometimes feels as if "a cat came at us speaking English." Her clean, clear, chiseled poems are some of the most fascinating and challenging in American literature.

Elements of any Fairy Tales: Propp's Schema

Directions: Are all folk stories composed of a set of common elements? If we counted them, how many would we see? Your task is to use the classification of fairy tales sheet on the back, from Russian critic Vladimir Propp, to break down the parts of the Grimm Brothers' tale "Godfather Death."

First, break the tale into its component parts. It has probably eight to ten of those breaks between one part of the story and another. Tell what happens in each part. Then see how many of Propp's categories fit the parts you just identified.

Godfather Death

A poor man had twelve children and was forced to work night and day to give them even bread. When therefore the thirteenth came into the world, he knew not what to do in his trouble, but ran out into the great highway, and resolved to ask the first person whom he met to be godfather. The first to meet him was the good God who already knew what filled his heart, and said to him, poor man, I pity you. I will hold your child at its christening, and will take charge of it and make it happy on earth. The man said, who are you. I am God. Then I do not desire to have you for a godfather, said the man, you give to the rich, and leave the poor to hunger. Thus spoke the man, for he did not know how wisely God apportions riches and poverty. He turned therefore away from the Lord, and went farther. Then the devil came to him and said, what do you seek. If you will take me as a godfather for your child, I will give him gold in plenty and all the joys of the world as well. The man asked, who are you. I am the devil. Then I do not desire to have you for godfather, said the man, you deceive men and lead them astray. He went onwards, and then came death striding up to him with withered legs, and said, take me as godfather. The man asked, who are you. I am death, and I make all equal. Then said the man, you are the right one, you take the rich as well as the poor, without distinction, you shall be godfather. Death answered, I will make your child rich and famous, for he who has me for a friend can lack nothing. The man said, next Sunday is the christening, be there at the right time. Death appeared as he had promised, and stood godfather quite in the usual way. When the boy had grown up, his godfather one day appeared and bade him go with him. He led him forth into a forest, and showed him a herb which grew there, and said, now you shall receive your godfather's present. I make you a celebrated physician. When you are called to a patient, I will always appear to you. If I stand by the head of the sick man, you may say with confidence that you will make him well again, and if you give him of this herb he will recover, but if I stand by the patient's feet, he is mine, and you must say that all remedies are in vain, and that no physician in the world could save him. But beware of using the herb against my will, or it might fare ill with you.

It was not long before the youth was the most famous physician in the whole world. He had only to look at the patient and he knew his condition at once, whether he would recover, or must needs die. So they said of him, and from far and wide people came to him, sent for him when they had anyone ill, and gave him so much money that he soon became a rich man. Now it so befell that the king became ill, and the physician was summoned, and was to say if recovery were possible. But when he came to the bed, death was standing by the feet of the sick man, and the herb did not grow which could save him. If I could but cheat death for once, thought the physician, he is sure to take it ill if I do but, as I am his godson, he will shut one eye, I will risk it. He therefore took up the sick man, and laid him the other way, so that now death was standing by his head. Then he gave the king some of the herbs, and he recovered and grew healthy again.

But death came to the physician, looking very black and angry, threatened him with his finger, and said, you have betrayed me, this time I will pardon it, as you are my godson, but if you venture it again, it will cost you your neck, for I will take you yourself away with me.

Soon afterwards the king's daughter fell into a severe illness. She was his only child, and he wept day and night, so that he began to lose the sight of his eyes, and he caused it to be made known that whosoever rescued her from death should be her husband and inherit the crown. When the physician came to the sick girl's bed, he saw death by her feet. He ought to have remembered the warning given by his godfather, but he was so infatuated by the great beauty of the king's daughter, and the happiness of becoming her husband, that he flung all thought to the winds. He did not see that death was casting angry glances on him, that he was raising his hand in the air, and threatening him with his withered fist. He raised up the sick girl, and placed her head where her feet had lain. Then he gave her some of the herb, and instantly her cheeks flushed red, and life stirred afresh in her.

When death saw that for a second time his own property had been misused, he walked up to the physician with long strides, and said, all is over with you, and now the lot falls on you, and seized him so firmly with his ice-cold hand, that he could not resist, and led him into a cave below the earth. There he saw how thousands and thousands of candles were burning in countless rows, some large, some medium-sized, others small. Every instant some were extinguished, and others again burnt up, so that the flames seemed to leap hither and thither in perpetual change. See, said death, these are the lights of men's lives. The large ones belong to children, the medium-sized ones to married people in their prime, the little ones belong to old people, but children and young folks likewise have often only a tiny candle. Show me the light of my life, said the physician, and he thought that it would be still very tall. Death pointed to a little end which was just threatening to go out, and said, behold, it is there. Ah, dear godfather, said the horrified physician, light a new one for me, do it for love of me, that I may enjoy my life, be king, and the husband of the king's beautiful daughter. I cannot, answered death, one must go out before a new one is lighted. Then place the old one on a new one, that will go on burning at once when the old one has come to an end, pleaded the physician. Death behaved as if he were going to fulfill his wish, and took hold of a tall new candle, but as he desired to revenge himself, he purposely made a mistake in fixing it, and the little piece fell down and was extinguished. Immediately the physician fell on the ground, and now he himself was in the hands of death.

Directions: In "Godfather Death, locate, identify, and prove the existence of at least eight of Propp's schema. They can be in any order, but you must prove how the event in the fairy tale fits the schema in order to earn any credit.

1.

2.

3.

4.

5.

6.

7.

8.

Propp's Schema—The 31 Elements into Which any Fairy Tale can be Broken

1. A member of a family leaves home (the hero is introduced);
2. An interdiction is addressed to the hero ('don't go there', 'go to this place');
3. The interdiction is violated (villain enters the tale);
4. The villain makes an attempt at reconnaissance (either villain tries to find the children/jewels etc; or intended victim questions the villain);
5. The villain gains information about the victim;
6. The villain attempts to deceive the victim to take possession of victim or victim's belongings (trickery; villain disguised, tries to win confidence of victim);
7. Victim taken in by deception, unwittingly helping the enemy;
8. Villain causes harm/injury to family member (by abduction, theft of magical agent, spoiling crops, plunders in other forms, causes a disappearance, expels someone, casts spell on someone, substitutes child etc, commits murder, imprisons/ detains someone, threatens forced marriage, provides nightly torments); Alternatively, a member of family lacks something

or desires something (magical potion etc);

9. Misfortune or lack is made known, (hero is dispatched, hears call for help etc/ alternative is that victimized hero is sent away, freed from imprisonment);

10. Seeker agrees to, or decides upon counter-action;

11. Hero leaves home;

12. Hero is tested, interrogated, attacked etc, preparing the way for his/her receiving magical agent or helper (donor);

13. Hero reacts to actions of future donor (withstands/fails the test, frees captive, reconciles disputants, performs service, uses adversary's powers against them);

14. Hero acquires use of a magical agent (directly transferred, located, purchased, prepared, spontaneously appears, eaten/ drunk, help offered by other characters);

15. Hero is transferred, delivered or led to whereabouts of an object of the search;

16. Hero and villain join in direct combat;

17. Hero is branded (wounded/marked, receives ring or scarf);

18. Villain is defeated (killed in combat, defeated in contest, killed while asleep, banished);

19. Initial misfortune or lack is resolved (object of search distributed, spell broken, slain person revived, captive freed);

20. Hero returns;

21. Hero is pursued (pursuer tries to kill, eat, undermine the hero);

22. Hero is rescued from pursuit (obstacles delay pursuer, hero hides or is hidden, hero transforms unrecognizably, hero saved from attempt on his/her life);

23. Hero unrecognized, arrives home or in another country;

24. False hero presents unfounded claims;

25. Difficult task proposed to the hero (trial by ordeal, riddles, test of strength/endurance, other tasks);

26. Task is resolved;

27. Hero is recognized (by mark, brand, or thing given to him/her);

28. False hero or villain is exposed;

29. Hero is given a new appearance (is made whole, handsome, new garments etc);

30. Villain is punished;

31. Hero marries and ascends the throne (is rewarded/promoted).

Critical Approaches to Literature Chart

Use the critical approaches discussed in the chart below to help you find an interesting angle from which to approach a text. Each approach is given a brief description **(Beliefs)**, some guidelines for studying a text **(Practices)** and prompts to inspire your discussion **(Questions)**.

Do not simply list and answer the questions for a particular critical approach. Instead, use the questions as a starting place for your actual analysis. The questions are intended to be thought-provoking, not a list to be completed.

Approach	Beliefs	Practices	Questions
Deconstructive Criticism	• Meaning is made by binary oppositions (happy/sad, man/woman, black/white); in every binary relationship, one item is favored over the other one • This favoring of one concept in the binary relationship can be questioned and reversed to open up new ideas and meanings	• Identify the binary oppositions in the text, and determine which items are favored	1. What are the binary oppositions that govern the text? 2. What ideas, concepts, and values are being established by these binaries? 3. Cite three different interpretations for the text by flipping a series of three major binaries.
Feminist Criticism	• Any interpretation of the text is influenced by the reader's own status, which includes gender and attitudes towards gender • Men and women are different: they write differently, read differently, and write about their reading differently	• Identify the gender of the author and narrator/main character of the text • Observe how sexual stereotypes might be reinforced or undermined in the text–specifically, how the text reflects, distorts, or supports the place of women (and men) in society	1. What types of roles do men/women have in the text? Do any stereotypical characterizations of men/women appear? 2. What are the attitudes toward women held by the male characters? 3. What is the author's attitude toward women in society? Explain your reasoning using detailed examples from the text.
Reader-Oriented Criticism	• The reader's response is what counts. We can't know for sure what an author intended, and the text is meaningless unless a reader responds • Responding to a text is a process. Descriptions of the process are valuable because one person's response may enrich another reader's response	• Focus on how particular details shape readers' expectations and responses	1. What did the author intend for you to feel while reading this work, and how did he or she make you feel it? 2. What kind of reader is implied by this text? For example, does it address you as if you are intelligent and well-informed, or as if you are inexperienced and innocent? 3. How is your response shaped by the text? For example, do the actions of a certain character bring you pleasure or displeasure? Why?
Historical Criticism	• Interpretation of a text should be based on an understanding of its context • The context includes information about the author; when the text was written; where the text was written	• Research the author's life and relate that information to the text • Research the author's time and location (the political history, economic history, etc.) and relate that information to the text	1. How can you connect the author's life to his or her text? Are there common issues, events, concerns? 2. Is the author part of a dominant culture, and how does that status affect the work? 3. What events occurred surrounding the original production of the text? How may these events be relevant to the text under investigation?

2. READING LITERATURE AS A CRITIC

Literary Criticism

By reading and discussing literature, we expand our imagination, our sense of what is possible, and our ability to empathize with others. Improve your ability to read critically and interpret texts while gaining appreciation for different literary genres and theories of interpretation. Read samples of literary interpretation. Write a critique of a literary work.

Texts that interpret literary works are usually persuasive texts. Literary critics may conduct a close reading of a literary work, critique a literary work from the stance of a particular literary theory, or debate the soundness of other critics' interpretations. The work of literary critics is similar to the work of authors writing evaluative texts. For example, the skills required to critique films, interpret laws, or evaluate artistic trends are similar to those skills required by literary critics.

Why Write Literary Criticism?

People have been telling stories and sharing responses to stories since the beginning of time. By reading and discussing literature, we expand our imagination, our sense of what is possible, and our ability to empathize with others. Reading and discussing literature can enhance our ability to write. It can sharpen our critical faculties, enabling us to assess works and better understand why literature can have such a powerful effect on our lives.

- http://writingcommons.org/open-text/genres/academic-writing/literary-criticism/28-literary-criticism

"Literary texts" include works of fiction and poetry. In school, English instructors ask students to critique literary texts, or works. Literary criticism refers to a genre of writing whereby an author critiques a literary text, either a work of fiction, a play, or poetry. Alternatively, some works of literary criticism address how a particular theory of interpretation informs a reading of a work or refutes some other critics' reading of a work.

Diverse Rhetorical Situations

The genre of literary interpretation is more specialized than most of the other genres addressed in this section, as suggested by the table below. People may discuss their reactions to literary works informally (at coffee houses, book clubs, or the gym) but the lion's share of literary criticism takes place more formally: in college classrooms, professional journals, academic magazines, and Web sites.

Students interpret literary works for English instructors or for students enrolled in English classes. In their interpretations, students may argue for a particular interpretation or they may dispute other critics' interpretations. Alternatively, students may read a text with a particular literary theory in mind, using the theory to explicate a particular point of view. For example, writers could critique The Story of an Hour by Kate Chopin from a feminist theoretical perspective. Thanks to the Internet, some English classes are now publishing students' interpretations on Web sites. In turn, some students and English faculty publish their work in academic literary criticism journals.

Over the years, literary critics have argued about the best ways to interpret literature. Accordingly, many "schools" or "theories of criticism" have emerged. As you can imagine—given that they were developed by sophisticated specialists—some of these theoretical approaches are quite sophisticated and abstract.

Below is a summary of some of the more popular literary theories. Because it is a summary, the following tends to oversimplify the theories. In any case, unless you are enrolled in a literary criticism course, you won't need to learn the particulars of all of these approaches. Instead, your teacher may ask you to take an eclectic approach, pulling interpretative questions from multiple literary theories.

Note: If you are interested in learning more about these theories, review either Skylar Hamilton Burris' Literary Criticism: An Overview of Approaches or Dino F. Felluga's Undergraduate Guide to Critical Theory

- Schools of Literary Criticism
- New Criticism: Focuses on "objectively" evaluating the text, identifying its underlying form. May study, for example, a text's use of imagery, metaphor, or symbolism. Isn't concerned with matters outside the text, such as biographical or contextual information. Online Examples: A Formalist Reading of Sandra Cisneros's "Woman Hollering Creek" , Sound in William Shakespeare's The Tempest by Skylar Hamilton Burris
- Reader-Respons: Criticism Focuses on each reader's personal reactions to a text, assuming meaning is created by a reader's or interpretive community's personal interaction with a text. Assumes no single, correct, universal meaning exists because meaning resides in the minds of readers. Online Examples:Theodore Roethke's "My Papa's Waltz": A Reader's Response (PDF)
- Feminism: Criticism Focuses on understanding ways gender roles are reflected or contradicted by texts, how dominance and submission play out in texts, and how gender roles evolve in texts. Online Example: "The Yellow Wall-Paper": A Twist on Conventional Symbols, Subverting the French Androcentric Influence by Jane Le Marquand
- New Historicism Focuses on understanding texts by viewing texts in the context of other texts. Seeks to understand economic, social, and political influences on texts. Tend to broadly define the term "text," so, for example, the Catholic Church could be defined as a "text." May adopt the perspectives of other interpretive communities—particularly reader-response criticism, feminist criticism, and Marxist approaches—to interpret texts. Online Example Monstrous Acts by Jonathan Lethem
- Media Criticism Focuses on writers' use of multimedia and hypertexts. Online Examples The Electronic Labyrinth by Christopher Keep, Tim McLaughlin, and Robin Parmar
- Psychoanalytical Criticism Focuses on psychological dimensions of the work. Online Examples: A Freudian Approach to Erin McGraw's "A Thief" by Skylar Hamilton Burris
- Marxist Criticism Focuses on ways texts reflect, reinforce, or challenge the effects of class, power relations, and social roles. Online Example: A Reading of Shirley Jackson's "The Lottery" by Peter Kosenko
- Archetypal Criticism Focuses on identifying the underlying myths in stories and archetypes, which reflect what the psychologist Carl Jung called the "collective unconsciousness." Online Example: A Catalogue of Symbols in The Awakening by Kate Chopin by Skylar Hamilton Burris
- Postcolonial Criticism Focuses on how Western culture's (mis)representation of third-world countries and peoples in stories, myths, and stereotypical images encourages repression and domination. Online Example: Other Voices
- Structuralism/Semiotics Focuses on literature as a system of signs where meaning is constructed in a context, where words are inscribed with meaning by being compared to other words and structures. Online Example: Applied Semiotics [Online journal with many samples]
- Post-Structuralism/Deconstruction Focuses, along with Structuralism, on viewing literature as a system of signs, yet rejects the Structuralist view that a critic can identify the inherent meaning of a text, suggesting, instead that literature has no center, no single interpretation, that literary language is inherently ambiguous

Powerful works of literature invoke multiple readings. In other words, we can all read the same story or poem (or watch the same movie or listen to the same song) and come up with different, even conflicting, interpretations about what the work means. Who we are reflects how we read texts. Our experiences inspire us to relate to and sympathize with characters and difficult situations. Have we read similar stories? Have we actually faced some of the same challenges the characters in the story face?

In addition, literary theories have unique ways to develop and substantiate arguments. Some theories draw extensively on the work of other critics, while others concentrate on the reader's thoughts and feelings. Some theories analyze a work from an historical perspective, while others focus solely on a close reading of a text.

Accordingly, as with other genres, the following key features need to be read as points of departure as opposed to a comprehensive blueprint:

Focus

Examine a subject from a rhetorical perspective. Identify the intended audience, purpose, context, media, voice, tone, and persona.Distinguish between summarizing the literary work and presenting your argument. Many students fall into the trap of spending too much time summarizing the literature being analyzed as opposed to critiquing it. As a result, it would be wise to check with your teacher regarding how much plot summary is expected. As you approach this project, remember to keep your eye on the ball: What, exactly (in one sentence) is the gist of your interpretation?

Development

You can develop your ideas by researching the work of other literary critics. How do other critics evaluate an author's work? What literary theories do literary critics use to interpret texts or particular moments in history? Reading sample proposals can help you find and adopt an appropriate voice and persona. By reading samples, you can learn how others have prioritized particular criteria.

Below are some of the questions invoked by popular literary theories. Consider these questions as you read a work, perhaps taking notes on your thoughts as you reread. You may focus on using one theory to "read and interpret" text or, more commonly, you may compare the critical concerns of different theories.

New Criticism/Formalism

- Character: How does the character evolve during the story? What is unique or interesting about a character? Is the character a stereotypical action hero, a patriarchal father figure, or Madonna? How does a character interact with other characters?
- Setting: How does the setting enhance tension within the work? Do any elements in the setting foreshadow the conclusion of the piece?
- Plot:What is the conflict? How do scenes lead to a suspenseful resolution? What scenes make the plot unusual, unexpected, suspenseful?
- Point of View: Who is telling the story? Is the narrator omniscient (all knowing) or does the narrator have limited understanding?

Reader-Response Criticism

How does the text make you feel? What memories or experiences come to mind when you read? If you were the central protagonist, would you have behaved differently? Why? What values or ethics do you believe are suggested by the story? As your reading of a text progresses, what surprises you, inspires you?

Feminist Criticism

How does the story re-inscribe or contradict traditional gender roles? For example, are the male characters in "power positions" while the women are "dominated"? Are the men prone to action, decisiveness, and leadership while the female characters are passive, subordinate? Do gender roles create tension within the story? Do characters' gender roles evolve over the course of the narrative?

New Historicism Criticism

How does the story reflect the aspirations and conditions of the lower classes or upper classes? Is tension created by juxtaposing privileged, powerful positions to subordinated, dominated positions? What information about the historical context of the story helps explain the character's motivations? Who benefits from the outcome of the story or from a given character's motivation?

Media Criticism

How does the medium alter readers' interactions with the text? Has the reader employed multimedia or hypertext? What traditions from print and page design have shaped the structure of the text? In what ways has the author deviated from traditional, deductively organized linear texts?

Cite from the Work

Literary criticism involves close reading of a literary work, regardless of whether you are arguing about a particular interpretation, comparing stories or poems, or using a theory to interpret literature. Do not summarize the story. The purpose of the document is not to inform the readers, but to argue a particular interpretation. You only need to cite parts of the work that support or relate to your argument and follow the citation format required by your instructor (see Using and Citing Sources).

Below is an example from Sample Essays for English 103: Introduction to Fiction, Professor Matthew Hurt. Note how the writer uses block quotes to highlight key elements and paraphrase and summarizes the original works, using quotation marks where necessary.

> ...Twain offers a long descriptive passage of Huck and Jim's life on the raft that seems, at first glance, to celebrate the idyllic freedom symbolized by the river and nature. . . A close reading of this passage, however, shows that the river is not a privileged natural space outside of and uncontaminated by society, but is inextricably linked to the social world on the shore, which itself has positive value for Huck. Instead of seeking to escape society, Huck wants to escape the dull routines of life.

The passage abounds with lyrical descriptions of the river's natural beauty. For example, Huck's long description of the sunrise over the river captures the peaceful stillness and the visual beauty of the scene:

The first thing to see, looking away over the water, was a kind of dull line — that was the woods on t'other side — you couldn't make nothing else out; then a pale place in the sky; then more paleness, spreading around; then the river softened up, away off, and warn't black any more, but gray; . . . sometimes you could hear a sweep screaking; or jumbled up voices, it was so still, and sounds come so far; and by-and-by you could see a streak on the water which you know by the look of the streak that there's a snag there in the swift current which breaks on it and makes the streak look that way; and you see the mist curl up off of the water, and the east reddens up, and the river, and you make out a log cabin in the edge of the woods, away on the bank on t'other side of the river, . . . then the nice breeze springs up, and comes fanning you from over there, so cool and fresh, and sweet to smell, on account of the woods and the flowers; . . . and next you've got the full day, and everything smiling in the sun, and the song-birds just going at it! (129-130)

Here Huck celebrates the beauty of the natural world coming to life at the beginning of a new day. The "paleness" gradually spreading across the sky makes new objects visible which he describes in loving detail for the reader. The "nice breeze" is "cool and fresh" and "sweet to smell," and the world seems to be "smiling in the sun" as the song-birds welcome the new day.

However, Huck includes a number of details within this passage that would seem to work against the language of natural beauty. After describing the gradually brightening sky, Huck notes that "you could see little dark spots drifting along, ever so far away — trading scows, and such things; and long black streaks — rafts." The sun rise reveals not only natural objects (the brightening sky, the "snag," the "mist"), but also brings into view man-made objects ("trading scows" and "rafts") that signify human society's presence in this natural environment. Similarly, Huck speculates that the picturesque "log cabin" on the distant shore is a "woodyard, likely, and piled by them cheats so you can throw a dog through it anywheres." Here the marker of human society takes on a sinister tone of corruption as Huck describes how unscrupulous wood sellers stack wood loosely to cheat their customers. Finally, although the breeze is "sweet to smell," Huck assures the reader that this isn't always the case: "but sometimes not that way, because they've left dead fish laying around, gars, and such, and they do get pretty rank."

These signs of society's presence on the river are largely negative. The woodyard is "piled by cheats" and the stacked fish pollute the "sweet" smell of the breeze. At this point, the opposition between "good nature" and "bad society" remains intact. The signs of human presence suggest a corruption of nature's beauty. In the paragraphs that follow, however, this opposition is subtly reversed. After Huck's account of the sunrise over the river, he describes how he and Jim watch the steamboats "coughing along up stream." But when there are no steamboats or rafts to watch, he describes the scene as "solid lonesomeness" (130). No songbirds, no sweet breezes. Without human activities to watch, the scene suddenly becomes empty and "lonesome," and nothing captures Huck's attention until more rafts and boats pass by and he can watch them chopping wood or listen to them beating pans in the fog.

Cite Other Critics' Interpretations of the Work

Criticism written by advanced English majors, graduate students, and literary critics may be more about what other critics have said than about the actual text. Indeed, many critics spend more time reading criticism and arguing about critical approaches than actually reading original works. However, unless you are enrolled in a literary theory course, your instructor probably wants you to focus more on interpreting the work than discussing other critical interpretations. This does not mean, however, that you should write about a literary work "blindly." Instead, you are wise to find out what other students and critics have said about the work.

Below is a sample passage that illustrates how other critics' works can inspire an author and guide him or her in constructing a counter argument, support an author's interpretation, and provide helpful biographical information.

In her critical biography of Shirley Jackson, Lenemaja Friedman notes that when Shirley Jackson's story "The Lottery" was published in the June 28, 1948 issue of the New Yorker it received a response that "no New Yorker story had ever received": hundreds of letters poured in that were characterized by "bewilderment, speculation, and old-fashioned abuse."1 It is not hard to account for this response: Jackson's story portrays an "average" New England village with "average" citizens engaged in a deadly rite, the annual selection of a sacrificial victim by means of a public lottery, and does so quite deviously: not until well along in the story do we suspect that the "winner" will be stoned to death by the rest of the villagers.

Organization

The format for literary critiques is fairly standard:

- State your claim(s).
- Forecast your organization.
- Marshal evidence for your claim.
- Reiterate argument and elaborate on its significance.

In English classes, you may be able to assume that your readers are familiar with the work you are critiquing. Perhaps, for example, the entire class is responding to one particular work after some class discussions about it. However, if your instructor asks you to address a broader audience, you may need to provide bibliographical information for the work. In other words, you may need to cite the title, publisher, date, and pages of the work (see Citing Sources).

Literary critiques are arguments. As such, your instructors expect you to state a claim in your introduction and then provide quotes and paraphrased statements from the text to serve as evidence for your claim. Ideally, your critique will be insightful and interesting. You'll want to come up with an interpretation that isn't immediately obvious. Below are some examples of "thesis statements" or "claims" from literary critiques:

- In "The Yellow Wallpaper," by Charlotte Perkins Gilman, the protagonist is oppressed and represents the effect of the oppression of women in society. This effect is created by the use of complex symbols such as the house, the window, and the wall-paper which facilitate her oppression as well as her self expression. ["'The Yellow Wall-Paper': A Twist on Conventional Symbols" by Liselle Sant]
- "The Yellow Wallpaper" by Charlotte Gilman is a sad story of the repression that women face in the days of the late 1800's as well as being representative of the turmoil that women face today. [Critique of "The Yellow Wallpaper" by Brandi Mahon]

- "The Yellow Wallpaper," written by Charlotte Perkins Gilman, is a story of a woman, her psychological difficulties and her husband's so called therapeutic treatment of her aliments during the late 1800s. . . Gilman does well throughout the story to show with descriptive phrases just how easily and effectively the man "seemingly" wields his "maleness" to control the woman. But, with further interpretation and insight I believe Gilman succeeds in nothing more than showing the weakness of women, of the day, as active persons in their own as well as society's decision making processes instead of the strength of men as women dominating machines. "The View from the Inside" by Timothy J. Decker
- In Adventures of Huckleberry Finn, Mark Twain creates a strong opposition between the freedom of Huck and Jim's life on the raft drifting down the Mississippi River, which represents "nature," and the confining and restrictive life on the shore, which represents "society." ["'All I wanted was a change': Positive Images of Nature and Society in Chapter 19 of Adventures of Huckleberry Finn" from Professor Matthew Hurt's "Sample Essays for English 103: Introduction to Fiction"]
- In Gabriel Garcia Marquez's short story, "A Very Old Man with Enormous Wings," an unexpected visitor comes down from the sky, and seems to test the faith of a community. The villagers have a difficult time figuring out just how the very old man with enormous wings fits into their lives. Because this character does not agree with their conception of what an angel should look like, they try to determine if the aged man could actually be an angel. In trying to prove the origin of their visitor, the villagers lose faith in the possibility of him being an angel because he does not adhere to their ordered world. Marquez keeps the identity of the very old man with enormous wings ambiguous to critique the villagers and, more generally, organized religion for having a lack of faith to believe in miracles that do not comply with their master narrative. ["Prove It: A Critique of the Villagers' Faith in 'A Very Old Man with Enormous Wings'" from Sample Essays for English 103: Introduction to Fiction, Professor Matthew Hurt]

Style

Literary criticism is a fairly specialized kind of writing. Instead of writing to a general lay audience, you are writing to members of a literary community who have read a work and who developed opinions about the work—as well as a vocabulary of interpretation.

Following are some common words used by literary critics. More specialized terms can be learned by reading criticism or by referring to a good encyclopedia for criticism or writing, including the Writer's Encyclopedia:

- Protagonist: The protagonist is the major character of the story; typically the character must overcome significant challenges.
- Antagonist: The protagonist's chief nemesis; in other words, the character whom the protagonist must overcome.
- Symbols: Metaphoric language; see A Catalogue of Symbols in The Awakening by Kate Chopin
- Viewpoint: Stories are told either in the first person or third person point of view. The first person is limited to a single character, although dialog can let you guess at other characters' intentions. The third person allows readers inside the character's mind so you know what the character feels and thinks.Viewpoint can be "limited," where the character knows less than the reader, or "omniscient," where the reader can hear the thoughts and feelings of all characters. Occasionally writers will use multiple character viewpoint, which takes you from one character's perspective to another.
- Plot: Plots are a series of scenes, typically moving from a conflict situation to a resolution. To surprise readers, authors will foreshadow "false plants," which lead readers to anticipate other resolutions. The term "denouement" refers to the unraveling of the plot in the conclusion.

Reader-Response Criticism

Summary

We have examined many schools of literary criticism. Here you will find an in-depth look at one of them: Reader-Response.

The Purpose of Reader-Response

Reader-response suggests that the role of the reader is essential to the meaning of a text, for only in the reading experience does the literary work come alive. For example, in Mary Wollstonecraft Shelley's *Frankenstein* (1818), the monster doesn't exist, so to speak, until the reader reads *Frankenstein* and reanimates it to life, becoming a co-creator of the text.
Thus, the purpose of a reading response is examining, explaining, and defending your personal reaction to a text.
Your critical reading of a text asks you to explore:

- why you like or dislike the text;
- explain whether you agree or disagree with the author;
- identify the text's purpose; and
- critique the text.

There is no right or wrong answer to a reading response. Nonetheless, it is important that you demonstrate an understanding of the reading and clearly explain and support your reactions. Do not use the standard approach of just writing: *"I liked this text because it is so cool and the ending made me feel happy,"* or *"I hated it because it was stupid, and had nothing at all to do with my life, and was too negative and boring."* In writing a response you may assume the reader has already read the text. Thus, do not summarize the contents of the text at length. Instead, take a systematic, analytical approach to the text.

Write as a Scholar

When writing a reader-response write as an educated adult addressing other adults or fellow scholars. As a beginning scholar, if you write that something has nothing to do with you or does not pass *your* "Who cares?" test, but many other people think that it is important and great, readers will probably *not* agree with you that the *text* is dull or boring. Instead, they may conclude that *you* are dull and boring, that you are too immature or uneducated to understand what important things the author wrote.

Criticize with Examples

If you did not like a text, that is fine, but criticize it either from:

- *principle*, for example:
  - Is the text racist?
  - Does the text unreasonably puts down things, such as religion, or groups of people, such as women or adolescents, conservatives or democrats, etc?
  - Does the text include factual errors or outright lies? It is too dark and despairing? Is it falsely positive?
- *form*, for example:
  - Is the text poorly written?
  - Does it contain too much verbal "fat"?
  - Is it too emotional or too childish?

- Does it have too many facts and figures?
- Are there typos or other errors in the text?
- Do the ideas wander around without making a point?

In each of these cases, do not simply criticize, but give examples. As a beginning scholar, be cautious of criticizing any text as "confusing" or "crazy," since readers might simply conclude that *you* are too ignorant or slow to understand and appreciate it.

The Structure of a Reader-Response Essay

Choosing a text to study is the first step in writing a reader-response essay. Once you have chosen the text, your challenge is to connect with it and have a "conversation" with the text.

In the beginning paragraph of your reader-response essay, be sure to mention the following:

- title of the work to which you are responding;
- the author; and
- the main thesis of the text.

Then, do your best to answer the questions below. Remember, however, that you are writing an essay, not filling out a short-answer worksheet. You do not need to work through these questions in order, one by one, in your essay. Rather, your paper as a whole should be sure to address these questions in some way.

- *What does the text have to do with you, personally, and with your life (past, present or future)?* It is not acceptable to write that the text has NOTHING to do with you, since just about everything humans can write has to do in some way with every other human.
- *How much does the text agree or clash with your view of the world, and what you consider right and wrong?* Use several quotes as examples of how it agrees with and supports what you think about the world, about right and wrong, and about what you think it is to be human. Use quotes and examples to discuss how the text disagrees with what you think about the world and about right and wrong.
- *What did you learn, and how much were your views and opinions challenged or changed by this text, if at all? Did the text communicate with you? Why or why not?* Give examples of how your views might have changed or been strengthened (or perhaps, of why the text failed to convince you, the way it is). Please do not write "I agree with everything the author wrote," since everybody disagrees about something, even if it is a tiny point. Use quotes to illustrate your points of challenge, or where you were persuaded, or where it left you cold.
- *How well does the text address things that you, personally, care about and consider important to the world? How does it address things that are important to your family, your community, your ethnic group, to people of your economic or social class or background, or your faith tradition? If not, who does or did the text serve? Did it pass the "Who cares?" test?* Use quotes from the text to illustrate.
- *What can you praise about the text? What problems did you have with it?* Reading and writing "critically" does not mean the same thing as "criticizing," in everyday language (complaining or griping, fault-finding, nit-picking). Your "critique" can and should be positive and praise the text if possible, as well as pointing out problems, disagreements and shortcomings.
- *How well did you enjoy the text (or not) as entertainment or as a work of art?* Use quotes or examples to illustrate the quality of the text as art or entertainment. Of course, be aware that some texts are not meant to be entertainment or art: a news report or textbook, for instance, may be neither entertaining or artistic, but may still be important and successful.

For the conclusion, you might want to discuss:

- your overall reaction to the text;
- whether you would read something else like this in the future;

- whether you would read something else by this author; and
- if would you recommend read this text to someone else and why.

Key Takeaways

- In reader-response, the reader is essential to the meaning of a text for they bring the text to life.
- The purpose of a reading response is examining, explaining, and defending your personal reaction to a text.
- When writing a reader-response, write as an educated adult addressing other adults or fellow scholars.
- As a beginning scholar, be cautious of criticizing any text as "boring," "crazy," or "dull." If you do criticize, base your criticism on the principles and form of the text itself.
- The challenge of a reader-response is to show how you connected with the text.

Examples

Reader-Response Essay Example

To Misread or to Rebel: A Woman's Reading of "The Secret Life of Walter Mitty"

At its simplest, reading is "an activity that is guided by the text; this must be processed by the reader who is then, in turn, affected by what he has processed" (Iser 63). The text is the compass and map, the reader is the explorer. However, the explorer cannot disregard those unexpected boulders in the path which he or she encounters along the journey that are not written on the map. Likewise, the woman reader does not come to the text without outside influences. She comes with her experiences as a woman—a professional woman, a divorcée, a single mother. Her reading, then, is influenced by her experiences. So when she reads a piece of literature like "The Secret Life of Walter Mitty" by James Thurber, which paints a highly negative picture of Mitty's wife, the woman reader is forced to either misread the story and accept Mrs. Mitty as a domineering, mothering wife, or rebel against that picture and become angry at the society which sees her that way.

Due to pre-existing sociosexual standards, women see characters, family structures, even societal structures from the bottom as an oppressed group rather than from a powerful position on the top, as men do. As Louise Rosenblatt states: a reader's "tendency toward identification [with characters or events] will certainly be guided by our preoccupations at the time we read. Our problems and needs may lead us to focus on those characters and situations through which we may achieve the satisfactions, the balanced vision, or perhaps merely the unequivocal motives unattained in our own lives" (38). A woman reader who feels chained by her role as a housewife is more likely to identify with an individual who is oppressed or feels trapped than the reader's executive husband is. Likewise, a woman who is unable to have children might respond to a story of a child's death more emotionally than a woman who does not want children. However, if the perspective of a woman does not match that of the male author whose work she is reading, a woman reader who has been shaped by a male-dominated society is forced to misread the text, reacting to the "words on the page in one way rather than another because she operates according to the same set of rules that the author used to generate them" (Tompkins xvii). By accepting the author's perspective and reading the text as he intended, the woman reader is forced to disregard her own, female perspective. This, in turn, leads to a concept called "asymmetrical contingency," described by Iser as that which occurs "when Partner A gives up trying to implement his own behavioral plan and without resistance follows that of Partner B. He adapts himself to and is absorbed by the behavioral strategy of B" (164). Using this argument, it becomes clear that a woman reader (Partner A) when faced with a text written by a man (Partner B) will most likely succumb to the perspective of the writer and she is thus forced to misread the text. Or, she could rebel against the text and raise an angry, feminist voice in protest.

James Thurber, in the eyes of most literary critics, is one of the foremost American humorists of the 20th century, and his short story "The Secret Life of Walter Mitty" is believed to have "ushered in a major [literary] period ... where the individual can maintain his self ... an appropriate way of assaulting rigid forms" (Elias 432). The rigid form in Thurber's story is Mrs. Mitty, the main character's wife. She is portrayed by Walter Mitty as a horrible, mothering nag. As a way of escaping her constant griping, he imagines fantastic daydreams which carry him away from Mrs. Mitty's voice. Yet she repeatedly interrupts his reveries and Mitty responds to her as though she is "grossly unfamiliar, like a strange woman who had yelled at him in the crowd" (286). Not only is his wife annoying to him, but she is also distant and removed from what he cares about, like a stranger. When she does speak to him, it seems reflective of the way a mother would speak to a child. For example, Mrs. Mitty asks, "'Why don't you wear your gloves? Have you lost your gloves?' Walter Mitty reached in a pocket and brought out the gloves. He put them on, but after she had turned and gone into the building and he had driven on to a red light, he took them off again" (286). Mrs. Mitty's care for her husband's health is seen as nagging to Walter Mitty, and the audience is amused that he responds like a child and does the opposite of what Mrs. Mitty asked of him. Finally, the clearest way in which Mrs. Mitty is portrayed as a burdensome wife is at the end of the piece when Walter, waiting for his wife to exit the store, imagines that he is facing "the firing squad; erect and motionless, proud and disdainful, Walter Mitty the Undefeated, inscrutable to the last" (289). Not only is Mrs. Mitty portrayed as a mothering, bothersome hen, but she is ultimately described as that which will be the death of Walter Mitty.

Mrs. Mitty is a direct literary descendant of the first woman to be stereotyped as a nagging wife, Dame Van Winkle, the creation of the American writer, Washington Irving. Likewise, Walter Mitty is a reflection of his dreaming predecessor, Rip Van Winkle, who falls into a deep sleep for a hundred years and awakes to the relief of finding out that his nagging wife has died. Judith Fetterley explains in her book, The Resisting Reader, how such a portrayal of women forces a woman who reads "Rip Van Winkle" and other such stories "to find herself excluded from the experience of the story" so that she "cannot read the story without being assaulted by the negative images of women it presents" (10). The result, it seems, is for a woman reader of a story like "Rip Van Winkle" or "The Secret Life of Walter Mitty" to either be excluded from the text, or accept the negative images of women the story puts forth. As Fetterley points out, "The consequence for the female reader is a divided self. She is asked to identify with Rip and against herself, to scorn the amiable sex and act just like it, to laugh at Dame Van Winkle and accept that she represents 'woman,' to be at once both repressor and repressed, and ultimately to realize that she is neither" (11). Thus, a woman is forced to misread the text and accept "woman as villain." as Fetterley names it, or rebel against both the story and its message.

So how does a woman reader respond to this portrayal of Mrs. Mitty? If she were to follow Iser's claim, she would defer to the male point of view presented by the author. She would sympathize with Mitty, as Thurber wants us to do, and see domineering women in her own life that resemble Mrs. Mitty. She may see her mother and remember all the times that she nagged her about zipping up her coat against the bitter winter wind. Or the female reader might identify Mrs. Mitty with her controlling mother-in-law and chuckle at Mitty's attempts to escape her control, just as her husband tries to escape the criticism and control of his own mother. Iser's ideal female reader would undoubtedly look at her own position as mother and wife and would vow to never become such a domineering person. This reader would probably also agree with a critic who says that "Mitty has a wife who embodies the authority of a society in which the husband cannot function" (Lindner 440). She could see the faults in a relationship that is too controlled by a woman and recognize that a man needs to feel important and dominant in his relationship with his wife. It could be said that the female reader would agree completely with Thurber's portrayal of the domineering wife. The female reader could simply misread the text.

Or, the female reader could rebel against the text. She could see Mrs. Mitty as a woman who is trying to do her best to keep her husband well and cared for. She could see Walter as a man with a fleeting grip on reality who daydreams that he is a fighter pilot, a brilliant surgeon, a gun expert, or a military hero, when he actually is a poor driver with a slow reaction time to a green traffic light. The female reader could read critics of Thurber who say that by allowing his wife to dominate him, Mitty becomes a "non-hero in a civilization in which women are winning the battle of the sexes" (Hasley 533) and become angry that a woman's fight for equality is seen merely as a battle between the sexes. She could read Walter's daydreams as his attempt to dominate his wife, since all of his fantasies center on him in traditional roles of power. This, for most women, would cause anger at Mitty (and indirectly Thurber) for creating and promoting a society which believes that women need to stay subservient to men. From a male point of view, it becomes a battle of the sexes. In a woman's eyes, her reading is simply a struggle for equality within the text and in the world outside that the text reflects.

It is certain that women misread "The Secret Life of Walter Mitty." I did. I found myself initially wishing that Mrs. Mitty would just let Walter daydream in peace. But after reading the story again and paying attention to the portrayal of Mrs. Mitty, I realized that it is imperative that women rebel against the texts that would oppress them. By misreading a text, the woman reader understands it in a way that is conventional and acceptable to the literary world. But in so doing, she is also distancing herself from the text, not fully embracing it or its meaning in her life. By rebelling against the text, the female reader not only has to understand the point of view of the author and the male audience, but she also has to formulate her own opinions and create a sort of dialogue between the text and herself. Rebelling against the text and the stereotypes encourages an active dialogue between the woman and the text which, in turn, guarantees an active and (most likely) angry reader response. I became a resisting reader.

Works Cited

Elias, Robert H. "James Thurber: The Primitive, the Innocent, and the Individual." *Contemporary Literary Criticism*. Vol. 5. Ed. Dedria Bryfonski. Detroit: Gale Research, 1980. 431–32. Print.

Fetterley, Judith. *The Resisting Reader*. Bloomington: Indiana UP, 1978. Print.

Hasley, Louis. "James Thurber: Artist in Humor." *Contemporary Literary Criticism*. Vol. 11. Ed. Dedria Bryfonski. Detroit: Gale Research, 1980. 532–34. Print.

Iser, Wolfgang. *The Act of Reading: A Theory of Aesthetic Response*. Baltimore: Johns Hopkins UP, 1981. Print.

Lindner, Carl M. "Thurber's Walter Mitty—The Underground American Hero." *Contemporary Literary Criticism*. Vol. 5. Ed. Dedria Bryfonski. Detroit: Gale Research, 1980. 440–41. Print.

Rosenblatt, Louise M. *Literature as Exploration*. New York: MLA, 1976. Print.

Thurber, James. "The Secret Life of Walter Mitty." *Literature: An Introduction to Critical Reading*. Ed. William Vesterman. Fort Worth: Harcourt Brace, 1993. 286–89. Print.

Tompkins, Jane P. "An Introduction to Reader-Response Criticism." *Reader Response Criticism: From Formalism to Post-Structuralism*. Ed. Jane P. Tompkins. Baltimore: Johns Hopkins UP, 1980. ix-xxvi. Print.

Troubleshoot Your Reading

Sometimes reading may **seem** difficult, you might have trouble getting started, or other challenges will surface. Here are some troubleshooting ideas.

Problem: "Sometimes I put my reading off or don't have time to do it, and then when I do have time, well, I'm out of time."

Suggestions: That's a problem, for sure. I always suggest to students that rather than trying to do a bunch of reading at once, they try to do a little bit every day. That makes it easier.

If you're stuck up against a deadline with no reading done, one suggestion is to do some good pre-reading. That should at least give you the idea of the main topic.

Another idea is to divide the total pages assigned by the number of available days, figuring out how many pages you'll need to read each day to finish the assignment. Sometimes approaching the text in smaller pieces like this can make it feel more doable. Also, once you figure out how long it takes you to read, say, five pages, you can predict how much time it will take to read a larger section.

Problem: "If I don't understand some part of the reading, I just skip over it and hope someone will explain it later in class."

Suggestions: Not understanding reading can be frustrating—and it can make it hard to succeed on your assignments. The best suggestion is to talk with your teacher. Let them know you don't understand the reading, and they should be able to help.

Another suggestion is to read sentence by sentence. Be sure you understand each word—if you don't, look them up. As you read, master each sentence before going on to the next one, and then, at the end of a paragraph, stop and summarize the entire paragraph, reflecting on what you just read.

Yet another idea: use the Web and do a search for the title of the reading followed by the word 'analysis.' Reading what other people have said about the text may help you get past your stuck points. If you're in a face-to-face classroom, asking a question in class will encourage discussion and will also help your fellow students, who may have the same confusions.

Problem: "I really don't like to read that much, so I read pretty fast and tend to stick with the obvious meanings. But then the teacher is always asking us to dig deeper and try to figure out what the author really meant. I get so frustrated with that!"

Suggestions: College-level writing tends to have multiple layers of significance. The easiest way to think about this is by separating the "obvious or surface meaning" from the "buried treasure meaning." This can actually be one of the most fun parts of a reading—you get to play detective. As you read, try to ask questions of the text: Why? Who? Where? For what reason? These questions will help you think more deeply about the text.

Problem: "Sometimes I jump to conclusions about what a text means and then later find out I wasn't understanding it completely."

Suggestions: This usually happens when we read too quickly and don't engage with the text. The best way to avoid this is to slow down and take time with the text, following all the guidelines for effective and critical reading.

Problem: "When a text suggests an idea I strongly disagree with, I can't seem to go any further."

Suggestions: Aristotle was known for saying, "It is the mark of an educated mind to be able to entertain a thought without accepting it." As a college student, you must be ready to explore and examine a wide range of ideas, whether you agree with them or not. In approaching texts with an open and willing mind, you leave yourself ready to engage with a wide world of ideas—many of which you may not have encountered before. This is what college is all about.

Problem: "I'm a slow reader. It takes me a long time to read material, and sometimes the amount of assigned reading panics me."

Suggestions: Two thoughts. One, the more you read, the easier it gets: like anything, reading improves with practice. And two, you'll probably find your reading is most effective if you try to do a little bit every day rather than several hours of reading all at one time. Plan ahead! Be aware of what you need to read and divide it up among the available days. Reading 100 pages in a week may seem overwhelming, but reading 15 pages a day will be easier. Be sure to read when you're fresh, too, rather than at day's end, when you're exhausted.

Problem: "Sometimes the teacher assigns content in an area I really know nothing about. I want to be an accountant. Why should I read philosophy or natural history, and how am I supposed to understand them?"

Suggestions: By reading a wide variety of texts, we don't just increase our knowledge base—we also make our minds work. This kind of "mental exercise" teaches the brain and prepares it to deal with all kinds of critical and innovative thinking. It also helps train us to different reading and writing tasks, even when they're not familiar to us.

Problem: "When I examine a text, I tend to automatically accept what it says. But the teacher is always encouraging us to ask questions and not make assumptions."

Suggestions:What you're doing is reading as a reader—reading for yourself and making your own assumptions. The teacher wants you to reach for the next level by reading critically. By engaging with the text and digging through it as if you're on an archaeological expedition, you'll discover even more about the text. This can be fun, and it also helps train your brain to explore texts with an analytic eye.

Problem: "I really hate reading. I've found I can skip the readings, read the Sparks Notes, and get by just fine."

Suggestions: First, if you aren't familiar with Sparks Notes, it's an online site that provides summary and analysis of many literary texts and other materials, and students often use this to either replace reading or to better understand materials. You may be able to get by, at least for a while, with reading Sparks Notes alone, for they do a decent basic job of summarizing content and talking about simple themes. But Sparks isn't good at reading texts deeply or considering deep analysis, which means a Sparks-only approach will result in your missing a lot of what the text includes.

You'll also be missing some great experiences. The more you read, the easier reading becomes. The more you read deeply and critically and the more comfortable you become with analyzing texts, the easier that process becomes. And as your textual skills become stronger, you'll find yourself more successful with all of your college studies, too. Reading remains a vital college (and life!) skill—the more you practice reading, the better you'll be at it. And honestly, reading can be fun, too– not to mention a great way to relax and an almost instant stress reducer.

Irony

Defining Irony

Irony is all about noticing contrast. No noticing by you = inaccurate interpretations.

Verbal irony occurs when the intended meaning and the stated meaning are different—and usually opposite. Huh? Let me clarify. Irony is when the connotation is the opposite of the denotation. Connotations are the contexts, the situations and feelings around a word. Denotations are the dictionary definitions surrounding a word.

When these don't match up, a space is created. You see that space, and you react to it by giving that situation meaning.

Exemplifying Verbal Irony

Irony is like sarcasm. For example, if I said "That's a **Great** tie" to someone with an extremely ugly tie, you would hear the tone in which I said it, right? You could look up "Great" in the dictionary and find that it means good, admirable, wonderful, etc. But "good" is opposite of the usage, right? I mean, I said it so he'd see it was **ugly and bad**. Some critics dispute this connection between sarcasm and irony.

How to Approach Irony

Ask questions about irony. Use the term in your discussions and your papers.

Do you think you'll see irony in the works we'll read? Will it be used in the same ways?

If irony is the difference between the stated meaning and the intended meaning, then is it used by all cultures?

Dramatic and Situation Irony: The Sidekick Types

Dramatic irony arises when an audience knows more about a situation than the character(s). The characters say or do something whose significance they don't know. For example, you go to *Oedipus the King* knowing that he has married his mom. You know this, he doesn't. So, as he discovers this, you watch and appreciate it.

Situational irony would result from a gapping—a difference—between what readers expect and what actually occurs. This is not to be confused with the popular misconception that irony occurs when something surprising or coincidental occurs. (Think of that 90s song by Alanis Morrissette, "Isn't it Ironic?" which actually featured nonexamples of irony. Now *that's* ironic!)

The Irony" by Jack Sirichumsaeng is licensed under CC BY 2.0

Binary Patterns: A Western Obsession

This or that? Me or you? I or thou? Subject or object?

Along with these basic either/or questions, Western thought is built on other key binaries.

A binary is an either/or choice like the zeroes and ones making up DVDs or other digital codes. While some things lend themselves to "this or that" choices, we know that the world is often much more complicated. The answer "Pepsi or Coke?" might define a person privately, but whether you like one or the other may not carry much public meaning. Ironically, it did carry meaning in the 80s during the Cola Wars.

These either/or choices often have strange histories. For instance, the tragedy/comedy binary informs genres on television and in literature. It is based on a thinker, Aristotle, who was not even approving of literature. Dig into the history of tragedy and comedy and you will find some strangeness. For instance, tragedy was supposed by Aristotle to feature someone making a choice which leads inevitably to their downfall, which we witness and feel *catharsis*, a sense of purging out of both ends. . .! Weird enough for you? It makes a certain amount of sense, just as listening to a blues song makes us feel happy, but it's what we'd call *contingent*: based on a quirky, particular set of happenings that did not have to occur. So binaries are contingent. (Call this the non-tragic theory of approaching binaries.) And comedy was supposed to involve a mating and joining offstage in early Greek comedies—which were held at the festival of the god Dionysus, at which, originally, his devotees called Maenads were said to mate with willing victims on mountainsides, after which they would rend apart the sacrificial victim. And this is what informs our genres—and has done so for 2,500 years. So I'd add necessary vs. contingent as a binary that can be useful.

For more on the strangeness of binaries, you might do a search for *humor theory* or look at the history of academia (gowns, gavels, graduations. . .). Or if you're talking good or evil, one might look at how evil always comes back (Sauron, Voldemort). Weirdly enough, this even contributes to a type of cannibalism whereby an enemy's body is eaten so that his soul can be erased–for a time–from the eternal battlefield. As the cliche goes, "The truth is stranger than fiction." In fields like literary analysis, there is no "capital-T Truth." That idea of there being one would go back to Plato and his theory of Forms.

So these issues have histories of which we should become aware. As a critical reader, it is important for you to take note of binaries and gauge their effects. Though they may exclude other choices, it is the case that humans notice contrasts and oppositions.

Binaries are crutches, tools. They can work but can put blinders on what we notice. Early in stages of the writing or critical thinking processes, they can be useful.

> Which side of a binary does the author notice or value more?
>
> Which views are portrayed as negative?
>
> What is undervalued or missing from a given text?

In a writing course, then, you might create a persuasive essay that argues one side against another. We contribute to these ongoing debates most thoughtfully if we realize that they arguments will continue, however well we write about them! Just don't fall into the trap of thinking that the world is either/or, comforting as that notion may be.

When Interpreting, Avoid Relativism (Because I Think So)

Get the title?

So that we avoid the major problem of relativism, heed the following warnings:

- If you don't happen to resemble an author's audience, don't attack the audience that writer appealed to
- What I often see in essays based on model reading assignments is reactive rather than flexible reading. For instance, I often teach skeptic Michael Shermer's book *The Science of Good and Evil*. In online discussion posts, I'll see people react with "Well, he is sarcastic but people already agreeing with him would find that funny. I just find it offensive." Then the student writer proceeds to do that Samuel L. Jackson "Allow me to retort" move from *Pulp Fiction* (Tarantino), trying to match snarkiness with Shermer or to refute him. When they get really desperate, they go to the web and find attack sites. "Allow me to retort!" is not our purpose in most academic writing. Later in the course, though, we will cover refutals, which are appropriately-handled counterarguments.
- "It's true for me" doesn't work here. I see this happen a lot in definition or rhetorical analysis essays that often start courses. If the writing is rhetorical analysis, cut out one's views from this process . . . it is supposed to be about form, not content, so if you start getting too much into content, you're not doing a formal analysis. In fact, to the extent that you go off (or gush in support) at the writer, you're not doing your job of analyzing. And definitions—while they may not seem arguable—actually contain areas of genuine, ongoing disagreement that we would do well to recognize.
- Academic writing is public, not private. Don't overuse *I* or *you*. Filtering this through the self is a bad idea. As Charlton Heston says of the mystery food in the movie *Soylent Green* "It's people!" (Fleischer). Don't serve us yourself . . . your friend Willie Wonka says "But that is called cannibalism, my dear children, and is in fact frowned upon in most societies" (Burton). I'm having fun with this, but the idea remains: The chapter is the source, not the self. Subjectivism pushes discussion only through our limited selves.

> I realize I am only going against the whole of American culture by stating this. . .

In interpreting literature, you may be right. . . just not only because you think so!

Finding Literary Criticism

Literary criticism is writing that explores the meaning of works of literature. Among other things, literary criticism analyzes works of literature in terms of their historical and literary context. It can also examine a particular type of literature or compare different works by the same author or works by different authors.

Literary criticism analyzes fiction, poetry, drama and some types of non-fiction by considering key issues such as plot, character, setting, theme, imagery, and voice. Literary criticism may also consider the effectiveness of a work of literature, but it's important to note that in this context the word "criticism" doesn't simply mean finding fault with the writing but rather looking at it from a critical or analytical viewpoint in order to understand it better.

It's also important to note that literary criticism involves more than just summarizing the plot or offering biographical information about the author.

Evaluating Sources of Literary Criticism

If you're asked to find *scholarly* sources of literary criticism, you should look for journals that are peer-reviewed. In other words, before articles are accepted for publication in the journal, they're reviewed by other scholars. Articles in a scholarly journal will also include citations for other works that are referenced. Scholarly books, likewise, will document their sources and are usually written by someone affiliated with a college or university and published by a university press. Sometimes a book of literary criticism is actually a compilation of articles that have previously appeared in journals. If that's the case, you can try to ascertain the nature of the journal in question.

Even if you know an article has come from a peer-reviewed journal, you may still wonder about its relevance, particularly if the work or author you're researching is one that's been studied extensively. One way to get more information about a source is to type the title of the article into Google Scholar and see how many times it's been cited. The higher the number, the more likely it is that the article is influential—or at least controversial. You can do a similar search to learn more about the reputation of a journal, book, or author.

Finally, when looking for critical work, don't rely on sources like SparkNotes, which provide help for students but are not considered reputable scholarly sources.

Sources of Literary Criticism

An ideal place to begin your search for literary criticism is the English subject guide on the TAMU libraries' website: library.tamu.edu/subject-guides/English. We also recommend their handout "Starting Points for Literary Criticism."

Here are some of the useful links you'll find on the library website:

ABELL (Annual Bibliography of English Language and Literature): This database includes English-language articles, books, and reviews published since 1920 on English language and literature, traditional culture and bibliography. It also includes unpublished dissertations from the years 1920-1999. It covers English, American and Commonwealth writers.

Academic Search Complete: EBSCO: This online database, a general source for scholarly works in a variety of disciplines, covers works on the literature of all languages. The database covers almost 11,000 publications and offers full text on about 5,000 of those.

Modern Language Association (MLA) International Bibliograghy: This is a key resource for information on literature, linguistics, and folklore. The database includes more than 4,000 journals in the field, as well as books, collections of essays, dissertations and other bibliographies. It covers work from 1920 to the present. When searching, you can specify the kind of references you want, i.e. books, journals, websites. You can also choose only those listings that link to a full text version of the material. You can also set the search parameters to show you only scholarly (peer reviewed) journals or you can request entries within a certain timeframe, such as only those published after the year 2000.

The TAMU library's English subject page also links to databases geared to specific time periods (such as Brepolis Medieval Bibliographies) and those pertaining to certain types of literature (such as the Children's Literature Database).

A few other resources you may want to investigate:

African American Review: This online journal specifically focuses on African American literature and ethnic studies, "[providing] a lively exchange between writers and scholars in the arts, humanities, and social sciences who hold diverse perspectives on African American literature and culture." The website features full-text online access to back issues.

American Literary Scholarship: This journal offers current critical analysis of American literature. Among the writers discussed are Whitman, Hawthorne, Poe, Melville, Twain, and Faulkner. It is available in print at PS3.A47 or electronically.

A Handbook to Literature: A collection of defined literary terms, movements, and theories, this text is edited by William Harmon and C. Hugh Holman and is easy to use. It is available in print at PN41 .H355 2000.

Literary Research: A Guide to Reference Sources for the Study of Literature in English and Related Topics: This book, published in 1993, is helpful for locating other bibliographies for English and American literature by period. It also provides a list of related topics (music, science, art, etc.) that may also be useful. The book is edited by James Harner and is available in print at Z2011.H34 1993.

The Year's Work in English Studies: This bibliography lists and assesses the scholarly literary criticism published in a given year. The information is presented according to major literary periods, such as "American Literature to 1900" and can also be searched by author. It can be accessed at: ywes.oxfordjournals.org/

Also recommended for you:

Literary Terms

Analyzing Novels & Short Stories

Analyzing Plays
Analyzing Poetry

3. WRITING ABOUT LITERATURE IN ACADEMIC SETTINGS

Academic Writing Review

Remember these items as you edit your essay. They can make a big difference. I hope this sort of things helps. It's incomplete, but it's a start.

Think of the purpose of your paper, and of how each paragraph helps you fulfill it. As I mentioned elsewhere, the essays in the book aren't pure models for the academic writing we will be doing. What we write should look more solid, even if it is less flashy. You'll need to cite details and quickly follow up on their meanings through strong interpretation of the cited material. Topic sentences and transitions are key elements as well.

Thesis/Introduction

- Set up your thesis; it's best to place it near/at the end of the introduction.
- Two-part introductions or other types of unconventional introductions tend not to work. Why? The writer tends not to do the jobs of the introduction. These include previewing the rest of the essay, setting up the thesis (and showing other sides to the point you're trying to prove).
- Make sure your introduction promises what you'll do. (Don't say "In this essay I'll. . ." or "First, I'll discuss," though. Just go ahead and start previewing the paper.)
- Avoid using "I" as much as possible.
- "Don't use don't." Avoid contractions—as I haven't in this posting!
- "Oh, I almost forgot." Be careful of the formal writing voice you need to use. Don't sound chatty. I want you to write more formally than you are in your postings.

Thesis Checklist

With the thesis statement, keep the following questions in mind. They might work for most academic writing. Get good at asking follow-up questions of your own so that you can edit your work.

- Is it a statement?
- Is it a complex sentence? (Most good thesis statements provide an overview of what you'll go into. Therefore, most good thesis statements need to be complex sentences.)
- Does it take into account your 2-3 main reasons? (These are usually your body paragraph topics, right?)
- Does it take different sides into account? You want to appear fair, and the thesis is a great place for you to frame the merits and weak points of contending sides.
- Where will you locate this statement? Usually, though not always, we put the thesis either at the end of the introduction, or near the end. This allows us to set up the thesis carefully. Your introduction should take care to preview what you'll get into in the body paragraphs, just as the conclusion reviews what you did.

Paragraphing

- Starting/ending paragraphs with quotes is often a warning sign. Why is that?
- When editing, check for strong topic sentences. Are they there? (Go a step further: did your major topics make it into the introduction as preview material, and into the conclusion as review?)
- Citing properly matters. If readers are wondering where a source begins or ends, they are not attending to the content you chose to cite. Their job of appreciating what you brought to the essay is made impossible by citing problems.
- Do interpret between quotes. Avoid stacking two or three quotes. I'm more interested in what you have to write about the quotes than what's in the quotes.

- Fix the problems with Smart Quotes. (See that mini-lecture in Module 1.)
- Are your paragraphs connected directly to the thesis? How? (Is the connection clear enough?)
- End paragraphs well. (Consider **transitions** as well as restatement of topic sentence.)

Interpretation

Perhaps the biggest frustration is that many of you include great quotes. They're promising, they're useful, they're. . . sitting there! Use the words in the quote. Get readers to see their meaning. If you aren't doing some work at this level, then you aren't interpreting. Good readers are waiting for you to prove your points through close reading of the text. (Sell us on what the words mean. That takes some time.)

Conclusion

- Lack of a conclusion will seriously affect your readers' reactions to the essay (and thus, your grade).
- I value strong conclusions that restate your points and remind readers about *how* you proved your claim(s).
- Do not add new information to the conclusion.
- Restate your thesis at a strategic point. Otherwise, readers will not remember your work soon afterwards—or a week from now.
- Be detailed: this is where you remind us of what you did.
- Don't write two or three sentences and "be done with it."

How to Avoid Plagiarizing

Tip #1: Make Sure You Are Very Certain about What Is and is Not Plagiarism

Tip #2: Give Yourself Plenty of Time to Complete an Assignment

Running out of time on an assignment is a main cause of plagiarism. Rushing to meet a deadline can result in carelessness (leading to unintentional plagiarism – see the next tip) and the desire to find a quick, easy solution such as copying someone else's work. Don't give in to that temptation! Plagiarism is a serious academic offense, and the chance of being caught (which is likely) is not worth it.

Avoid this situation entirely by starting your assignment far ahead of time and planning out when you will complete each phase of the writing process. Even if your teacher does not require you to turn in materials for each stage of the writing process (i.e. brainstorming, creating a thesis statement, outlining, drafting, revising, etc.), set your own personal deadlines for each step along the way and make sure to give yourself more than enough time to finish everything.

Tip #3: Document Everything

Plagiarism isn't always a conscious choice. Sometimes it can be unintentional, typically resulting from poor documentation of one's sources during the research phase. For example, sometimes students will write down an idea from a source using words identical to or very close to those in the original, but then when they go to write their paper forget that the material was not already in their own words. Adopting good research habits can prevent this type of plagiarism.

Print, photocopy, or scan the relevant pages of every source you are using (including the title and copyright pages, since they have the information you need for a bibliographic citation). When taking notes by hand (or typed into a file), list the bibliographic information for each source you use. Make sure to put quotation marks around any wordings taken directly from the source (and note the page where you found it), and remember to put everything else into your own words right away, so there is no danger of forgetting something is a quote. Documenting where all of your ideas, information, quotations, and so on come from is an important step in avoiding plagiarism.

Tip #4: Don't Include Too Much Material Taken from Other Sources

Writing assignments are about your ideas, your interpretations, and your ability to synthesize information. You should use relevant sources to support your ideas using evidence such as quotes, paraphrases, and summaries, as well as statistics and other data. But don't lose sight of the fact that your argument is central! Including too much material from other sources can result in a paper that feels like it has been pasted together from a variety of authors, rather than a cohesive essay. Such papers also run a much higher risk of setting off plagiarism warnings in SafeAssign or other plagiarism-detecting software. Try to find a balance: use enough evidence from credible sources to prove your points but don't let the ideas of others take the place of your own thoughts.

Tips for integrating sources into your research.

Tip #5: When in Doubt, Give a Citation

There are certain types of information – typically referred to as common knowledge – that don't require a citation when you include them in your writing. These are facts that are widely known and can be easily found in a number of sources. They are not ideas that originated with one particular source. Examples include scientific facts (for example, that solid, liquid, and gas are three states of matter), general historical information (for example, that George Washington was the first US president), or even information commonly known to certain groups of people but not others (for example, most musicians know that a C major triad includes the notes C, E, and G, even though many non-musicians would have no idea what a C major triad is).

For everything else, you need to include a citation, regardless of whether you are quoting directly from the source, paraphrasing it, or giving a summary. If you are at all unsure whether something qualifies as common knowledge or not, give a citation. You can also consult a more experienced figure in your field, such as your instructor, to find out if something counts as common knowledge or not.

In academic writing, the **"Quote Sandwich" approach** is useful for incorporating other writers' voices into your essays. It gives meaning and context to a quote, and helps you avoid plagiarism. This 3-step approach offers your readers a deeper understanding of what the quote is and how it relates to your essay's goals.

1. **Step 1**: Provide context for the source. If you haven't used it yet in the essay, tell us the source's title and author (if known), and any other information that's relevant, like the purpose of the organization that published it, for instance.
2. **Step 2**: Provide the quote itself. Be sure to format correctly and use quotation marks around exact language.
3. **Step 3**: Provide a summary and/or analysis of what the quote says, and how it relates to the subject matter of your essay and your thesis.

Self-Diagnosis of One's Writing Ailments can be Fun!

Is using plain language the law?

The following humorous site, "How to Write Good," is located on the *Plainlanguage.gov* page. It lists and breaks several writing rules. In breaking the rules, they illustrate them. It is an engaging way to learn the rules of English—especially since they always seem to have exceptions.

Note that not all of the rules are really rules anymore. For instance, the one about ending a sentence on a preposition is one we have largely gotten out of. (Get it?)

Introduction to Writing About Literature

The best of a book is not the thought which it contains, but the thought which it suggests; just as the charm of music dwells not in the tones but in the echoes of our hearts. – Oliver Wendell Holmes

Learning Outcomes

- Find and use historical sources to discuss the historical context of a literary work
- Find and use literary criticism in your analysis of literary works
- Cite sources correctly using MLA format

How not to Write the Introduction and Conclusion

Overview

The opening and closing of anything one writes become increasingly important with busy readers. The way a writers introduces the subject to readers could determine how they will approach the ideas or even if they will continue reading. The introduction of a research paper is especially important because research papers tend to be long and complex.

The Introduction

Your introduction should accomplish key goals:

- Grab attention. Open with a quote, fact, statistic, or short narrative.
- Convince readers that your paper is worth reading. Demonstrate the importance of your subject with details.
- Explain the basic context of your subject
- Narrow the topic to a specific thesis that clearly states your position

You may use the introduction to explain or justify research methods or address readers' objections.

The Conclusion

A conclusion should accomplish specific tasks:

- Bring the paper to an interesting, logical end
- End with a final fact, quote, or comment to provoke readers to accept your ideas and think about the topic on their own
- Reinforce the main points of the essay without unnecessary repetition
- Restate your thesis in a strategic spot where it will have the most effect on readers
- Speculate about future action

TRITE, CLICHED BEGINNINGS AND ENDINGS SEND MESSAGES

Remember, readers' memories are not very powerful. Remind them of the specific things they should take away from the reading of your essay. Just avoid saying "In conclusion, I will review _____ and _____," because this patterned ending sounds false. In fact, avoid every writing "In conclusion" to start a paragraph which is, obviously, the last!

Often, I mine the words for my introduction from the conclusion. By that point, I know more about what I have accomplished in those body paragraphs. I can copy and paste (and reword) my conclusion, which appears sharper than the original introduction. This process might work for you, and it's easy with the copy and paste commands. Then, go back and rewrite a conclusion, making sure it's not just parroting the wording of the introduction. Call this the Robin Hood Principle: Stealing from the rich to give to the poor.

Read aloud both your introduction and conclusion. Hear how they sound, and make sure they are of similar quality and length without seeming identical. Lastly, avoid "According to Dictionary.com, _____ is" or any "Society verbs _____" constructions. ("Society views the media as bad.") Provable? Arguable?)

Using Sources: Blending Source Material with Your Own Work

When working with sources, many students worry they are simply regurgitating ideas that others formulated. That is why it is important for you to develop your own assertions, organize your findings so that your own ideas are still the thrust of the paper, and take care not to rely too much on any one source, or your paper's content might be controlled too heavily by that source.

In practical terms, some ways to develop and back up your assertions include:

Blend sources with your assertions. Organize your sources before and as you write so that they blend, even within paragraphs. Your paper—both globally and at the paragraph level—should reveal relationships among your sources, and should also reveal the relationships between your own ideas and those of your sources.

Write an original introduction and conclusion. As much as is practical, make the paper's introduction and conclusion your own ideas or your own synthesis of the ideas inherent in your research. Use sources minimally in your introduction and conclusion.

Open and close paragraphs with originality. In general, use the openings and closing of your paragraphs to reveal your work—"enclose" your sources among your assertions. At a minimum, create your own topic sentences and wrap-up sentences for paragraphs.

Use transparent rhetorical strategies. When appropriate, outwardly practice such rhetorical strategies as analysis, synthesis, comparison, contrast, summary, description, definition, hierarchical structure, evaluation, hypothesis, generalization, classification, and even narration. Prove to your reader that you are thinking as you write.

Also, you must clarify where your own ideas end and the cited information begins. Part of your job is to help your reader draw the line between these two things, often by the way you create context for the cited information. A phrase such as "A 1979 study revealed that . . ." is an obvious announcement of citation to come. Another recommended technique is the insertion of the author's name into the text to announce the beginning of your cited information. You may worry that you are not allowed to give the actual names of sources you have studied in the paper's text, but just the opposite is true. In fact, the more respectable a source you cite, the more impressed your reader is likely to be with your material while reading. If you note that the source is the NASA Science website or an article by Stephen Jay Gould or a recent edition of *The Wall Street Journal* right in your text, you offer your readers immediate context without their having to guess or flip to the references page to look up the source.

What follows is an excerpt from a political science paper that clearly and admirably draws the line between writer and cited information:

The above political upheaval illuminates the reasons behind the growing Iranian hatred of foreign interference; as a result of this hatred, three enduring geopolitical patterns have evolved in Iran, as noted by John Limbert. First . . .

Note how the writer begins by redefining her previous paragraph's topic (political upheaval), then connects this to Iran's hatred of foreign interference, then suggests a causal relationship and ties her ideas into John Limbert's analysis—thereby announcing that a synthesis of Limbert's work is coming. This writer's work also becomes more credible and meaningful because, right in the text, she announces the name of a person who is a recognized authority in the field. Even in this short excerpt, it is obvious that this writer is using proper citation and backing up her own assertions with confidence and style.

Signal Phrases

Good readers will look for the way you set up your quotes as well as the way you interpret them. Use signal phrases to ensure smooth paragraphs.

As I keep mentioning, good writers are writers who know their options. Often, a well-placed word or phrase is necessary to guide readers. Signal phrases also separate your ideas from the source's ideas. This is crucial.

Here are some verbs you might use for strong signal phrases. Notice how they give away the author's tone. Of course, the catch is that you'll have to understand the quote and the author's tone, which is the author's attitude toward the work. This is the tough part! Here are some ready-made options for you:

Author is neutral

comments,describes, explains, illustrates, notes, observes, points out, records, relates, reports, says, sees, thinks, writes

Author infers or suggests

analyzes, asks, assesses, concludes, considers, finds, predicts, proposes, reveals, shows, speculates, suggests, supposes

Author argues

claims, contends, defends, holds, insists, maintains

Author agrees

avers, admits, grants, concedes, notes, agrees

Author is uneasy or disparaging

belittles, bemoans, complains, confesses, condemns, deplores, deprecates, derides, disagrees, laments, warns. (Notice how the de– prefix here lets us know that what follows goes away or from. These words have much different tones from the "togetherness" of co– com– prefixes. Little effects like this aren't lost on careful readers!)

Paragraph Menu Settings Use No Extra Vertical Spaces

MLA calls for double-spacing with no extra spaces (around titles, heading, between paragraphs). Avoid getting a significant penalty for multiple MLA errors.

Here's a screen shot of the proper Paragraph menu settings in Word:

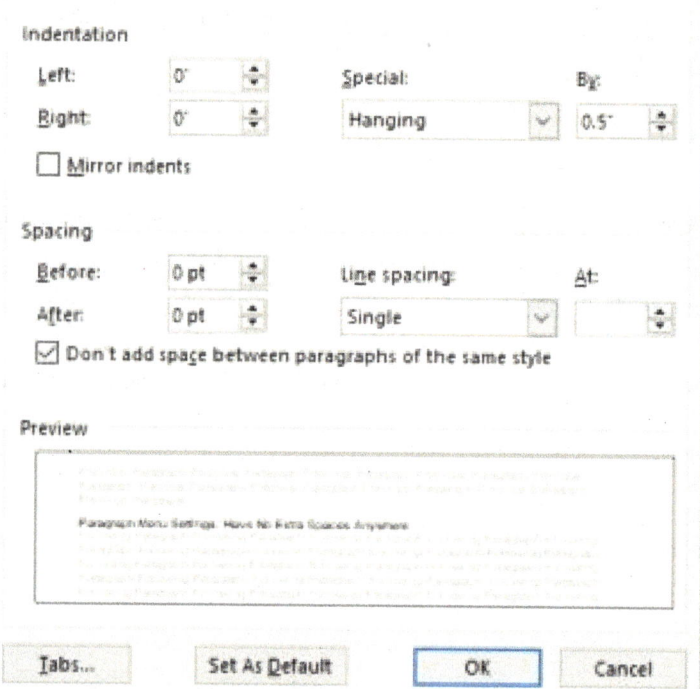

When managing the works cited page, use the Paragraph menu to create the hanging indent that indent the second or third lines of a given works cited entry.

The Paragraph Body: Supporting Your Ideas

Whether the drafting of a paragraph begins with a main idea or whether that idea surfaces in the revision process, once you have that main idea, you'll want to make sure that the idea has enough support. The job of the paragraph body is to develop and support the topic. Here's one way that you might think about it:

• Topic sentence: what is the main claim of your paragraph; what is the most important idea that you want your readers to take away from this paragraph?

• Support in the form of evidence: how can you prove that your claim or idea is true (or important, or noteworthy, or relevant)?

• Support in the form of analysis or evaluation: what discussion can you provide that helps your readers see the connection between the evidence and your claim?

• Transition: how can you help your readers move from the idea you're currently discussing to the next idea presented? (For more specific discussion about transitions, see the following section on "Developing Relationships between Ideas").

For more on methods of development that can help you to develop and organize your ideas within paragraphs, see "Patterns of Organization and Methods of Development" later in this section of this text.

Types of support might include

• Reasons.

• Facts.

• Statistics.

• Quotations.

• Examples.

Now that we have a good idea what it means to develop support for the main ideas of your paragraphs, let's talk about how to make sure that those supporting details are solid and convincing.

Good vs. Weak Support

What questions will your readers have? What will they need to know? What makes for good supporting details? Why might readers consider some evidence to be weak?

If you're already developing paragraphs, it's likely that you already have a plan for your essay, at least at the most basic level. You know what your topic is, you might have a working thesis, and you probably have at least a couple of supporting ideas in mind that will further develop and support your thesis.

So imagine you're developing a paragraph on one of these supporting ideas and you need to make sure that the support that you develop for this idea is solid. Considering some of the points about understanding and appealing to your audience (from the Audience and Purpose and the Prewriting sections of this text) can also be helpful in determining what your readers will consider good support and what they'll consider to be weak. Here are some tips on what to strive for and what to avoid when it comes to supporting details.

Good support

• Is relevant and focused (sticks to the point).

- Is well developed.
- Provides sufficient detail.
- Is vivid and descriptive.
- Is well organized.
- Is coherent and consistent.
- Highlights key terms and ideas.

Weak Support

- Lacks a clear connection to the point that it's meant to support.
- Lacks development.
- Lacks detail or gives too much detail.
- Is vague and imprecise.
- Lacks organization.
- Seems disjointed (ideas don't clearly relate to each other).
- Lacks emphasis of key terms and ideas.

Breaking, Combining, or Beginning New Paragraphs

Like sentence length, paragraph length varies. There is no single ideal length for "the perfect paragraph." There are some general guidelines, however. Some writing handbooks or resources suggest that a paragraph should be at least three or four sentences; others suggest that 100 to 200 words is a good target to shoot for. In academic writing, paragraphs tend to be longer, while in less formal or less complex writing, such as in a newspaper, paragraphs tend to be much shorter. Two-thirds to three-fourths of a page is usually a good target length for paragraphs at your current level of college writing. If your readers can't see a paragraph break on the page, they might wonder if the paragraph is ever going to end or they might lose interest.

The most important thing to keep in mind here is that the amount of space needed to develop one idea will likely be different than the amount of space needed to develop another. So when is a paragraph complete? The answer is, when it's fully developed. The guidelines above for providing good support should help.

Some signals that it's time to end a paragraph and start a new one include that

- You're ready to begin developing a new idea.
- You want to emphasize a point by setting it apart.
- You're getting ready to continue discussing the same idea but in a different way (e.g. shifting from comparison to contrast).
- You notice that your current paragraph is getting too long (more than three-fourths of a page or so), and you think your writers will need a visual break.

Some signals that you may want to combine paragraphs include that

- You notice that some of your paragraphs appear to be short and choppy.
- You have multiple paragraphs on the same topic.
- You have undeveloped material that needs to be united under a clear topic.

Finally, paragraph number is a lot like paragraph length. You may have been asked in the past to write a five paragraph essay. There's nothing inherently wrong with a five-paragraph essay, but just like sentence length and paragraph length, the number of paragraphs in an essay depends upon what's needed to get the job done. There's really no way to know that until you start writing. So try not to worry too much about the proper length and number of things. Just start writing and see where the essay and the paragraphs take you. There will be plenty of time to sort out the organization in the revision process. You're not trying to fit pegs into holes here. You're letting your ideas unfold. Give yourself—and them—the space to let that happen.

Developing Relationships Between Ideas

So you have a main idea, and you have supporting ideas, but how can you be sure that your readers will understand the relationships between them? How are the ideas tied to each other?

One way to emphasize these relationships is through the use of clear transitions between ideas. Like every other part of your essay, transitions have a job to do. They form logical connections between the ideas presented in an essay or paragraph, and they give readers clues that reveal how you want them to think about (process, organize, or use) the topics presented.

Why are Transitions Important?

Transitions signal the order of ideas, highlight relationships, unify concepts, and let readers know what's coming next or remind them about what's already been covered. When instructors or peers comment that your writing is choppy, abrupt, or needs to "flow better," those are some signals that you might need to work on building some better transitions into your writing. If a reader comments that she's not sure how something relates to your thesis or main idea, a transition is probably the right tool for the job.

When Is the Right Time to Build in Transitions?

There's no right answer to this question. Sometimes transitions occur spontaneously, but just as often (or maybe even more often) good transitions are developed in revision. While drafting, we often write what we think, sometimes without much reflection about how the ideas fit together or relate to one another. If your thought process jumps around a lot (and that's okay), it's more likely that you will need to pay careful attention to reorganization and to providing solid transitions as you revise.

When you're working on building transitions into an essay, consider the essay's overall organization. Consider using reverse outlining and other organizational strategies presented in this text to identify key ideas in your essay and to get a clearer look at how the ideas can be best organized. This can help you determine where transitions are needed.

Let's take some time to consider the importance of transitions at the sentence level and transitions between paragraphs.

Sentence-Level Transitions

Transitions between sentences often use "connecting words" to emphasize relationships between one sentence and another. A friend and coworker suggests the "something old something new" approach, meaning that the idea behind a transition is to introduce something new while connecting it to something old from an earlier point in the essay or paragraph. Here are some examples of ways that writers use connecting words (highlighted with red text and italicized) to show connections between ideas in adjacent sentences:

To Show Similarity

When I was growing up, my mother taught me to say "please" and "thank you" as one small way that I could show appreciation and respect for others. *In the same way*, I have tried to impress the importance of manners on my own children.

Other connecting words that show similarity include also, similarly, and likewise.

To Show Contrast

Some scientists take the existence of black holes for granted; however, in 2014, a physicist at the University of North Carolina claimed to have mathematically proven that they do not exist.

Other connecting words that show contrast include in spite of, on the other hand, in contrast, and yet.

To Exemplify

The cost of college tuition is higher than ever, so students are becoming increasingly motivated to keep costs as low as possible. For example, a rising number of students are signing up to spend their first two years at a less costly community college before transferring to a more expensive four-year school to finish their degrees.

Other connecting words that show example include for instance, specifically, and to illustrate.

To Show Cause and Effect

Where previously painters had to grind and mix their own dry pigments with linseed oil inside their studios, in the 1840s, new innovations in pigments allowed paints to be premixed in tubes. Consequently, this new technology facilitated the practice of painting outdoors and was a crucial tool for impressionist painters, such as Monet, Cezanne, Renoir, and Cassatt.

Other connecting words that show cause and effect include therefore, so, and thus.

To Show Additional Support

When choosing a good trail bike, experts recommend 120–140 millimeters of suspension travel; that's the amount that the frame or fork is able to flex or compress. Additionally, they recommend a 67–69 degree head-tube angle, as a steeper head-tube angle allows for faster turning and climbing.

Other connecting words that show additional support include also, besides, equally important, and in addition.

A Word of Caution

Single-word or short-phrase transitions can be helpful to signal a shift in ideas within a paragraph, rather than between paragraphs (see the discussion below about transitions between paragraphs). But it's also important to understand that these types of transitions shouldn't be frequent within a paragraph. As with anything else that happens in your writing, they should be used when they feel natural and feel like the right choice. Here are some examples to help you see the difference between transitions that feel like they occur naturally and transitions that seem forced and make the paragraph awkward to read:

Too Many Transitions: The Impressionist painters of the late 19th century are well known for their visible brush strokes, for their ability to convey a realistic sense of light, and for their everyday subjects portrayed in outdoor settings. In spite of this fact, many casual admirers of their work are unaware of the scientific innovations that made it possible this movement in art to take place. Then, In 1841, an American painter named John Rand invented the collapsible paint tube. To illustrate the importance of this invention, pigments previously had to be ground and mixed in a fairly complex process that made it difficult for artists to travel with them. For example, the mixtures were commonly stored in pieces of pig bladder to keep the paint from drying out. In addition, when working with their palettes, painters had to puncture the bladder, squeeze out some paint, and then mend the bladder again to keep the rest of the paint mixture from drying out. Thus, Rand's collapsible tube freed the painters from these cumbersome and messy processes, allowing artists to be more mobile and to paint in the open air.

Subtle Transitions that Aid Reader Understanding: The Impressionist painters of the late 19th century are well known for their visible brush strokes, for their ability to convey a realistic sense of light, for their everyday subjects portrayed in outdoor settings. However, many casual admirers of their work are unaware of the scientific innovations that made it possible for this movement in art to take place. In 1841, an American painter named John Rand invented the collapsible paint tube. Before this invention, pigments had to be ground and mixed in a fairly complex process that made it difficult for artists to travel with them. The mixtures were commonly stored in pieces of pig bladder to keep the paint from drying out. When working with their palettes, painters had to puncture the bladder, squeeze out some paint, and then mend the bladder again to keep the rest of the paint mixture from drying out. Rand's collapsible tube freed the painters from these cumbersome and messy processes, allowing artists to be more mobile and to paint in the open air.

Transitions between Paragraphs and Sections

It's important to consider how to emphasize the relationships not just between sentences but also between paragraphs in your essay. Here are a few strategies to help you show your readers how the main ideas of your paragraphs relate to each other and also to your thesis.

Use Signposts

Signposts are words or phrases that indicate where you are in the process of organizing an idea; for example, signposts might indicate that you are introducing a new concept, that you are summarizing an idea, or that you are concluding your thoughts. Some of the most common signposts include words and phrases like first, then, next, finally, in sum, and in conclusion. Be careful not to overuse these types of transitions in your writing. Your readers will quickly find them tiring or too obvious. Instead, think of more creative ways to let your readers know where they are situated within the ideas presented in your essay. You might say, "The first problem with this practice is…" Or you might say, "The next thing to consider is…" Or you might say, "Some final thoughts about this topic are…."

Use Forward-Looking Sentences at the End of Paragraphs

Sometimes, as you conclude a paragraph, you might want to give your readers a hint about what's coming next. For example, imagine that you're writing an essay about the benefits of trees to the environment and you've just wrapped up a paragraph about how trees absorb pollutants and provide oxygen. You might conclude with a forward-looking sentence like this: "Trees benefits to local air quality are important, but surely they have more to offer our communities than clean air." This might conclude a paragraph (or series of paragraphs) and then prepare your readers for additional paragraphs to come that cover the topics of trees' shade value and ability to slow water evaporation on hot summer days. This transitional strategy can be tricky to employ smoothly. Make sure that the conclusion of your paragraph doesn't sound like you're leaving your readers hanging with the introduction of a completely new or unrelated topic.

Use Backward-Looking Sentences at the Beginning of Paragraphs

Rather than concluding a paragraph by looking forward, you might instead begin a paragraph by looking back. Continuing with the example above of an essay about the value of trees, let's think about how we might begin a new paragraph or section by first taking a moment to look back. Maybe you just concluded a paragraph on the topic of trees' ability to decrease soil erosion and you're getting ready to talk about how they provide habitats for urban wildlife. Beginning the opening of a new paragraph or section of the essay with a backward-looking transition might look something like this: "While their benefits to soil and water conservation are great, the value that trees provide to our urban wildlife also cannot be overlooked."

Evaluate Transitions for Predictability or Conspicuousness

Finally, the most important thing about transitions is that you don't want them to become repetitive or too obvious. Reading your draft aloud is a great revision strategy for so many reasons, and revising your essay for transitions is no exception to this rule. If you read your essay aloud, you're likely to hear the areas that sound choppy or abrupt. This can help you make note of areas where transitions need to be added. Repetition is another problem that can be easier to spot if you read your essay aloud. If you notice yourself using the same transitions over and over again, take time to find some alternatives. And if the transitions frequently stand out as you read aloud, you may want to see if you can find some subtler strategies.

Using Modern Language Association (MLA) Style

We have addressed American Psychological Association (APA) style, as well as the importance of giving credit where credit is due, so now let's turn our attention to the formatting and citation style of the Modern Language Association, known as MLA style.

MLA style is often used in the liberal arts and humanities. Like APA style, it provides a uniform framework for consistency across a document in several areas. MLA style provides a format for the manuscript text and parenthetical citations, or in-text citations. It also provides the framework for the works cited area for references at the end of the essay. MLA style emphasizes brevity and clarity. As a student writer, it is to your advantage to be familiar with both major styles, and this section will outline the main points of MLA as well as offer specific examples of commonly used references. Remember that your writing represents you in your absence. The correct use of a citation style demonstrates your attention to detail and ability to produce a scholarly work in an acceptable style, and it can help prevent the appearance or accusations of plagiarism.

If you are taking an English, art history, or music appreciation class, chances are that you will be asked to write an essay in MLA format. One common question goes something like "What's the difference?" referring to APA and MLA style, and it deserves our consideration. The liberal arts and humanities often reflect works of creativity that come from individual and group effort, but they may adapt, change, or build on previous creative works. The inspiration to create something new, from a song to a music video, may contain elements of previous works. Drawing on your fellow artists and authors is part of the creative process, and so is giving credit where credit is due.

A reader interested in your subject wants not only to read what you wrote but also to be aware of the works that you used to create it. Readers want to examine your sources to see if you know your subject, to see if you missed anything, or if you offer anything new and interesting. Your new or up-to-date sources may offer the reader additional insight on the subject being considered. It also demonstrates that you, as the author, are up-to-date on what is happening in the field or on the subject. Giving credit where it is due enhances your credibility, and the MLA style offers a clear format to use.

Uncredited work that is incorporated into your own writing is considered plagiarism. In the professional world, plagiarism results in loss of credibility and often compensation, including future opportunities. In a classroom setting, plagiarism results in a range of sanctions, from loss of a grade to expulsion from a school or university. In both professional and academic settings, the penalties are severe. MLA offers artists and authors a systematic style of reference, again giving credit where credit is due, to protect MLA users from accusations of plagiarism.

MLA style uses a citation in the body of the essay that links to the works cited page at the end. The in-text citation is offset with parentheses, clearly calling attention to itself for the reader. The reference to the author or title is like a signal to the reader that information was incorporated from a separate source. It also provides the reader with information to then turn to the works cited section of your essay (at the end) where they can find the complete reference. If you follow the MLA style, and indicate your source both in your essay and in the works cited section, you will prevent the possibility of plagiarism. If you follow the MLA guidelines, pay attention to detail, and clearly indicate your sources, then this approach to formatting and citation offers a proven way to demonstrate your respect for other authors and artists.

Five Reasons to Use MLA Style

1. To demonstrate your ability to present a professional, academic essay in the correct style
2. To gain credibility and authenticity for your work
3. To enhance the ability of the reader to locate information discussed in your essay
4. To give credit where credit is due and prevent plagiarism
5. To get a good grade or demonstrate excellence in your writing

Before we transition to specifics, please consider one word of caution: consistency. If you are instructed to use the MLA style and need to indicate a date, you have options. For example, you could use an international or a US style:

- **International style:** 18 May 1980 (day/month/year)
- **US style:** May 18, 1980 (month/day/year)

If you are going to the US style, be consistent in its use. You'll find you have the option on page 83 of the *MLA Handbook for Writers of Research Papers*, 7th edition. You have many options when writing in English as the language itself has several conventions, or acceptable ways of writing particular parts of speech or information.

You are welcome to look in the *MLA Handbook* and see there is one preferred style or convention (you will also find the answer at end of this section marked by an asterisk [*]). Now you may say to yourself that you won't write that term and it may be true, but you will come to a term or word that has more than one way it can be written. In that case, what convention is acceptable in MLA style? This is where the *MLA Handbook* serves as an invaluable resource. Again, your attention to detail and the professional presentation of your work are aspects of learning to write in an academic setting.

Now let's transition from a general discussion on the advantages of MLA style to what we are required to do to write a standard academic essay. We will first examine a general "to do" list, then review a few "do not" suggestions, and finally take a tour through a sample of MLA features. Links to sample MLA papers are located at the end of this section.

General MLA List

1. Use standard white paper (8.5 × 11 inches).
2. Double space the essay and quotes.
3. Use Times New Roman 12-point font.
4. Use one-inch margins on all sides
5. Indent paragraphs (five spaces or 1.5 inches).
6. Include consecutive page numbers in the upper-right corner.
7. Use italics to indicate a title, as in *Writing for Success*.
8. On the first page, place your name, course, date, and instructor's name in the upper-left corner.
9. On the first page, place the title centered on the page, with no bold or italics and all words capitalized.
10. On all pages, place the header, student's name + one space + page number, 1.5 inches from the top, aligned on the right.

Tip

Depending on your field of study, you may sometimes write research papers in either APA or MLA style. Recognize that each has its advantages and preferred use in fields and disciplines. Learn to write and reference in both styles with proficiency.

Title Block Format

You never get a second chance to make a first impression, and your title block (not a separate title page; just a section at the top of the first page) makes an impression on the reader. If correctly formatted with each element of information in its proper place, form, and format, it says to the reader that you mean business, that you are a professional, and that you take your work seriously, so it should, in turn, be seriously considered. Your title block in MLA style contributes to your credibility. Remember that your writing represents you in your absence, and the title block is the tailored suit or outfit that represents you best. That said, sometimes a separate title page is necessary, but it is best both to know how to properly format a title block or page in MLA style and to ask your instructor if it is included as part of the assignment.

Your name

Instructor

Course number

Date

Title of Paper

Paragraphs and Indentation

Make sure you indent five spaces (from the left margin). You'll see that the indent offsets the beginning of a new paragraph. We use paragraphs to express single ideas or topics that reinforce our central purpose or thesis statement. Paragraphs include topic sentences, supporting sentences, and conclusion or transitional sentences that link paragraphs together to support the main focus of the essay.

Tables and Illustrations

Place tables and illustrations as close as possible to the text they reinforce or complement. Here's an example of a table in MLA.

Table 1

Sales Figures by Year	Sales Amount ($)
2007	100,000
2008	125,000
2009	185,000
2010	215,000

As we can see in Table 1, we have experienced significant growth since 2008.

This example demonstrates that the words that you write and the tables, figures, illustrations, or images that you include should be next to each other in your paper.

Parenthetical Citations

You must cite your sources as you use them. In the same way that a table or figure should be located right next to the sentence that discusses it (see the previous example), parenthetical citations, or citations enclosed in parenthesis that appear in the text, are required. You need to cite all your information. If someone else wrote it, said it, drew it, demonstrated it, or otherwise expressed it, you need to cite it. The exception to this statement is common, widespread knowledge. For example, if you search online for MLA resources, and specifically MLA sample papers, you will find many similar discussions on MLA style. MLA is a style and cannot be copyrighted because it is a style, but the seventh edition of the *MLA Handbook* can be copyright protected. If you reference a specific page in that handbook, you need to indicate it. If you write about a general MLA style issue that is commonly covered or addressed in multiple sources, you do not. When in doubt, reference the specific resource you used to write your essay.

Your in-text, or parenthetical, citations should do the following:

- Clearly indicate the specific sources also referenced in the works cited
- Specifically identify the location of the information that you used
- Keep the citation clear and concise, always confirming its accuracy

Works Cited Page

After the body of your paper comes the works cited page. It features the reference sources used in your essay. List the sources alphabetically by last name, or list them by title if the author is not known as is often the case of web-based articles. You will find links to examples of the works cited page in several of the sample MLA essays at the end of this section.

As a point of reference and comparison to our APA examples, let's examine the following three citations and the order of the information needed.

Citation Type	MLA Style	APA Style
Website	Author's Last Name, First Name. Title of the website. Publication Date. Name of Organization (if applicable). Date you accessed the website. <URL>.	Author's Last Name, First Initial. (Date of publication). Title of document. Retrieved from URL
Online article	Author's Last Name, First Name. "Title of Article." Title of the website. Date of publication. Organization that provides the website. Date you accessed the website.	Author's Last name, First Initial. (Date of publication). Title of article. *Title of Journal, Volume*(Issue). Retrieved from URL
Book	Author's Last Name, First Name. *Title of the Book*. Place of Publication: Publishing Company, Date of publication.	Author's Last Name, First Initial. (Date of publication). *Title of the book*. Place of Publication: Publishing Company.

Note: The items listed include proper punctuation and capitalization according to the style's guidelines.

Exercise 1

In Chapter 13 "APA and MLA Documentation and Formatting", Section 13.1 "Formatting a Research Paper", you created a sample essay in APA style. After reviewing this section and exploring the resources linked at the end of the section (including California State University–Sacramento's clear example of a paper in MLA format), please convert your paper to MLA style using the formatting and citation guidelines. You may find it helpful to use online applications that quickly, easily, and at no cost convert your citations to MLA format.

Exercise 2

Please convert the APA-style citations to MLA style. You may find that online applications can quickly, easily, and at no cost convert your citations to MLA format. There are several websites and applications available free (or as a free trial) that will allow you to input the information and will produce a correct citation in the style of your choice. Consider these two sites:

- http://www.noodletools.com
- http://citationmachine.net

Hint: You may need access to the Internet to find any missing information required to correctly cite in MLA style. This demonstrates an important difference between APA and MLA style—the information provided to the reader.

Sample Student Reference List in APA Style

1. Brent, D. A., Poling, K. D., & Goldstein, T. R. (2010). *Treating depressed and suicidal adolescents: A clinician's guide.* New York, NY: Guilford Press.

MLA

2. Dewan, S. (2007, September 17). Using crayons to exorcise Katrina. *The New York Times.*Retrieved from http://www.nytimes.com/2007/09/17/arts/design/17ther.html

MLA

3. Freud, S. (1955). Beyond the pleasure principle. In *The Complete Works of Sigmund Freud.* (Vol. XVII, pp. 3–66). London, England: Hogarth.

MLA

4. Henley, D. (2007). Naming the enemy: An art therapy intervention for children with bipolar and comorbid disorders. *Art Therapy: Journal of the American Art Therapy Association, 24*(3), 104–110.

MLA

5. Hutson, M. (2008). Art therapy: The healing arts. *Psychology Today.* Retrieved from http://www.psychologytoday.com/articles/200705/art-therapy-the-healing-arts

MLA

6. Isis, P. D., Bus, J., Siegel, C. A., & Ventura, Y. (2010). Empowering students through creativity: Art therapy in Miami-Dade County Public Schools. *Art Therapy: Journal of the American Art Therapy Association, 27*(2), 56–61.

MLA

7. Johnson, D. (1987). The role of the creative arts therapies in the diagnosis and treatment of psychological trauma. *The Arts in Psychotherapy, 14,* 7–13.

MLA

8. Malchiodi, C. (2006). *Art therapy sourcebook.* New York, NY: McGraw-Hill.

MLA

9. Markel, R. (Producer). (2010). *I'm an artist* [Motion picture]. United States: Red Pepper Films.

MLA

10. Kelley, S. J. (1984). The use of art therapy with sexually abused children. *Journal of Psychosocial Nursing and Mental Health, 22*(12), 12–28.

MLA

11. Pifalo, T. (2008). Why art therapy? *Darkness to light: Confronting child abuse with courage.* Retrieved from http://www.darkness2light.org/KnowAbout/articles_art_therapy.asp

MLA

12. Rubin, J. A. (2005). *Child art therapy* (25th ed.). New York, NY: Wiley.

MLA

13. Schimek, J. (1975). A critical re-examination of Freud's concept of unconscious mental representation. *International Review of Psychoanalysis, 2,* 171–187.

MLA

14. Strauss, M. B. (1999). *No talk therapy for children and adolescents.* New York, NY: Norton.

MLA

15. Thompson, T. (2008). *Freedom from meltdowns: Dr. Thompson's solutions for children with autism.* Baltimore, MD: Paul H. Brookes.

MLA

Useful Sources of Examples of MLA Style

- Arizona State University Libraries offers an excellent resource with clear examples.

  - http://libguides.asu.edu/content.php?pid=122697&sid=1132964

- Purdue Online Writing Lab includes sample pages and works cited.

  - http://owl.english.purdue.edu/owl/resource/747/01

- California State University–Sacramento's Online Writing Lab has an excellent visual description and example of an MLA paper.

  - http://www.csus.edu/owl/index/mla/mla_format.htm

- SUNY offers an excellent, brief, side-by-side comparison of MLA and APA citations.

  - http://www.sunywcc.edu/LIBRARY/research/MLA_APA_08.03.10.pdf

- Cornell University Library provides comprehensive MLA information on its Citation Management website.

  - http://www.library.cornell.edu/resrch/citmanage/mla

- The University of Kansas Writing Center is an excellent resource.

  - http://www.writing.ku.edu/guides

* (a) is the correct answer to the question at the beginning of this section. The *MLA Handbook* prefers "twentieth century."

KEY TAKEAWAYS

- MLA style is often used in the liberal arts and humanities.
- MLA style emphasizes brevity and clarity.
- A reader interested in your subject wants not only to read what you wrote but also to be informed of the works you used to create it.
- MLA style uses a citation in the body of the essay that refers to the works cited section at the end.
- If you follow MLA style, and indicate your source both in your essay and in the works cited section, you will prevent the possibility of plagiarism.

---

4. FICTION

How to Analyze a Short Story

What Is a Short Story?

A short story is a work of short, narrative prose that is usually centered around one single event. It is limited in scope and has an introduction, body and conclusion. Although a short story has much in common with a novel (See How to Analyze a Novel), it is written with much greater precision. You will often be asked to write a literary analysis. An analysis of a short story requires basic knowledge of literary elements. The following guide and questions may help you:

Old Fence. A short story has a structure and a message. Can you analyze this picture in much the same way as a short story?

Setting

Setting is a description of where and when the story takes place. In a short story there are fewer settings compared to a novel. The time is more limited. Ask yourself the following questions:

- How is the setting created? Consider geography, weather, time of day, social conditions, etc.
- What role does setting play in the story? Is it an important part of the plot or theme? Or is it just a backdrop against which the action takes place?

Study the time period, which is also part of the setting, and ask yourself the following:

- When was the story written?
- Does it take place in the present, the past, or the future?
- How does the time period affect the language, atmosphere or social circumstances of the short story?

Characterization

Characterization deals with how the characters in the story are described. In short stories there are usually fewer characters compared to a novel. They usually focus on one central character or protagonist. Ask yourself the following:

- Who is the main character?
- Are the main character and other characters described through dialogue – by the way they speak (dialect or slang for instance)?
- Has the author described the characters by physical appearance, thoughts and feelings, and interaction (the way they act towards others)?
- Are they static/flat characters who do not change?
- Are they dynamic/round characters who DO change?
- What type of characters are they? What qualities stand out? Are they stereotypes?
- Are the characters believable?

Plot and structure

The plot is the main sequence of events that make up the story. In short stories the plot is usually centered around one experience or significant moment. Consider the following questions:

- What is the most important event?
- How is the plot structured? Is it linear, chronological or does it move around?
- Is the plot believable?

Narrator and Point of view

The narrator is the person telling the story. Consider this question: Are the narrator and the main character the same?

By point of view we mean from whose eyes the story is being told. Short stories tend to be told through one character's point of view. The following are important questions to consider:

- Who is the narrator or speaker in the story?
- Does the author speak through the main character?
- Is the story written in the first person "I" point of view?
- Is the story written in a detached third person "he/she" point of view?
- Is there an "all-knowing" third person who can reveal what all the characters are thinking and doing at all times and in all places?

Conflict

Conflict or tension is usually the heart of the short story and is related to the main character. In a short story there is usually one main struggle.

- How would you describe the main conflict?
- Is it an internal conflict within the character?
- Is it an external conflict caused by the surroundings or environment the main character finds himself/herself in?

Climax

The climax is the point of greatest tension or intensity in the short story. It can also be the point where events take a major turn as the story races towards its conclusion. Ask yourself:

- Is there a turning point in the story?
- When does the climax take place?

Theme

The theme is the main idea, lesson, or message in the short story. It may be an abstract idea about the human condition, society, or life. Ask yourself:

- How is the theme expressed?
- Are any elements repeated and therefore suggest a theme?
- Is there more than one theme?

Style

The author's style has to do with the his or her vocabulary, use of imagery, tone, or the feeling of the story. It has to do with the author's attitude toward the subject. In some short stories the tone can be ironic, humorous, cold, or dramatic.

- Is the author's language full of figurative language?
- What images are used?
- Does the author use a lot of symbolism? Metaphors (comparisons that do not use "as" or "like") or similes (comparisons that use "as" or "like")?

Your literary analysis of a short story will often be in the form of an essay where you may be asked to give your opinions of the short story at the end. Choose the elements that made the greatest impression on you. Point out which character/characters you liked best or least and always support your arguments.

Native Voices Video

The Annenberg Learner series *American Passages* is a web-based literature class. Its resources include videos, links, and comprehension questions. The chapter on Native American mythology is particularly good, as is the chapter/video on the Gothic.

Unit 1 there is entitled "Resistance and Renewal in Native Literature." View the video.

Native Voices Video Questions

Review the following questions. Several of them bring up the themes that recur in the course readings. Be prepared to answer any of these questions after viewing the American Passages video *Native Voices*.

1. What is the relationship between Native American identity and American identity?
2. How does Native American literature reflect or help create a sense of what it means to be Native American in the United States?
3. What does this literature help reveal about the experience of having a multicultural identity?
4. How does the conception of American Indian identity depend upon the writer's identity?
5. What makes Native American traditions from different regions distinctive?
6. How has Native American literature been influenced by politics on and off the reservation?
7. How are Native American oral traditions shaped by the landscapes in which they are composed?
8. What role does the land play in oral tradition?
9. How does the notion of time in American Indian narratives compare with notions of time in Western cultures?
10. How does the chronology of particular narratives reflect differing notions of time?
11. How do Yellow Woman stories and the Nightway or Enemyway chant influence Leslie Marmon Silko's Ceremony and Storyteller?
12. How do Navajo chantways influence the poetry of Luci Tapahonso?
13. How does the Ghost Dance influence the vision of Black Elk?
14. How does the Ghost Dance challenge nineteenth-century European American notions of Manifest Destiny?
15. How do Yellow Woman stories subvert the genre of captivity narratives?
16. How do the poems of Simon J. Ortiz challenge the notion of what it means to be an American hero?

Navajo Origin Myth

Navajo Origin Myth

"NAVAJO ORIGIN LEGEND"

[It is Mythology, so I Renamed This]

BY A. M. STEPHEN.

Journal of American Folk-Lore, vol. 43, 1930, pp. 88-104.

The first (lowest) world was red, bare, barren ground, this was the earliest world. Etséhostin and Etséasun, his wife, existed there and they had nothing to eat till the fourth day, and on this day they began to think of eating. Hostjaishjiné stood up and rubbed his belly and some skin (*bitcin*) was loosened which formed in a roll under his hands and he laid this roll of cuticle on the ground. The woman stood up and followed his example. Then they each trampled on the rolls. Etséhostin reached over his shoulder, down his back, and formed another roll and laid it on the ground. The two rolls that he had formed turned into a man with a mask. This new-formed man stood up, and this is the origin of the first man (Navajo ?). Etséasun again followed the *hostin*'s example and from the rolls which she formed a woman arose: this was the virgin called Djosdelhazhy (biting vagina). The *hostin* (old man) then reached under his left arm and formed another roll of skin which he laid on the ground and it became (a water monster called) Téholtsody. The *hostin* then reached under his right arm and formed another roll of skin which, being laid upon the ground, became Usheenasun, Salt spirit, a woman who now lives at Nitcō (Salt Lake south of Zuñi).

Hostin then took the end of his tongue between his fingers and spat out a little piece of it (his tongue ? spittle ?) upon the ground before him and it became a wing which he placed upon his ear. The wind would shake this wing and tell everything in his ear. Etséasun then took a roll of skin from her scalp and laid it on the ground and placed a little feather beside it and this became the Thunder (with wings). On the left side the feathers were black on top and white underneath, on the right side the feathers were white above and black below. Etséhostin then rubbed the sole of his right foot and the roll of skin became a large frog, Tcalc. He rubbed the sole of his left foot, and a crane, Teklaliale was formed. This makes altogether twelve personages up to this time.

Etséhostin began thinking, "How can we get something to eat?" Etséasun said, "My husband, I know not." Hostin looked back and saw Hostjaishjiné and said to him, "You understand these things, tell us how we are to get food." Hostjaishjiné, who always looks stern and grim and angry, said, "I do not know," but he reached down on his neck and rolled a little skin in his hand and Wunushtcindy (locust ?) was produced. Then Etséasun looked far back and saw Nastjeasun and asked her how they could get something to eat. Nastjeasun rolled a little skin upon her breast and it became Ant, Nâzozi, which was then buried in the ground for four days and at the end of that time many little red (yellow) ants came forth. Hostjaishjiné then rolled some skin from his forehead and laid it on the ground when it turned into a horned toad, Nâshōngbitcijy. Etséhostin built a house and lived there and the red (yellow) ants built all round this big house, and annoyed him and the others, so that they could find no rest day or night. Teholtsody thought he would go off and find some place to rest so he travelled to the east. The world was very small at this time, and Teholtsody soon came to its utmost limit and as he could go no farther, he built his house there. In like manner, the frog being troubled with the ants, he travelled to the south to the utmost limit of the world, and built there. Then Salt Woman went similarly to the west and built a house, and Tulthklahallé went to the north. Each of these houses was fashioned from east to west like a rainbow (shabiklo), and from south to north of Sun-rays (jōnâaibikloth), when we build a house today we have four poles reaching from east west and from south to north, and these meet at the apex.

After these four had left him Etséhostin stayed in his own house. He said, "I wish we could get some clouds, I want rain," and he looked out of his house towards the East, where Teholtsody was and saw many clouds, for Teholtsody's house is of clouds. Etséasun then said, "I wish we had some kind of rain," and she looked to the south and saw a heavy fog, for this was the frog's house. Etséhostin wished that there was a mountain to stand on and look for rain, and he began to pray for rain; he looked west and saw a mirage, Hûtaonige, like a person. Etséasun now prayed on the north side, "Send rain so that everything may be wet." She saw a green scum on the water and made a house, 'Tutklitb'hogan, of this. This makes four houses.

Etséhostin sent Thunder naked to the cloud house of Teholtsody in the east, telling Thunder to stand right in the doorway of Teholtsody's house. Thunder went there and stood in the doorway naked and Teholtsody gave him a mantle of feathers which is the sheet (quick) lightning. On his head is the heat lightning, He had a tail feather which is Hajillkish, sheet lightning. Etséasun told the monster Tehlin (horn horse) to go to the south to Frog's house of fog. He went and stood in the doorway. Salt Woman had gone west and Etséhostin told Thonainilly to stand just outside the doorway of her house and watch her. He was to be her guardian. An old woman sat on the north side of the world and she sent a fish (turtle) to watch outside the doorway of Tulthklahale's house and guard it. After Teholtsody went east he made a water vessel (tositsa) of white clay. Frog in the south made one of blue clay; the Usheenasun in the west made one of yellow clay. Tultklehale on the north made one of spotted clay. It had variegated surface of black, blue, yellow and white.

Etséhostin began to travel and he went to Teholtsody's house, and in the middle of it he found the pot Teholtsody had made and it was covered. He lifted the cover and found it full of water. He went home and told his wife that Teholtsody was growing wiser than they were. Etséasun then went south to Frog's house and saw his pot full of water, and she returned to her house and told her husband. Jōsdelhazhy said she also would travel and she went west and found that Salt Woman also had a pot full of water. She returned and told what she had seen. Hashjaishjine then went north and found a pot of water in the house of Tulthkalhale and he returned very angry. He said, "They are all getting wiser than us. They are growing rich and we are still poor. We have nothing and cannot make anything." Etséhostin said, "Why should you be angry? We will grow wise like them and have many things some day." Then Etséhostin went to Teholtsody's house to get a little water, which he brought back to his own house. Etséasun went and brought some from the south. Next Hostin borrowed some from the west and Asun borrowed from the north. Having brought water from each of these four places Hostin planted it all together in the ground. In a few days he saw a damp, green spot there. He returned to look at the place in a few more days and saw that bushes had grown there. He made a third visit and found jointed grass. He made a fourth visit and found the reed grass, looka (arrow grass, tluka) but it had no pollen on the top, and there was a large spring also. Hostin again said, "I wish we had something more," and he went to the spring and found lookaitso growing right in the centre of it. Five different kinds of plants grew out of the spring and he pulled up some of each kind and took them home. One of these reeds had twelve joints and the wind came out of the other end and made music (a flageolet). The wind emerging from this reed whirled about on the ground all over the world and it went to the houses at the four quarters and caused them much trouble. The dweller at each house sent his guard out to trouble the wind. They took black clouds, fogs, and blue mould, also to each of them was given Thunder and Lightning and the guardians kept shooting at the little winds but these latter kept dodging about so that they could not be hit. But this only raised more wind and it rained heavily, then the guards stopped troubling the wind for they could not conquer it.

When the rain stopped Hostin said to his wife, "Everything looks beautiful, I wish we had something good to eat." He looked in all directions and saw Hajillkish (Glow-light Heat-Lightning) at the four points where people lived. Then he prayed for some kind of grass, or fruit, or seeds to live upon. He went to the spring and saw something green that had come up out of the ground and it was corn. He then went east to Teholtsody and found the pumpkin and squash and returned. Asun went south and found that Frog had raised watermelon and tobacco. She returned. Then Hostin went west to Salt Woman's house and found beans p. 91 and cotton growing, then she returned home. Hostin went north to Tulthkle's house and found muskmelon and gourds growing in great quantities. He then returned and said to Asun, "We have wished for these things (i.e. we have everything we prayed for). Now we have many things. Let us pray for something more." So he prayed and sang for more.

He went to the spring and saw a "fruit" in the middle of the water. He went back for Spider Woman and told her to get this fruit out of the water. She got it and gave it to Hostin who looked at it and saw it was Yolakaihatate, a big shell, big as a pan. He took this home and returned next day to the spring and found more fruit. Spider Woman again brought it out and it was Turquoise, Tedokiji. Hostin then went east to Teholtsody's house and went in and found a big black bow and arrow, also eagle feathers. These Hostin used as Thunder (the arrow for lightning, and the feathers to guide the arrows). Asun sent south to Frog's house, and Frog had stone knives (paishhathl). Spider Woman went to Salt Woman who had planted cotton and had been weaving it into cloth. Spider Woman got this and brought it home. Hashjaishjine went north to Tulthkle's house and found black cloth and fetched it home. On the first trip Hashjaishjine returned angry but this time he was in good humor. He said to Hostin, "The people at the four corners are growing rich." Hostin then prayed for more and went to the spring. The corn was growing ripe and each stalk carried twelve ears. Asun went over and gathered it and brought it home. They now had plenty of corn and much else besides. But those living at the four corners of the world had no corn so they came to Hostin's house and begged him for some. He told them to provide for themselves, but finally he gave them some of the pollen (taditin), but none of the ear corn. He told them to plant the pollen. They did so and it grew up small, like onions, but no ears grew upon it. Then they begged Hostin for some seed corn but he would not give them any. Teholtsody said, "When Hostin came borrowing water we all gave him some, and enabled him to raise water of his own." Hostin said, "Surely you let me have water and when you begged for corn I gave it to you and taught you how to plant it as best I could." Teholtsody was very angry and thought how he could destroy Hostin. Teholtsody gave Thunder a bow and arrow and told him to go and kill Hostin, "for," said he, "we must have some of this corn." Thunder went "to try and burst Hostin open with lightning," but Horned Toad was in the doorway of Hostin's house and the wind warned Hostin of his danger. Hostin told Horned Toad to stand in front of him always, for as he was so rough-coated lightning could not hurt him. Frog was also angry and assaulted Hostin. He sent his guardian Tehlinl (a water monster) to draw all the water away (to dry it up) from Hostin's spring. But Spider Woman wove an impenetrable web around it so that Frog and his guardian were foiled. (Hostjaishkine was the most powerful). Salt Woman gave Tiinainilly a lump p. 92 (double handful) of salt, and he also had some kind of lightning in his hands, and he came against Hostin. Hostjaishjine saw him coming and knew his harmful intent. Hostjaishjine had a long stone knife with a wooden handle. He ran into the house and made a fire by twirling a spindle of wood, etc. He made a small fire and scattered it all over Hostin's house. Tiinainilly (a young man) came close in order to throw his lightning on to the house and his salt upon the fire, which exploded, but no harm ensued, so he went back to the west and the Salt Woman was powerless. Tulthklahale, in the north, sent Mud Turtle (Black-mud Fish) to harm Hostin. Turtle had some kind of lightning of arrow, but could do no harm. Hastjaishjine made a big shirt of rawhide and gave it to Wunustcinde (locust) and this protected him against the lightning or arrows of the Turtle; no impression could be made on this shirt, and this is the origin of the shield. Hastjaishjini saw that all these people were jealous of the Hostin and were trying to destroy him. (They were envious of his possessing corn, etc.). Hostin then asked Hastjaishjini to do what he could against these people. Hashjaishjini's anger was roused against these people and he sallied forth to their houses. He went first to east, then south, then west, then north. He broke open their houses and successively broke the pot and spilled the water that was in them. The water that was in the pot in the east flowed to the south and the water that was in the pot in the north flowed toward the west, and all the waters met in the west and there was a great flood. Hostin had corn, white shells, turquoise and everything he wanted. He had large hollow reeds which would float on the water so he did not care when the flood should reach him. But all these eight persons who were envious and at enmity with Hostin were troubled and afraid of the flood. Hostin and his people were not afraid as they had the means of floating on the water.

Hostin and his family cut the great reeds and put all their corn and other possessions inside of these, and the whole world was gradually overflowed. Then Teholtsody and the others at the cardinal points began to wish that they could save themselves with Hostin and his family. Teholtsody made a bow and arrow and gave them to Thunder and told him to go to Hostin and give them to him and beg that there might be peace between them. Thunder went to Hostin's house and said, "Teholtsody sends you this bow and arrow and begs you to be his friend." Hostin would not look at them and said, "I have nothing to do with it. Go to Hostjaishjine. He is the one that broke the water vessels and brought on this flood." So Thunder took them to Hostjaishjine and made the same offer. Hostjaishjine would not listen to Thunder but said, "Go to Wunustcinde" (locust). Thunder went to him and he accepted the bow and arrow saying, "This is just what I want." There were two arrows and Wunustcinde thrust them into his breast, one at either side, and drew them completely through. You may see that this insect has the holes in its thorax to this day. Then he put them in his mouth and p. 93 thrust them down his throat into his stomach and withdrew them again, and there was blood adhering to them.

Next Frog sent Teklin to Hostin to say, "My house is overflowed and have lost everything except this tobacco bag which I wish you to accept that we may become friends." The bag was made from the green scum of the water and was embroidered with beads, etc. Hostin would not have it and referred him to Hostjaishjine who breathed upon it four times and there was some tobacco in it and he filled a clay pipe with it and smoked.

Next Salt Woman said, "We shall be killed by the water, we cannot live here, let us go to Hostin." She had a cotton blanket (*naskan*) and offered this through Tunelini (Salt Woman's guard) to Hostin. He would not have it, and said, "Go to Spider Woman and give her the blanket." She looked at it, put it around her waist, breathed from it four times and was satisfied. Next came Hakleale (Fish Guardian) who sent fish Hostin with a flint shirt and cap. He offered them, but Hostin sent him to second man (Nacûiditcije, Horned Toad). He took the shirt and cap, put the shirt on and wore the cap, and therefore all four groups (eight people) were now on peaceable terms with Hostin.

They were all friends. They stayed there a while but everything was flooded except on the east side. Little white mountains showed above the water. On the south side were little blue mountains; on the west side, little yellow mountains; on the north, little black mountains. All just barely showed their heads above water. Hostin went east to White mountains and picked up a little earth and returned. Spider Woman wove a web on the surface of the water near each of the four mountains. Hostin had a house of rainbow and sun rays in the form of a little mountain and he covered it with earth for a roof. The water had not yet covered the houses. Spider Woman wove a web so that the spring could not overflow yet. Old Man (Hostin) and Woman (Asun) went over to the spring and planted every growing thing, corn, melons, pumpkins, beans, all things, and they got all kinds of seeds and put them away. Those living in the various directions owned their water and had it with them. After the restoration of peace, Old Woman made new vessels for all these people in which they carried their water supply. When they made peace and were all united, the flood continued, so they put all their corn and property in the reeds and got inside themselves. All these people were inside the reeds and the water kept rising. Old Man and Woman went down to the spring. Old Man got on one side, Old Woman, on the other. He began to pray: "We are going to leave the spring, we will never come back again, but wherever I go I will always live as I have done here, do everything as I have done here."

When he finished praying, a young man came out of the spring and a little afterwards another. They did not look at the boys closely, but Old Woman took them in her arms and folded her blanket around them and went to the reeds. They made a hole in the reed in the side of the shaft and the people got inside and Old Man went in last, but Wunustcinde (locust) got up to the top of the reed and sat upon a leaf. As the reed began to move upward Wunustcinde began to make a noise through the holes in his thorax and as he did so the reed began to shake like wind. Black Wind shook it at the roots and made it move. The reed grew up higher and higher. The water now covered an the earth, everything except this reed which kept growing and Wunustcinde was always on the leaf at the top. As the reed grew, the water continued to rise; as Wunustcinde made his noise, the reed kept growing and Black Wind kept blowing at the roots and the people became aware that they were close to the roof of the world and did not know what to do as there was no space left for them between the surface of the water and the under side of this earth. Wunustcinde stopped his noise and Black Wind stopped blowing, and the reed stopped growing. They did not know what to do. Old Man then said to him of the north, "You begged me to bring you along, now come with me to look around and see if there is any way to get out of this world." But they could not find a hole anywhere nor any way to get out. They were frightened and thought they would all die there. But the Spider Woman wove a web on the surface of the water. It floated like a raft and an the people got out and sat upon it. They were puzzled what to do. Hostjaishjine picked up his *peshhath* (stone knife) and began to bore a hole in the roof over them. It was of clay which dropped and crumbled and when he could go no farther he called Wunustcinde to try, who soon bored a small hole through and came out upon the new world, but the water coming up through the hole which he had made was like to flood the new world also, so he stopped the hole up with mud.

No one saw him there as yet. Then he saw the water rising up from east, south, west, and north. He made the noise with his thorax. He saw a swan on the south side making much noise and the water was all in motion. Wunustcinde made such noise that the swan from the east, also one from the north and one from the west came to him. All four came to him but did not know what to think of him. They asked him where he came from. He told them from the world below. They would not believe him so he told them how he had come. The swans told him that neither he nor his people should come to this new place for it belonged to the swans only, and they would not let anyone else live here. Wunustcinde had a hard time with the swans, and they fought him. Finally they said, "If you want to stay here you must pay us." So Wunustcinde returned to his people and told them all this. Wunustcinde had the red substance that causes the sun to set red when it is going to storm and he offered this to the swans for their land. They put it on their wings and were so much pleased with it they said, "Well now, you can come and live here." Wunustcinde said to them that some of his people could not live in the water, although some of them could. Then the swans said p. 95 that after four days there would be some dry land. The swans had pots of clay and they placed one on the east side, one on the north side, one on the west side and in this way they carried off some of the water, and made some dry land. When the others came up to the new world they built little round houses again of the same red substance that had been given to the swans.

First Man made a man called Hosjelti and placed him on San Francisco Mountain; another called Hosjogwan (?) who lives on Ute Mountains; another called Navesrhuni (Nagenezgruni) who lives on Navajo Mountain; another called Hoshjaishjine who lives on San Mateo Mounitain, These four own all the game and other animals on these mountains. Old Man's people however lived close together. They took the earth gathered from the four mountains in the lower world and again they formed mountains as in lower world, at east, white; at south, blue; at west, yellow; at north, black. No one was allowed to see the boys who were found at the spring; they were left at the Ute Mountains when the people first came up. Old Man had brought seeds of all kinds with him and planted everything that grows, vegetables, plants, timber, sagebrush, flowers, everything. He found lots of people here who joined him. That was when bears, deer, antelope, rabbit, birds, all kinds of animals were people.

They (Old Man ?) made a white blanket for sunrise over Ute Mts., east; a blue blanket for the south sky, over San Mateo Mt., south; a yellow blanket for sunset over San Francisco Mt., west; a black blanket for Navajo Mt., north. There had been neither day nor night in the lower world, only sufficient light for existence. Old Man now said, "Let us arrange to have day and night, a time for work and a time for sleep," and so we see it is today. Just before sunrise comes a white streak in the east. Then the yellow of sunset and the white of the east meet in the middle so as to give light enough to work. And when the blue and the black meet in the middle this way it makes night, the time for sleep.

Then Old Man and Old Woman said, "We have nobody to talk to about ourselves (to worship us)." Old Man went off to the east to find people, or same as soon as they reached the upper world went toward the east. Old Man followed after these, and from east they brought back eagle feathers; from west, hawk feathers; from south, blue feathers; from north, speckled feathers (of whip-poor-will, night bird). When they got these altogether they laid them before them. Beside east feather they laid white corn and white shell; beside west feather, yellow corn and abalone shell; beside south feather, blue corn, and turquoise; beside north feather, all kinds of corn and shells and turquoise. All four were laid out together. Old man arranged all these for singing and praying to these things as he did at the spring, singing and praying. He and Old Woman and all his people moved about walking over these things several times in ceremonial manner.

East feather was for the wolf. The feather and corn and shell were prayed over and a wolf was raised. They prayed over the west objects, and Mountain Lion was raised; they prayed over the south objects and Tabastin, Otter, was raised; they prayed over the north objects, Bud (sic!) Beaver was raised. Old man said, "We need rulers," and he made these four rulers over these several regions. He planted all vegetable things and sprinkled them with the earth of the four mountains to give them power. These mountains had much wild tobacco growing on them. The four animals were the rulers of all the land. They smoked and felt good and began to teach the people to be farmers, to plant corn, wheat, melons, pumpkins, beans, chile, etc. and how to irrigate and take care of their crops. All four (animals) taught the people to use all kinds of grasses, timber, etc.

Old Man and Old Woman again talked about how they should get some more people, and they worked hard and made people. Joshdelhashi assisted them. She rubbed down the skin on her arms, and put the roll of cuticle on the ground, and it became a man (Repeat for various parts of the body, as in the first world, until twelve people are made).

They made six men and six women, and the offspring of these twelve people are all pueblo Indians, Moki, Oraibi, Zuñi, etc. men who cut their hair across the front of the face. When the white streak of daylight, the white of the east, met the yellow of sunset in mid heavens, and after they had each returned to their place (as they do daily) the white of the east had offspring which was

Coyote, and the yellow of the west a yellow fox. The blue and black met in mid heaven and returning had issue — the blue, a blue fox, and the black, a badger. On the east side is Coyote; on the west, Yellow Fox; on the south, Blue Fox; on the north, Badger.

The Coyote of the east came where the people were and asked Old Man where he came from. Old Man told him from three worlds down below and also told Coyote how he came up, also saying "If you (Coyote) are a clever man, I will teach you all we know about our religion, etc." So he taught him everything. Coyote got to know a great deal, and he went off to the Ute Mountains and got on the summit and commenced howling and making all sorts of noises. Old man had Guardian Wind and Wind went to Coyote and asked him what he was yelling about, and Coyote said, "It is none of your business." Coyote said he belonged to Old Man and had learned how to do everything, and that no roaring of the wind could frighten him. Wind said, "Keep on then, see if Old Man will not make a living without (after) you." Coyote said, "He will have to do more than he has been doing then." Coyote went back to Old Man and told him lies about the wind.

Blue and Yellow Foxes went together to the pueblos and belong to them. Coyote and Badger belong to the Navajos, but Great Wolf was the chief (ruler) of the whole. He gets up at daybreak, stands in the midst of the people's dwellings and calls to the people to go to work in the fields He advises them to get early to work planting corn, gardening and irrigating.[1]

He had a very smart woman for a wife and they had two children. After a time this woman made herself three small sticks for gambling and would go off all day long and leave the children helpless. Late in the afternoon Wolf chief, the man, came home and saw the state of the hogan, untidy, and one of the children lying in the ashes of the fireplace. He did not try to clean up for he was very tired and lay down. At sunset his wife came back with her sticks but she had gambled away everything she had. Then the husband expostulated with her on her conduct. She replied tartly that he could stay and take care of the hogan and children as he had nothing to do. He said he provided food, etc. but she was quarrelsome and continued scolding (like the Navaho women today!). She told her husband she could take care of herself and so continued scolding, etc. until time for the Corn dance. She carried off the corn to grind and make mush for the dance although her own children were crying with hunger. Finally she told her husband to go off and she could easily find another. She said she could do without assistance. The husband avoided replying to her and said nothing. He lay still all night feeling bad about her. In the morning he did not know what to do. He took his bow and arrow and walked off. Shortly he found some meat in the woods on a tree and he took some and ate it raw. That is why Wolf eats raw meat. He stole this meat (for it belonged to the second chief) but it was by reason of the trouble with his wife and he was muddled. At sunset he returned, said not a word to his wife, nor to his people who came to see him. In the night all his people came to see him for they thought he was sick. On the second night he said nothing, and next morning he would say nothing. The third chief came to see him, "Come out and do some work," said he. No answer. On the third night it was the same. On the fourth day the fourth chief called on him, still no result. On the fifth night, the three chiefs met together and said, "Let us go to First Chief's house and speak to him." So they went and said to him, "We called the people to work but they idle and gamble in the fields. Come into the house (lodge) and examine each separately, and find out who has spoken a bad word of you, our Chief," but they could find no one who had done so. Then they called in all the women to the lodge to find if any of them had given offense to the chief, still they found no one; by this time it was nearly daylight. Still the chief would say nothing. The women said there was none of them guilty. This was at daylight. "Who is the man? No man nor woman caused his trouble but the woman he was living with." On the sixth night the chief said, "I will speak a few words to you, and tomorrow I will go out to the fields." He went out and saw the crops neglected and weeds growing. On the following night he called the men into his house and they all assembled. He said "I am sorry. My wife alone is to blame, but every woman you have is liable to do the same as mine has done. Let them go and try to make a living for themselves and see how they like that. There is a wide, deep river, without a ford. Let us (men) find means to cross it, and leave all the women behind. Every man must leave his wife." Most of them felt sorry, and some said, "What will we do in the case of a nursing boy baby, shall we take him away from his mother? How about Nutlys, berdaches? They also like to gamble with the women. Let us see what the berdaches say?" The berdaches were the last to come in. They scratched the ground with a stick a long time trying to make up their minds. They did not care to go with the women, and what could they do? Finally they said, "We will go with the men." "Very well," the men said, "That is good, but you must take your own food with you." The men asked them also, "Have you your own grinding stones, pots, dippers, mush sticks, brushes, are all these your own?" "Yes, by my own hands." "All right," the men said, "We will take one berdache with us to cook for us."

The chief told the men to get ready to cross the river that day. They got ready to go. They had plenty of corn and all kinds of food, but he said, "We must go without anything, only a few kernels for seed." The berdache took along everything. Rafts were made and preparatians completed. Best hunters crossed first so that if they should find any antelope with milk they might bring it back for the children. The berdache remained behind (at the camp after crossing the river) and ground some corn and made a little mush for the children, and the hunters were to come back in the middle of the day with meat and milk. The hunters brought back deer and antelope but many did not feel like eating as they had just parted from their wives. All the men sat up during the night to talk about their trouble. Finally they said, "Let us go to work," and they began cutting trees for houses. The women camped on the opposite river bank and held out their privates (djocs) where the men could see them, calling out to them, "How would you like to have some?" etc. trying to tantalize them and entice them back. The hunters went out again and some cleared the ground for planting. At that time they had only stone implements for axes and broad sticks for hoes. The second night they camped out again and some brought in deer and antelope and they were better off than before. The fourth night they were all contented, they had plenty of game and food. The little children began to be contented as they grew accustomed to their separation from their mothers. The women camped on the river bank, and ground corn constantly in sight of the men on the opposite bank. The houses were strung along as the mealing stones were arranged. They had some square houses too, but these belonged to the Pueblo Indians. The men became quite indifferent to the women, but the women were becoming restless with increasing amatory desires. Four years this separation continued, and as the men had left plenty of corn and food of all kinds with the women they did not suffer much until the end of this time. By that time however, the fields had become overgrown with sagebrush and cottonwood as the women had planted nothing. Then they had to gather up bones and boil them for all their possessions were exhausted and they suffered greatly. Badger (of the north) wanted to copulate with the women but he had a bad penis, crooked like a hook. The first one he tried was Joshdelhashi, then all the others. It made them crazy and they went wild with desire to copulate continually. Some of them took a corn cob wrapped with any soft substance and continually performed the sexual act artificially. Some tried to swim the river to get to the men but were drowned. Some died crazy with wild desire. This and lack of food caused the death of most of the women. Coyote, Blue Fox, Yellow Fox and Badger copulated with the women continually, and licked the women between the legs. That is why dogs and these animals lick each other that way.

On the other side of the river, the children had grown up so that all could work. They had plenty of food as there were no idlers to consume it. When they killed an antelope they cut out the liver and made a hole in it and artificially performed the sexual act. Some who could overtake a doe would copulate with it, but these lightning struck and burst open. Some in like manner with an antelope doe, and the rattlesnake bit and killed them. Another man would do likewise with mountain sheep and a bear killed him.

Kideztizi was out hunting till late and as he could not reach home he camped. He lay down before the fire with a piece of liver in his hand, warming his penis to cause an erection. Nastja (owl) lit on branch above him and hooting called "Kitdeztizi, don't fornicate that liver," and then flew away. Another owl came from the same direction and lit crying "You go on and do so if you wish." He acted on the last suggestion and then went to sleep.

Very few women were left alive, but the men remained strong and well. The men came together one night and began to talk about the women and asked the chief what he thought ought to be done. Most of the men said, "We are here without women and when we begin to die we shall disappear very fast as we have no increase." They talked four nights and then the chief said, "One of you might go across the river and see how many of the women are left. Look for the woman who caused trouble and if she is dead, all will be well." She was found alive but could hardly lift her head. Scarcely any flesh remained on her bones and she defecated where she lay. All the four chiefs went over to see her. As the head chief went into his old house where she had abused him, she seized him, but he jerked away from her, and then she began to talk to him. She wept with sorrow and repentance, and acknowledged that she was unable to live alone as she had once thought. All the women came and begged piteously. But the men would not touch them for they all p. 100 smelled bad, like coyotes. The chiefs all returned across the river to discuss the matter. Most of them thought that they might as well keep the few women remaining, or else the race would disappear. The men had one berdache among them and they decided to leave the question to his decision. He said he was content to have the women come across because he was tired of cooking for them all. He said, "The best you can do is to bring these women over." He made a lot of small boats (rafts) and brought the women across in two days. After the women were brought over the men would give them nothing to eat for they smelled bad, and they put them in the sweathouses and gave them herbs to make them vomit. Some of the women ate too much and it killed them. On the fourth night the sweating ceremonies were over, and the women were fed. They grew fat and healthy again. Those whose wives had died became jealous of those whose wives rejoined them. This jealousy spread, and it has always continued. At the end of four years the young girls had grown fit for wives and those who had none took these. At the end of these four years they came from the east and crossed the ..... Mountains (omitted from mss.)

A long time before this when Teholtsody left, he built a house under the water upon the bottom of the river, and no one had seen him since. At night the cries of a baby were heard from the water house and Coyote tried to get the baby but failed. He went to Old Man and told him, and Old Man said, "Go to the Spider Woman." Spider Woman spun a web which spread over the river to the place where the house was beneath the water, and she got the baby and hid it away so that Teholtsody could not find the child. He is sad to this day because of the loss of the child. He is everybody's friend. Spider Woman took the baby and wrapped it in the web and placed it under her left arm and no one can find it to this day. Teholtsody being unable to find the baby grew crazy and said he would keep on killing everyone he met until he found this child. Being very angry he opened the earth at four corners and let the waters loose, and the rise of the water brought the people together and they saw the waters come up and out of the earth like the clouds and they could not understand it. Then they prayed for the winds, and they came up. White Wind being quick went to the east, Blue to the south, Yellow to west, and Black to the north, and they returned and said, "You are going to be drowned, for great bodies of water are coming together." Then one went to East Mountain to get some earth, one to San Francisco Mt., west; one to Navajo Mt., north; and one to San Mateo Mt., east. They brought earth from all these. When Old Man left the lower world Old Woman brought the springs up with her under her arms.

The two youths came back from the mountain called Tcolii. Everybody saw them. One had a piece of hollow reed with four holes in its side, the other a sunflower stem with four holes in its stem (i.e. flutes). And all the people came together. They had plenty of everything, but the water came so quickly upon them they had only time to take enough for seed and they began to climb the mountains but the waters still rose. So the people climbed up to the tops of the pine trees. The two youths who had the reed and sunflower planted the reed and the people got into it and the reed began to grow. Klishjo was at the bottom, then Thunder, then the Turkey whose tail dragged in the water, that is why his feathers are white. These flutes had four holes. The first hole was for Black Wind, second for Yellow, third for Blue, and fourth White, and these winds guarded the holes in the flute. The winds began to blow and the Great Fly also began to shake the flute, and it began to grow, and the rain kept falling. They had no rest for four nights and Badger began to dig upward but came back again. Wunusticinde then began to dig and shortly he penetrated through to another world, but he found nothing but water. Wunustcinde being small he was hard to see, but soon a man in the east who had an axe spied him and came and struck twelve times at him but could not hit him. Then came a man from the south and tried, then from the west, then from the north, but all failed to hurt him. So these four men went back in the directions they came from. The man who came with the axe first went back, but another man came from the east, Tcithkahilka with two arrows, one trimmed with gray eagle feathers and one with black. He came to Wunustcinde and threw the arrows at him. "What are you doing here?" he said. "You have no right here, this is my land." Wunustcinde said, "We shall see about that. We would like to live here at any rate." The man took his arrows and put one up his anus, the other down his throat and pushed them through, then drew them out and threw them to Wunustcinde saying, that if he could do that the land would be his. Wunustcinde said he could do better than that, so he pushed them through his breast, one from each side and taking them by the points drew them through. There was a little blood adhering to them but the act did not hurt him at all. Wunustcinde said, "If you do as I have done, you can have your ground back. It belongs to me now as I have won it from you." The man picked up his arrows and went home in sorrow. (Repeat for the men who came from the other three points). So Wunustcinde won that country.

He returned to his people and told of his new world, and four of his people went up. One of these with his flint knife cut the ground towards the east and made a little cañon. The next man went south, and dragged his black cane through the soft ground and made an arroyo. Mountain sheep, the third man, went west and formed an arroyo, ploughing up the ground. The fourth was Rhanskidde. He had a straight stick which he dragged along the ground and made an arroyo to the north side. All these four met again in the middle and then went down to their people. The four winds then came up on top and blew as hard as they could and by the fourth night everything was dry and the land beautiful. That is why water runs in all directions. When Badger came up, the ground was muddy in places and he being short-legged got stuck in the mud. That is why he has a black muzzle and black legs. The winds followed after Badger. The leader of the Winds was left-handed. The next one was the Striped Wind. Next the Spotted Wind, and fourth was Shiny Wind. These all raised a tempest which dried up the ground very quickly. They sent out big grey Fly who flew up and found everything beautiful. He returned and reported to his people, and they stayed yet another twelve days before the new world was dry enough for occupancy.

Spider Woman still carried Teholtsody's child under her arm wrapped in spider web. Everything being in readiness, long ladders were made to reach through the hole from the lower to the new upper world and the people all came up through by this means. The water of the lower world kept rising until it touched the bottom of new world and Turkey was last to come up. The foam touched his tail; that is why it is white on the end. Some water squirted up through the hole after all had got out, and it formed a lake. When all the people were up Hoskjelti (Hosdjeyelti) sought for the best place to build houses and he laid the foundations of the houses of all the Pueblo Indians. While he was working for these people his own people could not wait any longer without houses so they cut down poles and built hogans. Then they arranged their farms, planting all kinds of seed. Teholtsody was still searching for his child and followed these people. He wanted to come out upon this upper world and everyone was afraid and did not know what to do. While people were talking, Spider Woman came in with the child and they made her give the child back to Teholtsody, who then went down to the lower world and closed over the water.

To this latter world was brought from the former ones all the seeds of plants and of trees and of all things that grow.

Navajos and Mokis came up at the same time, (all this legend concerns them both).

Traditional Native Attitudes

Unfortunately, most Americans who read Indian literature aren't reading literature written by Indians. Instead, they are reading literature written by whites with an Indian setting. Why would such "fake" literature, which is not truly representing Native experiences, preferred over "the real thing"? I want to set these ideas out here for you so that we can avoid some silly-looking statements about "how Natives are" which might be based on the literature that poses as Native American. In this class, we'll read only authentic Native American literature, and we will come to understand the difference between it and the stuff that mass audiences and publishers prefer. We'll even look at why they might prefer the inauthentic literature.

So, let me outline some traditional Native American features in the debate over the what is and what was. . . .

Expect Native Authors to Play with the Traditional

We would be doing a disservice to the contemporary Native American authors we will read if we overlooked the flexible ways they make sense of the past. These authors are not relics, antiques. They are, I think, complex individuals whose writings reveal an ability to negotiate between vastly different cultures. They are interested in how cultures interact.

Each one of use negotiates with our past. I've noticed that, for some reason, students sometimes don't want to allow these authors to have a real, complex relationship with their culture and its traditions. It's much easier to read these authors as mere mouthpieces for past traditions. I hope that doesn't sound vague to you. It's just important that you read closely, looking for ways in which these authors characterize their relationship with their traditions.

Credit these authors with complexity. They are not hiding behind an Indian mysticism. Instead, they are creating characters and plots which are modern, complex, and alive with the problems we face today.

Using this Lecture

(The following progression is adapted from pages 24-5 of James Wilson's informative history, *The Earth Shall Weep: A Native History of North America*.) Note that the scope of our discussion (and the class) are incredibly general, so we can't take this too far. Still, here are some common threads you may see in traditional Native American poems, songs, and cultural beliefs:

Sacred Power

This is the idea that everything in the universe was interconnected and possessed a spiritual force or energy that could affect the lives of "the people" and of all other living things. Gaining power and the aid of powerful beings was absolutely vital: for success in hunting, plentiful crops, good health, thriving children and victory in battle. But power was also dangerous. By wrongdoing or negligence you could easily offend one of the spirits and see your food supply dwindle, your family stricken or your community defeated.

Orality

Experience and understanding are embodied in stories and legends that often offer the profoundest guide to how a people perceive reality. Stories may change greatly over time, but the fact that they are told over and over–and are memorized–gives the oral tradition a conservative cast. Also, think about the strength of a told story. It has a power that poetry has; the performance of a known story is a binding social event. On the other hand, think of how much tradition could be lost if key members of a group died due to disease or war. In this sense, Native American groups have lost much, and there is a need to re-search their culture for what has survived, for what is authentic and lasting.

Ritual & Ceremony

By following the prescribed instructions, "the people" were able to secure the favor and assistance of powerful spiritual forces. . . . Because everything in the universe was interrelated, and because "the people" were at the center of it, their rituals not only regulated their own relationship with the sacred and with other living beings but also ensured that the whole natural order was properly maintained.

What rituals do you go through in your own life? Do you think we have fewer rituals than traditional oral cultures?

Why is it important to do the ritual "just right"?

Do cultures with lots of rituals tend to be liberal or conservative?

The Animal Master

Animal masters are spiritual "masters" (or "keepers" or "owners") who controlled the game on which hunters depended for food. For example, there might be a buffalo king who tells his people where they are to graze, or when they should migrate.

Animal masters reflect the idea that the animal does not die.

Planting cultures had differing myths of dismemberment and ritual planting/sacrifice.

If game was killed *in the wrong way* or without the proper ritual, if the meat was treated disrespectfully, wasted or not shared generously among the whole group, then the animal masters would become angry and withhold food in the future.

Tricksters are often a play on the animal master. The trickster figure is found in many cultures, and constitutes a richly creative personality in folklore and myth.

Animal characters are often given human traits like the ability to speak. Animals are often characterized by a predominant personality trait.

Questions and Ideas

- To what extent is the view that Native Americans hold the land sacred a valid statement?
- What do you think about the land/area in which you live?
- In *The Power of Myth*, Joseph Campbell, a noted scholar of mythology, likens the 19th century Indian view of reality to calling everything a *Thou*. He contrasts this with a typical white attitude in which animals and the land were seen as merely *Its*. Consider this contrast as you read our assigned texts.
- *Is* ownership of land a ridiculous idea? From what point of view might it seem ridiculous? What "value" is there in this point of view? Do you "buy" it?

Gáqga', A Trickster Tale

Trickster tales are often told to establish the origin of an item or custom, or to impart a moral message. Review this Seneca story from Jeremiah Curtin's 1889 collection, *Seneca Indian Myths*(republished in 1922). *Consider how this relates to our unit discussion topics and the course objectives.*

GÁQGA´

Characters

GÁQGA´	Raven
DZODJÓGIS	Blackbirds
GAI´SGEn SE	Ground-birds
GANOGESHEGEA	Sparrows
DJEONYAIK	Robin
HÁNISHEONOn	Muck-worm

RAVEN was traveling but he didn't know whence he came or whither he was going. As he journeyed along he was thinking, "How did I come to be alive? Where did I come from? Where am I going?" After traveling a long time he saw a smoke and going toward it saw four hunters–blackbirds. Afraid to go near them he hid in the forest and watched.

The next morning after the hunters had started away, Raven crept up to their camp, stole their meat, carried it into the woods and made a camp for himself. He was lonely and he said, "I wish there were other people here." Looking around he saw a house west of his camp and going to it found Robin and his wife and five children. Raven ate the youngest child, then ate the other four. The father and mother tried to drive him away, but could not. When at last Raven went off he left old Rabin and his wife crying for their children.

Sometime after this, Raven saw a camp off in the southeast and going there found a family of Sparrows. He was afraid of the old people and he ran off, but they followed him, caught up and hit him on the head till they drove him far away.

"It is a shame to let such little people beat me!" thought Raven. But he was afraid to go back.

Now Raven had gone far from his camp; he hunted everywhere in the forest but couldn't find it. "Well," said he at last, "let it go, I don't care!" and he walked away toward the North. Just before dark, he found a camp and going towards it saw four men and a large quantity of meat. He hid in the forest and the next morning', looking toward the camp, he again saw the hunters.

"I'll wait till they go away," thought Raven, "then I'll steal their meat." Soon he heard the men moving around, then all was quiet and he knew that they had gone. He crept slowly toward the camp, but when he reached it be didn't find even one bite of meat–they were the hunters from whom he had stolen before. They had finished hunting, had packed their meat and started for home.

Raven was disappointed. He walked on and toward night found another camp. Creeping near it, he again saw the four hunters. He listened to what they were saying.

One said, "I wonder who stole our meat that day?"

Another said, "I think the thief is walking around in the woods, I think his name is Raven."

"Oh," thought Raven, "they are talking about me. They will be on the watch. How can I get their meat? Then he said, "Let them fall asleep and sleep soundly!"

That minute the four hunters fell asleep. Raven went up boldly, took their meat, carried it off into the woods and hid it, saying, "This is the kind of man I am!"

The next morning the four hunters missed their meat.

One said, "Somebody has stolen my meat!"

Another asked, "Who has stolen my meat?"

The third said, "I dreamed that I saw Raven around here and he started off toward the Southwest."

Then the four said, "Let us follow the direction given by the dream."

The hunters started to follow the thief. Soon they came to the place where he was camped. Raven had been out all night and now he was sleeping soundly.

One of the men said, "We must kill him."

"No," said another, "let him live, he didn't kill us while we were asleep."

They took their meat and went away.

When Raven woke up, he was very hungry, but the meat was gone. "Well," thought he, "I must hunt for something to eat." He traveled around in every direction but found no game. About midday he heard the noise of people. He listened a while then went on till he came to a house. A man inside the house was singing and the song said, "Raven is coming! Look out! Be careful! Raven is coming!"

"Why does he sing about me?" thought Raven, "I'll go in and find out."

He went into the house and found Ground-bird and his wife and four children.

"I have come to stay a few days with you," said Raven.

"Very well," said the man.

That night Raven ate the four children, then he lay down and slept.

The next morning the father and mother asked, "Where are our children?"

Raven said, "I dreamed that a man came and carried your children off, and my dream told me which way he went. I will go with you and hunt for them."

When the three had traveled some distance Raven said, "The man who stole your children lives on that high cliff over there. I can't go there with you, for I don't like that man. I will wait here till you come back."

As soon as the father and mother were out of sight, Raven ran off. He traveled till he came to where there were many of his own people. They were dancing and he sat down to watch them.

Soon Muck-worm was seen coming from the East. The people stopped dancing and ran in every direction, but Muck-worm pursued them and catching one after another by the neck he threw them aside dead.

Raven, who was watching, thought, "What sort of man is that? I wish he would see me. He can't throw me off dead, in that way."

Muck-worm, after killing many of the Raven people, started toward the West, Raven followed him. Muck-worm kept on for a long time without seeming to know that there was anyone behind him, but at last he stopped, looked back, and asked, "What do you want?"

"I don't want anything," said Raven, "I've come to be company for you."

"I don't want company," said Muck-worm.

Raven was frightened. Both men stood still for a minute then Muck-worm sprang at Raven and caught him. He would have killed him, but Raven screamed so loudly that many of his people heard the cry and came to his aid. They flew at Muck-worm and pecked him to death.

Washington Irving, The Legend of Sleepy Hollow

"The Legend of Sleepy Hollow" is a short story of speculative fiction by American author Washington Irving, contained in his collection of 34 essays and short stories entitled *The Sketch Book of Geoffrey Crayon, Gent.* Written while Irving was living abroad in Birmingham, England, "The Legend of Sleepy Hollow" was first published in 1820. Along with Irving's companion piece "Rip Van Winkle", "The Legend of Sleepy Hollow" is among the earliest examples of American fiction with enduring popularity, especially during the Halloween season.

Found among the papers of the late Diedrich Knickerbocker.

> A pleasing land of drowsy head it was,
>   Of dreams that wave before the half-shut eye;
> And of gay castles in the clouds that pass,
>   Forever flushing round a summer sky.
>   —Castle of Indolence.

In the bosom of one of those spacious coves which indent the eastern shore of the Hudson, at that broad expansion of the river denominated by the ancient Dutch navigators the Tappan Zee, and where they always prudently shortened sail and implored the protection of St. Nicholas when they crossed, there lies a small market town or rural port, which by some is called Greensburgh, but which is more generally and properly known by the name of Tarry Town. This name was given, we are told, in former days, by the good housewives of the adjacent country, from the inveterate propensity of their husbands to linger about the village tavern on market days. Be that as it may, I do not vouch for the fact, but merely advert to it, for the sake of being precise and authentic. Not far from this village, perhaps about two miles, there is a little valley or rather lap of land among high hills, which is one of the quietest places in the whole world. A small brook glides through it, with just murmur enough to lull one to repose; and the occasional whistle of a quail or tapping of a woodpecker is almost the only sound that ever breaks in upon the uniform tranquillity.

I recollect that, when a stripling, my first exploit in squirrel-shooting was in a grove of tall walnut-trees that shades one side of the valley. I had wandered into it at noontime, when all nature is peculiarly quiet, and was startled by the roar of my own gun, as it broke the Sabbath stillness around and was prolonged and reverberated by the angry echoes. If ever I should wish for a retreat whither I might steal from the world and its distractions, and dream quietly away the remnant of a troubled life, I know of none more promising than this little valley.

From the listless repose of the place, and the peculiar character of its inhabitants, who are descendants from the original Dutch settlers, this sequestered glen has long been known by the name of SLEEPY HOLLOW, and its rustic lads are called the Sleepy Hollow Boys throughout all the neighboring country. A drowsy, dreamy influence seems to hang over the land, and to pervade the very atmosphere. Some say that the place was bewitched by a High German doctor, during the early days of the settlement; others, that an old Indian chief, the prophet or wizard of his tribe, held his powwows there before the country was discovered by Master Hendrick Hudson. Certain it is, the place still continues under the sway of some witching power, that holds a spell over the minds of the good people, causing them to walk in a continual reverie. They are given to all kinds of marvellous beliefs, are subject to trances and visions, and frequently see strange sights, and hear music and voices in the air. The whole neighborhood abounds with local tales, haunted spots, and twilight superstitions; stars shoot and meteors glare oftener across the valley than in any other part of the country, and the nightmare, with her whole ninefold, seems to make it the favorite scene of her gambols.

The dominant spirit, however, that haunts this enchanted region, and seems to be commander-in-chief of all the powers of the air, is the apparition of a figure on horseback, without a head. It is said by some to be the ghost of a Hessian trooper, whose head had been carried away by a cannon-ball, in some nameless battle during the Revolutionary War, and who is ever and anon seen by the country folk hurrying along in the gloom of night, as if on the wings of the wind. His haunts are not confined to the valley, but extend at times to the adjacent roads, and especially to the vicinity of a church at no great distance. Indeed, certain of the most authentic historians of those parts, who have been careful in collecting and collating the floating facts concerning this spectre, allege that the body of the trooper having been buried in the churchyard, the ghost rides forth to the scene of battle in nightly quest of his head, and that the rushing speed with which he sometimes passes along the Hollow, like a midnight blast, is owing to his being belated, and in a hurry to get back to the churchyard before daybreak.

Such is the general purport of this legendary superstition, which has furnished materials for many a wild story in that region of shadows; and the spectre is known at all the country firesides, by the name of the Headless Horseman of Sleepy Hollow.

It is remarkable that the visionary propensity I have mentioned is not confined to the native inhabitants of the valley, but is unconsciously imbibed by every one who resides there for a time. However wide awake they may have been before they entered that sleepy region, they are sure, in a little time, to inhale the witching influence of the air, and begin to grow imaginative, to dream dreams, and see apparitions.

I mention this peaceful spot with all possible laud, for it is in such little retired Dutch valleys, found here and there embosomed in the great State of New York, that population, manners, and customs remain fixed, while the great torrent of migration and improvement, which is making such incessant changes in other parts of this restless country, sweeps by them unobserved. They are like those little nooks of still water, which border a rapid stream, where we may see the straw and bubble riding quietly at anchor, or slowly revolving in their mimic harbor, undisturbed by the rush of the passing current. Though many years have elapsed since I trod the drowsy shades of Sleepy Hollow, yet I question whether I should not still find the same trees and the same families vegetating in its sheltered bosom.

In this by-place of nature there abode, in a remote period of American history, that is to say, some thirty years since, a worthy wight of the name of Ichabod Crane, who sojourned, or, as he expressed it, "tarried," in Sleepy Hollow, for the purpose of instructing the children of the vicinity. He was a native of Connecticut, a State which supplies the Union with pioneers for the mind as well as for the forest, and sends forth yearly its legions of frontier woodmen and country schoolmasters. The cognomen of Crane was not inapplicable to his person. He was tall, but exceedingly lank, with narrow shoulders, long arms and legs, hands that dangled a mile out of his sleeves, feet that might have served for shovels, and his whole frame most loosely hung together. His head was small, and flat at top, with huge ears, large green glassy eyes, and a long snipe nose, so that it looked like a weather-cock perched upon his spindle neck to tell which way the wind blew. To see him striding along the profile of a hill on a windy day, with his clothes bagging and fluttering about him, one might have mistaken him for the genius of famine descending upon the earth, or some scarecrow eloped from a cornfield.

His schoolhouse was a low building of one large room, rudely constructed of logs; the windows partly glazed, and partly patched with leaves of old copybooks. It was most ingeniously secured at vacant hours, by a withe twisted in the handle of the door, and stakes set against the window shutters; so that though a thief might get in with perfect ease, he would find some embarrassment in getting out,—an idea most probably borrowed by the architect, Yost Van Houten, from the mystery of an eelpot. The schoolhouse stood in a rather lonely but pleasant situation, just at the foot of a woody hill, with a brook running close by, and a formidable birch-tree growing at one end of it. From hence the low murmur of his pupils' voices, conning over their lessons, might be heard in a drowsy summer's day, like the hum of a beehive; interrupted now and then by the authoritative voice of the master, in the tone of menace or command, or, peradventure, by the appalling sound of the birch, as he urged some tardy loiterer along the flowery path of knowledge. Truth to say, he was a conscientious man, and ever bore in mind the golden maxim, "Spare the rod and spoil the child." Ichabod Crane's scholars certainly were not spoiled.

I would not have it imagined, however, that he was one of those cruel potentates of the school who joy in the smart of their subjects; on the contrary, he administered justice with discrimination rather than severity; taking the burden off the backs of the weak, and laying it on those of the strong. Your mere puny stripling, that winced at the least flourish of the rod, was passed by with indulgence; but the claims of justice were satisfied by inflicting a double portion on some little tough wrong-headed, broad-skirted Dutch urchin, who sulked and swelled and grew dogged and sullen beneath the birch. All this he called "doing his duty by their parents;" and he never inflicted a chastisement without following it by the assurance, so consolatory to the smarting urchin, that "he would remember it and thank him for it the longest day he had to live."

When school hours were over, he was even the companion and playmate of the larger boys; and on holiday afternoons would convoy some of the smaller ones home, who happened to have pretty sisters, or good housewives for mothers, noted for the comforts of the cupboard. Indeed, it behooved him to keep on good terms with his pupils. The revenue arising from his school was small, and would have been scarcely sufficient to furnish him with daily bread, for he was a huge feeder, and, though lank, had the dilating powers of an anaconda; but to help out his maintenance, he was, according to country custom in those parts, boarded and lodged at the houses of the farmers whose children he instructed. With these he lived successively a week at a time, thus going the rounds of the neighborhood, with all his worldly effects tied up in a cotton handkerchief.

That all this might not be too onerous on the purses of his rustic patrons, who are apt to consider the costs of schooling a grievous burden, and schoolmasters as mere drones, he had various ways of rendering himself both useful and agreeable. He assisted the farmers occasionally in the lighter labors of their farms, helped to make hay, mended the fences, took the horses to water, drove the cows from pasture, and cut wood for the winter fire. He laid aside, too, all the dominant dignity and absolute sway with which he lorded it in his little empire, the school, and became wonderfully gentle and ingratiating. He found favor in the eyes of the mothers by petting the children, particularly the youngest; and like the lion bold, which whilom so magnanimously the lamb did hold, he would sit with a child on one knee, and rock a cradle with his foot for whole hours together.

In addition to his other vocations, he was the singing-master of the neighborhood, and picked up many bright shillings by instructing the young folks in psalmody. It was a matter of no little vanity to him on Sundays, to take his station in front of the church gallery, with a band of chosen singers; where, in his own mind, he completely carried away the palm from the parson. Certain it is, his voice resounded far above all the rest of the congregation; and there are peculiar quavers still to be heard in that church, and which may even be heard half a mile off, quite to the opposite side of the millpond, on a still Sunday morning, which are said to be legitimately descended from the nose of Ichabod Crane. Thus, by divers little makeshifts, in that ingenious way which is commonly denominated "by hook and by crook," the worthy pedagogue got on tolerably enough, and was thought, by all who understood nothing of the labor of headwork, to have a wonderfully easy life of it.

The schoolmaster is generally a man of some importance in the female circle of a rural neighborhood; being considered a kind of idle, gentlemanlike personage, of vastly superior taste and accomplishments to the rough country swains, and, indeed, inferior in learning only to the parson. His appearance, therefore, is apt to occasion some little stir at the tea-table of a farmhouse, and the addition of a supernumerary dish of cakes or sweetmeats, or, peradventure, the parade of a silver teapot. Our man of letters, therefore, was peculiarly happy in the smiles of all the country damsels. How he would figure among them in the churchyard, between services on Sundays; gathering grapes for them from the wild vines that overran the surrounding trees; reciting for their amusement all the epitaphs on the tombstones; or sauntering, with a whole bevy of them, along the banks of the adjacent millpond; while the more bashful country bumpkins hung sheepishly back, envying his superior elegance and address.

From his half-itinerant life, also, he was a kind of travelling gazette, carrying the whole budget of local gossip from house to house, so that his appearance was always greeted with satisfaction. He was, moreover, esteemed by the women as a man of great erudition, for he had read several books quite through, and was a perfect master of Cotton Mather's "History of New England Witchcraft," in which, by the way, he most firmly and potently believed.

He was, in fact, an odd mixture of small shrewdness and simple credulity. His appetite for the marvellous, and his powers of digesting it, were equally extraordinary; and both had been increased by his residence in this spell-bound region. No tale was too gross or monstrous for his capacious swallow. It was often his delight, after his school was dismissed in the afternoon, to stretch himself on the rich bed of clover bordering the little brook that whimpered by his schoolhouse, and there con over old Mather's direful tales, until the gathering dusk of evening made the printed page a mere mist before his eyes. Then, as he wended his way by swamp and stream and awful woodland, to the farmhouse where he happened to be quartered, every sound of nature, at that witching hour, fluttered his excited imagination,—the moan of the whip-poor-will from the hillside, the boding cry of the tree toad, that harbinger of storm, the dreary hooting of the screech owl, or the sudden rustling in the thicket of birds frightened from their roost. The fireflies, too, which sparkled most vividly in the darkest places, now and then startled him, as one of uncommon brightness would stream across his path; and if, by chance, a huge blockhead of a beetle came winging his blundering flight against him, the poor varlet was ready to give up the ghost, with the idea that he was struck with a witch's token. His only resource on such occasions, either to drown thought or drive away evil spirits, was to sing psalm tunes and the good people of Sleepy Hollow, as they sat by their doors of an evening, were often filled with awe at hearing his nasal melody, "in linked sweetness long drawn out," floating from the distant hill, or along the dusky road.

Another of his sources of fearful pleasure was to pass long winter evenings with the old Dutch wives, as they sat spinning by the fire, with a row of apples roasting and spluttering along the hearth, and listen to their marvellous tales of ghosts and goblins, and haunted fields, and haunted brooks, and haunted bridges, and haunted houses, and particularly of the headless horseman, or Galloping Hessian of the Hollow, as they sometimes called him. He would delight them equally by his anecdotes of witchcraft, and of the direful omens and portentous sights and sounds in the air, which prevailed in the earlier times of Connecticut; and would frighten them woefully with speculations upon comets and shooting stars; and with the alarming fact that the world did absolutely turn round, and that they were half the time topsy-turvy!

But if there was a pleasure in all this, while snugly cuddling in the chimney corner of a chamber that was all of a ruddy glow from the crackling wood fire, and where, of course, no spectre dared to show its face, it was dearly purchased by the terrors of his subsequent walk homewards. What fearful shapes and shadows beset his path, amidst the dim and ghastly glare of a snowy night! With what wistful look did he eye every trembling ray of light streaming across the waste fields from some distant window! How often was he appalled by some shrub covered with snow, which, like a sheeted spectre, beset his very path! How often did he shrink with curdling awe at the sound of his own steps on the frosty crust beneath his feet; and dread to look over his shoulder, lest he should behold some uncouth being tramping close behind him! And how often was he thrown into complete dismay by some rushing blast, howling among the trees, in the idea that it was the Galloping Hessian on one of his nightly scourings!

All these, however, were mere terrors of the night, phantoms of the mind that walk in darkness; and though he had seen many spectres in his time, and been more than once beset by Satan in divers shapes, in his lonely perambulations, yet daylight put an end to all these evils; and he would have passed a pleasant life of it, in despite of the Devil and all his works, if his path had not been crossed by a being that causes more perplexity to mortal man than ghosts, goblins, and the whole race of witches put together, and that was—a woman.

Among the musical disciples who assembled, one evening in each week, to receive his instructions in psalmody, was Katrina Van Tassel, the daughter and only child of a substantial Dutch farmer. She was a blooming lass of fresh eighteen; plump as a partridge; ripe and melting and rosy-cheeked as one of her father's peaches, and universally famed, not merely for her beauty, but her vast expectations. She was withal a little of a coquette, as might be perceived even in her dress, which was a mixture of ancient and modern fashions, as most suited to set off her charms. She wore the ornaments of pure yellow gold, which her great-great-grandmother had brought over from Saardam; the tempting stomacher of the olden time, and withal a provokingly short petticoat, to display the prettiest foot and ankle in the country round.

Ichabod Crane had a soft and foolish heart towards the sex; and it is not to be wondered at that so tempting a morsel soon found favor in his eyes, more especially after he had visited her in her paternal mansion. Old Baltus Van Tassel was a perfect picture of a thriving, contented, liberal-hearted farmer. He seldom, it is true, sent either his eyes or his thoughts beyond the boundaries of his own farm; but within those everything was snug, happy and well-conditioned. He was satisfied with his wealth, but not proud of it; and piqued himself upon the hearty abundance, rather than the style in which he lived. His stronghold was situated on the banks of the Hudson, in one of those green, sheltered, fertile nooks in which the Dutch farmers are so fond of nestling. A great elm tree spread its broad branches over it, at the foot of which bubbled up a spring of the softest and sweetest water, in a little well formed of a barrel; and then stole sparkling away through the grass, to a neighboring brook, that babbled along among alders and dwarf willows. Hard by the farmhouse was a vast barn, that might have served for a church; every window and crevice of which seemed bursting forth with the treasures of the farm; the flail was busily resounding within it from morning to night; swallows and martins skimmed twittering about the eaves; and rows of pigeons, some with one eye turned up, as if watching the weather, some with their heads under their wings or buried in their bosoms, and others swelling, and cooing, and bowing about their dames, were enjoying the sunshine on the roof. Sleek unwieldy porkers were grunting in the repose and abundance of their pens, from whence sallied forth, now and then, troops of sucking pigs, as if to snuff the air. A stately squadron of snowy geese were riding in an adjoining pond, convoying whole fleets of ducks; regiments of turkeys were gobbling through the farmyard, and Guinea fowls fretting about it, like ill-tempered housewives, with their peevish, discontented cry. Before the barn door strutted the gallant cock, that pattern of a husband, a warrior and a fine gentleman, clapping his burnished wings and crowing in the pride and gladness of his heart,—sometimes tearing up the earth with his feet, and then generously calling his ever-hungry family of wives and children to enjoy the rich morsel which he had discovered.

The pedagogue's mouth watered as he looked upon this sumptuous promise of luxurious winter fare. In his devouring mind's eye, he pictured to himself every roasting-pig running about with a pudding in his belly, and an apple in his mouth; the pigeons were snugly put to bed in a comfortable pie, and tucked in with a coverlet of crust; the geese were swimming in their own gravy; and the ducks pairing cosily in dishes, like snug married couples, with a decent competency of onion sauce. In the porkers he saw carved out the future sleek side of bacon, and juicy relishing ham; not a turkey but he beheld daintily trussed up, with its gizzard under its wing, and, peradventure, a necklace of savory sausages; and even bright chanticleer himself lay sprawling on his back, in a side dish, with uplifted claws, as if craving that quarter which his chivalrous spirit disdained to ask while living.

As the enraptured Ichabod fancied all this, and as he rolled his great green eyes over the fat meadow lands, the rich fields of wheat, of rye, of buckwheat, and Indian corn, and the orchards burdened with ruddy fruit, which surrounded the warm tenement of Van Tassel, his heart yearned after the damsel who was to inherit these domains, and his imagination expanded with the idea, how they might be readily turned into cash, and the money invested in immense tracts of wild land, and shingle palaces in the wilderness. Nay, his busy fancy already realized his hopes, and presented to him the blooming Katrina, with a whole family of children, mounted on the top of a wagon loaded with household trumpery, with pots and kettles dangling beneath; and he beheld himself bestriding a pacing mare, with a colt at her heels, setting out for Kentucky, Tennessee,—or the Lord knows where!

When he entered the house, the conquest of his heart was complete. It was one of those spacious farmhouses, with high-ridged but lowly sloping roofs, built in the style handed down from the first Dutch settlers; the low projecting eaves forming a piazza along the front, capable of being closed up in bad weather. Under this were hung flails, harness, various utensils of husbandry, and nets for fishing in the neighboring river. Benches were built along the sides for summer use; and a great spinning-wheel at one end, and a churn at the other, showed the various uses to which this important porch might be devoted. From this piazza the wondering Ichabod entered the hall, which formed the centre of the mansion, and the place of usual residence. Here rows of resplendent pewter, ranged on a long dresser, dazzled his eyes. In one corner stood a huge bag of wool, ready to be spun; in another, a quantity of linsey-woolsey just from the loom; ears of Indian corn, and strings of dried apples and peaches, hung in gay festoons along the walls, mingled with the gaud of red peppers; and a door left ajar gave him a peep into the best parlor, where the claw-footed chairs and dark mahogany tables shone like mirrors; andirons, with their accompanying shovel and tongs, glistened from their covert of asparagus tops; mock-oranges and conch-shells decorated the mantelpiece; strings of various-colored birds eggs were suspended above it; a great ostrich egg was hung from the centre of the room, and a corner cupboard, knowingly left open, displayed immense treasures of old silver and well-mended china.

From the moment Ichabod laid his eyes upon these regions of delight, the peace of his mind was at an end, and his only study was how to gain the affections of the peerless daughter of Van Tassel. In this enterprise, however, he had more real difficulties than generally fell to the lot of a knight-errant of yore, who seldom had anything but giants, enchanters, fiery dragons, and such like easily conquered adversaries, to contend with and had to make his way merely through gates of iron and brass, and walls of adamant to the castle keep, where the lady of his heart was confined; all which he achieved as easily as a man would carve his way to the centre of a Christmas pie; and then the lady gave him her hand as a matter of course. Ichabod, on the contrary, had to win his way to the heart of a country coquette, beset with a labyrinth of whims and caprices, which were forever presenting new difficulties and impediments; and he had to encounter a host of fearful adversaries of real flesh and blood, the numerous rustic admirers, who beset every portal to her heart, keeping a watchful and angry eye upon each other, but ready to fly out in the common cause against any new competitor.

Among these, the most formidable was a burly, roaring, roystering blade, of the name of Abraham, or, according to the Dutch abbreviation, Brom Van Brunt, the hero of the country round, which rang with his feats of strength and hardihood. He was broad-shouldered and double-jointed, with short curly black hair, and a bluff but not unpleasant countenance, having a mingled air of fun and arrogance. From his Herculean frame and great powers of limb he had received the nickname of BROM BONES, by which he was universally known. He was famed for great knowledge and skill in horsemanship, being as dexterous on horseback as a Tartar. He was foremost at all races and cock fights; and, with the ascendancy which bodily strength always acquires in rustic life, was the umpire in all disputes, setting his hat on one side, and giving his decisions with an air and tone that admitted of no gainsay or appeal. He was always ready for either a fight or a frolic; but had more mischief than ill-will in his composition; and with all his overbearing roughness, there was a strong dash of waggish good humor at bottom. He had three or four boon companions, who regarded him as their model, and at the head of whom he scoured the country, attending every scene of feud or merriment for miles round. In cold weather he was distinguished by a fur cap, surmounted with a flaunting fox's tail; and when the folks at a country gathering descried this well-known crest at a distance, whisking about among a squad of hard riders, they always stood by for a squall. Sometimes his crew would be heard dashing along past the farmhouses at midnight, with whoop and halloo, like a troop of Don Cossacks; and the old dames, startled out of their sleep, would listen for a moment till the hurry-scurry had clattered by, and then exclaim, "Ay, there goes Brom Bones and his gang!" The neighbors looked upon him with a mixture of awe, admiration, and good-will; and, when any madcap prank or rustic brawl occurred in the vicinity, always shook their heads, and warranted Brom Bones was at the bottom of it.

This rantipole hero had for some time singled out the blooming Katrina for the object of his uncouth gallantries, and though his amorous toyings were something like the gentle caresses and endearments of a bear, yet it was whispered that she did not altogether discourage his hopes. Certain it is, his advances were signals for rival candidates to retire, who felt no inclination to cross a lion in his amours; insomuch, that when his horse was seen tied to Van Tassel's paling, on a Sunday night, a sure sign that his master was courting, or, as it is termed, "sparking," within, all other suitors passed by in despair, and carried the war into other quarters.

Such was the formidable rival with whom Ichabod Crane had to contend, and, considering all things, a stouter man than he would have shrunk from the competition, and a wiser man would have despaired. He had, however, a happy mixture of pliability and perseverance in his nature; he was in form and spirit like a supple-jack—yielding, but tough; though he bent, he never broke; and though he bowed beneath the slightest pressure, yet, the moment it was away—jerk!—he was as erect, and carried his head as high as ever.

To have taken the field openly against his rival would have been madness; for he was not a man to be thwarted in his amours, any more than that stormy lover, Achilles. Ichabod, therefore, made his advances in a quiet and gently insinuating manner. Under cover of his character of singing-master, he made frequent visits at the farmhouse; not that he had anything to apprehend from the meddlesome interference of parents, which is so often a stumbling-block in the path of lovers. Balt Van Tassel was an easy indulgent soul; he loved his daughter better even than his pipe, and, like a reasonable man and an excellent father, let her have her way in everything. His notable little wife, too, had enough to do to attend to her housekeeping and manage her poultry; for, as she sagely observed, ducks and geese are foolish things, and must be looked after, but girls can take care of themselves. Thus, while the busy dame bustled about the house, or plied her spinning-wheel at one end of the piazza, honest Balt would sit smoking his evening pipe at the other, watching the achievements of a little wooden warrior, who, armed with a sword in each hand, was most valiantly fighting the wind on the pinnacle of the barn. In the mean time, Ichabod would carry on his suit with the daughter by the side of the spring under the great elm, or sauntering along in the twilight, that hour so favorable to the lover's eloquence.

I profess not to know how women's hearts are wooed and won. To me they have always been matters of riddle and admiration. Some seem to have but one vulnerable point, or door of access; while others have a thousand avenues, and may be captured in a thousand different ways. It is a great triumph of skill to gain the former, but a still greater proof of generalship to maintain possession of the latter, for man must battle for his fortress at every door and window. He who wins a thousand common hearts is therefore entitled to some renown; but he who keeps undisputed sway over the heart of a coquette is indeed a hero. Certain it is, this was not the case with the redoubtable Brom Bones; and from the moment Ichabod Crane made his advances, the interests of the former evidently declined: his horse was no longer seen tied to the palings on Sunday nights, and a deadly feud gradually arose between him and the preceptor of Sleepy Hollow.

Brom, who had a degree of rough chivalry in his nature, would fain have carried matters to open warfare and have settled their pretensions to the lady, according to the mode of those most concise and simple reasoners, the knights-errant of yore,—by single combat; but Ichabod was too conscious of the superior might of his adversary to enter the lists against him; he had overheard a boast of Bones, that he would "double the schoolmaster up, and lay him on a shelf of his own schoolhouse;" and he was too wary to give him an opportunity. There was something extremely provoking in this obstinately pacific system; it left Brom no alternative but to draw upon the funds of rustic waggery in his disposition, and to play off boorish practical jokes upon his rival. Ichabod became the object of whimsical persecution to Bones and his gang of rough riders. They harried his hitherto peaceful domains; smoked out his singing school by stopping up the chimney; broke into the schoolhouse at night, in spite of its formidable fastenings of withe and window stakes, and turned everything topsy-turvy, so that the poor schoolmaster began to think all the witches in the country held their meetings there. But what was still more annoying, Brom took all opportunities of turning him into ridicule in presence of his mistress, and had a scoundrel dog whom he taught to whine in the most ludicrous manner, and introduced as a rival of Ichabod's, to instruct her in psalmody.

In this way matters went on for some time, without producing any material effect on the relative situations of the contending powers. On a fine autumnal afternoon, Ichabod, in pensive mood, sat enthroned on the lofty stool from whence he usually watched all the concerns of his little literary realm. In his hand he swayed a ferule, that sceptre of despotic power; the birch of justice reposed on three nails behind the throne, a constant terror to evil doers, while on the desk before him might be seen sundry contraband articles and prohibited weapons, detected upon the persons of idle urchins, such as half-munched apples, popguns, whirligigs, fly-cages, and whole legions of rampant little paper gamecocks. Apparently there had been some appalling act of justice recently inflicted, for his scholars were all busily intent upon their books, or slyly whispering behind them with one eye kept upon the master; and a kind of buzzing stillness reigned throughout the schoolroom. It was suddenly interrupted by the appearance of a negro in tow-cloth jacket and trowsers, a round-crowned fragment of a hat, like the cap of Mercury, and mounted on the back of a ragged, wild, half-broken colt, which he managed with a rope by way of halter. He came clattering up to the school door with an invitation to Ichabod to attend a merry-making or "quilting frolic," to be held that evening at Mynheer Van Tassel's; and having delivered his message with that air of importance, and effort at fine language, which a negro is apt to display on petty embassies of the kind, he dashed over the brook, and was seen scampering away up the hollow, full of the importance and hurry of his mission.

All was now bustle and hubbub in the late quiet schoolroom. The scholars were hurried through their lessons without stopping at trifles; those who were nimble skipped over half with impunity, and those who were tardy had a smart application now and then in the rear, to quicken their speed or help them over a tall word. Books were flung aside without being put away on the shelves, inkstands were overturned, benches thrown down, and the whole school was turned loose an hour before the usual time, bursting forth like a legion of young imps, yelping and racketing about the green in joy at their early emancipation.

The gallant Ichabod now spent at least an extra half hour at his toilet, brushing and furbishing up his best, and indeed only suit of rusty black, and arranging his locks by a bit of broken looking-glass that hung up in the schoolhouse. That he might make his appearance before his mistress in the true style of a cavalier, he borrowed a horse from the farmer with whom he was domiciliated, a choleric old Dutchman of the name of Hans Van Ripper, and, thus gallantly mounted, issued forth like a knight-errant in quest of adventures. But it is meet I should, in the true spirit of romantic story, give some account of the looks and equipments of my hero and his steed. The animal he bestrode was a broken-down plow-horse, that had outlived almost everything but its viciousness. He was gaunt and shagged, with a ewe neck, and a head like a hammer; his rusty mane and tail were tangled and knotted with burs; one eye had lost its pupil, and was glaring and spectral, but the other had the gleam of a genuine devil in it. Still he must have had fire and mettle in his day, if we may judge from the name he bore of Gunpowder. He had, in fact, been a favorite steed of his master's, the choleric Van Ripper, who was a furious rider, and had infused, very probably, some of his own spirit into the animal; for, old and broken-down as he looked, there was more of the lurking devil in him than in any young filly in the country.

Ichabod was a suitable figure for such a steed. He rode with short stirrups, which brought his knees nearly up to the pommel of the saddle; his sharp elbows stuck out like grasshoppers'; he carried his whip perpendicularly in his hand, like a sceptre, and as his horse jogged on, the motion of his arms was not unlike the flapping of a pair of wings. A small wool hat rested on the top of his nose, for so his scanty strip of forehead might be called, and the skirts of his black coat fluttered out almost to the horses tail. Such was the appearance of Ichabod and his steed as they shambled out of the gate of Hans Van Ripper, and it was altogether such an apparition as is seldom to be met with in broad daylight.

It was, as I have said, a fine autumnal day; the sky was clear and serene, and nature wore that rich and golden livery which we always associate with the idea of abundance. The forests had put on their sober brown and yellow, while some trees of the tenderer kind had been nipped by the frosts into brilliant dyes of orange, purple, and scarlet. Streaming files of wild ducks began to make their appearance high in the air; the bark of the squirrel might be heard from the groves of beech and hickory-nuts, and the pensive whistle of the quail at intervals from the neighboring stubble field.

The small birds were taking their farewell banquets. In the fullness of their revelry, they fluttered, chirping and frolicking from bush to bush, and tree to tree, capricious from the very profusion and variety around them. There was the honest cock robin, the favorite game of stripling sportsmen, with its loud querulous note; and the twittering blackbirds flying in sable clouds; and the golden-winged woodpecker with his crimson crest, his broad black gorget, and splendid plumage; and the cedar bird, with its red-tipt wings and yellow-tipt tail and its little monteiro cap of feathers; and the blue jay, that noisy coxcomb, in his gay light blue coat and white underclothes, screaming and chattering, nodding and bobbing and bowing, and pretending to be on good terms with every songster of the grove.

As Ichabod jogged slowly on his way, his eye, ever open to every symptom of culinary abundance, ranged with delight over the treasures of jolly autumn. On all sides he beheld vast store of apples; some hanging in oppressive opulence on the trees; some gathered into baskets and barrels for the market; others heaped up in rich piles for the cider-press. Farther on he beheld great fields of Indian corn, with its golden ears peeping from their leafy coverts, and holding out the promise of cakes and hasty-pudding; and the yellow pumpkins lying beneath them, turning up their fair round bellies to the sun, and giving ample prospects of the most luxurious of pies; and anon he passed the fragrant buckwheat fields breathing the odor of the beehive, and as he beheld them, soft anticipations stole over his mind of dainty slapjacks, well buttered, and garnished with honey or treacle, by the delicate little dimpled hand of Katrina Van Tassel.

Thus feeding his mind with many sweet thoughts and "sugared suppositions," he journeyed along the sides of a range of hills which look out upon some of the goodliest scenes of the mighty Hudson. The sun gradually wheeled his broad disk down in the west. The wide bosom of the Tappan Zee lay motionless and glassy, excepting that here and there a gentle undulation waved and prolonged the blue shadow of the distant mountain. A few amber clouds floated in the sky, without a breath of air to move them. The horizon was of a fine golden tint, changing gradually into a pure apple green, and from that into the deep blue of the mid-heaven. A slanting ray lingered on the woody crests of the precipices that overhung some parts of the river, giving greater depth to the dark gray and purple of their rocky sides. A sloop was loitering in the distance, dropping slowly down with the tide, her sail hanging uselessly against the mast; and as the reflection of the sky gleamed along the still water, it seemed as if the vessel was suspended in the air.

It was toward evening that Ichabod arrived at the castle of the Heer Van Tassel, which he found thronged with the pride and flower of the adjacent country. Old farmers, a spare leathern-faced race, in homespun coats and breeches, blue stockings, huge shoes, and magnificent pewter buckles. Their brisk, withered little dames, in close-crimped caps, long-waisted short gowns, homespun petticoats, with scissors and pincushions, and gay calico pockets hanging on the outside. Buxom lasses, almost as antiquated as their mothers, excepting where a straw hat, a fine ribbon, or perhaps a white frock, gave symptoms of city innovation. The sons, in short square-skirted coats, with rows of stupendous brass buttons, and their hair generally queued in the fashion of the times, especially if they could procure an eel-skin for the purpose, it being esteemed throughout the country as a potent nourisher and strengthener of the hair.

Brom Bones, however, was the hero of the scene, having come to the gathering on his favorite steed Daredevil, a creature, like himself, full of mettle and mischief, and which no one but himself could manage. He was, in fact, noted for preferring vicious animals, given to all kinds of tricks which kept the rider in constant risk of his neck, for he held a tractable, well-broken horse as unworthy of a lad of spirit.

Fain would I pause to dwell upon the world of charms that burst upon the enraptured gaze of my hero, as he entered the state parlor of Van Tassel's mansion. Not those of the bevy of buxom lasses, with their luxurious display of red and white; but the ample charms of a genuine Dutch country tea-table, in the sumptuous time of autumn. Such heaped up platters of cakes of various and almost indescribable kinds, known only to experienced Dutch housewives! There was the doughty doughnut, the tender oly koek, and the crisp and crumbling cruller; sweet cakes and short cakes, ginger cakes and honey cakes, and the whole family of cakes. And then there were apple pies, and peach pies, and pumpkin pies; besides slices of ham and smoked beef; and moreover delectable dishes of preserved plums, and peaches, and pears, and quinces; not to mention broiled shad and roasted chickens; together with bowls of milk and cream, all mingled higgledy-piggledy, pretty much as I have enumerated them, with the motherly teapot sending up its clouds of vapor from the midst—Heaven bless the mark! I want breath and time to discuss this banquet as it deserves, and am too eager to get on with my story. Happily, Ichabod Crane was not in so great a hurry as his historian, but did ample justice to every dainty.

He was a kind and thankful creature, whose heart dilated in proportion as his skin was filled with good cheer, and whose spirits rose with eating, as some men's do with drink. He could not help, too, rolling his large eyes round him as he ate, and chuckling with the possibility that he might one day be lord of all this scene of almost unimaginable luxury and splendor. Then, he thought, how soon he'd turn his back upon the old schoolhouse; snap his fingers in the face of Hans Van Ripper, and every other niggardly patron, and kick any itinerant pedagogue out of doors that should dare to call him comrade!

Old Baltus Van Tassel moved about among his guests with a face dilated with content and good humor, round and jolly as the harvest moon. His hospitable attentions were brief, but expressive, being confined to a shake of the hand, a slap on the shoulder, a loud laugh, and a pressing invitation to "fall to, and help themselves."

And now the sound of the music from the common room, or hall, summoned to the dance. The musician was an old gray-headed negro, who had been the itinerant orchestra of the neighborhood for more than half a century. His instrument was as old and battered as himself. The greater part of the time he scraped on two or three strings, accompanying every movement of the bow with a motion of the head; bowing almost to the ground, and stamping with his foot whenever a fresh couple were to start.

Ichabod prided himself upon his dancing as much as upon his vocal powers. Not a limb, not a fibre about him was idle; and to have seen his loosely hung frame in full motion, and clattering about the room, you would have thought St. Vitus himself, that blessed patron of the dance, was figuring before you in person. He was the admiration of all the negroes; who, having gathered, of all ages and sizes, from the farm and the neighborhood, stood forming a pyramid of shining black faces at every door and window, gazing with delight at the scene, rolling their white eyeballs, and showing grinning rows of ivory from ear to ear. How could the flogger of urchins be otherwise than animated and joyous? The lady of his heart was his partner in the dance, and smiling graciously in reply to all his amorous oglings; while Brom Bones, sorely smitten with love and jealousy, sat brooding by himself in one corner.

When the dance was at an end, Ichabod was attracted to a knot of the sager folks, who, with Old Van Tassel, sat smoking at one end of the piazza, gossiping over former times, and drawing out long stories about the war.

This neighborhood, at the time of which I am speaking, was one of those highly favored places which abound with chronicle and great men. The British and American line had run near it during the war; it had, therefore, been the scene of marauding and infested with refugees, cowboys, and all kinds of border chivalry. Just sufficient time had elapsed to enable each storyteller to dress up his tale with a little becoming fiction, and, in the indistinctness of his recollection, to make himself the hero of every exploit.

There was the story of Doffue Martling, a large blue-bearded Dutchman, who had nearly taken a British frigate with an old iron nine-pounder from a mud breastwork, only that his gun burst at the sixth discharge. And there was an old gentleman who shall be nameless, being too rich a mynheer to be lightly mentioned, who, in the battle of White Plains, being an excellent master of defence, parried a musket-ball with a small sword, insomuch that he absolutely felt it whiz round the blade, and glance off at the hilt; in proof of which he was ready at any time to show the sword, with the hilt a little bent. There were several more that had been equally great in the field, not one of whom but was persuaded that he had a considerable hand in bringing the war to a happy termination.

But all these were nothing to the tales of ghosts and apparitions that succeeded. The neighborhood is rich in legendary treasures of the kind. Local tales and superstitions thrive best in these sheltered, long-settled retreats; but are trampled under foot by the shifting throng that forms the population of most of our country places. Besides, there is no encouragement for ghosts in most of our villages, for they have scarcely had time to finish their first nap and turn themselves in their graves, before their surviving friends have travelled away from the neighborhood; so that when they turn out at night to walk their rounds, they have no acquaintance left to call upon. This is perhaps the reason why we so seldom hear of ghosts except in our long-established Dutch communities.

The immediate cause, however, of the prevalence of supernatural stories in these parts, was doubtless owing to the vicinity of Sleepy Hollow. There was a contagion in the very air that blew from that haunted region; it breathed forth an atmosphere of dreams and fancies infecting all the land. Several of the Sleepy Hollow people were present at Van Tassel's, and, as usual, were doling out their wild and wonderful legends. Many dismal tales were told about funeral trains, and mourning cries and wailings heard and seen about the great tree where the unfortunate Major André was taken, and which stood in the neighborhood. Some mention was made also of the woman in white, that haunted the dark glen at Raven Rock, and was often heard to shriek on winter nights before a storm, having perished there in the snow. The chief part of the stories, however, turned upon the favorite spectre of Sleepy Hollow, the Headless Horseman, who had been heard several times of late, patrolling the country; and, it was said, tethered his horse nightly among the graves in the churchyard.

The sequestered situation of this church seems always to have made it a favorite haunt of troubled spirits. It stands on a knoll, surrounded by locust-trees and lofty elms, from among which its decent, whitewashed walls shine modestly forth, like Christian purity beaming through the shades of retirement. A gentle slope descends from it to a silver sheet of water, bordered by high trees, between which, peeps may be caught at the blue hills of the Hudson. To look upon its grass-grown yard, where the sunbeams seem to sleep so quietly, one would think that there at least the dead might rest in peace. On one side of the church extends a wide woody dell, along which raves a large brook among broken rocks and trunks of fallen trees. Over a deep black part of the stream, not far from the church, was formerly thrown a wooden bridge; the road that led to it, and the bridge itself, were thickly shaded by overhanging trees, which cast a gloom about it, even in the daytime; but occasioned a fearful darkness at night. Such was one of the favorite haunts of the Headless Horseman, and the place where he was most frequently encountered. The tale was told of old Brouwer, a most heretical disbeliever in ghosts, how he met the Horseman returning from his foray into Sleepy Hollow, and was obliged to get up behind him; how they galloped over bush and brake, over hill and swamp, until they reached the bridge; when the Horseman suddenly turned into a skeleton, threw old Brouwer into the brook, and sprang away over the tree-tops with a clap of thunder.

This story was immediately matched by a thrice marvellous adventure of Brom Bones, who made light of the Galloping Hessian as an arrant jockey. He affirmed that on returning one night from the neighboring village of Sing Sing, he had been overtaken by this midnight trooper; that he had offered to race with him for a bowl of punch, and should have won it too, for Daredevil beat the goblin horse all hollow, but just as they came to the church bridge, the Hessian bolted, and vanished in a flash of fire.

All these tales, told in that drowsy undertone with which men talk in the dark, the countenances of the listeners only now and then receiving a casual gleam from the glare of a pipe, sank deep in the mind of Ichabod. He repaid them in kind with large extracts from his invaluable author, Cotton Mather, and added many marvellous events that had taken place in his native State of Connecticut, and fearful sights which he had seen in his nightly walks about Sleepy Hollow.

The revel now gradually broke up. The old farmers gathered together their families in their wagons, and were heard for some time rattling along the hollow roads, and over the distant hills. Some of the damsels mounted on pillions behind their favorite swains, and their light-hearted laughter, mingling with the clatter of hoofs, echoed along the silent woodlands, sounding fainter and fainter, until they gradually died away,—and the late scene of noise and frolic was all silent and deserted. Ichabod only lingered behind, according to the custom of country lovers, to have a tête-à-tête with the heiress; fully convinced that he was now on the high road to success. What passed at this interview I will not pretend to say, for in fact I do not know. Something, however, I fear me, must have gone wrong, for he certainly sallied forth, after no very great interval, with an air quite desolate and chapfallen. Oh, these women! these women! Could that girl have been playing off any of her coquettish tricks? Was her encouragement of the poor pedagogue all a mere sham to secure her conquest of his rival? Heaven only knows, not I! Let it suffice to say, Ichabod stole forth with the air of one who had been sacking a henroost, rather than a fair lady's heart. Without looking to the right or left to notice the scene of rural wealth, on which he had so often gloated, he went straight to the stable, and with several hearty cuffs and kicks roused his steed most uncourteously from the comfortable quarters in which he was soundly sleeping, dreaming of mountains of corn and oats, and whole valleys of timothy and clover.

It was the very witching time of night that Ichabod, heavy-hearted and crestfallen, pursued his travels homewards, along the sides of the lofty hills which rise above Tarry Town, and which he had traversed so cheerily in the afternoon. The hour was as dismal as himself. Far below him the Tappan Zee spread its dusky and indistinct waste of waters, with here and there the tall mast of a sloop, riding quietly at anchor under the land. In the dead hush of midnight, he could even hear the barking of the watchdog from the opposite shore of the Hudson; but it was so vague and faint as only to give an idea of his distance from this faithful companion of man. Now and then, too, the long-drawn crowing of a cock, accidentally awakened, would sound far, far off, from some farmhouse away among the hills—but it was like a dreaming sound in his ear. No signs of life occurred near him, but occasionally the melancholy chirp of a cricket, or perhaps the guttural twang of a bullfrog from a neighboring marsh, as if sleeping uncomfortably and turning suddenly in his bed.

All the stories of ghosts and goblins that he had heard in the afternoon now came crowding upon his recollection. The night grew darker and darker; the stars seemed to sink deeper in the sky, and driving clouds occasionally hid them from his sight. He had never felt so lonely and dismal. He was, moreover, approaching the very place where many of the scenes of the ghost stories had been laid. In the centre of the road stood an enormous tulip-tree, which towered like a giant above all the other trees of the neighborhood, and formed a kind of landmark. Its limbs were gnarled and fantastic, large enough to form trunks for ordinary trees, twisting down almost to the earth, and rising again into the air. It was connected with the tragical story of the unfortunate André, who had been taken prisoner hard by; and was universally known by the name of Major André's tree. The common people regarded it with a mixture of respect and superstition, partly out of sympathy for the fate of its ill-starred namesake, and partly from the tales of strange sights, and doleful lamentations, told concerning it.

As Ichabod approached this fearful tree, he began to whistle; he thought his whistle was answered; it was but a blast sweeping sharply through the dry branches. As he approached a little nearer, he thought he saw something white, hanging in the midst of the tree: he paused and ceased whistling but, on looking more narrowly, perceived that it was a place where the tree had been scathed by lightning, and the white wood laid bare. Suddenly he heard a groan—his teeth chattered, and his knees smote against the saddle: it was but the rubbing of one huge bough upon another, as they were swayed about by the breeze. He passed the tree in safety, but new perils lay before him.

About two hundred yards from the tree, a small brook crossed the road, and ran into a marshy and thickly-wooded glen, known by the name of Wiley's Swamp. A few rough logs, laid side by side, served for a bridge over this stream. On that side of the road where the brook entered the wood, a group of oaks and chestnuts, matted thick with wild grape-vines, threw a cavernous gloom over it. To pass this bridge was the severest trial. It was at this identical spot that the unfortunate André was captured, and under the covert of those chestnuts and vines were the sturdy yeomen concealed who surprised him. This has ever since been considered a haunted stream, and fearful are the feelings of the schoolboy who has to pass it alone after dark.

As he approached the stream, his heart began to thump; he summoned up, however, all his resolution, gave his horse half a score of kicks in the ribs, and attempted to dash briskly across the bridge; but instead of starting forward, the perverse old animal made a lateral movement, and ran broadside against the fence. Ichabod, whose fears increased with the delay, jerked the reins on the other side, and kicked lustily with the contrary foot: it was all in vain; his steed started, it is true, but it was only to plunge to the opposite side of the road into a thicket of brambles and alder bushes. The schoolmaster now bestowed both whip and heel upon the starveling ribs of old Gunpowder, who dashed forward, snuffling and snorting, but came to a stand just by the bridge, with a suddenness that had nearly sent his rider sprawling over his head. Just at this moment a plashy tramp by the side of the bridge caught the sensitive ear of Ichabod. In the dark shadow of the grove, on the margin of the brook, he beheld something huge, misshapen and towering. It stirred not, but seemed gathered up in the gloom, like some gigantic monster ready to spring upon the traveller.

The hair of the affrighted pedagogue rose upon his head with terror. What was to be done? To turn and fly was now too late; and besides, what chance was there of escaping ghost or goblin, if such it was, which could ride upon the wings of the wind? Summoning up, therefore, a show of courage, he demanded in stammering accents, "Who are you?" He received no reply. He repeated his demand in a still more agitated voice. Still there was no answer. Once more he cudgelled the sides of the inflexible Gunpowder, and, shutting his eyes, broke forth with involuntary fervor into a psalm tune. Just then the shadowy object of alarm put itself in motion, and with a scramble and a bound stood at once in the middle of the road. Though the night was dark and dismal, yet the form of the unknown might now in some degree be ascertained. He appeared to be a horseman of large dimensions, and mounted on a black horse of powerful frame. He made no offer of molestation or sociability, but kept aloof on one side of the road, jogging along on the blind side of old Gunpowder, who had now got over his fright and waywardness.

Ichabod, who had no relish for this strange midnight companion, and bethought himself of the adventure of Brom Bones with the Galloping Hessian, now quickened his steed in hopes of leaving him behind. The stranger, however, quickened his horse to an equal pace. Ichabod pulled up, and fell into a walk, thinking to lag behind,—the other did the same. His heart began to sink within him; he endeavored to resume his psalm tune, but his parched tongue clove to the roof of his mouth, and he could not utter a stave. There was something in the moody and dogged silence of this pertinacious companion that was mysterious and appalling. It was soon fearfully accounted for. On mounting a rising ground, which brought the figure of his fellow-traveller in relief against the sky, gigantic in height, and muffled in a cloak, Ichabod was horror-struck on perceiving that he was headless!—but his horror was still more increased on observing that the head, which should have rested on his shoulders, was carried before him on the pommel of his saddle! His terror rose to desperation; he rained a shower of kicks and blows upon Gunpowder, hoping by a sudden movement to give his companion the slip; but the spectre started full jump with him. Away, then, they dashed through thick and thin; stones flying and sparks flashing at every bound. Ichabod's flimsy garments fluttered in the air, as he stretched his long lank body away over his horse's head, in the eagerness of his flight.

They had now reached the road which turns off to Sleepy Hollow; but Gunpowder, who seemed possessed with a demon, instead of keeping up it, made an opposite turn, and plunged headlong downhill to the left. This road leads through a sandy hollow shaded by trees for about a quarter of a mile, where it crosses the bridge famous in goblin story; and just beyond swells the green knoll on which stands the whitewashed church.

As yet the panic of the steed had given his unskilful rider an apparent advantage in the chase, but just as he had got half way through the hollow, the girths of the saddle gave way, and he felt it slipping from under him. He seized it by the pommel, and endeavored to hold it firm, but in vain; and had just time to save himself by clasping old Gunpowder round the neck, when the saddle fell to the earth, and he heard it trampled under foot by his pursuer. For a moment the terror of Hans Van Ripper's wrath passed across his mind,—for it was his Sunday saddle; but this was no time for petty fears; the goblin was hard on his haunches; and (unskilful rider that he was!) he had much ado to maintain his seat; sometimes slipping on one side, sometimes on another, and sometimes jolted on the high ridge of his horse's backbone, with a violence that he verily feared would cleave him asunder.

An opening in the trees now cheered him with the hopes that the church bridge was at hand. The wavering reflection of a silver star in the bosom of the brook told him that he was not mistaken. He saw the walls of the church dimly glaring under the trees beyond. He recollected the place where Brom Bones's ghostly competitor had disappeared. "If I can but reach that bridge," thought Ichabod, "I am safe." Just then he heard the black steed panting and blowing close behind him; he even fancied that he felt his hot breath. Another convulsive kick in the ribs, and old Gunpowder sprang upon the bridge; he thundered over the resounding planks; he gained the opposite side; and now Ichabod cast a look behind to see if his pursuer should vanish, according to rule, in a flash of fire and brimstone. Just then he saw the goblin rising in his stirrups, and in the very act of hurling his head at him. Ichabod endeavored to dodge the horrible missile, but too late. It encountered his cranium with a tremendous crash,—he was tumbled headlong into the dust, and Gunpowder, the black steed, and the goblin rider, passed by like a whirlwind.

The next morning the old horse was found without his saddle, and with the bridle under his feet, soberly cropping the grass at his master's gate. Ichabod did not make his appearance at breakfast; dinner-hour came, but no Ichabod. The boys assembled at the schoolhouse, and strolled idly about the banks of the brook; but no schoolmaster. Hans Van Ripper now began to feel some uneasiness about the fate of poor Ichabod, and his saddle. An inquiry was set on foot, and after diligent investigation they came upon his traces. In one part of the road leading to the church was found the saddle trampled in the dirt; the tracks of horses' hoofs deeply dented in the road, and evidently at furious speed, were traced to the bridge, beyond which, on the bank of a broad part of the brook, where the water ran deep and black, was found the hat of the unfortunate Ichabod, and close beside it a shattered pumpkin.

The brook was searched, but the body of the schoolmaster was not to be discovered. Hans Van Ripper as executor of his estate, examined the bundle which contained all his worldly effects. They consisted of two shirts and a half; two stocks for the neck; a pair or two of worsted stockings; an old pair of corduroy small-clothes; a rusty razor; a book of psalm tunes full of dog's-ears; and a broken pitch-pipe. As to the books and furniture of the schoolhouse, they belonged to the community, excepting Cotton Mather's "History of Witchcraft," a "New England Almanac," and a book of dreams and fortune-telling; in which last was a sheet of foolscap much scribbled and blotted in several fruitless attempts to make a copy of verses in honor of the heiress of Van Tassel. These magic books and the poetic scrawl were forthwith consigned to the flames by Hans Van Ripper; who, from that time forward, determined to send his children no more to school, observing that he never knew any good come of this same reading and writing. Whatever money the schoolmaster possessed, and he had received his quarter's pay but a day or two before, he must have had about his person at the time of his disappearance.

The mysterious event caused much speculation at the church on the following Sunday. Knots of gazers and gossips were collected in the churchyard, at the bridge, and at the spot where the hat and pumpkin had been found. The stories of Brouwer, of Bones, and a whole budget of others were called to mind; and when they had diligently considered them all, and compared them with the symptoms of the present case, they shook their heads, and came to the conclusion that Ichabod had been carried off by the Galloping Hessian. As he was a bachelor, and in nobody's debt, nobody troubled his head any more about him; the school was removed to a different quarter of the hollow, and another pedagogue reigned in his stead.

It is true, an old farmer, who had been down to New York on a visit several years after, and from whom this account of the ghostly adventure was received, brought home the intelligence that Ichabod Crane was still alive; that he had left the neighborhood partly through fear of the goblin and Hans Van Ripper, and partly in mortification at having been suddenly dismissed by the heiress; that he had changed his quarters to a distant part of the country; had kept school and studied law at the same time; had been admitted to the bar; turned politician; electioneered; written for the newspapers; and finally had been made a justice of the Ten Pound Court. Brom Bones, too, who, shortly after his rival's disappearance conducted the blooming Katrina in triumph to the altar, was observed to look exceedingly knowing whenever the story of Ichabod was related, and always burst into a hearty laugh at the mention of the pumpkin; which led some to suspect that he knew more about the matter than he chose to tell.

The old country wives, however, who are the best judges of these matters, maintain to this day that Ichabod was spirited away by supernatural means; and it is a favorite story often told about the neighborhood round the winter evening fire. The bridge became more than ever an object of superstitious awe; and that may be the reason why the road has been altered of late years, so as to approach the church by the border of the millpond. The schoolhouse being deserted soon fell to decay, and was reported to be haunted by the ghost of the unfortunate pedagogue and the plowboy, loitering homeward of a still summer evening, has often fancied his voice at a distance, chanting a melancholy psalm tune among the tranquil solitudes of Sleepy Hollow.

Postscript.

Found in the handwriting of Mr. Knickerbocker.

The preceding tale is given almost in the precise words in which I heard it related at a Corporation meeting at the ancient city of Manhattoes, at which were present many of its sagest and most illustrious burghers. The narrator was a pleasant, shabby, gentlemanly old fellow, in pepper-and-salt clothes, with a sadly humourous face, and one whom I strongly suspected of being poor—he made such efforts to be entertaining. When his story was concluded, there was much laughter and approbation, particularly from two or three deputy aldermen, who had been asleep the greater part of the time. There was, however, one tall, dry-looking old gentleman, with beetling eyebrows, who maintained a grave and rather severe face throughout, now and then folding his arms, inclining his head, and looking down upon the floor, as if turning a doubt over in his mind. He was one of your wary men, who never laugh but upon good grounds—when they have reason and law on their side. When the mirth of the rest of the company had subsided, and silence was restored, he leaned one arm on the elbow of his chair, and sticking the other akimbo, demanded, with a slight, but exceedingly sage motion of the head, and contraction of the brow, what was the moral of the story, and what it went to prove?

The story-teller, who was just putting a glass of wine to his lips, as a refreshment after his toils, paused for a moment, looked at his inquirer with an air of infinite deference, and, lowering the glass slowly to the table, observed that the story was intended most logically to prove—

"That there is no situation in life but has its advantages and pleasures—provided we will but take a joke as we find it:

"That, therefore, he that runs races with goblin troopers is likely to have rough riding of it.

"Ergo, for a country schoolmaster to be refused the hand of a Dutch heiress is a certain step to high preferment in the state."

The cautious old gentleman knit his brows tenfold closer after this explanation, being sorely puzzled by the ratiocination of the syllogism, while, methought, the one in pepper-and-salt eyed him with something of a triumphant leer. At length he observed that all this was very well, but still he thought the story a little on the extravagant—there were one or two points on which he had his doubts.

"Faith, sir," replied the story-teller, "as to that matter, I don't believe one-half of it myself." D. K.

Stephen Crane, An Episode of War

The lieutenant's rubber blanket lay on the ground, and upon it he had poured the company's supply of coffee. Corporals and other representatives of the grimy and hot-throated men who lined the breastwork had come for each squad's portion.

The lieutenant was frowning and serious at this task of division. His lips pursed as he drew with his sword various crevices in the heap until brown squares of coffee, astoundingly equal in size, appeared on the blanket. He was on the verge of a great triumph in mathematics, and the corporals were thronging forward, each to reap a little square, when suddenly the lieutenant cried out and looked quickly at a man near him as if he suspected it was a case of personal assault. The others cried out also when they saw blood upon the lieutenant's sleeve.

He had winced like a man stung, swayed dangerously, and then straightened. The sound of his hoarse breathing was plainly audible. He looked sadly, mystically, over the breastwork at the green face of a wood, where now were many little puffs of white smoke. During this moment the men about him gazed statue-like and silent, astonished and awed by this catastrophe which happened when catastrophes were not expected—when they had leisure to observe it.

As the lieutenant stared at the wood, they too swung their heads, so that for another instant all hands, still silent, contemplated the distant forest as if their minds were fixed upon the mystery of a bullet's journey.

The officer had, of course, been compelled to take his sword into his left hand. He did not hold it by the hilt. He gripped it at the middle of the blade, awkwardly. Turning his eyes from the hostile wood, he looked at the sword as he held it there, and seemed puzzled as to what to do with it, where to put it. In short, this weapon had of a sudden become a strange thing to him. He looked at it in a kind of stupefaction, as if he had been endowed with a trident, a sceptre, or a spade.

Finally he tried to sheath it. To sheath a sword held by the left hand, at the middle of the blade, in a scabbard hung at the left hip, is a feat worthy of a sawdust ring. This wounded officer engaged in a desperate struggle with the sword and the wobbling scabbard, and during the time of it he breathed like a wrestler.

But at this instant the men, the spectators, awoke from their stone-like poses and crowded forward sympathetically. The orderly-sergeant took the sword and tenderly placed it in the scabbard. At the time, he leaned nervously backward, and did not allow even his finger to brush the body of the lieutenant. A wound gives strange dignity to him who bears it.

Well men shy from this new and terrible majesty. It is as if the wounded man's hand is upon the curtain which hangs before the revelations of all existence—the meaning of ants, potentates, wars, cities, sunshine, snow, a feather dropped from a bird's wing; and the power of it sheds radiance upon a bloody form, and makes the other men understand sometimes that they are little. His comrades look at him with large eyes thoughtfully. Moreover, they fear vaguely that the weight of a finger upon him might send him headlong, precipitate the tragedy, hurl him at once into the dim, grey unknown. And so the orderly-sergeant, while sheathing the sword, leaned nervously backward.

There were others who proffered assistance. One timidly presented his shoulder and asked the lieutenant if he cared to lean upon it, but the latter waved him away mournfully. He wore the look of one who knows he is the victim of a terrible disease and understands his helplessness. He again stared over the breastwork at the forest, and then turning went slowly rearward. He held his right wrist tenderly in his left hand as if the wounded arm was made of very brittle glass.

And the men in silence stared at the wood, then at the departing lieutenant—then at the wood, then at the lieutenant.

As the wounded officer passed from the line of battle, he was enabled to see many things which as a participant in the fight were unknown to him. He saw a general on a black horse gazing over the lines of blue infantry at the green woods which veiled his problems. An aide galloped furiously, dragged his horse suddenly to a halt, saluted, and presented a paper. It was, for a wonder, precisely like an historical painting.

To the rear of the general and his staff a group, composed of a bugler, two or three orderlies, and the bearer of the corps standard, all upon maniacal horses, were working like slaves to hold their ground, preserve, their respectful interval, while the shells boomed in the air about them, and caused their chargers to make furious quivering leaps.

A battery, a tumultuous and shining mass, was swirling toward the right. The wild thud of hoofs, the cries of the riders shouting blame and praise, menace and encouragement, and, last the roar of the wheels, the slant of the glistening guns, brought the lieutenant to an intent pause. The battery swept in curves that stirred the heart; it made halts as dramatic as the crash of a wave on the rocks, and when it fled onward, this aggregation of wheels, levers, motors, had a beautiful unity, as if it were a missile. The sound of it was a war-chorus that reached into the depths of man's emotion.

The lieutenant, still holding his arm as if it were of glass, stood watching this battery until all detail of it was lost, save the figures of the riders, which rose and fell and waved lashes over the black mass.

Later, he turned his eyes toward the battle where the shooting sometimes crackled like bush-fires, sometimes sputtered with exasperating irregularity, and sometimes reverberated like the thunder. He saw the smoke rolling upward and saw crowds of men who ran and cheered, or stood and blazed away at the inscrutable distance.

He came upon some stragglers, and they told him how to find the field hospital. They described its exact location. In fact, these men, no longer having part in the battle, knew more of it than others. They told the performance of every corps, every division, the opinion of every general. The lieutenant, carrying his wounded arm rearward, looked upon them with wonder.

At the roadside a brigade was making coffee and buzzing with talk like a girls' boarding-school. Several officers came out to him and inquired concerning things of which he knew nothing. One, seeing his arm, began to scold. "Why, man, that's no way to do. You want to fix that thing." He appropriated the lieutenant and the lieutenant's wound. He cut the sleeve and laid bare the arm, every nerve of which softly fluttered under his touch. He bound his handkerchief over the wound, scolding away in the meantime. His tone allowed one to think that he was in the habit of being wounded every day. The lieutenant hung his head, feeling, in this presence, that he did not know how to be correctly wounded.

The low white tents of the hospital were grouped around an old school-house. There was here a singular commotion. In the foreground two ambulances interlocked wheels in the deep mud. The drivers were tossing the blame of it back and forth, gesticulating and berating, while from the ambulances, both crammed with wounded, there came an occasional groan. An interminable crowd of bandaged men were coming and going. Great numbers sat under the trees nursing heads or arms or legs. There was a dispute of some kind raging on the steps of the school-house. Sitting with his back against a tree a man with a face as grey as a new army blanket was serenely smoking a corn-cob pipe. The lieutenant wished to rush forward and inform him that he was dying.

A busy surgeon was passing near the lieutenant. "Good-morning," he said, with a friendly smile. Then he caught sight of the lieutenant's arm and his face at once changed. "Well, let's have a look at it." He seemed possessed suddenly of a great contempt for the lieutenant. This wound evidently placed the latter on a very low social plane. The doctor cried out impatiently, "What mutton-head had tied it up that way anyhow?" The lieutenant answered, "Oh, a man."

When the wound was disclosed the doctor fingered it disdainfully. "Humph," he said. "You come along with me and I'll 'tend to you." His voice contained the same scorn as if he were saying, "You will have to go to jail."

The lieutenant had been very meek, but now his face flushed, and he looked into the doctor's eyes. "I guess I won't have it amputated," he said.

"Nonsense, man! Nonsense! Nonsense!" cried the doctor. "Come along, now. I won't amputate it. Come along. Don't be a baby."

"Let go of me," said the lieutenant, holding back wrathfully, his glance fixed upon the door of the old school-house, as sinister to him as the portals of death.

And this is the story of how the lieutenant lost his arm. When he reached home, his sisters, his mother, his wife sobbed for a long time at the sight of the flat sleeve. "Oh, well," he said, standing shamefaced amid these tears, "I don't suppose it matters so much as all that."

Charles W. Chesnutt, The Goophered Grapevine

Charles W. Chesnutt's use of humor and dialect to send up the Northern character in this story open several lenses onto the workings of language, humor, and even magic in the American countryside following the Civil War.

Enjoy "The Goophered Grapevine."

The Goophered Grapevine

ABOUT ten years ago my wife was in poor health, and our family doctor, in whose skill and honesty I had implicit confidence, advised a change of climate. I was engaged in grape-culture in northern Ohio, and decided to look for a locality suitable for carrying on the same business in some Southern State. I wrote to a cousin who had gone into the turpentine business in central North Carolina, and he assured me that no better place could be found in the South than the State and neighborhood in which he lived: climate and soil were all that could be asked for, and land could be bought for a mere song. A cordial invitation to visit him while I looked into the matter was accepted. We found the weather delightful at that season, the end of the summer, and were most hospitably entertained. Our host placed a horse and buggy at our disposal, and himself acted as guide until I got somewhat familiar with the country.

I went several times to look at a place which I thought might suit me. It had been at one time a thriving plantation, but shiftless cultivation had well-night exhausted the soil. There had been a vineyard of some extent on the place, but it had not been attended to since the war, and had fallen into utter neglect. The vines — here partly supported by decayed and broken-down arbors, there twining themselves among the branches of the slender saplings which had sprung up among them — grew in wild and unpruned luxuriance, and the few scanty grapes which they bore were the undisputed prey of the first comer. The site was admirably adapted to grape-raising; the soil, with a little attention, could not have been better; and with the native grape, the luscious scuppernong, mainly to rely upon, I felt sure that I could introduce and cultivate successfully a number of other varieties.

One day I went over with my wife, to show her the place. We drove between the decayed gate-posts — the gate itself had long since disappeared — and up the straight, sandy lane to the open space where a dwelling-house had once stood. But the house had fallen a victim to the fortunes of war, and nothing remained of it except the brick pillars upon which the sills had rested. We alighted, and walked about the place for a while; but on Annie's complaining of weariness I led the way back to the yard, where a pine log, lying under a spreading elm, formed a shady though somewhat hard seat. One end of the log was already occupied by a venerable-looking colored man. He held on his knees a hat full of grapes, over which he was smacking his lips with great gusto, and a pile of grape-skins near him indicated that the performance was no new thing. He respectfully rose as we approached, and was moving away, when I begged him to keep his seat.

"Don't let us disturb you," I said. "There's plenty of room for us all."

He resumed his seat with somewhat of embarrassment.

"Do you live around here?" I asked, anxious to put him at his ease.

"Yas, suh. I lives des ober yander, behine de nex' san'-hill, on de Lumberton plank-road."

"Do you know anything about the time when this vineyard was cultivated?"

"Lawd bless yer, suh, I knows all about it. Dey ain' na'er a man in dis settlement w'at won' tell yer ole Julius McAdoo 'uz bawn an' raise' on dis yer same plantation. Is you de Norv'n gemman w'at's gwine ter buy de ole vimya'd?"

"I am looking at it," I replied; "but I don't know that I shall care to buy unless I can be reasonably sure of making something out of it."

"Well, suh, you is a stranger ter me, en I is a stranger ter you, en we is bofe strangers ter one anudder, but 'f I 'uz in yo' place, I wouldn' buy dis vimya'd."

"Why not?" I asked.

"Well, I dunner whe'r you b'lieves in cunj'in er not, — some er de w'ite folks don't, er says dey don't, — but de truf er de matter is dat dis yer ole vimya'd is goophered."

"Is what?" I asked, not grasping the meaning of this unfamiliar word.

"Is goophered, cunju'd, bewitch'."

He imparted this information with such solemn earnestness, and with such an air of confidential mystery, that I felt somewhat interested, while Annie was evidently much impressed, and drew closer to me.

"How do you know it is bewitched?" I asked.

"I wouldn' spec' fer you ter b'lieve me 'less you know all 'bout de fac's. But ef you en young miss dere doan' min' lis'n'in' ter a ole nigger run on a minute er two w'ile you er restin', I kin 'splain to yer how it all happen'."

We assured him that we would be glad to hear how it all happened, and he began to tell us. At first the current of his memory — or imagination — seemed somewhat sluggish; but as his embarrassment wore off, his language flowed more freely, and the story acquired perspective and coherence. As he became more and more absorbed in the narrative, his eyes assumed a dreamy expression, and he seemed to lose sight of his auditors, and to be living over again in monologue his life on the old plantation.

"Ole Mars Dugal' McAdoo bought dis place long many years befo' de wah, en I 'member well w'en he sot out all dis yer part er de plantation in scuppernon's. De vimes growed monst'us fas', en Mars Dugal' made a thousan' gallon er scuppernon' wine eve'y year.

"Now, ef dey's an'thing a nigger lub, nex' ter 'possum, en chick'n, en watermillyums, it's scuppernon's. Dey ain' nuffin dat kin stan' up side'n de scuppernon' fer sweetness; sugar ain't a suckumstance ter scuppernon'. W'en de season is nigh 'bout ober, en de grapes begin ter swivel up des a little wid de wrinkles er ole age, — w'en de skin git sof' en brown, — den de scuppernon' make you smack yo' lip en roll yo' eye en wush fer mo'; so I reckon it ain' very 'stonishin' dat niggers lub scuppernon'.

"Dey wuz a sight er niggers in de naberhood er de vimya'd. Dere wuz ole Mars Henry Brayboy's niggers, en ole Mars Dunkin McLean's niggers, en Mars Dugal's own niggers; den dey wuz a settlement er free niggers en po' buckrahs down by de Wim'l'ton Road, en Mars Dugal' had de only vimya'd in de naberhood. I reckon it ain' so much so nowadays, but befo' de wah, in slab'ry times, er nigger didn' mine goin' fi' er ten mile in a night, w'en dey wuz sump'n good ter eat at de yuther een.

"So atter a w'ile Mars Dugal' begin ter miss his scuppernon's. Co'se he 'cuse' de niggers er it, but dey all 'nied it ter de las'. Mars Dugal' sot spring guns en steel traps, en he en de oberseah sot up nights once't er twice't, tel one night Mars Dugal' — he 'uz a monst'us keerless man — got his leg shot full er cow-peas. But somehow er nudder dey couldn' nebber ketch none er de niggers. I dunner how it happen, but it happen des like I tell yer, en de grapes kep' on a-goin des de same.

"But bimeby ole Mars Dugal' fix' up a plan ter stop it. Dey 'uz a cunjuh 'ooman livin' down mongs' de free niggers on de Wim'l'ton Road, en all de darkies fum Rockfish ter Beaver Crick wuz feared uv her. She could wuk de mos' powerfulles' kind er goopher, — could make people hab fits er rheumatiz, er make 'em des dwinel away en die; en dey say she went out ridin' de niggers at night, for she wuz a witch 'sides bein' a cunjuh 'ooman. Mars Dugal' hearn 'bout Aun' Peggy's doin's, en begun ter 'flect whe'r er no he couldn' git her ter he'p him keep de niggers off'n de grapevimes. One day in de spring er de year, ole miss pack' up a basket er chick'n en poun'-cake, en a bottle er scuppernon' wine, en Mars Dugal' tuk it in his buggy en driv ober ter Aun' Peggy's cabin. He tuk de basket in, en had a long talk wid Aun' Peggy.

De nex' day Aun' Peggy come up ter de vimya'd. De niggers seed her slippin' 'roun', en dey soon foun' out what she 'uz doin' dere. Mars Dugal' had hi'ed her ter goopher de grapevimes. She sa'ntered 'roun' mongs' de vimes, en tuk a leaf fum dis one, en a grape-hull fum dat one, en a grape-seed fum anudder one; en den a little twig fum here, en a little pinch er dirt fum dere, — en put it all in a big black bottle, wid a snake's toof en a speckle' hen's gall en some ha's fum a black cat's tail, en den fill' de bottle wid scuppernon' wine. W'en she got de goopher all ready en fix', she tuk 'n went out in de woods en buried it under de root uv a red oak tree, en den come back en tole one er de niggers she done goopher de grapevimes, en a'er a nigger w'at eat dem grapes 'ud be sho ter die inside'n twel' mont's.

"Atter dat de niggers let de scuppernon's 'lone, en Mars Dugal' didn' hab no 'casion ter fine no mo' fault; en de season wuz mos' gone, w'en a strange gemman stop at de plantation one night ter see Mars Dugal' on some business; en his coachman, seein' de scuppernon's growin' so nice en sweet, slip 'roun' behine de smoke-house, en et all de scuppernon's he could hole. Nobody didn' notice it at de time, but dat night, on de way home, de gemman's hoss runned away en kill' de coachman. W'en we hearn de noos, Aun' Lucy, de cook, she up 'n say she seed de strange nigger eat'n' er de scuppernon's behine de smoke-house; en den we knowed de goopher had b'en er wukkin. Den one er de nigger chilluns runned away fum de quarters one day, en got in de scuppernon's, en died de nex' week. W'ite folks say he die' er de fevuh, but de niggers knowed it wuz de goopher. So you k'n be sho de darkies didn' hab much ter do wid dem scuppernon' vimes.

"W'en de scuppernon' season 'uz ober fer dat year, Mars Dugal' foun' he had made fifteen hund'ed gallon er wine; en one er de niggers hearn him laffin' wid de oberseah fit ter kill, en sayin' dem fifteen hund'ed gallon er wine wuz monst'us good intrus' on de ten dollars he laid out on de vimya'd. So I 'low ez he paid Aun' Peggy ten dollars fer to goopher de grapevimes.

"De goopher didn' wuk no mo' tel de nex' summer, w'en 'long to'ds de middle er de season one er de fiel' han's died; en ez dat lef' Mars Dugal' sho't er han's, he went off ter town fer ter buy anudder. He fotch de noo nigger home wid 'im. He wuz er ole nigger, er de color er a gingy-cake, en ball ez a hoss-apple on de top er his head. He wuz a peart ole nigger, do', en could do a big day's wuk.

"Now it happen dat one er de niggers on de nex' plantation, one er ole Mars Henry Brayboy's niggers, had runned away de day befo', en tuk ter de swamp, en ole Mars Dugal' en some er de yuther nabor w'ite folks had gone out wid dere guns en dere dogs fer ter he'p 'em hunt fer de nigger; en de han's on our own plantation wuz all so flusterated dat we fuhgot ter tell de noo han' 'bout de goopher on de scuppernon' vimes. Co'se he smell de grapes en see de vimes, an atter dahk de fus' thing he done wuz ter slip off ter de grapevimes 'dout sayin' nuffin ter nobody. Nex' mawnin' he tole some er de niggers 'bout de fine bait er scuppernon' he et de night befo'.

"W'en dey tole 'im 'bout de goopher on de grapevimes, he 'uz dat tarrified dat he turn pale, en look des like he gwine ter die right in his tracks. De oberseah come up en axed w'at 'uz de matter; en w'en dey tole 'im Henry be'n eatin' er de scuppernon's, en got de goopher on 'im, he gin Henry a big drink er w'iskey, en 'low dat de nex' rainy day he take 'im ober ter Aun' Peggy's, en see ef she wouldn' take de goopher off'n him, seein' ez he didn' know nuffin erbout it tel he done et de grapes.

"Sho nuff, it rain de nex' day, en de oberseah went ober ter Aun' Peggy's wid Henry. En Aun' Peggy say dat bein' ez Henry didn' know 'bout de goopher, en et de grapes in ign'ance er de quinseconces, she reckon she mought be able fer ter take de goopher off'n him. So she fotch out er bottle wid some cunjuh medicine in it, en po'd some out in a go'd fer Henry ter drink. He manage ter git it down; he say it tas'e like whiskey wid sump'n bitter in it. She 'lowed dat 'ud keep de goopher off'n him tel de spring; but w'en de sap begin ter rise in de grapevimes he ha' ter come en see her agin, en she tell him w'at e's ter do.

"Nex' spring, w'en de sap commence' ter rise in de scuppernon' vime, Henry tuk a ham one night. Whar'd he git de ham? I doan know; dey wa'nt no hams on de plantation 'cep'n' w'at 'uz in de smoke-house, but I never see Henry 'bout de smoke-house. But ez I wuz a-sayin', he tuk de ham ober ter Aun' Peggy's; en Aun' Peggy tole 'im dat w'en Mars Dugal' begin ter prume de grapevimes, he mus' go en take 'n scrape off de sap whar it ooze out'n de cut een's er de vimes, en 'n'int his ball head wid it; en ef he do dat once't a year de goopher wouldn' wuk agin 'im long ez he done it. En bein' ez he fotch her de ham, she fix' it so he kin eat all de scuppernon' he want.

"So Henry 'n'int his head wid de sap out'n de big grapevime des ha'f way 'twix' de quarters en de big house, en de goopher nebber wuk agin him dat summer. But de beatenes' thing you eber see happen ter Henry. Up ter dat time he wuz ez ball ez a sweeten' 'tater, but des ez soon ez de young leaves begun ter come out on de grapevimes de ha'r begun ter grow out on Henry's head, en by de middle er de summer he had de bigges' head er ha'r on de plantation. Befo' dat, Henry had tol'able good ha'r 'roun de aidges, but soon ez de young grapes begun ter come Henry's ha'r begun ter quirl all up in little balls, des like dis yer reg'lar grapy ha'r, en by de time de grapes got ripe his head look des like a bunch er grapes. Combin' it didn' do no good; he wuk at it ha'f de night wid er Jim Crow, en think he git it straighten' out, but in de mawnin' de grapes 'ud be dere des de same. So he gin it up, en tried ter keep de grapes down by havin' his ha'r cut sho't.

"But dat wa'nt de quares' thing 'bout de goopher. When Henry come ter de plantation, he wuz gittin' a little ole an stiff in de j'ints. But dat summer he got des ez spry en libely ez any young nigger on de plantation; fac' he got so biggity dat Mars Jackson, de oberseah, ha' ter th'eaten ter whip 'im, ef he didn' stop cuttin' up his didos en behave hisse'f. But de mos' cur'ouses' thing happen' in de fall, when de sap begin ter go down in de grapevimes. Fus', when de grapes 'uz gethered, de knots begun ter straighten out'n Henry's h'ar; en w'en de leaves begin ter fall, Henry's ha'r begin ter drap out; en w'en de vimes 'uz b'ar, Henry's head wuz baller 'n it wuz in de spring, en he begin ter git ole en stiff in de j'ints ag'in, en paid no mo' tention ter de gals dyoin' er de whole winter. En nex' spring, w'en he rub de sap on ag'in, he got young ag'in, en so soopl en libely dat none er de young niggers on de plantation couldn' jump, ner dance, ner hoe ez much cotton ez Henry. But in de fall er de year his grapes begun ter straighten out, en his j'ints ter git stiff, en his ha'r drap off, en de rheumatiz begin ter wrastle wid 'im.

"Now, ef you'd a knowed ole Mars Dugal' McAdoo, you'd a knowed dat it ha' ter be a mighty rainy day when he couldn' fine sump'n fer his niggers ter do, en it ha' ter be a mighty little hole he couldn' crawl thoo, en ha' ter be a monst'us cloudy night w'en a dollar git by him in de dahkness; en w'en he see how Henry git young in de spring en ole in de fall, he 'lowed ter hisse'f ez how he could make mo' money outen Henry dan by wukkin' him in de cotton fiel'. 'Long de nex' spring, atter de sap commence' ter rise, en Henry 'n'int 'is head en commence fer ter git young en soopl, Mars Dugal' up 'n tuk Henry ter town, en sole 'im fer fifteen hunder' dollars. Co'se de man w'at bought Henry didn' know nuffin 'bout de goopher, en Mars Dugal' didn' see no 'casion fer ter tell 'im. Long to'ds de fall, w'en de sap went down, Henry begin ter git ole again same ez yuzhal, en his noo marster begin ter git skeered les'n he gwine ter lose his fifteen-hunder'-dollar nigger. He sent fer a mighty fine doctor, but de med'cine didn' 'pear ter do no good; de goopher had a good holt. Henry tole de doctor 'bout de goopher, but de doctor des laff at 'im.

"One day in de winter Mars Dugal' went ter town, en wuz santerin' 'long de Main Street, when who should he meet but Henry's noo marster. Dey said 'Hoddy,' en Mars Dugal' ax 'im ter hab a seegyar; en atter dey run on awhile 'bout de craps en de weather, Mars Dugal' ax 'im, sorter keerless, like ez ef he des thought of it, —

"'How you like de nigger I sole you las' spring?'

"Henry's marster shuck his head en knock de ashes off'n his seegyar.

"'Spec' I made a bad bahgin when I bought dat nigger. Henry done good wuk all de summer, but sence de fall set in he 'pears ter be sorter pinin' away. Dey ain' nuffin pertickler de matter wid 'im — leastways de doctor say so — 'cep'n' a tech er de rheumatiz; but his ha'r is all fell out, en ef he don't pick up his strenk mighty soon, I spec' I'm gwine ter lose 'im.'

"Dey smoked on awhile, en bimeby ole mars say, 'Well, a bahgin's a bahgin, but you en me is good fren's, en I doan wan' ter see you lose all de money you paid fer dat digger [sic]; en ef w'at you say is so, en I ain't 'sputin' it, he ain't wuf much now. I spec's you wukked him too ha'd dis summer, er e'se de swamps down here don't agree wid de san'-hill nigger. So you des lemme know, en ef he gits any wusser I'll be willin' ter gib yer five hund'ed dollars fer 'im, en take my chances on his livin'.'

"Sho nuff, when Henry begun ter draw up wid de rheumatiz en it look like he gwine ter die fer sho, his noo marster sen' fer Mars Dugal', en Mars Dugal' gin him what he promus, en brung Henry home ag'in. He tuk good keer uv 'im dyoin' er de winter, — give 'im w'iskey ter rub his rheumatiz, en terbacker ter smoke, en all he want ter eat, — 'caze a nigger w'at he could make a thousan' dollars a year off'n didn' grow on eve'y huckleberry bush.

"Nex' spring, w'en de sap ris en Henry's ha'r commence' ter sprout, Mars Dugal' sole 'im ag'in, down in Robeson County dis time; en he kep' dat sellin' business up fer five year er mo'. Henry nebber say nuffin 'bout de goopher ter his noo marsters, 'caze he know he gwine ter be tuk good keer uv de nex' winter, w'en Mars Dugal' buy him back. En Mars Dugal' made 'nuff money off'n Henry ter buy anudder plantation ober on Beaver Crick.

"But long 'bout de een' er dat five year dey come a stranger ter stop at de plantation. De fus' day he 'uz dere he went out wid Mars Dugal' en spent all de mawnin' lookin' ober de vimya'd, en atter dinner dey spent all de evenin' playin' kya'ds. De niggers soon 'skiver' dat he wuz a Yankee, en dat he come down ter Norf C'lina fer ter learn de w'ite folks how to raise grapes en make wine. He promus Mars Dugal' he cud make de grapevimes b'ar twice't ez many grapes, en dat de noo wine-press he wuz a-sellin' would make mo' d'n twice't ez many gallons er wine. En ole Mars Dugal' des drunk it all in, des 'peared ter be bewitched wit dat Yankee. W'en de darkies see dat Yankee runnin' 'roun de vimya'd en diggin' under de grapevimes, dey shuk dere heads, en 'lowed dat dey feared Mars Dugal' losin' his min'. Mars Dugal' had all de dirt dug away fum under de roots er all de scuppernon' vimes, an' let 'em stan' dat away fer a week er mo'. Den dat Yankee made de niggers fix up a mixtry er lime en ashes en manyo, en po' it roun' de roots er de grapevimes. Den he 'vise' Mars Dugal' fer ter trim de vimes close't, en Mars Dugal' tuck 'n done eve'ything de Yankee tole him ter do. Dyoin' all er dis time, mind yer, 'e wuz libbin' off'n de fat er de lan', at de big house, en playin' kyards wid Mars Dugal' eve'y night; en dey say Mars Dugal' los' mo'n a thousan' dollars dyoin' er de week dat Yankee wuz a runnin' de grapevimes.

"W'en de sap ris nex' spring, ole Henry 'n'inted his head ez yuzhal, en his ha'r commence' ter grow des de same ez it done eve'y year. De scuppernon' vimes growed monst's fas', en de leaves wuz greener en thicker dan dey eber be'n dyowin my remem'ance; en Henry's ha'r growed out thicker dan eber, en he 'peared ter git younger 'n younger, en soopler 'n soopler; en seein' ez he wuz sho' er han's dat spring, havin' tuk in consid'able noo groun', Mars Dugal' 'cluded he wouldn' sell Henry 'tel he git de crap in en de cotton chop'. So he kep' Henry on de plantation.

"But 'long 'bout time fer de grapes ter come on de scuppernon' vimes, dey 'peared ter come a change ober dem; de leaves wivered en swivel' up, en de young grapes turn' yaller, en bimeby eve'ybody on de plantation could see dat de whole vimya'd wuz dyin'. Mars Dugal' tuck 'n water de vimes en done all he could, but 't wan' no use: dat Yankee done bus' de watermillyum. One time de vimes picked up a bit, en Mars Dugal' thought dey wuz gwine ter come out ag'in; but dat Yankee done dug too close unde' de roots, en prune de branches too close ter de vime, en all dat lime en ashes done burn' de life outen de vimes, en dey des kep' a with'in' en a swivelin'.

"All dis time de goopher wuz a-wukkin'. W'en de vimes commence' ter wither, Henry commence' ter complain er his rheumatiz, en when de leaves begin ter dry up his ha'r commence' ter drap out. When de vimes fresh up a bit Henry 'ud git peart agin, en when de vimes wither agin Henry 'ud git ole agin, en des kep' gittin' mo' en mo' fitten fer nuffin; he des pined away, en fine'ly tuk ter his cabin; en when de big vime whar he got de sap ter 'n'int his head withered en turned yaller en died, Henry died too, — des went out sorter like a cannel. Dey didn't 'pear ter be nuffin de matter wid 'im, 'cep'n de rheumatiz, but his strenk des dwinel' away 'tel he didn' hab ernuff lef' ter draw his bref. De goopher had got de under holt, en th'owed Henry fer good en all dat time.

"Mars Dugal' tuk on might'ly 'bout losin' his vimes en his nigger in de same year; en he swo' dat ef he could git hold er dat Yankee he'd wear 'im ter a frazzle, en den chaw up de frazzle; en he'd done it, too, for Mars Dugal' 'uz a monst'us brash man w'en he once git started. He sot de vimya'd out ober agin, but it wuz th'ee er fo' year befo' de vimes got ter b'arin' any scuppernon's.

"W'en de wah broke out, Mars Dugal' raise' a comp'ny, en went off ter fight de Yankees. He saw he wuz mighty glad dat wah come, en he des want ter kill a Yankee fer eve'y dollar he los' 'long er dat grape-raisin' Yankee. En I 'spec' he would a done it, too, ef de Yankees hadn' s'picioned sump'n, en killed him fus'. Atter de s'render ole miss move' ter town, de niggers all scattered 'way fum de plantation, en de vimya'd ain' be'n cultervated sence."

"Is that story true?" asked Annie, doubtfully, but seriously, as the old man concluded his narrative.

"It's des ez true ez I'm a-settin' here, miss. Dey's a easy way ter prove it: I kin lead de way right ter Henry's grave ober yander in de plantation buryin'-groun'. En I tell yer w'at, marster, I wouldn' 'vise yer to buy dis yer ole vimya'd, 'caze de goopher's on it yit, en dey ain' no tellin' w'en it's gwine ter crap out."

"But I thought you said all the old vines died."

"Dey did 'pear ter die, but a few ov 'em come out ag'in, en is mixed in mongs' de yuthers. I ain' skeered ter eat de grapes, 'caze I knows de old vimes fum de noo ones; but wid strangers dey ain' no tellin' w'at might happen. I wouldn' 'vise yer ter buy dis vimya'd."

I bought the vineyard, nevertheless, and it has been for a long time in a thriving condition, and is referred to by the local press as a striking illustration of the opportunities open to Northern capital in the development of Southern industries. The luscious scuppernong holds first rank among our grapes, though we cultivate a great many other varieties, and our income from grapes packed and shipped to the Northern markets is quite considerable. I have not noticed any developments of the goopher in the vineyard, although I have a mild suspicion that our colored assistants do not suffer from want of grapes during the season.

I found, when I bought the vineyard, that Uncle Julius had occupied a cabin on the place for many years, and derived a respectable revenue from the neglected grapevines. This, doubtless, accounted for his advice to me not to buy the vineyard, though whether it inspired the goopher story I am unable to state. I believe, however, that the wages I pay him for his services are more than an equivalent for anything he lost by the sale of the vineyard.

Hermann Hesse, Siddhartha

FIRST PART

THE SON OF THE BRAHMAN

In the shade of the house, in the sunshine of the riverbank near the boats, in the shade of the Sal-wood forest, in the shade of the fig tree is where Siddhartha grew up, the handsome son of the Brahman, the young falcon, together with his friend Govinda, son of a Brahman. The sun tanned his light shoulders by the banks of the river when bathing, performing the sacred ablutions, the sacred offerings. In the mango grove, shade poured into his black eyes, when playing as a boy, when his mother sang, when the sacred offerings were made, when his father, the scholar, taught him, when the wise men talked. For a long time, Siddhartha had been partaking in the discussions of the wise men, practising debate with Govinda, practising with Govinda the art of reflection, the service of meditation. He already knew how to speak the Om silently, the word of words, to speak it silently into himself while inhaling, to speak it silently out of himself while exhaling, with all the concentration of his soul, the forehead surrounded by the glow of the clear-thinking spirit. He already knew to feel Atman in the depths of his being, indestructible, one with the universe.

Joy leapt in his father's heart for his son who was quick to learn, thirsty for knowledge; he saw him growing up to become great wise man and priest, a prince among the Brahmans.

Bliss leapt in his mother's breast when she saw him, when she saw him walking, when she saw him sit down and get up, Siddhartha, strong, handsome, he who was walking on slender legs, greeting her with perfect respect.

Love touched the hearts of the Brahmans' young daughters when Siddhartha walked through the lanes of the town with the luminous forehead, with the eye of a king, with his slim hips.

But more than all the others he was loved by Govinda, his friend, the son of a Brahman. He loved Siddhartha's eye and sweet voice, he loved his walk and the perfect decency of his movements, he loved everything Siddhartha did and said and what he loved most was his spirit, his transcendent, fiery thoughts, his ardent will, his high calling. Govinda knew: he would not become a common Brahman, not a lazy official in charge of offerings; not a greedy merchant with magic spells; not a vain, vacuous speaker; not a mean, deceitful priest; and also not a decent, stupid sheep in the herd of the many. No, and he, Govinda, as well did not want to become one of those, not one of those tens of thousands of Brahmans. He wanted to follow Siddhartha, the beloved, the splendid. And in days to come, when Siddhartha would become a god, when he would join the glorious, then Govinda wanted to follow him as his friend, his companion, his servant, his spear-carrier, his shadow.

Siddhartha was thus loved by everyone. He was a source of joy for everybody, he was a delight for them all.

But he, Siddhartha, was not a source of joy for himself, he found no delight in himself. Walking the rosy paths of the fig tree garden, sitting in the bluish shade of the grove of contemplation, washing his limbs daily in the bath of repentance, sacrificing in the dim shade of the mango forest, his gestures of perfect decency, everyone's love and joy, he still lacked all joy in his heart. Dreams and restless thoughts came into his mind, flowing from the water of the river, sparkling from the stars of the night, melting from the beams of the sun, dreams came to him and a restlessness of the soul, fuming from the sacrifices, breathing forth from the verses of the Rig-Veda, being infused into him, drop by drop, from the teachings of the old Brahmans.

Siddhartha had started to nurse discontent in himself, he had started to feel that the love of his father and the love of his mother, and also the love of his friend, Govinda, would not bring him joy for ever and ever, would not nurse him, feed him, satisfy him. He had started to suspect that his venerable father and his other teachers, that the wise Brahmans had already revealed to him the most and best of their wisdom, that they had already filled his expecting vessel with their richness, and the vessel was not full, the spirit was not content, the soul was not calm, the heart was not satisfied. The ablutions were good, but they were water, they did not wash off the sin, they did not heal the spirit's thirst, they did not relieve the fear in his heart. The sacrifices and the invocation of the gods were excellent—but was that all? Did the sacrifices give a happy fortune? And what about the gods? Was it really Prajapati who had created the world? Was it not the Atman, He, the only one, the singular one? Were the gods not creations, created like me and you, subject to time, mortal? Was it therefore good, was it right, was it meaningful and the highest occupation to make offerings to the gods? For whom else were offerings to be made, who else was to be worshipped but Him, the only one, the Atman? And where was Atman to be found, where did He reside, where did his eternal heart beat, where else but in one's own self, in its innermost part, in its indestructible part, which everyone had in himself? But where, where was this self, this innermost part, this ultimate part? It was not flesh and bone, it was neither thought nor consciousness, thus the wisest ones taught. So, where, where was it? To reach this place, the self, myself, the Atman, there was another way, which was worthwhile looking for? Alas, and nobody showed this way, nobody knew it, not the father, and not the teachers and wise men, not the holy sacrificial songs! They knew everything, the Brahmans and their holy books, they knew everything, they had taken care of everything and of more than everything, the creation of the world, the origin of speech, of food, of inhaling, of exhaling, the arrangement of the senses, the acts of the gods, they knew infinitely much—but was it valuable to know all of this, not knowing that one and only thing, the most important thing, the solely important thing?

Surely, many verses of the holy books, particularly in the Upanishades of Samaveda, spoke of this innermost and ultimate thing, wonderful verses. "Your soul is the whole world", was written there, and it was written that man in his sleep, in his deep sleep, would meet with his innermost part and would reside in the Atman. Marvellous wisdom was in these verses, all knowledge of the wisest ones had been collected here in magic words, pure as honey collected by bees. No, not to be looked down upon was the tremendous amount of enlightenment which lay here collected and preserved by innumerable generations of wise Brahmans.— But where were the Brahmans, where the priests, where the wise men or penitents, who had succeeded in not just knowing this deepest of all knowledge but also to live it? Where was the knowledgeable one who wove his spell to bring his familiarity with the Atman out of the sleep into the state of being awake, into the life, into every step of the way, into word and deed? Siddhartha knew many venerable Brahmans, chiefly his father, the pure one, the scholar, the most venerable one. His father was to be admired, quiet and noble were his manners, pure his life, wise his words, delicate and noble thoughts lived behind its brow —but even he, who knew so much, did he live in blissfulness, did he have peace, was he not also just a searching man, a thirsty man? Did he not, again and again, have to drink from holy sources, as a thirsty man, from the offerings, from the books, from the disputes of the Brahmans? Why did he, the irreproachable one, have to wash off sins every day, strive for a cleansing every day, over and over every day? Was not Atman in him, did not the pristine source spring from his heart? It had to be found, the pristine source in one's own self, it had to be possessed! Everything else was searching, was a detour, was getting lost.

Thus were Siddhartha's thoughts, this was his thirst, this was his suffering.

Often he spoke to himself from a Chandogya-Upanishad the words: "Truly, the name of the Brahman is satyam—verily, he who knows such a thing, will enter the heavenly world every day." Often, it seemed near, the heavenly world, but never he had reached it completely, never he had quenched the ultimate thirst. And among all the wise and wisest men, he knew and whose instructions he had received, among all of them there was no one, who had reached it completely, the heavenly world, who had quenched it completely, the eternal thirst.

"Govinda," Siddhartha spoke to his friend, "Govinda, my dear, come with me under the Banyan tree, let's practise meditation."

They went to the Banyan tree, they sat down, Siddhartha right here, Govinda twenty paces away. While putting himself down, ready to speak the Om, Siddhartha repeated murmuring the verse:

Om is the bow, the arrow is soul, The Brahman is the arrow's target, That one should incessantly hit.

After the usual time of the exercise in meditation had passed, Govinda rose. The evening had come, it was time to perform the evening's ablution. He called Siddhartha's name. Siddhartha did not answer. Siddhartha sat there lost in thought, his eyes were rigidly focused towards a very distant target, the tip of his tongue was protruding a little between the teeth, he seemed not to breathe. Thus sat he, wrapped up in contemplation, thinking Om, his soul sent after the Brahman as an arrow.

Once, Samanas had travelled through Siddhartha's town, ascetics on a pilgrimage, three skinny, withered men, neither old nor young, with dusty and bloody shoulders, almost naked, scorched by the sun, surrounded by loneliness, strangers and enemies to the world, strangers and lank jackals in the realm of humans. Behind them blew a hot scent of quiet passion, of destructive service, of merciless self-denial.

In the evening, after the hour of contemplation, Siddhartha spoke to Govinda: "Early tomorrow morning, my friend, Siddhartha will go to the Samanas. He will become a Samana."

Govinda turned pale, when he heard these words and read the decision in the motionless face of his friend, unstoppable like the arrow shot from the bow. Soon and with the first glance, Govinda realized: Now it is beginning, now Siddhartha is taking his own way, now his fate is beginning to sprout, and with his, my own. And he turned pale like a dry banana-skin.

"O Siddhartha," he exclaimed, "will your father permit you to do that?"

Siddhartha looked over as if he was just waking up. Arrow-fast he read in Govinda's soul, read the fear, read the submission.

"O Govinda," he spoke quietly, "let's not waste words. Tomorrow, at daybreak I will begin the life of the Samanas. Speak no more of it."

Siddhartha entered the chamber, where his father was sitting on a mat of bast, and stepped behind his father and remained standing there, until his father felt that someone was standing behind him. Quoth the Brahman: "Is that you, Siddhartha? Then say what you came to say."

Quoth Siddhartha: "With your permission, my father. I came to tell you that it is my longing to leave your house tomorrow and go to the ascetics. My desire is to become a Samana. May my father not oppose this."

The Brahman fell silent, and remained silent for so long that the stars in the small window wandered and changed their relative positions, 'ere the silence was broken. Silent and motionless stood the son with his arms folded, silent and motionless sat the father on the mat, and the stars traced their paths in the sky. Then spoke the father: "Not proper it is for a Brahman to speak harsh and angry words. But indignation is in my heart. I wish not to hear this request for a second time from your mouth."

Slowly, the Brahman rose; Siddhartha stood silently, his arms folded.

"What are you waiting for?" asked the father.

Quoth Siddhartha: "You know what."

Indignant, the father left the chamber; indignant, he went to his bed and lay down.

After an hour, since no sleep had come over his eyes, the Brahman stood up, paced to and fro, and left the house. Through the small window of the chamber he looked back inside, and there he saw Siddhartha standing, his arms folded, not moving from his spot. Pale shimmered his bright robe. With anxiety in his heart, the father returned to his bed.

After another hour, since no sleep had come over his eyes, the Brahman stood up again, paced to and fro, walked out of the house and saw that the moon had risen. Through the window of the chamber he looked back inside; there stood Siddhartha, not moving from his spot, his arms folded, moonlight reflecting from his bare shins. With worry in his heart, the father went back to bed.

And he came back after an hour, he came back after two hours, looked through the small window, saw Siddhartha standing, in the moon light, by the light of the stars, in the darkness. And he came back hour after hour, silently, he looked into the chamber, saw him standing in the same place, filled his heart with anger, filled his heart with unrest, filled his heart with anguish, filled it with sadness.

And in the night's last hour, before the day began, he returned, stepped into the room, saw the young man standing there, who seemed tall and like a stranger to him.

"Siddhartha," he spoke, "what are you waiting for?"

"You know what."

"Will you always stand that way and wait, until it'll becomes morning, noon, and evening?"

"I will stand and wait.

"You will become tired, Siddhartha."

"I will become tired."

"You will fall asleep, Siddhartha."

"I will not fall asleep."

"You will die, Siddhartha."

"I will die."

"And would you rather die, than obey your father?"

"Siddhartha has always obeyed his father."

"So will you abandon your plan?"

"Siddhartha will do what his father will tell him to do."

The first light of day shone into the room. The Brahman saw that Siddhartha was trembling softly in his knees. In Siddhartha's face he saw no trembling, his eyes were fixed on a distant spot. Then his father realized that even now Siddhartha no longer dwelt with him in his home, that he had already left him.

The Father touched Siddhartha's shoulder.

"You will," he spoke, "go into the forest and be a Samana. When you'll have found blissfulness in the forest, then come back and teach me to be blissful. If you'll find disappointment, then return and let us once again make offerings to the gods together. Go now and kiss your mother, tell her where you are going to. But for me it is time to go to the river and to perform the first ablution."

He took his hand from the shoulder of his son and went outside. Siddhartha wavered to the side, as he tried to walk. He put his limbs back under control, bowed to his father, and went to his mother to do as his father had said.

As he slowly left on stiff legs in the first light of day the still quiet town, a shadow rose near the last hut, who had crouched there, and joined the pilgrim—Govinda.

"You have come," said Siddhartha and smiled.

"I have come," said Govinda.

WITH THE SAMANAS

In the evening of this day they caught up with the ascetics, the skinny Samanas, and offered them their companionship and—obedience. They were accepted.

Siddhartha gave his garments to a poor Brahman in the street. He wore nothing more than the loincloth and the earth-coloured, unsown cloak. He ate only once a day, and never something cooked. He fasted for fifteen days. He fasted for twenty-eight days. The flesh waned from his thighs and cheeks. Feverish dreams flickered from his enlarged eyes, long nails grew slowly on his parched fingers and a dry, shaggy beard grew on his chin. His glance turned to ice when he encountered women; his mouth twitched with contempt, when he walked through a city of nicely dressed people. He saw merchants trading, princes hunting, mourners wailing for their dead, whores offering themselves, physicians trying to help the sick, priests determining the most suitable day for seeding, lovers loving, mothers nursing their children—and all of this was not worthy of one look from his eye, it all lied, it all stank, it all stank of lies, it all pretended to be meaningful and joyful and beautiful, and it all was just concealed putrefaction. The world tasted bitter. Life was torture.

A goal stood before Siddhartha, a single goal: to become empty, empty of thirst, empty of wishing, empty of dreams, empty of joy and sorrow. Dead to himself, not to be a self any more, to find tranquility with an emptied heart, to be open to miracles in unselfish thoughts, that was his goal. Once all of my self was overcome and had died, once every desire and every urge was silent in the heart, then the ultimate part of me had to awake, the innermost of my being, which is no longer my self, the great secret.

Silently, Siddhartha exposed himself to burning rays of the sun directly above, glowing with pain, glowing with thirst, and stood there, until he neither felt any pain nor thirst any more. Silently, he stood there in the rainy season, from his hair the water was dripping over freezing shoulders, over freezing hips and legs, and the penitent stood there, until he could not feel the cold in his shoulders and legs any more, until they were silent, until they were quiet. Silently, he cowered in the thorny bushes, blood dripped from the burning skin, from festering wounds dripped pus, and Siddhartha stayed rigidly, stayed motionless, until no blood flowed any more, until nothing stung any more, until nothing burned any more.

Siddhartha sat upright and learned to breathe sparingly, learned to get along with only few breathes, learned to stop breathing. He learned, beginning with the breath, to calm the beat of his heart, leaned to reduce the beats of his heart, until they were only a few and almost none.

Instructed by the oldest of the Samanas, Siddhartha practised self-denial, practised meditation, according to a new Samana rules. A heron flew over the bamboo forest—and Siddhartha accepted the heron into his soul, flew over forest and mountains, was a heron, ate fish, felt the pangs of a heron's hunger, spoke the heron's croak, died a heron's death. A dead jackal was lying on the sandy bank, and Siddhartha's soul slipped inside the body, was the dead jackal, lay on the banks, got bloated, stank, decayed, was dismembered by hyaenas, was skinned by vultures, turned into a skeleton, turned to dust, was blown across the fields. And Siddhartha's soul returned, had died, had decayed, was scattered as dust, had tasted the gloomy intoxication of the cycle, awaited in new thirst like a hunter in the gap, where he could escape from the cycle, where the end of the causes, where an eternity without suffering began. He killed his senses, he killed his memory, he slipped out of his self into thousands of other forms, was an animal, was carrion, was stone, was wood, was water, and awoke every time to find his old self again, sun shone or moon, was his self again, turned round in the cycle, felt thirst, overcame the thirst, felt new thirst.

Siddhartha learned a lot when he was with the Samanas, many ways leading away from the self he learned to go. He went the way of self-denial by means of pain, through voluntarily suffering and overcoming pain, hunger, thirst, tiredness. He went the way of self-denial by means of meditation, through imagining the mind to be void of all conceptions. These and other ways he learned to go, a thousand times he left his self, for hours and days he remained in the non-self. But though the ways led away from the self, their end nevertheless always led back to the self. Though Siddhartha fled from the self a thousand times, stayed in nothingness, stayed in the animal, in the stone, the return was inevitable, inescapable was the hour, when he found himself back in the sunshine or in the moonlight, in the shade or in the rain, and was once again his self and Siddhartha, and again felt the agony of the cycle which had been forced upon him.

By his side lived Govinda, his shadow, walked the same paths, undertook the same efforts. They rarely spoke to one another, than the service and the exercises required. Occasionally the two of them went through the villages, to beg for food for themselves and their teachers.

"How do you think, Govinda," Siddhartha spoke one day while begging this way, "how do you think did we progress? Did we reach any goals?"

Govinda answered: "We have learned, and we'll continue learning. You'll be a great Samana, Siddhartha. Quickly, you've learned every exercise, often the old Samanas have admired you. One day, you'll be a holy man, oh Siddhartha."

Quoth Siddhartha: "I can't help but feel that it is not like this, my friend. What I've learned, being among the Samanas, up to this day, this, oh Govinda, I could have learned more quickly and by simpler means. In every tavern of that part of a town where the whorehouses are, my friend, among carters and gamblers I could have learned it."

Quoth Govinda: "Siddhartha is putting me on. How could you have learned meditation, holding your breath, insensitivity against hunger and pain there among these wretched people?"

And Siddhartha said quietly, as if he was talking to himself: "What is meditation? What is leaving one's body? What is fasting? What is holding one's breath? It is fleeing from the self, it is a short escape of the agony of being a self, it is a short numbing of the senses against the pain and the pointlessness of life. The same escape, the same short numbing is what the driver of an ox-cart finds in the inn, drinking a few bowls of rice-wine or fermented coconut-milk. Then he won't feel his self any more, then he won't feel the pains of life any more, then he finds a short numbing of the senses. When he falls asleep over his bowl of rice-wine, he'll find the same what Siddhartha and Govinda find when they escape their bodies through long exercises, staying in the non-self. This is how it is, oh Govinda."

Quoth Govinda: "You say so, oh friend, and yet you know that Siddhartha is no driver of an ox-cart and a Samana is no drunkard. It's true that a drinker numbs his senses, it's true that he briefly escapes and rests, but he'll return from the delusion, finds everything to be unchanged, has not become wiser, has gathered no enlightenment,—has not risen several steps."

And Siddhartha spoke with a smile: "I do not know, I've never been a drunkard. But that I, Siddhartha, find only a short numbing of the senses in my exercises and meditations and that I am just as far removed from wisdom, from salvation, as a child in the mother's womb, this I know, oh Govinda, this I know."

And once again, another time, when Siddhartha left the forest together with Govinda, to beg for some food in the village for their brothers and teachers, Siddhartha began to speak and said: "What now, oh Govinda, might we be on the right path? Might we get closer to enlightenment? Might we get closer to salvation? Or do we perhaps live in a circle— we, who have thought we were escaping the cycle?"

Quoth Govinda: "We have learned a lot, Siddhartha, there is still much to learn. We are not going around in circles, we are moving up, the circle is a spiral, we have already ascended many a level."

Siddhartha answered: "How old, would you think, is our oldest Samana, our venerable teacher?"

Quoth Govinda: "Our oldest one might be about sixty years of age."

And Siddhartha: "He has lived for sixty years and has not reached the nirvana. He'll turn seventy and eighty, and you and me, we will grow just as old and will do our exercises, and will fast, and will meditate. But we will not reach the nirvana, he won't and we won't. Oh Govinda, I believe out of all the Samanas out there, perhaps not a single one, not a single one, will reach the nirvana. We find comfort, we find numbness, we learn feats, to deceive others. But the most important thing, the path of paths, we will not find."

"If you only," spoke Govinda, "wouldn't speak such terrible words, Siddhartha! How could it be that among so many learned men, among so many Brahmans, among so many austere and venerable Samanas, among so many who are searching, so many who are eagerly trying, so many holy men, no one will find the path of paths?"

But Siddhartha said in a voice which contained just as much sadness as mockery, with a quiet, a slightly sad, a slightly mocking voice: "Soon, Govinda, your friend will leave the path of the Samanas, he has walked along your side for so long. I'm suffering of thirst, oh Govinda, and on this long path of a Samana, my thirst has remained as strong as ever. I always thirsted for knowledge, I have always been full of questions. I have asked the Brahmans, year after year, and I have asked the holy Vedas, year after year, and I have asked the devote Samanas, year after year. Perhaps, oh Govinda, it had been just as well, had been just as smart and just as profitable, if I had asked the hornbill-bird or the chimpanzee. It took me a long time and am not finished learning this yet, oh Govinda: that there is nothing to be learned! There is indeed no such thing, so I believe, as what we refer to as `learning'. There is, oh my friend, just one knowledge, this is everywhere, this is Atman, this is within me and within you and within every creature. And so I'm starting to believe that this knowledge has no worser enemy than the desire to know it, than learning."

At this, Govinda stopped on the path, rose his hands, and spoke: "If you, Siddhartha, only would not bother your friend with this kind of talk! Truly, you words stir up fear in my heart. And just consider: what would become of the sanctity of prayer, what of the venerability of the Brahmans' caste, what of the holiness of the Samanas, if it was as you say, if there was no learning?! What, oh Siddhartha, what would then become of all of this what is holy, what is precious, what is venerable on earth?!"

And Govinda mumbled a verse to himself, a verse from an Upanishad:

He who ponderingly, of a purified spirit, loses himself in the meditation of Atman, unexpressable by words is his blissfulness of his heart.

But Siddhartha remained silent. He thought about the words which Govinda had said to him and thought the words through to their end.

Yes, he thought, standing there with his head low, what would remain of all that which seemed to us to be holy? What remains? What can stand the test? And he shook his head.

At one time, when the two young men had lived among the Samanas for about three years and had shared their exercises, some news, a rumour, a myth reached them after being retold many times: A man had appeared, Gotama by name, the exalted one, the Buddha, he had overcome the suffering of the world in himself and had halted the cycle of rebirths. He was said to wander through the land, teaching, surrounded by disciples, without possession, without home, without a wife, in the yellow cloak of an ascetic, but with a cheerful brow, a man of bliss, and Brahmans and princes would bow down before him and would become his students.

This myth, this rumour, this legend resounded, its fragrants rose up, here and there; in the towns, the Brahmans spoke of it and in the forest, the Samanas; again and again, the name of Gotama, the Buddha reached the ears of the young men, with good and with bad talk, with praise and with defamation.

It was as if the plague had broken out in a country and news had been spreading around that in one or another place there was a man, a wise man, a knowledgeable one, whose word and breath was enough to heal everyone who had been infected with the pestilence, and as such news would go through the land and everyone would talk about it, many would believe, many would doubt, but many would get on their way as soon as possible, to seek the wise man, the helper, just like this this myth ran through the land, that fragrant myth of Gotama, the Buddha, the wise man of the family of Sakya. He possessed, so the believers said, the highest enlightenment, he remembered his previous lives, he had reached the nirvana and never returned into the cycle, was never again submerged in the murky river of physical forms. Many wonderful and unbelievable things were reported of him, he had performed miracles, had overcome the devil, had spoken to the gods. But his enemies and disbelievers said, this Gotama was a vain seducer, he would spent his days in luxury, scorned the offerings, was without learning, and knew neither exercises nor self-castigation.

The myth of Buddha sounded sweet. The scent of magic flowed from these reports. After all, the world was sick, life was hard to bear—and behold, here a source seemed to spring forth, here a messenger seemed to call out, comforting, mild, full of noble promises. Everywhere where the rumour of Buddha was heard, everywhere in the lands of India, the young men listened up, felt a longing, felt hope, and among the Brahmans' sons of the towns and villages every pilgrim and stranger was welcome, when he brought news of him, the exalted one, the Sakyamuni.

The myth had also reached the Samanas in the forest, and also Siddhartha, and also Govinda, slowly, drop by drop, every drop laden with hope, every drop laden with doubt. They rarely talked about it, because the oldest one of the Samanas did not like this myth. He had heard that this alleged Buddha used to be an ascetic before and had lived in the forest, but had then turned back to luxury and worldly pleasures, and he had no high opinion of this Gotama.

"Oh Siddhartha," Govinda spoke one day to his friend. "Today, I was in the village, and a Brahman invited me into his house, and in his house, there was the son of a Brahman from Magadha, who has seen the Buddha with his own eyes and has heard him teach. Verily, this made my chest ache when I breathed, and thought to myself: If only I would too, if only we both would too, Siddhartha and me, live to see the hour when we will hear the teachings from the mouth of this perfected man! Speak, friend, wouldn't we want to go there too and listen to the teachings from the Buddha's mouth?"

Quoth Siddhartha: "Always, oh Govinda, I had thought, Govinda would stay with the Samanas, always I had believed his goal was to live to be sixty and seventy years of age and to keep on practising those feats and exercises, which are becoming a Samana. But behold, I had not known Govinda well enough, I knew little of his heart. So now you, my faithful friend, want to take a new path and go there, where the Buddha spreads his teachings."

Quoth Govinda: "You're mocking me. Mock me if you like, Siddhartha! But have you not also developed a desire, an eagerness, to hear these teachings? And have you not at one time said to me, you would not walk the path of the Samanas for much longer?"

At this, Siddhartha laughed in his very own manner, in which his voice assumed a touch of sadness and a touch of mockery, and said: "Well, Govinda, you've spoken well, you've remembered correctly. If you only remembered the other thing as well, you've heard from me, which is that I have grown distrustful and tired against teachings and learning, and that my faith in words, which are brought to us by teachers, is small. But let's do it, my dear, I am willing to listen to these teachings—though in my heart I believe that we've already tasted the best fruit of these teachings."

Quoth Govinda: "Your willingness delights my heart. But tell me, how should this be possible? How should the Gotama's teachings, even before we have heard them, have already revealed their best fruit to us?"

Quoth Siddhartha: "Let us eat this fruit and wait for the rest, oh Govinda! But this fruit, which we already now received thanks to the Gotama, consisted in him calling us away from the Samanas! Whether he has also other and better things to give us, oh friend, let us await with calm hearts."

On this very same day, Siddhartha informed the oldest one of the Samanas of his decision, that he wanted to leave him. He informed the oldest one with all the courtesy and modesty becoming to a younger one and a student. But the Samana became angry, because the two young men wanted to leave him, and talked loudly and used crude swearwords.

Govinda was startled and became embarrassed. But Siddhartha put his mouth close to Govinda's ear and whispered to him: "Now, I want to show the old man that I've learned something from him."

Positioning himself closely in front of the Samana, with a concentrated soul, he captured the old man's glance with his glances, deprived him of his power, made him mute, took away his free will, subdued him under his own will, commanded him, to do silently, whatever he demanded him to do. The old man became mute, his eyes became motionless, his will was paralysed, his arms were hanging down; without power, he had fallen victim to Siddhartha's spell. But Siddhartha's thoughts brought the Samana under their control, he had to carry out, what they commanded. And thus, the old man made several bows, performed gestures of blessing, spoke stammeringly a godly wish for a good journey. And the young men returned the bows with thanks, returned the wish, went on their way with salutations.

On the way, Govinda said: "Oh Siddhartha, you have learned more from the Samanas than I knew. It is hard, it is very hard to cast a spell on an old Samana. Truly, if you had stayed there, you would soon have learned to walk on water."

"I do not seek to walk on water," said Siddhartha. "Let old Samanas be content with such feats!"

GOTAMA

In the town of Savathi, every child knew the name of the exalted Buddha, and every house was prepared to fill the alms-dish of Gotama's disciples, the silently begging ones. Near the town was Gotama's favourite place to stay, the grove of Jetavana, which the rich merchant Anathapindika, an obedient worshipper of the exalted one, had given him and his people for a gift.

All tales and answers, which the two young ascetics had received in their search for Gotama's abode, had pointed them towards this area. And arriving at Savathi, in the very first house, before the door of which they stopped to beg, food has been offered to them, and they accepted the food, and Siddhartha asked the woman, who handed them the food:

"We would like to know, oh charitable one, where the Buddha dwells, the most venerable one, for we are two Samanas from the forest and have come, to see him, the perfected one, and to hear the teachings from his mouth."

Quoth the woman: "Here, you have truly come to the right place, you Samanas from the forest. You should know, in Jetavana, in the garden of Anathapindika is where the exalted one dwells. There you pilgrims shall spent the night, for there is enough space for the innumerable, who flock here, to hear the teachings from his mouth."

This made Govinda happy, and full of joy he exclaimed: "Well so, thus we have reached our destination, and our path has come to an end! But tell us, oh mother of the pilgrims, do you know him, the Buddha, have you seen him with your own eyes?"

Quoth the woman: "Many times I have seen him, the exalted one. On many days, I have seen him, walking through the alleys in silence, wearing his yellow cloak, presenting his alms-dish in silence at the doors of the houses, leaving with a filled dish."

Delightedly, Govinda listened and wanted to ask and hear much more. But Siddhartha urged him to walk on. They thanked and left and hardly had to ask for directions, for rather many pilgrims and monks as well from Gotama's community were on their way to the Jetavana. And since they reached it at night, there were constant arrivals, shouts, and talk of those who sought shelter and got it. The two Samanas, accustomed to life in the forest, found quickly and without making any noise a place to stay and rested there until the morning.

At sunrise, they saw with astonishment what a large crowd of believers and curious people had spent the night here. On all paths of the marvellous grove, monks walked in yellow robes, under the trees they sat here and there, in deep contemplation—or in a conversation about spiritual matters, the shady gardens looked like a city, full of people, bustling like bees. The majority of the monks went out with their alms-dish, to collect food in town for their lunch, the only meal of the day. The Buddha himself, the enlightened one, was also in the habit of taking this walk to beg in the morning.

Siddhartha saw him, and he instantly recognised him, as if a god had pointed him out to him. He saw him, a simple man in a yellow robe, bearing the alms-dish in his hand, walking silently.

"Look here!" Siddhartha said quietly to Govinda. "This one is the Buddha."

Attentively, Govinda looked at the monk in the yellow robe, who seemed to be in no way different from the hundreds of other monks. And soon, Govinda also realized: This is the one. And they followed him and observed him.

The Buddha went on his way, modestly and deep in his thoughts, his calm face was neither happy nor sad, it seemed to smile quietly and inwardly. With a hidden smile, quiet, calm, somewhat resembling a healthy child, the Buddha walked, wore the robe and placed his feet just as all of his monks did, according to a precise rule. But his face and his walk, his quietly lowered glance, his quietly dangling hand and even every finger of his quietly dangling hand expressed peace, expressed perfection, did not search, did not imitate, breathed softly in an unwhithering calm, in an unwhithering light, an untouchable peace.

Thus Gotama walked towards the town, to collect alms, and the two Samanas recognised him solely by the perfection of his calm, by the quietness of his appearance, in which there was no searching, no desire, no imitation, no effort to be seen, only light and peace.

"Today, we'll hear the teachings from his mouth." said Govinda.

Siddhartha did not answer. He felt little curiosity for the teachings, he did not believe that they would teach him anything new, but he had, just as Govinda had, heard the contents of this Buddha's teachings again and again, though these reports only represented second- or third-hand information. But attentively he looked at Gotama's head, his shoulders, his feet, his quietly dangling hand, and it seemed to him as if every joint of every finger of this hand was of these teachings, spoke of, breathed of, exhaled the fragrant of, glistened of truth. This man, this Buddha was truthful down to the gesture of his last finger. This man was holy. Never before, Siddhartha had venerated a person so much, never before he had loved a person as much as this one.

They both followed the Buddha until they reached the town and then returned in silence, for they themselves intended to abstain from on this day. They saw Gotama returning—what he ate could not even have satisfied a bird's appetite, and they saw him retiring into the shade of the mango-trees.

But in the evening, when the heat cooled down and everyone in the camp started to bustle about and gathered around, they heard the Buddha teaching. They heard his voice, and it was also perfected, was of perfect calmness, was full of peace. Gotama taught the teachings of suffering, of the origin of suffering, of the way to relieve suffering. Calmly and clearly his quiet speech flowed on. Suffering was life, full of suffering was the world, but salvation from suffering had been found: salvation was obtained by him who would walk the path of the Buddha. With a soft, yet firm voice the exalted one spoke, taught the four main doctrines, taught the eightfold path, patiently he went the usual path of the teachings, of the examples, of the repetitions, brightly and quietly his voice hovered over the listeners, like a light, like a starry sky.

When the Buddha—night had already fallen—ended his speech, many a pilgrim stepped forward and asked to accepted into the community, sought refuge in the teachings. And Gotama accepted them by speaking: "You have heard the teachings well, it has come to you well. Thus join us and walk in holiness, to put an end to all suffering."

Behold, then Govinda, the shy one, also stepped forward and spoke: "I also take my refuge in the exalted one and his teachings," and he asked to accepted into the community of his disciples and was accepted.

Right afterwards, when the Buddha had retired for the night, Govinda turned to Siddhartha and spoke eagerly: "Siddhartha, it is not my place to scold you. We have both heard the exalted one, we have both perceived the teachings. Govinda has heard the teachings, he has taken refuge in it. But you, my honoured friend, don't you also want to walk the path of salvation? Would you want to hesitate, do you want to wait any longer?"

Siddhartha awakened as if he had been asleep, when he heard Govinda's words. For a long time, he looked into Govinda's face. Then he spoke quietly, in a voice without mockery: "Govinda, my friend, now you have taken this step, now you have chosen this path. Always, oh Govinda, you've been my friend, you've always walked one step behind me. Often I have thought: Won't Govinda for once also take a step by himself, without me, out of his own soul? Behold, now you've turned into a man and are choosing your path for yourself. I wish that you would go it up to its end, oh my friend, that you shall find salvation!"

Govinda, not completely understanding it yet, repeated his question in an impatient tone: "Speak up, I beg you, my dear! Tell me, since it could not be any other way, that you also, my learned friend, will take your refuge with the exalted Buddha!"

Siddhartha placed his hand on Govinda's shoulder: "You failed to hear my good wish for you, oh Govinda. I'm repeating it: I wish that you would go this path up to its end, that you shall find salvation!"

In this moment, Govinda realized that his friend had left him, and he started to weep.

"Siddhartha!" he exclaimed lamentingly.

Siddhartha kindly spoke to him: "Don't forget, Govinda, that you are now one of the Samanas of the Buddha! You have renounced your home and your parents, renounced your birth and possessions, renounced your free will, renounced all friendship. This is what the teachings require, this is what the exalted one wants. This is what you wanted for yourself. Tomorrow, oh Govinda, I'll leave you."

For a long time, the friends continued walking in the grove; for a long time, they lay there and found no sleep. And over and over again, Govinda urged his friend, he should tell him why he would not want to seek refuge in Gotama's teachings, what fault he would find in these teachings. But Siddhartha turned him away every time and said: "Be content, Govinda! Very good are the teachings of the exalted one, how could I find a fault in them?"

Very early in the morning, a follower of Buddha, one of his oldest monks, went through the garden and called all those to him who had as novices taken their refuge in the teachings, to dress them up in the yellow robe and to instruct them in the first teachings and duties of their position. Then Govinda broke loose, embraced once again his childhood friend and left with the novices.

But Siddhartha walked through the grove, lost in thought.

Then he happened to meet Gotama, the exalted one, and when he greeted him with respect and the Buddha's glance was so full of kindness and calm, the young man summoned his courage and asked the venerable one for the permission to talk to him. Silently the exalted one nodded his approval.

Quoth Siddhartha: "Yesterday, oh exalted one, I had been privileged to hear your wondrous teachings. Together with my friend, I had come from afar, to hear your teachings. And now my friend is going to stay with your people, he has taken his refuge with you. But I will again start on my pilgrimage."

"As you please," the venerable one spoke politely.

"Too bold is my speech," Siddhartha continued, "but I do not want to leave the exalted one without having honestly told him my thoughts. Does it please the venerable one to listen to me for one moment longer?"

Silently, the Buddha nodded his approval.

Quoth Siddhartha: "One thing, oh most venerable one, I have admired in your teachings most of all. Everything in your teachings is perfectly clear, is proven; you are presenting the world as a perfect chain, a chain which is never and nowhere broken, an eternal chain the links of which are causes and effects. Never before, this has been seen so clearly; never before, this has been presented so irrefutably; truly, the heart of every Brahman has to beat stronger with love, once he has seen the world through your teachings perfectly connected, without gaps, clear as a crystal, not depending on chance, not depending on gods. Whether it may be good or bad, whether living according to it would be suffering or joy, I do not wish to discuss, possibly this is not essential—but the uniformity of the world, that everything which happens is connected, that the great and the small things are all encompassed by the same forces of time, by the same law of causes, of coming into being and of dying, this is what shines brightly out of your exalted teachings, oh perfected one. But according to your very own teachings, this unity and necessary sequence of all things is nevertheless broken in one place, through a small gap, this world of unity is invaded by something alien, something new, something which had not been there before, and which cannot be demonstrated and cannot be proven: these are your teachings of overcoming the world, of salvation. But with this small gap, with this small breach, the entire eternal and uniform law of the world is breaking apart again and becomes void. Please forgive me for expressing this objection."

Quietly, Gotama had listened to him, unmoved. Now he spoke, the perfected one, with his kind, with his polite and clear voice: "You've heard the teachings, oh son of a Brahman, and good for you that you've thought about it thus deeply. You've found a gap in it, an error. You should think about this further. But be warned, oh seeker of knowledge, of the thicket of opinions and of arguing about words. There is nothing to opinions, they may be beautiful or ugly, smart or foolish, everyone can support them or discard them. But the teachings, you've heard from me, are no opinion, and their goal is not to explain the world to those who seek knowledge. They have a different goal; their goal is salvation from suffering. This is what Gotama teaches, nothing else."

"I wish that you, oh exalted one, would not be angry with me," said the young man. "I have not spoken to you like this to argue with you, to argue about words. You are truly right, there is little to opinions. But let me say this one more thing: I have not doubted in you for a single moment. I have not doubted for a single moment that you are Buddha, that you have reached the goal, the highest goal towards which so many thousands of Brahmans and sons of Brahmans are on their way. You have found salvation from death. It has come to you in the course of your own search, on your own path, through thoughts, through meditation, through realizations, through enlightenment. It has not come to you by means of teachings! And—thus is my thought, oh exalted one,—nobody will obtain salvation by means of teachings! You will not be able to convey and say to anybody, oh venerable one, in words and through teachings what has happened to you in the hour of enlightenment! The teachings of the enlightened Buddha contain much, it teaches many to live righteously, to avoid evil. But there is one thing which these so clear, these so venerable teachings do not contain: they do not contain the mystery of what the exalted one has experienced for himself, he alone among hundreds of thousands. This is what I have thought and realized, when I have heard the teachings. This is why I am continuing my travels—not to seek other, better teachings, for I know there are none, but to depart from all teachings and all teachers and to reach my goal by myself or to die. But often, I'll think of this day, oh exalted one, and of this hour, when my eyes beheld a holy man."

The Buddha's eyes quietly looked to the ground; quietly, in perfect equanimity his inscrutable face was smiling.

"I wish," the venerable one spoke slowly, "that your thoughts shall not be in error, that you shall reach the goal! But tell me: Have you seen the multitude of my Samanas, my many brothers, who have taken refuge in the teachings? And do you believe, oh stranger, oh Samana, do you believe that it would be better for them all the abandon the teachings and to return into the life the world and of desires?"

"Far is such a thought from my mind," exclaimed Siddhartha. "I wish that they shall all stay with the teachings, that they shall reach their goal! It is not my place to judge another person's life. Only for myself, for myself alone, I must decide, I must chose, I must refuse. Salvation from the self is what we Samanas search for, oh exalted one. If I merely were one of your disciples, oh venerable one, I'd fear that it might happen to me that only seemingly, only deceptively my self would be calm and be redeemed, but that in truth it would live on and grow, for then I had replaced my self with the teachings, my duty to follow you, my love for you, and the community of the monks!"

With half of a smile, with an unwavering openness and kindness, Gotama looked into the stranger's eyes and bid him to leave with a hardly noticeable gesture.

"You are wise, oh Samana.", the venerable one spoke.

"You know how to talk wisely, my friend. Be aware of too much wisdom!"

The Buddha turned away, and his glance and half of a smile remained forever etched in Siddhartha's memory.

I have never before seen a person glance and smile, sit and walk this way, he thought; truly, I wish to be able to glance and smile, sit and walk this way, too, thus free, thus venerable, thus concealed, thus open, thus child-like and mysterious. Truly, only a person who has succeeded in reaching the innermost part of his self would glance and walk this way. Well so, I also will seek to reach the innermost part of my self.

I saw a man, Siddhartha thought, a single man, before whom I would have to lower my glance. I do not want to lower my glance before any other, not before any other. No teachings will entice me any more, since this man's teachings have not enticed me.

I am deprived by the Buddha, thought Siddhartha, I am deprived, and even more he has given to me. He has deprived me of my friend, the one who had believed in me and now believes in him, who had been my shadow and is now Gotama's shadow. But he has given me Siddhartha, myself.

AWAKENING

When Siddhartha left the grove, where the Buddha, the perfected one, stayed behind, where Govinda stayed behind, then he felt that in this grove his past life also stayed behind and parted from him. He pondered about this sensation, which filled him completely, as he was slowly walking along. He pondered deeply, like diving into a deep water he let himself sink down to the ground of the sensation, down to the place where the causes lie, because to identify the causes, so it seemed to him, is the very essence of thinking, and by this alone sensations turn into realizations and are not lost, but become entities and start to emit like rays of light what is inside of them.

Slowly walking along, Siddhartha pondered. He realized that he was no youth any more, but had turned into a man. He realized that one thing had left him, as a snake is left by its old skin, that one thing no longer existed in him, which had accompanied him throughout his youth and used to be a part of him: the wish to have teachers and to listen to teachings. He had also left the last teacher who had appeared on his path, even him, the highest and wisest teacher, the most holy one, Buddha, he had left him, had to part with him, was not able to accept his teachings.

Slower, he walked along in his thoughts and asked himself: "But what is this, what you have sought to learn from teachings and from teachers, and what they, who have taught you much, were still unable to teach you?" And he found: "It was the self, the purpose and essence of which I sought to learn. It was the self, I wanted to free myself from, which I sought to overcome. But I was not able to overcome it, could only deceive it, could only flee from it, only hide from it. Truly, no thing in this world has kept my thoughts thus busy, as this my very own self, this mystery of me being alive, of me being one and being separated and isolated from all others, of me being Siddhartha! And there is no thing in this world I know less about than about me, about Siddhartha!"

Having been pondering while slowly walking along, he now stopped as these thoughts caught hold of him, and right away another thought sprang forth from these, a new thought, which was: "That I know nothing about myself, that Siddhartha has remained thus alien and unknown to me, stems from one cause, a single cause: I was afraid of myself, I was fleeing from myself! I searched Atman, I searched Brahman, I was willing to dissect my self and peel off all of its layers, to find the core of all peels in its unknown interior, the Atman, life, the divine part, the ultimate part. But I have lost myself in the process."

Siddhartha opened his eyes and looked around, a smile filled his face and a feeling of awakening from long dreams flowed through him from his head down to his toes. And it was not long before he walked again, walked quickly like a man who knows what he has got to do.

"Oh," he thought, taking a deep breath, "now I would not let Siddhartha escape from me again! No longer, I want to begin my thoughts and my life with Atman and with the suffering of the world. I do not want to kill and dissect myself any longer, to find a secret behind the ruins. Neither Yoga-Veda shall teach me any more, nor Atharva-Veda, nor the ascetics, nor any kind of teachings. I want to learn from myself, want to be my student, want to get to know myself, the secret of Siddhartha."

He looked around, as if he was seeing the world for the first time. Beautiful was the world, colourful was the world, strange and mysterious was the world! Here was blue, here was yellow, here was green, the sky and the river flowed, the forest and the mountains were rigid, all of it was beautiful, all of it was mysterious and magical, and in its midst was he, Siddhartha, the awakening one, on the path to himself. All of this, all this yellow and blue, river and forest, entered Siddhartha for the first time through the eyes, was no longer a spell of Mara, was no longer the veil of Maya, was no longer a pointless and coincidental diversity of mere appearances, despicable to the deeply thinking Brahman, who scorns diversity, who seeks unity. Blue was blue, river was river, and if also in the blue and the river, in Siddhartha, the singular and divine lived hidden, so it was still that very divinity's way and purpose, to be here yellow, here blue, there sky, there forest, and here Siddhartha. The purpose and the essential properties were not somewhere behind the things, they were in them, in everything.

"How deaf and stupid have I been!" he thought, walking swiftly along. "When someone reads a text, wants to discover its meaning, he will not scorn the symbols and letters and call them deceptions, coincidence, and worthless hull, but he will read them, he will study and love them, letter by letter. But I, who wanted to read the book of the world and the book of my own being, I have, for the sake of a meaning I had anticipated before I read, scorned the symbols and letters, I called the visible world a deception, called my eyes and my tongue coincidental and worthless forms without substance. No, this is over, I have awakened, I have indeed awakened and have not been born before this very day."

In thinking these thoughts, Siddhartha stopped once again, suddenly, as if there was a snake lying in front of him on the path.

Because suddenly, he had also become aware of this: He, who was indeed like someone who had just woken up or like a new-born baby, he had to start his life anew and start again at the very beginning. When he had left in this very morning from the grove Jetavana, the grove of that exalted one, already awakening, already on the path towards himself, he had every intention, regarded as natural and took for granted, that he, after years as an ascetic, would return to his home and his father. But now, only in this moment, when he stopped as if a snake was lying on his path, he also awoke to this realization: "But I am no longer the one I was, I am no ascetic any more, I am not a priest any more, I am no Brahman any more. Whatever should I do at home and at my father's place? Study? Make offerings? Practise meditation? But all this is over, all of this is no longer alongside my path."

Motionless, Siddhartha remained standing there, and for the time of one moment and breath, his heart felt cold, he felt a cold in his chest, as a small animal, a bird or a rabbit, would when seeing how alone he was. For many years, he had been without home and had felt nothing. Now, he felt it. Still, even in the deepest meditation, he had been his father's son, had been a Brahman, of a high caste, a cleric. Now, he was nothing but Siddhartha, the awoken one, nothing else was left. Deeply, he inhaled, and for a moment, he felt cold and shivered. Nobody was thus alone as he was. There was no nobleman who did not belong to the noblemen, no worker that did not belong to the workers, and found refuge with them, shared their life, spoke their language. No Brahman, who would not be regarded as Brahmans and lived with them, no ascetic who would not find his refuge in the caste of the Samanas, and even the most forlorn hermit in the forest was not just one and alone, he was also surrounded by a place he belonged to, he also belonged to a caste, in which he was at home. Govinda had become a monk, and a thousand monks were his brothers, wore the same robe as he, believed in his faith, spoke his language. But he, Siddhartha, where did he belong to? With whom would he share his life? Whose language would he speak?

Out of this moment, when the world melted away all around him, when he stood alone like a star in the sky, out of this moment of a cold and despair, Siddhartha emerged, more a self than before, more firmly concentrated. He felt: This had been the last tremor of the awakening, the last struggle of this birth. And it was not long until he walked again in long strides, started to proceed swiftly and impatiently, heading no longer for home, no longer to his father, no longer back.

SECOND PART

Dedicated to Wilhelm Gundert, my cousin in Japan

KAMALA

Siddhartha learned something new on every step of his path, for the world was transformed, and his heart was enchanted. He saw the sun rising over the mountains with their forests and setting over the distant beach with its palm-trees. At night, he saw the stars in the sky in their fixed positions and the crescent of the moon floating like a boat in the blue. He saw trees, stars, animals, clouds, rainbows, rocks, herbs, flowers, stream and river, the glistening dew in the bushes in the morning, distant high mountains which were blue and pale, birds sang and bees, wind silverishly blew through the rice-field. All of this, a thousand-fold and colourful, had always been there, always the sun and the moon had shone, always rivers had roared and bees had buzzed, but in former times all of this had been nothing more to Siddhartha than a fleeting, deceptive veil before his eyes, looked upon in distrust, destined to be penetrated and destroyed by thought, since it was not the essential existence, since this essence lay beyond, on the other side of, the visible. But now, his liberated eyes stayed on this side, he saw and became aware of the visible, sought to be at home in this world, did not search for the true essence, did not aim at a world beyond. Beautiful was this world, looking at it thus, without searching, thus simply, thus childlike. Beautiful were the moon and the stars, beautiful was the stream and the banks, the forest and the rocks, the goat and the gold-beetle, the flower and the butterfly. Beautiful and lovely it was, thus to walk through the world, thus childlike, thus awoken, thus open to what is near, thus without distrust. Differently the sun burnt the head, differently the shade of the forest cooled him down, differently the stream and the cistern, the pumpkin and the banana tasted. Short were the days, short the nights, every hour sped swiftly away like a sail on the sea, and under the sail was a ship full of treasures, full of joy. Siddhartha saw a group of apes moving through the high canopy of the forest, high in the branches, and heard their savage, greedy song. Siddhartha saw a male sheep following a female one and mating with her. In a lake of reeds, he saw the pike hungrily hunting for its dinner; propelling themselves away from it, in fear, wiggling and sparkling, the young fish jumped in droves out of the water; the scent of strength and passion came forcefully out of the hasty eddies of the water, which the pike stirred up, impetuously hunting.

All of this had always existed, and he had not seen it; he had not been with it. Now he was with it, he was part of it. Light and shadow ran through his eyes, stars and moon ran through his heart.

On the way, Siddhartha also remembered everything he had experienced in the Garden Jetavana, the teaching he had heard there, the divine Buddha, the farewell from Govinda, the conversation with the exalted one. Again he remembered his own words, he had spoken to the exalted one, every word, and with astonishment he became aware of the fact that there he had said things which he had not really known yet at this time. What he had said to Gotama: his, the Buddha's, treasure and secret was not the teachings, but the unexpressable and not teachable, which he had experienced in the hour of his enlightenment—it was nothing but this very thing which he had now gone to experience, what he now began to experience. Now, he had to experience his self. It is true that he had already known for a long time that his self was Atman, in its essence bearing the same eternal characteristics as Brahman. But never, he had really found this self, because he had wanted to capture it in the net of thought. With the body definitely not being the self, and not the spectacle of the senses, so it also was not the thought, not the rational mind, not the learned wisdom, not the learned ability to draw conclusions and to develop previous thoughts in to new ones. No, this world of thought was also still on this side, and nothing could be achieved by killing the random self of the senses, if the random self of thoughts and learned knowledge was fattened on the other hand. Both, the thoughts as well as the senses, were pretty things, the ultimate meaning was hidden behind both of them, both had to be listened to, both had to be played with, both neither had to be scorned nor overestimated, from both the secret voices of the innermost truth had to be attentively perceived. He wanted to strive for nothing, except for what the voice commanded him to strive for, dwell on nothing, except where the voice would advise him to do so. Why had Gotama, at that time, in the hour of all hours, sat down under the bo-tree, where the enlightenment hit him? He had heard a voice, a voice in his own heart, which had commanded him to seek rest under this tree, and he had neither preferred self-castigation, offerings, ablutions, nor prayer, neither food nor drink, neither sleep nor dream, he had obeyed the voice. To obey like this, not to an external command, only to the voice, to be ready like this, this was good, this was necessary, nothing else was necessary.

In the night when he slept in the straw hut of a ferryman by the river, Siddhartha had a dream: Govinda was standing in front of him, dressed in the yellow robe of an ascetic. Sad was how Govinda looked like, sadly he asked: Why have you forsaken me?

At this, he embraced Govinda, wrapped his arms around him, and as he was pulling him close to his chest and kissed him, it was not Govinda any more, but a woman, and a full breast popped out of the woman's dress, at which Siddhartha lay and drank, sweetly and strongly tasted the milk from this breast. It tasted of woman and man, of sun and forest, of animal and flower, of every fruit, of every joyful desire. It intoxicated him and rendered him unconscious.—When Siddhartha woke up, the pale river shimmered through the door of the hut, and in the forest, a dark call of an owl resounded deeply and pleasantly.

When the day began, Siddhartha asked his host, the ferryman, to get him across the river. The ferryman got him across the river on his bamboo-raft, the wide water shimmered reddishly in the light of the morning.

"This is a beautiful river," he said to his companion.

"Yes," said the ferryman, "a very beautiful river, I love it more than anything. Often I have listened to it, often I have looked into its eyes, and always I have learned from it. Much can be learned from a river."

"I thank you, my benefactor," spoke Siddhartha, disembarking on the other side of the river. "I have no gift I could give you for your hospitality, my dear, and also no payment for your work. I am a man without a home, a son of a Brahman and a Samana."

"I did see it," spoke the ferryman, "and I haven't expected any payment from you and no gift which would be the custom for guests to bear. You will give me the gift another time."

"Do you think so?" asked Siddhartha amusedly.

"Surely. This too, I have learned from the river: everything is coming back! You too, Samana, will come back. Now farewell! Let your friendship be my reward. Commemorate me, when you'll make offerings to the gods."

Smiling, they parted. Smiling, Siddhartha was happy about the friendship and the kindness of the ferryman. "He is like Govinda," he thought with a smile, "all I meet on my path are like Govinda. All are thankful, though they are the ones who would have a right to receive thanks. All are submissive, all would like to be friends, like to obey, think little. Like children are all people."

At about noon, he came through a village. In front of the mud cottages, children were rolling about in the street, were playing with pumpkin-seeds and sea-shells, screamed and wrestled, but they all timidly fled from the unknown Samana. In the end of the village, the path led through a stream, and by the side of the stream, a young woman was kneeling and washing clothes. When Siddhartha greeted her, she lifted her head and looked up to him with a smile, so that he saw the white in her eyes glistening. He called out a blessing to her, as it is the custom among travellers, and asked how far he still had to go to reach the large city. Then she got up and came to him, beautifully her wet mouth was shimmering in her young face. She exchanged humorous banter with him, asked whether he had eaten already, and whether it was true that the Samanas slept alone in the forest at night and were not allowed to have any women with them. While talking, she put her left foot on his right one and made a movement as a woman does who would want to initiate that kind of sexual pleasure with a man, which the textbooks call "climbing a tree". Siddhartha felt his blood heating up, and since in this moment he had to think of his dream again, he bend slightly down to the woman and kissed with his lips the brown nipple of her breast. Looking up, he saw her face smiling full of lust and her eyes, with contracted pupils, begging with desire.

Siddhartha also felt desire and felt the source of his sexuality moving; but since he had never touched a woman before, he hesitated for a moment, while his hands were already prepared to reach out for her. And in this moment he heard, shuddering with awe, the voice of his innermost self, and this voice said No. Then, all charms disappeared from the young woman's smiling face, he no longer saw anything else but the damp glance of a female animal in heat. Politely, he petted her cheek, turned away from her and disappeared away from the disappointed woman with light steps into the bamboo-wood.

On this day, he reached the large city before the evening, and was happy, for he felt the need to be among people. For a long time, he had lived in the forests, and the straw hut of the ferryman, in which he had slept that night, had been the first roof for a long time he has had over his head.

Before the city, in a beautifully fenced grove, the traveller came across a small group of servants, both male and female, carrying baskets. In their midst, carried by four servants in an ornamental sedan-chair, sat a woman, the mistress, on red pillows under a colourful canopy. Siddhartha stopped at the entrance to the pleasure-garden and watched the parade, saw the servants, the maids, the baskets, saw the sedan-chair and saw the lady in it. Under black hair, which made to tower high on her head, he saw a very fair, very delicate, very smart face, a brightly red mouth, like a freshly cracked fig, eyebrows which were well tended and painted in a high arch, smart and watchful dark eyes, a clear, tall neck rising from a green and golden garment, resting fair hands, long and thin, with wide golden bracelets over the wrists.

Siddhartha saw how beautiful she was, and his heart rejoiced. He bowed deeply, when the sedan-chair came closer, and straightening up again, he looked at the fair, charming face, read for a moment in the smart eyes with the high arcs above, breathed in a slight fragrant, he did not know. With a smile, the beautiful women nodded for a moment and disappeared into the grove, and then the servant as well.

Thus I am entering this city, Siddhartha thought, with a charming omen. He instantly felt drawn into the grove, but he thought about it, and only now he became aware of how the servants and maids had looked at him at the entrance, how despicable, how distrustful, how rejecting.

I am still a Samana, he thought, I am still an ascetic and beggar. I must not remain like this, I will not be able to enter the grove like this. And he laughed.

The next person who came along this path he asked about the grove and for the name of the woman, and was told that this was the grove of Kamala, the famous courtesan, and that, aside from the grove, she owned a house in the city.

Then, he entered the city. Now he had a goal.

Pursuing his goal, he allowed the city to suck him in, drifted through the flow of the streets, stood still on the squares, rested on the stairs of stone by the river. When the evening came, he made friends with barber's assistant, whom he had seen working in the shade of an arch in a building, whom he found again praying in a temple of Vishnu, whom he told about stories of Vishnu and the Lakshmi. Among the boats by the river, he slept this night, and early in the morning, before the first customers came into his shop, he had the barber's assistant shave his beard and cut his hair, comb his hair and anoint it with fine oil. Then he went to take his bath in the river.

When late in the afternoon, beautiful Kamala approached her grove in her sedan-chair, Siddhartha was standing at the entrance, made a bow and received the courtesan's greeting. But that servant who walked at the very end of her train he motioned to him and asked him to inform his mistress that a young Brahman would wish to talk to her. After a while, the servant returned, asked him, who had been waiting, to follow him conducted him, who was following him, without a word into a pavilion, where Kamala was lying on a couch, and left him alone with her.

"Weren't you already standing out there yesterday, greeting me?" asked Kamala.

"It's true that I've already seen and greeted you yesterday."

"But didn't you yesterday wear a beard, and long hair, and dust in your hair?"

"You have observed well, you have seen everything. You have seen Siddhartha, the son of a Brahman, who has left his home to become a Samana, and who has been a Samana for three years. But now, I have left that path and came into this city, and the first one I met, even before I had entered the city, was you. To say this, I have come to you, oh Kamala! You are the first woman whom Siddhartha is not addressing with his eyes turned to the ground. Never again I want to turn my eyes to the ground, when I'm coming across a beautiful woman."

Kamala smiled and played with her fan of peacocks' feathers. And asked: "And only to tell me this, Siddhartha has come to me?"

"To tell you this and to thank you for being so beautiful. And if it doesn't displease you, Kamala, I would like to ask you to be my friend and teacher, for I know nothing yet of that art which you have mastered in the highest degree."

At this, Kamala laughed aloud.

"Never before this has happened to me, my friend, that a Samana from the forest came to me and wanted to learn from me! Never before this has happened to me, that a Samana came to me with long hair and an old, torn loin-cloth! Many young men come to me, and there are also sons of Brahmans among them, but they come in beautiful clothes, they come in fine shoes, they have perfume in their hair and money in their pouches. This is, oh Samana, how the young men are like who come to me."

Quoth Siddhartha: "Already I am starting to learn from you. Even yesterday, I was already learning. I have already taken off my beard, have combed the hair, have oil in my hair. There is little which is still missing in me, oh excellent one: fine clothes, fine shoes, money in my pouch. You shall know, Siddhartha has set harder goals for himself than such trifles, and he has reached them. How shouldn't I reach that goal, which I have set for myself yesterday: to be your friend and to learn the joys of love from you! You'll see that I'll learn quickly, Kamala, I have already learned harder things than what you're supposed to teach me. And now let's get to it: You aren't satisfied with Siddhartha as he is, with oil in his hair, but without clothes, without shoes, without money?"

Laughing, Kamala exclaimed: "No, my dear, he doesn't satisfy me yet. Clothes are what he must have, pretty clothes, and shoes, pretty shoes, and lots of money in his pouch, and gifts for Kamala. Do you know it now, Samana from the forest? Did you mark my words?"

"Yes, I have marked your words," Siddhartha exclaimed. "How should I not mark words which are coming from such a mouth! Your mouth is like a freshly cracked fig, Kamala. My mouth is red and fresh as well, it will be a suitable match for yours, you'll see.—But tell me, beautiful Kamala, aren't you at all afraid of the Samana from the forest, who has come to learn how to make love?"

"Whatever for should I be afraid of a Samana, a stupid Samana from the forest, who is coming from the jackals and doesn't even know yet what women are?"

"Oh, he's strong, the Samana, and he isn't afraid of anything. He could force you, beautiful girl. He could kidnap you. He could hurt you."

"No, Samana, I am not afraid of this. Did any Samana or Brahman ever fear, someone might come and grab him and steal his learning, and his religious devotion, and his depth of thought? No, for they are his very own, and he would only give away from those whatever he is willing to give and to whomever he is willing to give. Like this it is, precisely like this it is also with Kamala and with the pleasures of love. Beautiful and red is Kamala's mouth, but just try to kiss it against Kamala's will, and you will not obtain a single drop of sweetness from it, which knows how to give so many sweet things! You are learning easily, Siddhartha, thus you should also learn this: love can be obtained by begging, buying, receiving it as a gift, finding it in the street, but it cannot be stolen. In this, you have come up with the wrong path. No, it would be a pity, if a pretty young man like you would want to tackle it in such a wrong manner."

Siddhartha bowed with a smile. "It would be a pity, Kamala, you are so right! It would be such a great pity. No, I shall not lose a single drop of sweetness from your mouth, nor you from mine! So it is settled: Siddhartha will return, once he'll have what he still lacks: clothes, shoes, money. But speak, lovely Kamala, couldn't you still give me one small advice?"

"An advice? Why not? Who wouldn't like to give an advice to a poor, ignorant Samana, who is coming from the jackals of the forest?"

"Dear Kamala, thus advise me where I should go to, that I'll find these three things most quickly?"

"Friend, many would like to know this. You must do what you've learned and ask for money, clothes, and shoes in return. There is no other way for a poor man to obtain money. What might you be able to do?"

"I can think. I can wait. I can fast."

"Nothing else?"

"Nothing. But yes, I can also write poetry. Would you like to give me a kiss for a poem?"

"I would like to, if I'll like your poem. What would be its title?"

Siddhartha spoke, after he had thought about it for a moment, these verses:

Into her shady grove stepped the pretty Kamala, At the grove's entrance stood the brown Samana. Deeply, seeing the lotus's blossom, Bowed that man, and smiling Kamala thanked. More lovely, thought the young man, than offerings for gods, More lovely is offering to pretty Kamala.

Kamala loudly clapped her hands, so that the golden bracelets clanged.

"Beautiful are your verses, oh brown Samana, and truly, I'm losing nothing when I'm giving you a kiss for them."

She beckoned him with her eyes, he tilted his head so that his face touched hers and placed his mouth on that mouth which was like a freshly cracked fig. For a long time, Kamala kissed him, and with a deep astonishment Siddhartha felt how she taught him, how wise she was, how she controlled him, rejected him, lured him, and how after this first one there was to be a long, a well ordered, well tested sequence of kisses, everyone different from the others, he was still to receive. Breathing deeply, he remained standing where he was, and was in this moment astonished like a child about the cornucopia of knowledge and things worth learning, which revealed itself before his eyes.

"Very beautiful are your verses," exclaimed Kamala, "if I was rich, I would give you pieces of gold for them. But it will be difficult for you to earn thus much money with verses as you need. For you need a lot of money, if you want to be Kamala's friend."

"The way you're able to kiss, Kamala!" stammered Siddhartha.

"Yes, this I am able to do, therefore I do not lack clothes, shoes, bracelets, and all beautiful things. But what will become of you? Aren't you able to do anything else but thinking, fasting, making poetry?"

"I also know the sacrificial songs," said Siddhartha, "but I do not want to sing them any more. I also know magic spells, but I do not want to speak them any more. I have read the scriptures—"

"Stop," Kamala interrupted him. "You're able to read? And write?"

"Certainly, I can do this. Many people can do this."

"Most people can't. I also can't do it. It is very good that you're able to read and write, very good. You will also still find use for the magic spells."

In this moment, a maid came running in and whispered a message into her mistress's ear.

"There's a visitor for me," exclaimed Kamala. "Hurry and get yourself away, Siddhartha, nobody may see you in here, remember this! Tomorrow, I'll see you again."

But to the maid she gave the order to give the pious Brahman white upper garments. Without fully understanding what was happening to him, Siddhartha found himself being dragged away by the maid, brought into a garden-house avoiding the direct path, being given upper garments as a gift, led into the bushes, and urgently admonished to get himself out of the grove as soon as possible without being seen.

Contently, he did as he had been told. Being accustomed to the forest, he managed to get out of the grove and over the hedge without making a sound. Contently, he returned to the city, carrying the rolled up garments under his arm. At the inn, where travellers stay, he positioned himself by the door, without words he asked for food, without a word he accepted a piece of rice-cake. Perhaps as soon as tomorrow, he thought, I will ask no one for food any more.

Suddenly, pride flared up in him. He was no Samana any more, it was no longer becoming to him to beg. He gave the rice-cake to a dog and remained without food.

"Simple is the life which people lead in this world here," thought Siddhartha. "It presents no difficulties. Everything was difficult, toilsome, and ultimately hopeless, when I was still a Samana. Now, everything is easy, easy like that lessons in kissing, which Kamala is giving me. I need clothes and money, nothing else; this a small, near goals, they won't make a person lose any sleep."

He had already discovered Kamala's house in the city long before, there he turned up the following day.

"Things are working out well," she called out to him. "They are expecting you at Kamaswami's, he is the richest merchant of the city. If he'll like you, he'll accept you into his service. Be smart, brown Samana. I had others tell him about you. Be polite towards him, he is very powerful. But don't be too modest! I do not want you to become his servant, you shall become his equal, or else I won't be satisfied with you. Kamaswami is starting to get old and lazy. If he'll like you, he'll entrust you with a lot."

Siddhartha thanked her and laughed, and when she found out that he had not eaten anything yesterday and today, she sent for bread and fruits and treated him to it.

"You've been lucky," she said when they parted, "I'm opening one door after another for you. How come? Do you have a spell?"

Siddhartha said: "Yesterday, I told you I knew how to think, to wait, and to fast, but you thought this was of no use. But it is useful for many things, Kamala, you'll see. You'll see that the stupid Samanas are learning and able to do many pretty things in the forest, which the likes of you aren't capable of. The day before yesterday, I was still a shaggy beggar, as soon as yesterday I have kissed Kamala, and soon I'll be a merchant and have money and all those things you insist upon."

"Well yes," she admitted. "But where would you be without me? What would you be, if Kamala wasn't helping you?"

"Dear Kamala," said Siddhartha and straightened up to his full height, "when I came to you into your grove, I did the first step. It was my resolution to learn love from this most beautiful woman. From that moment on when I had made this resolution, I also knew that I would carry it out. I knew that you would help me, at your first glance at the entrance of the grove I already knew it."

"But what if I hadn't been willing?"

"You were willing. Look, Kamala: When you throw a rock into the water, it will speed on the fastest course to the bottom of the water. This is how it is when Siddhartha has a goal, a resolution. Siddhartha does nothing, he waits, he thinks, he fasts, but he passes through the things of the world like a rock through water, without doing anything, without stirring; he is drawn, he lets himself fall. His goal attracts him, because he doesn't let anything enter his soul which might oppose the goal. This is what Siddhartha has learned among the Samanas. This is what fools call magic and of which they think it would be effected by means of the daemons. Nothing is effected by daemons, there are no daemons. Everyone can perform magic, everyone can reach his goals, if he is able to think, if he is able to wait, if he is able to fast."

Kamala listened to him. She loved his voice, she loved the look from his eyes.

"Perhaps it is so," she said quietly, "as you say, friend. But perhaps it is also like this: that Siddhartha is a handsome man, that his glance pleases the women, that therefore good fortune is coming towards him."

With one kiss, Siddhartha bid his farewell. "I wish that it should be this way, my teacher; that my glance shall please you, that always good fortune shall come to me out of your direction!"

WITH THE CHILDLIKE PEOPLE

Siddhartha went to Kamaswami the merchant, he was directed into a rich house, servants led him between precious carpets into a chamber, where he awaited the master of the house.

Kamaswami entered, a swiftly, smoothly moving man with very gray hair, with very intelligent, cautious eyes, with a greedy mouth. Politely, the host and the guest greeted one another.

"I have been told," the merchant began, "that you were a Brahman, a learned man, but that you seek to be in the service of a merchant. Might you have become destitute, Brahman, so that you seek to serve?"

"No," said Siddhartha, "I have not become destitute and have never been destitute. You should know that I'm coming from the Samanas, with whom I have lived for a long time."

"If you're coming from the Samanas, how could you be anything but destitute? Aren't the Samanas entirely without possessions?"

"I am without possessions," said Siddhartha, "if this is what you mean. Surely, I am without possessions. But I am so voluntarily, and therefore I am not destitute."

"But what are you planning to live of, being without possessions?"

"I haven't thought of this yet, sir. For more than three years, I have been without possessions, and have never thought about of what I should live."

"So you've lived of the possessions of others."

"Presumable this is how it is. After all, a merchant also lives of what other people own."

"Well said. But he wouldn't take anything from another person for nothing; he would give his merchandise in return."

"So it seems to be indeed. Everyone takes, everyone gives, such is life."

"But if you don't mind me asking: being without possessions, what would you like to give?"

"Everyone gives what he has. The warrior gives strength, the merchant gives merchandise, the teacher teachings, the farmer rice, the fisher fish."

"Yes indeed. And what is it now what you've got to give? What is it that you've learned, what you're able to do?"

"I can think. I can wait. I can fast."

"That's everything?"

"I believe, that's everything!"

"And what's the use of that? For example, the fasting—what is it good for?"

"It is very good, sir. When a person has nothing to eat, fasting is the smartest thing he could do. When, for example, Siddhartha hadn't learned to fast, he would have to accept any kind of service before this day is up, whether it may be with you or wherever, because hunger would force him to do so. But like this, Siddhartha can wait calmly, he knows no impatience, he knows no emergency, for a long time he can allow hunger to besiege him and can laugh about it. This, sir, is what fasting is good for."

"You're right, Samana. Wait for a moment."

Kamaswami left the room and returned with a scroll, which he handed to his guest while asking: "Can you read this?"

Siddhartha looked at the scroll, on which a sales-contract had been written down, and began to read out its contents.

"Excellent," said Kamaswami. "And would you write something for me on this piece of paper?"

He handed him a piece of paper and a pen, and Siddhartha wrote and returned the paper.

Kamaswami read: "Writing is good, thinking is better. Being smart is good, being patient is better."

"It is excellent how you're able to write," the merchant praised him. "Many a thing we will still have to discuss with one another. For today, I'm asking you to be my guest and to live in this house."

Siddhartha thanked and accepted, and lived in the dealers house from now on. Clothes were brought to him, and shoes, and every day, a servant prepared a bath for him. Twice a day, a plentiful meal was served, but Siddhartha only ate once a day, and ate neither meat nor did he drink wine. Kamaswami told him about his trade, showed him the merchandise and storage-rooms, showed him calculations. Siddhartha got to know many new things, he heard a lot and spoke little. And thinking of Kamala's words, he was never subservient to the merchant, forced him to treat him as an equal, yes even more than an equal. Kamaswami conducted his business with care and often with passion, but Siddhartha looked upon all of this as if it was a game, the rules of which he tried hard to learn precisely, but the contents of which did not touch his heart.

He was not in Kamaswami's house for long, when he already took part in his landlords business. But daily, at the hour appointed by her, he visited beautiful Kamala, wearing pretty clothes, fine shoes, and soon he brought her gifts as well. Much he learned from her red, smart mouth. Much he learned from her tender, supple hand. Him, who was, regarding love, still a boy and had a tendency to plunge blindly and insatiably into lust like into a bottomless pit, him she taught, thoroughly starting with the basics, about that school of thought which teaches that pleasure cannot be taken without giving pleasure, and that every gesture, every caress, every touch, every look, every spot of the body, however small it was, had its secret, which would bring happiness to those who know about it and unleash it. She taught him, that lovers must not part from one another after celebrating love, without one admiring the other, without being just as defeated as they have been victorious, so that with none of them should start feeling fed up or bored and get that evil feeling of having abused or having been abused. Wonderful hours he spent with the beautiful and smart artist, became her student, her lover, her friend. Here with Kamala was the worth and purpose of his present life, not with the business of Kamaswami.

The merchant passed to duties of writing important letters and contracts on to him and got into the habit of discussing all important affairs with him. He soon saw that Siddhartha knew little about rice and wool, shipping and trade, but that he acted in a fortunate manner, and that Siddhartha surpassed him, the merchant, in calmness and equanimity, and in the art of listening and deeply understanding previously unknown people. "This Brahman," he said to a friend, "is no proper merchant and will never be one, there is never any passion in his soul when he conducts our business. But he has that mysterious quality of those people to whom success comes all by itself, whether this may be a good star of his birth, magic, or something he has learned among Samanas. He always seems to be merely playing with out business-affairs, they never fully become a part of him, they never rule over him, he is never afraid of failure, he is never upset by a loss."

The friend advised the merchant: "Give him from the business he conducts for you a third of the profits, but let him also be liable for the same amount of the losses, when there is a loss. Then, he'll become more zealous."

Kamaswami followed the advice. But Siddhartha cared little about this. When he made a profit, he accepted it with equanimity; when he made losses, he laughed and said: "Well, look at this, so this one turned out badly!"

It seemed indeed, as if he did not care about the business. At one time, he travelled to a village to buy a large harvest of rice there. But when he got there, the rice had already been sold to another merchant. Nevertheless, Siddhartha stayed for several days in that village, treated the farmers for a drink, gave copper-coins to their children, joined in the celebration of a wedding, and returned extremely satisfied from his trip. Kamaswami held against him that he had not turned back right away, that he had wasted time and money. Siddhartha answered: "Stop scolding, dear friend! Nothing was ever achieved by scolding. If a loss has occurred, let me bear that loss. I am very satisfied with this trip. I have gotten to know many kinds of people, a Brahman has become my friend, children have sat on my knees, farmers have shown me their fields, nobody knew that I was a merchant."

"That's all very nice," exclaimed Kamaswami indignantly, "but in fact, you are a merchant after all, one ought to think! Or might you have only travelled for your amusement?"

"Surely," Siddhartha laughed, "surely I have travelled for my amusement. For what else? I have gotten to know people and places, I have received kindness and trust, I have found friendship. Look, my dear, if I had been Kamaswami, I would have travelled back, being annoyed and in a hurry, as soon as I had seen that my purchase had been rendered impossible, and time and money would indeed have been lost. But like this, I've had a few good days, I've learned, had joy, I've neither harmed myself nor others by annoyance and hastiness. And if I'll ever return there again, perhaps to buy an upcoming harvest, or for whatever purpose it might be, friendly people will receive me in a friendly and happy manner, and I will praise myself for not showing any hurry and displeasure at that time. So, leave it as it is, my friend, and don't harm yourself by scolding! If the day will come, when you will see: this Siddhartha is harming me, then speak a word and Siddhartha will go on his own path. But until then, let's be satisfied with one another."

Futile were also the merchant's attempts, to convince Siddhartha that he should eat his bread. Siddhartha ate his own bread, or rather they both ate other people's bread, all people's bread. Siddhartha never listened to Kamaswami's worries and Kamaswami had many worries. Whether there was a business-deal going on which was in danger of failing, or whether a shipment of merchandise seemed to have been lost, or a debtor seemed to be unable to pay, Kamaswami could never convince his partner that it would be useful to utter a few words of worry or anger, to have wrinkles on the forehead, to sleep badly. When, one day, Kamaswami held against him that he had learned everything he knew from him, he replied: "Would you please not kid me with such jokes! What I've learned from you is how much a basket of fish costs and how much interests may be charged on loaned money. These are your areas of expertise. I haven't learned to think from you, my dear Kamaswami, you ought to be the one seeking to learn from me."

Indeed his soul was not with the trade. The business was good enough to provide him with the money for Kamala, and it earned him much more than he needed. Besides from this, Siddhartha's interest and curiosity was only concerned with the people, whose businesses, crafts, worries, pleasures, and acts of foolishness used to be as alien and distant to him as the moon. However easily he succeeded in talking to all of them, in living with all of them, in learning from all of them, he was still aware that there was something which separated him from them and this separating factor was him being a Samana. He saw mankind going through life in a childlike or animallike manner, which he loved and also despised at the same time. He saw them toiling, saw them suffering, and becoming gray for the sake of things which seemed to him to entirely unworthy of this price, for money, for little pleasures, for being slightly honoured, he saw them scolding and insulting each other, he saw them complaining about pain at which a Samana would only smile, and suffering because of deprivations which a Samana would not feel.

He was open to everything, these people brought his way. Welcome was the merchant who offered him linen for sale, welcome was the debtor who sought another loan, welcome was the beggar who told him for one hour the story of his poverty and who was not half as poor as any given Samana. He did not treat the rich foreign merchant any different than the servant who shaved him and the street-vendor whom he let cheat him out of some small change when buying bananas. When Kamaswami came to him, to complain about his worries or to reproach him concerning his business, he listened curiously and happily, was puzzled by him, tried to understand him, consented that he was a little bit right, only as much as he considered indispensable, and turned away from him, towards the next person who would ask for him. And there were many who came to him, many to do business with him, many to cheat him, many to draw some secret out of him, many to appeal to his sympathy, many to get his advice. He gave advice, he pitied, he made gifts, he let them cheat him a bit, and this entire game and the passion with which all people played this game occupied his thoughts just as much as the gods and Brahmans used to occupy them.

At times he felt, deep in his chest, a dying, quiet voice, which admonished him quietly, lamented quietly; he hardly perceived it. And then, for an hour, he became aware of the strange life he was leading, of him doing lots of things which were only a game, of, though being happy and feeling joy at times, real life still passing him by and not touching him. As a ball-player plays with his balls, he played with his business-deals, with the people around him, watched them, found amusement in them; with his heart, with the source of his being, he was not with them. The source ran somewhere, far away from him, ran and ran invisibly, had nothing to do with his life any more. And at several times he suddenly became scared on account of such thoughts and wished that he would also be gifted with the ability to participate in all of this childlike-naive occupations of the daytime with passion and with his heart, really to live, really to act, really to enjoy and to live instead of just standing by as a spectator. But again and again, he came back to beautiful Kamala, learned the art of love, practised the cult of lust, in which more than in anything else giving and taking becomes one, chatted with her, learned from her, gave her advice, received advice. She understood him better than Govinda used to understand him, she was more similar to him.

Once, he said to her: "You are like me, you are different from most people. You are Kamala, nothing else, and inside of you, there is a peace and refuge, to which you can go at every hour of the day and be at home at yourself, as I can also do. Few people have this, and yet all could have it."

"Not all people are smart," said Kamala.

"No," said Siddhartha, "that's not the reason why. Kamaswami is just as smart as I, and still has no refuge in himself. Others have it, who are small children with respect to their mind. Most people, Kamala, are like a falling leaf, which is blown and is turning around through the air, and wavers, and tumbles to the ground. But others, a few, are like stars, they go on a fixed course, no wind reaches them, in themselves they have their law and their course. Among all the learned men and Samanas, of which I knew many, there was one of this kind, a perfected one, I'll never be able to forget him. It is that Gotama, the exalted one, who is spreading that teachings. Thousands of followers are listening to his teachings every day, follow his instructions every hour, but they are all falling leaves, not in themselves they have teachings and a law."

Kamala looked at him with a smile. "Again, you're talking about him," she said, "again, you're having a Samana's thoughts."

Siddhartha said nothing, and they played the game of love, one of the thirty or forty different games Kamala knew. Her body was flexible like that of a jaguar and like the bow of a hunter; he who had learned from her how to make love, was knowledgeable of many forms of lust, many secrets. For a long time, she played with Siddhartha, enticed him, rejected him, forced him, embraced him: enjoyed his masterful skills, until he was defeated and rested exhausted by her side.

The courtesan bent over him, took a long look at his face, at his eyes, which had grown tired.

"You are the best lover," she said thoughtfully, "I ever saw. You're stronger than others, more supple, more willing. You've learned my art well, Siddhartha. At some time, when I'll be older, I'd want to bear your child. And yet, my dear, you've remained a Samana, and yet you do not love me, you love nobody. Isn't it so?"

"It might very well be so," Siddhartha said tiredly. "I am like you. You also do not love—how else could you practise love as a craft? Perhaps, people of our kind can't love. The childlike people can; that's their secret."

SANSARA

For a long time, Siddhartha had lived the life of the world and of lust, though without being a part of it. His senses, which he had killed off in hot years as a Samana, had awoken again, he had tasted riches, had tasted lust, had tasted power; nevertheless he had still remained in his heart for a long time a Samana; Kamala, being smart, had realized this quite right. It was still the art of thinking, of waiting, of fasting, which guided his life; still the people of the world, the childlike people, had remained alien to him as he was alien to them.

Years passed by; surrounded by the good life, Siddhartha hardly felt them fading away. He had become rich, for quite a while he possessed a house of his own and his own servants, and a garden before the city by the river. The people liked him, they came to him, whenever they needed money or advice, but there was nobody close to him, except Kamala.

That high, bright state of being awake, which he had experienced that one time at the height of his youth, in those days after Gotama's sermon, after the separation from Govinda, that tense expectation, that proud state of standing alone without teachings and without teachers, that supple willingness to listen to the divine voice in his own heart, had slowly become a memory, had been fleeting; distant and quiet, the holy source murmured, which used to be near, which used to murmur within himself. Nevertheless, many things he had learned from the Samanas, he had learned from Gotama, he had learned from his father the Brahman, had remained within him for a long time afterwards: moderate living, joy of thinking, hours of meditation, secret knowledge of the self, of his eternal entity, which is neither body nor consciousness. Many a part of this he still had, but one part after another had been submerged and had gathered dust. Just as a potter's wheel, once it has been set in motion, will keep on turning for a long time and only slowly lose its vigour and come to a stop, thus Siddhartha's soul had kept on turning the wheel of asceticism, the wheel of thinking, the wheel of differentiation for a long time, still turning, but it turned slowly and hesitantly and was close to coming to a standstill. Slowly, like humidity entering the dying stem of a tree, filling it slowly and making it rot, the world and sloth had entered Siddhartha's soul, slowly it filled his soul, made it heavy, made it tired, put it to sleep. On the other hand, his senses had become alive, there was much they had learned, much they had experienced.

Siddhartha had learned to trade, to use his power over people, to enjoy himself with a woman, he had learned to wear beautiful clothes, to give orders to servants, to bathe in perfumed waters. He had learned to eat tenderly and carefully prepared food, even fish, even meat and poultry, spices and sweets, and to drink wine, which causes sloth and forgetfulness. He had learned to play with dice and on a chess-board, to watch dancing girls, to have himself carried about in a sedan-chair, to sleep on a soft bed. But still he had felt different from and superior to the others; always he had watched them with some mockery, some mocking disdain, with the same disdain which a Samana constantly feels for the people of the world. When Kamaswami was ailing, when he was annoyed, when he felt insulted, when he was vexed by his worries as a merchant, Siddhartha had always watched it with mockery. Just slowly and imperceptibly, as the harvest seasons and rainy seasons passed by, his mockery had become more tired, his superiority had become more quiet. Just slowly, among his growing riches, Siddhartha had assumed something of the childlike people's ways for himself, something of their childlikeness and of their fearfulness. And yet, he envied them, envied them just the more, the more similar he became to them. He envied them for the one thing that was missing from him and that they had, the importance they were able to attach to their lives, the amount of passion in their joys and fears, the fearful but sweet happiness of being constantly in love. These people were all of the time in love with themselves, with women, with their children, with honours or money, with plans or hopes. But he did not learn this from them, this out of all things, this joy of a child and this foolishness of a child; he learned from them out of all things the unpleasant ones, which he himself despised. It happened more and more often that, in the morning after having had company the night before, he stayed in bed for a long time, felt unable to think and tired. It happened that he became angry and impatient, when Kamaswami bored him with his worries. It happened that he laughed just too loud, when he lost a game of dice. His face was still smarter and more spiritual than others, but it rarely laughed, and assumed, one after another, those features which are so often found in the faces of rich people, those features of discontent, of sickliness, of ill-humour, of sloth, of a lack of love. Slowly the disease of the soul, which rich people have, grabbed hold of him.

Like a veil, like a thin mist, tiredness came over Siddhartha, slowly, getting a bit denser every day, a bit murkier every month, a bit heavier every year. As a new dress becomes old in time, loses its beautiful colour in time, gets stains, gets wrinkles, gets worn off at the seams, and starts to show threadbare spots here and there, thus Siddhartha's new life, which he had started after his separation from Govinda, had grown old, lost colour and splendour as the years passed by, was gathering wrinkles and stains, and hidden at bottom, already showing its ugliness here and there, disappointment and disgust were waiting. Siddhartha did not notice it. He only noticed that this bright and reliable voice inside of him, which had awoken in him at that time and had ever guided him in his best times, had become silent.

He had been captured by the world, by lust, covetousness, sloth, and finally also by that vice which he had used to despise and mock the most as the most foolish one of all vices: greed. Property, possessions, and riches also had finally captured him; they were no longer a game and trifles to him, had become a shackle and a burden. In a strange and devious way, Siddhartha had gotten into this final and most base of all dependencies, by means of the game of dice. It was since that time, when he had stopped being a Samana in his heart, that Siddhartha began to play the game for money and precious things, which he at other times only joined with a smile and casually as a custom of the childlike people, with an increasing rage and passion. He was a feared gambler, few dared to take him on, so high and audacious were his stakes. He played the game due to a pain of his heart, losing and wasting his wretched money in the game brought him an angry joy, in no other way he could demonstrate his disdain for wealth, the merchants' false god, more clearly and more mockingly. Thus he gambled with high stakes and mercilessly, hating himself, mocking himself, won thousands, threw away thousands, lost money, lost jewelry, lost a house in the country, won again, lost again. That fear, that terrible and petrifying fear, which he felt while he was rolling the dice, while he was worried about losing high stakes, that fear he loved and sought to always renew it, always increase it, always get it to a slightly higher level, for in this feeling alone he still felt something like happiness, something like an intoxication, something like an elevated form of life in the midst of his saturated, lukewarm, dull life.

And after each big loss, his mind was set on new riches, pursued the trade more zealously, forced his debtors more strictly to pay, because he wanted to continue gambling, he wanted to continue squandering, continue demonstrating his disdain of wealth. Siddhartha lost his calmness when losses occurred, lost his patience when he was not payed on time, lost his kindness towards beggars, lost his disposition for giving away and loaning money to those who petitioned him. He, who gambled away tens of thousands at one roll of the dice and laughed at it, became more strict and more petty in his business, occasionally dreaming at night about money! And whenever he woke up from this ugly spell, whenever he found his face in the mirror at the bedroom's wall to have aged and become more ugly, whenever embarrassment and disgust came over him, he continued fleeing, fleeing into a new game, fleeing into a numbing of his mind brought on by sex, by wine, and from there he fled back into the urge to pile up and obtain possessions. In this pointless cycle he ran, growing tired, growing old, growing ill.

Then the time came when a dream warned him. He had spent the hours of the evening with Kamala, in her beautiful pleasure-garden. They had been sitting under the trees, talking, and Kamala had said thoughtful words, words behind which a sadness and tiredness lay hidden. She had asked him to tell her about Gotama, and could not hear enough of him, how clear his eyes, how still and beautiful his mouth, how kind his smile, how peaceful his walk had been. For a long time, he had to tell her about the exalted Buddha, and Kamala had sighed and had said: "One day, perhaps soon, I'll also follow that Buddha. I'll give him my pleasure-garden for a gift and take my refuge in his teachings." But after this, she had aroused him, and had tied him to her in the act of making love with painful fervour, biting and in tears, as if, once more, she wanted to squeeze the last sweet drop out of this vain, fleeting pleasure. Never before, it had become so strangely clear to Siddhartha, how closely lust was akin to death. Then he had lain by her side, and Kamala's face had been close to him, and under her eyes and next to the corners of her mouth he had, as clearly as never before, read a fearful inscription, an inscription of small lines, of slight grooves, an inscription reminiscent of autumn and old age, just as Siddhartha himself, who was only in his forties, had already noticed, here and there, gray hairs among his black ones. Tiredness was written on Kamala's beautiful face, tiredness from walking a long path, which has no happy destination, tiredness and the beginning of withering, and concealed, still unsaid, perhaps not even conscious anxiety: fear of old age, fear of the autumn, fear of having to die. With a sigh, he had bid his farewell to her, the soul full of reluctance, and full of concealed anxiety.

Then, Siddhartha had spent the night in his house with dancing girls and wine, had acted as if he was superior to them towards the fellow-members of his caste, though this was no longer true, had drunk much wine and gone to bed a long time after midnight, being tired and yet excited, close to weeping and despair, and had for a long time sought to sleep in vain, his heart full of misery which he thought he could not bear any longer, full of a disgust which he felt penetrating his entire body like the lukewarm, repulsive taste of the wine, the just too sweet, dull music, the just too soft smile of the dancing girls, the just too sweet scent of their hair and breasts. But more than by anything else, he was disgusted by himself, by his perfumed hair, by the smell of wine from his mouth, by the flabby tiredness and listlessness of his skin. Like when someone, who has eaten and drunk far too much, vomits it back up again with agonising pain and is nevertheless glad about the relief, thus this sleepless man wished to free himself of these pleasures, these habits and all of this pointless life and himself, in an immense burst of disgust. Not until the light of the morning and the beginning of the first activities in the street before his city-house, he had slightly fallen asleep, had found for a few moments a half unconsciousness, a hint of sleep. In those moments, he had a dream:

Kamala owned a small, rare singing bird in a golden cage. Of this bird, he dreamt. He dreamt: this bird had become mute, who at other times always used to sing in the morning, and since this arose his attention, he stepped in front of the cage and looked inside; there the small bird was dead and lay stiff on the ground. He took it out, weighed it for a moment in his hand, and then threw it away, out in the street, and in the same moment, he felt terribly shocked, and his heart hurt, as if he had thrown away from himself all value and everything good by throwing out this dead bird.

Starting up from this dream, he felt encompassed by a deep sadness. Worthless, so it seemed to him, worthless and pointless was the way he had been going through life; nothing which was alive, nothing which was in some way delicious or worth keeping he had left in his hands. Alone he stood there and empty like a castaway on the shore.

With a gloomy mind, Siddhartha went to the pleasure-garden he owned, locked the gate, sat down under a mango-tree, felt death in his heart and horror in his chest, sat and sensed how everything died in him, withered in him, came to an end in him. By and by, he gathered his thoughts, and in his mind, he once again went the entire path of his life, starting with the first days he could remember. When was there ever a time when he had experienced happiness, felt a true bliss? Oh yes, several times he had experienced such a thing. In his years as a boy, he has had a taste of it, when he had obtained praise from the Brahmans, he had felt it in his heart: "There is a path in front of the one who has distinguished himself in the recitation of the holy verses, in the dispute with the learned ones, as an assistant in the offerings." Then, he had felt it in his heart: "There is a path in front of you, you are destined for, the gods are awaiting you." And again, as a young man, when the ever rising, upward fleeing, goal of all thinking had ripped him out of and up from the multitude of those seeking the same goal, when he wrestled in pain for the purpose of Brahman, when every obtained knowledge only kindled new thirst in him, then again he had, in the midst of the thirst, in the midst of the pain felt this very same thing: "Go on! Go on! You are called upon!" He had heard this voice when he had left his home and had chosen the life of a Samana, and again when he had gone away from the Samanas to that perfected one, and also when he had gone away from him to the uncertain. For how long had he not heard this voice any more, for how long had he reached no height any more, how even and dull was the manner in which his path had passed through life, for many long years, without a high goal, without thirst, without elevation, content with small lustful pleasures and yet never satisfied! For all of these many years, without knowing it himself, he had tried hard and longed to become a man like those many, like those children, and in all this, his life had been much more miserable and poorer than theirs, and their goals were not his, nor their worries; after all, that entire world of the Kamaswami-people had only been a game to him, a dance he would watch, a comedy. Only Kamala had been dear, had been valuable to him—but was she still thus? Did he still need her, or she him? Did they not play a game without an ending? Was it necessary to live for this? No, it was not necessary! The name of this game was Sansara, a game for children, a game which was perhaps enjoyable to play once, twice, ten times—but for ever and ever over again?

Then, Siddhartha knew that the game was over, that he could not play it any more. Shivers ran over his body, inside of him, so he felt, something had died.

That entire day, he sat under the mango-tree, thinking of his father, thinking of Govinda, thinking of Gotama. Did he have to leave them to become a Kamaswami? He still sat there, when the night had fallen. When, looking up, he caught sight of the stars, he thought: "Here I'm sitting under my mango-tree, in my pleasure-garden." He smiled a little —was it really necessary, was it right, was it not as foolish game, that he owned a mango-tree, that he owned a garden?

He also put an end to this, this also died in him. He rose, bid his farewell to the mango-tree, his farewell to the pleasure-garden. Since he had been without food this day, he felt strong hunger, and thought of his house in the city, of his chamber and bed, of the table with the meals on it. He smiled tiredly, shook himself, and bid his farewell to these things.

In the same hour of the night, Siddhartha left his garden, left the city, and never came back. For a long time, Kamaswami had people look for him, thinking that he had fallen into the hands of robbers. Kamala had no one look for him. When she was told that Siddhartha had disappeared, she was not astonished. Did she not always expect it? Was he not a Samana, a man who was at home nowhere, a pilgrim? And most of all, she had felt this the last time they had been together, and she was happy, in spite of all the pain of the loss, that she had pulled him so affectionately to her heart for this last time, that she had felt one more time to be so completely possessed and penetrated by him.

When she received the first news of Siddhartha's disappearance, she went to the window, where she held a rare singing bird captive in a golden cage. She opened the door of the cage, took the bird out and let it fly. For a long time, she gazed after it, the flying bird. From this day on, she received no more visitors and kept her house locked. But after some time, she became aware that she was pregnant from the last time she was together with Siddhartha.

BY THE RIVER

Siddhartha walked through the forest, was already far from the city, and knew nothing but that one thing, that there was no going back for him, that this life, as he had lived it for many years until now, was over and done away with, and that he had tasted all of it, sucked everything out of it until he was disgusted with it. Dead was the singing bird, he had dreamt of. Dead was the bird in his heart. Deeply, he had been entangled in Sansara, he had sucked up disgust and death from all sides into his body, like a sponge sucks up water until it is full. And full he was, full of the feeling of been sick of it, full of misery, full of death, there was nothing left in this world which could have attracted him, given him joy, given him comfort.

Passionately he wished to know nothing about himself anymore, to have rest, to be dead. If there only was a lightning-bolt to strike him dead! If there only was a tiger to devour him! If there only was a wine, a poison which would numb his senses, bring him forgetfulness and sleep, and no awakening from that! Was there still any kind of filth, he had not soiled himself with, a sin or foolish act he had not committed, a dreariness of the soul he had not brought upon himself? Was it still at all possible to be alive? Was it possible, to breathe in again and again, to breathe out, to feel hunger, to eat again, to sleep again, to sleep with a woman again? Was this cycle not exhausted and brought to a conclusion for him?

Siddhartha reached the large river in the forest, the same river over which a long time ago, when he had still been a young man and came from the town of Gotama, a ferryman had conducted him. By this river he stopped, hesitantly he stood at the bank. Tiredness and hunger had weakened him, and whatever for should he walk on, wherever to, to which goal? No, there were no more goals, there was nothing left but the deep, painful yearning to shake off this whole desolate dream, to spit out this stale wine, to put an end to this miserable and shameful life.

A hang bent over the bank of the river, a coconut-tree; Siddhartha leaned against its trunk with his shoulder, embraced the trunk with one arm, and looked down into the green water, which ran and ran under him, looked down and found himself to be entirely filled with the wish to let go and to drown in these waters. A frightening emptiness was reflected back at him by the water, answering to the terrible emptiness in his soul. Yes, he had reached the end. There was nothing left for him, except to annihilate himself, except to smash the failure into which he had shaped his life, to throw it away, before the feet of mockingly laughing gods. This was the great vomiting he had longed for: death, the smashing to bits of the form he hated! Let him be food for fishes, this dog Siddhartha, this lunatic, this depraved and rotten body, this weakened and abused soul! Let him be food for fishes and crocodiles, let him be chopped to bits by the daemons!

With a distorted face, he stared into the water, saw the reflection of his face and spit at it. In deep tiredness, he took his arm away from the trunk of the tree and turned a bit, in order to let himself fall straight down, in order to finally drown. With his eyes closed, he slipped towards death.

Then, out of remote areas of his soul, out of past times of his now weary life, a sound stirred up. It was a word, a syllable, which he, without thinking, with a slurred voice, spoke to himself, the old word which is the beginning and the end of all prayers of the Brahmans, the holy "Om", which roughly means "that what is perfect" or "the completion". And in the moment when the sound of "Om" touched Siddhartha's ear, his dormant spirit suddenly woke up and realized the foolishness of his actions.

Siddhartha was deeply shocked. So this was how things were with him, so doomed was he, so much he had lost his way and was forsaken by all knowledge, that he had been able to seek death, that this wish, this wish of a child, had been able to grow in him: to find rest by annihilating his body! What all agony of these recent times, all sobering realizations, all desperation had not brought about, this was brought on by this moment, when the Om entered his consciousness: he became aware of himself in his misery and in his error.

Om! he spoke to himself: Om! and again he knew about Brahman, knew about the indestructibility of life, knew about all that is divine, which he had forgotten.

But this was only a moment, flash. By the foot of the coconut-tree, Siddhartha collapsed, struck down by tiredness, mumbling Om, placed his head on the root of the tree and fell into a deep sleep.

Deep was his sleep and without dreams, for a long time he had not known such a sleep any more. When he woke up after many hours, he felt as if ten years had passed, he heard the water quietly flowing, did not know where he was and who had brought him here, opened his eyes, saw with astonishment that there were trees and the sky above him, and he remembered where he was and how he got here. But it took him a long while for this, and the past seemed to him as if it had been covered by a veil, infinitely distant, infinitely far away, infinitely meaningless. He only knew that his previous life (in the first moment when he thought about it, this past life seemed to him like a very old, previous incarnation, like an early pre-birth of his present self)—that his previous life had been abandoned by him, that, full of disgust and wretchedness, he had even intended to throw his life away, but that by a river, under a coconut-tree, he has come to his senses, the holy word Om on his lips, that then he had fallen asleep and had now woken up and was looking at the world as a new man. Quietly, he spoke the word Om to himself, speaking which he had fallen asleep, and it seemed to him as if his entire long sleep had been nothing but a long meditative recitation of Om, a thinking of Om, a submergence and complete entering into Om, into the nameless, the perfected.

What a wonderful sleep had this been! Never before by sleep, he had been thus refreshed, thus renewed, thus rejuvenated! Perhaps, he had really died, had drowned and was reborn in a new body? But no, he knew himself, he knew his hand and his feet, knew the place where he lay, knew this self in his chest, this Siddhartha, the eccentric, the weird one, but this Siddhartha was nevertheless transformed, was renewed, was strangely well rested, strangely awake, joyful and curious.

Siddhartha straightened up, then he saw a person sitting opposite to him, an unknown man, a monk in a yellow robe with a shaven head, sitting in the position of pondering. He observed the man, who had neither hair on his head nor a beard, and he had not observed him for long when he recognised this monk as Govinda, the friend of his youth, Govinda who had taken his refuge with the exalted Buddha. Govinda had aged, he too, but still his face bore the same features, expressed zeal, faithfulness, searching, timidness. But when Govinda now, sensing his gaze, opened his eyes and looked at him, Siddhartha saw that Govinda did not recognise him. Govinda was happy to find him awake; apparently, he had been sitting here for a long time and been waiting for him to wake up, though he did not know him.

"I have been sleeping," said Siddhartha. "However did you get here?"

"You have been sleeping," answered Govinda. "It is not good to be sleeping in such places, where snakes often are and the animals of the forest have their paths. I, oh sir, am a follower of the exalted Gotama, the Buddha, the Sakyamuni, and have been on a pilgrimage together with several of us on this path, when I saw you lying and sleeping in a place where it is dangerous to sleep. Therefore, I sought to wake you up, oh sir, and since I saw that your sleep was very deep, I stayed behind from my group and sat with you. And then, so it seems, I have fallen asleep myself, I who wanted to guard your sleep. Badly, I have served you, tiredness has overwhelmed me. But now that you're awake, let me go to catch up with my brothers."

"I thank you, Samana, for watching out over my sleep," spoke Siddhartha. "You're friendly, you followers of the exalted one. Now you may go then."

"I'm going, sir. May you, sir, always be in good health."

"I thank you, Samana."

Govinda made the gesture of a salutation and said: "Farewell."

"Farewell, Govinda," said Siddhartha.

The monk stopped.

"Permit me to ask, sir, from where do you know my name?"

Now, Siddhartha smiled.

"I know you, oh Govinda, from your father's hut, and from the school of the Brahmans, and from the offerings, and from our walk to the Samanas, and from that hour when you took your refuge with the exalted one in the grove Jetavana."

"You're Siddhartha," Govinda exclaimed loudly. "Now, I'm recognising you, and don't comprehend any more how I couldn't recognise you right away. Be welcome, Siddhartha, my joy is great, to see you again."

"It also gives me joy, to see you again. You've been the guard of my sleep, again I thank you for this, though I wouldn't have required any guard. Where are you going to, oh friend?"

"I'm going nowhere. We monks are always travelling, whenever it is not the rainy season, we always move from one place to another, live according to the rules if the teachings passed on to us, accept alms, move on. It is always like this. But you, Siddhartha, where are you going to?"

Quoth Siddhartha: "With me too, friend, it is as it is with you. I'm going nowhere. I'm just travelling. I'm on a pilgrimage."

Govinda spoke: "You're saying: you're on a pilgrimage, and I believe in you. But, forgive me, oh Siddhartha, you do not look like a pilgrim. You're wearing a rich man's garments, you're wearing the shoes of a distinguished gentleman, and your hair, with the fragrance of perfume, is not a pilgrim's hair, not the hair of a Samana."

"Right so, my dear, you have observed well, your keen eyes see everything. But I haven't said to you that I was a Samana. I said: I'm on a pilgrimage. And so it is: I'm on a pilgrimage."

"You're on a pilgrimage," said Govinda. "But few would go on a pilgrimage in such clothes, few in such shoes, few with such hair. Never I have met such a pilgrim, being a pilgrim myself for many years."

"I believe you, my dear Govinda. But now, today, you've met a pilgrim just like this, wearing such shoes, such a garment. Remember, my dear: Not eternal is the world of appearances, not eternal, anything but eternal are our garments and the style of our hair, and our hair and bodies themselves. I'm wearing a rich man's clothes, you've seen this quite right. I'm wearing them, because I have been a rich man, and I'm wearing my hair like the worldly and lustful people, for I have been one of them."

"And now, Siddhartha, what are you now?"

"I don't know it, I don't know it just like you. I'm travelling. I was a rich man and am no rich man any more, and what I'll be tomorrow, I don't know."

"You've lost your riches?"

"I've lost them or they me. They somehow happened to slip away from me. The wheel of physical manifestations is turning quickly, Govinda. Where is Siddhartha the Brahman? Where is Siddhartha the Samana? Where is Siddhartha the rich man? Non-eternal things change quickly, Govinda, you know it."

Govinda looked at the friend of his youth for a long time, with doubt in his eyes. After that, he gave him the salutation which one would use on a gentleman and went on his way.

With a smiling face, Siddhartha watched him leave, he loved him still, this faithful man, this fearful man. And how could he not have loved everybody and everything in this moment, in the glorious hour after his wonderful sleep, filled with Om! The enchantment, which had happened inside of him in his sleep and by means of the Om, was this very thing that he loved everything, that he was full of joyful love for everything he saw. And it was this very thing, so it seemed to him now, which had been his sickness before, that he was not able to love anybody or anything.

With a smiling face, Siddhartha watched the leaving monk. The sleep had strengthened him much, but hunger gave him much pain, for by now he had not eaten for two days, and the times were long past when he had been tough against hunger. With sadness, and yet also with a smile, he thought of that time. In those days, so he remembered, he had boasted of three things to Kamala, had been able to do three noble and undefeatable feats: fasting—waiting—thinking. These had been his possession, his power and strength, his solid staff; in the busy, laborious years of his youth, he had learned these three feats, nothing else. And now, they had abandoned him, none of them was his any more, neither fasting, nor waiting, nor thinking. For the most wretched things, he had given them up, for what fades most quickly, for sensual lust, for the good life, for riches! His life had indeed been strange. And now, so it seemed, now he had really become a childlike person.

Siddhartha thought about his situation. Thinking was hard on him, he did not really feel like it, but he forced himself.

Now, he thought, since all these most easily perishing things have slipped from me again, now I'm standing here under the sun again just as I have been standing here a little child, nothing is mine, I have no abilities, there is nothing I could bring about, I have learned nothing. How wondrous is this! Now, that I'm no longer young, that my hair is already half gray, that my strength is fading, now I'm starting again at the beginning and as a child! Again, he had to smile. Yes, his fate had been strange! Things were going downhill with him, and now he was again facing the world void and naked and stupid. But he could not feed sad about this, no, he even felt a great urge to laugh, to laugh about himself, to laugh about this strange, foolish world.

"Things are going downhill with you!" he said to himself, and laughed about it, and as he was saying it, he happened to glance at the river, and he also saw the river going downhill, always moving on downhill, and singing and being happy through it all. He liked this well, kindly he smiled at the river. Was this not the river in which he had intended to drown himself, in past times, a hundred years ago, or had he dreamed this?

Wondrous indeed was my life, so he thought, wondrous detours it has taken. As a boy, I had only to do with gods and offerings. As a youth, I had only to do with asceticism, with thinking and meditation, was searching for Brahman, worshipped the eternal in the Atman. But as a young man, I followed the penitents, lived in the forest, suffered of heat and frost, learned to hunger, taught my body to become dead. Wonderfully, soon afterwards, insight came towards me in the form of the great Buddha's teachings, I felt the knowledge of the oneness of the world circling in me like my own blood. But I also had to leave Buddha and the great knowledge. I went and learned the art of love with Kamala, learned trading with Kamaswami, piled up money, wasted money, learned to love my stomach, learned to please my senses. I had to spend many years losing my spirit, to unlearn thinking again, to forget the oneness. Isn't it just as if I had turned slowly and on a long detour from a man into a child, from a thinker into a childlike person? And yet, this path has been very good; and yet, the bird in my chest has not died. But what a path has this been! I had to pass through so much stupidity, through so much vices, through so many errors, through so much disgust and disappointments and woe, just to become a child again and to be able to start over. But it was right so, my heart says "Yes" to it, my eyes smile to it. I've had to experience despair, I've had to sink down to the most foolish one of all thoughts, to the thought of suicide, in order to be able to experience divine grace, to hear Om again, to be able to sleep properly and awake properly again. I had to become a fool, to find Atman in me again. I had to sin, to be able to live again. Where else might my path lead me to? It is foolish, this path, it moves in loops, perhaps it is going around in a circle. Let it go as it likes, I want to take it.

Wonderfully, he felt joy rolling like waves in his chest.

Wherever from, he asked his heart, where from did you get this happiness? Might it come from that long, good sleep, which has done me so good? Or from the word Om, which I said? Or from the fact that I have escaped, that I have completely fled, that I am finally free again and am standing like a child under the sky? Oh how good is it to have fled, to have become free! How clean and beautiful is the air here, how good to breathe! There, where I ran away from, there everything smelled of ointments, of spices, of wine, of excess, of sloth. How did I hate this world of the rich, of those who revel in fine food, of the gamblers! How did I hate myself for staying in this terrible world for so long! How did I hate myself, have deprive, poisoned, tortured myself, have made myself old and evil! No, never again I will, as I used to like doing so much, delude myself into thinking that Siddhartha was wise! But this one thing I have done well, this I like, this I must praise, that there is now an end to that hatred against myself, to that foolish and dreary life! I praise you, Siddhartha, after so many years of foolishness, you have once again had an idea, have done something, have heard the bird in your chest singing and have followed it!

Thus he praised himself, found joy in himself, listened curiously to his stomach, which was rumbling with hunger. He had now, so he felt, in these recent times and days, completely tasted and spit out, devoured up to the point of desperation and death, a piece of suffering, a piece of misery. Like this, it was good. For much longer, he could have stayed with Kamaswami, made money, wasted money, filled his stomach, and let his soul die of thirst; for much longer he could have lived in this soft, well upholstered hell, if this had not happened: the moment of complete hopelessness and despair, that most extreme moment, when he hung over the rushing waters and was ready to destroy himself. That he had felt this despair, this deep disgust, and that he had not succumbed to it, that the bird, the joyful source and voice in him was still alive after all, this was why he felt joy, this was why he laughed, this was why his face was smiling brightly under his hair which had turned gray.

"It is good," he thought, "to get a taste of everything for oneself, which one needs to know. That lust for the world and riches do not belong to the good things, I have already learned as a child. I have known it for a long time, but I have experienced only now. And now I know it, don't just know it in my memory, but in my eyes, in my heart, in my stomach. Good for me, to know this!"

For a long time, he pondered his transformation, listened to the bird, as it sang for joy. Had not this bird died in him, had he not felt its death? No, something else from within him had died, something which already for a long time had yearned to die. Was it not this what he used to intend to kill in his ardent years as a penitent? Was this not his self, his small, frightened, and proud self, he had wrestled with for so many years, which had defeated him again and again, which was back again after every killing, prohibited joy, felt fear? Was it not this, which today had finally come to its death, here in the forest, by this lovely river? Was it not due to this death, that he was now like a child, so full of trust, so without fear, so full of joy?

Now Siddhartha also got some idea of why he had fought this self in vain as a Brahman, as a penitent. Too much knowledge had held him back, too many holy verses, too many sacrificial rules, to much self-castigation, so much doing and striving for that goal! Full of arrogance, he had been, always the smartest, always working the most, always one step ahead of all others, always the knowing and spiritual one, always the priest or wise one. Into being a priest, into this arrogance, into this spirituality, his self had retreated, there it sat firmly and grew, while he thought he would kill it by fasting and penance. Now he saw it and saw that the secret voice had been right, that no teacher would ever have been able to bring about his salvation. Therefore, he had to go out into the world, lose himself to lust and power, to woman and money, had to become a merchant, a dice-gambler, a drinker, and a greedy person, until the priest and Samana in him was dead. Therefore, he had to continue bearing these ugly years, bearing the disgust, the teachings, the pointlessness of a dreary and wasted life up to the end, up to bitter despair, until Siddhartha the lustful, Siddhartha the greedy could also die. He had died, a new Siddhartha had woken up from the sleep. He would also grow old, he would also eventually have to die, mortal was Siddhartha, mortal was every physical form. But today he was young, was a child, the new Siddhartha, and was full of joy.

He thought these thoughts, listened with a smile to his stomach, listened gratefully to a buzzing bee. Cheerfully, he looked into the rushing river, never before he had liked a water so well as this one, never before he had perceived the voice and the parable of the moving water thus strongly and beautifully. It seemed to him, as if the river had something special to tell him, something he did not know yet, which was still awaiting him. In this river, Siddhartha had intended to drown himself, in it the old, tired, desperate Siddhartha had drowned today. But the new Siddhartha felt a deep love for this rushing water, and decided for himself, not to leave it very soon.

THE FERRYMAN

By this river I want to stay, thought Siddhartha, it is the same which I have crossed a long time ago on my way to the childlike people, a friendly ferryman had guided me then, he is the one I want to go to, starting out from his hut, my path had led me at that time into a new life, which had now grown old and is dead—my present path, my present new life, shall also take its start there!

Tenderly, he looked into the rushing water, into the transparent green, into the crystal lines of its drawing, so rich in secrets. Bright pearls he saw rising from the deep, quiet bubbles of air floating on the reflecting surface, the blue of the sky being depicted in it. With a thousand eyes, the river looked at him, with green ones, with white ones, with crystal ones, with sky-blue ones. How did he love this water, how did it delight him, how grateful was he to it! In his heart he heard the voice talking, which was newly awaking, and it told him: Love this water! Stay near it! Learn from it! Oh yes, he wanted to learn from it, he wanted to listen to it. He who would understand this water and its secrets, so it seemed to him, would also understand many other things, many secrets, all secrets.

But out of all secrets of the river, he today only saw one, this one touched his soul. He saw: this water ran and ran, incessantly it ran, and was nevertheless always there, was always at all times the same and yet new in every moment! Great be he who would grasp this, understand this! He understood and grasped it not, only felt some idea of it stirring, a distant memory, divine voices.

Siddhartha rose, the workings of hunger in his body became unbearable. In a daze he walked on, up the path by the bank, upriver, listened to the current, listened to the rumbling hunger in his body.

When he reached the ferry, the boat was just ready, and the same ferryman who had once transported the young Samana across the river, stood in the boat, Siddhartha recognised him, he had also aged very much.

"Would you like to ferry me over?" he asked.

The ferryman, being astonished to see such an elegant man walking along and on foot, took him into his boat and pushed it off the bank.

"It's a beautiful life you have chosen for yourself," the passenger spoke. "It must be beautiful to live by this water every day and to cruise on it."

With a smile, the man at the oar moved from side to side: "It is beautiful, sir, it is as you say. But isn't every life, isn't every work beautiful?"

"This may be true. But I envy you for yours."

"Ah, you would soon stop enjoying it. This is nothing for people wearing fine clothes."

Siddhartha laughed. "Once before, I have been looked upon today because of my clothes, I have been looked upon with distrust. Wouldn't you, ferryman, like to accept these clothes, which are a nuisance to me, from me? For you must know, I have no money to pay your fare."

"You're joking, sir," the ferryman laughed.

"I'm not joking, friend. Behold, once before you have ferried me across this water in your boat for the immaterial reward of a good deed. Thus, do it today as well, and accept my clothes for it."

"And do you, sir, intent to continue travelling without clothes?"

"Ah, most of all I wouldn't want to continue travelling at all. Most of all I would like you, ferryman, to give me an old loincloth and kept me with you as your assistant, or rather as your trainee, for I'll have to learn first how to handle the boat."

For a long time, the ferryman looked at the stranger, searching.

"Now I recognise you," he finally said. "At one time, you've slept in my hut, this was a long time ago, possibly more than twenty years ago, and you've been ferried across the river by me, and we parted like good friends. Haven't you've been a Samana? I can't think of your name any more."

"My name is Siddhartha, and I was a Samana, when you've last seen me."

"So be welcome, Siddhartha. My name is Vasudeva. You will, so I hope, be my guest today as well and sleep in my hut, and tell me, where you're coming from and why these beautiful clothes are such a nuisance to you."

They had reached the middle of the river, and Vasudeva pushed the oar with more strength, in order to overcome the current. He worked calmly, his eyes fixed in on the front of the boat, with brawny arms. Siddhartha sat and watched him, and remembered, how once before, on that last day of his time as a Samana, love for this man had stirred in his heart. Gratefully, he accepted Vasudeva's invitation. When they had reached the bank, he helped him to tie the boat to the stakes; after this, the ferryman asked him to enter the hut, offered him bread and water, and Siddhartha ate with eager pleasure, and also ate with eager pleasure of the mango fruits, Vasudeva offered him.

Afterwards, it was almost the time of the sunset, they sat on a log by the bank, and Siddhartha told the ferryman about where he originally came from and about his life, as he had seen it before his eyes today, in that hour of despair. Until late at night, lasted his tale.

Vasudeva listened with great attention. Listening carefully, he let everything enter his mind, birthplace and childhood, all that learning, all that searching, all joy, all distress. This was among the ferryman's virtues one of the greatest: like only a few, he knew how to listen. Without him having spoken a word, the speaker sensed how Vasudeva let his words enter his mind, quiet, open, waiting, how he did not lose a single one, awaited not a single one with impatience, did not add his praise or rebuke, was just listening. Siddhartha felt, what a happy fortune it is, to confess to such a listener, to bury in his heart his own life, his own search, his own suffering.

But in the end of Siddhartha's tale, when he spoke of the tree by the river, and of his deep fall, of the holy Om, and how he had felt such a love for the river after his slumber, the ferryman listened with twice the attention, entirely and completely absorbed by it, with his eyes closed.

But when Siddhartha fell silent, and a long silence had occurred, then Vasudeva said: "It is as I thought. The river has spoken to you. It is your friend as well, it speaks to you as well. That is good, that is very good. Stay with me, Siddhartha, my friend. I used to have a wife, her bed was next to mine, but she has died a long time ago, for a long time, I have lived alone. Now, you shall live with me, there is space and food for both."

"I thank you," said Siddhartha, "I thank you and accept. And I also thank you for this, Vasudeva, for listening to me so well! These people are rare who know how to listen. And I did not meet a single one who knew it as well as you did. I will also learn in this respect from you."

"You will learn it," spoke Vasudeva, "but not from me. The river has taught me to listen, from it you will learn it as well. It knows everything, the river, everything can be learned from it. See, you've already learned this from the water too, that it is good to strive downwards, to sink, to seek depth. The rich and elegant Siddhartha is becoming an oarsman's servant, the learned Brahman Siddhartha becomes a ferryman: this has also been told to you by the river. You'll learn that other thing from it as well."

Quoth Siddhartha after a long pause: "What other thing, Vasudeva?"

Vasudeva rose. "It is late," he said, "let's go to sleep. I can't tell you that other thing, oh friend. You'll learn it, or perhaps you know it already. See, I'm no learned man, I have no special skill in speaking, I also have no special skill in thinking. All I'm able to do is to listen and to be godly, I have learned nothing else. If I was able to say and teach it, I might be a wise man, but like this I am only a ferryman, and it is my task to ferry people across the river. I have transported many, thousands; and to all of them, my river has been nothing but an obstacle on their travels. They travelled to seek money and business, and for weddings, and on pilgrimages, and the river was obstructing their path, and the ferryman's job was to get them quickly across that obstacle. But for some among thousands, a few, four or five, the river has stopped being an obstacle, they have heard its voice, they have listened to it, and the river has become sacred to them, as it has become sacred to me. Let's rest now, Siddhartha."

Siddhartha stayed with the ferryman and learned to operate the boat, and when there was nothing to do at the ferry, he worked with Vasudeva in the rice-field, gathered wood, plucked the fruit off the banana-trees. He learned to build an oar, and learned to mend the boat, and to weave baskets, and was joyful because of everything he learned, and the days and months passed quickly. But more than Vasudeva could teach him, he was taught by the river. Incessantly, he learned from it. Most of all, he learned from it to listen, to pay close attention with a quiet heart, with a waiting, opened soul, without passion, without a wish, without judgement, without an opinion.

In a friendly manner, he lived side by side with Vasudeva, and occasionally they exchanged some words, few and at length thought about words. Vasudeva was no friend of words; rarely, Siddhartha succeeded in persuading him to speak.

"Did you," so he asked him at one time, "did you too learn that secret from the river: that there is no time?"

Vasudeva's face was filled with a bright smile.

"Yes, Siddhartha," he spoke. "It is this what you mean, isn't it: that the river is everywhere at once, at the source and at the mouth, at the waterfall, at the ferry, at the rapids, in the sea, in the mountains, everywhere at once, and that there is only the present time for it, not the shadow of the past, not the shadow of the future?"

"This it is," said Siddhartha. "And when I had learned it, I looked at my life, and it was also a river, and the boy Siddhartha was only separated from the man Siddhartha and from the old man Siddhartha by a shadow, not by something real. Also, Siddhartha's previous births were no past, and his death and his return to Brahma was no future. Nothing was, nothing will be; everything is, everything has existence and is present."

Siddhartha spoke with ecstasy; deeply, this enlightenment had delighted him. Oh, was not all suffering time, were not all forms of tormenting oneself and being afraid time, was not everything hard, everything hostile in the world gone and overcome as soon as one had overcome time, as soon as time would have been put out of existence by one's thoughts? In ecstatic delight, he had spoken, but Vasudeva smiled at him brightly and nodded in confirmation; silently he nodded, brushed his hand over Siddhartha's shoulder, turned back to his work.

And once again, when the river had just increased its flow in the rainy season and made a powerful noise, then said Siddhartha: "Isn't it so, oh friend, the river has many voices, very many voices? Hasn't it the voice of a king, and of a warrior, and of a bull, and of a bird of the night, and of a woman giving birth, and of a sighing man, and a thousand other voices more?"

"So it is," Vasudeva nodded, "all voices of the creatures are in its voice."

"And do you know," Siddhartha continued, "what word it speaks, when you succeed in hearing all of its ten thousand voices at once?"

Happily, Vasudeva's face was smiling, he bent over to Siddhartha and spoke the holy Om into his ear. And this had been the very thing which Siddhartha had also been hearing.

And time after time, his smile became more similar to the ferryman's, became almost just as bright, almost just as throughly glowing with bliss, just as shining out of thousand small wrinkles, just as alike to a child's, just as alike to an old man's. Many travellers, seeing the two ferrymen, thought they were brothers. Often, they sat in the evening together by the bank on the log, said nothing and both listened to the water, which was no water to them, but the voice of life, the voice of what exists, of what is eternally taking shape. And it happened from time to time that both, when listening to the river, thought of the same things, of a conversation from the day before yesterday, of one of their travellers, the face and fate of whom had occupied their thoughts, of death, of their childhood, and that they both in the same moment, when the river had been saying something good to them, looked at each other, both thinking precisely the same thing, both delighted about the same answer to the same question.

There was something about this ferry and the two ferrymen which was transmitted to others, which many of the travellers felt. It happened occasionally that a traveller, after having looked at the face of one of the ferrymen, started to tell the story of his life, told about pains, confessed evil things, asked for comfort and advice. It happened occasionally that someone asked for permission to stay for a night with them to listen to the river. It also happened that curious people came, who had been told that there were two wise men, or sorcerers, or holy men living by that ferry. The curious people asked many questions, but they got no answers, and they found neither sorcerers nor wise men, they only found two friendly little old men, who seemed to be mute and to have become a bit strange and gaga. And the curious people laughed and were discussing how foolishly and gullibly the common people were spreading such empty rumours.

The years passed by, and nobody counted them. Then, at one time, monks came by on a pilgrimage, followers of Gotama, the Buddha, who were asking to be ferried across the river, and by them the ferrymen were told that they were most hurriedly walking back to their great teacher, for the news had spread the exalted one was deadly sick and would soon die his last human death, in order to become one with the salvation. It was not long, until a new flock of monks came along on their pilgrimage, and another one, and the monks as well as most of the other travellers and people walking through the land spoke of nothing else than of Gotama and his impending death. And as people are flocking from everywhere and from all sides, when they are going to war or to the coronation of a king, and are gathering like ants in droves, thus they flocked, like being drawn on by a magic spell, to where the great Buddha was awaiting his death, where the huge event was to take place and the great perfected one of an era was to become one with the glory.

Often, Siddhartha thought in those days of the dying wise man, the great teacher, whose voice had admonished nations and had awoken hundreds of thousands, whose voice he had also once heard, whose holy face he had also once seen with respect. Kindly, he thought of him, saw his path to perfection before his eyes, and remembered with a smile those words which he had once, as a young man, said to him, the exalted one. They had been, so it seemed to him, proud and precocious words; with a smile, he remembered them. For a long time he knew that there was nothing standing between Gotama and him any more, though he was still unable to accept his teachings. No, there was no teaching a truly searching person, someone who truly wanted to find, could accept. But he who had found, he could approve of any teachings, every path, every goal, there was nothing standing between him and all the other thousand any more who lived in that what is eternal, who breathed what is divine.

On one of these days, when so many went on a pilgrimage to the dying Buddha, Kamala also went to him, who used to be the most beautiful of the courtesans. A long time ago, she had retired from her previous life, had given her garden to the monks of Gotama as a gift, had taken her refuge in the teachings, was among the friends and benefactors of the pilgrims. Together with Siddhartha the boy, her son, she had gone on her way due to the news of the near death of Gotama, in simple clothes, on foot. With her little son, she was travelling by the river; but the boy had soon grown tired, desired to go back home, desired to rest, desired to eat, became disobedient and started whining.

Kamala often had to take a rest with him, he was accustomed to having his way against her, she had to feed him, had to comfort him, had to scold him. He did not comprehend why he had to go on this exhausting and sad pilgrimage with his mother, to an unknown place, to a stranger, who was holy and about to die. So what if he died, how did this concern the boy?

The pilgrims were getting close to Vasudeva's ferry, when little Siddhartha once again forced his mother to rest. She, Kamala herself, had also become tired, and while the boy was chewing a banana, she crouched down on the ground, closed her eyes a bit, and rested. But suddenly, she uttered a wailing scream, the boy looked at her in fear and saw her face having grown pale from horror; and from under her dress, a small, black snake fled, by which Kamala had been bitten.

Hurriedly, they now both ran along the path, in order to reach people, and got near to the ferry, there Kamala collapsed, and was not able to go any further. But the boy started crying miserably, only interrupting it to kiss and hug his mother, and she also joined his loud screams for help, until the sound reached Vasudeva's ears, who stood at the ferry. Quickly, he came walking, took the woman on his arms, carried her into the boat, the boy ran along, and soon they all reached the hut, were Siddhartha stood by the stove and was just lighting the fire. He looked up and first saw the boy's face, which wondrously reminded him of something, like a warning to remember something he had forgotten. Then he saw Kamala, whom he instantly recognised, though she lay unconscious in the ferryman's arms, and now he knew that it was his own son, whose face had been such a warning reminder to him, and the heart stirred in his chest.

Kamala's wound was washed, but had already turned black and her body was swollen, she was made to drink a healing potion. Her consciousness returned, she lay on Siddhartha's bed in the hut and bent over her stood Siddhartha, who used to love her so much. It seemed like a dream to her; with a smile, she looked at her friend's face; just slowly she, realized her situation, remembered the bite, called timidly for the boy.

"He's with you, don't worry," said Siddhartha.

Kamala looked into his eyes. She spoke with a heavy tongue, paralysed by the poison. "You've become old, my dear," she said, "you've become gray. But you are like the young Samana, who at one time came without clothes, with dusty feet, to me into the garden. You are much more like him, than you were like him at that time when you had left me and Kamaswami. In the eyes, you're like him, Siddhartha. Alas, I have also grown old, old—could you still recognise me?"

Siddhartha smiled: "Instantly, I recognised you, Kamala, my dear."

Kamala pointed to her boy and said: "Did you recognise him as well? He is your son."

Her eyes became confused and fell shut. The boy wept, Siddhartha took him on his knees, let him weep, petted his hair, and at the sight of the child's face, a Brahman prayer came to his mind, which he had learned a long time ago, when he had been a little boy himself. Slowly, with a singing voice, he started to speak; from his past and childhood, the words came flowing to him. And with that singsong, the boy became calm, was only now and then uttering a sob and fell asleep. Siddhartha placed him on Vasudeva's bed. Vasudeva stood by the stove and cooked rice. Siddhartha gave him a look, which he returned with a smile.

"She'll die," Siddhartha said quietly.

Vasudeva nodded; over his friendly face ran the light of the stove's fire.

Once again, Kamala returned to consciousness. Pain distorted her face, Siddhartha's eyes read the suffering on her mouth, on her pale cheeks. Quietly, he read it, attentively, waiting, his mind becoming one with her suffering. Kamala felt it, her gaze sought his eyes.

Looking at him, she said: "Now I see that your eyes have changed as well. They've become completely different. By what do I still recognise that you're Siddhartha? It's you, and it's not you."

Siddhartha said nothing, quietly his eyes looked at hers.

"You have achieved it?" she asked. "You have found peace?"

He smiled and placed his hand on hers.

"I'm seeing it," she said, "I'm seeing it. I too will find peace."

"You have found it," Siddhartha spoke in a whisper.

Kamala never stopped looking into his eyes. She thought about her pilgrimage to Gotama, which she wanted to take, in order to see the face of the perfected one, to breathe his peace, and she thought that she had now found him in his place, and that it was good, just as good, as if she had seen the other one. She wanted to tell this to him, but the tongue no longer obeyed her will. Without speaking, she looked at him, and he saw the life fading from her eyes. When the final pain filled her eyes and made them grow dim, when the final shiver ran through her limbs, his finger closed her eyelids.

For a long time, he sat and looked at her peacefully dead face. For a long time, he observed her mouth, her old, tired mouth, with those lips, which had become thin, and he remembered, that he used to, in the spring of his years, compare this mouth with a freshly cracked fig. For a long time, he sat, read in the pale face, in the tired wrinkles, filled himself with this sight, saw his own face lying in the same manner, just as white, just as quenched out, and saw at the same time his face and hers being young, with red lips, with fiery eyes, and the feeling of this both being present and at the same time real, the feeling of eternity, completely filled every aspect of his being. Deeply he felt, more deeply than ever before, in this hour, the indestructibility of every life, the eternity of every moment.

When he rose, Vasudeva had prepared rice for him. But Siddhartha did not eat. In the stable, where their goat stood, the two old men prepared beds of straw for themselves, and Vasudeva lay himself down to sleep. But Siddhartha went outside and sat this night before the hut, listening to the river, surrounded by the past, touched and encircled by all times of his life at the same time. But occasionally, he rose, stepped to the door of the hut and listened, whether the boy was sleeping.

Early in the morning, even before the sun could be seen, Vasudeva came out of the stable and walked over to his friend.

"You haven't slept," he said.

"No, Vasudeva. I sat here, I was listening to the river. A lot it has told me, deeply it has filled me with the healing thought, with the thought of oneness."

"You've experienced suffering, Siddhartha, but I see: no sadness has entered your heart."

"No, my dear, how should I be sad? I, who have been rich and happy, have become even richer and happier now. My son has been given to me."

"Your son shall be welcome to me as well. But now, Siddhartha, let's get to work, there is much to be done. Kamala has died on the same bed, on which my wife had died a long time ago. Let us also build Kamala's funeral pile on the same hill on which I had then built my wife's funeral pile."

While the boy was still asleep, they built the funeral pile.

THE SON

Timid and weeping, the boy had attended his mother's funeral; gloomy and shy, he had listened to Siddhartha, who greeted him as his son and welcomed him at his place in Vasudeva's hut. Pale, he sat for many days by the hill of the dead, did not want to eat, gave no open look, did not open his heart, met his fate with resistance and denial.

Siddhartha spared him and let him do as he pleased, he honoured his mourning. Siddhartha understood that his son did not know him, that he could not love him like a father. Slowly, he also saw and understood that the eleven-year-old was a pampered boy, a mother's boy, and that he had grown up in the habits of rich people, accustomed to finer food, to a soft bed, accustomed to giving orders to servants. Siddhartha understood that the mourning, pampered child could not suddenly and willingly be content with a life among strangers and in poverty. He did not force him, he did many a chore for him, always picked the best piece of the meal for him. Slowly, he hoped to win him over, by friendly patience.

Rich and happy, he had called himself, when the boy had come to him. Since time had passed on in the meantime, and the boy remained a stranger and in a gloomy disposition, since he displayed a proud and stubbornly disobedient heart, did not want to do any work, did not pay his respect to the old men, stole from Vasudeva's fruit-trees, then Siddhartha began to understand that his son had not brought him happiness and peace, but suffering and worry. But he loved him, and he preferred the suffering and worries of love over happiness and joy without the boy. Since young Siddhartha was in the hut, the old men had split the work. Vasudeva had again taken on the job of the ferryman all by himself, and Siddhartha, in order to be with his son, did the work in the hut and the field.

For a long time, for long months, Siddhartha waited for his son to understand him, to accept his love, to perhaps reciprocate it. For long months, Vasudeva waited, watching, waited and said nothing. One day, when Siddhartha the younger had once again tormented his father very much with spite and an unsteadiness in his wishes and had broken both of his rice-bowls, Vasudeva took in the evening his friend aside and talked to him.

"Pardon me." he said, "from a friendly heart, I'm talking to you. I'm seeing that you are tormenting yourself, I'm seeing that you're in grief. Your son, my dear, is worrying you, and he is also worrying me. That young bird is accustomed to a different life, to a different nest. He has not, like you, ran away from riches and the city, being disgusted and fed up with it; against his will, he had to leave all this behind. I asked the river, oh friend, many times I have asked it. But the river laughs, it laughs at me, it laughs at you and me, and is shaking with laughter at our foolishness. Water wants to join water, youth wants to join youth, your son is not in the place where he can prosper. You too should ask the river; you too should listen to it!"

Troubled, Siddhartha looked into his friendly face, in the many wrinkles of which there was incessant cheerfulness.

"How could I part with him?" he said quietly, ashamed. "Give me some more time, my dear! See, I'm fighting for him, I'm seeking to win his heart, with love and with friendly patience I intent to capture it. One day, the river shall also talk to him, he also is called upon."

Vasudeva's smile flourished more warmly. "Oh yes, he too is called upon, he too is of the eternal life. But do we, you and me, know what he is called upon to do, what path to take, what actions to perform, what pain to endure? Not a small one, his pain will be; after all, his heart is proud and hard, people like this have to suffer a lot, err a lot, do much injustice, burden themselves with much sin. Tell me, my dear: you're not taking control of your son's upbringing? You don't force him? You don't beat him? You don't punish him?"

"No, Vasudeva, I don't do anything of this."

"I knew it. You don't force him, don't beat him, don't give him orders, because you know that 'soft' is stronger than 'hard', water stronger than rocks, love stronger than force. Very good, I praise you. But aren't you mistaken in thinking that you wouldn't force him, wouldn't punish him? Don't you shackle him with your love? Don't you make him feel inferior every day, and don't you make it even harder on him with your kindness and patience? Don't you force him, the arrogant and pampered boy, to live in a hut with two old banana-eaters, to whom even rice is a delicacy, whose thoughts can't be his, whose hearts are old and quiet and beats in a different pace than his? Isn't forced, isn't he punished by all this?"

Troubled, Siddhartha looked to the ground. Quietly, he asked: "What do you think should I do?"

Quoth Vasudeva: "Bring him into the city, bring him into his mother's house, there'll still be servants around, give him to them. And when there aren't any around any more, bring him to a teacher, not for the teachings' sake, but so that he shall be among other boys, and among girls, and in the world which is his own. Have you never thought of this?"

"You're seeing into my heart," Siddhartha spoke sadly. "Often, I have thought of this. But look, how shall I put him, who had no tender heart anyhow, into this world? Won't he become exuberant, won't he lose himself to pleasure and power, won't he repeat all of his father's mistakes, won't he perhaps get entirely lost in Sansara?"

Brightly, the ferryman's smile lit up; softly, he touched Siddhartha's arm and said: "Ask the river about it, my friend! Hear it laugh about it! Would you actually believe that you had committed your foolish acts in order to spare your son from committing them too? And could you in any way protect your son from Sansara? How could you? By means of teachings, prayer, admonition? My dear, have you entirely forgotten that story, that story containing so many lessons, that story about Siddhartha, a Brahman's son, which you once told me here on this very spot? Who has kept the Samana Siddhartha safe from Sansara, from sin, from greed, from foolishness? Were his father's religious devotion, his teachers warnings, his own knowledge, his own search able to keep him safe? Which father, which teacher had been able to protect him from living his life for himself, from soiling himself with life, from burdening himself with guilt, from drinking the bitter drink for himself, from finding his path for himself? Would you think, my dear, anybody might perhaps be spared from taking this path? That perhaps your little son would be spared, because you love him, because you would like to keep him from suffering and pain and disappointment? But even if you would die ten times for him, you would not be able to take the slightest part of his destiny upon yourself."

Never before, Vasudeva had spoken so many words. Kindly, Siddhartha thanked him, went troubled into the hut, could not sleep for a long time. Vasudeva had told him nothing, he had not already thought and known for himself. But this was a knowledge he could not act upon, stronger than the knowledge was his love for the boy, stronger was his tenderness, his fear to lose him. Had he ever lost his heart so much to something, had he ever loved any person thus, thus blindly, thus sufferingly, thus unsuccessfully, and yet thus happily?

Siddhartha could not heed his friend's advice, he could not give up the boy. He let the boy give him orders, he let him disregard him. He said nothing and waited; daily, he began the mute struggle of friendliness, the silent war of patience. Vasudeva also said nothing and waited, friendly, knowing, patient. They were both masters of patience.

At one time, when the boy's face reminded him very much of Kamala, Siddhartha suddenly had to think of a line which Kamala a long time ago, in the days of their youth, had once said to him. "You cannot love," she had said to him, and he had agreed with her and had compared himself with a star, while comparing the childlike people with falling leaves, and nevertheless he had also sensed an accusation in that line. Indeed, he had never been able to lose or devote himself completely to another person, to forget himself, to commit foolish acts for the love of another person; never he had been able to do this, and this was, as it had seemed to him at that time, the great distinction which set him apart from the childlike people. But now, since his son was here, now he, Siddhartha, had also become completely a childlike person, suffering for the sake of another person, loving another person, lost to a love, having become a fool on account of love. Now he too felt, late, once in his lifetime, this strongest and strangest of all passions, suffered from it, suffered miserably, and was nevertheless in bliss, was nevertheless renewed in one respect, enriched by one thing.

He did sense very well that this love, this blind love for his son, was a passion, something very human, that it was Sansara, a murky source, dark waters. Nevertheless, he felt at the same time, it was not worthless, it was necessary, came from the essence of his own being. This pleasure also had to be atoned for, this pain also had to be endured, these foolish acts also had to be committed.

Through all this, the son let him commit his foolish acts, let him court for his affection, let him humiliate himself every day by giving in to his moods. This father had nothing which would have delighted him and nothing which he would have feared. He was a good man, this father, a good, kind, soft man, perhaps a very devout man, perhaps a saint, all these were no attributes which could win the boy over. He was bored by this father, who kept him prisoner here in this miserable hut of his, he was bored by him, and for him to answer every naughtiness with a smile, every insult with friendliness, every viciousness with kindness, this very thing was the hated trick of this old sneak. Much more the boy would have liked it if he had been threatened by him, if he had been abused by him.

A day came, when what young Siddhartha had on his mind came bursting forth, and he openly turned against his father. The latter had given him a task, he had told him to gather brushwood. But the boy did not leave the hut, in stubborn disobedience and rage he stayed where he was, thumped on the ground with his feet, clenched his fists, and screamed in a powerful outburst his hatred and contempt into his father's face.

"Get the brushwood for yourself!" he shouted foaming at the mouth, "I'm not your servant. I do know, that you won't hit me, you don't dare; I do know, that you constantly want to punish me and put me down with your religious devotion and your indulgence. You want me to become like you, just as devout, just as soft, just as wise! But I, listen up, just to make you suffer, I rather want to become a highway-robber and murderer, and go to hell, than to become like you! I hate you, you're not my father, and if you've ten times been my mother's fornicator!"

Rage and grief boiled over in him, foamed at the father in a hundred savage and evil words. Then the boy ran away and only returned late at night.

But the next morning, he had disappeared. What had also disappeared was a small basket, woven out of bast of two colours, in which the ferrymen kept those copper and silver coins which they received as a fare. The boat had also disappeared, Siddhartha saw it lying by the opposite bank. The boy had ran away.

"I must follow him," said Siddhartha, who had been shivering with grief since those ranting speeches, the boy had made yesterday. "A child can't go through the forest all alone. He'll perish. We must build a raft, Vasudeva, to get over the water."

"We will build a raft," said Vasudeva, "to get our boat back, which the boy has taken away. But him, you shall let run along, my friend, he is no child any more, he knows how to get around. He's looking for the path to the city, and he is right, don't forget that. He's doing what you've failed to do yourself. He's taking care of himself, he's taking his course. Alas, Siddhartha, I see you suffering, but you're suffering a pain at which one would like to laugh, at which you'll soon laugh for yourself."

Siddhartha did not answer. He already held the axe in his hands and began to make a raft of bamboo, and Vasudeva helped him to tie the canes together with ropes of grass. Then they crossed over, drifted far off their course, pulled the raft upriver on the opposite bank.

"Why did you take the axe along?" asked Siddhartha.

Vasudeva said: "It might have been possible that the oar of our boat got lost."

But Siddhartha knew what his friend was thinking. He thought, the boy would have thrown away or broken the oar in order to get even and in order to keep them from following him. And in fact, there was no oar left in the boat. Vasudeva pointed to the bottom of the boat and looked at his friend with a smile, as if he wanted to say: "Don't you see what your son is trying to tell you? Don't you see that he doesn't want to be followed?" But he did not say this in words. He started making a new oar. But Siddhartha bid his farewell, to look for the run-away. Vasudeva did not stop him.

When Siddhartha had already been walking through the forest for a long time, the thought occurred to him that his search was useless. Either, so he thought, the boy was far ahead and had already reached the city, or, if he should still be on his way, he would conceal himself from him, the pursuer. As he continued thinking, he also found that he, on his part, was not worried for his son, that he knew deep inside that he had neither perished nor was in any danger in the forest. Nevertheless, he ran without stopping, no longer to save him, just to satisfy his desire, just to perhaps see him one more time. And he ran up to just outside of the city.

When, near the city, he reached a wide road, he stopped, by the entrance of the beautiful pleasure-garden, which used to belong to Kamala, where he had seen her for the first time in her sedan-chair. The past rose up in his soul, again he saw himself standing there, young, a bearded, naked Samana, the hair full of dust. For a long time, Siddhartha stood there and looked through the open gate into the garden, seeing monks in yellow robes walking among the beautiful trees.

For a long time, he stood there, pondering, seeing images, listening to the story of his life. For a long time, he stood there, looked at the monks, saw young Siddhartha in their place, saw young Kamala walking among the high trees. Clearly, he saw himself being served food and drink by Kamala, receiving his first kiss from her, looking proudly and disdainfully back on his Brahmanism, beginning proudly and full of desire his worldly life. He saw Kamaswami, saw the servants, the orgies, the gamblers with the dice, the musicians, saw Kamala's song-bird in the cage, lived through all this once again, breathed Sansara, was once again old and tired, felt once again disgust, felt once again the wish to annihilate himself, was once again healed by the holy Om.

After having been standing by the gate of the garden for a long time, Siddhartha realised that his desire was foolish, which had made him go up to this place, that he could not help his son, that he was not allowed to cling him. Deeply, he felt the love for the run-away in his heart, like a wound, and he felt at the same time that this wound had not been given to him in order to turn the knife in it, that it had to become a blossom and had to shine.

That this wound did not blossom yet, did not shine yet, at this hour, made him sad. Instead of the desired goal, which had drawn him here following the runaway son, there was now emptiness. Sadly, he sat down, felt something dying in his heart, experienced emptiness, saw no joy any more, no goal. He sat lost in thought and waited. This he had learned by the river, this one thing: waiting, having patience, listening attentively. And he sat and listened, in the dust of the road, listened to his heart, beating tiredly and sadly, waited for a voice. Many an hour he crouched, listening, saw no images any more, fell into emptiness, let himself fall, without seeing a path. And when he felt the wound burning, he silently spoke the Om, filled himself with Om. The monks in the garden saw him, and since he crouched for many hours, and dust was gathering on his gray hair, one of them came to him and placed two bananas in front of him. The old man did not see him.

From this petrified state, he was awoken by a hand touching his shoulder. Instantly, he recognised this touch, this tender, bashful touch, and regained his senses. He rose and greeted Vasudeva, who had followed him. And when he looked into Vasudeva's friendly face, into the small wrinkles, which were as if they were filled with nothing but his smile, into the happy eyes, then he smiled too. Now he saw the bananas lying in front of him, picked them up, gave one to the ferryman, ate the other one himself. After this, he silently went back into the forest with Vasudeva, returned home to the ferry. Neither one talked about what had happened today, neither one mentioned the boy's name, neither one spoke about him running away, neither one spoke about the wound. In the hut, Siddhartha lay down on his bed, and when after a while Vasudeva came to him, to offer him a bowl of coconut-milk, he already found him asleep.

OM

For a long time, the wound continued to burn. Many a traveller Siddhartha had to ferry across the river who was accompanied by a son or a daughter, and he saw none of them without envying him, without thinking: "So many, so many thousands possess this sweetest of good fortunes—why don't I? Even bad people, even thieves and robbers have children and love them, and are being loved by them, all except for me." Thus simply, thus without reason he now thought, thus similar to the childlike people he had become.

Differently than before, he now looked upon people, less smart, less proud, but instead warmer, more curious, more involved. When he ferried travellers of the ordinary kind, childlike people, businessmen, warriors, women, these people did not seem alien to him as they used to: he understood them, he understood and shared their life, which was not guided by thoughts and insight, but solely by urges and wishes, he felt like them. Though he was near perfection and was bearing his final wound, it still seemed to him as if those childlike people were his brothers, their vanities, desires for possession, and ridiculous aspects were no longer ridiculous to him, became understandable, became lovable, even became worthy of veneration to him. The blind love of a mother for her child, the stupid, blind pride of a conceited father for his only son, the blind, wild desire of a young, vain woman for jewelry and admiring glances from men, all of these urges, all of this childish stuff, all of these simple, foolish, but immensely strong, strongly living, strongly prevailing urges and desires were now no childish notions for Siddhartha any more, he saw people living for their sake, saw them achieving infinitely much for their sake, travelling, conducting wars, suffering infinitely much, bearing infinitely much, and he could love them for it, he saw life, that what is alive, the indestructible, the Brahman in each of their passions, each of their acts. Worthy of love and admiration were these people in their blind loyalty, their blind strength and tenacity. They lacked nothing, there was nothing the knowledgeable one, the thinker, had to put him above them except for one little thing, a single, tiny, small thing: the consciousness, the conscious thought of the oneness of all life. And Siddhartha even doubted in many an hour, whether this knowledge, this thought was to be valued thus highly, whether it might not also perhaps be a childish idea of the thinking people, of the thinking and childlike people. In all other respects, the worldly people were of equal rank to the wise men, were often far superior to them, just as animals too can, after all, in some moments, seem to be superior to humans in their tough, unrelenting performance of what is necessary.

Slowly blossomed, slowly ripened in Siddhartha the realisation, the knowledge, what wisdom actually was, what the goal of his long search was. It was nothing but a readiness of the soul, an ability, a secret art, to think every moment, while living his life, the thought of oneness, to be able to feel and inhale the oneness. Slowly this blossomed in him, was shining back at him from Vasudeva's old, childlike face: harmony, knowledge of the eternal perfection of the world, smiling, oneness.

But the wound still burned, longingly and bitterly Siddhartha thought of his son, nurtured his love and tenderness in his heart, allowed the pain to gnaw at him, committed all foolish acts of love. Not by itself, this flame would go out.

And one day, when the wound burned violently, Siddhartha ferried across the river, driven by a yearning, got off the boat and was willing to go to the city and to look for his son. The river flowed softly and quietly, it was the dry season, but its voice sounded strange: it laughed! It laughed clearly. The river laughed, it laughed brightly and clearly at the old ferryman. Siddhartha stopped, he bent over the water, in order to hear even better, and he saw his face reflected in the quietly moving waters, and in this reflected face there was something, which reminded him, something he had forgotten, and as he thought about it, he found it: this face resembled another face, which he used to know and love and also fear. It resembled his father's face, the Brahman. And he remembered how he, a long time ago, as a young man, had forced his father to let him go to the penitents, how he had bid his farewell to him, how he had gone and had never come back. Had his father not also suffered the same pain for him, which he now suffered for his son? Had his father not long since died, alone, without having seen his son again? Did he not have to expect the same fate for himself? Was it not a comedy, a strange and stupid matter, this repetition, this running around in a fateful circle?

The river laughed. Yes, so it was, everything came back, which had not been suffered and solved up to its end, the same pain was suffered over and over again. But Siddhartha went back into the boat and ferried back to the hut, thinking of his father, thinking of his son, laughed at by the river, at odds with himself, tending towards despair, and not less tending towards laughing along at himself and the entire world.

Alas, the wound was not blossoming yet, his heart was still fighting his fate, cheerfulness and victory were not yet shining from his suffering. Nevertheless, he felt hope, and once he had returned to the hut, he felt an undefeatable desire to open up to Vasudeva, to show him everything, the master of listening, to say everything.

Vasudeva was sitting in the hut and weaving a basket. He no longer used the ferry-boat, his eyes were starting to get weak, and not just his eyes; his arms and hands as well. Unchanged and flourishing was only the joy and the cheerful benevolence of his face.

Siddhartha sat down next to the old man, slowly he started talking. What they had never talked about, he now told him of, of his walk to the city, at that time, of the burning wound, of his envy at the sight of happy fathers, of his knowledge of the foolishness of such wishes, of his futile fight against them. He reported everything, he was able to say everything, even the most embarrassing parts, everything could be said, everything shown, everything he could tell. He presented his wound, also told how he fled today, how he ferried across the water, a childish run-away, willing to walk to the city, how the river had laughed.

While he spoke, spoke for a long time, while Vasudeva was listening with a quiet face, Vasudeva's listening gave Siddhartha a stronger sensation than ever before, he sensed how his pain, his fears flowed over to him, how his secret hope flowed over, came back at him from his counterpart. To show his wound to this listener was the same as bathing it in the river, until it had cooled and become one with the river. While he was still speaking, still admitting and confessing, Siddhartha felt more and more that this was no longer Vasudeva, no longer a human being, who was listening to him, that this motionless listener was absorbing his confession into himself like a tree the rain, that this motionless man was the river itself, that he was God himself, that he was the eternal itself. And while Siddhartha stopped thinking of himself and his wound, this realisation of Vasudeva's changed character took possession of him, and the more he felt it and entered into it, the less wondrous it became, the more he realised that everything was in order and natural, that Vasudeva had already been like this for a long time, almost forever, that only he had not quite recognised it, yes, that he himself had almost reached the same state. He felt, that he was now seeing old Vasudeva as the people see the gods, and that this could not last; in his heart, he started bidding his farewell to Vasudeva. Throughout all this, he talked incessantly.

When he had finished talking, Vasudeva turned his friendly eyes, which had grown slightly weak, at him, said nothing, let his silent love and cheerfulness, understanding and knowledge, shine at him. He took Siddhartha's hand, led him to the seat by the bank, sat down with him, smiled at the river.

"You've heard it laugh," he said. "But you haven't heard everything. Let's listen, you'll hear more."

They listened. Softly sounded the river, singing in many voices. Siddhartha looked into the water, and images appeared to him in the moving water: his father appeared, lonely, mourning for his son; he himself appeared, lonely, he also being tied with the bondage of yearning to his distant son; his son appeared, lonely as well, the boy, greedily rushing along the burning course of his young wishes, each one heading for his goal, each one obsessed by the goal, each one suffering. The river sang with a voice of suffering, longingly it sang, longingly, it flowed towards its goal, lamentingly its voice sang.

"Do you hear?" Vasudeva's mute gaze asked. Siddhartha nodded.

"Listen better!" Vasudeva whispered.

Siddhartha made an effort to listen better. The image of his father, his own image, the image of his son merged, Kamala's image also appeared and was dispersed, and the image of Govinda, and other images, and they merged with each other, turned all into the river, headed all, being the river, for the goal, longing, desiring, suffering, and the river's voice sounded full of yearning, full of burning woe, full of unsatisfiable desire. For the goal, the river was heading, Siddhartha saw it hurrying, the river, which consisted of him and his loved ones and of all people, he had ever seen, all of these waves and waters were hurrying, suffering, towards goals, many goals, the waterfall, the lake, the rapids, the sea, and all goals were reached, and every goal was followed by a new one, and the water turned into vapour and rose to the sky, turned into rain and poured down from the sky, turned into a source, a stream, a river, headed forward once again, flowed on once again. But the longing voice had changed. It still resounded, full of suffering, searching, but other voices joined it, voices of joy and of suffering, good and bad voices, laughing and sad ones, a hundred voices, a thousand voices.

Siddhartha listened. He was now nothing but a listener, completely concentrated on listening, completely empty, he felt, that he had now finished learning to listen. Often before, he had heard all this, these many voices in the river, today it sounded new. Already, he could no longer tell the many voices apart, not the happy ones from the weeping ones, not the ones of children from those of men, they all belonged together, the lamentation of yearning and the laughter of the knowledgeable one, the scream of rage and the moaning of the dying ones, everything was one, everything was intertwined and connected, entangled a thousand times. And everything together, all voices, all goals, all yearning, all suffering, all pleasure, all that was good and evil, all of this together was the world. All of it together was the flow of events, was the music of life. And when Siddhartha was listening attentively to this river, this song of a thousand voices, when he neither listened to the suffering nor the laughter, when he did not tie his soul to any particular voice and submerged his self into it, but when he heard them all, perceived the whole, the oneness, then the great song of the thousand voices consisted of a single word, which was Om: the perfection.

"Do you hear," Vasudeva's gaze asked again.

Brightly, Vasudeva's smile was shining, floating radiantly over all the wrinkles of his old face, as the Om was floating in the air over all the voices of the river. Brightly his smile was shining, when he looked at his friend, and brightly the same smile was now starting to shine on Siddhartha's face as well. His wound blossomed, his suffering was shining, his self had flown into the oneness.

In this hour, Siddhartha stopped fighting his fate, stopped suffering. On his face flourished the cheerfulness of a knowledge, which is no longer opposed by any will, which knows perfection, which is in agreement with the flow of events, with the current of life, full of sympathy for the pain of others, full of sympathy for the pleasure of others, devoted to the flow, belonging to the oneness.

When Vasudeva rose from the seat by the bank, when he looked into Siddhartha's eyes and saw the cheerfulness of the knowledge shining in them, he softly touched his shoulder with his hand, in this careful and tender manner, and said: "I've been waiting for this hour, my dear. Now that it has come, let me leave. For a long time, I've been waiting for this hour; for a long time, I've been Vasudeva the ferryman. Now it's enough. Farewell, hut, farewell, river, farewell, Siddhartha!"

Siddhartha made a deep bow before him who bid his farewell.

"I've known it," he said quietly. "You'll go into the forests?"

"I'm going into the forests, I'm going into the oneness," spoke Vasudeva with a bright smile.

With a bright smile, he left; Siddhartha watched him leaving. With deep joy, with deep solemnity he watched him leave, saw his steps full of peace, saw his head full of lustre, saw his body full of light.

GOVINDA

Together with other monks, Govinda used to spend the time of rest between pilgrimages in the pleasure-grove, which the courtesan Kamala had given to the followers of Gotama for a gift. He heard talk of an old ferryman, who lived one day's journey away by the river, and who was regarded as a wise man by many. When Govinda went back on his way, he chose the path to the ferry, eager to see the ferryman. Because, though he had lived his entire life by the rules, though he was also looked upon with veneration by the younger monks on account of his age and his modesty, the restlessness and the searching still had not perished from his heart.

He came to the river and asked the old man to ferry him over, and when they got off the boat on the other side, he said to the old man: "You're very good to us monks and pilgrims, you have already ferried many of us across the river. Aren't you too, ferryman, a searcher for the right path?"

Quoth Siddhartha, smiling from his old eyes: "Do you call yourself a searcher, oh venerable one, though you are already of an old in years and are wearing the robe of Gotama's monks?"

"It's true, I'm old," spoke Govinda, "but I haven't stopped searching. Never I'll stop searching, this seems to be my destiny. You too, so it seems to me, have been searching. Would you like to tell me something, oh honourable one?"

Quoth Siddhartha: "What should I possibly have to tell you, oh venerable one? Perhaps that you're searching far too much? That in all that searching, you don't find the time for finding?"

"How come?" asked Govinda.

"When someone is searching," said Siddhartha, "then it might easily happen that the only thing his eyes still see is that what he searches for, that he is unable to find anything, to let anything enter his mind, because he always thinks of nothing but the object of his search, because he has a goal, because he is obsessed by the goal. Searching means: having a goal. But finding means: being free, being open, having no goal. You, oh venerable one, are perhaps indeed a searcher, because, striving for your goal, there are many things you don't see, which are directly in front of your eyes."

"I don't quite understand yet," asked Govinda, "what do you mean by this?"

Quoth Siddhartha: "A long time ago, oh venerable one, many years ago, you've once before been at this river and have found a sleeping man by the river, and have sat down with him to guard his sleep. But, oh Govinda, you did not recognise the sleeping man."

Astonished, as if he had been the object of a magic spell, the monk looked into the ferryman's eyes.

"Are you Siddhartha?" he asked with a timid voice. "I wouldn't have recognised you this time as well! From my heart, I'm greeting you, Siddhartha; from my heart, I'm happy to see you once again! You've changed a lot, my friend.—And so you've now become a ferryman?"

In a friendly manner, Siddhartha laughed. "A ferryman, yes. Many people, Govinda, have to change a lot, have to wear many a robe, I am one of those, my dear. Be welcome, Govinda, and spend the night in my hut."

Govinda stayed the night in the hut and slept on the bed which used to be Vasudeva's bed. Many questions he posed to the friend of his youth, many things Siddhartha had to tell him from his life.

When in the next morning the time had come to start the day's journey, Govinda said, not without hesitation, these words: "Before I'll continue on my path, Siddhartha, permit me to ask one more question. Do you have a teaching? Do you have a faith, or a knowledge, you follow, which helps you to live and to do right?"

Quoth Siddhartha: "You know, my dear, that I already as a young man, in those days when we lived with the penitents in the forest, started to distrust teachers and teachings and to turn my back to them. I have stuck with this. Nevertheless, I have had many teachers since then. A beautiful courtesan has been my teacher for a long time, and a rich merchant was my teacher, and some gamblers with dice. Once, even a follower of Buddha, travelling on foot, has been my teacher; he sat with me when I had fallen asleep in the forest, on the pilgrimage. I've also learned from him, I'm also grateful to him, very grateful. But most of all, I have learned here from this river and from my predecessor, the ferryman Vasudeva. He was a very simple person, Vasudeva, he was no thinker, but he knew what is necessary just as well as Gotama, he was a perfect man, a saint."

Govinda said: "Still, oh Siddhartha, you love a bit to mock people, as it seems to me. I believe in you and know that you haven't followed a teacher. But haven't you found something by yourself, though you've found no teachings, you still found certain thoughts, certain insights, which are your own and which help you to live? If you would like to tell me some of these, you would delight my heart."

Quoth Siddhartha: "I've had thoughts, yes, and insight, again and again. Sometimes, for an hour or for an entire day, I have felt knowledge in me, as one would feel life in one's heart. There have been many thoughts, but it would be hard for me to convey them to you. Look, my dear Govinda, this is one of my thoughts, which I have found: wisdom cannot be passed on. Wisdom which a wise man tries to pass on to someone always sounds like foolishness."

"Are you kidding?" asked Govinda.

"I'm not kidding. I'm telling you what I've found. Knowledge can be conveyed, but not wisdom. It can be found, it can be lived, it is possible to be carried by it, miracles can be performed with it, but it cannot be expressed in words and taught. This was what I, even as a young man, sometimes suspected, what has driven me away from the teachers. I have found a thought, Govinda, which you'll again regard as a joke or foolishness, but which is my best thought. It says: The opposite of every truth is just as true! That's like this: any truth can only be expressed and put into words when it is one-sided. Everything is one-sided which can be thought with thoughts and said with words, it's all one-sided, all just one half, all lacks completeness, roundness, oneness. When the exalted Gotama spoke in his teachings of the world, he had to divide it into Sansara and Nirvana, into deception and truth, into suffering and salvation. It cannot be done differently, there is no other way for him who wants to teach. But the world itself, what exists around us and inside of us, is never one-sided. A person or an act is never entirely Sansara or entirely Nirvana, a person is never entirely holy or entirely sinful. It does really seem like this, because we are subject to deception, as if time was something real. Time is not real, Govinda, I have experienced this often and often again. And if time is not real, then the gap which seems to be between the world and the eternity, between suffering and blissfulness, between evil and good, is also a deception."

"How come?" asked Govinda timidly.

"Listen well, my dear, listen well! The sinner, which I am and which you are, is a sinner, but in times to come he will be Brahma again, he will reach the Nirvana, will be Buddha—and now see: these 'times to come' are a deception, are only a parable! The sinner is not on his way to become a Buddha, he is not in the process of developing, though our capacity for thinking does not know how else to picture these things. No, within the sinner is now and today already the future Buddha, his future is already all there, you have to worship in him, in you, in everyone the Buddha which is coming into being, the possible, the hidden Buddha. The world, my friend Govinda, is not imperfect, or on a slow path towards perfection: no, it is perfect in every moment, all sin already carries the divine forgiveness in itself, all small children already have the old person in themselves, all infants already have death, all dying people the eternal life. It is not possible for any person to see how far another one has already progressed on his path; in the robber and dice-gambler, the Buddha is waiting; in the Brahman, the robber is waiting. In deep meditation, there is the possibility to put time out of existence, to see all life which was, is, and will be as if it was simultaneous, and there everything is good, everything is perfect, everything is Brahman. Therefore, I see whatever exists as good, death is to me like life, sin like holiness, wisdom like foolishness, everything has to be as it is, everything only requires my consent, only my willingness, my loving agreement, to be good for me, to do nothing but work for my benefit, to be unable to ever harm me. I have experienced on my body and on my soul that I needed sin very much, I needed lust, the desire for possessions, vanity, and needed the most shameful despair, in order to learn how to give up all resistance, in order to learn how to love the world, in order to stop comparing it to some world I wished, I imagined, some kind of perfection I had made up, but to leave it as it is and to love it and to enjoy being a part of it.—These, oh Govinda, are some of the thoughts which have come into my mind."

Siddhartha bent down, picked up a stone from the ground, and weighed it in his hand.

"This here," he said playing with it, "is a stone, and will, after a certain time, perhaps turn into soil, and will turn from soil into a plant or animal or human being. In the past, I would have said: This stone is just a stone, it is worthless, it belongs to the world of the Maja; but because it might be able to become also a human being and a spirit in the cycle of transformations, therefore I also grant it importance. Thus, I would perhaps have thought in the past. But today I think: this stone is a stone, it is also animal, it is also god, it is also Buddha, I do not venerate and love it because it could turn into this or that, but rather because it is already and always everything— and it is this very fact, that it is a stone, that it appears to me now and today as a stone, this is why I love it and see worth and purpose in each of its veins and cavities, in the yellow, in the gray, in the hardness, in the sound it makes when I knock at it, in the dryness or wetness of its surface. There are stones which feel like oil or soap, and others like leaves, others like sand, and every one is special and prays the Om in its own way, each one is Brahman, but simultaneously and just as much it is a stone, is oily or juicy, and this is this very fact which I like and regard as wonderful and worthy of worship.—But let me speak no more of this. The words are not good for the secret meaning, everything always becomes a bit different, as soon as it is put into words, gets distorted a bit, a bit silly—yes, and this is also very good, and I like it a lot, I also very much agree with this, that this what is one man's treasure and wisdom always sounds like foolishness to another person."

Govinda listened silently.

"Why have you told me this about the stone?" he asked hesitantly after a pause.

"I did it without any specific intention. Or perhaps what I meant was, that love this very stone, and the river, and all these things we are looking at and from which we can learn. I can love a stone, Govinda, and also a tree or a piece of bark. This are things, and things can be loved. But I cannot love words. Therefore, teachings are no good for me, they have no hardness, no softness, no colours, no edges, no smell, no taste, they have nothing but words. Perhaps it are these which keep you from finding peace, perhaps it are the many words. Because salvation and virtue as well, Sansara and Nirvana as well, are mere words, Govinda. There is no thing which would be Nirvana; there is just the word Nirvana."

Quoth Govinda: "Not just a word, my friend, is Nirvana. It is a thought."

Siddhartha continued: "A thought, it might be so. I must confess to you, my dear: I don't differentiate much between thoughts and words. To be honest, I also have no high opinion of thoughts. I have a better opinion of things. Here on this ferry-boat, for instance, a man has been my predecessor and teacher, a holy man, who has for many years simply believed in the river, nothing else. He had noticed that the river's spoke to him, he learned from it, it educated and taught him, the river seemed to be a god to him, for many years he did not know that every wind, every cloud, every bird, every beetle was just as divine and knows just as much and can teach just as much as the worshipped river. But when this holy man went into the forests, he knew everything, knew more than you and me, without teachers, without books, only because he had believed in the river."

Govinda said: "But is that what you call 'things', actually something real, something which has existence? Isn't it just a deception of the Maja, just an image and illusion? Your stone, your tree, your river— are they actually a reality?"

"This too," spoke Siddhartha, "I do not care very much about. Let the things be illusions or not, after all I would then also be an illusion, and thus they are always like me. This is what makes them so dear and worthy of veneration for me: they are like me. Therefore, I can love them. And this is now a teaching you will laugh about: love, oh Govinda, seems to me to be the most important thing of all. To thoroughly understand the world, to explain it, to despise it, may be the thing great thinkers do. But I'm only interested in being able to love the world, not to despise it, not to hate it and me, to be able to look upon it and me and all beings with love and admiration and great respect."

"This I understand," spoke Govinda. "But this very thing was discovered by the exalted one to be a deception. He commands benevolence, clemency, sympathy, tolerance, but not love; he forbade us to tie our heart in love to earthly things."

"I know it," said Siddhartha; his smile shone golden. "I know it, Govinda. And behold, with this we are right in the middle of the thicket of opinions, in the dispute about words. For I cannot deny, my words of love are in a contradiction, a seeming contradiction with Gotama's words. For this very reason, I distrust in words so much, for I know, this contradiction is a deception. I know that I am in agreement with Gotama. How should he not know love, he, who has discovered all elements of human existence in their transitoriness, in their meaninglessness, and yet loved people thus much, to use a long, laborious life only to help them, to teach them! Even with him, even with your great teacher, I prefer the thing over the words, place more importance on his acts and life than on his speeches, more on the gestures of his hand than his opinions. Not in his speech, not in his thoughts, I see his greatness, only in his actions, in his life."

For a long time, the two old men said nothing. Then spoke Govinda, while bowing for a farewell: "I thank you, Siddhartha, for telling me some of your thoughts. They are partially strange thoughts, not all have been instantly understandable to me. This being as it may, I thank you, and I wish you to have calm days."

(But secretly he thought to himself: This Siddhartha is a bizarre person, he expresses bizarre thoughts, his teachings sound foolish. So differently sound the exalted one's pure teachings, clearer, purer, more comprehensible, nothing strange, foolish, or silly is contained in them. But different from his thoughts seemed to me Siddhartha's hands and feet, his eyes, his forehead, his breath, his smile, his greeting, his walk. Never again, after our exalted Gotama has become one with the Nirvana, never since then have I met a person of whom I felt: this is a holy man! Only him, this Siddhartha, I have found to be like this. May his teachings be strange, may his words sound foolish; out of his gaze and his hand, his skin and his hair, out of every part of him shines a purity, shines a calmness, shines a cheerfulness and mildness and holiness, which I have seen in no other person since the final death of our exalted teacher.)

As Govinda thought like this, and there was a conflict in his heart, he once again bowed to Siddhartha, drawn by love. Deeply he bowed to him who was calmly sitting.

"Siddhartha," he spoke, "we have become old men. It is unlikely for one of us to see the other again in this incarnation. I see, beloved, that you have found peace. I confess that I haven't found it. Tell me, oh honourable one, one more word, give me something on my way which I can grasp, which I can understand! Give me something to be with me on my path. It is often hard, my path, often dark, Siddhartha."

Siddhartha said nothing and looked at him with the ever unchanged, quiet smile. Govinda stared at his face, with fear, with yearning, suffering, and the eternal search was visible in his look, eternal not-finding.

Siddhartha saw it and smiled.

"Bend down to me!" he whispered quietly in Govinda's ear. "Bend down to me! Like this, even closer! Very close! Kiss my forehead, Govinda!"

But while Govinda with astonishment, and yet drawn by great love and expectation, obeyed his words, bent down closely to him and touched his forehead with his lips, something miraculous happened to him. While his thoughts were still dwelling on Siddhartha's wondrous words, while he was still struggling in vain and with reluctance to think away time, to imagine Nirvana and Sansara as one, while even a certain contempt for the words of his friend was fighting in him against an immense love and veneration, this happened to him:

He no longer saw the face of his friend Siddhartha, instead he saw other faces, many, a long sequence, a flowing river of faces, of hundreds, of thousands, which all came and disappeared, and yet all seemed to be there simultaneously, which all constantly changed and renewed themselves, and which were still all Siddhartha. He saw the face of a fish, a carp, with an infinitely painfully opened mouth, the face of a dying fish, with fading eyes—he saw the face of a new-born child, red and full of wrinkles, distorted from crying—he saw the face of a murderer, he saw him plunging a knife into the body of another person—he saw, in the same second, this criminal in bondage, kneeling and his head being chopped off by the executioner with one blow of his sword—he saw the bodies of men and women, naked in positions and cramps of frenzied love—he saw corpses stretched out, motionless, cold, void— he saw the heads of animals, of boars, of crocodiles, of elephants, of bulls, of birds—he saw gods, saw Krishna, saw Agni—he saw all of these figures and faces in a thousand relationships with one another, each one helping the other, loving it, hating it, destroying it, giving re-birth to it, each one was a will to die, a passionately painful confession of transitoriness, and yet none of them died, each one only transformed, was always re-born, received evermore a new face, without any time having passed between the one and the other face—and all of these figures and faces rested, flowed, generated themselves, floated along and merged with each other, and they were all constantly covered by something thin, without individuality of its own, but yet existing, like a thin glass or ice, like a transparent skin, a shell or mold or mask of water, and this mask was smiling, and this mask was Siddhartha's smiling face, which he, Govinda, in this very same moment touched with his lips. And, Govinda saw it like this, this smile of the mask, this smile of oneness above the flowing forms, this smile of simultaneousness above the thousand births and deaths, this smile of Siddhartha was precisely the same, was precisely of the same kind as the quiet, delicate, impenetrable, perhaps benevolent, perhaps mocking, wise, thousand-fold smile of Gotama, the Buddha, as he had seen it himself with great respect a hundred times. Like this, Govinda knew, the perfected ones are smiling.

Not knowing any more whether time existed, whether the vision had lasted a second or a hundred years, not knowing any more whether there existed a Siddhartha, a Gotama, a me and a you, feeling in his innermost self as if he had been wounded by a divine arrow, the injury of which tasted sweet, being enchanted and dissolved in his innermost self, Govinda still stood for a little while bent over Siddhartha's quiet face, which he had just kissed, which had just been the scene of all manifestations, all transformations, all existence. The face was unchanged, after under its surface the depth of the thousandfoldness had closed up again, he smiled silently, smiled quietly and softly, perhaps very benevolently, perhaps very mockingly, precisely as he used to smile, the exalted one.

Deeply, Govinda bowed; tears he knew nothing of, ran down his old face; like a fire burnt the feeling of the most intimate love, the humblest veneration in his heart. Deeply, he bowed, touching the ground, before him who was sitting motionlessly, whose smile reminded him of everything he had ever loved in his life, what had ever been valuable and holy to him in his life.

Arthur Conan Doyle, A Scandal in Bohemia

To Sherlock Holmes she is always *the* woman. I have seldom heard him mention her under any other name. In his eyes she eclipses and predominates the whole of her sex. It was not that he felt any emotion akin to love for Irene Adler. All emotions, and that one particularly, were abhorrent to his cold, precise, but admirably balanced mind. He was, I take it, the most perfect reasoning and observing machine that the world has seen; but, as a lover, he would have placed himself in a false position. He never spoke of the softer passions, save with a gibe and a sneer. They were admirable things for the observer—excellent for drawing the veil from men's motives and actions. But for the trained reasoner to admit such intrusions into his own delicate and finely adjusted temperament was to introduce a distracting factor which might throw a doubt upon all his mental results. Grit in a sensitive instrument, or a crack in one of his own high-power lenses, would not be more disturbing than a strong emotion in a nature such as his. And yet there was but one woman to him, and that woman was the late Irene Adler, of dubious and questionable memory.

I had seen little of Holmes lately. My marriage had drifted us away from each other. My own complete happiness, and the home-centred interests which rise up around the man who first finds himself master of his own establishment, were sufficient to absorb all my attention; while Holmes, who loathed every form of society with his whole Bohemian soul, remained in our lodgings in Baker-street, buried among his old books, and alternating from week to week between cocaine and ambition, the drowsiness of the drug, and the fierce energy of his own keen nature. He was still, as ever, deeply attracted by the study of crime, and occupied his immense faculties and extraordinary powers of observation in following out those clues, and clearing up those mysteries, which had been abandoned as hopeless by the official police. From time to time I heard some vague account of his doings: of his summons to Odessa in the case of the Trepoff murder, of his clearing up of the singular tragedy of the Atkinson brothers at Trincomalee, and finally of the mission which he had accomplished so delicately and successfully for the reigning family of Holland. Beyond these signs of his activity, however, which I merely shared with all the readers of the daily press, I knew little of my former friend and companion.

One night—it was on the 20th of March, 1888—I was returning from a journey to a patient (for I had now returned to civil practice), when my way led me through Baker-street. As I passed the well-remembered door, which must always be associated in my mind with my wooing, and with the dark incidents of the Study in Scarlet, I was seized with a keen desire to see Holmes again, and to know how he was employing his extraordinary powers. His rooms were brilliantly lit, and, even as I looked up, I saw his tall spare figure pass twice in a dark silhouette against the blind. He was pacing the room swiftly, eagerly, with his head sunk upon his chest and his hands clasped behind him. To me, who knew his every mood and habit, his attitude and manner told their own story. He was at work again. He had risen out of his drug-created dreams and was hot upon the scent of some new problem. I rang the bell, and was shown up to the chamber which had formerly been in part my own.

His manner was not effusive. It seldom was; but he was glad, I think, to see me. With hardly a word spoken, but with a kindly eye, he waved me to an armchair, threw across his case of cigars, and indicated a spirit case and a gasogene in the corner. Then he stood before the fire and looked me over in his singular introspective fashion.

"Wedlock suits you," he remarked. "I think, Watson, that you have put on seven and a half pounds since I saw you."

"Seven," I answered.

"Indeed, I should have thought a little more. Just a trifle more, I fancy, Watson. And in practice again, I observe. You did not tell me that you intended to go into harness."

"Then, how do you know?"

"I see it, I deduce it. How do I know that you have been getting yourself very wet lately, and that you have a most clumsy and careless servant girl?"

"My dear Holmes," said I, "this is too much. You would certainly have been burned, had you lived a few centuries ago. It is true that I had a country walk on Thursday and came home in a dreadful mess; but, as I have changed my clothes, I can't imagine how you deduce it. As to Mary Jane, she is incorrigible, and my wife has given her notice; but there again I fail to see how you work it out."

He chuckled to himself and rubbed his long nervous hands together.

"It is simplicity itself," said he; "my eyes tell me that on the inside of your left shoe, just where the firelight strikes it, the leather is scored by six almost parallel cuts. Obviously they have been caused by someone who has very carelessly scraped round the edges of the sole in order to remove crusted mud from it. Hence, you see, my double deduction that you had been out in vile weather, and that you had a particularly malignant boot-slitting specimen of the London slavey. As to your practice, if a gentleman walks into my rooms smelling of iodoform, with a black mark of nitrate of silver upon his right fore-finger, and a bulge on the side of his top-hat to show where he has secreted his stethoscope, I must be dull indeed, if I do not pronounce him to be an active member of the medical profession."

I could not help laughing at the ease with which he explained his process of deduction. "When I hear you give your reasons," I remarked, "the thing always appears to me to be so ridiculously simple that I could easily do it myself, though at each successive instance of your reasoning I am baffled until you explain your process. And yet I believe that my eyes are as good as yours."

"Quite so," he answered, lighting a cigarette, and throwing himself down into an armchair. "You see, but you do not observe. The distinction is clear. For example, you have frequently seen the steps which lead up from the hall to this room."

"Frequently."

"How often?"

"Well, some hundreds of times,"

"Then how many are there?"

"How many! I don't know."

"Quite so! You have not observed. And yet you have seen. That is just my point. Now, I know that there are seventeen steps, because I have both seen and observed. By the way, since you are interested in these little problems, and since you are good enough to chronicle one or two of my trifling experiences, you may be interested in this." He threw over a sheet of thick, pink-tinted notepaper which had been lying open upon the table. "It came by the last post," said he. "Read it aloud."

The note was undated, and without either signature or address.

"There will call upon you to-night, at a quarter to eight o'clock," it said, "a gentleman who desires to consult you upon a matter of the very deepest moment. Your recent services to one of the royal houses of Europe have shown that you are one who may safely be trusted with matters which are of an importance which can hardly be exaggerated. This account of you we have from all quarters received. Be in your chamber then at that hour, and do not take it amiss if your visitor wear a mask."

"This is indeed a mystery," I remarked. "What do you imagine that it means?"

"I have no data yet. It is a capital mistake to theorise before one has data. Insensibly one begins to twist facts to suit theories, instead of theories to suit facts. But the note itself. What do you deduce from it?"

I carefully examined the writing, and the paper upon which it was written.

"The man who wrote it was presumably well to do," I remarked, endeavouring to imitate my companion's processes. "Such paper could not be bought under half a crown a packet. It is peculiarly strong and stiff."

"Peculiar—that is the very word," said Holmes. "It is not an English paper at all. Hold it up to the light."

I did so, and saw a large *E* with a small *g*, a *P*, and a large *G* with a small *t* woven into the texture of the paper.

"What do you make of that?" asked Holmes.

"The name of the maker, no doubt; or his monogram, rather."

"Not at all. The *G* with the small *t* stands for 'Gesellschaft,' which is the German for 'Company.' It is a customary contraction like our 'Co.' *P*, of course, stands for 'Papier.' Now for the *Eg*. Let us glance at our Continental Gazetteer." He took down a heavy brown volume from his shelves. "Eglow, Eglonitz—here we are, Egria. It is in a German-speaking country—in Bohemia, not far from Carlsbad. 'Remarkable as being the scene of the death of Wallenstein, and for its numerous glass factories and paper mills.' Ha, ha, my boy, what do you make of that?" His eyes sparkled, and he sent up a great blue triumphant cloud from his cigarette.

"The paper was made in Bohemia," I said.

"Precisely. And the man who wrote the note is a German. Do you note the peculiar construction of the sentence—'This account of you we have from all quarters received.' A Frenchman or Russian could not have written that. It is the German who is so uncourteous to his verbs. It only remains, therefore, to discover what is wanted by this German who writes upon Bohemian paper, and prefers wearing a mask to showing his face. And here he comes, if I am not mistaken, to resolve all our doubts."

As he spoke there was the sharp sound of horses' hoofs and grating wheels against the curb, followed by a sharp pull at the bell. Holmes whistled.

"A pair, by the sound," said he. "Yes," he continued, glancing out of the window. "A nice little brougham and a pair of beauties. A hundred and fifty guineas apiece. There's money in this case, Watson, if there is nothing else."

"I think that I had better go, Holmes."

"Not a bit, Doctor. Stay where you are. I am lost without my Boswell. And this promises to be interesting. It would be a pity to miss it."

"But your client—"

"Never mind him. I may want your help, and so may he. Here he comes. Sit down in that armchair, Doctor, and give us your best attention."

A slow and heavy step, which had been heard upon the stairs and in the passage, paused immediately outside the door. Then there was a loud and authoritative tap.

"Come in!" said Holmes.

A man entered who could hardly have been less than six feet six inches in height, with the chest and limbs of a Hercules. His dress was rich with a richness which would, in England, be looked upon as akin to bad taste. Heavy bands of Astrakhan were slashed across the sleeves and fronts of his double-breasted coat, while the deep blue cloak which was thrown over his shoulders was lined with flame-coloured silk, and secured at the neck with a brooch which consisted of a single flaming beryl. Boots which extended half way up his calves, and which were trimmed at the tops with rich brown fur, completed the impression of barbaric opulence which was suggested by his whole appearance. He carried a broad-brimmed hat in his hand, while he wore across the upper part of his face, extending down past the cheek-bones, a black vizard mask, which he had apparently adjusted that very moment, for his hand was still raised to it as he entered. From the lower part of the face he appeared to be a man of strong character, with a thick, hanging lip, and a long, straight chin suggestive of resolution pushed to the length of obstinacy.

"You had my note?" he asked, with a deep harsh voice and a strongly marked German accent. "I told you that I would call." He looked from one to the other of us, as if uncertain which to address.

"Pray take a seat," said Holmes. "This is my friend and colleague, Dr. Watson, who is occasionally good enough to help me in my cases. Whom have I the honour to address?"

"You may address me as the Count Von Kramm, a Bohemian nobleman. I understand that this gentleman, your friend, is a man of honour and discretion, whom I may trust with a matter of the most extreme importance. If not, I should much prefer to communicate with you alone."

I rose to go, but Holmes caught me by the wrist and pushed me back into my chair. "It is both, or none," said he. "You may say before this gentleman anything which you may say to me."

The Count shrugged his broad shoulders. "Then I must begin," said he, "by binding you both to absolute secrecy for two years, at the end of that time the matter will be of no importance. At present it is not too much to say that it is of such weight it may have an influence upon European history."

"I promise," said Holmes.

"And I."

"You will excuse this mask," continued our strange visitor. "The august person who employs me wishes his agent to be unknown to you, and I may confess at once that the title by which I have just called myself is not exactly my own."

"I was aware of it," said Holmes dryly.

"The circumstances are of great delicacy, and every precaution has to be taken to quench what might grow to be an immense scandal and seriously compromise one of the reigning families of Europe. To speak plainly, the matter implicates the great House of Ormstein, hereditary kings of Bohemia."

"I was also aware of that," murmured Holmes, settling himself down in his armchair and closing his eyes.

Our visitor glanced with some apparent surprise at the languid, lounging figure of the man who had been no doubt depicted to him as the most incisive reasoner, and most energetic agent in Europe. Holmes slowly reopened his eyes, and looked impatiently at his gigantic client.

"If your Majesty would condescend to state your case," he remarked, "I should be better able to advise you."

The man sprang from his chair and paced up and down the room in uncontrollable agitation. Then, with a gesture of desperation, he tore the mask from his face and hurled it upon the ground. "You are right," he cried, "I am the King. Why should I attempt to conceal it?"

"Why, indeed?" murmured Holmes. "Your Majesty had not spoken before I was aware that I was addressing Wilhelm Gottsreich Sigismond von Ormstein, Grand Duke of Cassel-Felstein, and hereditary King of Bohemia."

"But you can understand," said our strange visitor, sitting down once more and passing his hand over his high white forehead, "you can understand that I am not accustomed to doing such business in my own person. Yet the matter was so delicate that I could not confide it to an agent without putting myself in his power. I have come *incognito* from Prague for the purpose of consulting you."

"Then, pray consult," said Holmes, shutting his eyes once more.

"The facts are briefly these: Some five years ago, during a lengthy visit to Warsaw, I made the acquaintance of the well-known adventuress, Irene Adler. The name is no doubt familiar to you."

"Kindly look her up in my index, Doctor," murmured Holmes, without opening his eyes. For many years he had adopted a system of docketing all paragraphs concerning men and things, so that it was difficult to name a subject or a person on which he could not at once furnish information. In this case I found her biography sandwiched in between that of a Hebrew Rabbi and that of a staff-commander who had written a monograph upon the deep sea fishes.

"Let me see?" said Holmes. "Hum! Born in New Jersey in the year 1858. Contralto—hum! La Scala, hum! Prima donna Imperial Opera of Warsaw—yes! Retired from operatic stage—ha! Living in London—quite so! Your Majesty, as I understand, became entangled with this young person, wrote her some compromising letters, and is now desirous of getting those letters back."

"Precisely so. But how—"

"Was there a secret marriage?"

"None."

"No legal papers or certificates?"

"None."

"Then I fail to follow your Majesty. If this young person should produce her letters for blackmailing or other purposes, how is she to prove their authenticity?"

"There is the writing."

"Pooh, pooh! Forgery."

"My private notepaper."

"Stolen."

"My own seal."

"Imitated."

"My photograph."

"Bought."

"We were both in the photograph."

"Oh, dear! That is very bad! Your Majesty has indeed committed an indiscretion."

"I was mad—insane."

"You have compromised yourself seriously."

"I was only Crown Prince then. I was young. I am but thirty now."

"It must be recovered."

"We have tried and failed."

"Your Majesty must pay. It must be bought."

"She will not sell."

"Stolen, then."

"Five attempts have been made. Twice burglars in my pay ransacked her house. Once we diverted her luggage when she travelled. Twice she has been waylaid. There has been no result."

"No sign of it?"

"Absolutely none."

Holmes laughed. "It is quite a pretty little problem," said he.

"But a very serious one to me," returned the King, reproachfully.

"Very, indeed. And what does she propose to do with the photograph?"

"To ruin me."

"But how?"

"I am about to be married."

"So I have heard."

"To Clotilde Lothman von Saxe-Meningen, second daughter of the King of Scandinavia. You may know the strict principles of her family. She is herself the very soul of delicacy. A shadow of a doubt as to my conduct would bring the matter to an end."

"And Irene Adler?"

"Threatens to send them the photograph. And she will do it. I know that she will do it. You do not know her, but she has a soul of steel. She has the face of the most beautiful of women, and the mind of the most resolute of men. Rather than I should marry another woman, there are no lengths to which she would not go—none."

"You are sure that she has not sent it yet?"

"I am sure."

"And why?"

"Because she has said that she would send it on the day when the betrothal was publicly proclaimed. That will be next Monday."

"Oh, then we have three days yet," said Holmes, with a yawn. "That is very fortunate, as I have one or two matters of importance to look into just at present. Your Majesty will, of course, stay in London for the present?"

"Certainly. You will find me at the Langham, under the name of the Count Von Kramm."

"Then I shall drop you a line to let you know how we progress."

"Pray do so. I shall be all anxiety."

"Then, as to money?"

"You have *carte blanche*."

"Absolutely?"

"I tell you that I would give one of the provinces of my kingdom to have that photograph."

"And for present expenses?"

The King took a heavy chamois leather bag from under his cloak, and laid it on the table.

"There are three hundred pounds in gold, and seven hundred in notes," he said.

Holmes scribbled a receipt upon a sheet of his note-book, and handed it to him.

"And mademoiselle's address?" he asked.

"Is Briony Lodge, Serpentine-avenue, St. John's Wood."

Holmes took a note of it. "One other question," said he. "Was the photograph a cabinet?"

"It was."

"Then, good night, your Majesty, and I trust that we shall soon have some good news for you. And good night, Watson," he added, as the wheels of the Royal brougham rolled down the street. "If you will be good enough to call to-morrow afternoon at three o'clock, I should like to chat this little matter over with you."

II.[edit]

At three o'clock precisely I was at Baker-street, but Holmes had not yet returned. The landlady informed me that he had left the house shortly after eight o'clock in the morning. I sat down beside the fire, however, with the intention of awaiting him, however long he might be. I was already deeply interested in his inquiry, for, though it was surrounded by none of the grim and strange features which were associated with the two crimes which I have already recorded, still, the nature of the case and the exalted station of his client gave it a character of its own. Indeed, apart from the nature of the investigation which my friend had on hand, there was something in his masterly grasp of a situation, and his keen, incisive reasoning, which made it a pleasure to me to study his system of work, and to follow the quick, subtle methods by which he disentangled the most inextricable mysteries. So accustomed was I to his invariable success that the very possibility of his failing had ceased to enter into my head.

It was close upon four before the door opened, and a drunken-looking groom, ill-kempt and side-whiskered, with an inflamed face and disreputable clothes, walked into the room. Accustomed as I was to my friend's amazing powers in the use of disguises, I had to look three times before I was certain that it was indeed he. With a nod he vanished into the bedroom, whence he emerged in five minutes tweed-suited and respectable, as of old. Putting his hands into his pockets, he stretched out his legs in front of the fire, and laughed heartily for some minutes.

"Well, really!" he cried, and then he choked; and laughed again until he was obliged to lie back, limp and helpless, in the chair.

"What is it?"

"It's quite too funny. I am sure you could never guess how I employed my morning, or what I ended by doing."

"I can't imagine. I suppose that you have been watching the habits, and perhaps the house, of Miss Irene Adler."

"Quite so, but the sequel was rather unusual. I will tell you, however. I left the house a little after eight o'clock this morning, in the character of a groom out of work. There is a wonderful sympathy and freemasonry among horsey men. Be one of them, and you will know all that there is to know. I soon found Briony Lodge. It is a *bijou* villa, with a garden at the back, but built out in front right up to the road, two stories. Chubb lock to the door. Large sitting-room on the right side, well furnished, with long windows almost to the floor, and those preposterous English window fasteners which a child could open. Behind there was nothing remarkable, save that the passage window could be reached from the top of the coach-house. I walked round it and examined it closely from every point of view, but without noting anything else of interest.

"I then lounged down the street, and found, as I expected, that there was a mews in a lane which runs down by one wall of the garden. I lent the ostlers a hand in rubbing down their horses, and I received in exchange twopence, a glass of half-and-half, two fills of shag tobacco, and as much information as I could desire about Miss Adler, to say nothing of half a dozen other people in the neighbourhood in whom I was not in the least interested, but whose biographies I was compelled to listen to."

"And what of Irene Adler?" I asked.

"Oh, she has turned all the men's heads down in that part. She is the daintiest thing under a bonnet on this planet. So say the Serpentine-mews, to a man. She lives quietly, sings at concerts, drives out at five every day, and returns at seven sharp for dinner. Seldom goes out at other times, except when she sings. Has only one male visitor, but a good deal of him. He is dark, handsome, and dashing; never calls less than once a day, and often twice. He is a Mr. Godfrey Norton, of the Inner Temple. See the advantages of a cabman as a confidant. They had driven him home a dozen times from Serpentine-mews, and knew all about him. When I had listened to all they had to tell, I began to walk up and down near Briony Lodge once more, and to think over my plan of campaign.

"This Godfrey Norton was evidently an important factor in the matter. He was a lawyer. That sounded ominous. What was the relation between them, and what the object of his repeated visits? Was she his client, his friend, or his mistress? If the former, she had probably transferred the photograph to his keeping. If the latter, it was less likely. On the issue of this question depended whether I should continue my work at Briony Lodge, or turn my attention to the gentleman's chambers in the Temple. It was a delicate point, and it widened the field of my inquiry. I fear that I bore you with these details, but I have to let you see my little difficulties, if you are to understand the situation."

"I am following you closely," I answered.

"I was still balancing the matter in my mind, when a hansom cab drove up to Briony Lodge, and a gentleman sprang out. He was a remarkably handsome man, dark, aquiline, and moustached—evidently the man of whom I had heard. He appeared to be in a great hurry, shouted to the cabman to wait, and brushed past the maid who opened the door with the air of a man who was thoroughly at home.

"He was in the house about half an hour, and I could catch glimpses of him, in the windows of the sitting-room, pacing up and down, talking excitedly and waving his arms. Of her I could see nothing. Presently he emerged, looking even more flurried than before. As he stepped up to the cab, he pulled a gold watch from his pocket and looked at it earnestly. 'Drive like the devil,' he shouted, 'first to Gross & Hankey's in Regent-street, and then to the Church of St. Monica in the Edgware-road. Half a guinea if you do it in twenty minutes!'

"Away they went, and I was just wondering whether I should not do well to follow them, when up the lane came a neat little landau, the coachman with his coat only half buttoned, and his tie under his ear, while all the tags of his harness were sticking out of the buckles. It hadn't pulled up before she shot out of the hall door and into it. I only caught a glimpse of her at the moment, but she was a lovely woman, with a face that a man might die for.

"'The Church of St. Monica, John,' she cried, 'and half a sovereign if you reach it in twenty minutes.'

"This was quite too good to lose, Watson. I was just balancing whether I should run for it, or whether I should perch behind her landau, when a cab came through the street. The driver looked twice at such a shabby fare; but I jumped in before he could object. 'The Church of St. Monica,' said I, 'and half a sovereign if you reach it in twenty minutes.' It was twenty-five minutes to twelve, and of course it was clear enough what was in the wind.

"My cabby drove fast. I don't think I ever drove faster, but the others were there before us. The cab and the landau with their steaming horses were in front of the door when I arrived. I paid the man, and hurried into the church. There was not a soul there save the two whom I had followed and a surpliced clergyman, who seemed to be expostulating with them. They were all three standing in a knot in front of the altar. I lounged up the side aisle like any other idler who has dropped into a church. Suddenly, to my surprise, the three at the altar faced round to me, and Godfrey Norton came running as hard as he could towards me."

"Thank God!" he cried. "You'll do. Come! Come!"

"What then?" I asked.

"Come man, come, only three minutes, or it won't be legal."

I was half dragged up to the altar, and, before I knew where I was, I found myself mumbling responses which were whispered in my ear, and vouching for things of which I knew nothing, and generally assisting in the secure tying up of Irene Adler, spinster, to Godfrey Norton, bachelor. It was all done in an instant, and there was the gentleman thanking me on the one side and the lady on the other, while the clergyman beamed on me in front. It was the most preposterous position in which I ever found myself in my life, and it was the thought of it that started me laughing just now. It seems that there had been some informality about their license, that the clergyman absolutely refused to marry them without a witness of some sort, and that my lucky appearance saved the bridegroom from having to sally out into the streets in search of a best man. The bride gave me a sovereign, and I mean to wear it on my watch chain in memory of the occasion."

"This is a very unexpected turn of affairs," said I; "and what then?"

"Well, I found my plans very seriously menaced. It looked as if the pair might take an immediate departure, and so necessitate very prompt and energetic measures on my part. At the church door, however, they separated, he driving back to the Temple, and she to her own house. 'I shall drive out in the Park at five as usual,' she said as she left him. I heard no more. They drove away in different directions, and I went off to make my own arrangements."

"Which are?"

"Some cold beef and a glass of beer," he answered, ringing the bell. "I have been too busy to think of food, and I am likely to be busier still this evening. By the way, Doctor, I shall want your co-operation."

"I shall be delighted."

"You don't mind breaking the law?"

"Not in the least."

"Nor running a chance of arrest?"

"Not in a good cause."

"Oh, the cause is excellent!"

"Then I am your man."

"I was sure that I might rely on you."

"But what is it you wish?"

"When Mrs. Turner has brought in the tray I will make it clear to you. Now," he said, as he turned hungrily on the simple fare that our landlady had provided, "I must discuss it while I eat, for I have not much time. It is nearly five now. In two hours we must be on the scene of action. Miss Irene, or Madame, rather, returns from her drive at seven. We must be at Briony Lodge to meet her."

"And what then?"

"You must leave that to me. I have already arranged what is to occur. There is only one point on which I must insist. You must not interfere, come what may. You understand?"

"I am to be neutral?"

"To do nothing whatever. There will probably be some small unpleasantness. Do not join in it. It will end in my being conveyed into the house. Four or five minutes afterwards the sitting-room window will open. You are to station yourself close to that open window."

"Yes."

"You are to watch me, for I will be visible to you."

"Yes."

"And when I raise my hand—so—you will throw into the room what I give you to throw, and will, at the same time, raise the cry of fire. You quite follow me?"

"Entirely."

"It is nothing very formidable," he said, taking a long cigar-shaped roll from his pocket. "It is an ordinary plumber's smoke-rocket, fitted with a cap at either end to make it self-lighting. Your task is confined to that. When you raise your cry of fire, it will be taken up by quite a number of people. You may then walk to the end of the street, and I will rejoin you in ten minutes. I hope that I have made myself clear?"

"I am to remain neutral, to get near the window, to watch you, and, at the signal, to throw in this object, then to raise the cry of fire, and to wait you at the corner of the street."

"Precisely."

"Then you may entirely rely on me."

"That is excellent. I think perhaps it is almost time that I prepare for the new *rôle* I have to play."

He disappeared into his bedroom, and returned in a few minutes in the character of an amiable and simple-minded Nonconformist clergyman. His broad black hat, his baggy trousers, his white tie, his sympathetic smile, and general look of peering and benevolent curiosity were such as Mr. John Hare alone could have equalled. It was not merely that Holmes changed his costume. His expression, his manner, his very soul seemed to vary with every fresh part that he assumed. The stage lost a fine actor, even as science lost an acute reasoner, when he became a specialist in crime.

It was a quarter past six when we left Baker-street, and it still wanted ten minutes to the hour when we found ourselves in Serpentine-avenue. It was already dusk, and the lamps were just being lighted as we paced up and down in front of Briony Lodge, waiting for the coming of its occupant. The house was just such as I had pictured it from Sherlock Holmes' succinct description, but the locality appeared to be less private than I expected. On the contrary, for a small street in a quiet neighbourhood, it was remarkably animated. There was a group of shabbily-dressed men smoking and laughing in a corner, a scissors grinder with his wheel, two guardsmen who were flirting with a nurse-girl, and several well-dressed young men who were lounging up and down with cigars in their mouths.

"You see," remarked Holmes, as we paced to and fro in front of the house, "this marriage rather simplifies matters. The photograph becomes a double-edged weapon now. The chances are that she would be as averse to its being seen by Mr. Godfrey Norton, as our client is to its coming to the eyes of his Princess. Now the question is—Where are we to find the photograph?"

"Where, indeed?"

"It is most unlikely that she carries it about with her. It is cabinet size. Too large for easy concealment about a woman's dress. She knows that the King is capable of having her waylaid and searched. Two attempts of the sort have already been made. We may take it then that she does not carry it about with her."

"Where, then?"

"Her banker or her lawyer. There is that double possibility. But I am inclined to think neither. Women are naturally secretive, and they like to do their own secreting. Why should she hand it over to anyone else? She could trust her own guardianship, but she could not tell what indirect or political influence might be brought to bear upon a business man. Besides, remember that she had resolved to use it within a few days. It must be where she can lay her hands upon it. It must be in her own house."

"But it has twice been burgled."

"Pshaw! They did not know how to look."

"But how will you look?"

"I will not look."

"What then?"

"I will get her to show me."

"But she will refuse."

"She will not be able to. But I hear the rumble of wheels. It is her carriage. Now carry out my orders to the letter."

As he spoke the gleam of the sidelights of a carriage came round the curve of the avenue. It was a smart little landau which rattled up to the door of Briony Lodge. As it pulled up one of the loafing men at the corner dashed forward to open the door in the hope of earning a copper, but was elbowed away by another loafer who had rushed up with the same intention. A fierce quarrel broke out, which was increased by the two guardsmen, who took sides with one of the loungers, and by the scissors grinder, who was equally hot upon the other side. A blow was struck, and in an instant the lady, who had stepped from her carriage, was the centre of a little knot of flushed and struggling men who struck savagely at each other with their fists and sticks. Holmes dashed into the crowd to protect the lady; but, just as he reached her, he gave a cry and dropped to the ground, with the blood running freely down his face. At his fall the guardsmen took to their heels in one direction and the loungers in the other, while a number of better dressed people, who had watched the scuffle without taking part in it, crowded in to help the lady and to attend to the injured man. Irene Adler, as I will still call her, had hurried up the steps; but she stood at the top with her superb figure outlined against the lights of the hall, looking back into the street.

"Is the poor gentleman much hurt?" she asked.

"He is dead," cried several voices.

"No, no, there's life in him," shouted another. "But he'll be gone before you can get him to hospital."

"He's a brave fellow," said a woman. "They would have had the lady's purse and watch if it hadn't been for him. They were a gang, and a rough one too. Ah, he's breathing now."

"He can't lie in the street. May we bring him in, marm?"

"Surely. Bring him into the sitting-room. There is a comfortable sofa. This way, please!"

Slowly and solemnly he was borne into Briony Lodge, and laid out in the principal room, while I still observed the proceedings from my post by the window. The lamps had been lit, but the blinds had not been drawn, so that I could see Holmes as he lay upon the couch. I do not know whether he was seized with compunction at that moment for the part he was playing, but I know that I never felt more heartily ashamed of myself in my life than when I saw the beautiful creature against whom I was conspiring, or the grace and kindliness with which she waited upon the injured man. And yet it would be the blackest treachery to Holmes to draw back now from the part which he had entrusted to me. I hardened my heart, and took the smoke-rocket from under my ulster. After all, I thought, we are not injuring her. We are but preventing her from injuring another.

Holmes had sat up upon the couch, and I saw him motion like a man who is in need of air. A maid rushed across and threw open the window. At the same instant I saw him raise his hand, and at the signal I tossed my rocket into the room with a cry of "Fire." The word was no sooner out of my mouth than the whole crowd of spectators, well dressed and ill—gentlemen, ostlers, and servant maids—joined in a general shriek of "Fire." Thick clouds of smoke curled through the room and out at the open window. I caught a glimpse of rushing figures, and a moment later the voice of Holmes from within, assuring them that it was a false alarm. Slipping through the shouting crowd I made my way to the corner of the street, and in ten minutes was rejoiced to find my friend's arm in mine, and to get away from the scene of uproar. He walked swiftly and in silence for some few minutes, until we had turned down one of the quiet streets which lead towards the Edgware-road.

"You did it very nicely, Doctor," he remarked. "Nothing could have been better. It is all right."

"You have the photograph!"

"I know where it is."

"And how did you find out?"

"She showed me, as I told you that she would."

"I am still in the dark."

"I do not wish to make a mystery," said he laughing. "The matter was perfectly simple. You, of course, saw that everyone in the street was an accomplice. They were all engaged for the evening."

"I guessed as much."

"Then, when the row broke out, I had a little moist red paint in the palm of my hand. I rushed forward, fell down, clapped my hand to my face, and became a piteous spectacle. It is an old trick."

"That also I could fathom."

"Then they carried me in. She was bound to have me in. What else could she do? And into her sitting-room, which was the very room which I suspected. It lay between that and her bedroom, and I was determined to see which. They laid me on a couch, I motioned for air, they were compelled to open the window, and you had your chance."

"How did that help you?"

"It was all-important. When a woman thinks that her house is on fire, her instinct is at once to rush to the thing which she values most. It is a perfectly overpowering impulse, and I have more than once taken advantage of it. In the case of the Darlington Substitution Scandal it was of use to me, and also in the Arnsworth Castle business. A married woman grabs at her baby—an unmarried one reaches for her jewel box. Now it was clear to me that our lady of to-day had nothing in the house more precious to her than what we are in quest of. She would rush to secure it. The alarm of fire was admirably done. The smoke and shouting were enough to shake nerves of steel. She responded beautifully. The photograph is in a recess behind a sliding panel just above the right bell pull. She was there in an instant, and I caught a glimpse of it as she half drew it out. When I cried out that it was a false alarm, she replaced it, glanced at the rocket, rushed from the room, and I have not seen her since. I rose, and, making my excuses, escaped from the house. I hesitated whether to attempt to secure the photograph at once; but the coachman had come in, and, as he was watching me narrowly, it seemed safer to wait. A little over-precipitance may ruin all."

"And now?" I asked.

"Our quest is practically finished. I shall call with the King to-morrow, and with you, if you care to come with us. We will be shown into the sitting-room to wait for the lady, but it is probable that when she comes she may find neither us nor the photograph. It might be a satisfaction to His Majesty to regain it with his own hands."

"And when will you call?"

"At eight in the morning. She will not be up, so that we shall have a clear field. Besides, we must be prompt, for this marriage may mean a complete change in her life and habits. I must wire to the King without delay."

We had reached Baker-street, and had stopped at the door. He was searching his pockets for the key, when someone passing said:—

"Good-night, Mister Sherlock Holmes."

There were several people on the pavement at the time, but the greeting appeared to come from a slim youth in an ulster who had hurried by.

"I've heard that voice before," said Holmes, staring down the dimly lit street. "Now, I wonder who the deuce that could have been."

III.[edit]

I slept at Baker-street that night, and we were engaged upon our toast and coffee in the morning when the King of Bohemia rushed into the room.

"You have really got it!" he cried, grasping Sherlock Holmes by either shoulder, and looking eagerly into his face.

"Not yet."

"But you have hopes?"

"I have hopes."

"Then, come. I am all impatience to be gone."

"We must have a cab."

"No, my brougham is waiting."

"Then that will simplify matters." We descended, and started off once more for Briony Lodge.

"Irene Adler is married," remarked Holmes.

"Married! When?"

"Yesterday."

"But to whom?"

"To an English lawyer named Norton."

"But she could not love him?"

"I am in hopes that she does."

"And why in hopes?"

"Because it would spare your Majesty all fear of future annoyance. If the lady loves her husband, she does not love your Majesty. If she does not love your Majesty, there is no reason why she should interfere with your Majesty's plan."

"It is true. And yet—! Well! I wish she had been of my own station! What a queen she would have made!" He relapsed into a moody silence which was not broken, until we drew up in Serpentine-avenue.

The door of Briony Lodge was open, and an elderly woman stood upon the steps. She watched us with a sardonic eye as we stepped from the brougham.

"Mr. Sherlock Holmes, I believe?" said she.

"I am Mr. Holmes," answered my companion, looking at her with a questioning and rather startled gaze.

"Indeed! My mistress told me that you were likely to call. She left this morning with her husband, by the 5.15 train from Charing-cross, for the Continent."

"What!" Sherlock Holmes staggered back, white with chagrin and surprise. "Do you mean that she has left England?"

"Never to return."

"And the papers?" asked the King, hoarsely. "All is lost."

"We shall see." He pushed past the servant, and rushed into the drawing-room, followed by the King and myself. The furniture was scattered about in every direction, with dismantled shelves, and open drawers, as if the lady had hurriedly ransacked them before her flight. Holmes rushed at the bell-pull, tore back a small sliding shutter, and, plunging in his hand, pulled out a photograph and a letter. The photograph was of Irene Adler herself in evening dress, the letter was superscribed to "Sherlock Holmes, Esq. To be left till called for." My friend tore it open, and we all three read it together. It was dated at midnight of the preceding night, and ran in this way:—

"My Dear Mr. Sherlock Holmes,—You really did it very well. You took me in completely. Until after the alarm of fire, I had not a suspicion. But then, when I found how I had betrayed myself, I began to think. I had been warned against you months ago. I had been told that, if the King employed an agent, it would certainly be you. And your address had been given me. Yet, with all this, you made me reveal what you wanted to know. Even after I became suspicious, I found it hard to think evil of such a dear, kind old clergyman. But, you know, I have been trained as an actress myself. Male costume is nothing new to me. I often take advantage of the freedom which it gives. I sent John, the coachman, to watch you, ran up stairs, got into my walking clothes, as I call them, and came down just as you departed.

"Well, I followed you to your door, and so made sure that I was really an object of interest to the celebrated Mr. Sherlock Holmes. Then I, rather imprudently, wished you good night, and started for the Temple to see my husband.

"We both thought the best resource was flight, when pursued by so formidable an antagonist; so you will find the nest empty when you call to-morrow. As to the photograph, your client may rest in peace. I love and am loved by a better man than he. The King may do what he will without hindrance from one whom he has cruelly wronged. I keep it only to safeguard myself, and to preserve a weapon which will always secure me from any steps which he might take in the future. I leave a photograph which he might care to possess; and I remain, dear Mr. Sherlock Holmes, very truly yours,
      "Irene Norton, *née* Adler."

"What a woman—oh, what a woman!" cried the King of Bohemia, when we had all three read this epistle. "Did I not tell you how quick and resolute she was? Would she not have made an admirable queen? Is it not a pity that she was not on my level?"

"From what I have seen of the lady, she seems, indeed, to be on a very different level to your Majesty," said Holmes, coldly. "I am sorry that I have not been able to bring your Majesty's business to a more successful conclusion."

"On the contrary, my dear sir," cried the King. "Nothing could be more successful. I know that her word is inviolate. The photograph is now as safe as if it were in the fire."

"I am glad to hear your Majesty say so."

"I am immensely indebted to you. Pray tell me in what way I can reward you. This ring—." He slipped an emerald snake ring from his finger, and held it out upon the palm of his hand.

"Your Majesty has something which I should value even more highly," said Holmes.

"You have but to name it."

"This photograph!"

The King stared at him in amazement.

"Irene's photograph!" he cried. "Certainly, if you wish it."

"I thank your Majesty. Then there is no more to be done in the matter. I have the honour to wish you a very good morning." He bowed, and, turning away without observing the hand which the King had stretched out to him, he set off in my company for his chambers.

And that was how a great scandal threatened to affect the kingdom of Bohemia, and how the best plans of Mr. Sherlock Holmes were beaten by a woman's wit. He used to make merry over the cleverness of women, but I have not heard him do it of late. And when he speaks of Irene Adler, or when he refers to her photograph, it is always under the honourable title of *the* woman.

Sir Arthur Ignatius Conan Doyle (22 May 1859 – 7 July 1930) was a Scottish writer and physician, most noted for creating the fictional detective Sherlock Holmes and writing stories about him which are generally considered milestones in the field of crime fiction.

He is also known for writing the fictional adventures of a second character he invented, Professor Challenger, and for popularizing the mystery of the *Mary Celeste*. He was a prolific writer whose other works include fantasy and science fiction stories, plays, romances, poetry, non-fiction and historical novels.

H. P. Lovecraft, The Shunned House

originally published in Weird Tales, *1937*

A posthumous story of immense power, written by a master of weird fiction—a tale of a revolting horror in the cellar of an old house in New England

1

From even the greatest of horrors irony is seldom absent. Sometimes it enters directly into the composition of the events, while sometimes it relates only to their fortuitous position among persons and places. The latter sort is splendidly exemplified by a case in the ancient city of Providence, where in the late forties Edgar Allan Poe used to sojourn often during his unsuccessful wooing of the gifted poetess, Mrs. Whitman. Poe generally stopped at the Mansion House in Benefit Street—the renamed Golden Ball Inn whose roof has sheltered Washington, Jefferson, and Lafayette—and his favorite walk led northward along the same street to Mrs. Whitman's home and the neighboring hillside churchyard of St. John's, whose hidden expanse of Eighteenth Century gravestones had for him a peculiar fascination.

Now the irony is this. In this walk, so many times repeated, the world's greatest master of the terrible and the bizarre was obliged to pass a particular house on the eastern side of the street; a dingy, antiquated structure perched on the abruptly rising side hill, with a great unkempt yard dating from a time when the region was partly open country. It does not appear that he ever wrote or spoke of it, nor is there any evidence that he even noticed it. And yet that house, to the two persons in possession of certain information, equals or outranks in horror the wildest fantasy of the genius who so often passed it unknowingly, and stands starkly leering as a symbol of all that is unutterably hideous.

The house was—and for that matter still is—of a kind to attract the attention of the curious. Originally a farm or semi-farm building, it followed the average New England colonial lines of the middle Eighteenth Century—the prosperous peaked-roof sort, with two stories and dormerless attic, and with the Georgian doorway and interior panelling dictated by the progress of taste at that time. It faced south, with one gable end buried to the lower windows in the eastward rising hill, and the other exposed to the foundations toward the street. Its construction, over a century and a half ago, had followed the grading and straightening of the road in that especial vicinity; for Benefit Street—at first called Back Street—was laid out as a lane winding amongst the graveyards of the first settlers, and straightened only when the removal of the bodies to the North Burial Ground made it decently possible to cut through the old family plots.

At the start, the western wall had lain some twenty feet up a precipitous lawn from the roadway; but a widening of the street at about the time of the Revolution sheared off most of the intervening space, exposing the foundations so that a brick basement wall had to be made, giving the deep cellar a street frontage with door and one window above ground, close to the new line of public travel. When the sidewalk was laid out a century ago the last of the intervening space was removed; and Poe in his walks must have seen only a sheer ascent of dull gray brick flush with the sidewalk and surmounted at a height of ten feet by the antique shingled bulk of the house proper.

"That awful door in Benefit Street which I had left ajar."

The farm-like ground extended back very deeply up the hill, almost to Wheaton Street. The space south of the house, abutting on Benefit Street, was of course greatly above the existing sidewalk level, forming a terrace bounded by a high bank wall of damp, mossy stone pierced by a steep flight of narrow steps which led inward between canyon-like surfaces to the upper region of mangy lawn, rheumy brick walks, and neglected gardens whose dismantled cement urns, rusted kettles fallen from tripods of knotty sticks, and similar paraphernalia set off the weather-beaten front door with its broken fanlight, rotting Ionic pilasters, and wormy triangular pediment.

What I heard in my youth about the shunned house was merely that people died there in alarmingly great numbers. That, I was told, was why the original owners had moved out some twenty years after building the place. It was plainly unhealthy, perhaps because of the dampness and fungous growths in the cellar, the general sickish smell, the drafts of the hallways, or the quality of the well and pump water. These things were bad enough, and these were all that gained belief among the persons whom I knew. Only the notebooks of my antiquarian uncle, Doctor Elihu Whipple, revealed to me at length the darker, vaguer surmises which formed an undercurrent of folklore among old-time servants and humble folk; surmises which never travelled far, and which were largely forgotten when Providence grew to be a metropolis with a shifting modern population.

The general fact is, that the house was never regarded by the solid part of the community as in any real sense "haunted." There were no widespread tales of rattling chains, cold currents of air, extinguished lights, or faces at the window. Extremists sometimes said the house was "unlucky," but that is as far as even they went. What was really beyond dispute is that a frightful proportion of persons died there; or more accurately, *had* died there, since after some peculiar happenings over sixty years ago the building had become deserted through the sheer impossibility of renting it. These persons were not all cut off suddenly by any one cause; rather did it seem that their vitality was insidiously sapped, so that each one died the sooner from whatever tendency to weakness he may have naturally had. And those who did not die displayed in varying degree a type of anemia or consumption, and sometimes a decline of the mental faculties, which spoke ill for the salubriousness of the building. Neighboring houses, it must be added, seemed entirely free from the noxious quality.

This much I knew before my insistent questioning led my uncle to show me the notes which finally embarked us both on our hideous investigation. In my childhood the shunned house was vacant, with barren, gnarled and terrible old trees, long, queerly pale grass and nightmarishly misshapen weeds in the high terraced yard where birds never lingered. We boys used to overrun the place, and I can still recall my youthful terror not only at the morbid strangeness of this sinister vegetation, but at the eldritch atmosphere and odor of the dilapidated house, whose unlocked front door was often entered in quest of shudders. The small-paned windows were largely broken, and a nameless air of desolation hung round the precarious panelling, shaky interior shutters, peeling wall-paper, falling plaster, rickety staircases, and such fragments of battered furniture as still remained. The dust and cobwebs added their touch of the fearful; and brave indeed was the boy who would voluntarily ascend the ladder to the attic, a vast raftered length lighted only by small blinking windows in the gable ends, and filled with a massed wreckage of chests, chairs, and spinning-wheels which infinite years of deposit had shrouded and festooned into monstrous and hellish shapes.

But after all, the attic was not the most terrible part of the house. It was the dank, humid cellar which somehow exerted the strongest repulsion on us, even though it was wholly above ground on the street side, with only a thin door and window-pierced brick wall to separate it from the busy sidewalk. We scarcely knew whether to haunt it in spectral fascination, or to shun it for the sake of our souls and our sanity. For one thing, the bad odor of the house was strongest there; and for another thing, we did not like the white fungous growths which occasionally sprang up in rainy summer weather from the hard earth floor. Those fungi, grotesquely like the vegetation in the yard outside, were truly horrible in their outlines; detestable parodies of toadstools and Indian-pipes, whose like we had never seen in any other situation. They rotted quickly, and at one stage became slightly phosphorescent; so that nocturnal passers-by sometimes spoke of witch-fires glowing behind the broken panes of the fetor-spreading windows.

We never—even in our wildest Halloween moods—visited this cellar by night, but in some of our daytime visits could detect the phosphorescence, especially when the day was dark and wet. There was also a subtler thing we often thought we detected—a very strange thing which was, however, merely suggestive at most. I refer to a sort of cloudy whitish pattern on the dirt floor—a vague, shifting deposit of mold or niter which we sometimes thought we could trace amidst the sparse fungous growths near the huge fireplace of the basement kitchen. Once in a while it struck us that this patch bore an uncanny resemblance to a doubled-up human figure, though generally no such kinship existed, and often there was no whitish deposit whatever.

On a certain rainy afternoon when this illusion seemed phenomenally strong, and when, in addition, I had fancied I glimpsed a kind of thin, yellowish, shimmering exhalation rising from the nitrous pattern toward the yawning fireplace, I spoke to my uncle about the matter. He smiled at this odd conceit, but it seemed that his smile was tinged with reminiscence. Later I heard that a similar notion entered into some of the wild ancient tales of the common folk—a notion likewise alluding to ghoulish, wolfish shapes taken by smoke from the great chimney, and queer contours assumed by certain of the sinuous tree-roots that thrust their way into the cellar through the loose foundation-stones.

2

Not till my adult years did my uncle set before me the notes and data which he had collected concerning the shunned house. Doctor Whipple was a sane, conservative physician of the old school, and for all his interest in the place was not eager to encourage young thoughts toward the abnormal. His own view, postulating simply a building and location of markedly unsanitary qualities, had nothing to do with abnormality; but he realized that the very picturesqueness which aroused his own interest would in a boy's fanciful mind take on all manner of gruesome imaginative associations.

The doctor was a bachelor; a white-haired, clean-shaven, old-fashioned gentleman, and a local historian of note, who had often broken a lance with such controversial guardians of tradition as Sidney S. Rider and Thomas W. Bicknell. He lived with one man-servant in a Georgian homestead with knocker and iron-railed steps, balanced eerily on the steep ascent of North Court Street beside the ancient brick court and colony house where his grandfather—a cousin of that celebrated privateersman, Captain Whipple, who burnt His Majesty's armed schooner *Gaspee* in 1772—had voted in the legislature on May 4, 1776, for the independence of the Rhode Island Colony. Around him in the damp, low-ceiled library with the musty white panelling, heavy carved overmantel and small-paned, vine-shaded windows, were the relics and records of his ancient family, among which were many dubious allusions to the shunned house in Benefit Street. That pest spot lies not far distant—for Benefit runs ledgewise just above the court house along the precipitous hill up which the first settlement climbed.

When, in the end, my insistent pestering and maturing years evoked from my uncle the hoarded lore I sought, there lay before me a strange enough chronicle. Long-winded, statistical, and drearily genealogical as some of the matter was, there ran through it a continuous thread of brooding, tenacious horror and preternatural malevolence which impressed me even more than it had impressed the good doctor. Separate events fitted together uncannily, and seemingly irrelevant details held mines of hideous possibilities. A new and burning curiosity grew in me, compared to which my boyish curiosity was feeble and inchoate.

The first revelation led to an exhaustive research, and finally to that shuddering quest which proved so disastrous to myself and mine. For at the last my uncle insisted on joining the search I had commenced, and after a certain night in that house he did not come away with me. I am lonely without that gentle soul whose long years were filled only with honor, virtue, good taste, benevolence, and learning. I have reared a marble urn to his memory in St. John's churchyard—the place that Poe loved—the hidden grove of giant willows on the hill, where tombs and headstones huddle quietly between the hoary bulk of the church and the houses and bank walls of Benefit Street.

The history of the house, opening amidst a maze of dates, revealed no trace of the sinister either about its construction or about the prosperous and honorable family who built it. Yet from the first a taint of calamity, soon increased to boding significance, was apparent. My uncle's carefully compiled record began with the building of the structure in 1763, and followed the theme with an unusual amount of detail. The shunned house, it seems, was first inhabited by William Harris and his wife Rhoby Dexter, with their children, Elkanah, born in 1755, Abigail, born in 1757, William, Jr., born in 1759, and Ruth, born in 1761. Harris was a substantial merchant and seaman in the West India trade, connected with the firm of Obadiah Brown and his nephews. After Brown's death in 1761, the new firm of Nicholas Brown & Company made him master of the brig *Prudence*, Providence-built, of 120 tons, thus enabling him to erect the new homestead he had desired ever since his marriage.

The site he had chosen—a recently straightened part of the new and fashionable Back Street, which ran along the side of the hill above crowded Cheapside—was all that could be wished, and the building did justice to the location. It was the best that moderate means could afford, and Harris hastened to move in before the birth of a fifth child which the family expected. That child, a boy, came in December; but was still-born. Nor was any child to be born alive in that house for a century and a half.

The next April, sickness occurred among the children, and Abigail and Ruth died before the month was over. Doctor Job Ives diagnosed the trouble as some infantile fever, though others declared it was more of a mere wasting-away or decline. It seemed, in any event, to be contagious; for Hannah Bowen, one of the two servants, died of it in the following June. Eli Lideason, the other servant, constantly complained of weakness; and would have returned to his father's farm in Rehoboth but for a sudden attachment for Mehitabel Pierce, who was hired to succeed Hannah. He died the next year—a sad year indeed, since it marked the death of William Harris himself, enfeebled as he was by the climate of Martinique, where his occupation had kept him for considerable periods during the preceding decade.

The widowed Rhoby Harris never recovered from the shock of her husband's death, and the passing of her first-born Elkanah two years later was the final blow to her reason. In 1768 she fell victim to a mild form of insanity, and was thereafter confined to the upper part of the house; her elder maiden sister, Mercy Dexter, having moved in to take charge of the family. Mercy was a plain, raw-boned woman of great strength; but her health visibly declined from the time of her advent. She was greatly devoted to her unfortunate sister, and had an especial affection for her only surviving nephew William, who from a sturdy infant had become a sickly, spindling lad. In this year the servant Mehitabel died, and the other servant, Preserved Smith, left without coherent explanation—or at least, with only some wild tales and a complaint that he disliked the smell of the place. For a time Mercy could secure no more help, since the seven deaths and case of madness, all occurring within five years' space, had begun to set in motion the body of fireside rumor which later became so bizarre. Ultimately, however, she obtained new servants from out of town; Ann White, a morose woman from that part of North Kingstown now set off as the township of Exeter, and a capable Boston man named Zenas Low.

It was Ann White who first gave definite shape to the sinister idle talk. Mercy should have known better than to hire anyone from the Nooseneck Hill country, for that remote bit of backwoods was then, as now, a seat of the most uncomfortable superstitions. As lately as 1892 an Exeter community exhumed a dead body and ceremoniously burnt its heart in order to prevent certain alleged visitations injurious to the public health and peace, and one may imagine the point of view of the same section in 1768. Ann's tongue was perniciously active, and within a few months Mercy discharged her, filling her place with a faithful and amiable Amazon from Newport, Maria Robbins.

Meanwhile poor Rhoby Harris, in her madness, gave voice to dreams and imaginings of the most hideous sort. At times her screams became insupportable, and for long periods she would utter shrieking horrors which necessitated her son's temporary residence with his cousin, Peleg Harris, in Presbyterian Lane near the new college building. The boy would seem to improve after these visits, and had Mercy been as wise as she was well-meaning, she would have let him live permanently with Peleg. Just what Mrs. Harris cried out in her fits of violence, tradition hesitates to say; or rather, presents such extravagant accounts that they nullify themselves through sheer absurdity. Certainly it sounds absurd to hear that a woman educated only in the rudiments of French often shouted for hours in a coarse and idiomatic form of that language, or that the same person, alone and guarded, complained wildly of a staring thing which bit and chewed at her. In 1772 the servant Zenas died, and when Mrs. Harris heard of it she laughed with a shocking delight utterly foreign to her. The next year she herself died, and was laid to rest in the North Burial Ground beside her husband.

Upon the outbreak of trouble with Great Britain in 1775, William Harris, despite his scant sixteen years and feeble constitution, managed to enlist in the Army of Observation under General Greene; and from that time on enjoyed a steady rise in health and prestige. In 1780, as a captain in the Rhode Island forces in New Jersey under Colonel Angell, he met and married Phebe Hetfield of Elizabethtown, whom he brought to Providence upon his honorable discharge in the following year.

The young soldier's return was not a thing of unmitigated happiness. The house, it is true, was still in good condition; and the street had been widened and changed in name from Back Street to Benefit Street. But Mercy Dexter's once robust frame had undergone a sad and curious decay, so that she was now a stooped and pathetic figure with hollow voice and disconcerting pallor—qualities shared to a singular degree by the one remaining servant Maria. In the autumn of 1782 Phebe Harris gave birth to a still-born daughter, and on the fifteenth of the next May Mercy Dexter took leave of a useful, austere, and virtuous life.

William Harris, at last thoroughly convinced of the radically unhealthful nature of his abode, now took steps toward quitting it and closing it for ever. Securing temporary quarters for himself and his wife at the newly opened Golden Ball Inn, he arranged for the building of a new and finer house in Westminster Street, in the growing part of the town across the Great Bridge. There, in 1785, his son Dutee was born; and there the family dwelt till the encroachments of commerce drove them back across the river and over the hill to Angell Street, in the newer East Side residence district, where the late Archer Harris built his sumptuous but hideous French-roofed mansion in 1876. William and Phebe both succumbed to the yellow fever epidemic of 1797, but Dutee was brought up by his cousin Rathbone Harris, Peleg's son.

Rathbone was a practical man, and rented the Benefit Street house despite William's wish to keep it vacant. He considered it an obligation to his ward to make the most of all the boy's property, nor did he concern himself with the deaths and illnesses which caused so many changes of tenants, or the steadily growing aversion with which the house was generally regarded. It is likely that he felt only vexation when, in 1804, the town council ordered him to fumigate the place with sulfur, tar, and gum camphor on account of the much-discussed deaths of four persons, presumably caused by the then diminishing fever epidemic. They said the place had a febrile smell.

Dutee himself thought little of the house, for he grew up to be a privateersman, and served with distinction on the *Vigilant* under Captain Cahoone in the War of 1812. He returned unharmed, married in 1814, and became a father on that memorable night of September 23, 1815, when a great gale drove the waters of the bay over half the town, and floated a tall sloop well up Westminster Street so that its masts almost tapped the Harris windows in symbolic affirmation that the new boy, Welcome, was a seaman's son.

Welcome did not survive his father, but lived to perish gloriously at Fredericksburg in 1862. Neither he nor his son Archer knew of the shunned house as other than a nuisance almost impossible to rent—perhaps on account of the mustiness and sickly odor of unkempt old age. Indeed, it never was rented after a series of deaths culminating in 1861, which the excitement of the war tended to throw into obscurity. Carrington Harris, last of the male line, knew it only as a deserted and somewhat picturesque center of legend until I told him my experience. He had meant to tear it down and build an apartment house on the site, but after my account decided to let it stand, install plumbing, and rent it. Nor has he yet had any difficulty in obtaining tenants. The horror has gone.

3

It may well be imagined how powerfully I was affected by the annals of the Harrises. In this continuous record there seemed to me to brood a persistent evil beyond anything in nature as I had known it; an evil clearly connected with the house and not with the family. This impression was confirmed by my uncle's less systematic array of miscellaneous data—legends transcribed from servant gossip, cuttings from the papers, copies of death certificates by fellow-physicians, and the like. All of this material I cannot hope to give, for my uncle was a tireless antiquarian and very deeply interested in the shunned house; but I may refer to several dominant points which earn notice by their recurrence through many reports from diverse sources. For example, the servant gossip was practically unanimous in attributing to the fungous and malodorous *cellar* of the house a vast supremacy in evil influence. There had been servants—Ann White especially—who would not use the cellar kitchen, and at least three well-defined legends bore upon the queer quasi-human or diabolic outlines assumed by tree-roots and patches of mold in that region. These latter narratives interested me profoundly, on account of what I had seen in my boyhood, but I felt that most of the significance had in each case been largely obscured by additions from the common stock of local ghost lore.

Ann White, with her Exeter superstition, had promulgated the most extravagant and at the same time most consistent tale; alleging that there must lie buried beneath the house one of those vampires—the dead who retain their bodily form and live on the blood or breath of the living—whose hideous legions send their preying shapes or spirits abroad by night. To destroy a vampire one must, the grandmothers say, exhume it and burn its heart, or at least drive a stake through that organ; and Ann's dogged insistence on a search under the cellar had been prominent in bringing about her discharge.

Her tales, however, commanded a wide audience, and were the more readily accepted because the house indeed stood on land once used for burial purposes. To me their interest depended less on this circumstance than on the peculiarly appropriate way in which they dovetailed with certain other things—the complaint of the departing servant Preserved Smith, who had preceded Ann and never heard of her, that something "sucked his breath" at night; the death-certificates of the fever victims of 1804, issued by Doctor Chad Hopkins, and showing the four deceased persons all unaccountably lacking in blood; and the obscure passages of poor Rhoby Harris's ravings, where she complained of the sharp teeth of a glassy-eyed, half-visible presence.

Free from unwarranted superstition though I am, these things produced in me an odd sensation, which was intensified by a pair of widely separated newspaper cuttings relating to deaths in the shunned house—one from the *Providence Gazette and Country-Journal* of April 12, 1815, and the other from the *Daily Transcript and Chronicle* of October 27, 1845—each of which detailed an appallingly grisly circumstance whose duplication was remarkable. It seems that in both instances the dying person, in 1815 a gentle old lady named Stafford and in 1845 a schoolteacher of middle age named Eleazar Durfee, became transfigured in a horrible way, glaring glassily and attempting to bite the throat of the attending physician. Even more puzzling, though, was the final case which put an end to the renting of the house—a series of anemia deaths preceded by progressive madnesses wherein the patient would craftily attempt the lives of his relatives by incisions in the neck or wrist.

This was in 1860 and 1861, when my uncle had just begun his medical practise; and before leaving for the front he heard much of it from his elder professional colleagues. The really inexplicable thing was the way in which the victims—ignorant people, for the ill-smelling and widely shunned house could now be rented to no others—would babble maledictions in French, a language they could not possibly have studied to any extent. It made one think of poor Rhoby Harris nearly a century before, and so moved my uncle that he commenced collecting historical data on the house after listening, some time subsequent to his return from the war, to the first-hand account of Doctors Chase and Whitmarsh. Indeed, I could see that my uncle had thought deeply on the subject, and that he was glad of my own interest—an open-minded and sympathetic interest which enabled him to discuss with me matters at which others would merely have laughed. His fancy had not gone so far as mine, but he felt that the place was rare in its imaginative potentialities, and worthy of note as an inspiration in the field of the grotesque and macabre.

For my part, I was disposed to take the whole subject with profound seriousness, and began at once not only to review the evidence, but to accumulate as much more as I could. I talked with the elderly Archer Harris, then owner of the house, many times before his death in 1916; and obtained from him and his still surviving maiden sister Alice an authentic corroboration of all the family data my uncle had collected. When, however, I asked them what connection with France or its language the house could have, they confessed themselves as frankly baffled and ignorant as I. Archer knew nothing, and all that Miss Harris could say was that an old allusion her grandfather, Dutee Harris, had heard of might have shed a little light. The old seaman, who had survived his son Welcome's death in battle by two years, had not himself known the legend, but recalled that his earliest nurse, the ancient Maria Robbins, seemed darkly aware of something that might have lent a weird significance to the French raving of Rhoby Harris, which she had so often heard during the last days of that hapless woman. Maria had been at the shunned house from 1769 till the removal of the family in 1783, and had seen Mercy Dexter die. Once she hinted to the child Dutee of a somewhat peculiar circumstance in Mercy's last moments, but he had soon forgotten all about it save that it was something peculiar. The granddaughter, moreover, recalled even this much with difficulty. She and her brother were not so much interested in the house as was Archer's son Carrington, the present owner, with whom I talked after my experience.

Having exhausted the Harris family of all the information it could furnish, I turned my attention to early town records and deeds with a zeal more penetrating than that which my uncle had occasionally shown in the same work. What I wished was a comprehensive history of the site from its very settlement in 1636—or even before, if any Narragansett Indian legend could be unearthed to supply the data. I found, at the start, that the land had been part of the long strip of home lot granted originally to John Throckmorton; one of many similar strips beginning at the Town Street beside the river and extending up over the hill to a line roughly corresponding with the modern Hope Street. The Throckmorton lot had later, of course, been much subdivided; and I became very assiduous in tracing that section through which Back or Benefit Street was later run. It had, as rumor indeed said, been the Throckmorton graveyard; but as I examined the records more carefully, I found that the graves had all been transferred at an early date to the North Burial Ground on the Pawtucket West Road.

Then suddenly I came—by a rare piece of chance, since it was not in the main body of records and might easily have been missed—upon something which aroused my keenest eagerness, fitting in as it did with several of the queerest phases of the affair. It was the record of a lease, in 1697, of a small tract of ground to an Etienne Roulet and wife. At last the French element had appeared—that, and another deeper element of horror which the name conjured up from the darkest recesses of my weird and heterogeneous reading—and I feverishly studied the platting of the locality as it had been before the cutting through and partial straightening of Back Street between 1747 and 1758. I found what I had half expected, that where the shunned house now stood the Roulets had laid out their graveyard behind a one-story and attic cottage, and that no record of any transfer of graves existed. The document, indeed, ended in much confusion; and I was forced to ransack both the Rhode Island Historical Society and Shepley Library before I could find a local door which the name of Etienne Roulet would unlock. In the end I did find something; something of such vague but monstrous import that I set about at once to examine the cellar of the shunned house itself with a new and excited minuteness.

The Roulets, it seemed, had come in 1696 from East Greenwich, down the west shore of Narragansett Bay. They were Huguenots from Caude, and had encountered much opposition before the Providence selectmen allowed them to settle in the town. Unpopularity had dogged them in East Greenwich, whither they had come in 1686, after the revocation of the Edict of Nantes, and rumor said that the cause of dislike extended beyond mere racial and national prejudice, or the land disputes which involved other French settlers with the English in rivalries which not even Governor Andros could quell. But their ardent Protestantism—too ardent, some whispered—and their evident distress when virtually driven from the village down the bay, had moved the sympathy of the town fathers. Here the strangers had been granted a haven; and the swarthy Etienne Roulet, less apt at agriculture than at reading queer books and drawing queer diagrams, was given a clerical post in the warehouse at Pardon Tillinghast's wharf, far south in Town Street. There had, however, been a riot of some sort later on—perhaps forty years later, after old Roulet's death—and no one seemed to hear of the family after that.

For a century and more, it appeared, the Roulets had been well remembered and frequently discussed as vivid incidents in the quiet life of a New England seaport. Etienne's son Paul, a surly fellow whose erratic conduct had probably provoked the riot which wiped out the family, was particularly a source of speculation; and though Providence never shared the witchcraft panics of her Puritan neighbors, it was freely intimated by old wives that his prayers were neither uttered at the proper time nor directed toward the proper object. All this had undoubtedly formed the basis of the legend known by old Maria Robbins. What relation it had to the French ravings of Rhoby Harris and other inhabitants of the shunned house, imagination or future discovery alone could determine. I wondered how many of those who had known the legends realized that additional link with the terrible which my wider reading had given me; that ominous item in the annals of morbid horror which tells of the creature *Jacques Roulet, of Caude*, who in 1598 was condemned to death as a demoniac but afterward saved from the stake by the Paris parliament and shut in a madhouse. He had been found covered with blood and shreds of flesh in a wood, shortly after the killing and rending of a boy by a pair of wolves. One wolf was seen to lope away unhurt. Surely a pretty hearthside tale, with a queer significance as to name and place; but I decided that the Providence gossips could not have generally known of it. Had they known, the coincidence of names would have brought some drastic and frightened action—indeed, might not its limited whispering have precipitated the final riot which erased the Roulets from the town?

I now visited the accursed place with increased frequency; studying the unwholesome vegetation of the garden, examining all the walls of the building, and poring over every inch of the earthen cellar floor. Finally, with Carrington Harris's permission, I fitted a key to the disused door opening from the cellar directly upon Benefit Street, preferring to have a more immediate access to the outside world than the dark stairs, ground-floor hall, and front door could give. There, where morbidity lurked most thickly, I searched and poked during long afternoons when the sunlight filtered in through the cobwebbed above-ground windows, and a sense of security glowed from the unlocked door which placed me only a few feet from the placid sidewalk outside. Nothing new rewarded my efforts—only the same depressing mustiness and faint suggestions of noxious odors and nitrous outlines on the floor—and I fancy that many pedestrians must have watched me curiously through the broken panes.

At length, upon a suggestion of my uncle's, I decided to try the spot nocturnally; and one stormy midnight ran the beams of an electric torch over the moldy floor with its uncanny shapes and distorted, half-phosphorescent fungi. The place had dispirited me curiously that evening, and I was almost prepared when I saw—or thought I saw—amidst the whitish deposits a particularly sharp definition of the "huddled form" I had suspected from boyhood. Its clearness was astonishing and unprecedented—and as I watched I seemed to see again the thin, yellowish, shimmering exhalation which had startled me on that rainy afternoon so many years before.

Above the anthropomorphic patch of mold by the fireplace it rose; a subtle, sickish, almost luminous vapor which as it hung trembling in the dampness seemed to develop vague and shocking suggestions of form, gradually trailing off into nebulous decay and passing up into the blackness of the great chimney with a fetor in its wake. It was truly horrible, and the more so to me because of what I knew of the spot. Refusing to flee, I watched it fade—and as I watched I felt that it was in turn watching me greedily with eyes more imaginable than visible. When I told my uncle about it he was greatly aroused; and after a tense hour of reflection, arrived at a definite and drastic decision. Weighing in his mind the importance of the matter, and the significance of our relation to it, he insisted that we both test—and if possible destroy—the horror of the house by a joint night or nights of aggressive vigil in that musty and fungus-cursed cellar.

4

On Wednesday, June 25, 1919, after a proper notification of Carrington Harris which did not include surmises as to what we expected to find, my uncle and I conveyed to the shunned house two camp chairs and a folding camp cot, together with some scientific mechanism of greater weight and intricacy. These we placed in the cellar during the day, screening the windows with paper and planning to return in the evening for our first vigil. We had locked the door from the cellar to the ground floor; and having a key to the outside cellar door, were prepared to leave our expensive and delicate apparatus—which we had obtained secretly and at great cost—as many days as our vigils might be protracted. It was our design to sit up together till very late, and then watch singly till dawn in two-hour stretches, myself first and then my companion; the inactive member resting on the cot.

The natural leadership with which my uncle procured the instruments from the laboratories of Brown University and the Cranston Street Armory, and instinctively assumed direction of our venture, was a marvelous commentary on the potential vitality and resilience of a man of eighty-one. Elihu Whipple had lived according to the hygienic laws he had preached as a physician, and but for what happened later would be here in full vigor today. Only two persons suspected what did happen—Carrington Harris and myself. I had to tell Harris because he owned the house and deserved to know what had gone out of it. Then too, we had spoken to him in advance of our quest; and I felt after my uncle's going that he would understand and assist me in some vitally necessary public explanations. He turned very pale, but agreed to help me, and decided that it would now be safe to rent the house.

To declare that we were not nervous on that rainy night of watching would be an exaggeration both gross and ridiculous. We were not, as I have said, in any sense childishly superstitious, but scientific study and reflection had taught us that the known universe of three dimensions embraces the merest fraction of the whole cosmos of substance and energy. In this case an overwhelming preponderance of evidence from numerous authentic sources pointed to the tenacious existence of certain forces of great power and, so far as the human point of view is concerned, exceptional malignancy. To say that we actually believed in vampires or werewolves would be a carelessly inclusive statement. Rather must it be said that we were not prepared to deny the possibility of certain unfamiliar and unclassified modifications of vital force and attenuated matter; existing very infrequently in three-dimensional space because of its more intimate connection with other spatial units, yet close enough to the boundary of our own to furnish us occasional manifestations which we, for lack of a proper vantage-point, may never hope to understand.

In short, it seemed to my uncle and me that an incontrovertible array of facts pointed to some lingering influence in the shunned house; traceable to one or another of the ill-favored French settlers of two centuries before, and still operative through rare and unknown laws of atomic and electronic motion. That the family of Roulet had possessed an abnormal affinity for outer circles of entity—dark spheres which for normal folk hold only repulsion and terror—their recorded history seemed to prove. Had not, then, the riots of those bygone seventeen-thirties set moving certain kinetic patterns in the morbid brain of one or more of them—notably the sinister Paul Roulet—which obscurely survived the bodies murdered and buried by the mob, and continued to function in some multiple-dimensioned space along the original lines of force determined by a frantic hatred of the encroaching community?

Such a thing was surely not a physical or biochemical impossibility in the light of a newer science which includes the theories of relativity and intra-atomic action. One might easily imagine an alien nucleus of substance or energy, formless or otherwise, kept alive by imperceptible or immaterial subtractions from the life-force or bodily tissue and fluids of other and more palpably living things into which it penetrates and with whose fabric it sometimes completely merges itself. It might be actively hostile, or it might be dictated merely by blind motives of self-preservation. In any case such a monster must of necessity be in our scheme of things an anomaly and an intruder, whose extirpation forms a primary duty with every man not an enemy to the world's life, health, and sanity.

What baffled us was our utter ignorance of the aspect in which we might encounter the thing. No sane person had ever seen it, and few had ever felt it definitely. It might be pure energy—a form ethereal and outside the realm of substance—or it might be partly material; some unknown and equivocal mass of plasticity, capable of changing at will to nebulous approximations of the solid, liquid, gaseous, or tenuously unparticled states. The anthropomorphic patch of mold on the floor, the form of the yellowish vapor, and the curvature of the tree-roots in some of the old tales, all argued at least a remote and reminiscent connection with the human shape; but how representative or permanent that similarity might be, none could say with any kind of certainty.

We had devised two weapons to fight it; a large and specially fitted Crookes tube operated by powerful storage batteries and provided with peculiar screens and reflectors, in case it proved intangible and opposable only by vigorously destructive ether radiations, and a pair of military flame-throwers of the sort used in the World War, in case it proved partly material and susceptible of mechanical destruction—for like the superstitious Exeter rustics, we were prepared to burn the thing's heart out if heart existed to burn. All this aggressive mechanism we set in the cellar in positions carefully arranged with reference to the cot and chairs, and to the spot before the fireplace where the mold had taken strange shapes. That suggestive patch, by the way, was only faintly visible when we placed our furniture and instruments, and when we returned that evening for the actual vigil. For a moment I half doubted that I had ever seen it in the more definitely limned form—but then I thought of the legends.

Our cellar vigil began at ten p. m., daylight saving time, and as it continued we found no promise of pertinent developments. A weak, filtered glow from the rain-harassed street-lamps outside, and a feeble phosphorescence from the detestable fungi within, showed the dripping stone of the walls, from which all traces of whitewash had vanished; the dank, fetid and mildew-tainted hard earth floor with its obscene fungi; the rotting remains of what had been stools, chairs, and tables, and other more shapeless furniture; the heavy planks and massive beams of the ground floor overhead; the decrepit plank door leading to bins and chambers beneath other parts of the house; the crumbling stone staircase with ruined wooden hand-rail; and the crude and cavernous fireplace of blackened brick where rusted iron fragments revealed the past presence of hooks, andirons, spit, crane, and a door to the Dutch oven—these things, and our austere cot and camp chairs, and the heavy and intricate destructive machinery we had brought.

We had, as in my own former explorations, left the door to the street unlocked; so that a direct and practical path of escape might lie open in case of manifestations beyond our power to deal with. It was our idea that our continued nocturnal presence would call forth whatever malign entity lurked there; and that being prepared, we could dispose of the thing with one or the other of our provided means as soon as we had recognized and observed it sufficiently. How long it might require to evoke and extinguish the thing, we had no notion. It occurred to us, too, that our venture was far from safe; for in what strength the thing might appear no one could tell. But we deemed the game worth the hazard, and embarked on it alone and unhesitatingly; conscious that the seeking of outside aid would only expose us to ridicule and perhaps defeat our entire purpose. Such was our frame of mind as we talked—far into the night, till my uncle's growing drowsiness made me remind him to lie down for his two-hour sleep.

Something like fear chilled me as I sat there in the small hours alone—I say alone, for one who sits by a sleeper is indeed alone; perhaps more alone than he can realize. My uncle breathed heavily, his deep inhalations and exhalations accompanied by the rain outside, and punctuated by another nerve-racking sound of distant dripping water within—for the house was repulsively damp even in dry weather, and in this storm positively swamp-like. I studied the loose, antique masonry of the walls in the fungus-light and the feeble rays which stole in from the street through the screened window; and once, when the noisome atmosphere of the place seemed about to sicken me, I opened the door and looked up and down the street, feasting my eyes on familiar sights and my nostrils on wholesome air. Still nothing occurred to reward my watching; and I yawned repeatedly, fatigue getting the better of apprehension.

Then the stirring of my uncle in his sleep attracted my notice. He had turned restlessly on the cot several times during the latter half of the first hour, but now he was breathing with unusual irregularity, occasionally heaving a sigh which held more than a few of the qualities of a choking moan.

I turned my electric flashlight on him and found his face averted; so rising and crossing to the other side of the cot, I again flashed the light to see if he seemed in any pain. What I saw unnerved me most surprisingly, considering its relative triviality. It must have been merely the association of any odd circumstance with the sinister nature of our location and mission, for surely the circumstance was not in itself frightful or unnatural. It was merely that my uncle's facial expression, disturbed no doubt by the strange dreams which our situation prompted, betrayed considerable agitation, and seemed not at all characteristic of him. His habitual expression was one of kindly and well-bred calm, whereas now a variety of emotions seemed struggling within him. I think, on the whole, that it was this *variety* which chiefly disturbed me. My uncle, as he gasped and tossed in increasing perturbation and with eyes that had now started open, seemed not one but many men, and suggested a curious quality of alienage from himself.

All at once he commenced to mutter, and I did not like the look of his mouth and teeth as he spoke. The words were at first indistinguishable, and then—with a tremendous start—I recognized something about them which filled me with icy fear till I recalled the breadth of my uncle's education and the interminable translations he had made from anthropological and antiquarian articles in the *Revue des Deux Mondes*. For the venerable Elihu Whipple was muttering *in French*, and the few phrases I could distinguish seemed connected with the darkest myths he had ever adapted from the famous Paris magazine.

Suddenly a perspiration broke out on the sleeper's forehead, and he leaped abruptly up, half awake. The jumble of French changed to a cry in English, and the hoarse voice shouted excitedly, "My breath, my breath!" Then the awakening became complete, and with a subsidence of facial expression to the normal state my uncle seized my hand and began to relate a dream whose nucleus of significance I could only surmise with a kind of awe.

He had, he said, floated off from a very ordinary series of dream-pictures into a scene whose strangeness was related to nothing he had ever read. It was of this world, and yet not of it—a shadowy geometrical confusion in which could be seen elements of familiar things in most unfamiliar and perturbing combinations. There was a suggestion of queerly disordered pictures superimposed one upon another; an arrangement in which the essentials of time as well as of space seemed dissolved and mixed in the most illogical fashion. In this kaleidoscopic vortex of phantasmal images were occasional snap-shots, if one might use the term, of singular clearness but unaccountable heterogeneity.

Once my uncle thought he lay in a carelessly dug open pit, with a crowd of angry faces framed by straggling locks and three-cornered hats frowning down on him. Again he seemed to be in the interior of a house—an old house, apparently—but the details and inhabitants were constantly changing, and he could never be certain of the faces or the furniture, or even of the room itself, since doors and windows seemed in just as great a state of flux as the presumably more mobile objects. It was queer—damnably queer—and my uncle spoke almost sheepishly, as if half expecting not to be believed, when he declared that of the strange faces many had unmistakably borne the features of the Harris family. And all the while there was a personal sensation of choking, as if some pervasive presence had spread itself through his body and sought to possess itself of his vital processes.

I shuddered at the thought of those vital processes, worn as they were by eighty-one years of continuous functioning, in conflict with unknown forces of which the youngest and strongest system might well be afraid; but in another moment reflected that dreams are only dreams, and that these uncomfortable visions could be, at most, no more than my uncle's reaction to the investigations and expectations which had lately filled our minds to the exclusion of all else.

Conversation, also, soon tended to dispel my sense of strangeness; and in time I yielded to my yawns and took my turn at slumber. My uncle seemed now very wakeful, and welcomed his period of watching even though the nightmare had aroused him far ahead of his allotted two hours.

Sleep seized me quickly, and I was at once haunted with dreams of the most disturbing kind. I felt, in my visions, a cosmic and abysmal loneness; with hostility surging from all sides upon some prison where I lay confined. I seemed bound and gagged, and taunted by the echoing yells of distant multitudes who thirsted for my blood. My uncle's face came to me with less pleasant association than in waking hours, and I recall many futile struggles and attempts to scream. It was not a pleasant sleep, and for a second I was not sorry for the echoing shriek which clove through the barriers of dream and flung me to a sharp and startled awakeness in which every actual object before my eyes stood out with more than natural clearness and reality.

5

I had been lying with my face away from my uncle's chair, so that in this sudden flash of awakening I saw only the door to the street, the window, and the wall and floor and ceiling toward the north of the room, all photographed with morbid vividness on my brain in a light brighter than the glow of the fungi or the rays from the street outside. It was not a strong or even a fairly strong light; certainly not nearly strong enough to read an average book by. But it cast a shadow of myself and the cot on the floor, and had a yellowish, penetrating force that hinted at things more potent than luminosity. This I perceived with unhealthy sharpness despite the fact that two of my other senses were violently assailed. For on my ears rang the reverberations of that shocking scream, while my nostrils revolted at the stench which filled the place. My mind, as alert as my senses, recognized the gravely unusual; and almost automatically I leaped up and turned about to grasp the destructive instruments which we had left trained on the moldy spot before the fireplace. As I turned, I dreaded what I was to see; for the scream had been in my uncle's voice, and I knew not against what menace I should have to defend him and myself.

Yet after all, the sight was worse than I had dreaded. There are horrors beyond horrors, and this was one of those nuclei of all dreamable hideousness which the cosmos saves to blast an accursed and unhappy few. Out of the fungus-ridden earth steamed up a vaporous corpse-light, yellow and diseased, which bubbled and lapped to a gigantic height in vague outlines half human and half monstrous, through which I could see the chimney and fireplace beyond. It was all eyes—wolfish and mocking—and the rugose insect-like head dissolved at the top to a thin stream of mist which curled putridly about and finally vanished up the chimney. I say that I saw this thing, but it is only in conscious retrospection that I ever definitely traced its damnable approach to form. At the time, it was to me only a seething, dimly phosphorescent cloud of fungous loathsomeness, enveloping and dissolving to an abhorrent plasticity the one object on which all my attention was focussed. That object was my uncle—the venerable Elihu Whipple—who with blackening and decaying features leered and gibbered at me, and reached out dripping claws to rend me in the fury which this horror had brought.

It was a sense of routine which kept me from going mad. I had drilled myself in preparation for the crucial moment, and blind training saved me. Recognizing the bubbling evil as no substance reachable by matter or material chemistry, and therefore ignoring the flame-thrower which loomed on my left, I threw on the current of the Crookes tube apparatus, and focussed toward that scene of immortal blasphemousness the strongest ether radiations which man's art can arouse from the spaces and fluids of nature. There was a bluish haze and a frenzied sputtering, and the yellowish phosphorescence grew dimmer to my eyes. But I saw the dimness was only that of contrast, and that the waves from the machine had no effect whatever.

Then, in the midst of that demoniac spectacle, I saw a fresh horror which brought cries to my lips and sent me fumbling and staggering toward that unlocked door to the quiet street, careless of what abnormal terrors I loosed upon the world, or what thoughts or judgments of men I brought down upon my head. In that dim blend of blue and yellow the form of my uncle had commenced a nauseous liquefaction whose essence eludes all description, and in which there played across his vanishing face such changes of identity as only madness can conceive. He was at once a devil and a multitude, a charnel-house and a pageant. Lit by the mixed and uncertain beams, that gelatinous face assumed a dozen—a score—a hundred—aspects; grinning, as it sank to the ground on a body that melted like tallow, in the caricatured likeness of legions strange and yet not strange.

I saw the features of the Harris line, masculine and feminine, adult and infantile, and other features old and young, coarse and refined, familiar and unfamiliar. For a second there flashed a degraded counterfeit of a miniature of poor mad Rhoby Harris that I had seen in the School of Design museum, and another time I thought I caught the raw-boned image of Mercy Dexter as I recalled her from a painting in Carrington Harris's house. It was frightful beyond conception; toward the last, when a curious blend of servant and baby visages flickered close to the fungous floor where a pool of greenish grease was spreading, it seemed as though the shifting features fought against themselves and strove to form contours like those of my uncle's kindly face. I like to think that he existed at that moment, and that he tried to bid me farewell. It seems to me I hiccupped a farewell from my own parched throat as I lurched out into the street; a thin stream of grease following me through the door to the rain-drenched sidewalk.

The rest is shadowy and monstrous. There was no one in the soaking street, and in all the world there was no one I dared tell. I walked aimlessly south past College Hill and the Athenæum, down Hopkins Street, and over the bridge to the business section where tall buildings seemed to guard me as modern material things guard the world from ancient and unwholesome wonder. Then gray dawn unfolded wetly from the east, silhouetting the archaic hill and its venerable steeples, and beckoning me to the place where my terrible work was still unfinished. And in the end I went, wet, hatless, and dazed in the morning light, and entered that awful door in Benefit Street which I had left ajar, and which still swung cryptically in full sight of the early householders to whom I dared not speak.

The grease was gone, for the moldy floor was porous. And in front of the fireplace was no vestige of the giant doubled-up form traced in niter. I looked at the cot, the chairs, the instruments, my neglected hat, and the yellowed straw hat of my uncle. Dazedness was uppermost, and I could scarcely recall what was dream and what was reality. Then thought trickled back, and I knew that I had witnessed things more horrible than I had dreamed.

Sitting down, I tried to conjecture as nearly as sanity would let me just what had happened, and how I might end the horror, if indeed it had been real. Matter it seemed not to be, nor ether, nor anything else conceivable by mortal mind. What, then, but some exotic *emanation*; some vampirish vapor such as Exeter rustics tell of as lurking over certain churchyards? This I felt was the clue, and again I looked at the floor before the fireplace where the mold and niter had taken strange forms.

In ten minutes my mind was made up, and taking my hat I set out for home, where I bathed, ate, and gave by telephone an order for a pickax, a spade, a military gas-mask, and six carboys of sulfuric acid, all to be delivered the next morning at the cellar door of the shunned house in Benefit Street. After that I tried to sleep; and failing, passed the hours in reading and in the composition of inane verses to counteract my mood.

At eleven a. m. the next day I commenced digging. It was sunny weather, and I was glad of that. I was still alone, for as much as I feared the unknown horror I sought, there was more fear in the thought of telling anybody. Later I told Harris only through sheer necessity, and because he had heard odd tales from old people which disposed him ever so little toward belief. As I turned up the stinking black earth in front of the fireplace, my spade causing a viscous yellow ichor to ooze from the white fungi which it severed, I trembled at the dubious thoughts of what I might uncover. Some secrets of inner earth are not good for mankind, and this seemed to me one of them.

My hand shook perceptibly, but still I delved; after a while standing in the large hole I had made. With the deepening of the hole, which was about six feet square, the evil smell increased; and I lost all doubt of my imminent contact with the hellish thing whose emanations had cursed the house for over a century and a half. I wondered what it would look like—what its form and substance would be, and how big it might have waxed through long ages of life-sucking. At length I climbed out of the hole and dispersed the heaped-up dirt, then arranging the great carboys of acid around and near two sides, so that when necessary I might empty them all down the aperture in quick succession. After that I dumped earth only along the other two sides; working more slowly and donning my gas-mask as the smell grew. I was nearly unnerved at my proximity to a nameless thing at the bottom of a pit.

Suddenly my spade struck something softer than earth. I shuddered, and made a motion as if to climb out of the hole, which was now as deep as my neck. Then courage returned, and I scraped away more dirt in the light of the electric torch I had provided. The surface I uncovered was fishy and glassy—a kind of semi-putrid congealed jelly with suggestions of translucency. I scraped further, and saw that it had form. There was a rift where a part of the substance was folded over. The exposed area was huge and roughly cylindrical; like a mammoth soft blue-white stovepipe doubled in two, its largest part some two feet in diameter. Still more I scraped, and then abruptly I leaped out of the hole and away from the filthy thing; frantically unstopping and tilting the heavy carboys, and precipitating their corrosive contents one after another down that charnel gulf and upon the unthinkable abnormality whose titan *elbow* I had seen.

The blinding maelstrom of greenish-yellow vapor which surged tempestuously up from that hole as the floods of acid descended, will never leave my memory. All along the hill people tell of the yellow day, when virulent and horrible fumes arose from the factory waste dumped in the Providence River, but I know how mistaken they are as to the source. They tell, too, of the hideous roar which at the same time came from some disordered water-pipe or gas main underground—but again I could correct them if I dared. It was unspeakably shocking, and I do not see how I lived through it. I did faint after emptying the fourth carboy, which I had to handle after the fumes had begun to penetrate my mask; but when I recovered I saw that the hole was emitting no fresh vapors.

The two remaining carboys I emptied down without particular result, and after a time I felt it safe to shovel the earth back into the pit. It was twilight before I was done, but fear had gone out of the place. The dampness was less fetid, and all the strange fungi had withered to a kind of harmless grayish powder which blew ash-like along the floor. One of earth's nethermost terrors had perished for ever; and if there be a hell, it had received at last the demon soul of an unhallowed thing. And as I patted down the last spadeful of mold, I shed the first of the many tears with which I have paid unaffected tribute to my beloved uncle's memory.

The next spring no more pale grass and strange weeds came up in the shunned house's terraced garden, and shortly afterward Carrington Harris rented the place. It is still spectral, but its strangeness fascinates me, and I shall find mixed with my relief a queer regret when it is torn down to make way for a tawdry shop or vulgar apartment building. The barren old trees in the yard have begun to bear small, sweet apples, and last year the birds nested in their gnarled boughs.

Near-Humans Freak Out Humans

If you're a gamer, you have likely heard of the uncanny valley. (Heck, it's even the name of a game.)

It's that near-humanness that can innately bother us. I think it's fascinating.

Here's a quick video on this.

- https://youtu.be/CNdAlPoh8a4

For more, check out *Blade Runner* in its entirety, or at least this little clip or some that follow:

- https://youtu.be/Umc9ezAyJv0

If we're in the mode of defining human, we can see the works of science fiction in a new light, since they are often about this, or about how technology affirms or denies our humanity.

And now you understand why I can never watch more than fifteen seconds of the PBS show *Sid the Science Kid.* . . !

5. DRAMA

Euripides, Medea

Translated by E. P. Coleridge

Dramatis Personae

NURSE OF MEDEA

ATTENDANT ON HER CHILDREN

MEDEA

CHORUS OF CORINTHIAN WOMEN

CREON, King of Corinth

JASON

AEGEUS, King of Athens

MESSENGER

Before MEDEA's house in Corinth, near the palace Of CREON. The NURSE enters from the house.

————————————————————-

NURSE Ah! Would to Heaven the good ship Argo ne'er had sped its course to the Colchian land through the misty blue Symplegades, nor ever in the glens of Pelion the pine been felled to furnish with oars the chieftain's hands, who went to fetch the golden fleece for Pelias; for then would my own mistress Medea never have sailed to the turrets of lolcos, her soul with love for Jason smitten, nor would she have beguiled the daughters of Pelias to slay their father and come to live here in the land of Corinth with her husband and children, where her exile found favour with the citizens to whose land she had come, and in all things of her own accord was she at one with Jason, the greatest safeguard this when wife and husband do agree; but now their love is all turned to hate, and tenderest ties are weak. For Jason hath betrayed his own children and my mistress dear for the love of a royal bride, for he hath wedded the daughter of Creon, lord of this land. While Medea, his hapless wife, thus scorned, appeals to the oaths he swore, recalls the strong pledge his right hand gave, and

bids heaven be witness what requital she is finding from Jason. And

here she lies fasting, yielding her body to her grief, wasting away

in tears ever since she learnt that she was wronged by her husband,

never lifting her eye nor raising her face from off the ground; and

she lends as deaf an ear to her friend's warning as if she were a

rock or ocean billow, save when she turns her snow-white neck aside

and softly to herself bemoans her father dear, her country and her

home, which she gave up to come hither with the man who now holds

her in dishonour. She, poor lady, hath by sad experience learnt how

good a thing it is never to quit one's native land. And she hates

her children now and feels no joy at seeing them; I fear she may contrive

some untoward scheme; for her mood is dangerous nor will she brook

her cruel treatment; full well I know her, and I much do dread that

she will plunge the keen sword through their hearts, stealing without

a word into the chamber where their marriage couch is spread, or else

that she will slay the prince and bridegroom too, and so find some

calamity still more grievous than the present; for dreadful is her

wrath; verily the man that doth incur her hate will have no easy task

to raise o'er her a song of triumph. Lo! where her sons come hither

from their childish sports; little they reck of their mother's woes,

for the soul of the young is no friend to sorrow. (The ATTENDANT

leads in MEDEA'S children.)

ATTENDANT Why dost thou, so long my lady's own handmaid, stand here

at the gate alone, loudly lamenting to thyself the piteous tale? how

comes it that Medea will have thee leave her to herself?

NURSE Old man, attendant on the sons of Jason, our masters' fortunes when they go awry make good slaves grieve and touch their hearts.

Oh! have come to such a pitch of grief that there stole a yearning

wish upon me to come forth hither and proclaim to heaven and earth

my mistress's hard fate.

ATTENDANT What! has not the poor lady ceased yet from her lamentation?

NURSE Would I were as thou art! the mischief is but now beginning;

it has not reached its climax yet.

ATTENDANT O foolish one, if I may call my mistress such a name; how

little she recks of evils yet more recent!

NURSE What mean'st, old man? grudge not to tell me.

ATTENDANT 'Tis naught; I do repent me even of the words I have spoken.

NURSE Nay, by thy beard I conjure thee, hide it not from thy fellow-slave;

will be silent, if need be, on that text.

ATTENDANT I heard one say, pretending not to listen as I approached

the place where our greybeards sit playing draughts near Pirene's

sacred spring, that Creon, the ruler of this land, is bent on driving

these children and their mother from the boundaries of Corinth; but

I know not whether the news is to be relied upon, and would fain it

were not.

NURSE What! will Jason brook such treatment of his sons, even though

he be at variance with their mother?

ATTENDANT Old ties give way to new; he bears no longer any love to

this family.

NURSE Undone, it seems, are we, if to old woes fresh ones we add,

ere we have drained the former to the dregs.

ATTENDANT Hold thou thy peace, say not a word of this; 'tis no time

for our mistress to learn hereof.

NURSE O children, do ye hear how your father feels towards you? Perdition

catch him, but no he is my master still; yet is he proved a very traitor

to his nearest and dearest.

ATTENDANT And who 'mongst men is not? Art learning only now, that

every single man cares for himself more than for his neighbour, some

from honest motives, others for mere gain's sake? seeing that to indulge

his passion their father has ceased to love these children.

NURSE Go, children, within the house; all will be well. Do thou keep

them as far away as may be, and bring them not near their mother in

her evil hour. For ere this have I seen her eyeing them savagely,

as though she were minded to do them some hurt, and well I know she

will not cease from her fury till she have pounced on some victim.

At least may she turn her hand against her foes, and not against her

friends.

MEDEA (chanting within) Ah, me! a wretched suffering woman I! O

would that I could die!

NURSE (chanting) 'Tis as I said, my dear children; wild fancies

stir your mother's heart, wild fury goads her on. Into the house without

delay, come not near her eye, approach her not, beware her savage

mood, the fell tempest of her reckless heart. In, in with what speed

ye may. For 'tis plain she will soon redouble her fury; that cry is

but the herald of the gathering storm-cloud whose lightning soon will

flash; what will her proud restless soul, in the anguish of despair,

be guilty of? (The ATTENDANT takes the children into the house. MEDEA (chanting within) Ah, me! the agony I have suffered, deep enough

to call for these laments! Curse you and your father too, ye children

damned, sons of a doomed mother! Ruin seize the whole family!

NURSE (chanting) Ah me! ah me! the pity of it! Why, pray, do thy

children share their father's crime? Why hatest thou them? Woe is

you, poor children, how do I grieve for you lest ye suffer some outrage!

Strange are the tempers of princes, and maybe because they seldom

have to obey, and mostly lord it over others, change they their moods

with difficulty. 'Tis better then to have been trained to live on

equal terms. Be it mine to reach old age, not in proud pomp, but in

security! Moderation wins the day first as a better word for men to

use, and likewise it is far the best course for them to pursue; but

greatness that doth o'erreach itself, brings no blessing to mortal

men; but pays a penalty of greater ruin whenever fortune is wroth

with a family. (The CHORUS enters. The following lines between the

NURSE, CHORUS, and MEDEA are sung.)

CHORUS I heard the voice, uplifted loud, of our poor Colchian lady,

nor yet is she quiet; speak, aged dame, for as I stood by the house

with double gates I heard a voice of weeping from within, and I do

grieve, lady, for the sorrows of this house, for it hath won my love.

NURSE 'Tis a house no more; all that is passed away long since; a

royal bride keeps Jason at her side, while our mistress pines away

in her bower, finding no comfort for her soul in aught her friends

can say.

MEDEA (within) Oh, oh! Would that Heaven's levin bolt would cleave this head in twain! What gain is life to me? Woe, woe is me! O, to

die and win release, quitting this loathed existence!

CHORUS Didst hear, O Zeus, thou earth, and thou, O light, the piteous

note of woe the hapless wife is uttering? How shall a yearning for

that insatiate resting-place ever hasten for thee, poor reckless one,

the end that death alone can bring? Never pray for that. And if thy

lord prefers a fresh love, be not angered with him for that; Zeus

will judge 'twixt thee and him herein. Then mourn not for thy husband's

loss too much, nor waste thyself away.

MEDEA (within) Great Themis, and husband of Themis, behold what

I am suffering now, though I did bind that accursed one, my husband,

by strong oaths to me! O, to see him and his bride some day brought

to utter destruction, they and their house with them, for that they

presume to wrong me thus unprovoked. O my father, my country, that

I have left to my shame, after slaying my own brother.

NURSE Do ye hear her words, how loudly she adjures Themis, oft invoked,

and Zeus, whom men regard as keeper of their oaths? On no mere trifle

surely will our mistress spend her rage.

CHORUS Would that she would come forth for us to see, and listen

to the words of counsel we might give, if haply she might lay aside

the fierce fury of her wrath, and her temper stern. Never be my zeal

at any rate denied my friends! But go thou and bring her hither outside

the house, and tell her this our friendly thought; haste thee ere

she do some mischief to those inside the house, for this sorrow of

hers is mounting high.

NURSE This will I do; but I doubt whether I shall persuade my mistress;

still willingly will I undertake this trouble for you; albeit, she

glares upon her servants with the look of a lioness with cubs, whenso

anyone draws nigh to speak to her. Wert thou to call the men of old

time rude uncultured boors thou wouldst not err, seeing that they

devised their hymns for festive occasions, for banquets, and to grace

the board, a pleasure to catch the ear, shed o'er our life, but no

man hath found a way to allay hated grief by music and the minstrel's

varied strain, whence arise slaughters and fell strokes of fate to

o'erthrow the homes of men. And yet this were surely a gain, to heal

men's wounds by music's spell, but why tune they their idle song where

rich banquets are spread? For of itself doth the rich banquet, set

before them, afford to men delight.

CHORUS I heard a bitter cry of lamentation! loudly, bitterly she

calls on the traitor of her marriage bed, her perfidious spouse; by

grievous wrongs oppressed she invokes Themis, bride of Zeus, witness

of oaths, who brought her unto Hellas, the land that fronts the strand

of Asia, o'er the sea by night through ocean's boundless gate. (As

the CHORUS finishes its song, MEDEA enters from the house.)

MEDEA From the house I have come forth, Corinthian ladies, for fear

lest you be blaming me; for well I know that amongst men many by showing

pride have gotten them an ill name and a reputation for indifference,

both those who shun men's gaze and those who move amid the stranger

crowd, and likewise they who choose a quiet walk in life. For there

is no just discernment in the eyes of men, for they, or ever they

have surely learnt their neighbour's heart, loathe him at first sight, though never wronged by him; and so a stranger most of all should adopt a city's views; nor do I commend that citizen, who, in the stubbornness of his heart, from churlishness resents the city's will.

But on me hath fallen this unforeseen disaster, and sapped my life; ruined I am, and long to resign the boon of existence, kind friends, and die. For he who was all the world to me, as well thou knowest, hath turned out the worst of men, my own husband. Of all things that have life and sense we women are the most hapless creatures; first must we buy a husband at a great price, and o'er ourselves a tyrant set which is an evil worse than the first; and herein lies the most important issue, whether our choice be good or bad. For divorce is not honourable to women, nor can we disown our lords. Next must the wife, coming as she does to ways and customs new, since she hath not learnt the lesson in her home, have a diviner's eye to see how best to treat the partner of her life. If haply we perform these tasks with thoroughness and tact, and the husband live with us, without resenting the yoke, our life is a happy one; if not, 'twere best to die. But when a man is vexed with what he finds indoors, he goeth forth and rids his soul of its disgust, betaking him to some friend or comrade of like age; whilst we must needs regard his single self.

And yet they say we live secure at home, while they are at the wars, with their sorry reasoning, for I would gladly take my stand in battle array three times o'er, than once give birth. But enough! this language suits not thee as it does me; thou hast a city here, a father's house, some joy in life, and friends to share thy thoughts, but I am destitute, without a city, and therefore scorned by my husband, a captive I from a foreign shore, with no mother, brother, or kinsman in whom to find a new haven of refuge from this calamity. Wherefore this one boon

and only this I wish to win from thee,-thy silence, if haply I can

some way or means devise to avenge me on my husband for this cruel

treatment, and on the man who gave to him his daughter, and on her

who is his wife. For though woman be timorous enough in all else,

and as regards courage, a coward at the mere sight of steel, yet in

the moment she finds her honour wronged, no heart is filled with deadlier

thoughts than hers.

LEADER OF THE CHORUS This will I do; for thou wilt be taking a just

vengeance on thy husband, Medea. That thou shouldst mourn thy lot

surprises me not. But lo! I see Creon, king of this land coming hither,

to announce some new resolve. (CREON enters, with his retinue.)

CREON Hark thee, Medea, I bid thee take those sullen looks and angry

thoughts against thy husband forth from this land in exile, and with

thee take both thy children and that without delay, for I am judge

in this sentence, and I will not return unto my house till I banish

thee beyond the borders of the land.

MEDEA Ah, me! now is utter destruction come upon me, unhappy that

I am! For my enemies are bearing down on me full sail, nor have I

any landing-place to come at in my trouble. Yet for all my wretched

plight I will ask thee, Creon, wherefore dost thou drive me from the

land?

CREON I fear thee,-no longer need I veil my dread 'neath words,-lest

thou devise against my child some cureless ill. Many things contribute

to this fear of mine; thou art a witch by nature, expert in countless

sorceries, and thou art chafing for the loss of thy husband's affection.
I hear, too, so they tell me, that thou dost threaten the father of
the bride, her husband, and herself with some mischief; wherefore
I will take precautions ere our troubles come. For 'tis better for
me to incur thy hatred now, lady, than to soften my heart and bitterly
repent it hereafter.

MEDEA Alas! this is not now the first time, but oft before, O Creon,
hath my reputation injured me and caused sore mischief. Wherefore
whoso is wise in his generation ought never to have his children taught
to be too clever; for besides the reputation they get for idleness,
they purchase bitter odium from the citizens. For if thou shouldst
import new learning amongst dullards, thou wilt be thought a useless
trifler, void of knowledge; while if thy fame in the city o'ertops
that of the pretenders to cunning knowledge, thou wilt win their dislike.
I too myself share in this ill-luck. Some think me clever and hate
me, others say I am too reserved, and some the very reverse; others
find me hard to please and not so very clever after all. Be that as
it may, thou dost fear me lest I bring on thee something to mar thy
harmony. Fear me not, Creon, my position scarce is such that should
seek to quarrel with princes. Why should I, for how hast thou injured
me? Thou hast betrothed thy daughter where thy fancy prompted thee.
No, 'tis my husband I hate, though I doubt not thou hast acted wisely
herein. And now I grudge not thy prosperity; betroth thy child, good
luck to thee, but let me abide in this land, for though I have been
wronged I will be still and yield to my superiors.

CREON Thy words are soft to hear, but much I dread lest thou art
devising some mischief in thy heart, and less than ever do I trust

thee now; for cunning woman, and man likewise, is easier to guard

against when quick-tempered than when taciturn. Nay, begone at once!

speak me no speeches, for this is decreed, nor hast thou any art whereby

thou shalt abide amongst us, since thou hatest me.

MEDEA O, say not so! by thy knees and by thy daughter newlywed, I

do implore!

CREON Thou wastest words; thou wilt never persuade me.

MEDEA What, wilt thou banish me, and to my prayers no pity yield?

CREON I will, for I love not thee above my own family.

MEDEA O my country! what fond memories I have of thee in this hour!

CREON Yea, for I myself love my city best of all things save my children.

MEDEA Ah me! ah me! to mortal man how dread a scourge is love!

CREON That, I deem, is according to the turn our fortunes take.

MEDEA O Zeus! let not the author of these my troubles escape thee.

CREON Begone, thou silly woman, and free me from my toil.

MEDEA The toil is mine, no lack of it.

CREON Soon wilt thou be thrust out forcibly by the hand of servants.

MEDEA Not that, not that, I do entreat thee, Creon

CREON Thou wilt cause disturbance yet, it seems.

MEDEA I will begone; I ask thee not this boon to grant.

CREON Why then this violence? why dost thou not depart?

MEDEA Suffer me to abide this single day and devise some plan for

the manner of my exile, and means of living for my children, since

their father cares not to provide his babes therewith. Then pity them;

thou too hast children of thine own; thou needs must have a kindly

heart. For my own lot I care naught, though I an exile am, but for those babes I weep, that they should learn what sorrow means.

CREON Mine is a nature anything but harsh; full oft by showing pity have suffered shipwreck; and now albeit I clearly see my error, yet shalt thou gain this request, lady; but I do forewarn thee, if tomorrow's rising sun shall find thee and thy children within the borders of this land, thou diest; my word is spoken and it will not lie. So now, if abide thou must, stay this one day only, for in it thou canst not do any of the fearful deeds I dread. (CREON and his retinue go out.)

CHORUS (chanting) Ah! poor lady, woe is thee! Alas, for thy sorrows! Whither wilt thou turn? What protection, what home or country to save thee from thy troubles wilt thou find? O Medea, in what a hopeless sea of misery heaven hath plunged thee!

MEDEA On all sides sorrow pens me in. Who shall gainsay this? But all is not yet lost! think not so. Still are there troubles in store for the new bride, and for her bridegroom no light toil. Dost think I would ever have fawned on yonder man, unless to gain some end or form some scheme? Nay, would not so much as have spoken to him or touched him with my hand. But he has in folly so far stepped in that, though he might have checked my plot by banishing me from the land, he hath allowed me to abide this day, in which I will lay low in death three of my enemies-a father and his daughter and my husband too. Now, though I have many ways to compass their death, I am not sure, friends, which I am to try first. Shall I set fire to the bridal mansion, or plunge the whetted sword through their hearts, softly stealing into the chamber where their couch is spread? One thing stands in my way. If I am caught making my way into the chamber, intent on my design, I shall be put to death and cause my foes to mock, 'Twere

best to take the shortest way-the way we women are most skilled in-by

poison to destroy them. Well, suppose them dead; what city will receive

me? What friendly host will give me a shelter in his land, a home

secure, and save my soul alive? None. So I will wait yet a little

while in case some tower of defence rise up for me; then will I proceed

to this bloody deed in crafty silence; but if some unexpected mischance

drive me forth, I will with mine own hand seize the sword, e'en though

I die for it, and slay them, and go forth on my bold path of daring.

By that dread queen whom I revere before all others and have chosen

to share my task, by Hecate who dwells within my inmost chamber, not

one of them shall wound my heart and rue it not. Bitter and sad will

I make their marriage for them; bitter shall be the wooing of it,

bitter my exile from the land. Up, then, Medea, spare not the secrets

of thy art in plotting and devising; on to the danger. Now comes a

struggle needing courage. Dost see what thou art suffering? 'Tis not

for thee to be a laughing-stock to the race of Sisyphus by reason

of this wedding of Jason, sprung, as thou art, from noble sire, and

of the Sun-god's race. Thou hast cunning; and, more than this, we

women, though by nature little apt for virtuous deeds, are most expert

to fashion any mischief.

CHORUS (singing, strophe 1)

Back to their source the holy rivers turn their tide. Order and the

universe are being reversed. 'Tis men whose counsels are treacherous,

whose oath by heaven is no longer sure. Rumour shall bring a change

o'er my life, bringing it into good repute. Honour's dawn is breaking

for woman's sex; no more shall the foul tongue of slander fix upon

us.

(antistrophe 1)

The songs of the poets of old shall cease to make our faithlessness

their theme. Phoebus, lord of minstrelsy, hath not implanted in our

mind the gift of heavenly song, else had I sung an answering strain

to the race of males, for time's long chapter affords many a theme

on their sex as well as ours.

(strophe 2)

With mind distraught didst thou thy father's house desert on thy

voyage betwixt ocean's twin rocks, and on a foreign strand thou dwellest

thy bed left husbandless, poor lady, and thou an exile from the land,

dishonoured, persecuted.

(antistrophe 2)

Gone is the grace that oaths once had. Through all the breadth of

Hellas honour is found no more; to heaven hath it sped away. For thee

no father's house is open, woe is thee! to be a haven from the troublous

storm, while o'er thy home is set another queen, the bride that is

preferred to thee. (As the CHORUS finishes its song, JASON enters,

alone. MEDEA comes out of the house.)

JASON It is not now I first remark, but oft ere this, how unruly

a pest is a harsh temper. For instance, thou, hadst thou but patiently

endured the will of thy superiors, mightest have remained here in

this land and house, but now for thy idle words wilt thou be banished.

Thy words are naught to me. Cease not to call Jason basest of men;

but for those words thou hast spoken against our rulers, count it

all gain that exile is thy only punishment. I ever tried to check the outbursts of the angry monarch, and would have had thee stay,

but thou wouldst not forego thy silly rage, always reviling our rulers,

and so thou wilt be banished. Yet even after all this I weary not

of my goodwill, but am come with thus much forethought, lady, that

thou mayst not be destitute nor want for aught, when, with thy sons,

thou art cast out. Many an evil doth exile bring in its train with

it; for even though thou hatest me, never will I harbour hard thoughts

of thee.

MEDEA Thou craven villain (for that is the only name my tongue can

find for thee, a foul reproach on thy unmanliness), comest thou to

me, thou, most hated foe of gods, of me, and of all mankind? 'Tis

no proof of courage or hardihood to confront thy friends after injuring

them, but that worst of all human diseases-loss of shame. Yet hast

thou done well to come; for I shall ease my soul by reviling thee,

and thou wilt be vexed at my recital. I will begin at the very beginning.

I saved thy life, as every Hellene knows who sailed with thee aboard

the good ship Argo, when thou wert sent to tame and yoke fire-breathing

bulls, and to sow the deadly tilth. Yea, and I slew the dragon which

guarded the golden fleece, keeping sleepless watch o'er it with many

a wreathed coil, and I raised for thee a beacon of deliverance. Father

and home of my free will I left and came with the to Iolcos, 'neath

Pelion's hills, for my love was stronger than my prudence. Next I

caused the death of Pelias by a doom most grievous, even by his own

children's hand, beguiling them of all their fear. All this have I

done for thee, thou traitor! and thou hast cast me over, taking to

thyself another wife, though children have been born to us. Hadst

thou been childless still, I could have pardoned thy desire for this

new union. Gone is now the trust I put in oaths. I cannot even understand whether thou thinkest that the gods of old no longer rule, or that

fresh decrees are now in vogue amongst mankind, for thy conscience

must tell thee thou hast not kept faith with me. Ah! poor right hand,

which thou didst often grasp. These knees thou didst embrace! All

in vain, I suffered a traitor to touch me! How short of my hopes I

am fallen! But come, I will deal with the as though thou wert my friend.

Yet what kindness can I expect from one so base as thee? But yet I

will do it, for my questioning will show thee yet more base. Whither

can I turn me now? to my father's house, to my own country, which

I for thee deserted to come hither? to the hapless daughters of Pelias?

A glad welcome, I trow, would they give me in their home, whose father's

death I compassed! My case stands even thus: I am become the bitter

foe to those of mine own home, and those whom I need ne'er have wronged

I have made mine enemies to pleasure thee. Wherefore to reward me

for this thou hast made me doubly blest in the eyes of many wife in

Hellas; and in thee I own a peerless, trusty lord. O woe is me, if

indeed I am to be cast forth an exile from the land, without one friend;

one lone woman with her babes forlorn! Yea, a fine reproach to thee

in thy bridal hour, that thy children and the wife who saved thy life

are beggars and vagabonds! O Zeus! why hast thou granted unto man

clear signs to know the sham in gold, while on man's brow no brand

is stamped whereby to gauge the villain's heart?

LEADER OF THE CHORUS There is a something terrible and past all cure,

when quarrels arise 'twixt those who are near and dear.

JASON Needs must I now, it seems, turn orator, and, like a good helmsman

on a ship with close-reefed sails, weather that wearisome tongue of

thine. Now, I believe, since thou wilt exaggerate thy favours, that to Cypri, alone of gods or men I owe the safety of my voyage. Thou

hast a subtle wit enough; yet were it a hateful thing for me to say

that the Love-god constrained thee by his resistless shaft to save

my life. However, I will not reckon this too nicely; 'twas kindly

done, however thou didst serve me. Yet for my safety hast thou received

more than ever thou gavest, as I will show. First, thou dwellest in

Hellas, instead of thy barbarian land, and hast learnt what justice

means and how to live by law, not by the dictates of brute force;

and all the Hellenes recognize thy cleverness, and thou hast gained

a name; whereas, if thou hadst dwelt upon the confines of the earth,

no tongue had mentioned thee. Give me no gold within my halls, nor

skill to sing a fairer strain than ever Orpheus sang, unless there-with

my fame be spread abroad! So much I say to thee about my own toils,

for 'twas thou didst challenge me to this retort. As for the taunts

thou urgest against my marriage with the princess, I will prove to

thee, first, that I am prudent herein, next chastened in my love,

and last powerful friend to thee and to thy sons; only hold thy peace.

Since I have here withdrawn from Iolcos with many a hopeless trouble

at my back, what happier device could I, an exile, frame than marriage

with the daughter of the king? 'Tis not because I loathe thee for

my wife-the thought that rankles in thy heart; 'tis not because I

am smitten with desire for a new bride, nor yet that I am eager to

vie with others in begetting many children, for those we have are

quite enough, and I do not complain. Nay, 'tis that we-and this is

most important-may dwell in comfort, instead of suffering want (for

well I know that every whilom friend avoids the poor) , and that

I might rear my sons as doth befit my house; further, that I might

be the father of brothers for the children thou hast borne, and raise

these to the same high rank, uniting the family in one,-to my lasting bliss. Thou, indeed, hast no need of more children, but me it profits

to help my present family by that which is to be. Have I miscarried

here? Not even thou wouldest say so unless a rival's charms rankled

in thy bosom. No, but you women have such strange ideas, that you

think all is well so long as your married life runs smooth; but if

some mischance occur to ruffle your love, all that was good and lovely

erst you reckon as your foes. Yea, men should have begotten children

from some other source, no female race existing; thus would no evil

ever have fallen on mankind.

LEADER This speech, O Jason, hast thou with specious art arranged;

but yet I think-albeit in speaking I am indiscreet-that thou hast

sinned in thy betrayal of thy wife.

MEDEA No doubt I differ from the mass of men on many points; for,

to my mind, whoso hath skill to fence with words in an unjust cause,

incurs the heaviest penalty; for such an one, confident that he can

cast a decent veil of words o'er his injustice, dares to practise

it; and yet he is not so very clever after all. So do not thou put

forth thy specious pleas and clever words to me now, for one word

of mine will lay thee low. Hadst thou not had a villain's heart, thou

shouldst have gained my consent, then made this match, instead of

hiding it from those who loved thee.

JASON Thou wouldest have lent me ready aid, no doubt, in this proposal,

if had told thee of my marriage, seeing that not even now canst thou

restrain thy soul's hot fury.

MEDEA This was not what restrained thee; but thine eye was turned towards old age, and a foreign wife began to appear a shame to thee.

JASON Be well assured of this: 'twas not for the woman's sake I wedded

the king's daughter, my present wife; but, as I have already told

thee, I wished to insure thy safety and to be the father of royal

sons bound by blood to my own children-a bulwark to our house.

MEDEA May that prosperity, whose end is woe, ne'er be mine, nor such

wealth as would ever sting my heart!

JASON Change that prayer as I will teach thee, and thou wilt show

more wisdom. Never let happiness appear in sorrow's guise, nor, when

thy fortune smiles, pretend she frowns!

MEDEA Mock on; thou hast a place of refuge; I am alone, an exile

soon to be.

JASON Thy own free choice was this; blame no one else.

MEDEA What did I do? Marry, then betray thee?

JASON Against the king thou didst invoke an impious curse.

MEDEA On thy house too maybe I bring the curse.

JASON Know this, I will no further dispute this point with thee.

But, if thou wilt of my fortune somewhat take for the children or

thyself to help thy exile, say on; for I am ready to grant it with

ungrudging hand, yea and to bend tokens to my friends elsewhere who

shall treat thee well. If thou refuse this offer, thou wilt do a foolish

deed, but if thou cease from anger the greater will be thy gain.

MEDEA I will have naught to do with friends of thine, naught will

I receive of thee, offer it not to me; a villain's gifts can bring no blessing.

JASON At least I call the gods to witness, that I am ready in all things to serve thee and thy children, but thou dost scorn my favours and thrustest thy friends stubbornly away; wherefore thy lot will be more bitter still.

MEDEA Away! By love for thy young bride entrapped, too long thou lingerest outside her chamber; go wed, for, if God will, thou shalt have such a marriage as thou wouldst fain refuse. (JASON goes out.)

CHORUS (singing, strophe 1)

When in excess and past all limits Love doth come, he brings not glory or repute to man; but if the Cyprian queen in moderate might approach, no goddess is so full of charm as she. Never, O never, lady mine, discharge at me from thy golden bow a shaft invincible, in passion's venom dipped.

(antistrophe 1)

On me may chastity, heaven's fairest gift, look with a favouring eye; never may Cypris, goddess dread, fasten on me a temper to dispute, or restless jealousy, smiting my soul with mad desire for unlawful love, but may she hallow peaceful married life and shrewdly decide whom each of us shall wed.

(strophe 2)

O my country, O my own dear home! God grant I may never be an outcast from my city, leading that cruel helpless life, whose every day is

misery. Ere that may I this life complete and yield to death, ay,

death; for there is no misery that doth surpass the loss of fatherland.

(antistrophe 2)

I have seen with mine eyes, nor from the lips of others have I the

lesson learnt; no city, not one friend doth pity thee in this thine

awful woe. May he perish and find no favour, whoso hath not in him

honour for his friends, freely unlocking his heart to them. Never

shall he be friend of mine. (MEDEA has been seated in despair on

her door-step during the choral song. AEGEUS and his attendants enter.)

AEGEUS All hail, Medea! no man knoweth fairer prelude to the greeting

of friends than this.

MEDEA All hail to thee likewise, Aegeus, son of wise Pandion. Whence

comest thou to this land?

AEGEUS From Phoebus' ancient oracle.

MEDEA What took thee on thy travels to the prophetic centre of the

earth?

AEGEUS The wish to ask how I might raise up seed unto myself.

MEDEA Pray tell me, hast thou till now dragged on a childless life?

AEGEUS I have no child owing to the visitation of some god.

MEDEA Hast thou a wife, or hast thou never known the married state?

AEGEUS I have a wife joined to me in wedlock's bond.

MEDEA What said Phoebus to thee as to children?

AEGEUS Words too subtle for man to comprehend.

MEDEA Surely I may learn the god's answer?

AEGEUS Most assuredly, for it is just thy subtle wit it needs.

MEDEA What said the god? speak, if I may hear it.

AEGEUS He bade me "not loose the wineskin's pendent neck."

MEDEA Till when? what must thou do first, what country visit?

AEGEUS Till I to my native home return.

MEDEA What object hast thou in sailing to this land?

AEGEUS O'er Troezen's realm is Pittheus king.

MEDEA Pelops' son, a man devout they say.

AEGEUS To him I fain would impart the oracle of the god.

MEDEA The man is shrewd and versed in such-like lore.

AEGEUS Aye, and to me the dearest of all my warrior friends.

MEDEA Good luck to thee! success to all thy wishes!

AEGEUS But why that downcast eye, that wasted cheek?

MEDEA O Aegeus, my husband has proved most evil.

AEGEUS What meanest thou? explain to me clearly the cause of thy

despondency.

MEDEA Jason is wronging me though I have given him no cause.

AEGEUS What hath he done? tell me more clearly.

MEDEA He is taking another wife to succeed me as mistress of his

house.

AEGEUS Can he have brought himself to such a dastard deed?

MEDEA Be assured thereof; I, whom he loved of yore, am in dishonour

now.

AEGEUS Hath he found a new love? or does he loathe thy bed?

MEDEA Much in love is he! A traitor to his friend is he become.

AEGEUS Enough! if he is a villain as thou sayest.

MEDEA The alliance he is so much enamoured of is with a princess.

AEGEUS Who gives his daughter to him? go on, I pray.

MEDEA Creon, who is lord of this land of Corinth.

AEGEUS Lady, I can well pardon thy grief.

MEDEA I am undone, and more than that, am banished from the land.

AEGEUS By whom? fresh woe this word of thine unfolds.

MEDEA Creon drives me forth in exile from Corinth.

AEGEUS Doth Jason allow it? This too I blame him for.

MEDEA Not in words, but he will not stand out against it. O, I implore thee by this beard and by thy knees, in suppliant posture, pity, O pity my sorrows; do not see me cast forth forlorn, but receive me in thy country, to a seat within thy halls. So may thy wish by heaven's grace be crowned with a full harvest of offspring, and may thy life close in happiness! Thou knowest not the rare good luck thou findest here, for I will make thy childlessness to cease and cause thee to beget fair issue; so potent are the spells I know.

AEGEUS Lady, on many grounds I am most fain to grant thee this thy boon, first for the gods' sake, next for the children whom thou dost promise I shall beget; for in respect of this I am completely lost. 'Tis thus with me; if e'er thou reach my land, I will attempt to champion thee as I am bound to do. Only one warning I do give thee first, lady; I will not from this land bear thee away, yet if of thyself thou reach my halls, there shalt thou bide in safety and I will never yield thee up to any man. But from this land escape without my aid, for I have no wish to incur the blame of my allies as well.

MEDEA It shall be even so; but wouldst thou pledge thy word to this, I should in all be well content with thee.

AEGEUS Surely thou dost trust me? or is there aught that troubles

thee?

MEDEA Thee I trust; but Pelias' house and Creon are my foes. Wherefore,

if thou art bound by an oath, thou wilt not give me up to them when

they come to drag me from the land, but, having entered into a compact

and sworn by heaven as well, thou wilt become my friend and disregard

their overtures. Weak is any aid of mine, whilst they have wealth

and a princely house.

AEGEUS Lady, thy words show much foresight, so if this is thy will,

I do not, refuse. For I shall feel secure and safe if I have some

pretext to offer to thy foes, and thy case too the firmer stands.

Now name thy gods.

MEDEA Swear by the plain of Earth, by Helios my father's sire, and,

in one comprehensive oath, by all the race of gods.

AEGEUS What shall I swear to do, from what refrain? tell me that.

MEDEA Swear that thou wilt never of thyself expel me from thy land,

nor, whilst life is thine, permit any other, one of my foes maybe,

to hale me thence if so he will.

AEGEUS By Earth I swear, by the Sun-god's holy beam and by all the

host of heaven that I will stand fast to the terms I hear thee make.

MEDEA 'Tis enough. If thou shouldst break this oath, what curse dost thou invoke upon thyself?

AEGEUS Whate'er betides the impious.

MEDEA Go in peace; all is well, and I with what speed I may, will

to thy city come, when I have wrought my purpose and obtained my wish.

(AEGEUS and his retinue depart.)

CHORUS (chanting) May Maia's princely son go with thee on thy way

to bring thee to thy home, and mayest thou attain that on which thy

soul is set so firmly, for to my mind thou seemest a generous man,

O Aegeus.

MEDEA O Zeus, and Justice, child of Zeus, and Sun-god's light, now

will triumph o'er my foes, kind friends; on victory's road have I

set forth; good hope have I of wreaking vengeance on those I hate.

For where we were in most distress this stranger hath appeared, to

be a haven in my counsels; to him will we make fast the cables of

our ship when we come to the town and citadel of Pallas. But now will

I explain to thee my plans in full; do not expect to hear a pleasant

tale. A servant of mine will I to Jason send and crave an interview;

then when he comes I will address him with soft words, say, "this

pleases me," and, "that is well," even the marriage with the princess,

which my treacherous lord is celebrating, and add "it suits us both,

'twas well thought out"; then will I entreat that here my children

may abide, not that I mean to leave them in a hostile land for foes

to flout, but that I may slay the king's daughter by guile. For I

will send them with gifts in their hands, carrying them unto the bride

to save them from banishment, a robe of finest woof and a chaplet

of gold. And if these ornaments she take and put them on, miserably

shall she die, and likewise everyone who touches her; with such fell poisons will I smear my gifts. And here I quit this theme; but I shudder

at the deed I must do next; for I will slay the children I have borne;

there is none shall take them from my toils; and when I have utterly

confounded Jason's house I will leave the land, escaping punishment

for my dear children's murder, after my most unholy deed. For I cannot

endure the taunts of enemies, kind friends; enough! what gain is life

to me? I have no country, home, or refuge left. O, I did wrong, that

hour I left my father's home, persuaded by that Hellene's words, who

now shall pay the penalty, so help me God, Never shall he see again

alive the children I bore to him, nor from his new bride shall he

beget issue, for she must die a hideous death, slain by my drugs.

Let no one deem me a poor weak woman who sits with folded hands, but

of another mould, dangerous to foes and well-disposed to friends;

for they win the fairest fame who live then, life like me.

LEADER OF THE CHORUS Since thou hast imparted this design to me,

I bid thee hold thy hand, both from a wish to serve thee and because

I would uphold the laws men make.

MEDEA It cannot but be so; thy words I pardon since thou art not

in the same sorry plight that I am.

LEADER O lady, wilt thou steel thyself to slay thy children twain?

MEDEA I will, for that will stab my husband to the heart.

LEADER It may, but thou wilt be the saddest wife alive.

MEDEA No matter; wasted is every word that comes 'twixt now and then.

Ho! (The NURSE enters in answer to her call.) Thou, go call me Jason

hither, for thee I do employ on every mission of trust. No word divulge

of all my purpose, as thou art to thy mistress loyal and likewise of my sex. (The NURSE goes out.)

CHORUS (singing, strophe 1)

Sons of Erechtheus, heroes happy from of yore, children of the blessed

gods, fed on wisdom's glorious food in a holy land ne'er pillaged

by its foes, ye who move with sprightly step through a climate ever

bright and clear, where, as legend tells, the Muses nine, Pieria's

holy maids, were brought to birth by Harmonia with the golden hair.

(antistrophe 1)

And poets sing how Cypris drawing water from the streams of fair-flowing

Cephissus breathes o'er the land a gentle breeze of balmy winds, and

ever as she crowns her tresses with a garland of sweet rose-buds sends

forth the Loves to sit by wisdom's side, to take part in every excellence.

(strophe 2)

How then shall the city of sacred streams, the land that welcomes

those it loves, receive thee, the murderess of thy children, thee

whose presence with others is a pollution? 'Think on the murder of

thy children, consider the bloody deed thou takest on thee. Nay, by

thy knees we, one and all, implore thee, slay not thy babes.

(antistrophe 2)

Where shall hand or heart find hardihood enough in wreaking such

a fearsome deed upon thy sons? How wilt thou look upon thy babes,

and still without a tear retain thy bloody purpose? Thou canst not,

when they fall at thy feet for mercy, steel thy heart and dip in their blood thy hand. (JASON enters.)

JASON I am come at thy bidding, for e'en though thy hate for me is
bitter thou shalt not fail in this small boon, but I will hear what
new request thou hast to make of me, lady.

MEDEA Jason, I crave thy pardon for the words I spoke, and well thou
mayest brook my burst of passion, for ere now we twain have shared
much love. For I have reasoned with my soul and railed upon me thus,
"Ah! poor heart! why am I thus distraught, why so angered 'gainst
all good advice, why have I come to hate the rulers of the land, my
husband too, who does the best for me he can, in wedding with a princess
and rearing for my children noble brothers? Shall I not cease to fret?
What possesses me, when heaven its best doth offer? Have I not my
children to consider? do I forget that we are fugitives, in need of
friends?" When I had thought all this I saw how foolish I had been,
how senselessly enraged. So now do commend thee and think thee most
wise in forming this connection for us; but I was mad, I who should
have shared in these designs, helped on thy plans, and lent my aid
to bring about the match, only too pleased to wait upon thy bride.
But what we are, we are, we women, evil I will not say; wherefore
thou shouldst not sink to our sorry level nor with our weapons meet
our childishness.

I yield and do confess that I was wrong then, but now have I come
to a better mind. Come hither, my children, come, leave the house,
step forth, and with me greet and bid farewell to your father, be
reconciled from all past bitterness unto your friends, as now your
mother is; for we have made a truce and anger is no more. (The ATTENDANT

comes out of the house with the children.) Take his right hand; ah

me! my sad fate! when I reflect, as now, upon the hidden future. O

my children, since there awaits you even thus a long, long life, stretch

forth the hand to take a fond farewell. Ah me! how new to tears am

I, how full of fear! For now that I have at last released me from

my quarrel with your father, I let the tear-drops stream adown my

tender cheek.

LEADER OF THE CHORUS From my eyes too bursts forth the copious tear;

O, may no greater ill than the present e'er befall!

JASON Lady, I praise this conduct, not that I blame what is past;

for it is but natural to the female sex to vent their spleen against

a husband when he trafficks in other marriages besides his own. But

thy heart is changed to wiser schemes and thou art determined on the

better course, late though it be; this is acting like a woman of sober

sense. And for you, my sons, hath your father provided with all good

heed a sure refuge, by God's grace; for ye, I trow, shall with your

brothers share hereafter the foremost rank in this Corinthian realm.

Only grow up, for all the rest your sire and whoso of the gods is

kind to us is bringing to pass. May I see you reach man's full estate,

high o'er the heads of those I hate! But thou, lady, why with fresh

tears dost thou thine eyelids wet, turning away thy wan cheek, with

no welcome for these my happy tidings?

MEDEA 'Tis naught; upon these children my thoughts were turned.

JASON Then take heart; for I will see that it is well with them.

MEDEA I will do so; nor will I doubt thy word; woman is a weak creature,

ever given to tears.

JASON Why prithee, unhappy one, dost moan o'er these children?

MEDEA I gave them birth; and when thou didst pray long life for them, pity entered into my soul to think that these things must be. But the reason of thy coming hither to speak with me is partly told, the rest will I now mention. Since it is the pleasure of the rulers of the land to banish me, and well I know 'twere best for me to stand not in the way of thee or of the rulers by dwelling here, enemy as I am thought unto their house, forth from this land in exile am I going, but these children,-that they may know thy fostering hand, beg Creon to remit their banishment.

JASON I doubt whether I can persuade him, yet must I attempt it.

MEDEA At least do thou bid thy wife ask her sire this boon, to remit the exile of the children from this land.

JASON Yea, that will I; and her methinks I shall persuade, since she is woman like the rest.

MEDEA I too will aid thee in this task, for by the children's hand I will send to her gifts that far surpass in beauty, I well know, aught that now is seen 'mongst men, a robe of finest tissue and a chaplet of chased gold. But one of my attendants must haste and bring the ornaments hither. (A servant goes into the house.) Happy shall she be not once alone but ten thousand-fold, for in thee she wins the noblest soul to share her love, and gets these gifts as well which on a day my father's sire, the Sun-god, bestowed on his descendants. (The servant returns and hands the gifts to the children.) My children, take in your hands these wedding gifts, and bear them as an offering

to the royal maid, the happy bride; for verily the gifts she shall

receive are not to be scorned.

JASON But why so rashly rob thyself of these gifts? Dost think a

royal palace wants for robes or gold? Keep them, nor give them to

another. For well I know that if my lady hold me in esteem, she will

set my price above all wealth.

MEDEA Say not so; 'tis said that gifts tempt even gods; and o'er

men's minds gold holds more potent sway than countless words. Fortune

smiles upon thy bride, and heaven now doth swell her triumph; youth

is hers and princely power; yet to save my children from exile I would

barter life, not dross alone. Children, when we are come to the rich

palace, pray your father's new bride, my mistress, with suppliant

voice to save you from exile, offering her these ornaments the while;

for it is most needful that she receive the gifts in her own hand.

Now go and linger not; may ye succeed and to your mother bring back

the glad tidings she fain would hear (JASON, the ATTENDANT, and the

children go out together.)

CHORUS (singing, strophe 1)

Gone, gone is every hope I had that the children yet might live;

forth to their doom they now proceed. The hapless bride will take,

ay, take the golden crown that is to be her ruin; with her own hand

will she lift and place upon her golden locks the garniture of death.

(antistrophe 1)

Its grace and sheen divine will tempt her to put on the robe and crown of gold, and in that act will she deck herself to be a bride

amid the dead. Such is the snare whereinto she will fall, such is

the deadly doom that waits the hapless maid, nor shall she from the

curse escape.

(strophe 2)

And thou, poor wretch, who to thy sorrow art wedding a king's daughter,

little thinkest of the doom thou art bringing on thy children's life,

or of the cruel death that waits thy bride. Woe is thee! how art thou

fallen from thy high estate!

(antistrophe 2)

Next do I bewail thy sorrows, O mother hapless in thy children, thou

who wilt slay thy babes because thou hast a rival, the babes thy husband

hath deserted impiously to join him to another bride. (The ATTENDANT

enters with the children.)

ATTENDANT Thy children, lady, are from exile freed, and gladly did

the royal bride accept thy gifts in her own hands, and so thy children

made their peace with her.

MEDEA Ah!

ATTENDANT Why art so disquieted in thy prosperous hour? Why turnest

thou thy cheek away, and hast no welcome for my glad news?

MEDEA Ah me!

ATTENDANT These groans but ill accord with the news I bring.

MEDEA Ah me! once more I say.

ATTENDANT Have I unwittingly announced some evil tidings? Have I

erred in thinking my news was good?

MEDEA Thy news is as it is; I blame thee not.

ATTENDANT Then why this downcast eye, these floods of tears?

MEDEA Old friend, needs must I weep; for the gods and I with fell

intent devised these schemes.

ATTENDANT Be of good cheer; thou too of a surety shalt by thy sons

yet be brought home again.

MEDEA Ere that shall I bring others to their home, ah! woe is me

ATTENDANT Thou art not the only mother from thy children reft. Bear

patiently thy troubles as a mortal must.

MEDEA I will obey; go thou within the house and make the day's provision

for the children. (The ATTENDANT enters the house. MEDEA turns to

the children.) O my babes, my babes, ye have still a city and a home,

where far from me and my sad lot you will live your lives, reft of

your mother for ever; while I must to another land in banishment,

or ever I have had my joy of you, or lived to see you happy, or ever

I have graced your marriage couch, your bride, your bridal bower,

or lifted high the wedding torch. Ah me! a victim of my own self-will.

So it was all in vain I reared you, O my sons; in vain did suffer,

racked with anguish, enduring the cruel pangs of childbirth. 'Fore

Heaven I once had hope, poor me! high hope of ye that you would nurse

me in my age and deck my corpse with loving hands, a boon we mortals

covet; but now is my sweet fancy dead and gone; for I must lose you

both and in bitterness and sorrow drag through life. And ye shall

never with fond eyes see your mother more for o'er your life there comes a change. Ah me! ah me! why do ye look at me so, my children? why smile that last sweet smile? Ah me! what am I to do? My heart gives way when I behold my children's laughing eyes. O, I cannot; farewell to all my former schemes; I will take the children from the land, the babes I bore. Why should I wound their sire by wounding them, and get me a twofold measure of sorrow? No, no, I will not do

1. Farewell my scheming! And yet what possesses me? Can I consent to let those foes of mine escape from punishment, and incur their mockery? I must face this deed. Out upon my craven heart! to think that I should even have let the soft words escape my soul. Into the house, children! (The children go into the house.) And whoso feels he must not be present at my sacrifice, must see to it himself; I will not spoil my handiwork. Ah! ah! do not, my heart, O do not do this deed! Let the children go, unhappy one, spare the babes! For if they live, they will cheer thee in our exile there. Nay, by the fiends of hell's abyss, never, never will I hand my children over to their foes to mock and flout. Die they must in any case, and since 'tis so, why I, the mother who bore them, will give the fatal blow. In any case their doom is fixed and there is no escape. Already the crown is on her head, the robe is round her, and she is dying, the royal bride; that do I know full well. But now since I have a piteous path to tread, and yet more piteous still the path I send my children on, fain would I say farewell to them. (The children come out at her call. She takes them in her arms.) O my babes, my babes, let your mother kiss your hands. Ah! hands I love so well, O lips most dear to me! O noble form and features of my children, I wish ye joy, but in that other land, for here your father robs you of your home. O the sweet embrace, the soft young cheek, the fragrant breath! my children! Go, leave me; I cannot bear to longer look upon ye; my sorrow

wins the day. At last I understand the awful deed I am to do; but

passion, that cause of direst woes to mortal man, hath triumphed o'er

my sober thoughts. (She goes into the house with the children.)

CHORUS (chanting) Oft ere now have I pursued subtler themes and

have faced graver issues than woman's sex should seek to probe; but

then e'en we aspire to culture, which dwells with us to teach us wisdom;

I say not all; for small is the class amongst women-(one maybe shalt

thou find 'mid many)-that is not incapable of wisdom. And amongst

mortals I do assert that they who are wholly without experience and

have never had children far surpass in happiness those who are parents.

The childless, because they have never proved whether children grow

up to be a blessing or curse to men are removed from all share in

many troubles; whilst those who have a sweet race of children growing

up in their houses do wear away, as I perceive, their whole life through;

first with the thought how they may train them up in virtue, next

how they shall leave their sons the means to live; and after all this

'tis far from clear whether on good or bad children they bestow their

toil. But one last crowning woe for every mortal man now will name;

suppose that they have found sufficient means to live, and seen their

children grow to man's estate and walk in virtue's path, still if

fortune so befall, comes Death and bears the children's bodies off

to Hades. Can it be any profit to the gods to heap upon us mortal

men beside our other woes this further grief for children lost, a

grief surpassing all? (MEDEA comes out of the house.)

MEDEA Kind friends, long have I waited expectantly to know how things

would at the palace chance. And lo! I see one of Jason's servants

coming hither, whose hurried gasps for breath proclaim him the bearer of some fresh tidings. (A MESSENGER rushes in.)

MESSENGER Fly, fly, Medea! who hast wrought an awful deed, transgressing

every law: nor leave behind or sea-borne bark or car that scours the

plain.

MEDEA Why, what hath chanced that calls for such a flight of mine?

MESSENGER The princess is dead, a moment gone, and Creon too, her

sire, slain by those drugs of thine.

MEDEA Tidings most fair are thine! Henceforth shalt thou be ranked

amongst my friends and benefactors.

MESSENGER Ha! What? Art sane? Art not distraught, lady, who hearest

with joy the outrage to our royal house done, and art not at the horrid

tale afraid?

MEDEA Somewhat have I, too, to say in answer to thy words. Be not

so hasty, friend, but tell the manner of their death, for thou wouldst

give me double joy, if so they perished miserably.

MESSENGER When the children twain whom thou didst bear came with

their father and entered the palace of the bride, right glad were

we thralls who had shared thy griefs, for instantly from ear to ear

a rumour spread that thou and thy lord had made up your former quarrel.

One kissed thy children's hands, another their golden hair, while

I for very joy went with them in person to the women's chambers. Our

mistress, whom now we do revere in thy room, cast a longing glance at Jason, ere she saw thy children twain; but then she veiled her

eyes and turned her blanching cheek away, disgusted at their coming;

but thy husband tried to check his young bride's angry humour with

these words: "O, be not angered 'gainst thy friends; cease from wrath

and turn once more thy face this way, counting as friends whomso thy

husband counts, and accept these gifts, and for my sake crave thy

sire to remit these children's exile." Soon as she saw the ornaments,

no longer she held out, but yielded to her lord in all; and ere the

father and his sons were far from the palace gone, she took the broidered

robe and put it on, and set the golden crown about her tresses, arranging

her hair at her bright mirror, with many a happy smile at her breathless

counterfeit. Then rising from her seat she passed across the chamber,

tripping lightly on her fair white foot, exulting in the gift, with

many a glance at her uplifted ankle. When lo! a scene of awful horror

did ensue. In a moment she turned pale, reeled backwards, trembling

in every limb, and sinks upon a seat scarce soon enough to save herself

from falling to the ground. An aged dame, one of her company, thinking

belike it was a fit from Pan or some god sent, raised a cry of prayer,

till from her mouth she saw the foam-flakes issue, her eyeballs rolling

in their sockets, and all the blood her face desert; then did she

raise a loud scream far different from her former cry. Forthwith one

handmaid rushed to her father's house, another to her new bridegroom

to tell his bride's sad fate, and the whole house echoed with their

running to and fro. By this time would a quick walker have made the

turn in a course of six plethra and reached the goal, when she with

one awful shriek awoke, poor sufferer, from her speechless trance

and oped her closed eyes, for against her a twofold anguish was warring.

The chaplet of gold about her head was sending forth a wondrous stream

of ravening flame, while the fine raiment, thy children's gift, was preying on the hapless maiden's fair white flesh; and she starts from

her seat in a blaze and seeks to fly, shaking her hair and head this

way and that, to cast the crown therefrom; but the gold held firm

to its fastenings, and the flame, as she shook her locks, blazed forth

the more with double fury. Then to the earth she sinks, by the cruel

blow o'ercome; past all recognition now save to a father's eye; for

her eyes had lost their tranquil gaze, her face no more its natural

look preserved, and from the crown of her head blood and fire in mingled

stream ran down; and from her bones the flesh kept peeling off beneath

the gnawing of those secret drugs, e'en as when the pine-tree weeps

its tears of pitch, a fearsome sight to see. And all were afraid to

touch the corpse, for we were warned by what had chanced. Anon came

her haples father unto the house, all unwitting of her doom, and stumbles

o'er the dead, and loud he cried, and folding his arms about her kissed

her, with words like these the while, "O my poor, poor child, which

of the gods hath destroyed thee thus foully? Who is robbing me of

thee, old as I am and ripe for death? O my child, alas! would I could

die with thee!" He ceased his sad lament, and would have raised his

aged frame, but found himself held fast by the fine-spun robe as ivy

that clings to the branches of the bay, and then ensued a fearful

struggle. He strove to rise, but she still held him back; and if ever

he pulled with all his might, from off his bones his aged flesh he

tore. At last he gave it up, and breathed forth his soul in awful

suffering; for he could no longer master the pain. So there they lie,

daughter and aged sire, dead side by side, a grievous sight that calls

for tears. And as for thee, I leave thee out of my consideration,

for thyself must discover a means to escape punishment. Not now for

the first time I think this human life a shadow; yea, and without

shrinking I will say that they amongst men who pretend to wisdom and expend deep thought on words do incur a serious charge of folly; for

amongst mortals no man is happy; wealth may pour in and make one luckier

than another, but none can happy be. (The MESSENGER departs.)

LEADER OF THE CHORUS This day the deity, it seems, will mass on Jason,

as he well deserves, heavy load of evils. Woe is thee, daughter of

Creon We pity thy sad fate, gone as thou art to Hades' halls as the

price of thy marriage with Jason.

MEDEA My friends, I am resolved upon the deed; at once will I slay

my children and then leave this land, without delaying long enough

to hand them over to some more savage hand to butcher. Needs must

they die in any case; and since they must, I will slay them-I, the

mother that bare them. O heart of mine, steel thyself! Why do I hesitate

to do the awful deed that must be done? Come, take the sword, thou

wretched hand of mine! Take it, and advance to the post whence starts

thy life of sorrow! Away with cowardice! Give not one thought to thy

babes, how dear they are or how thou art their mother. This one brief

day forget thy children dear, and after that lament; for though thou

wilt slay them yet they were thy darlings still, and I am a lady of

sorrows. (MEDEA enters the house.)

CHORUS (chanting) O earth, O sun whose beam illumines all, look,

look upon this lost woman, ere she stretch forth her murderous hand

upon her sons for blood; for lo! these are scions of thy own golden

seed, and the blood of gods is in danger of being shed by man. O light,

from Zeus proceeding, stay her, hold her hand, forth from the house

chase this fell bloody fiend by demons led. Vainly wasted were the

throes thy children cost thee; vainly hast thou borne, it seems, sweet babes, O thou who hast left behind thee that passage through the blue Symplegades, that strangers justly hate. Ah! hapless one, why doth fierce anger thy soul assail? Why in its place is fell murder growing up? For grievous unto mortal men are pollutions that come of kindred blood poured on the earth, woes to suit each crime hurled from heaven on the murderer's house.

FIRST SON (within) Ah, me; what can I do? Whither fly to escape my mother's blows?

SECOND SON (within) I know not, sweet brother mine; we are lost.

CHORUS (chanting) Didst hear, didst hear the children's cry? O lady, born to sorrow, victim of an evil fate! Shall I enter the house? For the children's sake I am resolved to ward off the murder.

FIRST SON (within) Yea, by heaven I adjure you; help, your aid is needed.

SECOND SON (within) Even now the toils of the sword are closing round us.

CHORUS (chanting) O hapless mother, surely thou hast a heart of stone or steel to slay the offspring of thy womb by such a murderous doom. Of all the wives of yore I know but one who laid her hand upon her children dear, even Ino, whom the gods did madden in the day that the wife of Zeus drove her wandering from her home. But she, poor sufferer, flung herself into the sea because of the foul murder of her children, leaping o'er the wave-beat cliff, and in her death was she united to her children twain. Can there be any deed of horror

left to follow this? Woe for the wooing of women fraught with disaster!

What sorrows hast thou caused for men ere now! (JASON and his attendants

enter.)

JASON Ladies, stationed near this house, pray tell me is the author

of these hideous deeds, Medea, still within, or hath she fled from

hence? For she must hide beneath the earth or soar on wings towards

heaven's vault, if she would avoid the vengeance of the royal house.

Is she so sure she will escape herself unpunished from this house,

when she hath slain the rulers of the land? But enough of this! I

am forgetting her children. As for her, those whom she hath wronged

will do the like by her; but I am come to save the children's life,

lest the victim's kin visit their wrath on me, in vengeance for the

murder foul, wrought by my children's mother.

LEADER OF THE CHORUS Unhappy man, thou knowest not the full extent

of thy misery, else had thou never said those words.

JASON How now? Can she want to kill me too?

LEADER Thy sons are dead; slain by their own mother's hand.

JASON O God! what sayest thou? Woman, thou hast sealed my doom.

LEADER Thy children are no more; be sure of this.

JASON Where slew she them; within the palace or outside?

LEADER Throw wide the doors and see thy children's murdered corpses.

JASON Haste, ye slaves, loose the bolts, undo the fastenings, that

I may see the sight of twofold woe, my murdered sons and her, whose

blood in vengeance I will shed. (MEDEA appears above the house, on

a chariot drawn by dragons; the children's corpses are beside her.)

MEDEA Why shake those doors and attempt to loose their bolts, in

quest of the dead and me their murderess? From such toil desist. If

thou wouldst aught with me, say on, if so thou wilt; but never shalt

thou lay hand on me, so swift the steeds the sun, my father's sire,

to me doth give to save me from the hand of my foes.

JASON Accursed woman! by gods, by me and all mankind abhorred as

never woman was, who hadst the heart to stab thy babes, thou their

mother, leaving me undone and childless; this hast thou done and still

dost gaze upon the sun and earth after this deed most impious. Curses

on thee! now perceive what then I missed in the day I brought thee,

fraught with doom, from thy home in a barbarian land to dwell in Hellas,

traitress to thy sire and to the land that nurtured thee. On me the

gods have hurled the curse that dogged thy steps, for thou didst slay

thy brother at his hearth ere thou cam'st aboard our fair ship, Argo.

Such was the outset of thy life of crime; then didst thou wed with

me, and having borne me sons to glut thy passion's lust, thou now

hast slain them. Not one amongst the wives of Hellas e'er had dared

this deed; yet before them all I chose thee for my wife, wedding a

foe to be my doom, no woman, but a lioness fiercer than Tyrrhene Scylla

in nature. But with reproaches heaped thousandfold I cannot wound

thee, so brazen is thy nature. Perish, vile sorceress, murderess of thy babes! Whilst I must mourn my luckless fate, for I shall ne'er

enjoy my new-found bride, nor shall I have the children, whom I bred

and reared, alive to say the last farewell to me; nay, I have lost

them.

MEDEA To this thy speech I could have made a long reply, but Father

Zeus knows well all I have done for thee, and the treatment thou hast

given me. Yet thou wert not ordained to scorn my love and lead a life

of joy in mockery of me, nor was thy royal bride nor Creon, who gave

thee a second wife, to thrust me from this land and rue it not. Wherefore,

if thou wilt, call me e'en a lioness, and Scylla, whose home is in

the Tyrrhene land; for I in turn have wrung thy heart, as well I might.

JASON Thou, too, art grieved thyself, and sharest in my sorrow.

MEDEA Be well assured I am; but it relieves my pain to know thou

canst not mock at me.

JASON O my children, how vile a mother ye have found!

MEDEA My sons, your father's feeble lust has been your ruin!

JASON 'Twas not my hand, at any rate, that slew them.

MEDEA No, but thy foul treatment of me, and thy new marriage.

JASON Didst think that marriage cause enough to murder them?

MEDEA Dost think a woman counts this a trifling injury?

JASON So she be self-restrained; but in thy eyes all is evil.

MEDEA Thy sons are dead and gone. That will stab thy heart.

JASON They live, methinks, to bring a curse upon thy head.

MEDEA The gods know, whoso of them began this troublous coil.

JASON Indeed, they know that hateful heart of thine.

MEDEA Thou art as hateful. I am aweary of thy bitter tongue.

JASON And I likewise of thine. But parting is easy.

MEDEA Say how; what am I to do? for I am fain as thou to go.

JASON Give up to me those dead, to bury and lament.

MEDEA No, never! I will bury them myself, bearing them to Hera's sacred field, who watches o'er the Cape, that none of their foes may insult them by pulling down their tombs; and in this land of Sisyphus I will ordain hereafter a solemn feast and mystic rites to atone for this impious murder. Myself will now to the land of Erechtheus, to dwell with Aegeus, Pandion's son. But thou, as well thou mayst, shalt die a caitiff's death, thy head crushed 'neath a shattered relic of Argo, when thou hast seen the bitter ending of my marriage.

JASON The curse of our sons' avenging spirit and of justice, that calls for blood, be on thee!

MEDEA What god or power divine hears thee, breaker of oaths and every law of hospitality?

JASON Fie upon thee! cursed witch! child-murderess!

MEDEA To thy house! go, bury thy wife.

JASON I go, bereft of both my sons.

MEDEA Thy grief is yet to come; wait till old age is with thee too.

JASON O my dear, dear children!

MEDEA Dear to their mother, not to thee.

JASON And yet thou didst slay them?

MEDEA Yea, to vex thy heart.

JASON One last fond kiss, ah me! I fain would on their lips imprint.

MEDEA Embraces now, and fond farewells for them; but then a cold

repulse!

JASON By heaven I do adjure thee, let me touch their tender skin.

MEDEA No, no! in vain this word has sped its flight.

JASON O Zeus, dost hear how I am driven hence; dost mark the treatment

I receive from this she-lion, fell murderess of her young? Yet so

far as I may and can, I raise for them a dirge, and do adjure the

gods to witness how thou hast slain my sons, and wilt not suffer me

to embrace or bury their dead bodies. Would I had never begotten them

to see thee slay them after all! (The chariot carries MEDEA away.)

CHORUS (chanting) Many a fate doth Zeus dispense, high on his Olympian

throne; oft do the gods bring things to pass beyond man's expectation;

that, which we thought would be, is not fulfilled, while for the unlooked-for

god finds out a way; and such hath been the issue of this matter.

THE END

Christopher Marlowe, The Tragical History of Doctor Faustus

From The Quarto of 1604

Edited by The Rev. Alexander Dyce

In reprinting this edition, I have here and there amended the text by means of the later 4tos,—1616, 1624, 1631.—Of 4to 1663, which contains various comparatively modern alterations and additions, I have made no use.THE TRAGICALL HISTORY OF D. FAUSTUS. AS IT HATH BENE ACTED BY THE RIGHT HONORABLE THE EARLE OF NOTTINGHAM HIS SERUANTS. WRITTEN BY CH. MARL.

DRAMATIS PERSONAE.

THE POPE.

CARDINAL OF LORRAIN.

THE EMPEROR OF GERMANY.

DUKE OF VANHOLT.

FAUSTUS.

VALDES,   ] friends to FAUSTUS.

CORNELIUS,]

WAGNER, servant to FAUSTUS.

Clown.

ROBIN.

RALPH.

Vintner.

Horse-courser.

A Knight.

An Old Man.

Scholars, Friars, and Attendants.

DUCHESS OF VANHOLT

LUCIFER.

BELZEBUB.

MEPHISTOPHILIS.

Good Angel.

Evil Angel.

The Seven Deadly Sins.

Devils.

Spirits in the shapes of ALEXANDER THE GREAT, of his Paramour
    and of HELEN.

Chorus.

THE TRAGICAL HISTORY OF DOCTOR FAUSTUS

FROM THE QUARTO OF 1604.

Enter CHORUS.

CHORUS. Not marching now in fields of Thrasymene,
Where Mars did mate1 the Carthaginians;
Nor sporting in the dalliance of love,
In courts of kings where state is overturn'd;
Nor in the pomp of proud audacious deeds,
Intends our Muse to vaunt2 her3 heavenly verse:
Only this, gentlemen,—we must perform
The form of Faustus' fortunes, good or bad:
To patient judgments we appeal our plaud,
And speak for Faustus in his infancy.
Now is he born, his parents base of stock,
In Germany, within a town call'd Rhodes:
Of riper years, to Wertenberg he went,
Whereas4 his kinsmen chiefly brought him up.
So soon he profits in divinity,
The fruitful plot of scholarism grac'd,
That shortly he was grac'd with doctor's name,
Excelling all whose sweet delight disputes
In heavenly matters of theology;
Till swoln with cunning,5 of a self-conceit,
His waxen wings did mount above his reach,
And, melting, heavens conspir'd his overthrow;
For, falling to a devilish exercise,
And glutted now6 with learning's golden gifts,
He surfeits upon cursed necromancy;
Nothing so sweet as magic is to him,
Which he prefers before his chiefest bliss:
And this the man that in his study sits.
    [Exit.]

FAUSTUS discovered in his study.7

FAUSTUS. Settle thy studies, Faustus, and begin
To sound the depth of that thou wilt profess:
Having commenc'd, be a divine in shew,
Yet level at the end of every art,
And live and die in Aristotle's works.
Sweet Analytics, 'tis thou8 hast ravish'd me!
Bene disserere est finis logices.
Is, to dispute well, logic's chiefest end?
Affords this art no greater miracle?

Then read no more; thou hast attain'd that9 end:
A greater subject fitteth Faustus' wit:
Bid Economy10 farewell, and11 Galen come,
Seeing, Ubi desinit philosophus, ibi incipit medicus:
Be a physician, Faustus; heap up gold,
And be eterniz'd for some wondrous cure:
Summum bonum medicinae sanitas,
The end of physic is our body's health.
Why, Faustus, hast thou not attain'd that end?
Is not thy common talk found aphorisms?
Are not thy bills hung up as monuments,
Whereby whole cities have escap'd the plague,
And thousand desperate maladies been eas'd?
Yet art thou still but Faustus, and a man.
Couldst12 thou make men13 to live eternally,
Or, being dead, raise them to life again,
Then this profession were to be esteem'd.
Physic, farewell! Where is Justinian?

　　[Reads.]
Si una eademque res legatur14 duobus, alter rem,
alter valorem rei, &c.

A pretty case of paltry legacies!

　　[Reads.]
Exhoereditare filium non potest pater, nisi, &c.15

Such is the subject of the institute,
And universal body of the law:16
This17 study fits a mercenary drudge,
Who aims at nothing but external trash;
Too servile18 and illiberal for me.
When all is done, divinity is best:
Jerome's Bible, Faustus; view it well.

　　[Reads.]
Stipendium peccati mors est.
　　　　　　　Ha!
　　　　　　　　Stipendium, &c.

The reward of sin is death: that's hard.

　　[Reads.]
Si peccasse negamus, fallimur, et nulla est in nobis veritas;

If we say that we have no sin, we deceive ourselves, and
there's no truth in us. Why, then, belike we must sin, and so

consequently die:

Ay, we must die an everlasting death.

What doctrine call you this, Che sera, sera,19

What will be, shall be? Divinity, adieu!

These metaphysics of magicians,

And necromantic books are heavenly;

Lines, circles, scenes,20 letters, and characters;

Ay, these are those that Faustus most desires.

O, what a world of profit and delight,

Of power, of honour, of omnipotence,

Is promis'd to the studious artizan!

All things that move between the quiet poles

Shall be at my command: emperors and kings

Are but obeyed in their several provinces,

Nor can they raise the wind, or rend the clouds;

But his dominion that exceeds in this,

Stretcheth as far as doth the mind of man;

A sound magician is a mighty god:

Here, Faustus, tire21 thy brains to gain a deity.

Enter WAGNER.22

Wagner, commend me to my dearest friends,

The German Valdes and Cornelius;

Request them earnestly to visit me.

WAGNER. I will, sir.

  [Exit.]

FAUSTUS. Their conference will be a greater help to me

Than all my labours, plod I ne'er so fast.

Enter GOOD ANGEL and EVIL ANGEL.

GOOD ANGEL. O, Faustus, lay that damned book aside,

And gaze not on it, lest it tempt thy soul,

And heap God's heavy wrath upon thy head!

Read, read the Scriptures:—that is blasphemy.

EVIL ANGEL. Go forward, Faustus, in that famous art

Wherein all Nature's treasure23 is contain'd:

Be thou on earth as Jove24 is in the sky,

Lord and commander of these elements.25

   [Exeunt Angels.]

FAUSTUS. How am I glutted with conceit of this!

Shall I make spirits fetch me what I please,

Resolve26 me of all ambiguities,

Perform what desperate enterprise I will?
I'll have them fly to India for gold,
Ransack the ocean for orient pearl,
And search all corners of the new-found world
For pleasant fruits and princely delicates;
I'll have them read me strange philosophy,
And tell the secrets of all foreign kings;
I'll have them wall all Germany with brass,
And make swift Rhine circle fair Wertenberg;
I'll have them fill the public schools with silk,27
Wherewith the students shall be bravely clad;
I'll levy soldiers with the coin they bring,
And chase the Prince of Parma from our land,
And reign sole king of all the28 provinces;
Yea, stranger engines for the brunt of war,
Than was the fiery keel at Antwerp's bridge,29
I'll make my servile spirits to invent.

    Enter VALDES and CORNELIUS.

Come, German Valdes, and Cornelius,
And make me blest with your sage conference.
Valdes, sweet Valdes, and Cornelius,
Know that your words have won me at the last
To practice magic and concealed arts:
Yet not your words only,30 but mine own fantasy,
That will receive no object; for my head
But ruminates on necromantic skill.
Philosophy is odious and obscure;
Both law and physic are for petty wits;
Divinity is basest of the three,
Unpleasant, harsh, contemptible, and vile:31
'Tis magic, magic, that hath ravish'd me.
Then, gentle friends, aid me in this attempt;
And I, that have with concise syllogisms32
Gravell'd the pastors of the German church,
And made the flowering pride of Wertenberg
Swarm to my problems, as the infernal spirits
On sweet Musaeus when he came to hell,
Will be as cunning33 as Agrippa34 was,
Whose shadow35 made all Europe honour him.

VALDES. Faustus, these books, thy wit, and our experience,
Shall make all nations to canonize us.
As Indian Moors obey their Spanish lords,
So shall the spirits36 of every element
Be always serviceable to us three;
Like lions shall they guard us when we please;

Like Almain rutters37 with their horsemen's staves,
Or Lapland giants, trotting by our sides;
Sometimes like women, or unwedded maids,
Shadowing more beauty in their airy brows
Than have the38 white breasts of the queen of love:
From39 Venice shall they drag huge argosies,
And from America the golden fleece
That yearly stuffs old Philip's treasury;
If learned Faustus will be resolute.

FAUSTUS. Valdes, as resolute am I in this
As thou to live: therefore object it not.

CORNELIUS. The miracles that magic will perform
Will make thee vow to study nothing else.
He that is grounded in astrology,
Enrich'd with tongues, well seen in40 minerals,
Hath all the principles magic doth require:
Then doubt not, Faustus, but to be renowm'd,41
And more frequented for this mystery
Than heretofore the Delphian oracle.
The spirits tell me they can dry the sea,
And fetch the treasure of all foreign wrecks,
Ay, all the wealth that our forefathers hid
Within the massy entrails of the earth:
Then tell me, Faustus, what shall we three want?

FAUSTUS. Nothing, Cornelius. O, this cheers my soul!
Come, shew me some demonstrations magical,
That I may conjure in some lusty grove,
And have these joys in full possession.

VALDES. Then haste thee to some solitary grove,
And bear wise Bacon's and Albertus'42 works,
The Hebrew Psalter, and New Testament;
And whatsoever else is requisite
We will inform thee ere our conference cease.

CORNELIUS. Valdes, first let him know the words of art;
And then, all other ceremonies learn'd,
Faustus may try his cunning43 by himself.

VALDES. First I'll instruct thee in the rudiments,
And then wilt thou be perfecter than I.

FAUSTUS. Then come and dine with me, and, after meat,
We'll canvass every quiddity thereof;
For, ere I sleep, I'll try what I can do:

This night I'll conjure, though I die therefore.

  [Exeunt.]

  Enter two SCHOLARS.44

FIRST SCHOLAR. I wonder what's become of Faustus, that was wont
to make our schools ring with sic probo.

SECOND SCHOLAR. That shall we know, for see, here comes his boy.

  Enter WAGNER.

FIRST SCHOLAR. How now, sirrah! where's thy master?

WAGNER. God in heaven knows.

SECOND SCHOLAR. Why, dost not thou know?

WAGNER. Yes, I know; but that follows not.

FIRST SCHOLAR. Go to, sirrah! leave your jesting, and tell us
where he is.

WAGNER. That follows not necessary by force of argument, that you,
being licentiates, should stand upon:45 therefore acknowledge
your error, and be attentive.

SECOND SCHOLAR. Why, didst thou not say thou knewest?

WAGNER. Have you any witness on't?

FIRST SCHOLAR. Yes, sirrah, I heard you.

WAGNER. Ask my fellow if I be a thief.

SECOND SCHOLAR. Well, you will not tell us?

WAGNER. Yes, sir, I will tell you: yet, if you were not dunces,
you would never ask me such a question; for is not he corpus
naturale? and is not that mobile? then wherefore should you
ask me such a question? But that I am by nature phlegmatic,
slow to wrath, and prone to lechery (to love, I would say),
it were not for you to come within forty foot of the place
of execution, although I do not doubt to see you both hanged
the next sessions. Thus having triumphed over you, I will set
my countenance like a precisian, and begin to speak thus:—
Truly, my dear brethren, my master is within at dinner,
with Valdes and Cornelius, as this wine, if it could speak,

would46 inform your worships: and so, the Lord bless you,
preserve you, and keep you, my dear brethren, my dear brethren!47
   [Exit.]

FIRST SCHOLAR. Nay, then, I fear he is fallen into that damned art
for which they two are infamous through the world.

SECOND SCHOLAR. Were he a stranger, and not allied to me, yet should
I grieve for him. But, come, let us go and inform the Rector,
and see if he by his grave counsel can reclaim him.

FIRST SCHOLAR. O, but I fear me nothing can reclaim him!

SECOND SCHOLAR. Yet let us try what we can do.
   [Exeunt.]

   Enter FAUSTUS to conjure.48

FAUSTUS. Now that the gloomy shadow of the earth,
Longing to view Orion's drizzling look,
Leaps from th' antartic world unto the sky,
And dims the welkin with her pitchy breath,
Faustus, begin thine incantations,
And try if devils will obey thy hest,
Seeing thou hast pray'd and sacrific'd to them.
Within this circle is Jehovah's name,
Forward and backward anagrammatiz'd,49
Th' abbreviated50 names of holy saints,
Figures of every adjunct to the heavens,
And characters of signs and erring51 stars,
By which the spirits are enforc'd to rise:
Then fear not, Faustus, but be resolute,
And try the uttermost magic can perform.—
Sint mihi dei Acherontis propitii! Valeat numen triplex Jehovoe!
Ignei, aerii, aquatani spiritus, salvete! Orientis princeps
Belzebub, inferni ardentis monarcha, et Demogorgon, propitiamus
vos, ut appareat et surgat Mephistophilis, quod tumeraris:52
per Jehovam, Gehennam, et consecratam aquam quam nunc spargo,
signumque crucis quod nunc facio, et per vota nostra, ipse nunc
surgat nobis dicatus53 Mephistophilis!

   Enter MEPHISTOPHILIS.

I charge thee to return, and change thy shape;
Thou art too ugly to attend on me:
Go, and return an old Franciscan friar;
That holy shape becomes a devil best.
   [Exit MEPHISTOPHILIS.]

I see there's virtue in my heavenly words:
Who would not be proficient in this art?
How pliant is this Mephistophilis,
Full of obedience and humility!
Such is the force of magic and my spells:
No, Faustus, thou art conjuror laureat,
That canst command great Mephistophilis:
Quin regis Mephistophilis fratris imagine.

    Re-enter MEPHISTOPHILIS like a Franciscan friar.54

MEPHIST. Now, Faustus, what wouldst thou have me do?

FAUSTUS. I charge thee wait upon me whilst I live,
To do whatever Faustus shall command,
Be it to make the moon drop from her sphere,
Or the ocean to overwhelm the world.

MEPHIST. I am a servant to great Lucifer,
And may not follow thee without his leave:
No more than he commands must we perform.

FAUSTUS. Did not he charge thee to appear to me?

MEPHIST. No, I came hither55 of mine own accord.

FAUSTUS. Did not my conjuring speeches raise thee? speak.

MEPHIST. That was the cause, but yet per accidens;56
For, when we hear one rack the name of God,
Abjure the Scriptures and his Saviour Christ,
We fly, in hope to get his glorious soul;
Nor will we come, unless he use such means
Whereby he is in danger to be damn'd.
Therefore the shortest cut for conjuring
Is stoutly to abjure the Trinity,
And pray devoutly to the prince of hell.

FAUSTUS. So Faustus hath
Already done; and holds this principle,
There is no chief but only Belzebub;
To whom Faustus doth dedicate himself.
This word "damnation" terrifies not him,
For he confounds hell in Elysium:
His ghost be with the old philosophers!
But, leaving these vain trifles of men's souls,
Tell me what is that Lucifer thy lord?

MEPHIST. Arch-regent and commander of all spirits.

FAUSTUS. Was not that Lucifer an angel once?

MEPHIST. Yes, Faustus, and most dearly lov'd of God.

FAUSTUS. How comes it, then, that he is prince of devils?

MEPHIST. O, by aspiring pride and insolence;
For which God threw him from the face of heaven.

FAUSTUS. And what are you that live with Lucifer?

MEPHIST. Unhappy spirits that fell with Lucifer,
Conspir'd against our God with Lucifer,
And are for ever damn'd with Lucifer.

FAUSTUS. Where are you damn'd?

MEPHIST. In hell.

FAUSTUS. How comes it, then, that thou art out of hell?

MEPHIST. Why, this is hell, nor am I out of it:57
Think'st thou that I, who saw the face of God,
And tasted the eternal joys of heaven,
Am not tormented with ten thousand hells,
In being depriv'd of everlasting bliss?
O, Faustus, leave these frivolous demands,
Which strike a terror to my fainting soul!

FAUSTUS. What, is great Mephistophilis so passionate
For being deprived of the joys of heaven?
Learn thou of Faustus manly fortitude,
And scorn those joys thou never shalt possess.
Go bear these58 tidings to great Lucifer:
Seeing Faustus hath incurr'd eternal death
By desperate thoughts against Jove's59 deity,
Say, he surrenders up to him his soul,
So he will spare him four and twenty60 years,
Letting him live in all voluptuousness;
Having thee ever to attend on me,
To give me whatsoever I shall ask,
To tell me whatsoever I demand,
To slay mine enemies, and aid my friends,
And always be obedient to my will.
Go and return to mighty Lucifer,

And meet me in my study at midnight,
And then resolve61 me of thy master's mind.

MEPHIST. I will, Faustus.
　　[Exit.]

FAUSTUS. Had I as many souls as there be stars,
I'd give them all for Mephistophilis.
By him I'll be great emperor of the world,
And make a bridge thorough62 the moving air,
To pass the ocean with a band of men;
I'll join the hills that bind the Afric shore,
And make that country63 continent to Spain,
And both contributory to my crown:
The Emperor shall not live but by my leave,
Nor any potentate of Germany.
Now that I have obtain'd what I desir'd,64
I'll live in speculation of this art,
Till Mephistophilis return again.
　　[Exit.]

　　Enter WAGNER65 and CLOWN.

WAGNER. Sirrah boy, come hither.

CLOWN. How, boy! swowns, boy! I hope you have seen many boys
with such pickadevaunts66 as I have: boy, quotha!

WAGNER. Tell me, sirrah, hast thou any comings in?

CLOWN. Ay, and goings out too; you may see else.

WAGNER. Alas, poor slave! see how poverty jesteth in his nakedness!
the villain is bare and out of service, and so hungry, that I know
he would give his soul to the devil for a shoulder of mutton,
though it were blood-raw.

CLOWN. How! my soul to the devil for a shoulder of mutton, though
'twere blood-raw! not so, good friend: by'r lady,67 I had need
have it well roasted, and good sauce to it, if I pay so dear.

WAGNER. Well, wilt thou serve me, and I'll make thee go like
Qui mihi discipulus?68

CLOWN. How, in verse?

WAGNER. No, sirrah; in beaten silk and staves-acre.69

CLOWN. How, how, knaves-acre! ay, I thought that was all the land his father left him. Do you hear? I would be sorry to rob you of your living.

WAGNER. Sirrah, I say in staves-acre.

CLOWN. Oho, oho, staves-acre! why, then, belike, if I were your man, I should be full of vermin.70

WAGNER. So thou shalt, whether thou beest with me or no. But, sirrah, leave your jesting, and bind yourself presently unto me for seven years, or I'll turn all the lice about thee into familiars,71 and they shall tear thee in pieces.

CLOWN. Do you hear, sir? you may save that labour; they are too familiar with me already: swowns, they are as bold with my flesh as if they had paid for their72 meat and drink.

WAGNER. Well, do you hear, sirrah? hold, take these guilders.
  [Gives money.]

CLOWN. Gridirons! what be they?

WAGNER. Why, French crowns.

CLOWN. Mass, but for the name of French crowns, a man were as good have as many English counters. And what should I do with these?

WAGNER. Why, now, sirrah, thou art at an hour's warning, whensoever or wheresoever the devil shall fetch thee.

CLOWN. No, no; here, take your gridirons again.

WAGNER. Truly, I'll none of them.

CLOWN. Truly, but you shall.

WAGNER. Bear witness I gave them him.

CLOWN. Bear witness I give them you again.

WAGNER. Well, I will cause two devils presently to fetch thee away.—Baliol and Belcher!

CLOWN. Let your Baliol and your Belcher come here, and I'll knock them, they were never so knocked since they were devils: say I should kill one of them, what would folks say? "Do ye see yonder tall fellow in the round slop?73 he has killed the devil."

So I should be called Kill-devil all the parish over.

    Enter two DEVILS; and the CLOWN runs up and down crying.

WAGNER. Baliol and Belcher,—spirits, away!
    [Exeunt DEVILS.]

CLOWN. What, are they gone? a vengeance on them! they have vile74
long nails. There was a he-devil and a she-devil: I'll tell you
how you shall know them; all he-devils has horns, and all
she-devils has clifts and cloven feet.

WAGNER. Well, sirrah, follow me.

CLOWN. But, do you hear? if I should serve you, would you teach
me to raise up Banios and Belcheos?

WAGNER. I will teach thee to turn thyself to any thing, to a dog,
or a cat, or a mouse, or a rat, or any thing.

CLOWN. How! a Christian fellow to a dog, or a cat, a mouse,
or a rat! no, no, sir; if you turn me into any thing, let it be
in the likeness of a little pretty frisking flea, that I may be
here and there and every where: O, I'll tickle the pretty wenches'
plackets! I'll be amongst them, i'faith.

WAGNER. Well, sirrah, come.

CLOWN. But, do you hear, Wagner?

WAGNER. How!—Baliol and Belcher!

CLOWN. O Lord! I pray, sir, let Banio and Belcher go sleep.

WAGNER. Villain, call me Master Wagner, and let thy left eye be
diametarily fixed upon my right heel, with quasi vestigiis
nostris75 insistere.
    [Exit.]

CLOWN. God forgive me, he speaks Dutch fustian. Well, I'll follow
him; I'll serve him, that's flat.
    [Exit.]

    FAUSTUS discovered in his study.

FAUSTUS. Now, Faustus, must
Thou needs be damn'd, and canst thou not be sav'd:
What boots it, then, to think of God or heaven?

Away with such vain fancies, and despair;
Despair in God, and trust in Belzebub:
Now go not backward; no, Faustus, be resolute:
Why waver'st thou? O, something soundeth in mine ears,
"Abjure this magic, turn to God again!"
Ay, and Faustus will turn to God again.
To God? he loves thee not;
The god thou serv'st is thine own appetite,
Wherein is fix'd the love of Belzebub:
To him I'll build an altar and a church,
And offer lukewarm blood of new-born babes.

    Enter GOOD ANGEL and EVIL ANGEL.

GOOD ANGEL. Sweet Faustus, leave that execrable art.

FAUSTUS. Contrition, prayer, repentance—what of them?

GOOD ANGEL. O, they are means to bring thee unto heaven!

EVIL ANGEL. Rather illusions, fruits of lunacy,
That make men foolish that do trust them most.

GOOD ANGEL. Sweet Faustus, think of heaven and heavenly things.

EVIL ANGEL. No, Faustus; think of honour and of76 wealth.
    [Exeunt ANGELS.]

FAUSTUS. Of wealth!
Why, the signiory of Embden shall be mine.
When Mephistophilis shall stand by me,
What god can hurt thee, Faustus? thou art safe
Cast no more doubts.—Come, Mephistophilis,
And bring glad tidings from great Lucifer;—
Is't not midnight?—come, Mephistophilis,
Veni, veni, Mephistophile!

    Enter MEPHISTOPHILIS.

Now tell me77 what says Lucifer, thy lord?

MEPHIST. That I shall wait on Faustus whilst he lives,78
So he will buy my service with his soul.

FAUSTUS. Already Faustus hath hazarded that for thee.

MEPHIST. But, Faustus, thou must bequeath it solemnly,
And write a deed of gift with thine own blood;

For that security craves great Lucifer.
If thou deny it, I will back to hell.

FAUSTUS. Stay, Mephistophilis, and tell me, what good will my soul
do thy lord?

MEPHIST. Enlarge his kingdom.

FAUSTUS. Is that the reason why79 he tempts us thus?

MEPHIST. Solamen miseris socios habuisse doloris.80

FAUSTUS. Why,81 have you any pain that torture82 others!

MEPHIST. As great as have the human souls of men.
But, tell me, Faustus, shall I have thy soul?
And I will be thy slave, and wait on thee,
And give thee more than thou hast wit to ask.

FAUSTUS. Ay, Mephistophilis, I give it thee.

MEPHIST. Then, Faustus,83 stab thine arm courageously,
And bind thy soul, that at some certain day
Great Lucifer may claim it as his own;
And then be thou as great as Lucifer.

FAUSTUS. [Stabbing his arm] Lo, Mephistophilis, for love of thee,
I cut mine arm, and with my proper blood
Assure my soul to be great Lucifer's,
Chief lord and regent of perpetual night!
View here the blood that trickles from mine arm,
And let it be propitious for my wish.

MEPHIST. But, Faustus, thou must
Write it in manner of a deed of gift.

FAUSTUS. Ay, so I will [Writes]. But, Mephistophilis,
My blood congeals, and I can write no more.

MEPHIST. I'll fetch thee fire to dissolve it straight.
   [Exit.]

FAUSTUS. What might the staying of my blood portend?
Is it unwilling I should write this bill?84
Why streams it not, that I may write afresh?
FAUSTUS GIVES TO THEE HIS SOUL: ah, there it stay'd!
Why shouldst thou not? is not thy soul shine own?
Then write again, FAUSTUS GIVES TO THEE HIS SOUL.

Re-enter MEPHISTOPHILIS with a chafer of coals.

MEPHIST. Here's fire; come, Faustus, set it on.85

FAUSTUS. So, now the blood begins to clear again;
Now will I make an end immediately.
  [Writes.]

MEPHIST. O, what will not I do to obtain his soul?
  [Aside.]

FAUSTUS. Consummatum est; this bill is ended,
And Faustus hath bequeath'd his soul to Lucifer.
But what is this inscription86 on mine arm?
Homo, fuge: whither should I fly?
If unto God, he'll throw me87 down to hell.
My senses are deceiv'd; here's nothing writ:—
I see it plain; here in this place is writ,
Homo, fuge: yet shall not Faustus fly.

MEPHIST. I'll fetch him somewhat to delight his mind.
  [Aside, and then exit.]

  Re-enter MEPHISTOPHILIS with DEVILS, who give crowns
  and rich apparel to FAUSTUS, dance, and then depart.

FAUSTUS. Speak, Mephistophilis, what means this show?

MEPHIST. Nothing, Faustus, but to delight thy mind withal,
And to shew thee what magic can perform.

FAUSTUS. But may I raise up spirits when I please?

MEPHIST. Ay, Faustus, and do greater things than these.

FAUSTUS. Then there's enough for a thousand souls.
Here, Mephistophilis, receive this scroll,
A deed of gift of body and of soul:
But yet conditionally that thou perform
All articles prescrib'd between us both.

MEPHIST. Faustus, I swear by hell and Lucifer
To effect all promises between us made!

FAUSTUS. Then hear me read them. [Reads] ON THESE CONDITIONS
FOLLOWING. FIRST, THAT FAUSTUS MAY BE A SPIRIT IN FORM AND
SUBSTANCE. SECONDLY, THAT MEPHISTOPHILIS SHALL BE HIS SERVANT,

AND AT HIS COMMAND. THIRDLY, THAT MEPHISTOPHILIS SHALL DO FOR HIM, AND BRING HIM WHATSOEVER HE DESIRES.88 FOURTHLY, THAT HE SHALL BE IN HIS CHAMBER OR HOUSE INVISIBLE. LASTLY, THAT HE SHALL APPEAR TO THE SAID JOHN FAUSTUS, AT ALL TIMES, IN WHAT FORM OR SHAPE SOEVER HE PLEASE. I, JOHN FAUSTUS, OF WERTENBERG, DOCTOR, BY THESE PRESENTS, DO GIVE BOTH BODY AND SOUL TO LUCIFER PRINCE OF THE EAST, AND HIS MINISTER MEPHISTOPHILIS; AND FURTHERMORE GRANT UNTO THEM, THAT,89 TWENTY-FOUR YEARS BEING EXPIRED, THE ARTICLES ABOVE-WRITTEN INVIOLATE, FULL POWER TO FETCH OR CARRY THE SAID JOHN FAUSTUS, BODY AND SOUL, FLESH, BLOOD, OR GOODS, INTO THEIR HABITATION WHERESOEVER. BY ME, JOHN FAUSTUS.

MEPHIST. Speak, Faustus, do you deliver this as your deed?

FAUSTUS. Ay, take it, and the devil give thee good on't!

MEPHIST. Now, Faustus, ask what thou wilt.

FAUSTUS. First will I question with thee about hell.
Tell me, where is the place that men call hell?

MEPHIST. Under the heavens.

FAUSTUS. Ay, but whereabout?

MEPHIST. Within the bowels of these90 elements,
Where we are tortur'd and remain for ever:
Hell hath no limits, nor is circumscrib'd
In one self place; for where we are is hell,
And where hell is, there91 must we ever be:
And, to conclude, when all the world dissolves,
And every creature shall be purified,
All places shall be hell that are92 not heaven.

FAUSTUS. Come, I think hell's a fable.

MEPHIST. Ay, think so still, till experience change thy mind.

FAUSTUS. Why, think'st thou, then, that Faustus shall be damn'd?

MEPHIST. Ay, of necessity, for here's the scroll
Wherein thou hast given thy soul to Lucifer.

FAUSTUS. Ay, and body too: but what of that?
Think'st thou that Faustus is so fond93 to imagine
That, after this life, there is any pain?
Tush, these are trifles and mere old wives' tales.

MEPHIST. But, Faustus, I am an instance to prove the contrary,
For I am damn'd, and am now in hell.

FAUSTUS. How! now in hell!
Nay, an this be hell, I'll willingly be damn'd here:
What! walking, disputing, &c.94
But, leaving off this, let me have a wife,95
The fairest maid in Germany;
For I am wanton and lascivious,
And cannot live without a wife.

MEPHIST. How! a wife!
I prithee, Faustus, talk not of a wife.

FAUSTUS. Nay, sweet Mephistophilis, fetch me one, for I will have
one.

MEPHIST. Well, thou wilt have one? Sit there till I come: I'll
fetch thee a wife in the devil's name.
  [Exit.]

  Re-enter MEPHISTOPHILIS with a DEVIL drest like a WOMAN,
  with fire-works.

MEPHIST. Tell me,96 Faustus, how dost thou like thy wife?

FAUSTUS. A plague on her for a hot whore!

MEPHIST. Tut, Faustus,
Marriage is but a ceremonial toy;
If thou lovest me, think no97 more of it.
I'll cull thee out the fairest courtezans,
And bring them every morning to thy bed:
She whom thine eye shall like, thy heart shall have,
Be she as chaste as was Penelope,
As wise as Saba,98 or as beautiful
As was bright Lucifer before his fall.
Hold, take this book, peruse it thoroughly:
  [Gives book.]

The iterating99 of these lines brings gold;
The framing of this circle on the ground
Brings whirlwinds, tempests, thunder, and lightning;
Pronounce this thrice devoutly to thyself,
And men in armour shall appear to thee,
Ready to execute what thou desir'st.

FAUSTUS. Thanks, Mephistophilis: yet fain would I have a book

wherein I might behold all spells and incantations, that I
might raise up spirits when I please.

MEPHIST. Here they are in this book.
  [Turns to them.]

FAUSTUS. Now would I have a book where I might see all characters
and planets of the heavens, that I might know their motions and
dispositions.

MEPHIST. Here they are too.
  [Turns to them.]

FAUSTUS. Nay, let me have one book more,—and then I have done,—
wherein I might see all plants, herbs, and trees, that grow upon
the earth.

MEPHIST. Here they be.

FAUSTUS. O, thou art deceived.

MEPHIST. Tut, I warrant thee.
  [Turns to them.]

FAUSTUS. When I behold the heavens, then I repent,
And curse thee, wicked Mephistophilis,
Because thou hast depriv'd me of those joys.

MEPHIST. Why, Faustus,
Thinkest thou heaven is such a glorious thing?
I tell thee, 'tis not half so fair as thou,
Or any man that breathes on earth.

FAUSTUS. How prov'st thou that?

MEPHIST. 'Twas made for man, therefore is man more excellent.

FAUSTUS. If it were made for man, 'twas made for me:
I will renounce this magic and repent.

  Enter GOOD ANGEL and EVIL ANGEL.

GOOD ANGEL. Faustus, repent; yet God will pity thee.

EVIL ANGEL. Thou art a spirit; God cannot pity thee.

FAUSTUS. Who buzzeth in mine ears I am a spirit?
Be I a devil, yet God may pity me;

Ay, God will pity me, if I repent.

EVIL ANGEL. Ay, but Faustus never shall repent.
   [Exeunt ANGELS.]

FAUSTUS. My heart's so harden'd, I cannot repent:
Scarce can I name salvation, faith, or heaven,
But fearful echoes thunder in mine ears,
"Faustus, thou art damn'd!" then swords, and knives,
Poison, guns, halters, and envenom'd steel
Are laid before me to despatch myself;
And long ere this I should have slain myself,
Had not sweet pleasure conquer'd deep despair.
Have not I made blind Homer sing to me
Of Alexander's love and Oenon's death?
And hath not he, that built the walls of Thebes
With ravishing sound of his melodious harp,
Made music with my Mephistophilis?
Why should I die, then, or basely despair?
I am resolv'd; Faustus shall ne'er repent.—
Come, Mephistophilis, let us dispute again,
And argue of divine astrology.100
Tell me, are there many heavens above the moon
Are all celestial bodies but one globe,
As is the substance of this centric earth?

MEPHIST. As are the elements, such are the spheres,
Mutually folded in each other's orb,
And, Faustus,
All jointly move upon one axletree,
Whose terminine is term'd the world's wide pole;
Nor are the names of Saturn, Mars, or Jupiter
Feign'd, but are erring101 stars.

FAUSTUS. But, tell me, have they all one motion, both situ et
tempore?

MEPHIST. All jointly move from east to west in twenty-four hours
upon the poles of the world; but differ in their motion upon
the poles of the zodiac.

FAUSTUS. Tush,
These slender trifles Wagner can decide:
Hath Mephistophilis no greater skill?
Who knows not the double motion of the planets?
The first is finish'd in a natural day;
The second thus; as Saturn in thirty years; Jupiter in twelve;
Mars in four; the Sun, Venus, and Mercury in a year; the Moon in

twenty-eight days. Tush, these are freshmen's102 suppositions.
But, tell me, hath every sphere a dominion or intelligentia?

MEPHIST. Ay.

FAUSTUS. How many heavens or spheres are there?

MEPHIST. Nine; the seven planets, the firmament, and the empyreal
heaven.

FAUSTUS. Well, resolve103 me in this question; why have we not
conjunctions, oppositions, aspects, eclipses, all at one time,
but in some years we have more, in some less?

MEPHIST. Per inoequalem motum respectu totius.

FAUSTUS. Well, I am answered. Tell me who made the world?

MEPHIST. I will not.

FAUSTUS. Sweet Mephistophilis, tell me.

MEPHIST. Move me not, for I will not tell thee.

FAUSTUS. Villain, have I not bound thee to tell me any thing?

MEPHIST. Ay, that is not against our kingdom; but this is. Think
thou on hell, Faustus, for thou art damned.

FAUSTUS. Think, Faustus, upon God that made the world.

MEPHIST. Remember this.
   [Exit.]

FAUSTUS. Ay, go, accursed spirit, to ugly hell!
'Tis thou hast damn'd distressed Faustus' soul.
Is't not too late?

   Re-enter GOOD ANGEL and EVIL ANGEL.

EVIL ANGEL. Too late.

GOOD ANGEL. Never too late, if Faustus can repent.

EVIL ANGEL. If thou repent, devils shall tear thee in pieces.

GOOD ANGEL. Repent, and they shall never raze thy skin.
   [Exeunt ANGELS.]

FAUSTUS. Ah, Christ, my Saviour,
Seek to save104 distressed Faustus' soul!

Enter LUCIFER, BELZEBUB, and MEPHISTOPHILIS.

LUCIFER. Christ cannot save thy soul, for he is just:
There's none but I have interest in the same.

FAUSTUS. O, who art thou that look'st so terrible?

LUCIFER. I am Lucifer,
And this is my companion-prince in hell.

FAUSTUS. O, Faustus, they are come to fetch away thy soul!

LUCIFER. We come to tell thee thou dost injure us;
Thou talk'st of Christ, contrary to thy promise:
Thou shouldst not think of God: think of the devil,
And of his dam too.

FAUSTUS. Nor will I henceforth: pardon me in this,
And Faustus vows never to look to heaven,
Never to name God, or to pray to him,
To burn his Scriptures, slay his ministers,
And make my spirits pull his churches down.

LUCIFER. Do so, and we will highly gratify thee. Faustus, we are
come from hell to shew thee some pastime: sit down, and thou
shalt see all the Seven Deadly Sins appear in their proper shapes.

FAUSTUS. That sight will be as pleasing unto me,
As Paradise was to Adam, the first day
Of his creation.

LUCIFER. Talk not of Paradise nor creation; but mark this show:
talk of the devil, and nothing else.—Come away!

Enter the SEVEN DEADLY SINS.105

Now, Faustus, examine them of their several names and dispositions.

FAUSTUS. What art thou, the first?

PRIDE. I am Pride. I disdain to have any parents. I am like to
Ovid's flea; I can creep into every corner of a wench; sometimes,
like a perriwig, I sit upon her brow; or, like a fan of feathers,
I kiss her lips; indeed, I do—what do I not? But, fie, what a

scent is here! I'll not speak another word, except the ground
were perfumed, and covered with cloth of arras.

FAUSTUS. What art thou, the second?

COVETOUSNESS. I am Covetousness, begotten of an old churl, in an
old leathern bag: and, might I have my wish, I would desire that
this house and all the people in it were turned to gold, that I
might lock you up in my good chest: O, my sweet gold!

FAUSTUS. What art thou, the third?

WRATH. I am Wrath. I had neither father nor mother: I leapt out
of a lion's mouth when I was scarce half-an-hour old; and ever
since I have run up and down the world with this case106
of rapiers, wounding myself when I had nobody to fight withal.
I was born in hell; and look to it, for some of you shall be
my father.

FAUSTUS. What art thou, the fourth?

ENVY. I am Envy, begotten of a chimney-sweeper and an oyster-wife.
I cannot read, and therefore wish all books were burnt. I am lean
with seeing others eat. O, that there would come a famine through
all the world, that all might die, and I live alone! then thou
shouldst see how fat I would be. But must thou sit, and I stand?
come down, with a vengeance!

FAUSTUS. Away, envious rascal!—What art thou, the fifth?

GLUTTONY. Who I, sir? I am Gluttony. My parents are all dead,
and the devil a penny they have left me, but a bare pension, and
that is thirty meals a-day and ten bevers,107—a small trifle
to suffice nature. O, I come of a royal parentage! my grandfather
was a Gammon of Bacon, my grandmother a Hogshead of Claret-wine;
my godfathers were these, Peter Pickle-herring and Martin
Martlemas-beef; O, but my godmother, she was a jolly gentlewoman,
and well-beloved in every good town and city; her name was Mistress
Margery March-beer. Now, Faustus, thou hast heard all my progeny;
wilt thou bid me to supper?

FAUSTUS. No, I'll see thee hanged: thou wilt eat up all my victuals.

GLUTTONY. Then the devil choke thee!

FAUSTUS. Choke thyself, glutton!—What art thou, the sixth?

SLOTH. I am Sloth. I was begotten on a sunny bank, where I have lain ever since; and you have done me great injury to bring me from thence: let me be carried thither again by Gluttony and Lechery. I'll not speak another word for a king's ransom.

FAUSTUS. What are you, Mistress Minx, the seventh and last?

LECHERY. Who I, sir? I am one that loves an inch of raw mutton better than an ell of fried stock-fish; and the first letter of my name begins with L.108

FAUSTUS. Away, to hell, to hell!109
   [Exeunt the SINS.]

LUCIFER. Now, Faustus, how dost thou like this?

FAUSTUS. O, this feeds my soul!

LUCIFER. Tut, Faustus, in hell is all manner of delight.

FAUSTUS. O, might I see hell, and return again,
How happy were I then!

LUCIFER. Thou shalt; I will send for thee at midnight.110
In meantime take this book; peruse it throughly,
And thou shalt turn thyself into what shape thou wilt.

FAUSTUS. Great thanks, mighty Lucifer!
This will I keep as chary as my life.

LUCIFER. Farewell, Faustus, and think on the devil.

FAUSTUS. Farewell, great Lucifer.
   [Exeunt LUCIFER and BELZEBUB.]

Come, Mephistophilis.
   [Exeunt.]

   Enter CHORUS.111

CHORUS. Learned Faustus,
To know the secrets of astronomy112
Graven in the book of Jove's high firmament,
Did mount himself to scale Olympus' top,
Being seated in a chariot burning bright,
Drawn by the strength of yoky dragons' necks.
He now is gone to prove cosmography,
And, as I guess, will first arrive at Rome,
To see the Pope and manner of his court,

And take some part of holy Peter's feast,
That to this day is highly solemniz'd.
  [Exit.]

  Enter FAUSTUS and MEPHISTOPHILIS.113

FAUSTUS. Having now, my good Mephistophilis,
Pass'd with delight the stately town of Trier,114
Environ'd round with airy mountain-tops,
With walls of flint, and deep-entrenched lakes,
Not to be won by any conquering prince;
From Paris next,115 coasting the realm of France,
We saw the river Maine fall into Rhine,
Whose banks are set with groves of fruitful vines;
Then up to Naples, rich Campania,
Whose buildings fair and gorgeous to the eye,
The streets straight forth, and pav'd with finest brick,
Quarter the town in four equivalents:
There saw we learned Maro's golden tomb,
The way he cut,116 an English mile in length,
Thorough a rock of stone, in one night's space;
From thence to Venice, Padua, and the rest,
In one of which a sumptuous temple stands,117
That threats the stars with her aspiring top.
Thus hitherto hath Faustus spent his time:
But tell me now what resting-place is this?
Hast thou, as erst I did command,
Conducted me within the walls of Rome?

MEPHIST. Faustus, I have; and, because we will not be unprovided,
I have taken up his Holiness' privy-chamber for our use.

FAUSTUS. I hope his Holiness will bid us welcome.

MEPHIST.
Tut, 'tis no matter; man; we'll be bold with his good cheer.
And now, my Faustus, that thou mayst perceive
What Rome containeth to delight thee with,
Know that this city stands upon seven hills
That underprop the groundwork of the same:
Just through the midst118 runs flowing Tiber's stream
With winding banks that cut it in two parts;
Over the which four stately bridges lean,
That make safe passage to each part of Rome:
Upon the bridge call'd Ponte119 Angelo
Erected is a castle passing strong,
Within whose walls such store of ordnance are,
And double cannons fram'd of carved brass,

As match the days within one complete year;
Besides the gates, and high pyramides,
Which Julius Caesar brought from Africa.

FAUSTUS. Now, by the kingdoms of infernal rule,
Of Styx, of120 Acheron, and the fiery lake
Of ever-burning Phlegethon, I swear
That I do long to see the monuments
And situation of bright-splendent Rome:
Come, therefore, let's away.

MEPHIST. Nay, Faustus, stay: I know you'd fain see the Pope,
And take some part of holy Peter's feast,
Where thou shalt see a troop of bald-pate friars,
Whose summum bonum is in belly-cheer.

FAUSTUS. Well, I'm content to compass then some sport,
And by their folly make us merriment.
Then charm me, that I121
May be invisible, to do what I please,
Unseen of any whilst I stay in Rome.
    [Mephistophilis charms him.]

MEPHIST. So, Faustus; now
Do what thou wilt, thou shalt not be discern'd.

    Sound a Sonnet.122 Enter the POPE and the CARDINAL OF
    LORRAIN to the banquet, with FRIARS attending.

POPE. My Lord of Lorrain, will't please you draw near?

FAUSTUS. Fall to, and the devil choke you, an you spare!

POPE. How now! who's that which spake?—Friars, look about.

FIRST FRIAR. Here's nobody, if it like your Holiness.

POPE. My lord, here is a dainty dish was sent me from the Bishop
of Milan.

FAUSTUS. I thank you, sir.
    [Snatches the dish.]

POPE. How now! who's that which snatched the meat from me? will
no man look?—My lord, this dish was sent me from the Cardinal
of Florence.

FAUSTUS. You say true; I'll ha't.

[Snatches the dish.]

POPE. What, again!—My lord, I'll drink to your grace.

FAUSTUS. I'll pledge your grace.
  [Snatches the cup.]

C. OF LOR. My lord, it may be some ghost, newly crept out of
Purgatory, come to beg a pardon of your Holiness.

POPE. It may be so.—Friars, prepare a dirge to lay the fury
of this ghost.—Once again, my lord, fall to.
  [The POPE crosses himself.]

FAUSTUS. What, are you crossing of yourself?
Well, use that trick no more, I would advise you.
  [The POPE crosses himself again.]

Well, there's the second time. Aware the third;
I give you fair warning.
  [The POPE crosses himself again, and FAUSTUS hits him a box
   of the ear; and they all run away.]

Come on, Mephistophilis; what shall we do?

MEPHIST. Nay, I know not: we shall be cursed with bell, book,
and candle.

FAUSTUS. How! bell, book, and candle,—candle, book, and bell,—
Forward and backward, to curse Faustus to hell!
Anon you shall hear a hog grunt, a calf bleat, and an ass bray,
Because it is Saint Peter's holiday.

  Re-enter all the FRIARS to sing the Dirge.

FIRST FRIAR.
Come, brethren, let's about our business with good devotion.

  They sing.

CURSED BE HE THAT STOLE AWAY HIS HOLINESS' MEAT FROM THE
TABLE! maledicat Dominus!
CURSED BE HE THAT STRUCK HIS HOLINESS A BLOW ON THE FACE!
maledicat Dominus!
CURSED BE HE THAT TOOK FRIAR SANDELO A BLOW ON THE PATE!
maledicat Dominus!
CURSED BE HE THAT DISTURBETH OUR HOLY DIRGE! maledicat
Dominus!

CURSED BE HE THAT TOOK AWAY HIS HOLINESS' WINE! maledicat
Dominus? ['?' sic]

    Et omnes Sancti! Amen!

    [MEPHISTOPHILIS and FAUSTUS beat the FRIARS, and fling
     fire-works among them; and so exeunt.]

    Enter CHORUS.

CHORUS. When Faustus had with pleasure ta'en the view
Of rarest things, and royal courts of kings,
He stay'd his course, and so returned home;
Where such as bear his absence but with grief,
I mean his friends and near'st companions,
Did gratulate his safety with kind words,
And in their conference of what befell,
Touching his journey through the world and air,
They put forth questions of astrology,
Which Faustus answer'd with such learned skill
As they admir'd and wonder'd at his wit.
Now is his fame spread forth in every land:
Amongst the rest the Emperor is one,
Carolus the Fifth, at whose palace now
Faustus is feasted 'mongst his noblemen.
What there he did, in trial of his art,
I leave untold; your eyes shall see['t] perform'd.
   [Exit.]

    Enter ROBIN123 the Ostler, with a book in his hand.

ROBIN. O, this is admirable! here I ha' stolen one of Doctor
Faustus' conjuring-books, and, i'faith, I mean to search some
circles for my own use. Now will I make all the maidens in our
parish dance at my pleasure, stark naked, before me; and so
by that means I shall see more than e'er I felt or saw yet.

    Enter RALPH, calling ROBIN.

RALPH. Robin, prithee, come away; there's a gentleman tarries
to have his horse, and he would have his things rubbed and made
clean: he keeps such a chafing with my mistress about it; and
she has sent me to look thee out; prithee, come away.

ROBIN. Keep out, keep out, or else you are blown up, you are
dismembered, Ralph: keep out, for I am about a roaring piece
of work.

RALPH. Come, what doest thou with that same book? thou canst not read?

ROBIN. Yes, my master and mistress shall find that I can read,
he for his forehead, she for her private study; she's born to
bear with me, or else my art fails.

RALPH. Why, Robin, what book is that?

ROBIN. What book! why, the most intolerable book for conjuring
that e'er was invented by any brimstone devil.

RALPH. Canst thou conjure with it?

ROBIN. I can do all these things easily with it; first, I can
make thee drunk with ippocras124 at any tabern125 in Europe
for nothing; that's one of my conjuring works.

RALPH. Our Master Parson says that's nothing.

ROBIN. True, Ralph: and more, Ralph, if thou hast any mind to
Nan Spit, our kitchen-maid, then turn her and wind her to thy own
use, as often as thou wilt, and at midnight.

RALPH. O, brave, Robin! shall I have Nan Spit, and to mine own
use? On that condition I'll feed thy devil with horse-bread as
long as he lives, of free cost.

ROBIN. No more, sweet Ralph: let's go and make clean our boots,
which lie foul upon our hands, and then to our conjuring in the
devil's name.
  [Exeunt.]

  Enter ROBIN and RALPH126 with a silver goblet.

ROBIN. Come, Ralph: did not I tell thee, we were for ever made
by this Doctor Faustus' book? ecce, signum! here's a simple
purchase127 for horse-keepers: our horses shall eat no hay as
long as this lasts.

RALPH. But, Robin, here comes the Vintner.

ROBIN. Hush! I'll gull him supernaturally.

  Enter VINTNER.

Drawer,128 I hope all is paid; God be with you!—Come, Ralph.

VINTNER. Soft, sir; a word with you. I must yet have a goblet paid from you, ere you go.

ROBIN. I a goblet, Ralph, I a goblet!—I scorn you; and you are
but a, &c. I a goblet! search me.

VINTNER. I mean so, sir, with your favour.
   [Searches ROBIN.]

ROBIN. How say you now?

VINTNER. I must say somewhat to your fellow.—You, sir!

RALPH. Me, sir! me, sir! search your fill. [VINTNER searches him.]
Now, sir, you may be ashamed to burden honest men with a matter
of truth.

VINTNER. Well, tone129 of you hath this goblet about you.

ROBIN. You lie, drawer, 'tis afore me [Aside].—Sirrah you, I'll
teach you to impeach honest men;—stand by;—I'll scour you for
a goblet;—stand aside you had best, I charge you in the name of
Belzebub.—Look to the goblet, Ralph [Aside to RALPH].

VINTNER. What mean you, sirrah?

ROBIN. I'll tell you what I mean. [Reads from a book] Sanctobulorum
Periphrasticon—nay, I'll tickle you, Vintner.—Look to the goblet,
Ralph [Aside to RALPH].—[Reads] Polypragmos Belseborams framanto
pacostiphos tostu, Mephistophilis, &c.

   Enter MEPHISTOPHILIS, sets squibs at their backs, and then
   exit. They run about.

VINTNER. O, nomine Domini! what meanest thou, Robin? thou hast no
goblet.

RALPH. Peccatum peccatorum!—Here's thy goblet, good Vintner.
   [Gives the goblet to VINTNER, who exit.]

ROBIN. Misericordia pro nobis! what shall I do? Good devil, forgive
me now, and I'll never rob thy library more.

   Re-enter MEPHISTOPHILIS.

MEPHIST. Monarch of Hell,130 under whose black survey
Great potentates do kneel with awful fear,
Upon whose altars thousand souls do lie,
How am I vexed with these villains' charms?

From Constantinople am I hither come,
Only for pleasure of these damned slaves.

ROBIN. How, from Constantinople! you have had a great journey:
will you take sixpence in your purse to pay for your supper, and
be gone?

MEPHIST. Well, villains, for your presumption, I transform thee
into an ape, and thee into a dog; and so be gone!
   [Exit.]

ROBIN. How, into an ape! that's brave: I'll have fine sport with
the boys; I'll get nuts and apples enow.

RALPH. And I must be a dog.

ROBIN. I'faith, thy head will never be out of the pottage-pot.
   [Exeunt.]

   Enter EMPEROR,131 FAUSTUS, and a KNIGHT, with ATTENDANTS.

EMPEROR. Master Doctor Faustus,132 I have heard strange report
of thy knowledge in the black art, how that none in my empire
nor in the whole world can compare with thee for the rare effects
of magic: they say thou hast a familiar spirit, by whom thou canst
accomplish what thou list. This, therefore, is my request, that
thou let me see some proof of thy skill, that mine eyes may be
witnesses to confirm what mine ears have heard reported: and here
I swear to thee, by the honour of mine imperial crown, that,
whatever thou doest, thou shalt be no ways prejudiced or endamaged.

KNIGHT. I'faith, he looks much like a conjurer.
   [Aside.]

FAUSTUS. My gracious sovereign, though I must confess myself far
inferior to the report men have published, and nothing answerable
to the honour of your imperial majesty, yet, for that love and duty
binds me thereunto, I am content to do whatsoever your majesty
shall command me.

EMPEROR. Then, Doctor Faustus, mark what I shall say.
As I was sometime solitary set
Within my closet, sundry thoughts arose
About the honour of mine ancestors,
How they had won133 by prowess such exploits,
Got such riches, subdu'd so many kingdoms,
As we that do succeed,134 or they that shall
Hereafter possess our throne, shall

(I fear me) ne'er attain to that degree
Of high renown and great authority:
Amongst which kings is Alexander the Great,
Chief spectacle of the world's pre-eminence,
The bright135 shining of whose glorious acts
Lightens the world with his reflecting beams,
As when I hear but motion made of him,
It grieves my soul I never saw the man:
If, therefore, thou, by cunning of thine art,
Canst raise this man from hollow vaults below,
Where lies entomb'd this famous conqueror,
And bring with him his beauteous paramour,
Both in their right shapes, gesture, and attire
They us'd to wear during their time of life,
Thou shalt both satisfy my just desire,
And give me cause to praise thee whilst I live.

FAUSTUS. My gracious lord, I am ready to accomplish your request,
so far forth as by art and power of my spirit I am able to perform.

KNIGHT. I'faith, that's just nothing at all.
    [Aside.]

FAUSTUS. But, if it like your grace, it is not in my ability136
to present before your eyes the true substantial bodies of those
two deceased princes, which long since are consumed to dust.

KNIGHT. Ay, marry, Master Doctor, now there's a sign of grace in
you, when you will confess the truth.
    [Aside.]

FAUSTUS. But such spirits as can lively resemble Alexander and
his paramour shall appear before your grace, in that manner that
they both137 lived in, in their most flourishing estate; which
I doubt not shall sufficiently content your imperial majesty.

EMPEROR. Go to, Master Doctor; let me see them presently.

KNIGHT. Do you hear, Master Doctor? you bring Alexander and his
paramour before the Emperor!

FAUSTUS. How then, sir?

KNIGHT. I'faith, that's as true as Diana turned me to a stag.

FAUSTUS. No, sir; but, when Actaeon died, he left the horns for
you.—Mephistophilis, be gone.
    [Exit MEPHISTOPHILIS.]

KNIGHT. Nay, an you go to conjuring, I'll be gone.
   [Exit.]

FAUSTUS. I'll meet with you anon for interrupting me so.
—Here they are, my gracious lord.

   Re-enter MEPHISTOPHILIS with SPIRITS in the shapes of ALEXANDER
   and his PARAMOUR.

EMPEROR. Master Doctor, I heard this lady, while she lived, had a
wart or mole in her neck: how shall I know whether it be so or no?

FAUSTUS. Your highness may boldly go and see.

EMPEROR. Sure, these are no spirits, but the true substantial
bodies of those two deceased princes.
   [Exeunt Spirits.]

FAUSTUS. Wilt please your highness now to send for the knight
that was so pleasant with me here of late?

EMPEROR. One of you call him forth.
   [Exit ATTENDANT.]

   Re-enter the KNIGHT with a pair of horns on his head.

How now, sir knight! why, I had thought thou hadst been a bachelor,
but now I see thou hast a wife, that not only gives thee horns,
but makes thee wear them. Feel on thy head.

KNIGHT. Thou damned wretch and execrable dog,
Bred in the concave of some monstrous rock,
How dar'st thou thus abuse a gentleman?
Villain, I say, undo what thou hast done!

FAUSTUS. O, not so fast, sir! there's no haste: but, good, are
you remembered how you crossed me in my conference with the
Emperor? I think I have met with you for it.

EMPEROR. Good Master Doctor, at my entreaty release him: he hath
done penance sufficient.

FAUSTUS. My gracious lord, not so much for the injury he offered
me here in your presence, as to delight you with some mirth, hath
Faustus worthily requited this injurious knight; which being all
I desire, I am content to release him of his horns:—and,
sir knight, hereafter speak well of scholars.—Mephistophilis,

transform him straight.138 [MEPHISTOPHILIS removes the horns.]
—Now, my good lord, having done my duty, I humbly take my leave.

EMPEROR. Farewell, Master Doctor: yet, ere you go,
Expect from me a bounteous reward.
    [Exeunt EMPEROR, KNIGHT, and ATTENDANTS.]

FAUSTUS. Now, Mephistophilis,139 the restless course
That time doth run with calm and silent foot,
Shortening my days and thread of vital life,
Calls for the payment of my latest years:
Therefore, sweet Mephistophilis, let us
Make haste to Wertenberg.

MEPHIST. What, will you go on horse-back or on foot[?]

FAUSTUS. Nay, till I'm past this fair and pleasant green,
I'll walk on foot.

    Enter a HORSE-COURSER.140

HORSE-COURSER. I have been all this day seeking one Master Fustian:
mass, see where he is!—God save you, Master Doctor!

FAUSTUS. What, horse-courser! you are well met.

HORSE-COURSER. Do you hear, sir? I have brought you forty dollars
for your horse.

FAUSTUS. I cannot sell him so: if thou likest him for fifty, take
him.

HORSE-COURSER. Alas, sir, I have no more!—I pray you, speak for
me.

MEPHIST. I pray you, let him have him: he is an honest fellow,
and he has a great charge, neither wife nor child.

FAUSTUS. Well, come, give me your money [HORSE-COURSER gives
FAUSTUS the money]: my boy will deliver him to you. But I must
tell you one thing before you have him; ride him not into the
water, at any hand.

HORSE-COURSER. Why, sir, will he not drink of all waters?

FAUSTUS. O, yes, he will drink of all waters; but ride him not
into the water: ride him over hedge or ditch, or where thou wilt,
but not into the water.

HORSE-COURSER. Well, sir.—Now am I made man for ever: I'll not
leave my horse for forty:141 if he had but the quality of
hey-ding-ding, hey-ding-ding, I'd make a brave living on him:
he has a buttock as slick as an eel [Aside].—Well, God b'wi'ye,
sir: your boy will deliver him me: but, hark you, sir; if my horse
be sick or ill at ease, if I bring his water to you, you'll tell
me what it is?

FAUSTUS. Away, you villain! what, dost think I am a horse-doctor?
    [Exit HORSE-COURSER.]

What art thou, Faustus, but a man condemn'd to die?
Thy fatal time doth draw to final end;
Despair doth drive distrust into142 my thoughts:
Confound these passions with a quiet sleep:
Tush, Christ did call the thief upon the Cross;
Then rest thee, Faustus, quiet in conceit.
    [Sleeps in his chair.]

    Re-enter HORSE-COURSER, all wet, crying.

HORSE-COURSER. Alas, alas! Doctor Fustian, quoth a? mass, Doctor
Lopus143 was never such a doctor: has given me a purgation, has
purged me of forty dollars; I shall never see them more. But yet,
like an ass as I was, I would not be ruled by him, for he bade me
I should ride him into no water: now I, thinking my horse had had
some rare quality that he would not have had me know of,144 I,
like a venturous youth, rid him into the deep pond at the town's
end. I was no sooner in the middle of the pond, but my horse
vanished away, and I sat upon a bottle of hay, never so near
drowning in my life. But I'll seek out my doctor, and have my
forty dollars again, or I'll make it the dearest horse!—O,
yonder is his snipper-snapper.—Do you hear? you, hey-pass,145
where's your master?

MEPHIST. Why, sir, what would you? you cannot speak with him.

HORSE-COURSER. But I will speak with him.

MEPHIST. Why, he's fast asleep: come some other time.

HORSE-COURSER. I'll speak with him now, or I'll break his
glass-windows about his ears.

MEPHIST. I tell thee, he has not slept this eight nights.

HORSE-COURSER. An he have not slept this eight weeks, I'll

speak with him.

MEPHIST. See, where he is, fast asleep.

HORSE-COURSER. Ay, this is he.—God save you, Master Doctor,
Master Doctor, Master Doctor Fustian! forty dollars, forty dollars
for a bottle of hay!

MEPHIST. Why, thou seest he hears thee not.

HORSE-COURSER. So-ho, ho! so-ho, ho! [Hollows in his ear.] No,
will you not wake? I'll make you wake ere I go. [Pulls FAUSTUS
by the leg, and pulls it away.] Alas, I am undone! what shall
I do?

FAUSTUS. O, my leg, my leg!—Help, Mephistophilis! call the
officers.—My leg, my leg!

MEPHIST. Come, villain, to the constable.

HORSE-COURSER. O Lord, sir, let me go, and I'll give you forty
dollars more!

MEPHIST. Where be they?

HORSE-COURSER. I have none about me: come to my ostry,146
and I'll give them you.

MEPHIST. Be gone quickly.
   [HORSE-COURSER runs away.]

FAUSTUS. What, is he gone? farewell he! Faustus has his leg again,
and the Horse-courser, I take it, a bottle of hay for his labour:
well, this trick shall cost him forty dollars more.

   Enter WAGNER.

How now, Wagner! what's the news with thee?

WAGNER. Sir, the Duke of Vanholt doth earnestly entreat your
company.

FAUSTUS. The Duke of Vanholt! an honourable gentleman, to whom
I must be no niggard of my cunning.147—Come, Mephistophilis,
let's away to him.
   [Exeunt.]

   Enter the DUKE OF VANHOLT, the DUCHESS, and FAUSTUS.148

DUKE. Believe me, Master Doctor, this merriment hath much pleased me.

FAUSTUS. My gracious lord, I am glad it contents you so well.
—But it may be, madam, you take no delight in this. I have heard
that great-bellied women do long for some dainties or other: what
is it, madam? tell me, and you shall have it.

DUCHESS. Thanks, good Master Doctor: and, for I see your courteous
intent to pleasure me, I will not hide from you the thing my heart
desires; and, were it now summer, as it is January and the dead
time of the winter, I would desire no better meat than a dish
of ripe grapes.

FAUSTUS. Alas, madam, that's nothing!—Mephistophilis, be gone.
[Exit MEPHISTOPHILIS.] Were it a greater thing than this, so it
would content you, you should have it.

   Re-enter MEPHISTOPHILIS with grapes.

Here they be, madam: wilt please you taste on them?

DUKE. Believe me, Master Doctor, this makes me wonder above the
rest, that being in the dead time of winter and in the month of
January, how you should come by these grapes.

FAUSTUS. If it like your grace, the year is divided into two
circles over the whole world, that, when it is here winter with
us, in the contrary circle it is summer with them, as in India,
Saba,149 and farther countries in the east; and by means of a
swift spirit that I have, I had them brought hither, as you see.
—How do you like them, madam? be they good?

DUCHESS. Believe me, Master Doctor, they be the best grapes that
e'er I tasted in my life before.

FAUSTUS. I am glad they content you so, madam.

DUKE. Come, madam, let us in, where you must well reward this
learned man for the great kindness he hath shewed to you.

DUCHESS. And so I will, my lord; and, whilst I live, rest
beholding150 for this courtesy.

FAUSTUS. I humbly thank your grace.

DUKE. Come, Master Doctor, follow us, and receive your reward.

[Exeunt.]

Enter WAGNER.151

WAGNER. I think my master means to die shortly,
For he hath given to me all his goods:152
And yet, methinks, if that death were near,
He would not banquet, and carouse, and swill
Amongst the students, as even now he doth,
Who are at supper with such belly-cheer
As Wagner ne'er beheld in all his life.
See, where they come! belike the feast is ended.
    [Exit.]

Enter FAUSTUS with two or three SCHOLARS, and MEPHISTOPHILIS.

FIRST SCHOLAR. Master Doctor Faustus, since our conference about
fair ladies, which was the beautifulest in all the world, we have
determined with ourselves that Helen of Greece was the admirablest
lady that ever lived: therefore, Master Doctor, if you will do us
that favour, as to let us see that peerless dame of Greece, whom
all the world admires for majesty, we should think ourselves much
beholding unto you.

FAUSTUS. Gentlemen,
For that I know your friendship is unfeign'd,
And Faustus' custom is not to deny
The just requests of those that wish him well,
You shall behold that peerless dame of Greece,
No otherways for pomp and majesty
Than when Sir Paris cross'd the seas with her,
And brought the spoils to rich Dardania.
Be silent, then, for danger is in words.
    [Music sounds, and HELEN passeth over the stage.] 153

SECOND SCHOLAR. Too simple is my wit to tell her praise,
Whom all the world admires for majesty.

THIRD SCHOLAR. No marvel though the angry Greeks pursu'd
With ten years' war the rape of such a queen,
Whose heavenly beauty passeth all compare.

FIRST SCHOLAR. Since we have seen the pride of Nature's works,
And only paragon of excellence,
Let us depart; and for this glorious deed
Happy and blest be Faustus evermore!

FAUSTUS. Gentlemen, farewell: the same I wish to you.

[Exeunt SCHOLARS.]

Enter an OLD MAN.154

OLD MAN. Ah, Doctor Faustus, that I might prevail
To guide thy steps unto the way of life,
By which sweet path thou mayst attain the goal
That shall conduct thee to celestial rest!
Break heart, drop blood, and mingle it with tears,
Tears falling from repentant heaviness
Of thy most vile155 and loathsome filthiness,
The stench whereof corrupts the inward soul
With such flagitious crimes of heinous sin156
As no commiseration may expel,
But mercy, Faustus, of thy Saviour sweet,
Whose blood alone must wash away thy guilt.

FAUSTUS. Where art thou, Faustus? wretch, what hast thou done?
Damn'd art thou, Faustus, damn'd; despair and die!
Hell calls for right, and with a roaring voice
Says, "Faustus, come; thine hour is almost157 come;"
And Faustus now158 will come to do thee right.
    [MEPHISTOPHILIS gives him a dagger.]

OLD MAN. Ah, stay, good Faustus, stay thy desperate steps!
I see an angel hovers o'er thy head,
And, with a vial full of precious grace,
Offers to pour the same into thy soul:
Then call for mercy, and avoid despair.

FAUSTUS. Ah, my sweet friend, I feel
Thy words to comfort my distressed soul!
Leave me a while to ponder on my sins.

OLD MAN. I go, sweet Faustus; but with heavy cheer,
Fearing the ruin of thy hopeless soul.
    [Exit.]

FAUSTUS. Accursed Faustus, where is mercy now?
I do repent; and yet I do despair:
Hell strives with grace for conquest in my breast:
What shall I do to shun the snares of death?

MEPHIST. Thou traitor, Faustus, I arrest thy soul
For disobedience to my sovereign lord:
Revolt, or I'll in piece-meal tear thy flesh.

FAUSTUS. Sweet Mephistophilis, entreat thy lord

To pardon my unjust presumption,
And with my blood again I will confirm
My former vow I made to Lucifer.

MEPHIST. Do it, then, quickly,159 with unfeigned heart,
Lest greater danger do attend thy drift.

FAUSTUS. Torment, sweet friend, that base and crooked age,
That durst dissuade me from thy Lucifer,
With greatest torments that our hell affords.

MEPHIST. His faith is great; I cannot touch his soul;
But what I may afflict his body with
I will attempt, which is but little worth.

FAUSTUS. One thing, good servant,160 let me crave of thee,
To glut the longing of my heart's desire,—
That I might have unto my paramour
That heavenly Helen which I saw of late,
Whose sweet embracings may extinguish clean
Those161 thoughts that do dissuade me from my vow,
And keep mine oath I made to Lucifer.

MEPHIST. Faustus, this,162 or what else thou shalt desire,
Shall be perform'd in twinkling of an eye.

   Re-enter HELEN.

FAUSTUS. Was this the face that launch'd a thousand ships,
And burnt the topless163 towers of Ilium—
Sweet Helen, make me immortal with a kiss.—
  [Kisses her.]
Her lips suck forth my soul: see, where it flies!—
Come, Helen, come, give me my soul again.
Here will I dwell, for heaven is164 in these lips,
And all is dross that is not Helena.
I will be Paris, and for love of thee,
Instead of Troy, shall Wertenberg be sack'd;
And I will combat with weak Menelaus,
And wear thy colours on my plumed crest;
Yea, I will wound Achilles in the heel,
And then return to Helen for a kiss.
O, thou art fairer than the evening air
Clad in the beauty of a thousand stars;
Brighter art thou than flaming Jupiter
When he appear'd to hapless Semele;
More lovely than the monarch of the sky
In wanton Arethusa's azur'd arms;

And none but thou shalt165 be my paramour!
    [Exeunt.]

    Enter the OLD MAN.166

OLD MAN. Accursed Faustus, miserable man,
That from thy soul exclud'st the grace of heaven,
And fly'st the throne of his tribunal-seat!

    Enter DEVILS.

Satan begins to sift me with his pride:
As in this furnace God shall try my faith,
My faith, vile hell, shall triumph over thee.
Ambitious fiends, see how the heavens smile
At your repulse, and laugh your state to scorn!
Hence, hell! for hence I fly unto my God.
    [Exeunt,—on one side, DEVILS, on the other, OLD MAN.]

    Enter FAUSTUS,167 with SCHOLARS.

FAUSTUS. Ah, gentlemen!

FIRST SCHOLAR. What ails Faustus?

FAUSTUS. Ah, my sweet chamber-fellow, had I lived with thee,
then had I lived still! but now I die eternally. Look, comes
he not? comes he not?

SECOND SCHOLAR. What means Faustus?

THIRD SCHOLAR. Belike he is grown into some sickness by being
over-solitary.

FIRST SCHOLAR. If it be so, we'll have physicians to cure him.
—'Tis but a surfeit; never fear, man.

FAUSTUS. A surfeit of deadly sin, that hath damned both body
and soul.

SECOND SCHOLAR. Yet, Faustus, look up to heaven; remember God's
mercies are infinite.

FAUSTUS. But Faustus' offence can ne'er be pardoned: the serpent
that tempted Eve may be saved, but not Faustus. Ah, gentlemen,
hear me with patience, and tremble not at my speeches! Though
my heart pants and quivers to remember that I have been a student
here these thirty years, O, would I had never seen Wertenberg,

never read book! and what wonders I have done, all Germany can witness, yea, all the world; for which Faustus hath lost both Germany and the world, yea, heaven itself, heaven, the seat of God, the throne of the blessed, the kingdom of joy; and must remain in hell for ever, hell, ah, hell, for ever! Sweet friends, what shall become of Faustus, being in hell for ever?

THIRD SCHOLAR. Yet, Faustus, call on God.

FAUSTUS. On God, whom Faustus hath abjured! on God, whom Faustus hath blasphemed! Ah, my God, I would weep! but the devil draws in my tears. Gush forth blood, instead of tears! yea, life and soul! O, he stays my tongue! I would lift up my hands; but see, they hold them, they hold them!

ALL. Who, Faustus?

FAUSTUS. Lucifer and Mephistophilis. Ah, gentlemen, I gave them my soul for my cunning!168

ALL. God forbid!

FAUSTUS. God forbade it, indeed; but Faustus hath done it: for vain pleasure of twenty-four years hath Faustus lost eternal joy and felicity. I writ them a bill with mine own blood: the date is expired; the time will come, and he will fetch me.

FIRST SCHOLAR. Why did not Faustus tell us of this before,169 that divines might have prayed for thee?

FAUSTUS. Oft have I thought to have done so; but the devil threatened to tear me in pieces, if I named God, to fetch both body and soul, if I once gave ear to divinity: and now 'tis too late. Gentlemen, away, lest you perish with me.

SECOND SCHOLAR. O, what shall we do to save170 Faustus?

FAUSTUS. Talk not of me, but save yourselves, and depart.

THIRD SCHOLAR. God will strengthen me; I will stay with Faustus.

FIRST SCHOLAR. Tempt not God, sweet friend; but let us into the next room, and there pray for him.

FAUSTUS. Ay, pray for me, pray for me; and what noise soever ye hear,171 come not unto me, for nothing can rescue me.

SECOND SCHOLAR. Pray thou, and we will pray that God may have mercy upon thee.

FAUSTUS. Gentlemen, farewell: if I live till morning, I'll visit you; if not, Faustus is gone to hell.

ALL. Faustus, farewell.
   [Exeunt SCHOLARS.—The clock strikes eleven.]

FAUSTUS. Ah, Faustus,
Now hast thou but one bare hour to live,
And then thou must be damn'd perpetually!
Stand still, you ever-moving spheres of heaven,
That time may cease, and midnight never come;
Fair Nature's eye, rise, rise again, and make
Perpetual day; or let this hour be but
A year, a month, a week, a natural day,
That Faustus may repent and save his soul!
O lente,172 lente currite, noctis equi!
The stars move still, time runs, the clock will strike,
The devil will come, and Faustus must be damn'd.
O, I'll leap up to my God!—Who pulls me down?—
See, see, where Christ's blood streams in the firmament!
One drop would save my soul, half a drop: ah, my Christ!—
Ah, rend not my heart for naming of my Christ!
Yet will I call on him: O, spare me, Lucifer!—
Where is it now? 'tis gone: and see, where God
Stretcheth out his arm, and bends his ireful brows!
Mountains and hills, come, come, and fall on me,
And hide me from the heavy wrath of God!
No, no!
Then will I headlong run into the earth:
Earth, gape! O, no, it will not harbour me!
You stars that reign'd at my nativity,
Whose influence hath allotted death and hell,
Now draw up Faustus, like a foggy mist.
Into the entrails of yon labouring cloud[s],
That, when you173 vomit forth into the air,
My limbs may issue from your smoky mouths,
So that my soul may but ascend to heaven!
   [The clock strikes the half-hour.]
Ah, half the hour is past! 'twill all be past anon
O God,
If thou wilt not have mercy on my soul,
Yet for Christ's sake, whose blood hath ransom'd me,
Impose some end to my incessant pain;
Let Faustus live in hell a thousand years,
A hundred thousand, and at last be sav'd!
O, no end is limited to damned souls!

Why wert thou not a creature wanting soul?

Or why is this immortal that thou hast?

Ah, Pythagoras' metempsychosis, were that true,

This soul should fly from me, and I be chang'd

Unto some brutish beast!174 all beasts are happy,

For, when they die,

Their souls are soon dissolv'd in elements;

But mine must live still to be plagu'd in hell.

Curs'd be the parents that engender'd me!

No, Faustus, curse thyself, curse Lucifer

That hath depriv'd thee of the joys of heaven.

    [The clock strikes twelve.]

O, it strikes, it strikes! Now, body, turn to air,

Or Lucifer will bear thee quick to hell!

    [Thunder and lightning.]

O soul, be chang'd into little water-drops,

And fall into the ocean, ne'er be found!

    Enter DEVILS.

My God, my god, look not so fierce on me!

Adders and serpents, let me breathe a while!

Ugly hell, gape not! come not, Lucifer!

I'll burn my books!—Ah, Mephistophilis!

    [Exeunt DEVILS with FAUSTUS.] 175

    Enter CHORUS.

CHORUS. Cut is the branch that might have grown full straight,

And burned is Apollo's laurel-bough,

That sometime grew within this learned man.

Faustus is gone: regard his hellish fall,

Whose fiendful fortune may exhort the wise,

Only to wonder at unlawful things,

Whose deepness doth entice such forward wits

To practice more than heavenly power permits.

    [Exit.]

Terminat hora diem; terminat auctor opus.

William Shakespeare, Henry IV Part I

ACT I

SCENE I. London. The palace.

Enter KING HENRY, LORD JOHN OF LANCASTER, the EARL of WESTMORELAND, SIR WALTER BLUNT, and others

KING HENRY IV

So shaken as we are, so wan with care,
Find we a time for frighted peace to pant,
And breathe short-winded accents of new broils
To be commenced in strands afar remote.
No more the thirsty entrance of this soil
Shall daub her lips with her own children's blood;
Nor more shall trenching war channel her fields,
Nor bruise her flowerets with the armed hoofs
Of hostile paces: those opposed eyes,
Which, like the meteors of a troubled heaven,
All of one nature, of one substance bred,
Did lately meet in the intestine shock
And furious close of civil butchery
Shall now, in mutual well-beseeming ranks,
March all one way and be no more opposed
Against acquaintance, kindred and allies:
The edge of war, like an ill-sheathed knife,
No more shall cut his master. Therefore, friends,
As far as to the sepulchre of Christ,
Whose soldier now, under whose blessed cross
We are impressed and engaged to fight,
Forthwith a power of English shall we levy;
Whose arms were moulded in their mothers' womb
To chase these pagans in those holy fields
Over whose acres walk'd those blessed feet
Which fourteen hundred years ago were nail'd
For our advantage on the bitter cross.
But this our purpose now is twelve month old,
And bootless 'tis to tell you we will go:
Therefore we meet not now. Then let me hear
Of you, my gentle cousin Westmoreland,
What yesternight our council did decree
In forwarding this dear expedience.

WESTMORELAND

My liege, this haste was hot in question,
And many limits of the charge set down

But yesternight: when all athwart there came
A post from Wales loaden with heavy news;
Whose worst was, that the noble Mortimer,
Leading the men of Herefordshire to fight
Against the irregular and wild Glendower,
Was by the rude hands of that Welshman taken,
A thousand of his people butchered;
Upon whose dead corpse there was such misuse,
Such beastly shameless transformation,
By those Welshwomen done as may not be
Without much shame retold or spoken of.

KING HENRY IV

It seems then that the tidings of this broil
Brake off our business for the Holy Land.

WESTMORELAND

This match'd with other did, my gracious lord;
For more uneven and unwelcome news
Came from the north and thus it did import:
On Holy-rood day, the gallant Hotspur there,
Young Harry Percy and brave Archibald,
That ever-valiant and approved Scot,
At Holmedon met,
Where they did spend a sad and bloody hour,
As by discharge of their artillery,
And shape of likelihood, the news was told;
For he that brought them, in the very heat
And pride of their contention did take horse,
Uncertain of the issue any way.

KING HENRY IV

Here is a dear, a true industrious friend,
Sir Walter Blunt, new lighted from his horse.
Stain'd with the variation of each soil
Betwixt that Holmedon and this seat of ours;
And he hath brought us smooth and welcome news.
The Earl of Douglas is discomfited:
Ten thousand bold Scots, two and twenty knights,
Balk'd in their own blood did Sir Walter see
On Holmedon's plains. Of prisoners, Hotspur took
Mordake the Earl of Fife, and eldest son
To beaten Douglas; and the Earl of Athol,
Of Murray, Angus, and Menteith:
And is not this an honourable spoil?
A gallant prize? ha, cousin, is it not?

WESTMORELAND

In faith,
It is a conquest for a prince to boast of.

KING HENRY IV

Yea, there thou makest me sad and makest me sin
In envy that my Lord Northumberland
Should be the father to so blest a son,
A son who is the theme of honour's tongue;
Amongst a grove, the very straightest plant;
Who is sweet Fortune's minion and her pride:
Whilst I, by looking on the praise of him,
See riot and dishonour stain the brow
Of my young Harry. O that it could be proved
That some night-tripping fairy had exchanged
In cradle-clothes our children where they lay,
And call'd mine Percy, his Plantagenet!
Then would I have his Harry, and he mine.
But let him from my thoughts. What think you, coz,
Of this young Percy's pride? the prisoners,
Which he in this adventure hath surprised,
To his own use he keeps; and sends me word,
I shall have none but Mordake Earl of Fife.

WESTMORELAND

This is his uncle's teaching; this is Worcester,
Malevolent to you in all aspects;
Which makes him prune himself, and bristle up
The crest of youth against your dignity.

KING HENRY IV

But I have sent for him to answer this;
And for this cause awhile we must neglect
Our holy purpose to Jerusalem.
Cousin, on Wednesday next our council we
Will hold at Windsor; so inform the lords:
But come yourself with speed to us again;
For more is to be said and to be done
Than out of anger can be uttered.

WESTMORELAND

I will, my liege.

Exeunt

SCENE II. London. An apartment of the Prince's.

Enter the PRINCE OF WALES and FALSTAFF

FALSTAFF

Now, Hal, what time of day is it, lad?

PRINCE HENRY

Thou art so fat-witted, with drinking of old sack
and unbuttoning thee after supper and sleeping upon
benches after noon, that thou hast forgotten to
demand that truly which thou wouldst truly know.
What a devil hast thou to do with the time of the
day? Unless hours were cups of sack and minutes
capons and clocks the tongues of bawds and dials the
signs of leaping-houses and the blessed sun himself
a fair hot wench in flame-coloured taffeta, I see no
reason why thou shouldst be so superfluous to demand
the time of the day.

FALSTAFF

Indeed, you come near me now, Hal; for we that take
purses go by the moon and the seven stars, and not
by Phoebus, he,'that wandering knight so fair.' And,
I prithee, sweet wag, when thou art king, as, God
save thy grace,—majesty I should say, for grace
thou wilt have none,—

PRINCE HENRY

What, none?

FALSTAFF

No, by my troth, not so much as will serve to
prologue to an egg and butter.

PRINCE HENRY

Well, how then? come, roundly, roundly.

FALSTAFF

Marry, then, sweet wag, when thou art king, let not
us that are squires of the night's body be called
thieves of the day's beauty: let us be Diana's
foresters, gentlemen of the shade, minions of the
moon; and let men say we be men of good government,
being governed, as the sea is, by our noble and
chaste mistress the moon, under whose countenance we steal.

PRINCE HENRY

Thou sayest well, and it holds well too; for the
fortune of us that are the moon's men doth ebb and
flow like the sea, being governed, as the sea is,
by the moon. As, for proof, now: a purse of gold
most resolutely snatched on Monday night and most
dissolutely spent on Tuesday morning; got with
swearing 'Lay by' and spent with crying 'Bring in;'
now in as low an ebb as the foot of the ladder
and by and by in as high a flow as the ridge of the gallows.

FALSTAFF

By the Lord, thou sayest true, lad. And is not my
hostess of the tavern a most sweet wench?

PRINCE HENRY

As the honey of Hybla, my old lad of the castle. And
is not a buff jerkin a most sweet robe of durance?

FALSTAFF

How now, how now, mad wag! what, in thy quips and
thy quiddities? what a plague have I to do with a
buff jerkin?

PRINCE HENRY

Why, what a pox have I to do with my hostess of the tavern?

FALSTAFF

Well, thou hast called her to a reckoning many a
time and oft.

PRINCE HENRY

Did I ever call for thee to pay thy part?

FALSTAFF

No; I'll give thee thy due, thou hast paid all there.

PRINCE HENRY

Yea, and elsewhere, so far as my coin would stretch;
and where it would not, I have used my credit.

FALSTAFF

Yea, and so used it that were it not here apparent
that thou art heir apparent—But, I prithee, sweet
wag, shall there be gallows standing in England when

thou art king? and resolution thus fobbed as it is
with the rusty curb of old father antic the law? Do
not thou, when thou art king, hang a thief.

PRINCE HENRY

No; thou shalt.

FALSTAFF

Shall I? O rare! By the Lord, I'll be a brave judge.

PRINCE HENRY

Thou judgest false already: I mean, thou shalt have
the hanging of the thieves and so become a rare hangman.

FALSTAFF

Well, Hal, well; and in some sort it jumps with my
humour as well as waiting in the court, I can tell
you.

PRINCE HENRY

For obtaining of suits?

FALSTAFF

Yea, for obtaining of suits, whereof the hangman
hath no lean wardrobe. 'Sblood, I am as melancholy
as a gib cat or a lugged bear.

PRINCE HENRY

Or an old lion, or a lover's lute.

FALSTAFF

Yea, or the drone of a Lincolnshire bagpipe.

PRINCE HENRY

What sayest thou to a hare, or the melancholy of
Moor-ditch?

FALSTAFF

Thou hast the most unsavoury similes and art indeed
the most comparative, rascalliest, sweet young
prince. But, Hal, I prithee, trouble me no more
with vanity. I would to God thou and I knew where a
commodity of good names were to be bought. An old
lord of the council rated me the other day in the

street about you, sir, but I marked him not; and yet
he talked very wisely, but I regarded him not; and
yet he talked wisely, and in the street too.

PRINCE HENRY

Thou didst well; for wisdom cries out in the
streets, and no man regards it.

FALSTAFF

O, thou hast damnable iteration and art indeed able
to corrupt a saint. Thou hast done much harm upon
me, Hal; God forgive thee for it! Before I knew
thee, Hal, I knew nothing; and now am I, if a man
should speak truly, little better than one of the
wicked. I must give over this life, and I will give
it over: by the Lord, and I do not, I am a villain:
I'll be damned for never a king's son in
Christendom.

PRINCE HENRY

Where shall we take a purse tomorrow, Jack?

FALSTAFF

'Zounds, where thou wilt, lad; I'll make one; an I
do not, call me villain and baffle me.

PRINCE HENRY

I see a good amendment of life in thee; from praying
to purse-taking.

FALSTAFF

Why, Hal, 'tis my vocation, Hal; 'tis no sin for a
man to labour in his vocation.

Enter POINS

Poins! Now shall we know if Gadshill have set a
match. O, if men were to be saved by merit, what
hole in hell were hot enough for him? This is the
most omnipotent villain that ever cried 'Stand' to
a true man.

PRINCE HENRY

Good morrow, Ned.

POINS

Good morrow, sweet Hal. What says Monsieur Remorse?
what says Sir John Sack and Sugar? Jack! how
agrees the devil and thee about thy soul, that thou
soldest him on Good-Friday last for a cup of Madeira
and a cold capon's leg?

PRINCE HENRY

Sir John stands to his word, the devil shall have
his bargain; for he was never yet a breaker of
proverbs: he will give the devil his due.

POINS

Then art thou damned for keeping thy word with the devil.

PRINCE HENRY

Else he had been damned for cozening the devil.

POINS

But, my lads, my lads, to-morrow morning, by four
o'clock, early at Gadshill! there are pilgrims going
to Canterbury with rich offerings, and traders
riding to London with fat purses: I have vizards
for you all; you have horses for yourselves:
Gadshill lies to-night in Rochester: I have bespoke
supper to-morrow night in Eastcheap: we may do it
as secure as sleep. If you will go, I will stuff
your purses full of crowns; if you will not, tarry
at home and be hanged.

FALSTAFF

Hear ye, Yedward; if I tarry at home and go not,
I'll hang you for going.

POINS

You will, chops?

FALSTAFF

Hal, wilt thou make one?

PRINCE HENRY

Who, I rob? I a thief? not I, by my faith.

FALSTAFF

There's neither honesty, manhood, nor good fellowship in thee, nor thou camest not of the blood royal, if thou darest not stand for ten shillings.

PRINCE HENRY

Well then, once in my days I'll be a madcap.

FALSTAFF

Why, that's well said.

PRINCE HENRY

Well, come what will, I'll tarry at home.

FALSTAFF

By the Lord, I'll be a traitor then, when thou art king.

PRINCE HENRY

I care not.

POINS

Sir John, I prithee, leave the prince and me alone: I will lay him down such reasons for this adventure that he shall go.

FALSTAFF

Well, God give thee the spirit of persuasion and him the ears of profiting, that what thou speakest may move and what he hears may be believed, that the true prince may, for recreation sake, prove a false thief; for the poor abuses of the time want countenance. Farewell: you shall find me in Eastcheap.

PRINCE HENRY

Farewell, thou latter spring! farewell, All-hallown summer!

Exit Falstaff

POINS

Now, my good sweet honey lord, ride with us to-morrow: I have a jest to execute that I cannot manage alone. Falstaff, Bardolph, Peto and Gadshill shall rob those men that we have already waylaid: yourself and I will not be there; and when they have the booty, if you and I do not rob them, cut this head off from my shoulders.

PRINCE HENRY

How shall we part with them in setting forth?

POINS

Why, we will set forth before or after them, and
appoint them a place of meeting, wherein it is at
our pleasure to fail, and then will they adventure
upon the exploit themselves; which they shall have
no sooner achieved, but we'll set upon them.

PRINCE HENRY

Yea, but 'tis like that they will know us by our
horses, by our habits and by every other
appointment, to be ourselves.

POINS

Tut! our horses they shall not see: I'll tie them
in the wood; our vizards we will change after we
leave them: and, sirrah, I have cases of buckram
for the nonce, to immask our noted outward garments.

PRINCE HENRY

Yea, but I doubt they will be too hard for us.

POINS

Well, for two of them, I know them to be as
true-bred cowards as ever turned back; and for the
third, if he fight longer than he sees reason, I'll
forswear arms. The virtue of this jest will be, the
incomprehensible lies that this same fat rogue will
tell us when we meet at supper: how thirty, at
least, he fought with; what wards, what blows, what
extremities he endured; and in the reproof of this
lies the jest.

PRINCE HENRY

Well, I'll go with thee: provide us all things
necessary and meet me to-morrow night in Eastcheap;
there I'll sup. Farewell.

POINS

Farewell, my lord.

Exit Poins

PRINCE HENRY

I know you all, and will awhile uphold
The unyoked humour of your idleness:
Yet herein will I imitate the sun,
Who doth permit the base contagious clouds
To smother up his beauty from the world,
That, when he please again to be himself,
Being wanted, he may be more wonder'd at,
By breaking through the foul and ugly mists
Of vapours that did seem to strangle him.
If all the year were playing holidays,
To sport would be as tedious as to work;
But when they seldom come, they wish'd for come,
And nothing pleaseth but rare accidents.
So, when this loose behavior I throw off
And pay the debt I never promised,
By how much better than my word I am,
By so much shall I falsify men's hopes;
And like bright metal on a sullen ground,
My reformation, glittering o'er my fault,
Shall show more goodly and attract more eyes
Than that which hath no foil to set it off.
I'll so offend, to make offence a skill;
Redeeming time when men think least I will.

Exit

SCENE III. London. The palace.

Enter the KING, NORTHUMBERLAND, WORCESTER, HOTSPUR, SIR WALTER BLUNT, with others

KING HENRY IV

My blood hath been too cold and temperate,
Unapt to stir at these indignities,
And you have found me; for accordingly
You tread upon my patience: but be sure
I will from henceforth rather be myself,
Mighty and to be fear'd, than my condition;
Which hath been smooth as oil, soft as young down,
And therefore lost that title of respect
Which the proud soul ne'er pays but to the proud.

EARL OF WORCESTER

Our house, my sovereign liege, little deserves
The scourge of greatness to be used on it;
And that same greatness too which our own hands
Have help to make so portly.

NORTHUMBERLAND

My lord.—

KING HENRY IV

Worcester, get thee gone; for I do see
Danger and disobedience in thine eye:
O, sir, your presence is too bold and peremptory,
And majesty might never yet endure
The moody frontier of a servant brow.
You have good leave to leave us: when we need
Your use and counsel, we shall send for you.

Exit Worcester

You were about to speak.

To North

NORTHUMBERLAND

Yea, my good lord.
Those prisoners in your highness' name demanded,
Which Harry Percy here at Holmedon took,
Were, as he says, not with such strength denied
As is deliver'd to your majesty:
Either envy, therefore, or misprison
Is guilty of this fault and not my son.

HOTSPUR

My liege, I did deny no prisoners.
But I remember, when the fight was done,
When I was dry with rage and extreme toil,
Breathless and faint, leaning upon my sword,
Came there a certain lord, neat, and trimly dress'd,
Fresh as a bridegroom; and his chin new reap'd
Show'd like a stubble-land at harvest-home;
He was perfumed like a milliner;
And 'twixt his finger and his thumb he held
A pouncet-box, which ever and anon
He gave his nose and took't away again;
Who therewith angry, when it next came there,
Took it in snuff; and still he smiled and talk'd,
And as the soldiers bore dead bodies by,
He call'd them untaught knaves, unmannerly,
To bring a slovenly unhandsome corse
Betwixt the wind and his nobility.
With many holiday and lady terms
He question'd me; amongst the rest, demanded
My prisoners in your majesty's behalf.
I then, all smarting with my wounds being cold,

To be so pester'd with a popinjay,
Out of my grief and my impatience,
Answer'd neglectingly I know not what,
He should or he should not; for he made me mad
To see him shine so brisk and smell so sweet
And talk so like a waiting-gentlewoman
Of guns and drums and wounds,—God save the mark!—
And telling me the sovereign'st thing on earth
Was parmaceti for an inward bruise;
And that it was great pity, so it was,
This villanous salt-petre should be digg'd
Out of the bowels of the harmless earth,
Which many a good tall fellow had destroy'd
So cowardly; and but for these vile guns,
He would himself have been a soldier.
This bald unjointed chat of his, my lord,
I answer'd indirectly, as I said;
And I beseech you, let not his report
Come current for an accusation
Betwixt my love and your high majesty.

SIR WALTER BLUNT

The circumstance consider'd, good my lord,
Whate'er Lord Harry Percy then had said
To such a person and in such a place,
At such a time, with all the rest retold,
May reasonably die and never rise
To do him wrong or any way impeach
What then he said, so he unsay it now.

KING HENRY IV

Why, yet he doth deny his prisoners,
But with proviso and exception,
That we at our own charge shall ransom straight
His brother-in-law, the foolish Mortimer;
Who, on my soul, hath wilfully betray'd
The lives of those that he did lead to fight
Against that great magician, damn'd Glendower,
Whose daughter, as we hear, the Earl of March
Hath lately married. Shall our coffers, then,
Be emptied to redeem a traitor home?
Shall we but treason? and indent with fears,
When they have lost and forfeited themselves?
No, on the barren mountains let him starve;
For I shall never hold that man my friend
Whose tongue shall ask me for one penny cost
To ransom home revolted Mortimer.

HOTSPUR

Revolted Mortimer!
He never did fall off, my sovereign liege,
But by the chance of war; to prove that true
Needs no more but one tongue for all those wounds,
Those mouthed wounds, which valiantly he took
When on the gentle Severn's sedgy bank,
In single opposition, hand to hand,
He did confound the best part of an hour
In changing hardiment with great Glendower:
Three times they breathed and three times did
they drink,
Upon agreement, of swift Severn's flood;
Who then, affrighted with their bloody looks,
Ran fearfully among the trembling reeds,
And hid his crisp head in the hollow bank,
Bloodstained with these valiant combatants.
Never did base and rotten policy
Colour her working with such deadly wounds;
Nor could the noble Mortimer
Receive so many, and all willingly:
Then let not him be slander'd with revolt.

KING HENRY IV

Thou dost belie him, Percy, thou dost belie him;
He never did encounter with Glendower:
I tell thee,
He durst as well have met the devil alone
As Owen Glendower for an enemy.
Art thou not ashamed? But, sirrah, henceforth
Let me not hear you speak of Mortimer:
Send me your prisoners with the speediest means,
Or you shall hear in such a kind from me
As will displease you. My Lord Northumberland,
We licence your departure with your son.
Send us your prisoners, or you will hear of it.

Exeunt King Henry, Blunt, and train

HOTSPUR

An if the devil come and roar for them,
I will not send them: I will after straight
And tell him so; for I will ease my heart,
Albeit I make a hazard of my head.

NORTHUMBERLAND

What, drunk with choler? stay and pause awhile:
Here comes your uncle.

Re-enter WORCESTER

HOTSPUR

Speak of Mortimer!
'Zounds, I will speak of him; and let my soul
Want mercy, if I do not join with him:
Yea, on his part I'll empty all these veins,
And shed my dear blood drop by drop in the dust,
But I will lift the down-trod Mortimer
As high in the air as this unthankful king,
As this ingrate and canker'd Bolingbroke.

NORTHUMBERLAND

Brother, the king hath made your nephew mad.

EARL OF WORCESTER

Who struck this heat up after I was gone?

HOTSPUR

He will, forsooth, have all my prisoners;
And when I urged the ransom once again
Of my wife's brother, then his cheek look'd pale,
And on my face he turn'd an eye of death,
Trembling even at the name of Mortimer.

EARL OF WORCESTER

I cannot blame him: was not he proclaim'd
By Richard that dead is the next of blood?

NORTHUMBERLAND

He was; I heard the proclamation:
And then it was when the unhappy king,
—Whose wrongs in us God pardon!—did set forth
Upon his Irish expedition;
From whence he intercepted did return
To be deposed and shortly murdered.

EARL OF WORCESTER

And for whose death we in the world's wide mouth
Live scandalized and foully spoken of.

HOTSPUR

But soft, I pray you; did King Richard then
Proclaim my brother Edmund Mortimer
Heir to the crown?

NORTHUMBERLAND

He did; myself did hear it.

HOTSPUR

Nay, then I cannot blame his cousin king,
That wished him on the barren mountains starve.
But shall it be that you, that set the crown
Upon the head of this forgetful man
And for his sake wear the detested blot
Of murderous subornation, shall it be,
That you a world of curses undergo,
Being the agents, or base second means,
The cords, the ladder, or the hangman rather?
O, pardon me that I descend so low,
To show the line and the predicament
Wherein you range under this subtle king;
Shall it for shame be spoken in these days,
Or fill up chronicles in time to come,
That men of your nobility and power
Did gage them both in an unjust behalf,
As both of you—God pardon it!—have done,
To put down Richard, that sweet lovely rose,
An plant this thorn, this canker, Bolingbroke?
And shall it in more shame be further spoken,
That you are fool'd, discarded and shook off
By him for whom these shames ye underwent?
No; yet time serves wherein you may redeem
Your banish'd honours and restore yourselves
Into the good thoughts of the world again,
Revenge the jeering and disdain'd contempt
Of this proud king, who studies day and night
To answer all the debt he owes to you
Even with the bloody payment of your deaths:
Therefore, I say—

EARL OF WORCESTER

Peace, cousin, say no more:
And now I will unclasp a secret book,
And to your quick-conceiving discontents
I'll read you matter deep and dangerous,
As full of peril and adventurous spirit
As to o'er-walk a current roaring loud
On the unsteadfast footing of a spear.

HOTSPUR

If he fall in, good night! or sink or swim:
Send danger from the east unto the west,
So honour cross it from the north to south,
And let them grapple: O, the blood more stirs
To rouse a lion than to start a hare!

NORTHUMBERLAND

Imagination of some great exploit
Drives him beyond the bounds of patience.

HOTSPUR

By heaven, methinks it were an easy leap,
To pluck bright honour from the pale-faced moon,
Or dive into the bottom of the deep,
Where fathom-line could never touch the ground,
And pluck up drowned honour by the locks;
So he that doth redeem her thence might wear
Without corrival, all her dignities:
But out upon this half-faced fellowship!

EARL OF WORCESTER

He apprehends a world of figures here,
But not the form of what he should attend.
Good cousin, give me audience for a while.

HOTSPUR

I cry you mercy.

EARL OF WORCESTER

Those same noble Scots
That are your prisoners,—

HOTSPUR

I'll keep them all;
By God, he shall not have a Scot of them;
No, if a Scot would save his soul, he shall not:
I'll keep them, by this hand.

EARL OF WORCESTER

You start away
And lend no ear unto my purposes.
Those prisoners you shall keep.

HOTSPUR

Nay, I will; that's flat:
He said he would not ransom Mortimer;
Forbad my tongue to speak of Mortimer;
But I will find him when he lies asleep,
And in his ear I'll holla 'Mortimer!'
Nay,
I'll have a starling shall be taught to speak
Nothing but 'Mortimer,' and give it him
To keep his anger still in motion.

EARL OF WORCESTER

Hear you, cousin; a word.

HOTSPUR

All studies here I solemnly defy,
Save how to gall and pinch this Bolingbroke:
And that same sword-and-buckler Prince of Wales,
But that I think his father loves him not
And would be glad he met with some mischance,
I would have him poison'd with a pot of ale.

EARL OF WORCESTER

Farewell, kinsman: I'll talk to you
When you are better temper'd to attend.

NORTHUMBERLAND

Why, what a wasp-stung and impatient fool
Art thou to break into this woman's mood,
Tying thine ear to no tongue but thine own!

HOTSPUR

Why, look you, I am whipp'd and scourged with rods,
Nettled and stung with pismires, when I hear
Of this vile politician, Bolingbroke.
In Richard's time,—what do you call the place?—
A plague upon it, it is in Gloucestershire;
'Twas where the madcap duke his uncle kept,
His uncle York; where I first bow'd my knee
Unto this king of smiles, this Bolingbroke,—
'Sblood!—
When you and he came back from Ravenspurgh.

NORTHUMBERLAND

At Berkley castle.

HOTSPUR

You say true:
Why, what a candy deal of courtesy
This fawning greyhound then did proffer me!
Look,'when his infant fortune came to age,'
And 'gentle Harry Percy,' and 'kind cousin;'
O, the devil take such cozeners! God forgive me!
Good uncle, tell your tale; I have done.

EARL OF WORCESTER

Nay, if you have not, to it again;
We will stay your leisure.

HOTSPUR

I have done, i' faith.

EARL OF WORCESTER

Then once more to your Scottish prisoners.
Deliver them up without their ransom straight,
And make the Douglas' son your only mean
For powers in Scotland; which, for divers reasons
Which I shall send you written, be assured,
Will easily be granted. You, my lord,

To Northumberland

Your son in Scotland being thus employ'd,
Shall secretly into the bosom creep
Of that same noble prelate, well beloved,
The archbishop.

HOTSPUR

Of York, is it not?

EARL OF WORCESTER

True; who bears hard
His brother's death at Bristol, the Lord Scroop.
I speak not this in estimation,
As what I think might be, but what I know
Is ruminated, plotted and set down,
And only stays but to behold the face
Of that occasion that shall bring it on.

HOTSPUR

I smell it: upon my life, it will do well.

NORTHUMBERLAND

Before the game is afoot, thou still let'st slip.

HOTSPUR

Why, it cannot choose but be a noble plot;
And then the power of Scotland and of York,
To join with Mortimer, ha?

EARL OF WORCESTER

And so they shall.

HOTSPUR

In faith, it is exceedingly well aim'd.

EARL OF WORCESTER

And 'tis no little reason bids us speed,
To save our heads by raising of a head;
For, bear ourselves as even as we can,
The king will always think him in our debt,
And think we think ourselves unsatisfied,
Till he hath found a time to pay us home:
And see already how he doth begin
To make us strangers to his looks of love.

HOTSPUR

He does, he does: we'll be revenged on him.

EARL OF WORCESTER

Cousin, farewell: no further go in this
Than I by letters shall direct your course.
When time is ripe, which will be suddenly,
I'll steal to Glendower and Lord Mortimer;
Where you and Douglas and our powers at once,
As I will fashion it, shall happily meet,
To bear our fortunes in our own strong arms,
Which now we hold at much uncertainty.

NORTHUMBERLAND

Farewell, good brother: we shall thrive, I trust.

HOTSPUR

Uncle, Adieu: O, let the hours be short
Till fields and blows and groans applaud our sport!

Exeunt

ACT II

SCENE I. Rochester. An inn yard.

Enter a Carrier with a lantern in his hand

First Carrier

Heigh-ho! an it be not four by the day, I'll be
hanged: Charles' wain is over the new chimney, and
yet our horse not packed. What, ostler!

Ostler

[Within] Anon, anon.

First Carrier

I prithee, Tom, beat Cut's saddle, put a few flocks
in the point; poor jade, is wrung in the withers out
of all cess.

Enter another Carrier

Second Carrier

Peas and beans are as dank here as a dog, and that
is the next way to give poor jades the bots: this
house is turned upside down since Robin Ostler died.

First Carrier

Poor fellow, never joyed since the price of oats
rose; it was the death of him.

Second Carrier

I think this be the most villanous house in all
London road for fleas: I am stung like a tench.

First Carrier

Like a tench! by the mass, there is ne'er a king
christen could be better bit than I have been since
the first cock.

Second Carrier

Why, they will allow us ne'er a jordan, and then we
leak in your chimney; and your chamber-lie breeds
fleas like a loach.

First Carrier

What, ostler! come away and be hanged!

Second Carrier

I have a gammon of bacon and two razors of ginger,
to be delivered as far as Charing-cross.

First Carrier

God's body! the turkeys in my pannier are quite
starved. What, ostler! A plague on thee! hast thou
never an eye in thy head? canst not hear? An
'twere not as good deed as drink, to break the pate
on thee, I am a very villain. Come, and be hanged!
hast thou no faith in thee?

Enter GADSHILL

GADSHILL

Good morrow, carriers. What's o'clock?

First Carrier

I think it be two o'clock.

GADSHILL

I pray thee lend me thy lantern, to see my gelding
in the stable.

First Carrier

Nay, by God, soft; I know a trick worth two of that, i' faith.

GADSHILL

I pray thee, lend me thine.

Second Carrier

Ay, when? can'st tell? Lend me thy lantern, quoth
he? marry, I'll see thee hanged first.

GADSHILL

Sirrah carrier, what time do you mean to come to London?

Second Carrier

Time enough to go to bed with a candle, I warrant
thee. Come, neighbour Mugs, we'll call up the
gentleman: they will along with company, for they
have great charge.

Exeunt carriers

GADSHILL

What, ho! chamberlain!

Chamberlain

[Within] At hand, quoth pick-purse.

GADSHILL

That's even as fair as—at hand, quoth the
chamberlain; for thou variest no more from picking
of purses than giving direction doth from labouring;
thou layest the plot how.

Enter Chamberlain

Chamberlain

Good morrow, Master Gadshill. It holds current that
I told you yesternight: there's a franklin in the
wild of Kent hath brought three hundred marks with
him in gold: I heard him tell it to one of his
company last night at supper; a kind of auditor; one
that hath abundance of charge too, God knows what.
They are up already, and call for eggs and butter;
they will away presently.

GADSHILL

Sirrah, if they meet not with Saint Nicholas'
clerks, I'll give thee this neck.

Chamberlain

No, I'll none of it: I pray thee keep that for the
hangman; for I know thou worshippest St. Nicholas
as truly as a man of falsehood may.

GADSHILL

What talkest thou to me of the hangman? if I hang,
I'll make a fat pair of gallows; for if I hang, old
Sir John hangs with me, and thou knowest he is no
starveling. Tut! there are other Trojans that thou
dreamest not of, the which for sport sake are
content to do the profession some grace; that would,
if matters should be looked into, for their own
credit sake, make all whole. I am joined with no
foot-land rakers, no long-staff sixpenny strikers,
none of these mad mustachio purple-hued malt-worms;
but with nobility and tranquillity, burgomasters and
great oneyers, such as can hold in, such as will

strike sooner than speak, and speak sooner than drink, and drink sooner than pray: and yet, zounds, I lie; for they pray continually to their saint, the commonwealth; or rather, not pray to her, but prey on her, for they ride up and down on her and make her their boots.

Chamberlain

What, the commonwealth their boots? will she hold out water in foul way?

GADSHILL

She will, she will; justice hath liquored her. We steal as in a castle, cocksure; we have the receipt of fern-seed, we walk invisible.

Chamberlain

Nay, by my faith, I think you are more beholding to the night than to fern-seed for your walking invisible.

GADSHILL

Give me thy hand: thou shalt have a share in our purchase, as I am a true man.

Chamberlain

Nay, rather let me have it, as you are a false thief.

GADSHILL

Go to; 'homo' is a common name to all men. Bid the ostler bring my gelding out of the stable. Farewell, you muddy knave.

Exeunt

SCENE II. The highway, near Gadshill.

Enter PRINCE HENRY and POINS

POINS

Come, shelter, shelter: I have removed Falstaff's horse, and he frets like a gummed velvet.

PRINCE HENRY

Stand close.

Enter FALSTAFF

FALSTAFF

Poins! Poins, and be hanged! Poins!

PRINCE HENRY

Peace, ye fat-kidneyed rascal! what a brawling dost
thou keep!

FALSTAFF

Where's Poins, Hal?

PRINCE HENRY

He is walked up to the top of the hill: I'll go seek him.

FALSTAFF

I am accursed to rob in that thief's company: the
rascal hath removed my horse, and tied him I know
not where. If I travel but four foot by the squier
further afoot, I shall break my wind. Well, I doubt
not but to die a fair death for all this, if I
'scape hanging for killing that rogue. I have
forsworn his company hourly any time this two and
twenty years, and yet I am bewitched with the
rogue's company. If the rascal hath not given me
medicines to make me love him, I'll be hanged; it
could not be else: I have drunk medicines. Poins!
Hal! a plague upon you both! Bardolph! Peto!
I'll starve ere I'll rob a foot further. An 'twere
not as good a deed as drink, to turn true man and to
leave these rogues, I am the veriest varlet that
ever chewed with a tooth. Eight yards of uneven
ground is threescore and ten miles afoot with me;
and the stony-hearted villains know it well enough:
a plague upon it when thieves cannot be true one to another!

They whistle

Whew! A plague upon you all! Give me my horse, you
rogues; give me my horse, and be hanged!

PRINCE HENRY

Peace, ye fat-guts! lie down; lay thine ear close
to the ground and list if thou canst hear the tread
of travellers.

FALSTAFF

Have you any levers to lift me up again, being down?
'Sblood, I'll not bear mine own flesh so far afoot
again for all the coin in thy father's exchequer.
What a plague mean ye to colt me thus?

PRINCE HENRY

Thou liest; thou art not colted, thou art uncolted.

FALSTAFF

I prithee, good Prince Hal, help me to my horse,
good king's son.

PRINCE HENRY

Out, ye rogue! shall I be your ostler?

FALSTAFF

Go, hang thyself in thine own heir-apparent
garters! If I be ta'en, I'll peach for this. An I
have not ballads made on you all and sung to filthy
tunes, let a cup of sack be my poison: when a jest
is so forward, and afoot too! I hate it.

Enter GADSHILL, BARDOLPH and PETO

GADSHILL

Stand.

FALSTAFF

So I do, against my will.

POINS

O, 'tis our setter: I know his voice. Bardolph,
what news?

BARDOLPH

Case ye, case ye; on with your vizards: there 's
money of the king's coming down the hill; 'tis going
to the king's exchequer.

FALSTAFF

You lie, ye rogue; 'tis going to the king's tavern.

GADSHILL

There's enough to make us all.

FALSTAFF

To be hanged.

PRINCE HENRY

Sirs, you four shall front them in the narrow lane;
Ned Poins and I will walk lower: if they 'scape
from your encounter, then they light on us.

PETO

How many be there of them?

GADSHILL

Some eight or ten.

FALSTAFF

'Zounds, will they not rob us?

PRINCE HENRY

What, a coward, Sir John Paunch?

FALSTAFF

Indeed, I am not John of Gaunt, your grandfather;
but yet no coward, Hal.

PRINCE HENRY

Well, we leave that to the proof.

POINS

Sirrah Jack, thy horse stands behind the hedge:
when thou needest him, there thou shalt find him.
Farewell, and stand fast.

FALSTAFF

Now cannot I strike him, if I should be hanged.

PRINCE HENRY

Ned, where are our disguises?

POINS

Here, hard by: stand close.

Exeunt PRINCE HENRY and POINS

FALSTAFF

Now, my masters, happy man be his dole, say I:
every man to his business.

Enter the Travellers

First Traveller

Come, neighbour: the boy shall lead our horses down
the hill; we'll walk afoot awhile, and ease our legs.

Thieves

Stand!

Travellers

Jesus bless us!

FALSTAFF

Strike; down with them; cut the villains' throats:
ah! whoreson caterpillars! bacon-fed knaves! they
hate us youth: down with them: fleece them.

Travellers

O, we are undone, both we and ours for ever!

FALSTAFF

Hang ye, gorbellied knaves, are ye undone? No, ye
fat chuffs: I would your store were here! On,
bacons, on! What, ye knaves! young men must live.
You are Grand-jurors, are ye? we'll jure ye, 'faith.

Here they rob them and bind them. Exeunt

Re-enter PRINCE HENRY and POINS

PRINCE HENRY

The thieves have bound the true men. Now could thou
and I rob the thieves and go merrily to London, it
would be argument for a week, laughter for a month
and a good jest for ever.

POINS

Stand close; I hear them coming.

Enter the Thieves again

FALSTAFF

Come, my masters, let us share, and then to horse
before day. An the Prince and Poins be not two
arrant cowards, there's no equity stirring: there's
no more valour in that Poins than in a wild-duck.

PRINCE HENRY

Your money!

POINS

Villains!

As they are sharing, the Prince and Poins set upon them; they all run away; and Falstaff, after a blow or two, runs away too, leaving the booty behind them

PRINCE HENRY

Got with much ease. Now merrily to horse:
The thieves are all scatter'd and possess'd with fear
So strongly that they dare not meet each other;
Each takes his fellow for an officer.
Away, good Ned. Falstaff sweats to death,
And lards the lean earth as he walks along:
Were 't not for laughing, I should pity him.

POINS

How the rogue roar'd!

Exeunt

SCENE III. Warkworth castle

Enter HOTSPUR, solus, reading a letter

HOTSPUR

'But for mine own part, my lord, I could be well
contented to be there, in respect of the love I bear
your house.' He could be contented: why is he not,
then? In respect of the love he bears our house:
he shows in this, he loves his own barn better than
he loves our house. Let me see some more. 'The
purpose you undertake is dangerous;'—why, that's
certain: 'tis dangerous to take a cold, to sleep, to
drink; but I tell you, my lord fool, out of this
nettle, danger, we pluck this flower, safety. 'The
purpose you undertake is dangerous; the friends you
have named uncertain; the time itself unsorted; and
your whole plot too light for the counterpoise of so
great an opposition.' Say you so, say you so? I say
unto you again, you are a shallow cowardly hind, and
you lie. What a lack-brain is this! By the Lord,
our plot is a good plot as ever was laid; our
friends true and constant: a good plot, good
friends, and full of expectation; an excellent plot,

very good friends. What a frosty-spirited rogue is
this! Why, my lord of York commends the plot and the
general course of action. 'Zounds, an I were now by
this rascal, I could brain him with his lady's fan.
Is there not my father, my uncle and myself? lord
Edmund Mortimer, My lord of York and Owen Glendower?
is there not besides the Douglas? have I not all
their letters to meet me in arms by the ninth of the
next month? and are they not some of them set
forward already? What a pagan rascal is this! an
infidel! Ha! you shall see now in very sincerity
of fear and cold heart, will he to the king and lay
open all our proceedings. O, I could divide myself
and go to buffets, for moving such a dish of
skim milk with so honourable an action! Hang him!
let him tell the king: we are prepared. I will set
forward to-night.

Enter LADY PERCY

How now, Kate! I must leave you within these two hours.

LADY PERCY

O, my good lord, why are you thus alone?
For what offence have I this fortnight been
A banish'd woman from my Harry's bed?
Tell me, sweet lord, what is't that takes from thee
Thy stomach, pleasure and thy golden sleep?
Why dost thou bend thine eyes upon the earth,
And start so often when thou sit'st alone?
Why hast thou lost the fresh blood in thy cheeks;
And given my treasures and my rights of thee
To thick-eyed musing and cursed melancholy?
In thy faint slumbers I by thee have watch'd,
And heard thee murmur tales of iron wars;
Speak terms of manage to thy bounding steed;
Cry 'Courage! to the field!' And thou hast talk'd
Of sallies and retires, of trenches, tents,
Of palisadoes, frontiers, parapets,
Of basilisks, of cannon, culverin,
Of prisoners' ransom and of soldiers slain,
And all the currents of a heady fight.
Thy spirit within thee hath been so at war
And thus hath so bestirr'd thee in thy sleep,
That beads of sweat have stood upon thy brow
Like bubbles in a late-disturbed stream;
And in thy face strange motions have appear'd,
Such as we see when men restrain their breath

On some great sudden hest. O, what portents are these?
Some heavy business hath my lord in hand,
And I must know it, else he loves me not.

HOTSPUR

What, ho!

Enter Servant

Is Gilliams with the packet gone?

Servant

He is, my lord, an hour ago.

HOTSPUR

Hath Butler brought those horses from the sheriff?

Servant

One horse, my lord, he brought even now.

HOTSPUR

What horse? a roan, a crop-ear, is it not?

Servant

It is, my lord.

HOTSPUR

That roan shall by my throne.
Well, I will back him straight: O esperance!
Bid Butler lead him forth into the park.

Exit Servant

LADY PERCY

But hear you, my lord.

HOTSPUR

What say'st thou, my lady?

LADY PERCY

What is it carries you away?

HOTSPUR

Why, my horse, my love, my horse.

LADY PERCY

Out, you mad-headed ape!
A weasel hath not such a deal of spleen
As you are toss'd with. In faith,
I'll know your business, Harry, that I will.
I fear my brother Mortimer doth stir
About his title, and hath sent for you
To line his enterprise: but if you go,–

HOTSPUR

So far afoot, I shall be weary, love.

LADY PERCY

Come, come, you paraquito, answer me
Directly unto this question that I ask:
In faith, I'll break thy little finger, Harry,
An if thou wilt not tell me all things true.

HOTSPUR

Away,
Away, you trifler! Love! I love thee not,
I care not for thee, Kate: this is no world
To play with mammets and to tilt with lips:
We must have bloody noses and crack'd crowns,
And pass them current too. God's me, my horse!
What say'st thou, Kate? what would'st thou
have with me?

LADY PERCY

Do you not love me? do you not, indeed?
Well, do not then; for since you love me not,
I will not love myself. Do you not love me?
Nay, tell me if you speak in jest or no.

HOTSPUR

Come, wilt thou see me ride?
And when I am on horseback, I will swear
I love thee infinitely. But hark you, Kate;
I must not have you henceforth question me
Whither I go, nor reason whereabout:
Whither I must, I must; and, to conclude,
This evening must I leave you, gentle Kate.
I know you wise, but yet no farther wise
Than Harry Percy's wife: constant you are,
But yet a woman: and for secrecy,
No lady closer; for I well believe
Thou wilt not utter what thou dost not know;
And so far will I trust thee, gentle Kate.

LADY PERCY

How! so far?

HOTSPUR

Not an inch further. But hark you, Kate:
Whither I go, thither shall you go too;
To-day will I set forth, to-morrow you.
Will this content you, Kate?

LADY PERCY

It must of force.

Exeunt

SCENE IV. The Boar's-Head Tavern, Eastcheap.

Enter PRINCE HENRY and POINS

PRINCE HENRY

Ned, prithee, come out of that fat room, and lend me
thy hand to laugh a little.

POINS

Where hast been, Hal?

PRINCE HENRY

With three or four loggerheads amongst three or four
score hogsheads. I have sounded the very
base-string of humility. Sirrah, I am sworn brother
to a leash of drawers; and can call them all by
their christen names, as Tom, Dick, and Francis.
They take it already upon their salvation, that
though I be but the prince of Wales, yet I am king
of courtesy; and tell me flatly I am no proud Jack,
like Falstaff, but a Corinthian, a lad of mettle, a
good boy, by the Lord, so they call me, and when I
am king of England, I shall command all the good
lads in Eastcheap. They call drinking deep, dyeing
scarlet; and when you breathe in your watering, they
cry 'hem!' and bid you play it off. To conclude, I
am so good a proficient in one quarter of an hour,
that I can drink with any tinker in his own language
during my life. I tell thee, Ned, thou hast lost
much honour, that thou wert not with me in this sweet
action. But, sweet Ned,—to sweeten which name of
Ned, I give thee this pennyworth of sugar, clapped

even now into my hand by an under-skinker, one that
never spake other English in his life than 'Eight
shillings and sixpence' and 'You are welcome,' with
this shrill addition, 'Anon, anon, sir! Score a pint
of bastard in the Half-Moon,' or so. But, Ned, to
drive away the time till Falstaff come, I prithee,
do thou stand in some by-room, while I question my
puny drawer to what end he gave me the sugar; and do
thou never leave calling 'Francis,' that his tale
to me may be nothing but 'Anon.' Step aside, and
I'll show thee a precedent.

POINS

Francis!

PRINCE HENRY

Thou art perfect.

POINS

Francis!

Exit POINS

Enter FRANCIS

FRANCIS

Anon, anon, sir. Look down into the Pomgarnet, Ralph.

PRINCE HENRY

Come hither, Francis.

FRANCIS

My lord?

PRINCE HENRY

How long hast thou to serve, Francis?

FRANCIS

Forsooth, five years, and as much as to—

POINS

[Within] Francis!

FRANCIS

Anon, anon, sir.

PRINCE HENRY

Five year! by'r lady, a long lease for the clinking
of pewter. But, Francis, darest thou be so valiant
as to play the coward with thy indenture and show it
a fair pair of heels and run from it?

FRANCIS

O Lord, sir, I'll be sworn upon all the books in
England, I could find in my heart.

POINS

[Within] Francis!

FRANCIS

Anon, sir.

PRINCE HENRY

How old art thou, Francis?

FRANCIS

Let me see—about Michaelmas next I shall be—

POINS

[Within] Francis!

FRANCIS

Anon, sir. Pray stay a little, my lord.

PRINCE HENRY

Nay, but hark you, Francis: for the sugar thou
gavest me,'twas a pennyworth, wast't not?

FRANCIS

O Lord, I would it had been two!

PRINCE HENRY

I will give thee for it a thousand pound: ask me
when thou wilt, and thou shalt have it.

POINS

[Within] Francis!

FRANCIS

Anon, anon.

PRINCE HENRY

Anon, Francis? No, Francis; but to-morrow, Francis;
or, Francis, o' Thursday; or indeed, Francis, when
thou wilt. But, Francis!

FRANCIS

My lord?

PRINCE HENRY

Wilt thou rob this leathern jerkin, crystal-button,
not-pated, agate-ring, puke-stocking, caddis-garter,
smooth-tongue, Spanish-pouch,—

FRANCIS

O Lord, sir, who do you mean?

PRINCE HENRY

Why, then, your brown bastard is your only drink;
for look you, Francis, your white canvas doublet
will sully: in Barbary, sir, it cannot come to so much.

FRANCIS

What, sir?

POINS

[Within] Francis!

PRINCE HENRY

Away, you rogue! dost thou not hear them call?

Here they both call him; the drawer stands amazed, not knowing which way to go

Enter Vintner

Vintner

What, standest thou still, and hearest such a
calling? Look to the guests within.

Exit Francis

My lord, old Sir John, with half-a-dozen more, are
at the door: shall I let them in?

PRINCE HENRY

Let them alone awhile, and then open the door.

Exit Vintner

Poins!

Re-enter POINS

POINS

Anon, anon, sir.

PRINCE HENRY

Sirrah, Falstaff and the rest of the thieves are at
the door: shall we be merry?

POINS

As merry as crickets, my lad. But hark ye; what
cunning match have you made with this jest of the
drawer? come, what's the issue?

PRINCE HENRY

I am now of all humours that have showed themselves
humours since the old days of goodman Adam to the
pupil age of this present twelve o'clock at midnight.

Re-enter FRANCIS

What's o'clock, Francis?

FRANCIS

Anon, anon, sir.

Exit

PRINCE HENRY

That ever this fellow should have fewer words than a
parrot, and yet the son of a woman! His industry is
upstairs and downstairs; his eloquence the parcel of
a reckoning. I am not yet of Percy's mind, the
Hotspur of the north; he that kills me some six or
seven dozen of Scots at a breakfast, washes his
hands, and says to his wife 'Fie upon this quiet
life! I want work.' 'O my sweet Harry,' says she,
'how many hast thou killed to-day?' 'Give my roan
horse a drench,' says he; and answers 'Some
fourteen,' an hour after; 'a trifle, a trifle.' I
prithee, call in Falstaff: I'll play Percy, and
that damned brawn shall play Dame Mortimer his
wife. 'Rivo!' says the drunkard. Call in ribs, call in tallow.

Enter FALSTAFF, GADSHILL, BARDOLPH, and PETO; FRANCIS following with wine

POINS

Welcome, Jack: where hast thou been?

FALSTAFF

A plague of all cowards, I say, and a vengeance too!
marry, and amen! Give me a cup of sack, boy. Ere I
lead this life long, I'll sew nether stocks and mend
them and foot them too. A plague of all cowards!
Give me a cup of sack, rogue. Is there no virtue extant?

He drinks

PRINCE HENRY

Didst thou never see Titan kiss a dish of butter?
pitiful-hearted Titan, that melted at the sweet tale
of the sun's! if thou didst, then behold that compound.

FALSTAFF

You rogue, here's lime in this sack too: there is
nothing but roguery to be found in villanous man:
yet a coward is worse than a cup of sack with lime
in it. A villanous coward! Go thy ways, old Jack;
die when thou wilt, if manhood, good manhood, be
not forgot upon the face of the earth, then am I a
shotten herring. There live not three good men
unhanged in England; and one of them is fat and
grows old: God help the while! a bad world, I say.
I would I were a weaver; I could sing psalms or any
thing. A plague of all cowards, I say still.

PRINCE HENRY

How now, wool-sack! what mutter you?

FALSTAFF

A king's son! If I do not beat thee out of thy
kingdom with a dagger of lath, and drive all thy
subjects afore thee like a flock of wild-geese,
I'll never wear hair on my face more. You Prince of Wales!

PRINCE HENRY

Why, you whoreson round man, what's the matter?

FALSTAFF

Are not you a coward? answer me to that: and Poins there?

POINS

'Zounds, ye fat paunch, an ye call me coward, by the Lord, I'll stab thee.

FALSTAFF

I call thee coward! I'll see thee damned ere I call thee coward: but I would give a thousand pound I could run as fast as thou canst. You are straight enough in the shoulders, you care not who sees your back: call you that backing of your friends? A plague upon such backing! give me them that will face me. Give me a cup of sack: I am a rogue, if I drunk to-day.

PRINCE HENRY

O villain! thy lips are scarce wiped since thou drunkest last.

FALSTAFF

All's one for that.

He drinks

A plague of all cowards, still say I.

PRINCE HENRY

What's the matter?

FALSTAFF

What's the matter! there be four of us here have ta'en a thousand pound this day morning.

PRINCE HENRY

Where is it, Jack? where is it?

FALSTAFF

Where is it! taken from us it is: a hundred upon poor four of us.

PRINCE HENRY

What, a hundred, man?

FALSTAFF

I am a rogue, if I were not at half-sword with a dozen of them two hours together. I have 'scaped by miracle. I am eight times thrust through the doublet, four through the hose; my buckler cut

through and through; my sword hacked like a
hand-saw—ecce signum! I never dealt better since
I was a man: all would not do. A plague of all
cowards! Let them speak: if they speak more or
less than truth, they are villains and the sons of darkness.

PRINCE HENRY

Speak, sirs; how was it?

GADSHILL

We four set upon some dozen—

FALSTAFF

Sixteen at least, my lord.

GADSHILL

And bound them.

PETO

No, no, they were not bound.

FALSTAFF

You rogue, they were bound, every man of them; or I
am a Jew else, an Ebrew Jew.

GADSHILL

As we were sharing, some six or seven fresh men set upon us—

FALSTAFF

And unbound the rest, and then come in the other.

PRINCE HENRY

What, fought you with them all?

FALSTAFF

All! I know not what you call all; but if I fought
not with fifty of them, I am a bunch of radish: if
there were not two or three and fifty upon poor old
Jack, then am I no two-legged creature.

PRINCE HENRY

Pray God you have not murdered some of them.

FALSTAFF

Nay, that's past praying for: I have peppered two
of them; two I am sure I have paid, two rogues
in buckram suits. I tell thee what, Hal, if I tell
thee a lie, spit in my face, call me horse. Thou
knowest my old ward; here I lay and thus I bore my
point. Four rogues in buckram let drive at me—

PRINCE HENRY

What, four? thou saidst but two even now.

FALSTAFF

Four, Hal; I told thee four.

POINS

Ay, ay, he said four.

FALSTAFF

These four came all a-front, and mainly thrust at
me. I made me no more ado but took all their seven
points in my target, thus.

PRINCE HENRY

Seven? why, there were but four even now.

FALSTAFF

In buckram?

POINS

Ay, four, in buckram suits.

FALSTAFF

Seven, by these hilts, or I am a villain else.

PRINCE HENRY

Prithee, let him alone; we shall have more anon.

FALSTAFF

Dost thou hear me, Hal?

PRINCE HENRY

Ay, and mark thee too, Jack.

FALSTAFF

Do so, for it is worth the listening to. These nine
in buckram that I told thee of—

PRINCE HENRY

So, two more already.

FALSTAFF

Their points being broken,–

POINS

Down fell their hose.

FALSTAFF

Began to give me ground: but I followed me close,
came in foot and hand; and with a thought seven of
the eleven I paid.

PRINCE HENRY

O monstrous! eleven buckram men grown out of two!

FALSTAFF

But, as the devil would have it, three misbegotten
knaves in Kendal green came at my back and let drive
at me; for it was so dark, Hal, that thou couldst
not see thy hand.

PRINCE HENRY

These lies are like their father that begets them;
gross as a mountain, open, palpable. Why, thou
clay-brained guts, thou knotty-pated fool, thou
whoreson, obscene, grease tallow-catch,–

FALSTAFF

What, art thou mad? art thou mad? is not the truth
the truth?

PRINCE HENRY

Why, how couldst thou know these men in Kendal
green, when it was so dark thou couldst not see thy
hand? come, tell us your reason: what sayest thou to this?

POINS

Come, your reason, Jack, your reason.

FALSTAFF

What, upon compulsion? 'Zounds, an I were at the
strappado, or all the racks in the world, I would

not tell you on compulsion. Give you a reason on compulsion! If reasons were as plentiful as blackberries, I would give no man a reason upon compulsion, I.

PRINCE HENRY

I'll be no longer guilty of this sin; this sanguine coward, this bed-presser, this horseback-breaker, this huge hill of flesh,—

FALSTAFF

'Sblood, you starveling, you elf-skin, you dried neat's tongue, you bull's pizzle, you stock-fish! O for breath to utter what is like thee! you tailor's-yard, you sheath, you bowcase; you vile standing-tuck,—

PRINCE HENRY

Well, breathe awhile, and then to it again: and when thou hast tired thyself in base comparisons, hear me speak but this.

POINS

Mark, Jack.

PRINCE HENRY

We two saw you four set on four and bound them, and were masters of their wealth. Mark now, how a plain tale shall put you down. Then did we two set on you four; and, with a word, out-faced you from your prize, and have it; yea, and can show it you here in the house: and, Falstaff, you carried your guts away as nimbly, with as quick dexterity, and roared for mercy and still run and roared, as ever I heard bull-calf. What a slave art thou, to hack thy sword as thou hast done, and then say it was in fight! What trick, what device, what starting-hole, canst thou now find out to hide thee from this open and apparent shame?

POINS

Come, let's hear, Jack; what trick hast thou now?

FALSTAFF

By the Lord, I knew ye as well as he that made ye. Why, hear you, my masters: was it for me to kill the heir-apparent? should I turn upon the true prince? why, thou knowest I am as valiant as Hercules: but beware instinct; the lion will not touch the true prince. Instinct is a great matter; I was now a coward on instinct. I shall think the better of myself and thee during my life; I for a valiant lion, and thou for a true prince. But, by the Lord, lads, I am glad you have the money. Hostess, clap to the doors: watch to-night, pray to-morrow. Gallants, lads, boys, hearts of gold, all the titles of good fellowship come to you! What, shall we be merry? shall we have a play extempore?

PRINCE HENRY

Content; and the argument shall be thy running away.

FALSTAFF

Ah, no more of that, Hal, an thou lovest me!

Enter Hostess

Hostess

O Jesu, my lord the prince!

PRINCE HENRY

How now, my lady the hostess! what sayest thou to me?

Hostess

Marry, my lord, there is a nobleman of the court at door would speak with you: he says he comes from your father.

PRINCE HENRY

Give him as much as will make him a royal man, and send him back again to my mother.

FALSTAFF

What manner of man is he?

Hostess

An old man.

FALSTAFF

What doth gravity out of his bed at midnight? Shall I give him his answer?

PRINCE HENRY

Prithee, do, Jack.

FALSTAFF

'Faith, and I'll send him packing.

Exit FALSTAFF

PRINCE HENRY

Now, sirs: by'r lady, you fought fair; so did you,
Peto; so did you, Bardolph: you are lions too, you
ran away upon instinct, you will not touch the true
prince; no, fie!

BARDOLPH

'Faith, I ran when I saw others run.

PRINCE HENRY

'Faith, tell me now in earnest, how came Falstaff's
sword so hacked?

PETO

Why, he hacked it with his dagger, and said he would
swear truth out of England but he would make you
believe it was done in fight, and persuaded us to do the like.

BARDOLPH

Yea, and to tickle our noses with spear-grass to
make them bleed, and then to beslubber our garments
with it and swear it was the blood of true men. I
did that I did not this seven year before, I blushed
to hear his monstrous devices.

PRINCE HENRY

O villain, thou stolest a cup of sack eighteen years
ago, and wert taken with the manner, and ever since
thou hast blushed extempore. Thou hadst fire and
sword on thy side, and yet thou rannest away: what
instinct hadst thou for it?

BARDOLPH

My lord, do you see these meteors? do you behold
these exhalations?

PRINCE HENRY

I do.

BARDOLPH

What think you they portend?

PRINCE HENRY

Hot livers and cold purses.

BARDOLPH

Choler, my lord, if rightly taken.

PRINCE HENRY

No, if rightly taken, halter.

Re-enter FALSTAFF

Here comes lean Jack, here comes bare-bone.
How now, my sweet creature of bombast!
How long is't ago, Jack, since thou sawest thine own knee?

FALSTAFF

My own knee! when I was about thy years, Hal, I was
not an eagle's talon in the waist; I could have
crept into any alderman's thumb-ring: a plague of
sighing and grief! it blows a man up like a
bladder. There's villanous news abroad: here was
Sir John Bracy from your father; you must to the
court in the morning. That same mad fellow of the
north, Percy, and he of Wales, that gave Amamon the
bastinado and made Lucifer cuckold and swore the
devil his true liegeman upon the cross of a Welsh
hook—what a plague call you him?

POINS

O, Glendower.

FALSTAFF

Owen, Owen, the same; and his son-in-law Mortimer,
and old Northumberland, and that sprightly Scot of
Scots, Douglas, that runs o' horseback up a hill
perpendicular,—

PRINCE HENRY

He that rides at high speed and with his pistol
kills a sparrow flying.

FALSTAFF

You have hit it.

PRINCE HENRY

So did he never the sparrow.

FALSTAFF

Well, that rascal hath good mettle in him; he will not run.

PRINCE HENRY

Why, what a rascal art thou then, to praise him so
for running!

FALSTAFF

O' horseback, ye cuckoo; but afoot he will not budge a foot.

PRINCE HENRY

Yes, Jack, upon instinct.

FALSTAFF

I grant ye, upon instinct. Well, he is there too,
and one Mordake, and a thousand blue-caps more:
Worcester is stolen away to-night; thy father's
beard is turned white with the news: you may buy
land now as cheap as stinking mackerel.

PRINCE HENRY

Why, then, it is like, if there come a hot June and
this civil buffeting hold, we shall buy maidenheads
as they buy hob-nails, by the hundreds.

FALSTAFF

By the mass, lad, thou sayest true; it is like we
shall have good trading that way. But tell me, Hal,
art not thou horrible afeard? thou being
heir-apparent, could the world pick thee out three
such enemies again as that fiend Douglas, that
spirit Percy, and that devil Glendower? Art thou
not horribly afraid? doth not thy blood thrill at
it?

PRINCE HENRY

Not a whit, i' faith; I lack some of thy instinct.

FALSTAFF

Well, thou wert be horribly chid tomorrow when thou
comest to thy father: if thou love me, practise an answer.

PRINCE HENRY

Do thou stand for my father, and examine me upon the
particulars of my life.

FALSTAFF

Shall I? content: this chair shall be my state,
this dagger my sceptre, and this cushion my crown.

PRINCE HENRY

Thy state is taken for a joined-stool, thy golden
sceptre for a leaden dagger, and thy precious rich
crown for a pitiful bald crown!

FALSTAFF

Well, an the fire of grace be not quite out of thee,
now shalt thou be moved. Give me a cup of sack to
make my eyes look red, that it may be thought I have
wept; for I must speak in passion, and I will do it
in King Cambyses' vein.

PRINCE HENRY

Well, here is my leg.

FALSTAFF

And here is my speech. Stand aside, nobility.

Hostess

O Jesu, this is excellent sport, i' faith!

FALSTAFF

Weep not, sweet queen; for trickling tears are vain.

Hostess

O, the father, how he holds his countenance!

FALSTAFF

For God's sake, lords, convey my tristful queen;
For tears do stop the flood-gates of her eyes.

Hostess

O Jesu, he doth it as like one of these harlotry
players as ever I see!

FALSTAFF

Peace, good pint-pot; peace, good tickle-brain.
Harry, I do not only marvel where thou spendest thy
time, but also how thou art accompanied: for though
the camomile, the more it is trodden on the faster
it grows, yet youth, the more it is wasted the
sooner it wears. That thou art my son, I have
partly thy mother's word, partly my own opinion,
but chiefly a villanous trick of thine eye and a
foolish-hanging of thy nether lip, that doth warrant
me. If then thou be son to me, here lies the point;
why, being son to me, art thou so pointed at? Shall
the blessed sun of heaven prove a micher and eat
blackberries? a question not to be asked. Shall
the sun of England prove a thief and take purses? a
question to be asked. There is a thing, Harry,
which thou hast often heard of and it is known to
many in our land by the name of pitch: this pitch,
as ancient writers do report, doth defile; so doth
the company thou keepest: for, Harry, now I do not
speak to thee in drink but in tears, not in
pleasure but in passion, not in words only, but in
woes also: and yet there is a virtuous man whom I
have often noted in thy company, but I know not his name.

PRINCE HENRY

What manner of man, an it like your majesty?

FALSTAFF

A goodly portly man, i' faith, and a corpulent; of a
cheerful look, a pleasing eye and a most noble
carriage; and, as I think, his age some fifty, or,
by'r lady, inclining to three score; and now I
remember me, his name is Falstaff: if that man
should be lewdly given, he deceiveth me; for, Harry,
I see virtue in his looks. If then the tree may be
known by the fruit, as the fruit by the tree, then,
peremptorily I speak it, there is virtue in that
Falstaff: him keep with, the rest banish. And tell
me now, thou naughty varlet, tell me, where hast
thou been this month?

PRINCE HENRY

Dost thou speak like a king? Do thou stand for me,
and I'll play my father.

FALSTAFF

Depose me? if thou dost it half so gravely, so majestically, both in word and matter, hang me up by the heels for a rabbit-sucker or a poulter's hare.

PRINCE HENRY

Well, here I am set.

FALSTAFF

And here I stand: judge, my masters.

PRINCE HENRY

Now, Harry, whence come you?

FALSTAFF

My noble lord, from Eastcheap.

PRINCE HENRY

The complaints I hear of thee are grievous.

FALSTAFF

'Sblood, my lord, they are false: nay, I'll tickle ye for a young prince, i' faith.

PRINCE HENRY

Swearest thou, ungracious boy? henceforth ne'er look on me. Thou art violently carried away from grace: there is a devil haunts thee in the likeness of an old fat man; a tun of man is thy companion. Why dost thou converse with that trunk of humours, that bolting-hutch of beastliness, that swollen parcel of dropsies, that huge bombard of sack, that stuffed cloak-bag of guts, that roasted Manningtree ox with the pudding in his belly, that reverend vice, that grey iniquity, that father ruffian, that vanity in years? Wherein is he good, but to taste sack and drink it? wherein neat and cleanly, but to carve a capon and eat it? wherein cunning, but in craft? wherein crafty, but in villany? wherein villanous, but in all things? wherein worthy, but in nothing?

FALSTAFF

I would your grace would take me with you: whom means your grace?

PRINCE HENRY

That villanous abominable misleader of youth,
Falstaff, that old white-bearded Satan.

FALSTAFF

My lord, the man I know.

PRINCE HENRY

I know thou dost.

FALSTAFF

But to say I know more harm in him than in myself,
were to say more than I know. That he is old, the
more the pity, his white hairs do witness it; but
that he is, saving your reverence, a whoremaster,
that I utterly deny. If sack and sugar be a fault,
God help the wicked! if to be old and merry be a
sin, then many an old host that I know is damned: if
to be fat be to be hated, then Pharaoh's lean kine
are to be loved. No, my good lord; banish Peto,
banish Bardolph, banish Poins: but for sweet Jack
Falstaff, kind Jack Falstaff, true Jack Falstaff,
valiant Jack Falstaff, and therefore more valiant,
being, as he is, old Jack Falstaff, banish not him
thy Harry's company, banish not him thy Harry's
company: banish plump Jack, and banish all the world.

PRINCE HENRY

I do, I will.

A knocking heard

Exeunt Hostess, FRANCIS, and BARDOLPH

Re-enter BARDOLPH, running

BARDOLPH

O, my lord, my lord! the sheriff with a most
monstrous watch is at the door.

FALSTAFF

Out, ye rogue! Play out the play: I have much to
say in the behalf of that Falstaff.

Re-enter the Hostess

Hostess

O Jesu, my lord, my lord!

PRINCE HENRY

Heigh, heigh! the devil rides upon a fiddlestick:
what's the matter?

Hostess

The sheriff and all the watch are at the door: they
are come to search the house. Shall I let them in?

FALSTAFF

Dost thou hear, Hal? never call a true piece of
gold a counterfeit: thou art essentially mad,
without seeming so.

PRINCE HENRY

And thou a natural coward, without instinct.

FALSTAFF

I deny your major: if you will deny the sheriff,
so; if not, let him enter: if I become not a cart
as well as another man, a plague on my bringing up!
I hope I shall as soon be strangled with a halter as another.

PRINCE HENRY

Go, hide thee behind the arras: the rest walk up
above. Now, my masters, for a true face and good
conscience.

FALSTAFF

Both which I have had: but their date is out, and
therefore I'll hide me.

PRINCE HENRY

Call in the sheriff.

Exeunt all except PRINCE HENRY and PETO

Enter Sheriff and the Carrier

Now, master sheriff, what is your will with me?

Sheriff

First, pardon me, my lord. A hue and cry
Hath follow'd certain men unto this house.

PRINCE HENRY

What men?

Sheriff

One of them is well known, my gracious lord,
A gross fat man.

Carrier

As fat as butter.

PRINCE HENRY

The man, I do assure you, is not here;
For I myself at this time have employ'd him.
And, sheriff, I will engage my word to thee
That I will, by to-morrow dinner-time,
Send him to answer thee, or any man,
For any thing he shall be charged withal:
And so let me entreat you leave the house.

Sheriff

I will, my lord. There are two gentlemen
Have in this robbery lost three hundred marks.

PRINCE HENRY

It may be so: if he have robb'd these men,
He shall be answerable; and so farewell.

Sheriff

Good night, my noble lord.

PRINCE HENRY

I think it is good morrow, is it not?

Sheriff

Indeed, my lord, I think it be two o'clock.

Exeunt Sheriff and Carrier

PRINCE HENRY

This oily rascal is known as well as Paul's. Go,
call him forth.

PETO

Falstaff!—Fast asleep behind the arras, and
snorting like a horse.

PRINCE HENRY

Hark, how hard he fetches breath. Search his pockets.

He searcheth his pockets, and findeth certain papers

What hast thou found?

PETO

Nothing but papers, my lord.

PRINCE HENRY

Let's see what they be: read them.

PETO

[Reads] Item, A capon,. . 2s. 2d.
Item, Sauce,. . . 4d.
Item, Sack, two gallons, 5s. 8d.
Item, Anchovies and sack after supper, 2s. 6d.
Item, Bread, ob.

PRINCE HENRY

O monstrous! but one half-penny-worth of bread to
this intolerable deal of sack! What there is else,
keep close; we'll read it at more advantage: there
let him sleep till day. I'll to the court in the
morning. We must all to the wars, and thy place
shall be honourable. I'll procure this fat rogue a
charge of foot; and I know his death will be a
march of twelve-score. The money shall be paid
back again with advantage. Be with me betimes in
the morning; and so, good morrow, Peto.

Exeunt

PETO

Good morrow, good my lord.

ACT III

SCENE I. Bangor. The Archdeacon's house.

Enter HOTSPUR, WORCESTER, MORTIMER, and GLENDOWER

MORTIMER

These promises are fair, the parties sure,
And our induction full of prosperous hope.

HOTSPUR

Lord Mortimer, and cousin Glendower,
Will you sit down?
And uncle Worcester: a plague upon it!
I have forgot the map.

GLENDOWER

No, here it is.
Sit, cousin Percy; sit, good cousin Hotspur,
For by that name as oft as Lancaster
Doth speak of you, his cheek looks pale and with
A rising sigh he wisheth you in heaven.

HOTSPUR

And you in hell, as oft as he hears Owen Glendower spoke of.

GLENDOWER

I cannot blame him: at my nativity
The front of heaven was full of fiery shapes,
Of burning cressets; and at my birth
The frame and huge foundation of the earth
Shaked like a coward.

HOTSPUR

Why, so it would have done at the same season, if
your mother's cat had but kittened, though yourself
had never been born.

GLENDOWER

I say the earth did shake when I was born.

HOTSPUR

And I say the earth was not of my mind,
If you suppose as fearing you it shook.

GLENDOWER

The heavens were all on fire, the earth did tremble.

HOTSPUR

O, then the earth shook to see the heavens on fire,
And not in fear of your nativity.
Diseased nature oftentimes breaks forth
In strange eruptions; oft the teeming earth
Is with a kind of colic pinch'd and vex'd
By the imprisoning of unruly wind
Within her womb; which, for enlargement striving,
Shakes the old beldam earth and topples down

Steeples and moss-grown towers. At your birth
Our grandam earth, having this distemperature,
In passion shook.

GLENDOWER

Cousin, of many men
I do not bear these crossings. Give me leave
To tell you once again that at my birth
The front of heaven was full of fiery shapes,
The goats ran from the mountains, and the herds
Were strangely clamorous to the frighted fields.
These signs have mark'd me extraordinary;
And all the courses of my life do show
I am not in the roll of common men.
Where is he living, clipp'd in with the sea
That chides the banks of England, Scotland, Wales,
Which calls me pupil, or hath read to me?
And bring him out that is but woman's son
Can trace me in the tedious ways of art
And hold me pace in deep experiments.

HOTSPUR

I think there's no man speaks better Welsh.
I'll to dinner.

MORTIMER

Peace, cousin Percy; you will make him mad.

GLENDOWER

I can call spirits from the vasty deep.

HOTSPUR

Why, so can I, or so can any man;
But will they come when you do call for them?

GLENDOWER

Why, I can teach you, cousin, to command
The devil.

HOTSPUR

And I can teach thee, coz, to shame the devil
By telling truth: tell truth and shame the devil.
If thou have power to raise him, bring him hither,
And I'll be sworn I have power to shame him hence.
O, while you live, tell truth and shame the devil!

MORTIMER

Come, come, no more of this unprofitable chat.

GLENDOWER

Three times hath Henry Bolingbroke made head
Against my power; thrice from the banks of Wye
And sandy-bottom'd Severn have I sent him
Bootless home and weather-beaten back.

HOTSPUR

Home without boots, and in foul weather too!
How 'scapes he agues, in the devil's name?

GLENDOWER

Come, here's the map: shall we divide our right
According to our threefold order ta'en?

MORTIMER

The archdeacon hath divided it
Into three limits very equally:
England, from Trent and Severn hitherto,
By south and east is to my part assign'd:
All westward, Wales beyond the Severn shore,
And all the fertile land within that bound,
To Owen Glendower: and, dear coz, to you
The remnant northward, lying off from Trent.
And our indentures tripartite are drawn;
Which being sealed interchangeably,
A business that this night may execute,
To-morrow, cousin Percy, you and I
And my good Lord of Worcester will set forth
To meet your father and the Scottish power,
As is appointed us, at Shrewsbury.
My father Glendower is not ready yet,
Not shall we need his help these fourteen days.
Within that space you may have drawn together
Your tenants, friends and neighbouring gentlemen.

GLENDOWER

A shorter time shall send me to you, lords:
And in my conduct shall your ladies come;
From whom you now must steal and take no leave,
For there will be a world of water shed
Upon the parting of your wives and you.

HOTSPUR

Methinks my moiety, north from Burton here,
In quantity equals not one of yours:
See how this river comes me cranking in,
And cuts me from the best of all my land
A huge half-moon, a monstrous cantle out.
I'll have the current in this place damm'd up;
And here the smug and silver Trent shall run
In a new channel, fair and evenly;
It shall not wind with such a deep indent,
To rob me of so rich a bottom here.

GLENDOWER

Not wind? it shall, it must; you see it doth.

MORTIMER

Yea, but
Mark how he bears his course, and runs me up
With like advantage on the other side;
Gelding the opposed continent as much
As on the other side it takes from you.

EARL OF WORCESTER

Yea, but a little charge will trench him here
And on this north side win this cape of land;
And then he runs straight and even.

HOTSPUR

I'll have it so: a little charge will do it.

GLENDOWER

I'll not have it alter'd.

HOTSPUR

Will not you?

GLENDOWER

No, nor you shall not.

HOTSPUR

Who shall say me nay?

GLENDOWER

Why, that will I.

HOTSPUR

Let me not understand you, then; speak it in Welsh.

GLENDOWER

I can speak English, lord, as well as you;
For I was train'd up in the English court;
Where, being but young, I framed to the harp
Many an English ditty lovely well
And gave the tongue a helpful ornament,
A virtue that was never seen in you.

HOTSPUR

Marry,
And I am glad of it with all my heart:
I had rather be a kitten and cry mew
Than one of these same metre ballad-mongers;
I had rather hear a brazen canstick turn'd,
Or a dry wheel grate on the axle-tree;
And that would set my teeth nothing on edge,
Nothing so much as mincing poetry:
'Tis like the forced gait of a shuffling nag.

GLENDOWER

Come, you shall have Trent turn'd.

HOTSPUR

I do not care: I'll give thrice so much land
To any well-deserving friend;
But in the way of bargain, mark ye me,
I'll cavil on the ninth part of a hair.
Are the indentures drawn? shall we be gone?

GLENDOWER

The moon shines fair; you may away by night:
I'll haste the writer and withal
Break with your wives of your departure hence:
I am afraid my daughter will run mad,
So much she doteth on her Mortimer.

Exit GLENDOWER

MORTIMER

Fie, cousin Percy! how you cross my father!

HOTSPUR

I cannot choose: sometime he angers me
With telling me of the mouldwarp and the ant,

Of the dreamer Merlin and his prophecies,
And of a dragon and a finless fish,
A clip-wing'd griffin and a moulten raven,
A couching lion and a ramping cat,
And such a deal of skimble-skamble stuff
As puts me from my faith. I tell you what;
He held me last night at least nine hours
In reckoning up the several devils' names
That were his lackeys: I cried 'hum,' and 'well, go to,'
But mark'd him not a word. O, he is as tedious
As a tired horse, a railing wife;
Worse than a smoky house: I had rather live
With cheese and garlic in a windmill, far,
Than feed on cates and have him talk to me
In any summer-house in Christendom.

MORTIMER

In faith, he is a worthy gentleman,
Exceedingly well read, and profited
In strange concealments, valiant as a lion
And as wondrous affable and as bountiful
As mines of India. Shall I tell you, cousin?
He holds your temper in a high respect
And curbs himself even of his natural scope
When you come 'cross his humour; faith, he does:
I warrant you, that man is not alive
Might so have tempted him as you have done,
Without the taste of danger and reproof:
But do not use it oft, let me entreat you.

EARL OF WORCESTER

In faith, my lord, you are too wilful-blame;
And since your coming hither have done enough
To put him quite beside his patience.
You must needs learn, lord, to amend this fault:
Though sometimes it show greatness, courage, blood,–
And that's the dearest grace it renders you,–
Yet oftentimes it doth present harsh rage,
Defect of manners, want of government,
Pride, haughtiness, opinion and disdain:
The least of which haunting a nobleman
Loseth men's hearts and leaves behind a stain
Upon the beauty of all parts besides,
Beguiling them of commendation.

HOTSPUR

Well, I am school'd: good manners be your speed!
Here come our wives, and let us take our leave.

Re-enter GLENDOWER with the ladies

MORTIMER

This is the deadly spite that angers me;
My wife can speak no English, I no Welsh.

GLENDOWER

My daughter weeps: she will not part with you;
She'll be a soldier too, she'll to the wars.

MORTIMER

Good father, tell her that she and my aunt Percy
Shall follow in your conduct speedily.

Glendower speaks to her in Welsh, and she answers him in the same

GLENDOWER

She is desperate here; a peevish self-wind harlotry,
one that no persuasion can do good upon.

The lady speaks in Welsh

MORTIMER

I understand thy looks: that pretty Welsh
Which thou pour'st down from these swelling heavens
I am too perfect in; and, but for shame,
In such a parley should I answer thee.

The lady speaks again in Welsh

I understand thy kisses and thou mine,
And that's a feeling disputation:
But I will never be a truant, love,
Till I have learned thy language; for thy tongue
Makes Welsh as sweet as ditties highly penn'd,
Sung by a fair queen in a summer's bower,
With ravishing division, to her lute.

GLENDOWER

Nay, if you melt, then will she run mad.

The lady speaks again in Welsh

MORTIMER

O, I am ignorance itself in this!

GLENDOWER

She bids you on the wanton rushes lay you down
And rest your gentle head upon her lap,
And she will sing the song that pleaseth you
And on your eyelids crown the god of sleep.
Charming your blood with pleasing heaviness,
Making such difference 'twixt wake and sleep
As is the difference betwixt day and night
The hour before the heavenly-harness'd team
Begins his golden progress in the east.

MORTIMER

With all my heart I'll sit and hear her sing:
By that time will our book, I think, be drawn

GLENDOWER

Do so;
And those musicians that shall play to you
Hang in the air a thousand leagues from hence,
And straight they shall be here: sit, and attend.

HOTSPUR

Come, Kate, thou art perfect in lying down: come,
quick, quick, that I may lay my head in thy lap.

LADY PERCY

Go, ye giddy goose.

The music plays

HOTSPUR

Now I perceive the devil understands Welsh;
And 'tis no marvel he is so humorous.
By'r lady, he is a good musician.

LADY PERCY

Then should you be nothing but musical for you are
altogether governed by humours. Lie still, ye thief,
and hear the lady sing in Welsh.

HOTSPUR

I had rather hear Lady, my brach, howl in Irish.

LADY PERCY

Wouldst thou have thy head broken?

HOTSPUR

No.

LADY PERCY

Then be still.

HOTSPUR

Neither;'tis a woman's fault.

LADY PERCY

Now God help thee!

HOTSPUR

To the Welsh lady's bed.

LADY PERCY

What's that?

HOTSPUR

Peace! she sings.

Here the lady sings a Welsh song

HOTSPUR

Come, Kate, I'll have your song too.

LADY PERCY

Not mine, in good sooth.

HOTSPUR

Not yours, in good sooth! Heart! you swear like a
comfit-maker's wife. 'Not you, in good sooth,' and
'as true as I live,' and 'as God shall mend me,' and
'as sure as day,'
And givest such sarcenet surety for thy oaths,
As if thou never walk'st further than Finsbury.
Swear me, Kate, like a lady as thou art,
A good mouth-filling oath, and leave 'in sooth,'
And such protest of pepper-gingerbread,
To velvet-guards and Sunday-citizens.
Come, sing.

LADY PERCY

I will not sing.

HOTSPUR

'Tis the next way to turn tailor, or be red-breast
teacher. An the indentures be drawn, I'll away
within these two hours; and so, come in when ye will.

Exit

GLENDOWER

Come, come, Lord Mortimer; you are as slow
As hot Lord Percy is on fire to go.
By this our book is drawn; we'll but seal,
And then to horse immediately.

MORTIMER

With all my heart.

Exeunt

SCENE II. London. The palace.

Enter KING HENRY IV, PRINCE HENRY, and others

KING HENRY IV

Lords, give us leave; the Prince of Wales and I
Must have some private conference; but be near at hand,
For we shall presently have need of you.

Exeunt Lords

I know not whether God will have it so,
For some displeasing service I have done,
That, in his secret doom, out of my blood
He'll breed revengement and a scourge for me;
But thou dost in thy passages of life
Make me believe that thou art only mark'd
For the hot vengeance and the rod of heaven
To punish my mistreadings. Tell me else,
Could such inordinate and low desires,
Such poor, such bare, such lewd, such mean attempts,
Such barren pleasures, rude society,
As thou art match'd withal and grafted to,
Accompany the greatness of thy blood
And hold their level with thy princely heart?

PRINCE HENRY

So please your majesty, I would I could
Quit all offences with as clear excuse
As well as I am doubtless I can purge

Myself of many I am charged withal:
Yet such extenuation let me beg,
As, in reproof of many tales devised,
which oft the ear of greatness needs must hear,
By smiling pick-thanks and base news-mongers,
I may, for some things true, wherein my youth
Hath faulty wander'd and irregular,
Find pardon on my true submission.

KING HENRY IV

God pardon thee! yet let me wonder, Harry,
At thy affections, which do hold a wing
Quite from the flight of all thy ancestors.
Thy place in council thou hast rudely lost.
Which by thy younger brother is supplied,
And art almost an alien to the hearts
Of all the court and princes of my blood:
The hope and expectation of thy time
Is ruin'd, and the soul of every man
Prophetically doth forethink thy fall.
Had I so lavish of my presence been,
So common-hackney'd in the eyes of men,
So stale and cheap to vulgar company,
Opinion, that did help me to the crown,
Had still kept loyal to possession
And left me in reputeless banishment,
A fellow of no mark nor likelihood.
By being seldom seen, I could not stir
But like a comet I was wonder'd at;
That men would tell their children 'This is he;'
Others would say 'Where, which is Bolingbroke?'
And then I stole all courtesy from heaven,
And dress'd myself in such humility
That I did pluck allegiance from men's hearts,
Loud shouts and salutations from their mouths,
Even in the presence of the crowned king.
Thus did I keep my person fresh and new;
My presence, like a robe pontifical,
Ne'er seen but wonder'd at: and so my state,
Seldom but sumptuous, showed like a feast
And won by rareness such solemnity.
The skipping king, he ambled up and down
With shallow jesters and rash bavin wits,
Soon kindled and soon burnt; carded his state,
Mingled his royalty with capering fools,
Had his great name profaned with their scorns
And gave his countenance, against his name,
To laugh at gibing boys and stand the push

Of every beardless vain comparative,
Grew a companion to the common streets,
Enfeoff'd himself to popularity;
That, being daily swallow'd by men's eyes,
They surfeited with honey and began
To loathe the taste of sweetness, whereof a little
More than a little is by much too much.
So when he had occasion to be seen,
He was but as the cuckoo is in June,
Heard, not regarded; seen, but with such eyes
As, sick and blunted with community,
Afford no extraordinary gaze,
Such as is bent on sun-like majesty
When it shines seldom in admiring eyes;
But rather drowzed and hung their eyelids down,
Slept in his face and render'd such aspect
As cloudy men use to their adversaries,
Being with his presence glutted, gorged and full.
And in that very line, Harry, standest thou;
For thou has lost thy princely privilege
With vile participation: not an eye
But is a-weary of thy common sight,
Save mine, which hath desired to see thee more;
Which now doth that I would not have it do,
Make blind itself with foolish tenderness.

PRINCE HENRY

I shall hereafter, my thrice gracious lord,
Be more myself.

KING HENRY IV

For all the world
As thou art to this hour was Richard then
When I from France set foot at Ravenspurgh,
And even as I was then is Percy now.
Now, by my sceptre and my soul to boot,
He hath more worthy interest to the state
Than thou the shadow of succession;
For of no right, nor colour like to right,
He doth fill fields with harness in the realm,
Turns head against the lion's armed jaws,
And, being no more in debt to years than thou,
Leads ancient lords and reverend bishops on
To bloody battles and to bruising arms.
What never-dying honour hath he got
Against renowned Douglas! whose high deeds,
Whose hot incursions and great name in arms

Holds from all soldiers chief majority

And military title capital

Through all the kingdoms that acknowledge Christ:

Thrice hath this Hotspur, Mars in swathling clothes,

This infant warrior, in his enterprises

Discomfited great Douglas, ta'en him once,

Enlarged him and made a friend of him,

To fill the mouth of deep defiance up

And shake the peace and safety of our throne.

And what say you to this? Percy, Northumberland,

The Archbishop's grace of York, Douglas, Mortimer,

Capitulate against us and are up.

But wherefore do I tell these news to thee?

Why, Harry, do I tell thee of my foes,

Which art my near'st and dearest enemy?

Thou that art like enough, through vassal fear,

Base inclination and the start of spleen

To fight against me under Percy's pay,

To dog his heels and curtsy at his frowns,

To show how much thou art degenerate.

PRINCE HENRY

Do not think so; you shall not find it so:

And God forgive them that so much have sway'd

Your majesty's good thoughts away from me!

I will redeem all this on Percy's head

And in the closing of some glorious day

Be bold to tell you that I am your son;

When I will wear a garment all of blood

And stain my favours in a bloody mask,

Which, wash'd away, shall scour my shame with it:

And that shall be the day, whene'er it lights,

That this same child of honour and renown,

This gallant Hotspur, this all-praised knight,

And your unthought-of Harry chance to meet.

For every honour sitting on his helm,

Would they were multitudes, and on my head

My shames redoubled! for the time will come,

That I shall make this northern youth exchange

His glorious deeds for my indignities.

Percy is but my factor, good my lord,

To engross up glorious deeds on my behalf;

And I will call him to so strict account,

That he shall render every glory up,

Yea, even the slightest worship of his time,

Or I will tear the reckoning from his heart.

This, in the name of God, I promise here:

The which if He be pleased I shall perform,

I do beseech your majesty may salve
The long-grown wounds of my intemperance:
If not, the end of life cancels all bands;
And I will die a hundred thousand deaths
Ere break the smallest parcel of this vow.

KING HENRY IV

A hundred thousand rebels die in this:
Thou shalt have charge and sovereign trust herein.

Enter BLUNT

How now, good Blunt? thy looks are full of speed.

SIR WALTER BLUNT

So hath the business that I come to speak of.
Lord Mortimer of Scotland hath sent word
That Douglas and the English rebels met
The eleventh of this month at Shrewsbury
A mighty and a fearful head they are,
If promises be kept on every hand,
As ever offer'd foul play in the state.

KING HENRY IV

The Earl of Westmoreland set forth to-day;
With him my son, Lord John of Lancaster;
For this advertisement is five days old:
On Wednesday next, Harry, you shall set forward;
On Thursday we ourselves will march: our meeting
Is Bridgenorth: and, Harry, you shall march
Through Gloucestershire; by which account,
Our business valued, some twelve days hence
Our general forces at Bridgenorth shall meet.
Our hands are full of business: let's away;
Advantage feeds him fat, while men delay.

Exeunt

Scene III

Eastcheap. The Boar's-Head Tavern.

Enter FALSTAFF and BARDOLPH

FALSTAFF

Bardolph, am I not fallen away vilely since this last
action? do I not bate? do I not dwindle? Why my
skin hangs about me like an like an old lady's loose

gown; I am withered like an old apple-john. Well,
I'll repent, and that suddenly, while I am in some
liking; I shall be out of heart shortly, and then I
shall have no strength to repent. An I have not
forgotten what the inside of a church is made of, I
am a peppercorn, a brewer's horse: the inside of a
church! Company, villanous company, hath been the
spoil of me.

BARDOLPH

Sir John, you are so fretful, you cannot live long.

FALSTAFF

Why, there is it: come sing me a bawdy song; make
me merry. I was as virtuously given as a gentleman
need to be; virtuous enough; swore little; diced not
above seven times a week; went to a bawdy-house once
in a quarter–of an hour; paid money that I
borrowed, three of four times; lived well and in
good compass: and now I live out of all order, out
of all compass.

BARDOLPH

Why, you are so fat, Sir John, that you must needs
be out of all compass, out of all reasonable
compass, Sir John.

FALSTAFF

Do thou amend thy face, and I'll amend my life:
thou art our admiral, thou bearest the lantern in
the poop, but 'tis in the nose of thee; thou art the
Knight of the Burning Lamp.

BARDOLPH

Why, Sir John, my face does you no harm.

FALSTAFF

No, I'll be sworn; I make as good use of it as many
a man doth of a Death's-head or a memento mori: I
never see thy face but I think upon hell-fire and
Dives that lived in purple; for there he is in his
robes, burning, burning. If thou wert any way
given to virtue, I would swear by thy face; my oath
should be 'By this fire, that's God's angel:' but
thou art altogether given over; and wert indeed, but
for the light in thy face, the son of utter

darkness. When thou rannest up Gadshill in the
night to catch my horse, if I did not think thou
hadst been an ignis fatuus or a ball of wildfire,
there's no purchase in money. O, thou art a
perpetual triumph, an everlasting bonfire-light!
Thou hast saved me a thousand marks in links and
torches, walking with thee in the night betwixt
tavern and tavern: but the sack that thou hast
drunk me would have bought me lights as good cheap
at the dearest chandler's in Europe. I have
maintained that salamander of yours with fire any
time this two and thirty years; God reward me for
it!

BARDOLPH

'Sblood, I would my face were in your belly!

FALSTAFF

God-a-mercy! so should I be sure to be heart-burned.

Enter Hostess

How now, Dame Partlet the hen! have you inquired
yet who picked my pocket?

Hostess

Why, Sir John, what do you think, Sir John? do you
think I keep thieves in my house? I have searched,
I have inquired, so has my husband, man by man, boy
by boy, servant by servant: the tithe of a hair
was never lost in my house before.

FALSTAFF

Ye lie, hostess: Bardolph was shaved and lost many
a hair; and I'll be sworn my pocket was picked. Go
to, you are a woman, go.

Hostess

Who, I? no; I defy thee: God's light, I was never
called so in mine own house before.

FALSTAFF

Go to, I know you well enough.

Hostess

No, Sir John; You do not know me, Sir John. I know
you, Sir John: you owe me money, Sir John; and now
you pick a quarrel to beguile me of it: I bought
you a dozen of shirts to your back.

FALSTAFF

Dowlas, filthy dowlas: I have given them away to
bakers' wives, and they have made bolters of them.

Hostess

Now, as I am a true woman, holland of eight
shillings an ell. You owe money here besides, Sir
John, for your diet and by-drinkings, and money lent
you, four and twenty pound.

FALSTAFF

He had his part of it; let him pay.

Hostess

He? alas, he is poor; he hath nothing.

FALSTAFF

How! poor? look upon his face; what call you rich?
let them coin his nose, let them coin his cheeks:
Ill not pay a denier. What, will you make a younker
of me? shall I not take mine case in mine inn but I
shall have my pocket picked? I have lost a
seal-ring of my grandfather's worth forty mark.

Hostess

O Jesu, I have heard the prince tell him, I know not
how oft, that ring was copper!

FALSTAFF

How! the prince is a Jack, a sneak-cup: 'sblood, an
he were here, I would cudgel him like a dog, if he
would say so.

Enter PRINCE HENRY and PETO, marching, and FALSTAFF meets them playing on his truncheon like a life

How now, lad! is the wind in that door, i' faith?
must we all march?

BARDOLPH

Yea, two and two, Newgate fashion.

Hostess

My lord, I pray you, hear me.

PRINCE HENRY

What sayest thou, Mistress Quickly? How doth thy husband? I love him well; he is an honest man.

Hostess

Good my lord, hear me.

FALSTAFF

Prithee, let her alone, and list to me.

PRINCE HENRY

What sayest thou, Jack?

FALSTAFF

The other night I fell asleep here behind the arras and had my pocket picked: this house is turned bawdy-house; they pick pockets.

PRINCE HENRY

What didst thou lose, Jack?

FALSTAFF

Wilt thou believe me, Hal? three or four bonds of forty pound apiece, and a seal-ring of my grandfather's.

PRINCE HENRY

A trifle, some eight-penny matter.

Hostess

So I told him, my lord; and I said I heard your grace say so: and, my lord, he speaks most vilely of you, like a foul-mouthed man as he is; and said he would cudgel you.

PRINCE HENRY

What! he did not?

Hostess

There's neither faith, truth, nor womanhood in me else.

FALSTAFF

There's no more faith in thee than in a stewed prune; nor no more truth in thee than in a drawn fox; and for womanhood, Maid Marian may be the deputy's wife of the ward to thee. Go, you thing, go

Hostess

Say, what thing? what thing?

FALSTAFF

What thing! why, a thing to thank God on.

Hostess

I am no thing to thank God on, I would thou shouldst know it; I am an honest man's wife: and, setting thy knighthood aside, thou art a knave to call me so.

FALSTAFF

Setting thy womanhood aside, thou art a beast to say otherwise.

Hostess

Say, what beast, thou knave, thou?

FALSTAFF

What beast! why, an otter.

PRINCE HENRY

An otter, Sir John! Why an otter?

FALSTAFF

Why, she's neither fish nor flesh; a man knows not where to have her.

Hostess

Thou art an unjust man in saying so: thou or any man knows where to have me, thou knave, thou!

PRINCE HENRY

Thou sayest true, hostess; and he slanders thee most grossly.

Hostess

So he doth you, my lord; and said this other day you ought him a thousand pound.

PRINCE HENRY

Sirrah, do I owe you a thousand pound?

FALSTAFF

A thousand pound, Ha! a million: thy love is worth
a million: thou owest me thy love.

Hostess

Nay, my lord, he called you Jack, and said he would
cudgel you.

FALSTAFF

Did I, Bardolph?

BARDOLPH

Indeed, Sir John, you said so.

FALSTAFF

Yea, if he said my ring was copper.

PRINCE HENRY

I say 'tis copper: darest thou be as good as thy word now?

FALSTAFF

Why, Hal, thou knowest, as thou art but man, I dare:
but as thou art prince, I fear thee as I fear the
roaring of a lion's whelp.

PRINCE HENRY

And why not as the lion?

FALSTAFF

The king is to be feared as the lion: dost thou
think I'll fear thee as I fear thy father? nay, an
I do, I pray God my girdle break.

PRINCE HENRY

O, if it should, how would thy guts fall about thy
knees! But, sirrah, there's no room for faith,
truth, nor honesty in this bosom of thine; it is all
filled up with guts and midriff. Charge an honest
woman with picking thy pocket! why, thou whoreson,
impudent, embossed rascal, if there were anything in
thy pocket but tavern-reckonings, memorandums of

bawdy-houses, and one poor penny-worth of
sugar-candy to make thee long-winded, if thy pocket
were enriched with any other injuries but these, I
am a villain: and yet you will stand to if; you will
not pocket up wrong: art thou not ashamed?

FALSTAFF

Dost thou hear, Hal? thou knowest in the state of
innocency Adam fell; and what should poor Jack
Falstaff do in the days of villany? Thou seest I
have more flesh than another man, and therefore more
frailty. You confess then, you picked my pocket?

PRINCE HENRY

It appears so by the story.

FALSTAFF

Hostess, I forgive thee: go, make ready breakfast;
love thy husband, look to thy servants, cherish thy
guests: thou shalt find me tractable to any honest
reason: thou seest I am pacified still. Nay,
prithee, be gone.

Exit Hostèss

Now Hal, to the news at court: for the robbery,
lad, how is that answered?

PRINCE HENRY

O, my sweet beef, I must still be good angel to
thee: the money is paid back again.

FALSTAFF

O, I do not like that paying back; 'tis a double labour.

PRINCE HENRY

I am good friends with my father and may do any thing.

FALSTAFF

Rob me the exchequer the first thing thou doest, and
do it with unwashed hands too.

BARDOLPH

Do, my lord.

PRINCE HENRY

I have procured thee, Jack, a charge of foot.

FALSTAFF

I would it had been of horse. Where shall I find
one that can steal well? O for a fine thief, of the
age of two and twenty or thereabouts! I am
heinously unprovided. Well, God be thanked for
these rebels, they offend none but the virtuous: I
laud them, I praise them.

PRINCE HENRY

Bardolph!

BARDOLPH

My lord?

PRINCE HENRY

Go bear this letter to Lord John of Lancaster, to my
brother John; this to my Lord of Westmoreland.

Exit Bardolph

Go, Peto, to horse, to horse; for thou and I have
thirty miles to ride yet ere dinner time.

Exit Peto

Jack, meet me to-morrow in the temple hall at two
o'clock in the afternoon.
There shalt thou know thy charge; and there receive
Money and order for their furniture.
The land is burning; Percy stands on high;
And either we or they must lower lie.

Exit PRINCE HENRY

FALSTAFF

Rare words! brave world! Hostess, my breakfast, come!
O, I could wish this tavern were my drum!

Exit

ACT IV

SCENE I. The rebel camp near Shrewsbury.

Enter HOTSPUR, WORCESTER, and DOUGLAS

HOTSPUR

Well said, my noble Scot: if speaking truth
In this fine age were not thought flattery,
Such attribution should the Douglas have,
As not a soldier of this season's stamp
Should go so general current through the world.
By God, I cannot flatter; I do defy
The tongues of soothers; but a braver place
In my heart's love hath no man than yourself:
Nay, task me to my word; approve me, lord.

EARL OF DOUGLAS

Thou art the king of honour:
No man so potent breathes upon the ground
But I will beard him.

HOTSPUR

Do so, and 'tis well.

Enter a Messenger with letters

What letters hast thou there?—I can but thank you.

Messenger

These letters come from your father.

HOTSPUR

Letters from him! why comes he not himself?

Messenger

He cannot come, my lord; he is grievous sick.

HOTSPUR

'Zounds! how has he the leisure to be sick
In such a rustling time? Who leads his power?
Under whose government come they along?

Messenger

His letters bear his mind, not I, my lord.

EARL OF WORCESTER

I prithee, tell me, doth he keep his bed?

Messenger

He did, my lord, four days ere I set forth;
And at the time of my departure thence
He was much fear'd by his physicians.

EARL OF WORCESTER

I would the state of time had first been whole
Ere he by sickness had been visited:
His health was never better worth than now.

HOTSPUR

Sick now! droop now! this sickness doth infect
The very life-blood of our enterprise;
'Tis catching hither, even to our camp.
He writes me here, that inward sickness—
And that his friends by deputation could not
So soon be drawn, nor did he think it meet
To lay so dangerous and dear a trust
On any soul removed but on his own.
Yet doth he give us bold advertisement,
That with our small conjunction we should on,
To see how fortune is disposed to us;
For, as he writes, there is no quailing now.
Because the king is certainly possess'd
Of all our purposes. What say you to it?

EARL OF WORCESTER

Your father's sickness is a maim to us.

HOTSPUR

A perilous gash, a very limb lopp'd off:
And yet, in faith, it is not; his present want
Seems more than we shall find it: were it good
To set the exact wealth of all our states
All at one cast? to set so rich a main
On the nice hazard of one doubtful hour?
It were not good; for therein should we read
The very bottom and the soul of hope,
The very list, the very utmost bound
Of all our fortunes.

EARL OF DOUGLAS

'Faith, and so we should;
Where now remains a sweet reversion:
We may boldly spend upon the hope of what
Is to come in:
A comfort of retirement lives in this.

HOTSPUR

A rendezvous, a home to fly unto.
If that the devil and mischance look big
Upon the maidenhead of our affairs.

EARL OF WORCESTER

But yet I would your father had been here.
The quality and hair of our attempt
Brooks no division: it will be thought
By some, that know not why he is away,
That wisdom, loyalty and mere dislike
Of our proceedings kept the earl from hence:
And think how such an apprehension
May turn the tide of fearful faction
And breed a kind of question in our cause;
For well you know we of the offering side
Must keep aloof from strict arbitrement,
And stop all sight-holes, every loop from whence
The eye of reason may pry in upon us:
This absence of your father's draws a curtain,
That shows the ignorant a kind of fear
Before not dreamt of.

HOTSPUR

You strain too far.
I rather of his absence make this use:
It lends a lustre and more great opinion,
A larger dare to our great enterprise,
Than if the earl were here; for men must think,
If we without his help can make a head
To push against a kingdom, with his help
We shall o'erturn it topsy-turvy down.
Yet all goes well, yet all our joints are whole.

EARL OF DOUGLAS

As heart can think: there is not such a word
Spoke of in Scotland as this term of fear.

Enter SIR RICHARD VERNON

HOTSPUR

My cousin Vernon, welcome, by my soul.

VERNON

Pray God my news be worth a welcome, lord.
The Earl of Westmoreland, seven thousand strong,
Is marching hitherwards; with him Prince John.

HOTSPUR

No harm: what more?

VERNON

And further, I have learn'd,
The king himself in person is set forth,
Or hitherwards intended speedily,
With strong and mighty preparation.

HOTSPUR

He shall be welcome too. Where is his son,
The nimble-footed madcap Prince of Wales,
And his comrades, that daff'd the world aside,
And bid it pass?

VERNON

All furnish'd, all in arms;
All plumed like estridges that with the wind
Baited like eagles having lately bathed;
Glittering in golden coats, like images;
As full of spirit as the month of May,
And gorgeous as the sun at midsummer;
Wanton as youthful goats, wild as young bulls.
I saw young Harry, with his beaver on,
His cuisses on his thighs, gallantly arm'd
Rise from the ground like feather'd Mercury,
And vaulted with such ease into his seat,
As if an angel dropp'd down from the clouds,
To turn and wind a fiery Pegasus
And witch the world with noble horsemanship.

HOTSPUR

No more, no more: worse than the sun in March,
This praise doth nourish agues. Let them come:
They come like sacrifices in their trim,
And to the fire-eyed maid of smoky war
All hot and bleeding will we offer them:
The mailed Mars shall on his altar sit
Up to the ears in blood. I am on fire
To hear this rich reprisal is so nigh
And yet not ours. Come, let me taste my horse,
Who is to bear me like a thunderbolt
Against the bosom of the Prince of Wales:
Harry to Harry shall, hot horse to horse,
Meet and ne'er part till one drop down a corse.
O that Glendower were come!

VERNON

There is more news:
I learn'd in Worcester, as I rode along,
He cannot draw his power this fourteen days.

EARL OF DOUGLAS

That's the worst tidings that I hear of yet.

WORCESTER

Ay, by my faith, that bears a frosty sound.

HOTSPUR

What may the king's whole battle reach unto?

VERNON

To thirty thousand.

HOTSPUR

Forty let it be:
My father and Glendower being both away,
The powers of us may serve so great a day
Come, let us take a muster speedily:
Doomsday is near; die all, die merrily.

EARL OF DOUGLAS

Talk not of dying: I am out of fear
Of death or death's hand for this one-half year.

Exeunt

SCENE II. A public road near Coventry.

Enter FALSTAFF and BARDOLPH

FALSTAFF

Bardolph, get thee before to Coventry; fill me a
bottle of sack: our soldiers shall march through;
we'll to Sutton Co'fil' tonight.

BARDOLPH

Will you give me money, captain?

FALSTAFF

Lay out, lay out.

BARDOLPH

This bottle makes an angel.

FALSTAFF

An if it do, take it for thy labour; and if it make
twenty, take them all; I'll answer the coinage. Bid
my lieutenant Peto meet me at town's end.

BARDOLPH

I will, captain: farewell.

Exit

FALSTAFF

If I be not ashamed of my soldiers, I am a soused
gurnet. I have misused the king's press damnably.
I have got, in exchange of a hundred and fifty
soldiers, three hundred and odd pounds. I press me
none but good house-holders, yeoman's sons; inquire
me out contracted bachelors, such as had been asked
twice on the banns; such a commodity of warm slaves,
as had as lieve hear the devil as a drum; such as
fear the report of a caliver worse than a struck
fowl or a hurt wild-duck. I pressed me none but such
toasts-and-butter, with hearts in their bellies no
bigger than pins' heads, and they have bought out
their services; and now my whole charge consists of
ancients, corporals, lieutenants, gentlemen of
companies, slaves as ragged as Lazarus in the
painted cloth, where the glutton's dogs licked his
sores; and such as indeed were never soldiers, but
discarded unjust serving-men, younger sons to
younger brothers, revolted tapsters and ostlers
trade-fallen, the cankers of a calm world and a
long peace, ten times more dishonourable ragged than
an old faced ancient: and such have I, to fill up
the rooms of them that have bought out their
services, that you would think that I had a hundred
and fifty tattered prodigals lately come from
swine-keeping, from eating draff and husks. A mad
fellow met me on the way and told me I had unloaded
all the gibbets and pressed the dead bodies. No eye
hath seen such scarecrows. I'll not march through
Coventry with them, that's flat: nay, and the
villains march wide betwixt the legs, as if they had
gyves on; for indeed I had the most of them out of
prison. There's but a shirt and a half in all my

company; and the half shirt is two napkins tacked
together and thrown over the shoulders like an
herald's coat without sleeves; and the shirt, to say
the truth, stolen from my host at Saint Alban's, or
the red-nose innkeeper of Daventry. But that's all
one; they'll find linen enough on every hedge.

Enter the PRINCE and WESTMORELAND

PRINCE HENRY

How now, blown Jack! how now, quilt!

FALSTAFF

What, Hal! how now, mad wag! what a devil dost thou
in Warwickshire? My good Lord of Westmoreland, I
cry you mercy: I thought your honour had already been
at Shrewsbury.

WESTMORELAND

Faith, Sir John,'tis more than time that I were
there, and you too; but my powers are there already.
The king, I can tell you, looks for us all: we must
away all night.

FALSTAFF

Tut, never fear me: I am as vigilant as a cat to
steal cream.

PRINCE HENRY

I think, to steal cream indeed, for thy theft hath
already made thee butter. But tell me, Jack, whose
fellows are these that come after?

FALSTAFF

Mine, Hal, mine.

PRINCE HENRY

I did never see such pitiful rascals.

FALSTAFF

Tut, tut; good enough to toss; food for powder, food
for powder; they'll fill a pit as well as better:
tush, man, mortal men, mortal men.

WESTMORELAND

Ay, but, Sir John, methinks they are exceeding poor and bare, too beggarly.

FALSTAFF

'Faith, for their poverty, I know not where they had that; and for their bareness, I am sure they never learned that of me.

PRINCE HENRY

No I'll be sworn; unless you call three fingers on the ribs bare. But, sirrah, make haste: Percy is already in the field.

FALSTAFF

What, is the king encamped?

WESTMORELAND

He is, Sir John: I fear we shall stay too long.

FALSTAFF

Well,
To the latter end of a fray and the beginning of a feast
Fits a dull fighter and a keen guest.

Exeunt

SCENE III. The rebel camp near Shrewsbury.

Enter HOTSPUR, WORCESTER, DOUGLAS, and VERNON

HOTSPUR

We'll fight with him to-night.

EARL OF WORCESTER

It may not be.

EARL OF DOUGLAS

You give him then the advantage.

VERNON

Not a whit.

HOTSPUR

Why say you so? looks he not for supply?

VERNON

So do we.

HOTSPUR

His is certain, ours is doubtful.

EARL OF WORCESTER

Good cousin, be advised; stir not tonight.

VERNON

Do not, my lord.

EARL OF DOUGLAS

You do not counsel well:
You speak it out of fear and cold heart.

VERNON

Do me no slander, Douglas: by my life,
And I dare well maintain it with my life,
If well-respected honour bid me on,
I hold as little counsel with weak fear
As you, my lord, or any Scot that this day lives:
Let it be seen to-morrow in the battle
Which of us fears.

EARL OF DOUGLAS

Yea, or to-night.

VERNON

Content.

HOTSPUR

To-night, say I.

VERNON

Come, come it nay not be. I wonder much,
Being men of such great leading as you are,
That you foresee not what impediments
Drag back our expedition: certain horse
Of my cousin Vernon's are not yet come up:
Your uncle Worcester's horse came but today;
And now their pride and mettle is asleep,
Their courage with hard labour tame and dull,
That not a horse is half the half of himself.

HOTSPUR

So are the horses of the enemy
In general, journey-bated and brought low:
The better part of ours are full of rest.

EARL OF WORCESTER

The number of the king exceedeth ours:
For God's sake. cousin, stay till all come in.

The trumpet sounds a parley

Enter SIR WALTER BLUNT

SIR WALTER BLUNT

I come with gracious offers from the king,
if you vouchsafe me hearing and respect.

HOTSPUR

Welcome, Sir Walter Blunt; and would to God
You were of our determination!
Some of us love you well; and even those some
Envy your great deservings and good name,
Because you are not of our quality,
But stand against us like an enemy.

SIR WALTER BLUNT

And God defend but still I should stand so,
So long as out of limit and true rule
You stand against anointed majesty.
But to my charge. The king hath sent to know
The nature of your griefs, and whereupon
You conjure from the breast of civil peace
Such bold hostility, teaching his duteous land
Audacious cruelty. If that the king
Have any way your good deserts forgot,
Which he confesseth to be manifold,
He bids you name your griefs; and with all speed
You shall have your desires with interest
And pardon absolute for yourself and these
Herein misled by your suggestion.

HOTSPUR

The king is kind; and well we know the king
Knows at what time to promise, when to pay.
My father and my uncle and myself
Did give him that same royalty he wears;
And when he was not six and twenty strong,
Sick in the world's regard, wretched and low,

A poor unminded outlaw sneaking home,
My father gave him welcome to the shore;
And when he heard him swear and vow to God
He came but to be Duke of Lancaster,
To sue his livery and beg his peace,
With tears of innocency and terms of zeal,
My father, in kind heart and pity moved,
Swore him assistance and perform'd it too.
Now when the lords and barons of the realm
Perceived Northumberland did lean to him,
The more and less came in with cap and knee;
Met him in boroughs, cities, villages,
Attended him on bridges, stood in lanes,
Laid gifts before him, proffer'd him their oaths,
Gave him their heirs, as pages follow'd him
Even at the heels in golden multitudes.
He presently, as greatness knows itself,
Steps me a little higher than his vow
Made to my father, while his blood was poor,
Upon the naked shore at Ravenspurgh;
And now, forsooth, takes on him to reform
Some certain edicts and some strait decrees
That lie too heavy on the commonwealth,
Cries out upon abuses, seems to weep
Over his country's wrongs; and by this face,
This seeming brow of justice, did he win
The hearts of all that he did angle for;
Proceeded further; cut me off the heads
Of all the favourites that the absent king
In deputation left behind him here,
When he was personal in the Irish war.

SIR WALTER BLUNT

Tut, I came not to hear this.

HOTSPUR

Then to the point.
In short time after, he deposed the king;
Soon after that, deprived him of his life;
And in the neck of that, task'd the whole state:
To make that worse, suffer'd his kinsman March,
Who is, if every owner were well placed,
Indeed his king, to be engaged in Wales,
There without ransom to lie forfeited;
Disgraced me in my happy victories,
Sought to entrap me by intelligence;
Rated mine uncle from the council-board;

In rage dismiss'd my father from the court;
Broke oath on oath, committed wrong on wrong,
And in conclusion drove us to seek out
This head of safety; and withal to pry
Into his title, the which we find
Too indirect for long continuance.

SIR WALTER BLUNT

Shall I return this answer to the king?

HOTSPUR

Not so, Sir Walter: we'll withdraw awhile.
Go to the king; and let there be impawn'd
Some surety for a safe return again,
And in the morning early shall my uncle
Bring him our purposes: and so farewell.

SIR WALTER BLUNT

I would you would accept of grace and love.

HOTSPUR

And may be so we shall.

SIR WALTER BLUNT

Pray God you do.

Exeunt

SCENE IV. York. The ARCHBISHOP'S palace.

Enter the ARCHBISHOP OF YORK and SIR MICHAEL

ARCHBISHOP OF YORK

Hie, good Sir Michael; bear this sealed brief
With winged haste to the lord marshal;
This to my cousin Scroop, and all the rest
To whom they are directed. If you knew
How much they do to import, you would make haste.

SIR MICHAEL

My good lord,
I guess their tenor.

ARCHBISHOP OF YORK

Like enough you do.
To-morrow, good Sir Michael, is a day

Wherein the fortune of ten thousand men
Must bide the touch; for, sir, at Shrewsbury,
As I am truly given to understand,
The king with mighty and quick-raised power
Meets with Lord Harry: and, I fear, Sir Michael,
What with the sickness of Northumberland,
Whose power was in the first proportion,
And what with Owen Glendower's absence thence,
Who with them was a rated sinew too
And comes not in, o'er-ruled by prophecies,
I fear the power of Percy is too weak
To wage an instant trial with the king.

SIR MICHAEL

Why, my good lord, you need not fear;
There is Douglas and Lord Mortimer.

ARCHBISHOP OF YORK

No, Mortimer is not there.

SIR MICHAEL

But there is Mordake, Vernon, Lord Harry Percy,
And there is my Lord of Worcester and a head
Of gallant warriors, noble gentlemen.

ARCHBISHOP OF YORK

And so there is: but yet the king hath drawn
The special head of all the land together:
The Prince of Wales, Lord John of Lancaster,
The noble Westmoreland and warlike Blunt;
And moe corrivals and dear men
Of estimation and command in arms.

SIR MICHAEL

Doubt not, my lord, they shall be well opposed.

ARCHBISHOP OF YORK

I hope no less, yet needful 'tis to fear;
And, to prevent the worst, Sir Michael, speed:
For if Lord Percy thrive not, ere the king
Dismiss his power, he means to visit us,
For he hath heard of our confederacy,
And 'tis but wisdom to make strong against him:
Therefore make haste. I must go write again
To other friends; and so farewell, Sir Michael.

Exeunt

ACT V

SCENE I. KING HENRY IV's camp near Shrewsbury.

Enter KING HENRY, PRINCE HENRY, Lord John of LANCASTER, EARL OF WESTMORELAND, SIR WALTER BLUNT, and FALSTAFF

KING HENRY IV

How bloodily the sun begins to peer
Above yon busky hill! the day looks pale
At his distemperature.

PRINCE HENRY

The southern wind
Doth play the trumpet to his purposes,
And by his hollow whistling in the leaves
Foretells a tempest and a blustering day.

KING HENRY IV

Then with the losers let it sympathize,
For nothing can seem foul to those that win.

The trumpet sounds

Enter WORCESTER and VERNON

How now, my Lord of Worcester! 'tis not well
That you and I should meet upon such terms
As now we meet. You have deceived our trust,
And made us doff our easy robes of peace,
To crush our old limbs in ungentle steel:
This is not well, my lord, this is not well.
What say you to it? will you again unknit
This curlish knot of all-abhorred war?
And move in that obedient orb again
Where you did give a fair and natural light,
And be no more an exhaled meteor,
A prodigy of fear and a portent
Of broached mischief to the unborn times?

EARL OF WORCESTER

Hear me, my liege:
For mine own part, I could be well content
To entertain the lag-end of my life
With quiet hours; for I do protest,
I have not sought the day of this dislike.

KING HENRY IV

You have not sought it! how comes it, then?

FALSTAFF

Rebellion lay in his way, and he found it.

PRINCE HENRY

Peace, chewet, peace!

EARL OF WORCESTER

It pleased your majesty to turn your looks
Of favour from myself and all our house;
And yet I must remember you, my lord,
We were the first and dearest of your friends.
For you my staff of office did I break
In Richard's time; and posted day and night
to meet you on the way, and kiss your hand,
When yet you were in place and in account
Nothing so strong and fortunate as I.
It was myself, my brother and his son,
That brought you home and boldly did outdare
The dangers of the time. You swore to us,
And you did swear that oath at Doncaster,
That you did nothing purpose 'gainst the state;
Nor claim no further than your new-fall'n right,
The seat of Gaunt, dukedom of Lancaster:
To this we swore our aid. But in short space
It rain'd down fortune showering on your head;
And such a flood of greatness fell on you,
What with our help, what with the absent king,
What with the injuries of a wanton time,
The seeming sufferances that you had borne,
And the contrarious winds that held the king
So long in his unlucky Irish wars
That all in England did repute him dead:
And from this swarm of fair advantages
You took occasion to be quickly woo'd
To gripe the general sway into your hand;
Forget your oath to us at Doncaster;
And being fed by us you used us so
As that ungentle hull, the cuckoo's bird,
Useth the sparrow; did oppress our nest;
Grew by our feeding to so great a bulk
That even our love durst not come near your sight
For fear of swallowing; but with nimble wing
We were enforced, for safety sake, to fly
Out of sight and raise this present head;
Whereby we stand opposed by such means

As you yourself have forged against yourself
By unkind usage, dangerous countenance,
And violation of all faith and troth
Sworn to us in your younger enterprise.

KING HENRY IV

These things indeed you have articulate,
Proclaim'd at market-crosses, read in churches,
To face the garment of rebellion
With some fine colour that may please the eye
Of fickle changelings and poor discontents,
Which gape and rub the elbow at the news
Of hurlyburly innovation:
And never yet did insurrection want
Such water-colours to impaint his cause;
Nor moody beggars, starving for a time
Of pellmell havoc and confusion.

PRINCE HENRY

In both your armies there is many a soul
Shall pay full dearly for this encounter,
If once they join in trial. Tell your nephew,
The Prince of Wales doth join with all the world
In praise of Henry Percy: by my hopes,
This present enterprise set off his head,
I do not think a braver gentleman,
More active-valiant or more valiant-young,
More daring or more bold, is now alive
To grace this latter age with noble deeds.
For my part, I may speak it to my shame,
I have a truant been to chivalry;
And so I hear he doth account me too;
Yet this before my father's majesty—
I am content that he shall take the odds
Of his great name and estimation,
And will, to save the blood on either side,
Try fortune with him in a single fight.

KING HENRY IV

And, Prince of Wales, so dare we venture thee,
Albeit considerations infinite
Do make against it. No, good Worcester, no,
We love our people well; even those we love
That are misled upon your cousin's part;
And, will they take the offer of our grace,
Both he and they and you, every man
Shall be my friend again and I'll be his:

So tell your cousin, and bring me word
What he will do: but if he will not yield,
Rebuke and dread correction wait on us
And they shall do their office. So, be gone;
We will not now be troubled with reply:
We offer fair; take it advisedly.

Exeunt WORCESTER and VERNON

PRINCE HENRY

It will not be accepted, on my life:
The Douglas and the Hotspur both together
Are confident against the world in arms.

KING HENRY IV

Hence, therefore, every leader to his charge;
For, on their answer, will we set on them:
And God befriend us, as our cause is just!

Exeunt all but PRINCE HENRY and FALSTAFF

FALSTAFF

Hal, if thou see me down in the battle and bestride
me, so; 'tis a point of friendship.

PRINCE HENRY

Nothing but a colossus can do thee that friendship.
Say thy prayers, and farewell.

FALSTAFF

I would 'twere bed-time, Hal, and all well.

PRINCE HENRY

Why, thou owest God a death.

Exit PRINCE HENRY

FALSTAFF

'Tis not due yet; I would be loath to pay him before
his day. What need I be so forward with him that
calls not on me? Well, 'tis no matter; honour pricks
me on. Yea, but how if honour prick me off when I
come on? how then? Can honour set to a leg? no: or
an arm? no: or take away the grief of a wound? no.
Honour hath no skill in surgery, then? no. What is
honour? a word. What is in that word honour? what
is that honour? air. A trim reckoning! Who hath it?

he that died o' Wednesday. Doth he feel it? no.
Doth he hear it? no. 'Tis insensible, then. Yea,
to the dead. But will it not live with the living?
no. Why? detraction will not suffer it. Therefore
I'll none of it. Honour is a mere scutcheon: and so
ends my catechism.

Exit

SCENE II. The rebel camp.

Enter WORCESTER and VERNON

EARL OF WORCESTER

O, no, my nephew must not know, Sir Richard,
The liberal and kind offer of the king.

VERNON

'Twere best he did.

EARL OF WORCESTER

Then are we all undone.
It is not possible, it cannot be,
The king should keep his word in loving us;
He will suspect us still and find a time
To punish this offence in other faults:
Suspicion all our lives shall be stuck full of eyes;
For treason is but trusted like the fox,
Who, ne'er so tame, so cherish'd and lock'd up,
Will have a wild trick of his ancestors.
Look how we can, or sad or merrily,
Interpretation will misquote our looks,
And we shall feed like oxen at a stall,
The better cherish'd, still the nearer death.
My nephew's trespass may be well forgot;
it hath the excuse of youth and heat of blood,
And an adopted name of privilege,
A hair-brain'd Hotspur, govern'd by a spleen:
All his offences live upon my head
And on his father's; we did train him on,
And, his corruption being ta'en from us,
We, as the spring of all, shall pay for all.
Therefore, good cousin, let not Harry know,
In any case, the offer of the king.

VERNON

Deliver what you will; I'll say 'tis so.
Here comes your cousin.

Enter HOTSPUR and DOUGLAS

HOTSPUR

My uncle is return'd:
Deliver up my Lord of Westmoreland.
Uncle, what news?

EARL OF WORCESTER

The king will bid you battle presently.

EARL OF DOUGLAS

Defy him by the Lord of Westmoreland.

HOTSPUR

Lord Douglas, go you and tell him so.

EARL OF DOUGLAS

Marry, and shall, and very willingly.

Exit

EARL OF WORCESTER

There is no seeming mercy in the king.

HOTSPUR

Did you beg any? God forbid!

EARL OF WORCESTER

I told him gently of our grievances,
Of his oath-breaking; which he mended thus,
By now forswearing that he is forsworn:
He calls us rebels, traitors; and will scourge
With haughty arms this hateful name in us.

Re-enter the EARL OF DOUGLAS

EARL OF DOUGLAS

Arm, gentlemen; to arms! for I have thrown
A brave defiance in King Henry's teeth,
And Westmoreland, that was engaged, did bear it;
Which cannot choose but bring him quickly on.

EARL OF WORCESTER

The Prince of Wales stepp'd forth before the king,
And, nephew, challenged you to single fight.

HOTSPUR

O, would the quarrel lay upon our heads,
And that no man might draw short breath today
But I and Harry Monmouth! Tell me, tell me,
How show'd his tasking? seem'd it in contempt?

VERNON

No, by my soul; I never in my life
Did hear a challenge urged more modestly,
Unless a brother should a brother dare
To gentle exercise and proof of arms.
He gave you all the duties of a man;
Trimm'd up your praises with a princely tongue,
Spoke to your deservings like a chronicle,
Making you ever better than his praise
By still dispraising praise valued in you;
And, which became him like a prince indeed,
He made a blushing cital of himself;
And chid his truant youth with such a grace
As if he master'd there a double spirit.
Of teaching and of learning instantly.
There did he pause: but let me tell the world,
If he outlive the envy of this day,
England did never owe so sweet a hope,
So much misconstrued in his wantonness.

HOTSPUR

Cousin, I think thou art enamoured
On his follies: never did I hear
Of any prince so wild a libertine.
But be he as he will, yet once ere night
I will embrace him with a soldier's arm,
That he shall shrink under my courtesy.
Arm, arm with speed: and, fellows, soldiers, friends,
Better consider what you have to do
Than I, that have not well the gift of tongue,
Can lift your blood up with persuasion.

Enter a Messenger

Messenger

My lord, here are letters for you.

HOTSPUR

I cannot read them now.
O gentlemen, the time of life is short!
To spend that shortness basely were too long,
If life did ride upon a dial's point,
Still ending at the arrival of an hour.
An if we live, we live to tread on kings;
If die, brave death, when princes die with us!
Now, for our consciences, the arms are fair,
When the intent of bearing them is just.

Enter another Messenger

Messenger

My lord, prepare; the king comes on apace.

HOTSPUR

I thank him, that he cuts me from my tale,
For I profess not talking; only this—
Let each man do his best: and here draw I
A sword, whose temper I intend to stain
With the best blood that I can meet withal
In the adventure of this perilous day.
Now, Esperance! Percy! and set on.
Sound all the lofty instruments of war,
And by that music let us all embrace;
For, heaven to earth, some of us never shall
A second time do such a courtesy.

The trumpets sound. They embrace, and exeunt

SCENE III. Plain between the camps.

KING HENRY enters with his power. Alarum to the battle. Then enter DOUGLAS and SIR WALTER BLUNT

SIR WALTER BLUNT

What is thy name, that in the battle thus
Thou crossest me? what honour dost thou seek
Upon my head?

EARL OF DOUGLAS

Know then, my name is Douglas;
And I do haunt thee in the battle thus
Because some tell me that thou art a king.

SIR WALTER BLUNT

They tell thee true.

EARL OF DOUGLAS

The Lord of Stafford dear to-day hath bought
Thy likeness, for instead of thee, King Harry,
This sword hath ended him: so shall it thee,
Unless thou yield thee as my prisoner.

SIR WALTER BLUNT

I was not born a yielder, thou proud Scot;
And thou shalt find a king that will revenge
Lord Stafford's death.

They fight. DOUGLAS kills SIR WALTER BLUNT. Enter HOTSPUR

HOTSPUR

O Douglas, hadst thou fought at Holmedon thus,
never had triumph'd upon a Scot.

EARL OF DOUGLAS

All's done, all's won; here breathless lies the king.

HOTSPUR

Where?

EARL OF DOUGLAS

Here.

HOTSPUR

This, Douglas? no: I know this face full well:
A gallant knight he was, his name was Blunt;
Semblably furnish'd like the king himself.

EARL OF DOUGLAS

A fool go with thy soul, whither it goes!
A borrow'd title hast thou bought too dear:
Why didst thou tell me that thou wert a king?

HOTSPUR

The king hath many marching in his coats.

EARL OF DOUGLAS

Now, by my sword, I will kill all his coats;
I'll murder all his wardrobe, piece by piece,
Until I meet the king.

HOTSPUR

Up, and away!
Our soldiers stand full fairly for the day.

Exeunt

Alarum. Enter FALSTAFF, solus

FALSTAFF

Though I could 'scape shot-free at London, I fear
the shot here; here's no scoring but upon the pate.
Soft! who are you? Sir Walter Blunt: there's honour
for you! here's no vanity! I am as hot as moulten
lead, and as heavy too: God keep lead out of me! I
need no more weight than mine own bowels. I have
led my ragamuffins where they are peppered: there's
not three of my hundred and fifty left alive; and
they are for the town's end, to beg during life.
But who comes here?

Enter PRINCE HENRY

PRINCE HENRY

What, stand'st thou idle here? lend me thy sword:
Many a nobleman lies stark and stiff
Under the hoofs of vaunting enemies,
Whose deaths are yet unrevenged: I prithee,
lend me thy sword.

FALSTAFF

O Hal, I prithee, give me leave to breathe awhile.
Turk Gregory never did such deeds in arms as I have
done this day. I have paid Percy, I have made him sure.

PRINCE HENRY

He is, indeed; and living to kill thee. I prithee,
lend me thy sword.

FALSTAFF

Nay, before God, Hal, if Percy be alive, thou get'st
not my sword; but take my pistol, if thou wilt.

PRINCE HENRY

Give it to me: what, is it in the case?

FALSTAFF

Ay, Hal; 'tis hot, 'tis hot; there's that will sack a city.

PRINCE HENRY draws it out, and finds it to be a bottle of sack

PRINCE HENRY

What, is it a time to jest and dally now?

He throws the bottle at him. Exit

FALSTAFF

Well, if Percy be alive, I'll pierce him. If he do
come in my way, so: if he do not, if I come in his
willingly, let him make a carbonado of me. I like
not such grinning honour as Sir Walter hath: give me
life: which if I can save, so; if not, honour comes
unlooked for, and there's an end.

Exit FALSTAFF

SCENE IV. Another part of the field.

Alarum. Excursions. Enter PRINCE HENRY, LORD JOHN OF LANCASTER, and EARL OF WESTMORELAND

KING HENRY IV

I prithee,
Harry, withdraw thyself; thou bleed'st too much.
Lord John of Lancaster, go you with him.

LANCASTER

Not I, my lord, unless I did bleed too.

PRINCE HENRY

I beseech your majesty, make up,
Lest your retirement do amaze your friends.

KING HENRY IV

I will do so.
My Lord of Westmoreland, lead him to his tent.

WESTMORELAND

Come, my lord, I'll lead you to your tent.

PRINCE HENRY

Lead me, my lord? I do not need your help:
And God forbid a shallow scratch should drive
The Prince of Wales from such a field as this,
Where stain'd nobility lies trodden on,
and rebels' arms triumph in massacres!

LANCASTER

We breathe too long: come, cousin Westmoreland,
Our duty this way lies; for God's sake come.

Exeunt LANCASTER and WESTMORELAND

PRINCE HENRY

By God, thou hast deceived me, Lancaster;
I did not think thee lord of such a spirit:
Before, I loved thee as a brother, John;
But now, I do respect thee as my soul.

KING HENRY IV

I saw him hold Lord Percy at the point
With lustier maintenance than I did look for
Of such an ungrown warrior.

PRINCE HENRY

O, this boy
Lends mettle to us all!

Exit

Enter DOUGLAS

EARL OF DOUGLAS

Another king! they grow like Hydra's heads:
I am the Douglas, fatal to all those
That wear those colours on them: what art thou,
That counterfeit'st the person of a king?

KING HENRY IV

The king himself; who, Douglas, grieves at heart
So many of his shadows thou hast met
And not the very king. I have two boys
Seek Percy and thyself about the field:
But, seeing thou fall'st on me so luckily,
I will assay thee: so, defend thyself.

EARL OF DOUGLAS

I fear thou art another counterfeit;
And yet, in faith, thou bear'st thee like a king:
But mine I am sure thou art, whoe'er thou be,
And thus I win thee.

They fight. KING HENRY being in danger, PRINCE HENRY enters

PRINCE HENRY

Hold up thy head, vile Scot, or thou art like
Never to hold it up again! the spirits
Of valiant Shirley, Stafford, Blunt, are in my arms:
It is the Prince of Wales that threatens thee;
Who never promiseth but he means to pay.

They fight: DOUGLAS flies

Cheerly, my lord how fares your grace?
Sir Nicholas Gawsey hath for succor sent,
And so hath Clifton: I'll to Clifton straight.

KING HENRY IV

Stay, and breathe awhile:
Thou hast redeem'd thy lost opinion,
And show'd thou makest some tender of my life,
In this fair rescue thou hast brought to me.

PRINCE HENRY

O God! they did me too much injury
That ever said I hearken'd for your death.
If it were so, I might have let alone
The insulting hand of Douglas over you,
Which would have been as speedy in your end
As all the poisonous potions in the world
And saved the treacherous labour of your son.

KING HENRY IV

Make up to Clifton: I'll to Sir Nicholas Gawsey.

Exit

Enter HOTSPUR

HOTSPUR

If I mistake not, thou art Harry Monmouth.

PRINCE HENRY

Thou speak'st as if I would deny my name.

HOTSPUR

My name is Harry Percy.

PRINCE HENRY

Why, then I see
A very valiant rebel of the name.

I am the Prince of Wales; and think not, Percy,
To share with me in glory any more:
Two stars keep not their motion in one sphere;
Nor can one England brook a double reign,
Of Harry Percy and the Prince of Wales.

HOTSPUR

Nor shall it, Harry; for the hour is come
To end the one of us; and would to God
Thy name in arms were now as great as mine!

PRINCE HENRY

I'll make it greater ere I part from thee;
And all the budding honours on thy crest
I'll crop, to make a garland for my head.

HOTSPUR

I can no longer brook thy vanities.

They fight

Enter FALSTAFF

FALSTAFF

Well said, Hal! to it Hal! Nay, you shall find no
boy's play here, I can tell you.

Re-enter DOUGLAS; he fights with FALSTAFF, who falls down as if he were dead, and exit DOUGLAS. HOTSPUR is wounded, and falls

HOTSPUR

O, Harry, thou hast robb'd me of my youth!
I better brook the loss of brittle life
Than those proud titles thou hast won of me;
They wound my thoughts worse than sword my flesh:
But thought's the slave of life, and life time's fool;
And time, that takes survey of all the world,
Must have a stop. O, I could prophesy,
But that the earthy and cold hand of death
Lies on my tongue: no, Percy, thou art dust
And food for—

Dies

PRINCE HENRY

For worms, brave Percy: fare thee well, great heart!
Ill-weaved ambition, how much art thou shrunk!
When that this body did contain a spirit,

A kingdom for it was too small a bound;
But now two paces of the vilest earth
Is room enough: this earth that bears thee dead
Bears not alive so stout a gentleman.
If thou wert sensible of courtesy,
I should not make so dear a show of zeal:
But let my favours hide thy mangled face;
And, even in thy behalf, I'll thank myself
For doing these fair rites of tenderness.
Adieu, and take thy praise with thee to heaven!
Thy ignominy sleep with thee in the grave,
But not remember'd in thy epitaph!

He spieth FALSTAFF on the ground

What, old acquaintance! could not all this flesh
Keep in a little life? Poor Jack, farewell!
I could have better spared a better man:
O, I should have a heavy miss of thee,
If I were much in love with vanity!
Death hath not struck so fat a deer to-day,
Though many dearer, in this bloody fray.
Embowell'd will I see thee by and by:
Till then in blood by noble Percy lie.

Exit PRINCE HENRY

FALSTAFF

[Rising up] Embowelled! if thou embowel me to-day,
I'll give you leave to powder me and eat me too
to-morrow. 'Sblood,'twas time to counterfeit, or
that hot termagant Scot had paid me scot and lot too.
Counterfeit? I lie, I am no counterfeit: to die,
is to be a counterfeit; for he is but the
counterfeit of a man who hath not the life of a man:
but to counterfeit dying, when a man thereby
liveth, is to be no counterfeit, but the true and
perfect image of life indeed. The better part of
valour is discretion; in the which better part I
have saved my life.'Zounds, I am afraid of this
gunpowder Percy, though he be dead: how, if he
should counterfeit too and rise? by my faith, I am
afraid he would prove the better counterfeit.
Therefore I'll make him sure; yea, and I'll swear I
killed him. Why may not he rise as well as I?
Nothing confutes me but eyes, and nobody sees me.
Therefore, sirrah,

Stabbing him

with a new wound in your thigh, come you along with me.

Takes up HOTSPUR on his back

Re-enter PRINCE HENRY and LORD JOHN OF LANCASTER

PRINCE HENRY

Come, brother John; full bravely hast thou flesh'd
Thy maiden sword.

LANCASTER

But, soft! whom have we here?
Did you not tell me this fat man was dead?

PRINCE HENRY

I did; I saw him dead,
Breathless and bleeding on the ground. Art
thou alive?
Or is it fantasy that plays upon our eyesight?
I prithee, speak; we will not trust our eyes
Without our ears: thou art not what thou seem'st.

FALSTAFF

No, that's certain; I am not a double man: but if I
be not Jack Falstaff, then am I a Jack. There is Percy:

Throwing the body down

if your father will do me any honour, so; if not, let
him kill the next Percy himself. I look to be either
earl or duke, I can assure you.

PRINCE HENRY

Why, Percy I killed myself and saw thee dead.

FALSTAFF

Didst thou? Lord, Lord, how this world is given to
lying! I grant you I was down and out of breath;
and so was he: but we rose both at an instant and
fought a long hour by Shrewsbury clock. If I may be
believed, so; if not, let them that should reward
valour bear the sin upon their own heads. I'll take
it upon my death, I gave him this wound in the
thigh: if the man were alive and would deny it,
'zounds, I would make him eat a piece of my sword.

LANCASTER

This is the strangest tale that ever I heard.

PRINCE HENRY

This is the strangest fellow, brother John.
Come, bring your luggage nobly on your back:
For my part, if a lie may do thee grace,
I'll gild it with the happiest terms I have.

A retreat is sounded

The trumpet sounds retreat; the day is ours.
Come, brother, let us to the highest of the field,
To see what friends are living, who are dead.

Exeunt PRINCE HENRY and LANCASTER

FALSTAFF

I'll follow, as they say, for reward. He that
rewards me, God reward him! If I do grow great,
I'll grow less; for I'll purge, and leave sack, and
live cleanly as a nobleman should do.

Exit

SCENE V. Another part of the field.

The trumpets sound. Enter KING HENRY IV, PRINCE HENRY, LORD JOHN LANCASTER, EARL OF WESTMORELAND, with WORCESTER and VERNON prisoners

KING HENRY IV

Thus ever did rebellion find rebuke.
Ill-spirited Worcester! did not we send grace,
Pardon and terms of love to all of you?
And wouldst thou turn our offers contrary?
Misuse the tenor of thy kinsman's trust?
Three knights upon our party slain to-day,
A noble earl and many a creature else
Had been alive this hour,
If like a Christian thou hadst truly borne
Betwixt our armies true intelligence.

EARL OF WORCESTER

What I have done my safety urged me to;
And I embrace this fortune patiently,
Since not to be avoided it falls on me.

KING HENRY IV

Bear Worcester to the death and Vernon too:
Other offenders we will pause upon.

Exeunt WORCESTER and VERNON, guarded

How goes the field?

PRINCE HENRY

The noble Scot, Lord Douglas, when he saw
The fortune of the day quite turn'd from him,
The noble Percy slain, and all his men
Upon the foot of fear, fled with the rest;
And falling from a hill, he was so bruised
That the pursuers took him. At my tent
The Douglas is; and I beseech your grace
I may dispose of him.

KING HENRY IV

With all my heart.

PRINCE HENRY

Then, brother John of Lancaster, to you
This honourable bounty shall belong:
Go to the Douglas, and deliver him
Up to his pleasure, ransomless and free:
His valour shown upon our crests to-day
Hath taught us how to cherish such high deeds
Even in the bosom of our adversaries.

LANCASTER

I thank your grace for this high courtesy,
Which I shall give away immediately.

KING HENRY IV

Then this remains, that we divide our power.
You, son John, and my cousin Westmoreland
Towards York shall bend you with your dearest speed,
To meet Northumberland and the prelate Scroop,
Who, as we hear, are busily in arms:
Myself and you, son Harry, will towards Wales,
To fight with Glendower and the Earl of March.
Rebellion in this land shall lose his sway,
Meeting the cheque of such another day:
And since this business so fair is done,
Let us not leave till all our own be won.

Exeunt

6. POETRY

Approaching Poetry

Introduction

This reading is designed to develop the analytical skills you need for a more in-depth study of literary texts. You will learn about rhythm, alliteration, rhyme, poetic inversion, voice and line lengths and endings. You will examine poems that do not rhyme and learn how to compare and contrast poetry.

By the end of this reading you should be able to:

- have an awareness of the role of analysis to inform appreciation and understanding of poetry;
- be able to identify and discuss the main analytical concepts used in analyzing poetry.

What is the point of analyzing poetry? One simple answer is that the more we know about anything the more interesting it becomes: listening to music or looking at paintings with someone who can tell us a little about what we hear or see – or what we're reading – is one way of increasing our understanding and pleasure. That may mean learning something about the people who produced the writing, music, painting that we are interested in, and why they produced it. But it may also mean understanding why one particular form was chosen rather than another: why, for example, did the poet choose to write a sonnet rather than an ode, a ballad, or a villanelle? To appreciate the appropriateness of one form, we need to be aware of a range of options available to that particular writer at that particular time. In the same

way, we also need to pay attention to word choice. Why was this particular word chosen from a whole range of words that might have said much the same? Looking at manuscript drafts can be really enlightening, showing how much effort was expended in order to find the most appropriate or most evocative expression.

ACTIVITY 1

Click on William Blake's "Tyger" to read and compare the two versions of the poem. The one on the left is a draft; the other is the final published version.

Discussion

The most obvious difference between the two is that stanza 4 of the draft does not survive in the published version, and an entirely new stanza, "When the stars threw down their spears," appears in the finished poem. Significantly, this introduces the idea of "the Lamb," a dramatic contrast to the tiger, as well as the idea of a "he" who made the lamb. One similarity between the draft and final version is that each is made up entirely of unanswered questions. But if you look at the manuscript stanza 5, you can see revisions from "What" to "Where," and the struggle with the third line, where Blake eventually decided that the idea of an arm was redundant, subsumed in the notions of grasping and clasping. The two rhyme words are decided—grasp/clasp—but in which order should they come? 'Clasp' is a less aggressive word than 'grasp'; 'clasp' is not quite as gentle as an embrace, but it is closer to embracing than 'grasp' is – so it must be for deliberate effect that we end up with 'What dread grasp/Dare its deadly terrors clasp?

It is rare to have manuscript drafts to examine in this way, but I hope that this convinces you of the kind of attention writers pay to word choice. Let us take one more example. Think about this first stanza of Thomas Hardy's 'Neutral Tones' (1867):

> We stood by a pond that winter day,
>
> And the sun was white, as though chidden of God,
>
> And a few leaves lay on the starving sod;
>
> —They had fallen from an ash, and were gray. (Gibson, 1976, p. 12)

Notice that, in the last line, 'oak' or 'elm' would work just as well as far as the rhythm or music of the line is concerned, but 'ash' has extra connotations of grayness, of something burnt out, dead, finished ('ashes to ashes', too, perhaps?), all of which contribute to the mood that Hardy conveys in a way that 'oak' or 'elm' wouldn't.

To return to my original question then, 'what is the point of analyzing poetry?', one answer is that only an analytical approach can help us arrive at an informed appreciation and understanding of the poem. Whether we like a poem or not, we should be able to recognize the craftsmanship that has gone into making it, the ways in which stylistic techniques and devices have worked to create meaning. General readers may be entirely happy to find a poem pleasing, or unsatisfactory, without stopping to ask why. But
studying poetry is a different matter and requires some background understanding of what those stylistic techniques might be, as well as an awareness of constraints and conventions within which poets have written throughout different periods of history.

You may write poetry yourself. If so, you probably know only too well how difficult it is to produce something you feel really expresses what you want to convey. Writing an essay presents enough problems – a poem is a different matter, but certainly no easier. Thinking of poetry as a discipline and a craft which, to some extent, can be learned, is another useful way of approaching analysis. After all, how successful are emotional outpourings on paper? Words one might scribble down in the heat of an intense moment may have some validity in conveying that intensity, but in general might they not be more satisfactory if they were later revised? My own feeling is that a remark Wordsworth made 200 years ago has become responsible for a number of misconceptions about what poetry should do. In the Preface to a volume of poems called
Lyrical Ballads (1802) he wrote that 'all good poetry is the spontaneous overflow of powerful feelings' (Owens and Johnson, 1998, p.85,11.105–6). The second time he uses the same phrase he says something that I think is often forgotten today: 'poetry is the spontaneous overflow of powerful feelings; it takes its origin from emotion *recollected in tranquillity*' (my italics) (ibid., p. 95, ll.557–8). Notice the significant time lapse implied there – the idea that, however powerful or spontaneous the emotion, it needs to be carefully considered before you start writing. He goes on:

> The emotion is contemplated till, by a species of reaction, the tranquillity gradually disappears, and an emotion kindred to that which was before the subject of contemplation is gradually reproduced, and does itself actually exist in the mind. In this mood successful composition generally begins.

You don't have to agree with Wordsworth about what poetry is or how best to achieve it. (Would you always want a poem to express powerful emotion, for example? I referred to Hardy's 'Neutral Tones' above, where the whole point is that neither of the two characters described feels anything much at all.) But the idea of contemplation is a useful and important one: it implies distance, perhaps detachment, but above all re-creation, not the thing itself. And if we try to re-create something, we must choose our methods and our words carefully in order to convey what we experienced as closely as possible. A word of warning though: writers do not always aim to express personal experiences; often a persona is created.

The poet Ezra Pound offered this advice to other poets in an essay written in 1913: 'Use no superfluous word, no adjective, which does not reveal something' (Gray, 1990, p. 56). And in the 1950s William Carlos Williams advised, 'cut and cut again whatever you write'. In his opinion, the 'test of the artist is to be able to revise without showing a seam' (loc. cit.). That sewing image he uses appeals to me particularly because it stresses the notion of skilled craftsmanship. Pound and Williams were American, writing long after Wordsworth, but, as you can see, like countless other poets they too reflected very seriously on their own poetic practice. I hope this helps convince you that as students we owe it to the poems we read to give them close analytical attention.

Note About Organization

In what follows, section headings like 'Rhyme', 'Rhythm', 'Line lengths and line endings', 'Alliteration', and so on, are intended to act as signposts to help you (if terms are unfamiliar, look them up in the glossary at the end). But these headings indicate only the *main* technique being discussed. While it is something we need to attempt, it is very difficult to try to isolate devices in this way – to separate out, for example, the effects of rhythm from rhyme. This doesn't mean that we shouldn't look for particular techniques at work in a poem, but we need to be aware that they will be interdependent and the end product effective or not because of the way such elements work together.

As you work through this reading, don't be discouraged if your response to exercises differs from mine. Remember that I had the advantage of choosing my own examples and that I've long been familiar with the poems I've used. On a daily basis, we probably read much less poetry than we do prose. This is perhaps one reason why many people say they find poetry difficult – unfamiliarity and lack of practice. But, like anything else, the more effort we put in, the wider the range of experiences we have to draw on. I hope that when you come across an unfamiliar extract in the discussions that follow you might decide to look up the whole poem on your own account, widening your own experience and enjoying it too.

Remember that language changes over the years. I've deliberately chosen to discuss poems from different periods, and given dates of first publication. Do keep this in mind, especially as you may find some examples more accessible than others. The idiom and register of a poem written in the eighteenth century will usually be quite different from one written in the twentieth. Different verse forms are popular at different times: while sonnets have been written for centuries, they were especially fashionable in Elizabethan times, for example. Don't expect to find free verse written much before the twentieth century.

If you are working on a poem, it can be a good idea to print it, maybe even enlarge it, and then write anything you find particularly striking in the margins. Use highlighters or colored pens to underline repetitions and link rhyme words. Patterns may well emerge that will help you understand the way the poem develops. Make the poems your own in this way, and then, if you are the kind of person who doesn't mind writing in books, you can insert notes in a more restrained way in the margins of your book.

If you prefer to work on your computer, you can do a similar thing by using an annotation tool on your word processor.

Whatever you do, always ask yourself what the effect of a particular technique that you identify is. Noticing an unusual choice of words, a particular rhyme scheme or use of alliteration is an important first step, but you need to take another one. Unless you go on to say why what you have noticed is effective, what it contributes to the rest of the poem, how it endorses or changes things, then you are doing less than half the job. Get into the habit of asking yourself questions, even if you can't always answer them satisfactorily.

Rhythm

All speech has rhythm because we naturally stress some words or syllables more than others. The rhythm can sometimes be very regular and pronounced, as in a children's nursery rhyme – 'JACK and JILL went UP the HILL' – but even in the most ordinary sentence the important words are given more stress. In poetry, rhythm is extremely important: patterns are deliberately created and repeated for varying effects. The rhythmical pattern of a poem is called its meter, and we can analyze, or 'scan' lines of poetry to identify stressed and unstressed syllables. In marking the text to show this, the mark '/' is used to indicate a stressed syllable, and 'x' to indicate an unstressed syllable. Each complete unit of stressed and unstressed syllables is called a 'foot', which usually has one stressed and one or two unstressed syllables.

The most common foot in English is known as the iamb, which is an unstressed syllable followed by a stressed one (x /). Many words in English are iambic: a simple example is the word 'forgot'. When we say this, the stresses naturally fall in the sequence:

$$\overset{x}{} \quad \overset{/}{}$$
'forgot'.

Iambic rhythm is in fact the basic sound pattern in ordinary English speech. If you say the following line aloud you will hear what I mean:

x / x / x / x / x / x /
I went across the road and bought a pair of shoes.

The next most common foot is the trochee, a stressed syllable (or 'beat', if you like) followed by an unstressed one (/x), as in the word

/ x
'mountain'.

Both the iamb and the trochee have two syllables, the iamb being a 'rising' rhythm and the trochee a 'falling' rhythm. Another two-syllable foot known as the spondee has two equally stressed beats (/ /), as in

/ /
'blue spurt'.

Other important feet have three syllables. The most common are the anapest (x x /) and the dactyl (/ x x), which are triple rhythms, rising and falling respectively, as in the words

x x / / x x
'unimpressed' and 'probably'.

Here are some fairly regular examples of the four main kinds of meter used in poetry. (I have separated the feet by using a vertical slash.) You should say the lines aloud, listening for the stress patterns and noting how the 'beats' fall on particular syllables or words.

Iambic meter

```
   x    /    x    /       x    /      x    /      x    /
The cur- | few tolls | the knell | of part- | ing day
```

Trochaic meter

```
 /  x    /  x      /   x        /
Tiger | tiger | burning | bright
```

Anapestic meter

```
 x  x   /       x    x    /       x    x   /       x  x    /
She is far | from the land | where her young | hero sleeps
```

Dactylic meter

```
 /   x    x        /    x    x      /   x   x     /    x    x
Woman much | missed how you | call to me, | call to me
```

The other technical point that you need to know about is the way the lengths of lines of verse are described. This is done according to the number of feet they contain, and the names given to different lengths of lines are as follows:

monometer	a line of one foot
dimeter	a line of two feet
trimeter	a line of three feet
tetrameter	a line of four feet
pentameter	a line of five feet
hexameter	a line of six feet
heptameter	a line of seven feet
octameter	a line of eight feet.

By far the most widely used of these are the tetrameter and the pentameter. If you look back at the four lines of poetry given as examples above, you can count the feet. You will see that the first one has five feet, so it is an iambic pentameter line; the second one has four feet, so it is a trochaic tetrameter line; the fourth and fifth also have four feet, so are anapestic and dactylic tetrameter lines respectively. Lines do not always have exactly the 'right' number of beats. Sometimes a pentameter line will have an extra 'beat', as in the famous line from *Hamlet*, 'To be or not to be: that is the question', where the 'tion' of question is an eleventh, unstressed beat. (It is worth asking yourself why Shakespeare wrote the line like this. Why did he not write what would have been a perfectly regular ten-syllable line, such as 'The question is, to be or not to be'?)

Having outlined some of the basic meters of English poetry, it is important to say at once that very few poems would ever conform to a perfectly regular metrical pattern. The effect of that would be very boring indeed: imagine being restricted to using only iambic words, or trying to keep up a regular trochaic rhythm. Poets therefore often include trochaic or anapestic or dactylic words or phrases within what are basically iambic lines, in order to make them more interesting and suggestive, and to retain normal pronunciation. Here is a brief example from Shakespeare to show you what I mean. I have chosen a couple of lines spoken by Rosalind in

As You Like It, Act 1, scene 2, and have marked this first version to show you the basic iambic meter:

```
  x   /      x    /        x     /      x    /      x    /
My fa- | ther loved | Sir Row- | land as | his soul,
  x   /    x     /       x    /     x . /     x       /
And all | the world | was of | my fa | ther's mind.
```

If you say the lines out loud in this regular way you can hear that the effect is very unnatural. Here is one way the lines might be scanned to show how the stresses would fall in speech (though there are other ways of scanning them):

```
  /  /  x  /      x   x   x   x   x    /
My father loved Sir Rowland as his soul,
  x   /  x   /     x   x   x  /  x     /
And all the world was of my father's mind.
```

It must be emphasized that there is no need to feel that you must try to remember all the technical terms I have been introducing here. The purpose has been to help you to become aware of the importance of rhythmic effects in poetry, and it can be just as effective to try to describe these in your own words. The thing to hang on to when writing about the rhythm of a poem is that, as Ezra Pound put it, 'Rhythm MUST have meaning': 'It can't be merely a careless dash off with no grip and no real hold to the words and sense, a tumty tum tumpty tum tum ta' (quoted in Gray, 1990, p. 56). There are occasions, of course, when a tum-ty-ty-tum rhythm may be appropriate, and 'have meaning'. When Tennyson wrote 'The Charge of the Light Brigade', he recreated the sound, pace, and movement of horses thundering along with the emphatic dactyls of 'Half a league, half a league, half a league onward / Into the valley of death rode the six hundred'. But for a very different example we might take a short two-line poem by Pound himself. This time there is no fixed meter: like much twentieth-century poetry, this poem is in 'free verse'. Its title is 'In a Station of the Metro' (the Metro being the Paris underground railway), and it was written in 1916:

```
  x   x    x x x    x    /    /   x   x    /
The apparition of these faces in the crowd;
  / x   x   x   /     /      /
Petals on a wet, black bough.
```

Here you can see that the rhythm plays a subtle part in conveying the meaning. The poem is comparing the faces of people in a crowded underground to petals that have fallen on to a wet bough. The rhythm not only highlights the key words in each line, but produces much of the emotional feeling of the poem by slowing down the middle words of the first line and the final three words of the second.

For our final example of rhythm I've chosen a passage from Alexander Pope's *An Essay on Criticism* (1711).

ACTIVITY 2

Take a look at this excerpt from An Essay on Criticism. Read it aloud if you can. Listen to the rhythm, and identify why the rhythm is appropriate to the meaning.

Discussion

Pope here uses a basic structure of iambic pentameters with variations, so that the lines sound as if they have a different pace, faster or slower, depending on what is being described. It is not just rhythm that contributes to the effect here: rhyme and alliteration (successive words beginning with the same sound) recreate smooth, rough, slow and swift movement. Rhythm is entirely dependent on word choice, but is also influenced by other interdependent stylistic devices. Pope's lines enact what they describe simply because of the care that has gone into choosing the right words. It doesn't matter if you don't recognise the classical allusions: from the descriptions it is clear that Ajax is a strong man and Camilla is quick and light. If you count the beats of each line, you'll notice that, in spite of the variety of sound and effect, all have five stresses, except the last, which has six. Strangely enough it is the last and longest line that creates an impression of speed. How is this achieved? Try to hear the lines by reading them again out loud.

There is really only one way, and that is through the words chosen to represent movement: the repeated 's' sounds associated with Camilla trip swiftly off the tip of the tongue, whereas Ajax's lines demand real physical effort from mouth, lips, and tongue. You will get a much stronger sense of this if you form the words in this way, even if you are unable to say them out loud. In an exam, for instance, silent articulation of a poem will help you grasp many poetic techniques and effects that may otherwise be missed.

This extract from Pope's *An Essay on Criticism*, like the whole poem, is written in rhyming couplets (lines rhyming in pairs). They confer a formal, regular quality to the verse. The punctuation helps to control the way in which we read: notice that there is a pause at the end of each line, either a comma, a semi-colon, or a full stop. This use of the end-stopped line is characteristic of eighteenth-century heroic couplets (iambic pentameter lines rhyming in pairs), where the aim was to reproduce classical qualities of balance, harmony, and proportion.

Get into the habit of looking at rhyme words. Are any of Pope's rhymes particularly interesting here? One thing I noticed was what is known as poetic inversion. The rhyme 'shore'/'roar' is clearly important to the sound sense of the verse, but the more natural word order (were this ordinary speech) would be 'The hoarse rough verse should roar like the torrent'. Had he written this, Pope would have lost the sound qualities of the rhyme 'shore'/'roar'. He would have had to find a word such as 'abhorrent' to rhyme with 'torrent' and the couplet would have had a very different meaning. He would also have lost the rhythm of the line, in spite of the fact that the words are exactly the same.

Before we leave *An Essay on Criticism*, did you notice that Pope's subject in this poem is really poetry itself? Like Wordsworth, Pound, and William Carlos Williams, all of whom I've quoted earlier, Pope too was concerned with poetry as a craft.

Alliteration

Alliteration is the term used to describe successive words beginning with the same sound – usually, then, with the same letter.

To illustrate this I would like to use a stanza from Arthur Hugh Clough's poem, 'Natura naturans'. There is not enough space to quote the whole poem, but to give you some idea of the context of this stanza so that you can more fully appreciate what Clough is doing, it is worth explaining that 'Natura naturans' describes the sexual tension between a young man and woman who sit next to each other in a railway carriage. They have not been introduced, and they neither speak nor exchange so much as a glance. The subject matter and its treatment is unusual and also extraordinarily frank for the time of writing (about 1849), but you need to know what is being described in order to appreciate the physicality of the lines I quote.

ACTIVITY 3

Read the attached stanza from Arthur Hugh Clough's poem "Natura Naturans" and consider the following questions:

1. What is the single most striking technique used, and what are the effects?
2. How would you describe the imagery, and what does it contribute to the overall effect?

Discussion

1. Visually the use of alliteration is striking, particularly in the first line and almost equally so in the second. If you took the advice above about paying attention to the physical business of articulating the words too, you should be in a good position to discriminate between the rapidity of the flies and the heavier movement of the bees, and to notice how tactile the language is. The effect is actually to create sensuality in the stanza.

2. Notice that though we begin with flies, bees and rooks, all of which are fairly common flying creatures, we move to the more romantic lark with its 'wild' song, and then to the positively exotic gazelle, leopard, and dolphin. From the rather homely English air (flies, bees, birds), we move to foreign locations 'Libyan dell' and 'Indian glade', and from there to 'tropic seas'. (Cod in the North Sea would have very different connotations from dolphins in the tropics.) Air, earth, and sea are all invoked to help express the variety of changing highly charged erotic feelings that the speaker remembers. The images are playful and preposterous, joyfully expressing the familiar poetic subject of sexual attraction and arousal in a way that makes it strange and new. Notice that in each case the image is more effective because the alliteration emphasizes it.

Rhyme

If a poem rhymes, then considering how the rhyme works is always important.

Rhyme schemes can be simple or highly intricate and complex; it will always be worth considering why a particular rhyme pattern was chosen and trying to assess its effects.

ACTIVITY 4

Read "Love from the North" (1862) by Christina Rossetti. What is the poem about, and how does the rhyme contribute to the meaning and overall effect?

Discussion

'Love From the North' tells a simple story. A woman about to marry one man is whisked away by another, just as she is about to exchange vows. The form of the poem is very simple: the second and fourth lines of each of the eight 4-line stanzas rhyme. More significantly, because the last word of each stanza is 'nay', there is only one rhyme sound throughout. There are more internal rhymes relying on the same repeated sound, however, aren't there? Look at the last lines of stanzas 1, 2, 6, 7 and 8 where 'say' 'nay'; 'nay' 'nay'; 'say' 'nay'; 'yea' 'nay'; and 'say' 'nay' appear. In the second stanza, 'gay' occurs twice in line 2; stanza five and six both have 'yea' in line 3. What is the effect of this?

Do you think the effect might be to help over-simplify the story? Clearly the woman has doubts about the man from the south's devotion: he 'never dared' to say no to her. He seems to have no will of his own: he 'saddens' when she does, is 'gay' when she is, wants only what she does. On her wedding day she thinks: 'It's quite too late to think of nay'. But is she any happier with the strong man from the north? Who is he? Has he carried her off against her will? And what exactly do you make of the last stanza? Do the 'links of love' imply a chain? This strong-minded woman who imposed her will on the man from the south has 'neither heart nor power/Nor will nor wish' to say no to the man from the north. Is that good, or bad? And what do you make of the 'book and bell' with which she's made to stay? Certainly they imply something different from the conventional Christian marriage she was about to embark on in the middle of the poem – witchcraft, perhaps, or magic? And are the words 'Till now' particularly significant at the beginning of line 3 in the last stanza? Might they suggest a new resolve to break free?

How important is it to resolve such questions? It is very useful to ask them, but not at all easy to find answers. In fact, that is one of the reasons I like the poem so much. The language is very simple and so is the form – eight quatrains (or four-line stanzas) – and yet the more I think about the poem, the more interesting and ambiguous it seems. In my opinion, that is its strength. After all, do we always know exactly what we want or how we feel about relationships? Even if we do, is it always possible to put such feelings into words? Aren't feelings often ambivalent rather than straightforward?

It is also worth bearing in mind the fact that the poem is written in ballad form. A ballad tells a story, but it does only recount events – part of the convention is that ballads don't go into psychological complexities. It is likely that Rossetti chose this ancient oral verse form because she was interested in raising ambiguities. But perhaps the point of the word 'nay' chiming throughout 'Love From the North' is to indicate the female speaker saying no to both men – the compliant lover and his opposite, the demon lover, alike? After all, 'nay' is the sound which gives the poem striking unity and coherence.

Keats's 'Eve of St Agnes' (1820) also tells a tale of lovers, but it isn't a ballad, even though the rhyme scheme of the first four lines is the same as Rossetti's quatrains. The stanzas are longer, and the form more complex and sophisticated. The rhyme pattern is the same throughout all 42 stanzas, the first two of which are reproduced for the following activity:

ACTIVITY 5

Read the first two stanzas of Keats's "Eve of St Agnes." How would you describe the rhyme scheme, and does it seem appropriate for the subject matter?

Discussion

In comparison to the Rossetti poem the rhyme sounds form complex patterns, don't they? While 'was'/'grass' in the first stanza and 'man'/'wan' in the second do not quite produce a full rhyme (depending on your accent), the first and third lines do rhyme in subsequent stanzas. Using a letter of the alphabet to describe each new rhyme sound, we could describe the pattern like this: a b a b b c b c c (imagine sustaining that intricate patterning for 42 stanzas). This kind of formula is useful up to a point for showing how often the same sounds recur, and it does show how complicated the interweaving of echoing sounds is. But it says nothing about how the sounds relate to what is being said – and, as I have been arguing all along, it is the relationship between meaning and word choice that is of particular interest. To give a full answer to my own question, I'd really need to consider the function of rhyme throughout the poem. It would not be necessary to describe what happens in each stanza, but picking out particular pertinent examples would help me argue a case. With only the first two stanzas to work with, I could say that, if nothing else, the intricate rhyme pattern seems appropriate not only for the detailed descriptions but also for the medieval, slightly gothic setting of the chapel where the holy man prays.

ACTIVITY 6

Read the extract from Tennyson's "Mariana" (1830). Again, this comes from a longer poem, so it would be useful to look it up and read the rest if you have the opportunity.

Read the extract and consider the following questions:

1. Describe the rhyme in the stanza from Tennyson's 'Mariana'.
2. What is the first stanza about?

Discussion

1. As with the Keats poem, the rhyme scheme here is quite complicated. Using the same diagrammatic formula of a letter for each new rhyme sound, we could describe this as 'a b a b c d d c e f e f. You might notice too that indentations at the beginning of each line emphasise lines that rhyme with each other: usually the indentations are alternate, except for lines 6 and 7, which form a couplet in the middle of the stanza. It is worth telling you too that each of the stanzas ends with a variation of the line 'I would that I were dead' (this is known as a refrain) so – as in Christina Rossetti's 'Love From the North' – a dominant sound or series of sounds throughout helps to control the mood of the poem.
2. We may not know who Mariana is, or why she is in the lonely, crumbling grange, but she is obviously waiting for a man who is slow in arriving. The 'dreary'/'aweary' and 'dead'/'said' rhymes, which, if you read the rest of the poem, you will see are repeated in each stanza, convey her dejection and express the boredom of endless waiting. As with the stanzas from Keats's 'Eve of St Agnes', there is plenty of carefully observed detail – black moss on the flower-plots, rusty nails, a clinking latch on a gate or door – all of which description contributes to the desolation of the scene and Mariana's mood. Were the moated grange a lively, sociable household, the poem would be very different. Either Mariana would be cheerful, or her suicidal misery would be in sharp contrast to her surroundings. It is always worth considering what settings contribute to the overall mood of a poem.

Poetic Inversion

Poetic inversion, or changing the usual word order of speech, is often linked to the need to maintain a rhythm or to find a rhyme. We noticed Pope's poetic inversion in *An Essay on Criticism* and saw how the rhyme was intimately linked to the rhythm of the verse. The song 'Dancing in the Street', first recorded by Martha and the Vandellas in the 1960s, does violence to word order in the interests of rhyme – 'There'll be dancing in the street/ A chance new folk to meet' – but, because the words are sung to a driving rhythm, we are unlikely to notice how awkward they are. There's a convention that we recognise, however unconsciously, that prevents us from mentally re-writing the line as 'a chance to meet new people'. ('People' rather than 'folk' would be more usual usage for me, but, as with the Pope example, this would mean that the rhythm too would be lost.)

Poems That Don't Rhyme

Are poems that don't rhyme prose? Not necessarily. Virginia Woolf (1882–1941), a novelist rather than a poet, and T.S. Eliot (1888–1965), known particularly for his poetry, both wrote descriptive pieces best described as 'prose poems'. These look like short prose passages since there is no attention to line lengths or layout on the page, as there was, for example, in 'Mariana'. When you study Shakespeare you will come across blank verse. 'Blank' here means 'not rhyming', but the term 'blank verse' is used specifically to describe verse in unrhyming iambic pentameters.

Although iambic pentameters resemble our normal speech patterns, in ordinary life we speak in prose. You'll notice if you look through Shakespeare's plays that blank verse is reserved for kings, nobles, heroes and heroines. They may *also* speak in prose, as lesser characters do, but commoners don't ever have speeches in blank verse. Shakespeare – and other playwrights like him – used the form to indicate status. It is important to recognise this convention, which would have been understood by his contemporaries – writers, readers, and audiences alike. So choosing to write a poem in blank verse is an important decision: it will elevate the subject. One such example is Milton's epic *Paradise Lost*(1667), a long poem in twelve Books describing Creation, Adam and Eve's temptation, disobedience and expulsion from Paradise. It sets out to justify the ways of God to man, so blank verse is entirely appropriate. This great epic was in Wordsworth's mind when he chose the same form for his autobiographical poem, *The Prelude*.

ACTIVITY 7

Read and compare these extracts. One is from Book XIII of *The Prelude*, where Wordsworth is walking up Mount Snowdon; the other is from "The Idiot Boy," one of his *Lyrical Ballads*. What effects are achieved by the different forms?

Discussion

Both poems use iambic meter – an unstressed followed by a stressed syllable. The extract from *The Prelude* uses iambic pentameters, five metrical feet in each line, whereas 'The Idiot Boy' (like the ballad, 'Love From the North') is in tetrameters, only four, establishing a more sing-song rhythm. Other stylistic techniques contribute to the difference in tone too: the language of *The Prelude* is formal (Wordsworth's 'Ascending' rather than 'going up'), whereas 'The Idiot Boy' uses deliberately homely diction, and rhyme. Three simple rhyme words ring out throughout the 92 stanzas of the latter: 'Foy', 'boy' and 'joy' stand at the heart of the poem, expressing the mother's pride in her son. The moon features in each extract. In *The Prelude*, as Wordsworth climbs, the ground lightens, as it does in The Old Testament before a prophet appears. Far from being a meaningless syllable to fill the rhythm of a line, 'lo' heightens the religious parallel, recalling the biblical 'Lo, I bring you tidings of great joy': this episode from *The Prelude* describes a moment of spiritual illumination. Wordsworth's intentions in these two poems were quite different, and the techniques reflect that.

Other poems that don't use rhyme are discussed later ('Wherever I Hang'; 'Mona Lisa'; 'Poem'). Notice that they use a variety of rhythms, and because of that none can be described as blank verse.

Voice

Is the speaker in a poem one and the same as the writer? Stop and consider this for a few moments. Can you think of any poems you have read where a writer has created a character, or persona, whose voice we hear when we read?

Wordsworth's *The Prelude* was written as an autobiographical poem, but there are many instances where it is obvious that poet and persona are different. Charlotte Mew's poem, 'The Farmer's Bride' (1916) begins like this:

Three summers since I chose a maid,
Too young maybe – but more's to do
At harvest-time than bide and woo.
When us was wed she turned afraid

Of love and me and all things human;

(Warner, 1981, pp. 1–2)

Mew invents a male character here, and clearly separates herself as a writer from the voice in her poem. Some of the most well-known created characters – or personae – in poetry are Browning's dramatic monologues.

ACTIVITY 8

Consider the opening lines from three Robert Browning poems. Who do you think is speaking?

Discussion

Well, the first speaker isn't named, but we can infer that, like Brother Lawrence whom he hates, he's a monk. The second must be a Duke since he refers to his 'last Duchess' and, if we read to the end of the third poem, we discover that the speaker is a man consumed with such jealousy that he strangles his beloved Porphyria with her own hair. Each of the poems is written in the first person ('

my heart's abhorrence'; 'That's *my* last Duchess'; *I* listened with heart fit to break'). None of the characters Browning created in these poems bears any resemblance to him: the whole point of a dramatic monologue is the creation of a character who is most definitely not the poet. Charlotte Mew's poem can be described in the same way.

Line Lengths and Line Endings

Read the following prose extract taken from Walter Pater's discussion of the *Mona Lisa*, written in 1893, and then complete the activity:

> She is older than the rocks among which she sits; like the vampire, she has been dead many times, and learned the secrets of the grave; and has been a diver in deep seas, and keeps their fallen day about her; and trafficked for strange webs with Eastern merchants: and, as Leda, was the mother of Helen of Troy, and, as Saint Anne, the mother of Mary; and all this has been to her but as the sound of lyres and flutes, and lives only in the delicacy with which it has moulded the changing lineaments, and tinged the eyelids and the hands.

When W.B. Yeats was asked to edit *The Oxford Book of Modern Verse 1892–1935* (1936), he chose to begin with this passage from Pater, but he set it out quite differently on the page. Before you read his version, write out the extract as a poem yourself. The exercise is designed to make you think about line lengths, where to start a new line and where to end it when there is no rhyme to give you a clue. There is no *regular* rhythm either, though I'm sure you will discover rhythms in the words, as well as repeated patterns. How can you best bring out these poetic features?

Discussion

Of course, there is no right answer to this exercise, but you should compare your version to Yeats's, printed below, to see if you made similar decisions.

> *She is older than the rocks among which she sits;*
> *Like the Vampire,*
> *She has been dead many times,*
> *And learned the secrets of the grave;*
> *And has been a diver in deep seas,*
> *And keeps their fallen day about her;*
> *And trafficked for strange webs with Eastern merchants;*
> *And, as Leda,*
> *Was the mother of Helen of Troy,*
> *And, as St Anne,*
> *Was the mother of Mary;*
> *And all this has been to her but as the sound of lyres and flutes,*
> *And lives*
> *Only in the delicacy*
> *With which it has moulded the changing lineaments,*
>
> *And tinged the eyelids and the hands.*

View the document as a PDF.

I wonder whether you used upper case letters for the first word of each line, as Yeats did? You may have changed the punctuation, or perhaps have left it out altogether. Like Yeats, you may have used 'And' at the beginnings of lines to draw attention to the repetitions: nine of the lines begin in this way, emphasising the way the clauses pile up, defining and redefining the mysterious Mona Lisa. Two lines begin with 'She': while there was no choice about the first, beginning the third in the same way focuses attention on her right at the start of the poem. Yeats has used Pater's punctuation to guide his line endings in all but two places: lines 13 and 14 run on – a stylistic device known as enjambment. The effect is an interesting interaction between eyes and ears. While we may be tempted to read on without pausing to find the sense, the line endings and white space of the page impose pauses on our reading, less than the commas and semi-colons that mark off the other lines, but significant nevertheless.

Yeats's arrangement of the words makes the structure and movement of Pater's long sentence clearer than it appears when written as prose. The poem begins with age – she is 'older than the rocks' – and refers to 'Vampire', death, and 'grave' in the first lines. The decision to single out the two words 'And lives' in a line by themselves towards the end of the poem sets them in direct opposition to the opening; we have moved from great age and living death to life. The arrangement of lines 8–11 highlights her links with both pagan and Christian religions: the Mona Lisa was the mother of Helen of Troy and the Virgin Mary. The wisdom and knowledge she has acquired is worn lightly, nothing more than 'the sound of lyres and flutes', apparent only in the 'delicacy' of colour on 'eyelids and hands'.

The aim of the preceding exercise was to encourage you to think about form and structure even when a poem does not appear to follow a conventional pattern. Because you have now 'written' a poem and had the opportunity to compare it with someone else's version of the same words, you should begin to realise the importance of decisions about where exactly to place a word for maximum effect, and how patterns can emerge which will control our reading when, for example, successive lines begin with repetitions. It should have made you think about the importance of the beginnings of lines, as well as line endings. What has been achieved by using a short line here, a longer one there? How do these decisions relate to what is being said? These are questions that can usefully be asked of any poem.

Earlier, discussing the extract from Pope's *An Essay on Criticism*, I asked you to concentrate on the sound qualities of the poetry. Here, I want you to consider the visual impact of the poem on the page. It is a good thing to be aware of what a complex task reading is, and to be alive to the visual as well as the aural qualities of the verse.

ACTIVITY 10

When W.B. Yeats was asked to edit *The Oxford Book of Modern Verse 1892–1935* (1936), he chose to begin with this passage from Pater, but he set it out quite differently on the page. Before you read his version, write out the extract as a poem yourself. The exercise is designed to make you think about line lengths, where to start a new line and where to end it when there is no rhyme to give you a clue. There is no *regular* rhythm either, though I'm sure you will discover rhythms in the words, as well as repeated patterns. How can you best bring out these poetic features?

Further exercise: taking Grace Nichols's 'Wherever I Hang', discussed in Activity 10, you could reverse the process carried out in the previous exercise by writing out the poem as prose. Then, covering up the original, you could rewrite it as verse and compare your version with the original.

Comparing and Contrasting

Often you will find that an assignment asks you to 'compare and contrast' poems. There's a very good reason for this, for often it is only by considering different treatments of similar subjects that we become aware of a range of possibilities, and begin to understand why particular choices have been made. You will have realised that often in the previous discussions I've used a similar strategy, showing, for example, how we can describe the rhyme scheme of 'Love From the North' as simple once we have looked at the more intricate patterning of Keats's 'The Eve of St Agnes' or Tennyson's 'Mariana'. Anne Brontë's 'Home' and Grace Nichols's 'Wherever I Hang' treat the subject of exile in quite different ways, and looking at one can sharpen our understanding of what the other does.

ACTIVITY 11

Read the opening lines from these two poems commemorating deaths. What can you explain why they sound so very different?

Discussion

If I had to identify one thing, I would say that the first begins more elaborately and with a more formal tone than the second. 'Felix Randal' tends to use language in an unusual way, but you would probably agree that the first sentence is quite straightforward and sounds colloquial (or informal), as if the speaker has just overheard someone talking about Randal's death and wants to confirm his impression. 'Lycidas' opens quite differently. It is not immediately apparent what evergreens have to do with anything (in fact they work to establish an appropriately melancholy atmosphere or tone), and it isn't until line 8 that we learn of a death. The word 'dead' is repeated, and the following line tells us that Lycidas was a young man. While 'Felix Randal' has an immediacy, the speaker of 'Lycidas' seems to find it hard to get going.

Both poems are elegies – poems written to commemorate death – and both poets are aware of writing within this convention, although they treat it differently.

ACTIVITY 12

What do the titles of the poems used in Activity 13 tell us about each poem, and how might they help us understand the different uses of the elegiac convention?

Discussion

I think it would be apparent to most readers that 'Felix Randall' is simply a man's name, while 'Lycidas' is more mysterious. In fact Lycidas is a traditional pastoral name, but unless you know something about the classical pastoral tradition it might mean very little to you. The young man whose death Milton was commemorating was actually called Edward King, but, at the time he was writing, elegies were formal, public and impersonal poems rather than private expressions of grief. 'Lycidas' commemorates a member of a prominent family rather than a close friend of the poet's. Over two hundred years later, Hopkins, while working loosely within the same elegiac convention, adapts it. Felix Randal is an ordinary working man, not a public figure. In the seventeenth century it would have been unlikely that he would have been considered worthy of a poem like this.

If you were making a special study of elegies, there would be a great deal more to say. That's not the idea here, though. The point is that by comparing and contrasting the tone of the opening lines and the titles, and considering when the poems were written, we have come up with a number of significant differences.

ACTIVITY 13

Read this poem by Robert Browning carefully. Who is speaking, and who is being addressed?

Discussion

From the evidence of the poem we know that the speaker once walked across a moor, found an eagle's feather, and has a high regard for the poet Shelley (1792–1822). The person being addressed is not named, but we discover that he (or she) once met Shelley, and this alone confers status by association. The word 'you' ('your' in one instance) is repeated in 6 out of the first 8 lines. 'You' becomes a rhyme word at the end of the second line, so when we reach the word 'new' in line four – one of the two lines in the first stanzas that doesn't contain 'you' – the echo supplies the deficiency. 'You' clearly represents an important focus in the first half of the poem, but who exactly is 'you' ?

Thinking about this apparently straightforward question of who is being addressed takes us into an important area of critical debate: for each one of us who has just read the poem has, in one sense, become a person who not only knows who Shelley is (which may not necessarily be the case) but lived when he did, met him, listened to him, and indeed exchanged at least a couple of words with him. Each of us reads the poem as an individual, but the poem itself constructs a reader who is not identical to any of us. We are so used to adopting 'reading' roles dictated by texts like this that often we don't even notice the way in which the text has manipulated us.

ACTIVITY 14

Now read the Robert Browning poem again, this time asking yourself if the speaking voice changes in the last two stanzas, and if the person who is being addressed remains the same.

Discussion

If the first half of the poem is characterised by the repetition of 'you' and the sense of an audience that pronoun creates, then the second half seems quite different in content and tone. The speaker is trying to find a parallel in his experience to make sense of and explain his feeling of awe; the change of tone is subtle. Whereas someone is undoubtedly being addressed directly in the first stanza, in the third and fourth, readers overhear – as if the speaker is talking to himself.

At first the connection between the man who met Shelley and the memory of finding an eagle's feather may not be obvious, but there is a point of comparison. As stanza 2 explains, part of the speaker's sense of wonder stems from the fact that time did not stand still: 'you were living before that, / And also you are living after'. The moor in stanza 3, like the listener, is anonymous – it has 'a name of its own … no doubt' – but where it is or what it is called is unimportant: only one 'hand's-breadth' is memorable, the spot that 'shines alone' where the feather was found. The poem is about moments that stand out in our memories while the ordinary daily stuff of life fades. It also acknowledges that we don't all value the same things.

ACTIVITY 15

Take another look at the poem. How would you describe its form?

Discussion

The structure of the poem is perfectly balanced: of the four quatrains, two deal with each memory, so, although the nature of each seems quite different, implicitly the form invites us to compare them. Think about the way in which Browning introduces the eagle feather. How does he convince us that this is a rare find?

To begin with, the third and fourth stanzas make up one complete sentence, with a colon at the end of the third announcing the fourth; this helps to achieve a sense of building up to something important. Then we move from the visual image of a large space of moor to the very circumscribed place where the feather is found, but the reason why this 'hand's-breadth' shines out is delayed for the next two lines 'For there I picked up on the heather' – yes? what? – 'And there I put inside my breast' – well? – 'A moulted feather', ah (and notice the internal rhyme there of 'feather' with 'heather' which draws attention to and emphasises the harmony of the moment), and then the word 'feather' is repeated and expanded: 'an eagle-feather' Clearly the feather of no other bird would do, for ultimately the comparison is of eagle to the poet; Browning knows Shelley through his poetry as he knows the eagle through its feather, and that feather presents a striking visual image.

There is an immediacy about the conversational opening of the poem which, I have suggested, deliberately moves into a more contemplative tone, possibly in the second stanza (think about it), but certainly by the third. We have considered some of the poetic techniques that Browning employs to convince us of the rarity of his find in the third and fourth stanzas. You might like to think more analytically about the word sounds, not just the rhyme but, for example, the repeated 'ae' sound in 'breadth' 'heather' 'breast' and 'feather'. What, however, do you make of the tone of the last line? Try saying the last lines of each stanza out loud. Whether you can identify the meter with technical language or not is beside the point. The important thing is that 'Well, I forget the rest' sounds deliberately lame. After the intensity of two extraordinary memories, everything else pales into insignificance and, to reiterate this, the rhythm tails off. While the tone throughout is informal, the last remark is deliberately casual.

Glossary

Alliteration	repetition of sounds, usually the first letters of successive words, or words that are close together. Alliteration usually applies only to consonants.
Anapest	*see under* foot.
Assonance	repetition of identical or similar vowel sounds.
Ballad	originally a song which tells a story, often involving dialogue. Characteristically, the storyteller's own feelings are not expressed.
Caesura	strong pause in a line of verse, usually appearing in the middle of a line and marked with a comma, semi-colon, or a full stop.
Couplet	pair of rhymed lines, often used as a way of rounding off a sonnet; hence the term 'closing couplet'.
Dactyl	*see under* foot.
Dialogue	spoken exchange between characters, usually in drama and fiction but also sometimes in poetry.
Diction	writer's choice of words. Poetic diction might be described, for instance, as formal or informal, elevated or colloquial.
Elegy	poem of loss, usually mourning the death of a public figure, or someone close to the poet.
Ellipsis	omission of words from a sentence to achieve brevity and compression.
Enjambment	the use of run-on lines in poetry. Instead of stopping or pausing at the end of a line of poetry, we have to carry on reading until we complete the meaning in a later line. The term comes from the French for 'striding'.
Epic	a long narrative poem dealing with events on a grand scale, often with a hero above average in qualities and exploits.
Epigram	witty, condensed expression. The closing couplet in some of Shakespeare's sonnets is often described as an epigram.
Foot	a unit of meter with a pattern of stressed and unstressed syllables. In the examples that follow, a stressed syllable is indicated by '/', and an unstressed syllable by 'x': anapest: xx/; dactyl: /xx; iamb: x/; spondee: //; trochee: /x

Heroic couplet	iambic pentameter lines rhyming in pairs, most commonly used for satiric or didactic poetry, and particularly favoured in the eighteenth century.
Iamb	*see under* foot.
Iambic pentameter	a line consisting of five iambs.
Imagery	special use of language in a way that evokes sense impressions (usually visual). Many poetic images function as mental pictures that give shape and appeal to something otherwise vague and abstract; for example, 'yonder before us lie/ Deserts of vast Eternity'. Simile and metaphor are two types of imagery.
Metaphor	image in which one thing is substituted for another, or the quality of one object is identified with another. The sun, for Shakespeare, becomes 'the eye of heaven'.
Meter	(from the Greek *metron*, 'measure') measurement of a line of poetry, including its length and its pattern of stressed and unstressed syllables. There are different meter in poetry. Most sonnets, for example, written in English are divided into lines of ten syllables with five stresses – a measure known as pentameter (from the Greek *pente* for 'five'). The sonnet also tends to use a line (known as the iambic line) in which an unstressed syllable is followed by a stressed one, as in this line: 'If I should die, think only this of me'. Most sonnets, then are written in iambic pentameters.
Narrative	the telling of a series of events (either true or fictitious). The person relating these events is the narrator. However, it is often more usual in poetry to refer to 'the speaker'.
Octave	group of eight lines of poetry, often forming the first part of a sonnet.
Ode	a poem on a serious subject, usually written in an elevated formal style; often written to commemorate public events.
Onomatopoeia	a word that seems to imitate the sound or sounds associated with the object or action, for example, 'cuckoo'.
Ottava rima	a poem in eight-line stanzas, rhyming a b a b a b c c.
Personification	writing about something not human as if it were a person, for example 'Busy old fool, unruly Sun,/Why dost thou thus,/Through windows and through curtains call onus?'.
Poetic inversion	reversing the order of normal speech in order to make the words fit a particular rhythm, or rhyme, or both.
Pun	double meaning or ambiguity in a word, often employed in a witty way. Puns are often associated with wordplay.
Quatrain	group of four lines of poetry, usually rhymed.
Refrain	a line or phrase repeated throughout a poem, sometimes with variations, often at the end of each stanza.
Rhyme	echo of a similar sound, usually at the end of a line of poetry. Occasionally, internal rhymes can be found, as in: 'Sister, my sister, O *fleet, sweet* swallow'.
Rhyme scheme	pattern of rhymes established in a poem. The pattern of rhymes in a quatrain, for instance, might be 'a b a b' or 'a b b a'.
Rhythm	the pattern of beats or stresses in a line creating a sense of movement. Sestet: group of six lines of poetry, often forming the second part of a sonnet.
Simile	image in which one thing is likened to another. The similarity is usually pointed out with the word 'like' or 'as': 'My love is like a red, red rose'.
Sonnet	fourteen iambic pentameter lines with varying rhyme schemes.
Spondee	*see under* foot.
Syllable	single unit of pronunciation. 'Sun' is one syllable; 'sunshine' is two syllables.
Tercet	group of three lines in poetry, sometimes referred to as a triplet. Trochee: *see under* foot.
Turn	distinctive movement of change in mood or thought or feeling. In the sonnet, the turn usually occurs between the octave and the sestet, though the closing couplet in Shakespeare's sonnets often constitutes the turn.
Villanelle	an intricate French verse form with some lines repeated, and only two rhyme sounds throughout the five three-line stanzas and the final four-line stanza.

References

Abrams, M.H. (1971) *A Glossary of Literary Terms*, Holt, Rinehart and Winston.

Barker, J.R.V. (ed.) (1985) *The Brontes: Selected Poems*, Dent.

Bush, D. (ed.) (1966) *Milton: Poetical Works*, Oxford University Press.

Bygrave, S. (ed.) (1998) *Romantic Writings*, The Open University.

Clough, A.H. (1890) *Poems*, Macmillan.

Gardner, W.H. (1953) *Poems and Prose of Gerard Manley Hopkins*, Penguin.

Gibson, J. (ed.) (1976) *The Complete Poems of Thomas Hardy*, Macmillan.

Goodman, L. (1996) *Literature and Gender*, The Open University.

Gray, R. (1990) *American Poetry of the Twentieth Century*, Longman.

Hutchinson, T. (ed.) (1936) (revised 1969 by E. De Selincourt) *Wordsworth: Poetical Works*, Oxford University Press.

Jack, I. and Fowler, R. (eds) (1988) *The Poetical Works of Robert Browning*, vol. III *Bells and Pomegranates*, Clarendon Press.

Matterson, S. and Jones, D. (2000) *Studying Poetry*, Arnold. O'Hara, F. (1964) *Lunch Poems*, City Lights Books.

Owens, W.R. and Johnson, H. (eds) (1998) *Romantic Writings: An Anthology*, The Open University.

Pater, W. (1893) (1998) *The Renaissance: Studies in Art and Poetry*, ed. Adam Phillips, Oxford University Press.

Regan, S. (1997) 'Form and Meaning in Poetry: The Sonnet', in *A103 An Introduction to the Humanities*, Block 1 'Form and Reading', The Open University.

Sisson, C.H. (1984) *Christina Rossetti: Selected Poems*, Carcanet.

Trilling, T. and Bloom, H. (1973) *Victorian Prose and Poetry*, Oxford University Press.

Wain, J. (ed.) (1990) *The Oxford Library of English Poetry*, vol.II, Oxford University Press / Guild Publishing.

Warner, V. (ed.) (1981)
Charlotte Mew: Collected Poems and Prose, Virago Press. Yeats, W.B. (1936) *The Oxford Book of Modern Verse 1892–1935*, Clarendon Press.

Stress in Poetry

Overview

Stresses allow poets to focus readers' attention on the meaning of their poetry. We all know that poetry is different from everyday language. A lot of that sense of *difference* resides in the stresses good poets manipulate in order to create meaningful experiences for readers. I don't expect you to start counting stresses. Most of the poetry we'll read is not in formal meter; however, you should become attuned to the sound of the words.

How does the poet choose to use stresses in a given line?

For what purpose does this word get used?

How does this sound?

These are all legitimate questions. I expect you to become aware (in a general way) of the way poets use sound for their purposes. You won't get to these questions unless you reread the poems. Reading aloud helps, too!

If you get the idea that stresses are relative and that poets play with patterns, you're in good shape. I also want you to see *if* the NA poets we read follow iambic patterns. Don't expect them to rhyme—most contemporary poets couldn't rhyme if you paid them. (Hah, most contemporary poets couldn't get paid for their work, either, but that's another story.)

Stressed Yet?

Okay: read aloud, reread, transitions. What else is there? Lots, actually!

Take stresses, for example. In a heavily accented language like English, words have relative stresses. Here's an example:"A man, a plan, a canal, Panama." Not exactly poetry, but it reads the same backwards as it does forwards (it's a palindrome). We can give this line stresses: put / in for a stressed syllable, and U above the syllable that's not as stressed.

U / U / UU / / U U

A man, a plan, a canal, Panama

Try an easier one, now:

The rain in Spain falls mainly on the plain.

Where would the stresses go?

U / U / U / U / U /

The rain in Spain falls mainly on the plain.

That's right!

Form and Content

Now, you might disagree with my stresses here. It's somewhat open to interpretation. Words have stress patterns (just look in any dictionary). If you wanted to give mainly two stresses in a row, you'd probably avoid stressing "on." Here's a major point about reading: **Change the form and you change the content**.

I don't like using all caps, but that statement above is the big deal about poetry! Above, you changed the form (the stress pattern you saw), and that changed the content of the poem (its meaning). Form and content—it's all about form and content. When you look for a change in meaning, you'll probably also find a change in the form.

Metric Feet? Huh? Are we in Canada?

Poetry is all about patterns. The unstressed-stressed pattern here is very important.

A foot is a measure of stressed. Usually, feet have two syllables (though some have three).

An iamb is a pattern of unstressed stressed syllables. Is the second example iambic? (If you said "yes," you're right.)

A trochee is a foot where the first syllable is stressed and the second is unstressed.

Poetry would be pretty boring if poets didn't vary the pattern. Just like in soccer or hockey, where players make certain moves, poets have moves.

The second example has how many feet? (5)

The second example has _____ syllables? (10)

It's called **iambic pentameter**. Its overall pattern is iambic, and it has five feet of two syllables each.

Questions

Why would five-foot lines be a good choice in poetry?

What do ten-syllable (five-foot) lines allow poets to do?

Why would two-foot lines or ten-foot lines have major drawbacks?

Religion and Spiritual Beliefs

The White Buffalo Woman (Brule Sioux)

One summer so long ago that nobody remembers how long, the Oceti-Shakowin, the seven sacred councils fires of the Lakota Oyate, the nation, came together and camped. The sun shone all the time, but there was no game and the people were starving. Every day they sent scouts to look for game, but the scouts found nothing.

Among the bands assembled were the Itazipcho, the Without-Bows, who had their own camp circle under their chief, Standing Hollow Horn. Early one morning the chief sent two of his young men to hunt for game. They went on foot, because at that time the Sioux didn't yet have horses. They searched everywhere but could find nothing. Seeing a high hill, they decided to climb it in order to look over the whole country. Halfway up, they saw something coming toward them from far off, but the figure was floating instead of walking. From this they knew that the person was wakan, holy.

At first they could make out only a small moving speck and had to squint to see that it was a human form. But as it came nearer, they realized it was a beautiful young woman, more beautiful than any they had ever seen, with two round, red dots of face paint on her cheeks. She wore a wonderful white buckskin outfit, tanned until it shone a long way in the sun. It was embroidered with sacred and marvelous designs of porcupine quill, in radiant colors no ordinary woman could have made. This wakan stranger was Ptesan-Wi, White Buffalo Woman. In her hands she carried a large bundle and a fan of sage leaves. She wore her blue-black hair loose except for a strand at the left side, which was tied up with buffalo fur. Her eyes shone dark and sparkling with great power in them.

The young men looked at her open-mouthed. One was overawed, but the other desired her body and stretched his hand out to touch her. This woman was lila wakan, very sacred, and could not be treated with disrespect. Lightning instantly struck the brash young man and burned him up, so that only a small heap of blackened bones was left. Or some say that he was suddenly covered by a cloud, and within it he was eaten up by snakes that left only his skeleton, just as a man can be eaten up by lust.

To the other scout who behaved rightly, the White Buffalo Woman said: "Good things I am bringing, something holy to your nation. A message I carry for your people from the buffalo nation. Go back to the camp and tell your people to prepare for my arrival. Tell your chief to put up a medicine lodge with twenty-four poles. Let it be made holy for my coming."

This young hunter returned to the camp. He told the chief, he told the people, what the sacred woman had commanded. The chief told the eyapaha, the crier, and the crier went through the camp circle calling: "Someone sacred is coming. A holy woman approaches. Make all things ready for her." So the people put up the big medicine tipi and waited. After four days they saw the White Buffalo Woman approaching, carrying her bundle before her. Her wonderful white buckskin dress shone from afar. The chief, Standing Hollow Horn, invited her to enter the medicine lodge. She went in and circled the interior sunwise. The chief addressed her respectfully, saying: "Sister, we are glad you have come to instruct us."

She told them what she wanted done. In the center of tipi they were to put up an owanka wakan, a sacred alter, made of red earth, with a buffalo skull and a three-stick rack for a holy thing she was bringing. They did what she directed, and she traced with her finger on the smoothed earth of the altar. She showed them how to do all this, then circled the lodge again sunwise. Halting before the chief, she now opened the bundle. The holy thing it contained was the chanunpa, the sacred pipe. She held it out to the people and let them look at it. She was grasping the stem with her right hand and the bowl with her left, and thus the pipe has been held ever since.

Again the chief spoke, saying: "Sister, we are glad. We have had no meat for some time. All we can give you is water." They dipped some wacanga, sweet grass, into a skin bag of water and gave it to her, and to this day the people dip sweet grass or an eagle feather in water and sprinkle it on a person to be purified.

The White Buffalo Woman showed the people how to use the pipe. She filled it with chan-shasha, red willow bark tobacco. She walked around the lodge four times after the manner of Anpetu-Wi, the great sun. This represented the circle without end, the flame to be passed on from generation to generation. She told them that the smoke rising from the bowl was Tunkashila's breath, the living breath of the great Grandfather Mystery.

The White Buffalo Woman showed the people the right way to pray, the right words and right gestures. She taught them how to sing the pipe-filling song and how to lift the pipe up to the sky, toward Grandfather, and down toward Grandmother Earth, to Unci, and then to the four directions of the universe.

"With this holy pipe," she said, "You will walk like a living prayer. With your feet resting upon the earth and pipestem reaching into the sky, your body forms a living bridge between the Sacred Beneath and the Sacred Above. Wakan Takan smiles upon us, because now we are as one: earth, sky, all living things, the two-legged, the four-legged, the winged ones, the trees and grasses. Together with the people, they are all related, one family. The pipe holds them all together.

"Look at this bowl," said the White Buffalo Woman. "Its stone represents the buffalo, but also the flesh and blood of the red man. The buffalo represents the universe and the four directions, because he stands on four legs, for the four ages of creation. The buffalo was put in the west by Wakan Tanka at the making of the world, to hold back the waters. Every year he loses one hair, and in every one of the four ages he loses a leg. The sacred hoop will end when all the hair and legs of the great buffalo are gone, and the water comes back to cover the earth.

The wooden stem of this chanunpa stands for all that grows on the earth. Twelve feathers hanging from where the stem—the backbone—joins the bowl—the skull—are from Wanblee Galeshka, the spotted eagle, the very sacred bird who is the Great Spirit's messenger and the wisest of all flying ones. You are joined to all things of the universe, for they all cry out to Tunkashila. Look at the bowl: engraved in it are seven circles of various sizes. They stand for the seven sacred ceremonies you will practice with this pipe, and for the Ocheit Shakowin, the seven sacred campfires of our Lakota nation."

The White Buffalo Woman then spoke to the women, telling them that it was the work of their hands and the fruit of their bodies which kept the people alive. "You are from mother earth," she told them. "What you are doing is as great as what the warriors do."

And therefore the sacred pipe is also something that binds men and women together in a circle of love. It is the one holy object in the making of which both men and women have a hand. The men carved the bowl and make the stem; the women decorate it with bands of colored porcupine quills. When a man takes a wife, they both hold the pipe at the same time and red trade cloth is wound around their hands, thus tying them together for life.

The White Buffalo Woman had many things for her Lakota sister in her sacred womb bag—corn, wasna (pemmican), wild turnip. She taught them how to make the hearth fire. She filled a buffalo paunch with cold water and dropped a red-hot stone into it. "This way you shall cook the corn and meat," she told them.

The White Buffalo Woman also talked to the children, because they have an understanding beyond their years. She told them that what their fathers and mothers did was for them, that their parents could remember being little once, and that they, the children, would grow up to have little ones of their own. She told them: "You are the coming generation, that's why you are the most important and precious ones. Some day you will hold this pipe and smoke it. Some day you will pray with it."

She spoke once more to all the people: "The pipe is alive; it is a red being showing you a red life and a red road. And this is the first ceremony for which you will use the pipe. You will use it to keep the soul of a dead person, because through it you can talk to Wakan Tanka, the Great Mystery Spirit. The day a human dies is always a sacred day. The day when the soul is released to the Great Spirit is another. Four women will become sacred on such a day. They will be the ones to cut the sacred tree—the can-wakan—for the sun dance.

She told the Lakota that they were the purest among the tribes, and for that reason Tunkashila had bestowed upon them the holy chanunpa. They had been chosen to take care of it for all the Indian people on this turtle island.

She spoke one last time to Standing Hollow Horn, the chief, saying, "Remember: this pipe is very sacred. Respect it and it will take you to the end of the road. The four ages of creation are in me; I am the four ages. I will come to see you in every generation cycle. I shall come back to you."

The sacred woman then took leave of the people, saying: "Toksha ake wacinyanktin ktelo—I shall see you again."

The people saw her walking off in the same direction from which she had come, outlined against the red ball of the setting sun. As she went, she stopped and rolled over four times. The first time she turned into a black buffalo; the second time into a brown one; the third time into a red one; and finally, the fourth time she rolled over, she turned into a white female buffalo calf. A white buffalo is the most sacred living thing you could ever encounter.

The White Buffalo Woman disappeared over the horizon. Sometime she might come back. As soon as she had vanished, buffalo in great herds appeared, allowing themselves to be killed so that the people might survive. And from that day on, our relations, the buffalo, furnished the people with everything they needed-meat for food, skins for their clothes and tipis, bones for their many tools.

Told by Lame Deer at Winner, Rosebud Reservation, South Dakota, 1967 (Erdoes and Ortiz)

This story is a **genesis** or **origin story.** Such a story tells people of the societies from which they come where they come from, their origins. They tell people of the society to whom they belong, how they are expected to interact with each other, with other elements of creation or nature, and with spiritual beings. Origin stories are an important part of the religious or spiritual beliefs of any society. This story is quite different than the Judeo-Christian story of the Garden of Eden that you may be familiar with. The origin stories of Native peoples throughout North America are also quite different from each other. Each Native American society has its own origin story; there is no one story as there is in Christianity and Judaism.

Origin stories are just one aspect of religious or spiritual beliefs for any society. Spiritual beliefs tell us where we come from, where we are going after death, and what is expected from us while we are in this world. Spiritual beliefs function on an individual and community level. They tell individuals what they must do to be considered a good person by their family, society, and by the spiritual beings. Spiritual beliefs also tell societies what is expected from them as a community: how individuals within the community should be treated, what qualities are needed for leadership, and how outsiders should be treated. Spiritual beliefs also tell kin groups and communities the consequences of inappropriate behavior. In this way, spiritual beliefs function as a form of social control. They tell individuals within a community what behavior is desired and appropriate, and the consequences of inappropriate behavior.

In Native American origin stories, animals, plants, and even forces of nature like the snakes that ate the disrespectful young man, are active participants in the story. Unlike the Judeo-Christian story in which the serpent is the only animal to have a part mentioned, in Native American stories the animals are very important to the action of the story; often they help humans to survive. Animals may sometimes be **tricksters**, like Coyote of southwestern stories or the Great Hare of the Southeast, but even they sometimes help humans. You may notice from many of the stories included in this book, humans and animals cooperate and work together. Many Native American societies believe that all things in the world have souls or spirits: therefore all things in the world must be treated respectfully. Anthropologists and others who study religious beliefs call this **animism,** the belief that key parts of nature have spirits. In foraging societies there are thanksgiving rituals for the animals that give their lives for us to eat. Failing to enact the rituals may result in the animals **withdrawing** themselves. For all living things there are expectations of behavior, and when humans or animals do not meet these expectations, there are consequences. For example, in the Apache story told at the beginning of Chapter 1, the gray crow eats carrion and is turned black for this inappropriate behavior.

The stories from Native American societies included in this book are parts of much longer cycles of stories that tell what all religious texts tell its followers: where people came from; what will happen to you in the afterlife; and what is expected from you while you are in this world. In telling people what is expected from them while they are in this world, religious or spiritual beliefs function as part of the larger social order. People behave properly because their families and their spiritual beliefs tell them what is appropriate behavior and what will happen to them if they don't behave appropriately. In any society the stories that relate religious beliefs also tell what is considered appropriate behavior in a society. Origin stories are told and retold within family and community groups. In Native American societies, if a child misbehaves, they are told a story about the consequences of similar behavior for a human or animal.

Ceremonies and rituals are another important part of any religious tradition. Ceremonies are formal religious or public occasions that are performed according to a traditional or prescribed form. There are secular ceremonies like the inauguration of a new president or prime minister, as well as sacred ceremonies that mark religious occasions such as Easter and Passover. Among many Native American societies there are rituals or ceremonies that re-enact aspects of origin stories. Among the Hidatsa this ceremony is called the **Naxpike** or **hide beating**, and has many of the elements common to the Sun Dance practiced by societies throughout the plains. The ceremonial grounds where the ritual will take place are prepared and blessed by the elder women, then a post made from a cottonwood tree is placed in the middle of the grounds by the elder men Young men volunteer to re-enact the suffering and torture of **Spring Boy**, the first to person to do the Naxpike. By doing so they achieve individual visions and help renew the earth for their community (Bonvillain 2001). As with origin stories, rituals and ceremonies vary from society to society.

In many predominately Christian countries, new governmental leaders often take an oath of office with their hand on the Bible. Among many Native American societies, such as the Haundenosaune or the southwestern societies, the raising up of a new leader also has heavy religious overtones; the chiefs are fulfilling religious obligations laid out in their origin stories.

A ritual is much like a ceremony, except there is an emphasis on the actions that are done according to a prescribed order. Think about the order of rituals you might be familiar with, like a wedding or services at your church, temple, or mosque. Everyone knows what is coming next in the ritual and there is significance to the order. Among foraging societies, there are rituals to thank the animals, birds, and fish that gave up their lives to be killed for food, and rituals to ensure there will continue to be animals, fish, and birds for the coming years. These rituals are called **renewal ceremonies**. Foraging societies may also have rituals for the growth of plants, particularly plants that are important for medicines. If the rituals are not done, or done incorrectly, the animals or plants may withdraw themselves and no longer be available.

Rituals and ceremonies can meet the needs of individuals and the community. For instance, horticultural or agricultural societies have ceremonies or rituals to ensure the growth of their crops. Among the Haundenosaune, there are ceremonies for the coming of maple sap and strawberries. There are several for corn: the planting of the seeds, the "greening of the corn," when the plant "tassels," and the harvesting of the crop. Many societies also have rituals that renew the earth itself, such as the Hidatsa's Naxpike or the Sun Dance practiced by many Plains societies. The Naxpike or Sun Dance may be done to fulfill an individual's vow or to invoke a vision. These rituals also fulfill community needs, bringing the community together and renewing the earth for the upcoming year.

Some rituals are done as called for, a thanksgiving ritual when an animal is killed, for example. Additionally, foraging, horticultural, and agricultural Native American societies typically have a cycle of ceremonies that are done on a yearly or **calendric** basis. The cycle of ceremonies includes those having to do with important foods and crops, such as the **Mid-Winter Ceremony**, typically held in January. Many Native American societies have yearly rituals to renew the earth. The Plains' Sun Dance is an example of such a ritual. Foraging societies have yearly rituals done to ensure the renewal of needed animals. Horticultural and agricultural societies have ceremonies, of which feasts were an important part, to celebrate and thank the earth for a successful growing season and to ask for a successful succeeding year. These feast-ceremonies often included speeches by leaders about community responsibilities, speeches by ordinary people about the responsibility of the leaders, and games. An important game among many Native societies was a ball game, from which the modern game of lacrosse is probably derived.

In addition to offering thanks, these ceremonies were and are also an opportunity for the community to come together, iron out grievances, have a good time, and look for potential marriage partners. Modern-day **pow-wows** function in a similar way for contemporary Native American communities. While the traditional ceremonies are still practiced by many societies, pow-wows are an opportunity for those who no longer live on the reservation or reserve to come home to celebrate their culture and family connections. Pow-wows are used to honor respected members of the community, and currently are often held to welcome returning war veterans and incorporate them back into the community. These gatherings are an example of how rituals function on a societal level, bringing the community together for mutual purposes and benefits.

Among Native American societies, rituals and ceremonies may be carried out by ordinary people, or they may be officiated by religious specialists. For example: everyone is expected to do a thanksgiving ritual when hunting or fishing. Any man may pledge himself to do the Sun Dance; but respected women bless and prepare the dance grounds. Respected older men who have already participated in the Sun Dance chop down the cottonwood tree that will be used for the dance pole, and they erect of the pole. Among the Dine' important rituals are performed by a **singer**, a man (women have recently started assuming this role as well) who has spent his life learning a cycle of over 250 chants or songs that are used in curing and other ceremonies, along with the technique and designs of sand paintings that are a part of the rituals. Many of the songs or chants are **curing** ceremonies, used to help cure an individual or even the community. People in Native American societies generally know what available plants are useful in treating illnesses or diseases. As Jack Weatherford has pointed out in *Indian Givers* and *Native Gifts,* a number of these plants are now essential to many modern-day medicines. In addition to these medicinal plants, religious practitioners could call upon spiritual powers for help in curing someone. Many medicinal plants themselves were thought to have spiritual powers.

Among the most specialized of spiritual roles is that of a **shaman.** The word "shaman" is Siberian in origin and refers to a man or woman who is able to travel to the spirit world through a trance state. In Native American societies, all people have some access to spiritual power and knowledge. Shamans typically work for the entire community to find out why the crops have failed or why hunting has been unsuccessful. In many Arctic societies, it is believed that the animals they depend on were made from the fingers of a woman named Sedna, the guardian of the animals. Sedna will withdraw or remove the animals if hunters have not treated them respectfully and done the thanksgiving rituals after killing them. If hunting becomes unsuccessful, the community's shaman will enter a trance state and travel underwater to where Sedna lives to find out why the animals have been withdrawn and what must be done to bring them back. To appease Sedna, the shaman will comb her hair, which she can no longer do because of the loss of her fingers.

Shamans and trances are part of the spiritual traditions of many societies around the world. In some societies, anyone may attain a trance through dancing, drumming, chanting, or the use of hallucinate drugs, but they are not recognized as shamans because their trances are typically for individual purposes, while a shaman typically goes into a trance state to benefit his/her community. Shamans are usually called to what can be very difficult roles in their society. An individual may be called through dreams. In many Native American societies, people who have nearly died, particularly through an illness, are thought to have the power to become a shaman because they have already traveled to the spirit world and returned. Among the societies of the Northwest coast, individuals might spend their lifetimes training to become a shaman, often apprenticing themselves to a shaman and inheriting their teacher's powers upon their death.

As with the specialized, religious practitioners of any society, shamans undergo much training and must live according to many **taboos** (also spelled **tabu**). Taboos are things shamans are not suppose to do, though other members of their society may do them. For example, Catholic nuns and priests take vows of celibacy, something the rest of us are not expected to do. Some taboos apply to everybody, such as the taboos prohibiting incest or cannibalism. Taboos may also be temporary. For example, Catholics used to not eat meat on Fridays. In some foraging societies, pregnant women will not eat rabbit meat because they believe it will cause their children to be timid and fearful. In the United States and Canada, athletes may abstain from certain foods or behaviors, believing they will be weakened. For shamans, taboos are usually life long.

In addition to abiding by the taboos, shamans typically live very solitary lives. They must spend much time learning their skills. In turn, their skills make them very powerful, and potentially vary dangerous. Those who have the power to heal, also have the power to injure or kill. As a result, shamans are often feared and somewhat distrusted by their societies. Among the Northwest coast societies, who typically live in large, extended families, shamans live alone in the woods. When they die, their homes are abandoned and allowed to decay. Because of their power, special funeral rites and burial methods are often accorded to shamans. Despite the power a shaman may have, it is not a life to which many people aspire.

While shamans have special spiritual powers, Native American societies believe all people—indeed, all living things—have access to spiritual power. One of the ways spiritual power is attained is through dreams. Revitalization movements were often started in response to dreams. Dreams are seen as a conduit between people and the spirit realm. Through dreams the spirits tell people how to live their lives, what they're doing wrong, even warning them of danger. Many Native American societies have rituals in which people seek advice about their dreams. A person with a troubling dream may go to a shaman; or, as among the Haundenosaune, they may tell it to the entire community for advice about its meaning. The Iroquois, and many other Native American societies, believe the messages of dreams must be acted upon or there will be negative consequences for the individual and the entire community.

Another way individuals have access to spiritual power is through visions. Men and women will undertake a **vision quest** as a way to attain spiritual power. In a vision quest individuals will go to a solitary place and go without food, water, and sleep in order to obtain a vision. It is believed the spirits will tell individuals what is expected from them through visions.

The vision quest can be part of **life cycle rituals**—rituals that mark important transitions in a person's life. Not all Native American societies have the same life cycle rituals, but there are typically rituals to mark birth, the attainment of **personhood**, adulthood, marriage, and death. A mother (and sometimes the father) may begin rituals before a child is born. A mother may abstain from some foods, such as rabbit, to ensure the child will be brave and not run away from danger. Rituals are done to ensure an easy delivery and a healthy child. Among the Dine', a **blessingway** song is sung over the mother to ensure an easy birth and protect the child and mother from evil spirits. The mother may also be given medicinals, and the women in her family may manipulate her abdomen to aid in the birth. After birth and bathing, the baby is sprinkled with white and yellow corn pollen, and the women of the mother's family will gently press the baby's body to ensure good health.

It is a sad fact that not all children who are born survive. Factors like malnutrition, diseases, and poor water supplies can all affect the survival rates of infants. In non-industrial societies, infants who die are generally not given their society's typical burial rituals. Many societies believed the infant's soul enters the body of another newborn, went into an animal or bird, or returned to the spirit world until it could be born again. So while ceremonies may be done at birth, a child is often not considered a person or given a name until she or he has lived for a time. Such rituals are **personhood** rituals, as they incorporate the child into his or her society. Among the Tewa Pueblo, for example, children are incorporated into their moiety and given a moiety-specific name during the **water-giving** ritual when they are eight days old. The Zunis believe a newborn child is **soft** or not yet ripened, so it is kept in the house away from the sun for eight days after birth. Before dawn on the eighth day the child's umbilical cord is buried, connecting the child to Mother Earth and the underworld from which its ancestors emerged. The baby is washed, put in its cradleboard, and cornmeal is put in its hands. Its paternal grandmother will carry the baby outside, facing the rising sun. The baby usually does not receive a name then. Its family will wait until the baby has **hardened** and are confident the child will survive (Bonvillain 2001).

Among the most important rituals for any individual are **coming of age rituals.** Adolescence (teen years), when one is not a child but not yet an adult, is the invention of industrial societies in which young people are not suppose to engage in adult behaviors and are not supposed to be engaged in wage-labor, but instead go to school. In non-industrial societies, individuals are considered either children or adults. Even children may engage in labor that provides resources for their families and communities. Coming of age rituals mark the transition from childhood to adulthood. The vision quest is an example of a coming of age ritual for young men. Often, for the first time, they must go into the woods, mountains, or desert by themselves, fast, and try to stay awake until they receive a vision. Killing an animal for food or fighting an enemy may also be part of a young man's coming of age ritual. The young man's family will hold a feast and often give-aways, in which goods and resources are given away, to mark his transition to adulthood.

Young women also go through coming of age rituals, usually when they start menstruating. Among the most elaborate is the **kinaalda**, girl's puberty rite, of the Dine'. The kinaalda is a four-day ceremony. At dawn and noon on each day, the young woman, accompanied by friends and family members, races to the east to build up her strength and endurance. A respected older woman will knead her body (as newborn babies are kneaded) to mold her to also become a respected woman. The young woman and her family prepare large amounts of food, particularly corn, to be part of a community feast held on the fourth day. On this day the young woman washes, and then her face is painted with white lines. She then distributes food to all the guests (Schwarz 1997).

Coming of age rituals have several purposes. They show that young men and women have acquired the skills and knowledge needed for adulthood. They mark the transition from childhood to adulthood in front of the entire community. Historically, after a coming of age ritual, newly anointed men and women are able to marry. Thus, like many religious beliefs and rituals, it functions on the individual and societal level.

In historical Native American societies, marriage ceremonies were not as elaborate as those of contemporary U.S. and Canadian societies. The ceremony would often consist of the exchange of gifts between the bride and groom and their families and a feast. Of more importance were death or funeral rituals. Like birth and adulthood, death is a transition, so anthropologists often call rituals that mark them **rites of passage**. For many Native American societies, birth is the transition from the spirit world; death is a transition back to the spirit world. Death rituals may be started before the individual dies to help in this transition. Among the Dine', for example, a **night way** ceremony may be held to help prepare the individual and his/her family for the death. The Dine' have a great fear of ghosts; so much of the behavior at the funeral ritual is to ensure the ghost of the dead does not stay around kin members. The body is carefully washed and dressed by kin members, but the left moccasin is put on the right foot and the right moccasin is put on the left foot, to make it difficult for the ghost to walk. If the person dies at home, the body is carried out through a hole cut into the wall so as to not contaminate the usual paths of the living. If the deceased dies in a **hogan**, the traditional house-structure of the Dine', the hogan is abandoned or burnt down. The body is transported in silence to a remote spot. Burial typically takes place in the ground, or a rock niche that is then sealed. The mourners return by a different path, go through a purification ceremony, and never speak the name of the deceased. These observances help to ensure that the ghost of the deceased does not follow or return to haunt family members (Bonvillain 2001). The Dine' believe the deceased must become part of nature or the cosmos, "as a drop of water is part of a rain cloud."

Unlike the Dine', the Lakota have a ritual to keep the spirit of the beloved family member close, at least a period of time. Called the **Ghost Bundle** ritual, the belongings, cloths, hair, tools, or ornaments of the deceased are kept in a bundle. The keeping of a Ghost Bundle requires a great commitment on the part of the family. A woman of the family is required to always be with the Ghost Bundle. When the Lakota were on the plains and living in teepees, the Ghost Bundle was the first item to be removed, and held by the woman in charge of it when the community moved. She then carried it to the new living site. The first thing to go into the teepee when it was re-erected was the Ghost Bundle. After the end of a year the bundle is opened, the spirit or ghost released to the spirit world, and the items distributed to family members (Deloria 1988). A give-away usually occurs during the opening of the bundle, so the family must also have economic resources to conduct this ritual. The time and resources required for keeping a Ghost Bundle all serve to prohibit families from holding such a ceremony for all deceased family members, only their most honored members, such as grandparents.

Missionaries and government agents all strove to convert Native American societies to Christianity, or to at least to stop them from practicing their own religious traditions. In the United States, from the 1880s until John Collier's administration of the Bureau of Indian Affairs in the 1930s, Native American religious practices were openly prohibited. It was not until 1978 that The American Indian Religious Freedom Act, which guaranteed the rights of American Indians to practice their religions, was passed by the U. S. government. The act was amended in 1993 and 1994, largely to protect the right of Native Americans, particularly those who are members of the **American Indian Church** to use **peyote** as part of their rituals. Peyote is a hallucinogenic cactus found in the Southwest. The **Huichol** people of northern Mexico have used peyote for thousands of years to attain a trance state to commune with **Brother Deer**, the creator-spirit of the Huichol. Members of the American Indian Church also use peyote to attain a trance state. In 1999 the Religious Freedom Act was further amended to allow Native American prisoners the right to have their own religious rituals while in jail.

The American Indian Church is a part of the **Pan-Indian Movement** in the United States. Because of population loss, the loss or removal from traditional lands, and the boarding school experience, many Native peoples have lost parts of their culture, such as language and religious rituals. When Native peoples from across Canada and the United States would meet through boarding schools, the military, and college, they would practice what they remembered of their rituals and combine them with those from other Native peoples they encountered who might have very different practices. For instance, not all Native peoples partook in **sweat baths**, the practice of enduring a very hot steam bath for an extended period of time for both physical and spiritual cleansing. Sweat baths, like pow-wows, are practices that have been adopted by many Native American groups throughout North America and are part of the American Indian Church. Through a process called **syncretism,** the amalgamation or combining of religions or cultures, practices of the American Indian Church may also include Christian beliefs. Some people who have taken peyote as part of rituals in the American Indian Church say they see Jesus Christ while in a trance.

Christian missionaries of all denominations liked to think they were successfully converting Native Americans to their churches. But in many instances the traditional religions went "underground," and were practiced secretly in isolated spots. In other instances, Native American religious traditions were combined with Christian traditions, as in the American Indian Church. The Christian celebration of Christmas is an example of syncretism. We have no idea when Jesus Christ was born; but Christians celebrate it on December 25 because that date coincides with the Roman holiday of Saturnia, a winter solstice ceremony in which gifts are exchanged. Many attributes of Christmas, such as lights, trees, and mistletoe are northern European traditions also associated with the winter solstice. As Christianity spread throughout Europe, its leaders found it was often better to incorporate these **pagan** (which simply means "of or from the country") traditions into their own, rather than try to eliminate them. The same process of syncretism happened in Native American societies.

In the Southwest, pueblos where churches were built with Native slave labor are found the Stations of Cross, statues or paintings that depict events from the crucifixion of Christ. In the Pueblo churches, in front of each station is a small pot or bowl that contains the corn pollen that is essential to all Pueblo rituals. In front of grave markers and crosses there are small bowls containing corn pollen. So while the Puebloan peoples may attend the Catholic churches, it contains elements of the pre-Christian Pueblo traditions. In the Northeast, at the St. Regis Catholic Church at the Akwesase, Mohawk church hymns are often sung in Mohawk, and sweet grass is burnt during Mass instead of incense.

These are just a few examples of the syncretism found in many Native American communities. People might attend Christian church on Sunday, but they will also attend the cycle of rituals to thank the earth for its plants and animals, and people will still have potlatches or kinaaldas to mark the coming of age of their sons and daughters. People do not randomly adopt new traditions alongside old beliefs. The people of a society will adopt or accept new traditions and beliefs that best fit with their existing beliefs and traditions. The Pueblo peoples of the Southwest used corn pollen as part of religious rituals for thousands of years before the arrival of Christian missionaries, and they still use corn pollen within the Catholic churches. Just as Christians around the world may celebrate Christmas, they celebrate it differently because the Christmas celebrations are combined with the celebrations of previous societies. In the United States and Canada people from all over the world have settled here and brought their traditions with them, which through syncretism have become part of the Christmas traditions practiced here. **(Chapter excerpt ends here.)**

Free Verse

Free verse refers to poetry that does not follow standard or regularized meter (the organization of stressed and unstressed syllables) or rhyme scheme. As opposed to more traditional poetry, which tends to use recurring line lengths, metrical patterns, and rhyme to unify individual lines of verse and tie them to other lines within the same poem, free verse can, at times, seem to be random, having no pattern or organization at all. Yet in the hands of many poets, free verse enables a different kind of organization, as they balance free verse's openness, its ability to provide elements of the poem with a different amount of emphasis, with the use of repeated imagery or syntactic patterns (parallel organization of grammatical elements) to maintain coherence and create a sense of connection among lines. Even as it eschews regular meter and rhyme schemes, free verse does, at times, draw on metrical patterns and occasional rhyme to tie lines together. What distinguishes free verse from other traditional forms of verse is that it only uses these elements occasionally—for a few lines here and there in a longer poem—and does not use them to structure the poem as a whole. A poem in free verse, then, does not lack structure—or, in many cases, some instances of metrical organization or rhyme—it simply does not maintain or use a regular pattern of meter or rhyme to structure the poem as a whole. Instead, free verse relies more on thematic, syntactic, or semantic repetition and development to create coherence.

Walt Whitman's *Leaves of Grass* is often credited as introducing free verse into English-language poetry. While not quite true (other experiments and uses preceded his), Whitman's poetry helped to establish free verse's potential for exploring a broad range of topics and its ability to embrace an extensive number of ways of organizing verse lines. Later-nineteenth-century poets, such as Matthew Arnold in England, further explored the use of free verse, but it was the French symbolists (Jules Laforgue, Gustave Kahn, and Arthur Rimbaud) who practiced what they called vers libre most fully during this period. In the twentieth century, free verse came to dominate much poetic production in English, beginning with the modernists (such as T. S. Eliot, Ezra Pound, and William Carlos Williams) who saw the open form as allowing for the more nimble representation of a modern fragmented and accelerated world.

The Homeric Hymn to Hermes

Available readily online through a search for "Homeric Hymn to Hermes." This version is from: http://www.perseus.tufts.edu/hopper/textdoc=Perseus%3Atext%3A1999.01.0138%3Ahymn%3D4

To Hermes

[1] Muse, sing of Hermes, the son of Zeus and Maia, lord of Cyllene and Arcadia rich in flocks, the luck-bringing messenger of the immortals whom Maia bare, the rich-tressed nymph, when she was joined in love with Zeus, [5] —a shy goddess, for she avoided the company of the blessed gods, and lived within a deep, shady cave. There the son of Cronos used to lie with the rich-tressed nymph, unseen by deathless gods and mortal men, at dead of night while sweet sleep should hold white-armed Hera fast. [10] And when the purpose of great Zeus was fulfilled, and the tenth moon with her was fixed in heaven, she was delivered and a notable thing was come to pass. For then she bare a son, of many shifts, blandly cunning, a robber, a cattle driver, a bringer of dreams, [15] a watcher by night, a thief at the gates, one who was soon to show forth wonderful deeds among the deathless gods. Born with the dawning, at mid-day he played on the lyre, and in the evening he stole the cattle of far-shooting Apollo on the fourth day of the month; for on that day queenly Maia bare him. [20] So soon as he had leaped from his mother's heavenly womb, he lay not long waiting in his holy cradle, but he sprang up and sought the oxen of Apollo. But as he stepped over the threshold of the high-roofed cave, he found a tortoise there and gained endless delight. [25] For it was Hermes who first made the tortoise a singer. The creature fell in his way at the courtyard gate, where it was feeding on the rich grass before the dwelling, waddling along. When he saw it, the luck-bringing son of Zeus laughed and said:[30] "An omen of great luck for me so soon! I do not slight it. Hail, comrade of the feast, lovely in shape, sounding at the dance! With joy I meet you! Where got you that rich gaud for covering, that spangled shell —a tortoise living in the mountains? But I will take and carry you within: you shall help me [35] and I will do you no disgrace, though first of all you must profit me. It is better to be at home: harm may come out of doors. Living, you shall be a spell against mischievous witchcraft[1]; but if you die, then you shall make sweetest song."

Thus speaking, he took up the tortoise in both hands [40] and went back into the house carrying his charming toy. Then he cut off its limbs and scooped out the marrow of the mountain-tortoise with a scoop of grey iron. As a swift thought darts through the heart of a man when thronging cares haunt him, [45] or as bright glances flash from the eye, so glorious Hermes planned both thought and deed at once. He cut stalks of reed to measure and fixed them, fastening their ends across the back and through the shell of the tortoise, and then stretched ox hide all over it by his skill. [50] Also he put in the horns and fitted a cross-piece upon the two of them, and stretched seven strings of sheep-gut. But when he had made it he proved each string in turn with the key, as he held the lovely thing. [55] At the touch of his hand it sounded marvelously; and, as he tried it, the god sang sweet random snatches, even as youths bandy taunts at festivals. He sang of Zeus the son of Cronos and neat-shod Maia, the converse which they had before in the comradeship of love, telling all the glorious tale of his own begetting. [60] He celebrated, too, the handmaids of the nymph, and her bright home, and the tripods all about the house, and the abundant cauldrons.

But while he was singing of all these, his heart was bent on other matters. And he took the hollow lyre and laid it in his sacred cradle, [65] and sprang from the sweet-smelling hall to a watch-place, pondering sheer trickery in his heart —deeds such as knavish folk pursue in the dark night-time; for he longed to taste flesh.

The Sun was going down beneath the earth towards Ocean with his horses and chariot when Hermes [70] came hurrying to the shadowy mountains of Pieria, where the divine cattle of the blessed gods had their steads and grazed the pleasant, unmown meadows. Of these the Son of Maia, the sharp-eyed slayer of Argus then cut off from the herd fifty loud-lowing kine, [75] and drove them straggling-wise across a sandy place, turning their hoof-prints aside. Also, he bethought him of a crafty ruse and reversed the marks of their hoofs, making the front behind and the hind before, while he himself walked the other way.[2] Then he wove sandals with wicker-work by the sand of the sea, [80] wonderful things, unthought of, unimagined; for he mixed together tamarisk and myrtle-twigs, fastening together an armful of their fresh, young wood, and tied them, leaves and all securely under his feet as light sandals. That brushwood the glorious Slayer of Argus [85] plucked in Pieria as he was preparing for his journey, making shift[3] as one making haste for a long journey.

But an old man tilling his flowering vineyard saw him as he was hurrying down the plain through grassy Onchestus. So the Son of Maia began and said to him:

[90] "Old man, digging about your vines with bowed shoulders, surely you shall have much wine when all these bear fruit, [91a] if you obey me and strictly remember not to have seen what you have seen, and not to have heard what you have heard, and to keep silent when nothing of your own is harmed."

When he had said this much, he hurried the strong cattle on together: [95] through many shadowy mountains and echoing gorges and flowery plains glorious Hermes drove them. And now the divine night, his dark ally, was mostly passed, and dawn that sets folk to work was quickly coming on, while bright Selene, [100] daughter of the lord Pallas, Megamedes' son, had just climbed her watch-post, when the strong Son of Zeus drove the wide-browed cattle of Phoebus Apollo to the river Alpheus. And they came unwearied to the high-roofed byres and the drinking-troughs that were before the noble meadow. [105] Then, after he had well-fed the loud-bellowing cattle with fodder and driven them into the byre, close-packed and chewing lotus and dewy galingal, he gathered a pile of wood and began to seek the art of fire. He chose a stout laurel branch and trimmed it with the knife ...

[4] [110] held firmly in his hand: and the hot smoke rose up. For it was Hermes who first invented fire-sticks and fire. Next he took many dried sticks and piled them thick and plenty in a sunken trench: and flame began to glow, spreading afar the blast of fierce-burning fire.

[115] And while the strength of glorious Hephaestus was beginning to kindle the fire, he dragged out two lowing, horned cows close to the fire; for great strength was with him. He threw them both panting upon their backs on the ground, and rolled them on their sides, bending their necks over,[5] and pierced their vital chord. [120] Then he went on from task to task: first he cut up the rich, fatted meat, and pierced it with wooden spits, and roasted flesh and the honorable chine and the paunch full of dark blood all together. He laid them there upon the ground, and spread out the hides on a rugged rock: [125] and so they are still there many ages afterwards, a long, long time after all this, and are continually[6]. Next glad-hearted Hermes dragged the rich meats he had prepared and put them on a smooth, flat stone, and divided them into twelve portions distributed by lot, making each portion wholly honorable. [130] Then glorious Hermes longed for the sacrificial meat, for the sweet savour wearied him, god though he was; nevertheless his proud heart was not prevailed upon to devour the flesh, although he greatly desired.[7] But he put away in the high-roofed byre [135] the fat and all the flesh, placing them high up to be a token of his youthful theft. And after that he gathered dry sticks and utterly destroyed with fire all the hoofs and all the heads.

And when the god had duly finished all, he threw his sandals into deep-eddying Alpheus, [140] and quenched the embers, covering the black ashes with sand, and so spent the night while Selene's soft light shone down. Then the god went straight back again at dawn to the bright crests of Cyllene, and no one met him on the long journey either of the blessed gods or mortal men, [145] nor did any dog bark. And luck-bringing Hermes, the son of Zeus, passed edgeways through the key-hole of the hall like the autumn breeze, even as mist: straight through the cave he went and came to the rich inner chamber, walking softly, and making no noise as one might upon the floor. [150] Then glorious Hermes went hurriedly to his cradle, wrapping his swaddling clothes about his shoulders as though he were a feeble babe, and lay playing with the covering about his knees; but at his left hand he kept close his sweet lyre.

But the god did not pass unseen by the goddess his mother; but she said to him: [155] "How now, you rogue! Whence come you back so at night-time, you that wear shamelessness as a garment? And now I surely believe the son of Leto will soon have you forth out of doors with unbreakable cords about your ribs, or you will live a rogue's life in the glens robbing by whiles. [160] Go to, then; your father got you to be a great worry to mortal men and deathless gods."

Then Hermes answered her with crafty words: "Mother, why do you seek to frighten me like a feeble child whose heart knows few words of blame, [165] a fearful babe that fears its mother's scolding? Nay, but I will try whatever plan is best, and so feed myself and you continually. We will not be content to remain here, as you bid, alone of all the gods unfee'd with offerings and prayers. [170] Better to live in fellowship with the deathless gods continually, rich, wealthy, and enjoying stores of grain, than to sit always in a gloomy cave: and, as regards honor, I too will enter upon the rite that Apollo has. If my father will not give it me, [175] I will seek —and I am able —to be a prince of robbers. And if Leto's most glorious son shall seek me out, I think another and a greater loss will befall him. For I will go to Pytho to break into his great house, and will plunder therefrom splendid tripods, and cauldrons, [180] and gold, and plenty of bright iron, and much apparel; and you shall see it if you will."

With such words they spoke together, the son of Zeus who holds the aegis, and the lady Maia. Now Eos the early born, bringing light to men, [185] was rising from deep-flowing Ocean, when Apollo, as he went, came to Onchestus, the lovely grove and sacred place of the loud-roaring Holder of the Earth. There he found an old man grazing his beast along the pathway from his court-yard fence, and the all-glorious Son of Leto began and said to him.

[190] "Old man, weeder[8] of grassy Onchestus, I am come here from Pieria seeking cattle, cows all of them, all with curving horns, from my herd. The black bull was grazing alone away from the rest, but fierce-eyed hounds followed the cows, [195] four of them, all of one mind, like men. These were left behind, the dogs and the bull —which is a great marvel; but the cows strayed out of the soft meadow, away from the pasture when the sun was just going down. Now tell me this, old man born long ago: have you seen [200] one passing along behind those cows?"

Then the old man answered him and said: "My son, it is hard to tell all that one's eyes see; for many wayfarers pass to and fro this way, some bent on much evil, and some on good: [205] it is difficult to know each one. However, I was digging about my plot of vineyard all day long until the sun went down, and I thought, good sir, but I do not know for certain, that I marked a child, whoever the child was, that followed long-horned cattle— [210] an infant who had a staff and kept walking from side to side: he was driving them backwards way, with their heads towards him."

So said the old man. And when Apollo heard this report, he went yet more quickly on his way, and presently, seeing a long-winged bird, he knew at once by that omen that the thief was the child of Zeus the son of Cronos. [215] So the lord Apollo, son of Zeus, hurried on to goodly Pylos seeking his shambling oxen, and he had his broad shoulders covered with a dark cloud. But when the Far-Shooter perceived the tracks, he cried:

"Oh, oh! Truly this is a great marvel that my eyes behold! [220] These are indeed the tracks of straight-horned oxen, but they are turned backwards towards the flowery meadow. But these others are not the footprints of man or woman or grey wolves or bears or lions, nor do I think they are the tracks of a rough-maned Centaur — [225] whoever it be that with swift feet makes such monstrous footprints; wonderful are the tracks on this side of the way, but yet more wonderful are those on that."

When he had so said, the lord Apollo, the Son of Zeus hastened on and came to the forest-clad mountain of Cyllene and the deep-shadowed cave in the rock where the divine nymph [230] brought forth the child of Zeus who is the son of Cronos. A sweet odor spread over the lovely hill, and many thin-shanked sheep were grazing on the grass. Then far-shooting Apollo himself stepped down in haste over the stone threshold into the dusky cave.

[235] Now when the Son of Zeus and Maia saw Apollo in a rage about his cattle, he snuggled down in his fragrant swaddling-clothes; and as wood-ash covers over the deep embers of tree-stumps, so Hermes cuddled himself up when he saw the Far-Shooter. [240] He squeezed head and hands and feet together in a small space, like a new born child seeking sweet sleep, though in truth he was wide awake, and he kept his lyre under his armpit. But the Son of Leto was aware and failed not to perceive the beautiful mountain-nymph and her dear son, [245] albeit a little child and swathed so craftily. He peered in every corner of the great dwelling and, taking a bright key, he opened three closets full of nectar and lovely ambrosia. And much gold and silver was stored in them, [250] and many garments of the nymph, some purple and some silvery white, such as are kept in the sacred houses of the blessed gods. Then, after the Son of Leto had searched out the recesses of the great house, he spake to glorious Hermes:

"Child, lying in the cradle, make haste and tell me of my cattle, [255] or we two will soon fall out angrily. For I will take and cast you into dusky Tartarus and awful hopeless darkness, and neither your mother nor your father shall free you or bring you up again to the light, but you will wander under the earth and be the leader amongst little folk."[9]

[260] Then Hermes answered him with crafty words: "Son of Leto, what harsh words are these you have spoken? And is it cattle of the field you are come here to seek? I have not seen them: I have not heard of them: no one has told me of them. I cannot give news of them, nor win the reward for news. [265] Am I like a cattle-lifter, a stalwart person? This is no task for me: rather I care for other things: I care for sleep, and milk of my mother's breast, and wrappings round my shoulders, and warm baths. Let no one hear the cause of this dispute; [270] for this would be a great marvel indeed among the deathless gods, that a child newly born should pass in through the forepart of the house with cattle of the field: herein you speak extravagantly. I was born yesterday, and my feet are soft and the ground beneath is rough; nevertheless, if you will have it so, I will swear a great oath by my father's head and vow that [275] neither am I guilty myself, neither have I seen any other who stole your cows —whatever cows may be; for I know them only by hearsay."

So, then, said Hermes, shooting quick glances from his eyes: and he kept raising his brows and looking this way and that, [280] whistling long and listening to Apollo's story as to an idle tale.

But far-working Apollo laughed softly and said to him: "O rogue, deceiver, crafty in heart, you talk so innocently that I most surely believe that you have broken into many a well-built house and stripped more than one poor wretch bare this night, [285] [10] gathering his goods together all over the house without noise. You will plague many a lonely herdsman in mountain glades, when you come on herds and thick-fleeced sheep, and have a hankering after flesh. But come now, if you would not sleep your last and latest sleep, [290] get out of your cradle, you comrade of dark night. Surely hereafter this shall be your title amongst the deathless gods, to be called the prince of robbers continually."

So said Phoebus Apollo, and took the child and began to carry him. But at that moment the strong Slayer of Argus [295] had his plan, and, while Apollo held him in his hands, sent forth an omen, a hard-worked belly-serf, a rude messenger, and sneezed directly after. And when Apollo heard it, he dropped glorious Hermes out of his hands on the ground: [300] then sitting down before him, though he was eager to go on his way, he spoke mockingly to Hermes:

"Fear not, little swaddling baby, son of Zeus and Maia. I shall find the strong cattle presently by these omens, and you shall lead the way."

When Apollo had so said, Cyllenian Hermes sprang up quickly, [305] starting in haste. With both hands he pushed up to his ears the covering that he had wrapped about his shoulders, and said:

"Where are you carrying me, Far-Worker, hastiest of all the gods? Is it because of your cattle that you are so angry and harass me? O dear, would that all the sort of oxen might perish; for it is not I [310] who stole your cows, nor did I see another steal them —whatever cows may be, and of that I have only heard report. Nay, give right and take it before Zeus, the Son of Cronos."

So Hermes the shepherd and Leto's glorious son [315] kept stubbornly disputing each article of their quarrel: Apollo, speaking truly …

not unfairly sought to seize glorious Hermes because of the cows; but he, the Cyllenian, tried to deceive the God of the Silver Bow with tricks and cunning words. But when, though he had many wiles, he found the other had as many shifts, [320] he began to walk across the sand, himself in front, while the Son of Zeus and Leto came behind. Soon they came, these lovely children of Zeus, to the top of fragrant Olympus, to their father, the Son of Cronos; for there were the scales of judgement set for them both. [325] There was an assembly on snowy Olympus, and the immortals who perish not were gathering after the hour of gold-throned Dawn.

Then Hermes and Apollo of the Silver Bow stood at the knees of Zeus: and Zeus who thunders on high spoke to his glorious son and asked him:

[330] "Phoebus, whence come you driving this great spoil, a child new born that has the look of a herald? This is a weighty matter that is come before the council of the gods."

Then the lord, far-working Apollo, answered him: "O my father, you shall soon hear no trifling tale though you reproach me [335] that I alone am fond of spoil. Here is a child, a burgling robber, whom I found after a long journey in the hills of Cyllene: for my part I have never seen one so pert either among the gods or all men that catch folk unawares throughout the world. [340] He stole away my cows from their meadow and drove them off in the evening along the shore of the loud-roaring sea, making straight for Pylos. There were double tracks, and wonderful they were, such as one might marvel at, the doing of a clever sprite; for as for the cows, the dark dust kept and showed their footprints leading towards the flowery meadow; [345] but he himself —bewildering creature —crossed the sandy ground outside the path, not on his feet nor yet on his hands; but, furnished with some other means he trudged his way —wonder of wonders! —as though one walked on slender oak-trees. [350] Now while he followed the cattle across sandy ground, all the tracks showed quite clearly in the dust; but when he had finished the long way across the sand, presently the cows' track and his own could not be traced over the hard ground. But a mortal man noticed him [355] as he drove the wide-browed kine straight towards Pylos. And as soon as he had shut them up quietly, and had gone home by crafty turns and twists, he lay down in his cradle in the gloom of a dim cave, as still as dark night, so that not even [360] an eagle keenly gazing would have spied him. Much he rubbed his eyes with his hands as he prepared falsehood, and himself straightway said roundly: `I have not seen them: I have not heard of them: no man has told me of them. I could not tell you of them, nor win the reward of telling.'"

[365] When he had so spoken, Phoebus Apollo sat down. But Hermes on his part answered and said, pointing at the Son of Cronos, the lord of all the gods:

"Zeus, my father, indeed I will speak truth to you; for I am truthful and I cannot tell a lie. [370] He came to our house to-day looking for his shambling cows, as the sun was newly rising. He brought no witnesses with him nor any of the blessed gods who had seen the theft, but with great violence ordered me to confess, threatening much to throw me into wide Tartarus. [375] For he has the rich bloom of glorious youth, while I was born but yesterday —as he too knows —, nor am I like a cattle-lifter, a sturdy fellow. Believe my tale (for you claim to be my own father), that I did not drive his cows to my house —so may I prosper— [380] nor crossed the threshold: this I say truly. I reverence Helios greatly and the other gods, and you I love and him I dread. You yourself know that I am not guilty: and I will swear a great oath upon it:—No! by these rich-decked porticoes of the gods. [385] And some day I will punish him, strong as he is, for this pitiless inquisition; but now do you help the younger."

So spake the Cyllenian, the Slayer of Argus, while he kept shooting sidelong glances and kept his swaddling-clothes upon his arm, and did not cast them away. But Zeus laughed out loud to see his evil-plotting child [390] well and cunningly denying guilt about the cattle. And he bade them both to be of one mind and search for the cattle, and guiding Hermes to lead the way and, without mischievousness of heart, to show the place where now he had hidden the strong cattle. [395] Then the Son of Cronos bowed his head: and goodly Hermes obeyed him; for the will of Zeus who holds the aegis easily prevailed with him.

Then the two all-glorious children of Zeus hastened both to sandy Pylos, and reached the ford of Alpheus, and came to the fields and the high-roofed byre [400] where the beasts were cherished at night-time. Now while Hermes went to the cave in the rock and began to drive out the strong cattle, the son of Leto, looking aside, saw the cowhides on the sheer rock. And he asked glorious Hermes at once:

[405] "How were you able, you crafty rogue, to flay two cows, new-born and babyish as you are? For my part, I dread the strength that will be yours: there is no need you should keep growing long, Cyllenian, son of Maia!"

So saying, Apollo twisted strong withes with his hands [409a] meaning to bind Hermes with firm bands; [409b] but the bands would not hold him, and the withes of osier fell far from him [410] and began to grow at once from the ground beneath their feet in that very place. And intertwining with one another, they quickly grew and covered all the wild-roving cattle by the will of thievish Hermes, so that Apollo was astonished as he gazed.

Then the strong slayer of Argus [415] looked furtively upon the ground with eyes flashing fire ...

desiring to hide ...

Very easily he softened the son of all-glorious Leto as he would, stern though the Far-shooter was. He took the lyre upon his left arm and tried each string in turn with the key, so that at his touch [420] it sounded awesomely. And Phoebus Apollo laughed for joy; for the sweet throb of the marvellous music went to his heart, and a soft longing took hold on his soul as he listened. Then the son of Maia, harping sweetly upon his lyre, took courage and stood at the left hand [425] of Phoebus Apollo; and soon, while he played shrilly on his lyre, he lifted up his voice and sang, and lovely was the sound of his voice that followed. He sang the story of the deathless gods and of the dark earth, how at the first they came to be, and how each one received his portion. First among the gods he honored Mnemosyne, [430] mother of the Muses, in his song; for the son of Maia was of her following. And next the goodly son of Zeus hymned the rest of the immortals according to their order in age, and told how each was born, mentioning all in order as he struck the lyre upon his arm. But Apollo was seized with a longing not to be allayed, [435] and he opened his mouth and spoke winged words to Hermes:

"Slayer of oxen, trickster, busy one, comrade of the feast, this song of yours is worth fifty cows, and I believe that presently we shall settle our quarrel peacefully. But come now, tell me this, resourceful son of Maia: [440] has this marvellous thing been with you from your birth, or did some god or mortal man give it you —a noble gift —and teach you heavenly song? For wonderful is this new-uttered sound I hear, the like of which I vow that no man [445] nor god dwelling on Olympus ever yet has known but you,O thievish son of Maia. What skill is this? What song for desperate cares? What way of song? For verily here are three things to hand all at once from which to choose, —mirth, and love, and sweet sleep. [450] And though I am a follower of the Olympian Muses who love dances and the bright path of song —the full-toned chant and ravishing thrill of flutes —yet I never cared for any of those feats of skill at young men's revels, as I do now for this: [455] I am filled with wonder, O son of Zeus, at your sweet playing. But now, since you, though little, have such glorious skill, sit down, dear boy, and respect the words of your elders For now you shall have renown among the deathless gods, you and your mother also. This I will declare to you exactly: [460] by this shaft of cornel wood I will surely make you a leader renowned among the deathless gods, and fortunate, and will give you glorious gifts and will not deceive you from first to last."

Then Hermes answered him with artful words: "You question me carefully, O Far-worker; yet I am [465] not jealous that you should enter upon my art: this day you shall know it. For I seek to be friendly with you both in thought and word. Now you well know all things in your heart, since you sit foremost among the deathless gods, O son of Zeus, and are goodly and strong. And wise Zeus loves you [470] as all right is, and has given you splendid gifts. And they say that from the utterance of Zeus you have learned both the honors due to the gods, O Far-worker, and oracles from Zeus, even all his ordinances. Of all these I myself have already learned that you have great wealth. Now, you are free to learn whatever you please; [475] but since, as it seems, your heart is so strongly set on playing the lyre, chant, and play upon it, and give yourself to merriment, taking this as a gift from me, and do you, my friend, bestow glory on me. Sing well with this clear-voiced companion in your hands; for you are skilled in good, well-ordered utterance. [480] From now on bring it confidently to the rich feast and lovely dance and glorious revel, a joy by night and by day. Whoso with wit and wisdom enquires of it cunningly, him it teaches [485] through its sound all manner of things that delight the mind, being easily played with gentle familiarities, for it abhors toilsome drudgery; but whoso in ignorance enquires of it violently, to him it chatters mere vanity and foolishness. But you are able to learn whatever you please. [490] So then, I will give you this lyre, glorious son of Zeus, while I for my part will graze down with wild-roving cattle the pastures on hill and horse-feeding plain: so shall the cows covered by the bulls calve abundantly both males and females. And now there is no need for you, [495] bargainer though you are, to be furiously angry."

When Hermes had said this, he held out the lyre: and Phoebus Apollo took it, and readily put his shining whip in Hermes' hand, and ordained him keeper of herds. The son of Maia received it joyfully, [500] while the glorious son of Leto, the lord far-working Apollo, took the lyre upon his left arm and tried each string with the key. Awesomely it sounded at the touch of the god, while he sang sweetly to its note.

Afterwards they two, the all-glorious sons of Zeus turned the cows back towards the sacred meadow, [505] but themselves hastened back to snowy Olympus, delighting in the lyre. Then wise Zeus was glad and made them both friends. And Hermes loved the son of Leto continually, even as he does now, when he had given the lyre as token to the Far-shooter, [510] who played it skilfully, holding it upon his arm. But for himself Hermes found out another cunning art and made himself the pipes whose sound is heard afar.

Then the son of Leto said to Hermes: "Son of Maia, guide and cunning one, I fear [515] you may steal from me the lyre and my curved bow together; for you have an office from Zeus, to establish deeds of barter amongst men throughout the fruitful earth. Now if you would only swear me the great oath of the gods, either by nodding your head, or by the potent water of Styx, [520] you would do all that can please and ease my heart."

Then Maia's son nodded his head and promised that he would never steal anything of all the Far-shooter possessed, and would never go near his strong house; but Apollo, son of Leto, swore to be fellow and friend to Hermes, [525] vowing that he would love no other among the immortals, neither god nor man sprung from Zeus, better than Hermes: [526a] and the Father sent forth an eagle in confirmation. And Apollo swear also: "Verily I will make you only to be an omen for the immortals and all alike, trusted and honored by my heart. Moreover, I will give you a splendid staff of riches and wealth: [530] it is of gold, with three branches, and will keep you scatheless, accomplishing every task, whether of words or deeds that are good, which I claim to know through the utterance of Zeus. But as for sooth-saying, noble, heaven-born child, of which you ask, it is not lawful for you to learn it, nor for any other [535] of the deathless gods: only the mind of Zeus knows that. I am pledged and have vowed and sworn a strong oath that no other of the eternal gods save I should know the wise-hearted counsel of Zeus. And do not you, my brother, bearer of the golden wand, bid me [540] tell those decrees which all-seeing Zeus intends. As for men, I will harm one and profit another, sorely perplexing the tribes of unenviable men. Whosoever shall come guided by the call and flight of birds of sure omen, [545] that man shall have advantage through my voice, and I will not deceive him. But whoso shall trust to idly-chattering birds and shall seek to invoke my prophetic art contrary to my will, and to understand more than the eternal gods, I declare that he shall come on an idle journey; yet his gifts I would take.

[550] But I will tell you another thing, Son of all-glorious Maia and Zeus who holds the aegis, luck-bringing genius of the gods. There are certain holy ones, sisters born —three virgins[11] gifted with wings: their heads are besprinkled with white meal, [555] and they dwell under a ridge of Parnassus. These are teachers of divination apart from me, the art which I practised while yet a boy following herds, though my father paid no heed to it. From their home they fly now here, now there, feeding on honey-comb and bringing all things to pass. [560] And when they are inspired through eating yellow honey, they are willing to speak truth; but if they be deprived of the gods' sweet food, then they speak falsely, as they swarm in and out together. These, then, I give you; enquire of them strictly [565] and delight your heart: and if you should teach any mortal so to do, often will he hear your response —if he have good fortune. Take these, Son of Maia, and tend the wild roving, horned oxen and horses and patient mules."

[568a] So he spake. And from heaven father Zeus himself gave confirmation to his words, [568b] and commanded that glorious Hermes should be lord over all birds of omen and grim-eyed lions, and boars with gleaming tusks, [570] and over dogs and all flocks that the wide earth nourishes, and over all sheep; also that he only should be the appointed messenger to Hades, who, though he takes no gift, shall give him no mean prize.

Thus the lord Apollo showed his kindness for the Son of Maia [575] by all manner of friendship: and the Son of Cronos gave him grace besides. He consorts with all mortals and immortals: a little he profits, but continually throughout the dark night he cozens the tribes of mortal men.

And so, farewell, Son of Zeus and Maia; [580] but I will remember you and another song also.

1 Pliny notices the efficacy of the flesh of a tortoise against witchcraft. In Geoponica i. 14. 8 the living tortoise is prescribed as a charm to preserve vineyards from hail.

2 Hermes makes the cattle walk backwards way, so that they seem to be going towards the meadow instead of leaving it (cp. 1. 345) ; he himself walks in the normal manner, relying on his sandals as a disguise.

3 Such seems to be the meaning indicated by the context, though the verb is taken by Allen and Sikes to mean, "to be like oneself," and so "to be original."

4 Kuhn points out that there is a lacuna here. In 1. 109 the borer is described, but the friction of this upon the fire-block (to which the phrase "held firmly" clearly belongs) must also have been mentioned.

5 The cows being on their sides on the ground, Hermes bends their heads back towards their flanks and so can reach their backbones.

6 O. Muller thinks the "hides" were a stalactite formation in the "Cave of Nestor" near Messenian Pylos, —though the cave of Hermes is near the Alpheus (1. 139) . Others suggest that actual skins were shown as relics before some cave near Triphylian Pylos.

7 Gemoll explains that Hermes, having offered all the meat as sacrifice to the Twelve Gods, remembers that he himself as one of them must be content with the savour instead of the substance of the sacrifice. Can it be that by eating he would have forfeited the position he claimed as one of the Twelve Gods?

8 *Lit.* "thorn-plucker."

9 Hermes is ambitious (1.175) , but if he is cast into Hades he will have to be content with the leadership of mere babies like himself, since those in Hades retain the state of growth —whether childhood or manhood —in which they are at the moment of leaving the upper world.

10 Literally, "you have made him sit on the floor," i.e. "you have stolen everything down to his last chair."

11 The Thriae, who practised divination by means of pebbles (also calledθριαί) . In this hymn they are represented as aged maidens (ll. 553-4) , but are closely associated with bees (ll. 559-563) and possibly are here conceived as having human heads and breasts with the bodies and wings of bees. See the edition of Allen and Sikes, Appendix III.

Anonymous. The Homeric Hymns and Homerica with an English Translation by Hugh G. Evelyn-White. Homeric Hymns. Cambridge, MA.,Harvard University Press; London, William Heinemann Ltd. 1914.The Annenberg CPB/Project provided support for entering this text.

Anne Bradstreet

The poems of Anne Bradstreet are remarkable for their seeming contemporary. . . with us, that is! The voice is so recognizable and fresh that it undercuts many stereotypes of Puritanism. There is plenty of irony combining with varied tones, so read these linked poems from The Poetry Foundation aloud.

- The Author to Her Book

- Before the Birth of One of Her Children
- By Night when Others Soundly Slept
- Contemplations
- A Dialogue between Old England and New
- The Four Ages of Man
- In Honour of that High and Mighty Princess, Queen Elizabeth
- In Reference to her Children, 23 June 1659
- A Letter to her Husband, absent upon Publick employment
- Prologue
- To Her Father with Some Verses

- To My Dear and Loving Husband

Painting of Anne Bradstreet.

Anne Bradstreet, Verses upon the Burning of Our House

> **Verses upon the Burning of our House** (full title: **Here follow some verses upon the burning of our house, July 10, 1666**) is a poem by Anne Bradstreet. She wrote it to express the traumatic loss of her home and most of her material. However, she expands the understanding that God had taken them away in order for her family to live a more pious life.
>
> The poem has a couplet-based rhyme scheme. It has many lines with an inverted syntax, making lines sound "odd".

In silent night when rest I took,
For sorrow near I did not look,
I waken'd was with thund'ring noise
And piteous shrieks of dreadful voice.
That fearful sound of "Fire" and "Fire," 5
Let no man know is my Desire.
I starting up, the light did spy,
And to my God my heart did cry
To straighten me in my Distress 9
And not to leave me succourless.
Then coming out, behold a space
The flame consume my dwelling place. 12
And when I could no longer look,
I blest his grace that gave and took,
That laid my goods now in the dust. 15
Yea, so it was, and so 'twas just.
It was his own; it was not mine.
Far be it that I should repine,
He might of all justly bereft
But yet sufficient for us left. 20
When by the Ruins oft I past
My sorrowing eyes aside did cast
And here and there the places spy
Where oft I sate and long did lie.
Here stood that Trunk, and there that chest, 25
There lay that store I counted best,
My pleasant things in ashes lie
And them behold no more shall I.
Under the roof no guest shall sit,
Nor at thy Table eat a bit. 30
No pleasant talk shall 'ere be told
Nor things recounted done of old.
No Candle 'ere shall shine in Thee,
Nor bridegroom's voice ere heard shall bee. 34

In silence ever shalt thou lie. 35

Adieu, Adieu, All's Vanity.

Then straight I 'gin my heart to chide:

And did thy wealth on earth abide,

Didst fix thy hope on mouldring dust,

The arm of flesh didst make thy trust? 40

Raise up thy thoughts above the sky

That dunghill mists away may fly.

Thou hast a house on high erect

Fram'd by that mighty Architect,

With glory richly furnished 45

Stands permanent, though this be fled.

It's purchased and paid for too

By him who hath enough to do.

A price so vast as is unknown,

Yet by his gift is made thine own. 50

There's wealth enough; I need no more.

Farewell, my pelf; farewell, my store.

The world no longer let me love;

My hope and Treasure lies above. 54

William Cullen Bryant, Thanatopsis

"Thanatopsis" is a poem by the American poet William Cullen Bryant.

The title comes from the Greek *thanatos* ("death") and *opsis* ("sight"); it has often been translated as "Meditation upon Death." Bryant wrote the bulk of the poem in 1811 at age 17, and it was first published in 1817 by the *North American Review*. He added the introductory and concluding lines 10 years later in 1821.

To him who in the love of Nature holds
Communion with her visible forms, she speaks
A various language; for his gayer hours
She has a voice of gladness, and a smile
And eloquence of beauty, and she glides
Into his darker musings, with a mild
And healing sympathy, that steals away
Their sharpness, ere he is aware. When thoughts
Of the last bitter hour come like a blight
Over thy spirit, and sad images
Of the stern agony, and shroud, and pall,
And breathless darkness, and the narrow house,
Make thee to shudder, and grow sick at heart;—
Go forth, under the open sky, and list
To Nature's teachings, while from all around—
Earth and her waters, and the depths of air—
Comes a still voice—Yet a few days, and thee
The all-beholding sun shall see no more
In all his course; nor yet in the cold ground,
Where thy pale form was laid, with many tears,
Nor in the embrace of ocean, shall exist
Thy image. Earth, that nourished thee, shall claim
Thy growth, to be resolved to earth again,
And, lost each human trace, surrendering up
Thine individual being, shalt thou go
To mix for ever with the elements,
To be a brother to the insensible rock
And to the sluggish clod, which the rude swain
Turns with his share, and treads upon. The oak
Shall send his roots abroad, and pierce thy mould.

Yet not to thine eternal resting-place
Shalt thou retire alone, nor couldst thou wish
Couch more magnificent. Thou shalt lie down
With patriarchs of the infant world—with kings,
The powerful of the earth—the wise, the good,
Fair forms, and hoary seers of ages past,
All in one mighty sepulchre. The hills

Rock-ribbed and ancient as the sun,—the vales
Stretching in pensive quietness between;
The venerable woods—rivers that move
In majesty, and the complaining brooks
That make the meadows green; and, poured round all,
Old Ocean's gray and melancholy waste,—
Are but the solemn decorations all
Of the great tomb of man. The golden sun,
The planets, all the infinite host of heaven,
Are shining on the sad abodes of death,
Through the still lapse of ages. All that tread
The globe are but a handful to the tribes
That slumber in its bosom.—- Take the wings
Of morning, pierce the Barean wilderness,
Or lose thyself in the continuous woods
Where rolls the Oregon, and hears no sound,
Save his own dashings—yet the dead are there:
And millions in those solitudes, since first
The flight of years began, have laid them down
In their last sleep—the dead reign there alone,
So shalt thou rest, and what if thou withdraw
In silence from the living, and no friend
Take note of thy departure? All that breathe
Will share thy destiny. The gay will laugh
When thou art gone, the solemn brood of care
Plod on, and each one as before will chase
His favorite phantom; yet all these shall leave
Their mirth and their employments, and shall come
And make their bed with thee. As the long train
Of ages glide away, the sons of men,
The youth in life's green spring, and he who goes
In the full strength of years, matron and maid,
The speechless babe, and the gray-headed man—
Shall one by one be gathered to thy side,
By those, who in their turn shall follow them.

So live, that when thy summons comes to join
The innumerable caravan, which moves
To that mysterious realm, where each shall take
His chamber in the silent halls of death,
Thou go not, like the quarry-slave at night,
Scourged to his dungeon, but, sustained and soothed
By an unfaltering trust, approach thy grave,
Like one who wraps the drapery of his couch
About him, and lies down to pleasant dreams.

Public domain content

The Raven

"The Raven" is a narrative poem by American writer Edgar Allan Poe. First published in January 1845, the poem is often noted for its musicality, stylized language, and supernatural atmosphere. It tells of a talking raven's mysterious visit to a distraught lover, tracing the man's slow fall into madness. The lover, often identified as being a student, is lamenting the loss of his love, Lenore. Sitting on a bust of Pallas, the raven seems to further instigate his distress with its constant repetition of the word "Nevermore." The poem makes use of a number of folk and classical references.

Poe claimed to have written the poem very logically and methodically, intending to create a poem that would appeal to both critical and popular tastes, as he explained in his 1846 follow-up essay, "The Philosophy of Composition." The poem was inspired in part by a talking raven in the novel *Barnaby Rudge: A Tale of the Riots of 'Eighty* by Charles Dickens. Poe borrows the complex rhythm and meter of Elizabeth Barrett's poem "Lady Geraldine's Courtship," and makes use of internal rhyme as well as alliteration throughout.

Once upon a midnight dreary, while I pondered, weak and weary,
Over many a quaint and curious volume of forgotten lore—
While I nodded, nearly napping, suddenly there came a tapping,
As of some one gently rapping, rapping at my chamber door.
"'Tis some visiter," I muttered, "tapping at my chamber door—
Only this and nothing more."

Ah, distinctly I remember it was in the bleak December,
And each separate dying ember wrought its ghost upon the floor.
Eagerly I wished the morrow;—vainly I had sought to borrow
From my books surcease of sorrow—sorrow for the lost Lenore—
For the rare and radiant maiden whom the angels name Lenore—
Nameless here for evermore.

And the silken sad uncertain rustling of each purple curtain
Thrilled me—filled me with fantastic terrors never felt before;
So that now, to still the beating of my heart, I stood repeating
"'Tis some visiter entreating entrance at my chamber door—
Some late visiter entreating entrance at my chamber door;
This it is and nothing more."

Presently my soul grew stronger; hesitating then no longer,
"Sir," said I, "or Madam, truly your forgiveness I implore;
But the fact is I was napping, and so gently you came rapping,
And so faintly you came tapping, tapping at my chamber door,
That I scarce was sure I heard you"—here I opened wide the door—
Darkness there and nothing more.

Deep into that darkness peering, long I stood there wondering, fearing,
Doubting, dreaming dreams no mortals ever dared to dream before;

But the silence was unbroken, and the stillness gave no token,
And the only word there spoken was the whispered word, "Lenore?"
This I whispered, and an echo murmured back the word, "Lenore!"—
Merely this and nothing more.

Back into the chamber turning, all my soul within me burning,
Soon again I heard a tapping something louder than before.
"Surely," said I, "surely that is something at my window lattice;
Let me see, then, what thereat is and this mystery explore—
Let my heart be still a moment and this mystery explore;—
'Tis the wind and nothing more.

Open here I flung the shutter, when, with many a flirt and flutter,
In there stepped a stately Raven of the saintly days of yore.
Not the least obeisance made he; not a minute stopped or stayed he,
But, with mien of lord or lady, perched above my chamber door—
Perched upon a bust of Pallas just above my chamber door—
Perched, and sat, and nothing more.

Then the ebony bird beguiling my sad fancy into smiling,
By the grave and stern decorum of the countenance it wore,
"Though thy crest be shorn and shaven, thou," I said, "art sure no craven,
Ghastly grim and ancient Raven wandering from the Nightly shore—
Tell me what thy lordly name is on the Night's Plutonian shore!"
Quoth the Raven, "Nevermore."

Much I marvelled this ungainly fowl to hear discourse so plainly,
Though its answer little meaning—little relevancy bore;
For we cannot help agreeing that no living human being
Ever yet was blessed with seeing bird above his chamber door—
Bird or beast upon the sculptured bust above his chamber door,
With such name as "Nevermore."

But the Raven, sitting lonely on that placid bust, spoke only
That one word, as if its soul in that one word he did outpour
Nothing farther then he uttered; not a feather then he fluttered—
Till I scarcely more than muttered: "Other friends have flown before—
On the morrow he will leave me, as my Hopes have flown before."
Then the bird said "Nevermore."

Startled at the stillness broken by reply so aptly spoken,
"Doubtless," said I, "what it utters is its only stock and store,
Caught from some unhappy master whom unmerciful Disaster
Followed fast and followed faster till his songs one burden bore—
Till the dirges of his Hope that melancholy burden bore
Of 'Never—nevermore.'"

But the Raven still beguiling all my sad soul into smiling,
Straight I wheeled a cushioned seat in front of bird and bust and door;
Then, upon the velvet sinking, I betook myself to linking

Fancy unto fancy, thinking what this ominous bird of yore—
What this grim, ungainly, ghastly, gaunt, and ominous bird of yore
Meant in croaking "Nevermore."

This I sat engaged in guessing, but no syllable expressing
To the fowl whose fiery eyes now burned into my bosom's core;
This and more I sat divining, with my head at ease reclining
On the cushion's velvet lining that the lamp-light gloated o'er,
But whose velvet violet lining with the lamp-light gloating o'er
She shall press, ah, nevermore!

Then, methought, the air grew denser, perfumed from an unseen censer
Swung by Seraphim whose foot-falls tinkled on the tufted floor.
"Wretch," I cried, "thy God hath lent thee—by these angels he hath sent thee
Respite—respite and nepenthe from thy memories of Lenore!
Quaff, oh quaff this kind nepenthe and forget this lost Lenore!"
Quoth the Raven, "Nevermore."

"Prophet!" said I, "thing of evil!—prophet still, if bird or devil!—
Whether Tempter sent, or whether tempest tossed thee here ashore,
Desolate, yet all undaunted, on this desert land enchanted—
On this home by Horror haunted—tell me truly, I implore—
Is there—is there balm in Gilead?—tell me—tell me, I implore!"
Quoth the Raven, "Nevermore."

"Prophet!" said I, "thing of evil!—prophet still, if bird or devil!
By that Heaven that bends above us—by that God we both adore—
Tell this soul with sorrow laden if, within the distant Aidenn,
It shall clasp a sainted maiden whom the angels name Lenore—
Clasp a rare and radiant maiden whom the angels name Lenore."
Quoth the Raven, "Nevermore."

"Be that word our sign of parting, bird or fiend!" I shrieked, upstarting—
"Get thee back into the tempest and the Night's Plutonian shore!
Leave no black plume as a token of that lie thy soul has spoken!
Leave my loneliness unbroken!—quit the bust above my door!
Take thy beak from out my heart, and take thy form from off my door!"
Quoth the Raven, "Nevermore."

And the Raven, never flitting, still is sitting, still is sitting
On the pallid bust of Pallas just above my chamber door;
And his eyes have all the seeming of a demon's that is dreaming
And the lamp-light o'er him streaming throws his shadows on the floor;
And my soul from out that shadow that lies floating on the floor
Shall be lifted—nevermore!

7. LITERARY NONFICTION

Nature

"Nature" is an essay written by Ralph Waldo Emerson, and published by James Munroe and Company in 1836. In this essay Emerson put forth the foundation of transcendentalism, a belief system that espouses a non-traditional appreciation of nature. Transcendentalism suggests that the divine, or God, suffuses nature, and suggests that reality can be understood by studying nature. Emerson's visit to the Muséum National d'Histoire Naturelle in Paris inspired a set of lectures he later delivered in Boston which were then published.

Within the essay, Emerson divides nature into four usages: Commodity, Beauty, Language and Discipline. These distinctions define the ways by which humans use nature for their basic needs, their desire for delight, their communication with one another and their understanding of the world. Emerson followed the success of "Nature" with a speech, "The American Scholar," which together with his previous lectures laid the foundation for transcendentalism and his literary career.

Introduction

OUR age is retrospective. It builds the sepulchres of the fathers. It writes biographies, histories, and criticism. The foregoing generations beheld God and nature face to face; we, through their eyes. Why should not we also enjoy an original relation to the universe? Why should not we have a poetry and philosophy of insight and not of tradition, and a religion by revelation to us, and not the history of theirs? Embosomed for a season in nature, whose floods of life stream around and through us, and invite us by the powers they supply, to action proportioned to nature, why should we grope among the dry bones of the past, or put the living generation into masquerade out of its faded wardrobe? The sun shines to-day also. There is more wool and flax in the fields. There are new lands, new men, new thoughts. Let us demand our own works and laws and worship.

Undoubtedly we have no questions to ask which are unanswerable. We must trust the perfection of the creation so far, as to believe that whatever curiosity the order of things has awakened in our minds, the order of things can satisfy. Every man's condition is a solution in hieroglyphic to those inquiries he would put. He acts it as life, before he apprehends it as truth. In like manner, nature is already, in its forms and tendencies, describing its own design. Let us interrogate the great apparition, that shines so peacefully around us. Let us inquire, to what end is nature?

All science has one aim, namely, to find a theory of nature. We have theories of races and of functions, but scarcely yet a remote approach to an idea of creation. We are now so far from the road to truth, that religious teachers dispute and hate each other, and speculative men are esteemed unsound and frivolous. But to a sound judgment, the most abstract truth is the most practical. Whenever a true theory appears, it will be its own evidence. Its test is, that it will explain all phenomena. Now many are thought not only unexplained but inexplicable; as language, sleep, madness, dreams, beasts, sex.

Philosophically considered, the universe is composed of Nature and the Soul. Strictly speaking, therefore, all that is separate from us, all which Philosophy distinguishes as the NOT ME, that is, both nature and art, all other men and my own body, must be ranked under this name, NATURE. In enumerating the values of nature and casting up their sum, I shall use the word in both senses;—in its common and in its philosophical import. In inquiries so general as our present one, the inaccuracy is not material; no confusion of thought will occur. *Nature*, in the common sense, refers to essences unchanged by man; space, the air, the river, the leaf. *Art* is applied to the mixture of his will with the same things, as in a house, a canal, a statue, a picture. But his operations taken together are so insignificant, a little chipping, baking, patching, and washing, that in an impression so grand as that of the world on the human mind, they do not vary the result.

Nature

TO go into solitude, a man needs to retire as much from his chamber as from society. I am not solitary whilst I read and write, though nobody is with me. But if a man would be alone, let him look at the stars. The rays that come from those heavenly worlds, will separate between him and what he touches. One might think the atmosphere was made transparent with this design, to give man, in the heavenly bodies, the perpetual presence of the sublime. Seen in the streets of cities, how great they are! If the stars should appear one night in a thousand years, how would men believe and adore; and preserve for many generations the remembrance of the city of God which had been shown! But every night come out these envoys of beauty, and light the universe with their admonishing smile.

The stars awaken a certain reverence, because though always present, they are inaccessible; but all natural objects make a kindred impression, when the mind is open to their influence. Nature never wears a mean appearance. Neither does the wisest man extort her secret, and lose his curiosity by finding out all her perfection. Nature never became a toy to a wise spirit. The flowers, the animals, the mountains, reflected the wisdom of his best hour, as much as they had delighted the simplicity of his childhood.

When we speak of nature in this manner, we have a distinct but most poetical sense in the mind. We mean the integrity of impression made by manifold natural objects. It is this which distinguishes the stick of timber of the wood-cutter, from the tree of the poet. The charming landscape which I saw this morning, is indubitably made up of some twenty or thirty farms. Miller owns this field, Locke that, and Manning the woodland beyond. But none of them owns the landscape. There is a property in the horizon which no man has but he whose eye can integrate all the parts, that is, the poet. This is the best part of these men's farms, yet to this their warranty-deeds give no title.

To speak truly, few adult persons can see nature. Most persons do not see the sun. At least they have a very superficial seeing. The sun illuminates only the eye of the man, but shines into the eye and the heart of the child. The lover of nature is he whose inward and outward senses are still truly adjusted to each other; who has retained the spirit of infancy even into the era of manhood. His intercourse with heaven and earth, becomes part of his daily food. In the presence of nature, a wild delight runs through the man, in spite of real sorrows. Nature says,—he is my creature, and maugre all his impertinent griefs, he shall be glad with me. Not the sun or the summer alone, but every hour and season yields its tribute of delight; for every hour and change corresponds to and authorizes a different state of the mind, from breathless noon to grimmest midnight. Nature is a setting that fits equally well a comic or a mourning piece. In good health, the air is a cordial of incredible virtue. Crossing a bare common, in snow puddles, at twilight, under a clouded sky, without having in my thoughts any occurrence of special good fortune, I have enjoyed a perfect exhilaration. I am glad to the brink of fear. In the woods too, a man casts off his years, as the snake his slough, and at what period soever of life, is always a child. In the woods, is perpetual youth. Within these plantations of God, a decorum and sanctity reign, a perennial festival is dressed, and the guest sees not how he should tire of them in a thousand years. In the woods, we return to reason and faith. There I feel that nothing can befall me in life,—no disgrace, no calamity, (leaving me my eyes,) which nature cannot repair. Standing on the bare ground,—my head bathed by the blithe air, and uplifted into infinite space,—all mean egotism vanishes. I become a transparent eye-ball; I am nothing; I see all; the currents of the Universal Being circulate through me; I am part or particle of God. The name of the nearest friend sounds then foreign and accidental: to be brothers, to be acquaintances,—master or servant, is then a trifle and a disturbance. I am the lover of uncontained and immortal beauty. In the wilderness, I find something more dear and connate than in streets or villages. In the tranquil landscape, and especially in the distant line of the horizon, man beholds somewhat as beautiful as his own nature.

The greatest delight which the fields and woods minister, is the suggestion of an occult relation between man and the vegetable. I am not alone and unacknowledged. They nod to me, and I to them. The waving of the boughs in the storm, is new to me and old. It takes me by surprise, and yet is not unknown. Its effect is like that of a higher thought or a better emotion coming over me, when I deemed I was thinking justly or doing right.

Yet it is certain that the power to produce this delight, does not reside in nature, but in man, or in a harmony of both. It is necessary to use these pleasures with great temperance. For, nature is not always tricked in holiday attire, but the same scene which yesterday breathed perfume and glittered as for the frolic of the nymphs, is overspread with melancholy today. Nature always wears the colors of the spirit. To a man laboring under calamity, the heat of his own fire hath sadness in it. Then, there is a kind of contempt of the landscape felt by him who has just lost by death a dear friend. The sky is less grand as it shuts down over less worth in the population.

The American Scholar

"The American Scholar" was a speech given by Ralph Waldo Emerson on August 31, 1837, to the Phi Beta Kappa Society at Cambridge, Massachusetts. He was invited to speak in recognition of his groundbreaking work *Nature*, published a year earlier, in which he established a new way for America's fledgling society to regard the world. Sixty years after declaring independence, American culture was still heavily influenced by Europe, and Emerson, for possibly the first time in the country's history, provided a visionary philosophical framework for escaping "from under its iron lids" and building a new, distinctly American cultural identity.

Emerson uses Transcendentalist and Romantic views to get his points across by explaining a true American scholar's relationship to nature.

This address was delivered at Cambridge in 1837, before the Harvard Chapter of the Phi Beta Kappa Society, a college fraternity composed of the first twenty-five men in each graduating class. The society has annual meetings, which have been the occasion for addresses from the most distinguished scholars and thinkers of the day.

Mr. President and Gentlemen,

I greet you on the recommencement of our literary year. Our anniversary is one of hope, and, perhaps, not enough of labor. We do not meet for games of strength[1] or skill, for the recitation of histories, tragedies, and odes, like the ancient Greeks; for parliaments of love and poesy, like the Troubadours;[2] nor for the advancement of science, like our co-temporaries in the British and European capitals. Thus far, our holiday has been simply a friendly sign of the survival of the love of letters amongst a people too busy to give to letters any more. As such it is precious as the sign of an indestructible instinct. Perhaps the time is already come when it ought to be, and will be, something else; when the sluggard intellect [20]of this continent will look from under its iron lids and fill the postponed expectation of the world with something better than the exertions of mechanical skill. Our day of dependence, our long apprenticeship to the learning of other lands, draws to a close. The millions that around us are rushing into life cannot always be fed on the sere remains of foreign harvests.[3] Events, actions arise that must be sung, that will sing themselves. Who can doubt that poetry will revive and lead in a new age, as the star in the constellation Harp, which now flames in our zenith, astronomers announce, shall one day be the pole-star[4] for a thousand years?

In the light of this hope I accept the topic which not only usage but the nature of our association seem to prescribe to this day,—the American Scholar. Year by year we come up hither to read one more chapter of his biography. Let us inquire what new lights, new events, and more days have thrown on his character, his duties, and his hopes.

It is one of those fables which out of an unknown antiquity convey an unlooked-for wisdom, that the gods, in the beginning, divided Man into men, that he might be more helpful to himself; just as the hand was divided into fingers, the better to answer its end.[5]

The old fable covers a doctrine ever new and sublime; that there is One Man,—present to all particular men only partially, or through one faculty; and that you must take the whole society to find the [21]whole man. Man is not a farmer, or a professor, or an engineer, but he is all. Man is priest, and scholar, and statesman, and producer, and soldier. In the *divided* or social state these functions are parceled out to individuals, each of whom aims to do his stint[6] of the joint work, whilst each other performs his. The fable implies that the individual, to possess himself, must sometimes return from his own labor to embrace all the other laborers. But, unfortunately, this original unit, this fountain of power, has been so distributed to multitudes, has been so minutely subdivided and peddled out, that it is spilled into drops, and cannot be gathered. The state of society is one in which the members have suffered amputation from the trunk and strut about so many walking monsters,—a good finger, a neck, a stomach, an elbow, but never a man.

Man is thus metamorphosed into a thing, into many things. The planter, who is Man sent out into the field to gather food, is seldom cheered by any idea of the true dignity of his ministry. He sees his bushel and his cart, and nothing beyond, and sinks into the farmer, instead of Man on the farm. The tradesman scarcely ever gives an ideal worth to his work, but is ridden[7] by the routine of his craft, and the soul is subject to dollars. The priest becomes a form; the attorney a statute-book; the mechanic a machine; the sailor a rope of the ship.

In this distribution of functions the scholar is the delegated intellect. In the right state he is *Man [22]Thinking*. In the degenerate state, when the victim of society, he tends to become a mere thinker, or, still worse, the parrot of other men's thinking.

In this view of him, as Man Thinking, the whole theory of his office is contained. Him Nature solicits with all her placid, all her monitory pictures.[8] Him the past instructs. Him the future invites. Is not indeed every man a student, and do not all things exist for the student's behoof? And, finally, is not the true scholar the only true master? But as the old oracle said, "All things have two handles: Beware of the wrong one."[9] In life, too often, the scholar errs with mankind and forfeits his privilege. Let us see him in his school, and consider him in reference to the main influences he receives.

I. The first in time and the first in importance of the influences upon the mind is that of nature. Every day, the sun;[10] and, after sunset, Night and her stars. Ever the winds blow; ever the grass grows. Every day, men and women, conversing, beholding and beholden.[11] The scholar must needs stand wistful and admiring before this great spectacle. He must settle its value in his mind. What is nature to him? There is never a beginning, there is never an end, to the inexplicable continuity of this web of God, but always circular power returning into itself.[12] Therein it resembles his own spirit, whose beginning, whose ending, he never can find,—so entire, so boundless. Far too as her splendors shine, system on system shooting [23]like rays, upward, downward, without center, without circumference,—in the mass and in the particle, Nature hastens to render account of herself to the mind. Classification begins. To the young mind everything is individual, stands by itself. By and by it finds how to join two things and see in them one nature; then three, then three thousand; and so, tyrannized over by its own unifying instinct, it goes on tying things together, diminishing anomalies, discovering roots running under ground whereby contrary and remote things cohere and flower out from one stem. It presently learns that since the dawn of history there has been a constant accumulation and classifying of facts. But what is classification but the perceiving that these objects are not chaotic, and are not foreign, but have a law which is also a law of the human mind? The astronomer discovers that geometry, a pure abstraction of the human mind, is the measure of planetary motion. The chemist finds proportions and intelligible method throughout matter; and science is nothing but the finding of analogy, identity, in the most remote parts. The ambitious soul sits down before each refractory fact; one after another reduces all strange constitutions, all new powers, to their class and their law, and goes on forever to animate the last fiber of organization, the outskirts of nature, by insight.

Thus to him, to this school-boy under the bending dome of day, is suggested that he and it proceed from one Root; one is leaf and one is flower; relation, [24]sympathy, stirring in every vein. And what is that root? Is not that the soul of his soul?—A thought too bold?—A dream too wild? Yet when this spiritual light shall have revealed the law of more earthly natures,—when he has learned to worship the soul, and to see that the natural philosophy that now is, is only the first gropings of its gigantic hand,—he shall look forward to an ever-expanding knowledge as to a becoming creator.[13] He shall see that nature is the opposite of the soul, answering to it part for part. One is seal and one is print. Its beauty is the beauty of his own mind. Its laws are the laws of his own mind. Nature then becomes to him the measure of his attainments. So much of nature as he is ignorant of, so much of his own mind does he not yet possess. And, in fine, the ancient precept, "Know thyself,"[14] and the modern precept, "Study nature," become at last one maxim.

II. The next great influence into the spirit of the scholar is the mind of the Past,—in whatever form, whether of literature, of art, of institutions, that mind is inscribed. Books are the best type of the influence of the past, and perhaps we shall get at the truth,—learn the amount of this influence more conveniently,—by considering their value alone.

The theory of books is noble. The scholar of the first age received into him the world around; brooded thereon; gave it the new arrangement of his own mind, and uttered it again. It came into him life; [25]it went out from him truth. It came to him short-lived actions; it went out from him immortal thoughts. It came to him business; it went from him poetry. It was dead fact; now, it is quick thought. It can stand, and it can go. It now endures, it now flies, it now inspires.[15] Precisely in proportion to the depth of mind from which it issued, so high does it soar, so long does it sing.

Or, I might say, it depends on how far the process had gone, of transmuting life into truth. In proportion to the completeness of the distillation, so will the purity and imperishableness of the product be. But none is quite perfect. As no air-pump can by any means make a perfect vacuum,[16] so neither can any artist entirely exclude the conventional, the local, the perishable from his book, or write a book of pure thought, that shall be as efficient, in all respects, to a remote posterity, as to contemporaries, or rather to the second age. Each age, it is found, must write its own books; or rather, each generation for the next succeeding. The books of an older period will not fit this.

Yet hence arises a grave mischief. The sacredness which attaches to the act of creation, the act of thought, is instantly transferred to the record. The poet chanting was felt to be a divine man. Henceforth the chant is divine also. The writer was a just and wise spirit. Henceforward it is settled the book is perfect; as love of the hero corrupts into worship of his statue. Instantly the book becomes noxious.[17][26]The guide is a tyrant. We sought a brother, and lo, a governor. The sluggish and perverted mind of the multitude, always slow to open to the incursions of Reason, having once so opened, having once received this book, stands upon it, and makes an outcry if it is disparaged. Colleges are built on it. Books are written on it by thinkers, not by Man Thinking, by men of talent, that is, who start wrong, who set out from accepted dogmas, not from their own sight of principles. Meek young men grow up in libraries, believing it their duty to accept the views which Cicero, which Locke,[18] which Bacon,[19] have given; forgetful that Cicero, Locke and Bacon were only young men in libraries when they wrote these books.

Hence, instead of Man Thinking, we have the bookworm. Hence the book-learned class, who value books, as such; not as related to nature and the human constitution, but as making a sort of Third Estate[20] with the world and soul. Hence the restorers of readings,[21] the emendators,[22] the bibliomaniacs[23] of all degrees. This is bad; this is worse than it seems.

Books are the best of things, well used; abused, among the worst. What is the right use? What is the one end which all means go to effect? They are for nothing but to inspire.[24] I had better never see a book than to be warped by its attraction clean out of my own orbit, and made a satellite instead of a system. The one thing in the world of value is the [27]active soul,—the soul, free, sovereign, active. This every man is entitled to; this every man contains within him, although in almost all men obstructed, and as yet unborn. The soul active sees absolute truth and utters truth, or creates. In this action it is genius; not the privilege of here and there a favorite, but the sound estate of every man.[25] In its essence it is progressive. The book, the college, the school of art, the institution of any kind, stop with some past utterance of genius. This is good, say they,—let us hold by this. They pin me down.[26] They look backward and not forward. But genius always looks forward. The eyes of man are set in his forehead, not in his hindhead. Man hopes. Genius creates. To create,—to create,—is the proof of a divine presence. Whatever talents may be, if the man create not, the pure efflux of the Deity is not his;[27]—cinders and smoke there may be, but not yet flame. There are creative manners, there are creative actions, and creative words; manners, actions, words, that is, indicative of no custom or authority, but springing spontaneous from the mind's own sense of good and fair.

On the other part, instead of being its own seer, let it receive always from another mind its truth, though it were in torrents of light, without periods of solitude, inquest, and self-recovery; and a fatal disservice[28] is done. Genius is always sufficiently the enemy of genius by over-influence.[29] The literature of [28]every nation bear me witness. The English dramatic poets have Shakespearized now for two hundred years.[30]

Undoubtedly there is a right way of reading, so it be sternly subordinated. Man Thinking must not be subdued by his instruments. Books are for the scholar's idle times. When he can read God directly, the hour is too precious to be wasted in other men's transcripts of their readings.[31] But when the intervals of darkness come, as come they must,—when the soul seeth not, when the sun is hid and the stars withdraw their shining,—we repair to the lamps which were kindled by their ray, to guide our steps to the East again, where the dawn is.[32] We hear, that we may speak. The Arabian proverb says, "A fig-tree, looking on a fig-tree, becometh fruitful."

It is remarkable, the character of the pleasure we derive from the best books. They impress us ever with the conviction that one nature wrote and the same reads. We read the verses of one of the great English poets, of Chaucer,[33] of Marvell,[34] of Dryden,[35] with the most modern joy,—with a pleasure, I mean, which is in great part caused by the abstraction of all *time* from their verses. There is some awe mixed with the joy of our surprise, when this poet, who lived in some past world, two or three hundred years ago, says that which lies close to my own soul, that which I also had well-nigh thought and said. But for the evidence thence afforded to the philosophical doctrine of the identity of all minds, we should [29]suppose some pre-established harmony, some foresight of souls that were to be, and some preparation of stores for their future wants, like the fact observed in insects, who lay up food before death for the young grub they shall never see.

I would not be hurried by any love of system, by any exaggeration of instincts, to underrate the Book. We all know that as the human body can be nourished on any food, though it were boiled grass and the broth of shoes, so the human mind can be fed by any knowledge. And great and heroic men have existed who had almost no other information than by the printed page. I only would say that it needs a strong head to bear that diet. One must be an inventor to read well. As the proverb says, "He that would bring home the wealth of the Indies must carry out the wealth of the Indies." There is then creative reading as well as creative writing. When the mind is braced by labor and invention, the page of whatever book we read becomes luminous with manifold allusion. Every sentence is doubly significant, and the sense of our author is as broad as the world. We then see, what is always true, that as the seer's hour of vision is short and rare among heavy days and months, so is its record, perchance, the least part of his volume. The discerning will read, in his Plato[36] or Shakespeare, only that least part,—only the authentic utterances of the oracle;—all the rest he rejects, were it never so many times Plato's and Shakespeare's.

[30]

Of course there is a portion of reading quite indispensable to a wise man. History and exact science he must learn by laborious reading. Colleges, in like manner, have their indispensable office,—to teach elements. But they can only highly serve us when they aim not to drill, but to create; when they gather from far every ray of various genius to their hospitable halls, and by the concentrated fires set the hearts of their youth on flame. Thought and knowledge are natures in which apparatus and pretension avail nothing. Gowns[37] and pecuniary foundations,[38] though of towns of gold, can never countervail the least sentence or syllable of wit.[39] Forget this, and our American colleges will recede in their public importance, whilst they grow richer every year.

III. There goes in the world a notion that the scholar should be a recluse, a valetudinarian,[40]—as unfit for any handiwork or public labor as a penknife for an axe. The so-called "practical men" sneer at speculative men, as if, because they speculate or *see*, they could do nothing. I have heard it said that the clergy—who are always, more universally than any other class, the scholars of their day—are addressed as women; that the rough, spontaneous conversation of men they do not hear, but only a mincing[41] and diluted speech. They are often virtually disfranchised; and indeed there are advocates for their celibacy. As far as this is true of the studious classes, it is not just and wise. Action is [31]with the scholar subordinate, but it is essential. Without it he is not yet man. Without it thought can never ripen into truth. Whilst the world hangs before the eye as a cloud of beauty, we cannot even see its beauty. Inaction is cowardice, but there can be no scholar without the heroic mind. The preamble[42] of thought, the transition through which it passes from the unconscious to the conscious, is action. Only so much do I know, as I have lived. Instantly we know whose words are loaded with life, and whose not.

The world—this shadow of the soul, or *other me*, lies wide around. Its attractions are the keys which unlock my thoughts and make me acquainted with myself. I launch eagerly into this resounding tumult. I grasp the hands of those next me, and take my place in the ring to suffer and to work, taught by an instinct that so shall the dumb abyss[43] be vocal with speech. I pierce its order; I dissipate its fear;[44] I dispose of it within the circuit of my expanding life. So much only of life as I know by experience, so much of the wilderness have I vanquished and planted, or so far have I extended my being, my dominion. I do not see how any man can afford, for the sake of his nerves and his nap, to spare any action in which he can partake. It is pearls and rubies to his discourse. Drudgery, calamity, exasperation, want, are instructors in eloquence and wisdom. The true scholar grudges every opportunity of action passed by, as a loss of power.

[32]

It is the raw material out of which the intellect molds her splendid products. A strange process too, this by which experience is converted into thought, as a mulberry-leaf is converted into satin.[45] The manufacture goes forward at all hours.

The actions and events of our childhood and youth are now matters of calmest observation. They lie like fair pictures in the air. Not so with our recent actions,—with the business which we now have in hand. On this we are quite unable to speculate. Our affections as yet circulate through it. We no more feel or know it than we feel the feet, or the hand, or the brain of our body. The new deed is yet a part of life,—remains for a time immersed in our unconscious life. In some contemplative hour it detaches itself from the life like a ripe fruit,[46] to become a thought of the mind. Instantly it is raised, transfigured; the corruptible has put on incorruption.[47] Henceforth it is an object of beauty, however base its origin and neighborhood. Observe, too, the impossibility of antedating this act. In its grub state it cannot fly, it cannot shine, it is a dull grub. But suddenly, without observation, the selfsame thing unfurls beautiful wings, and is an angel of wisdom. So is there no fact, no event, in our private history, which shall not, sooner or later, lose its adhesive, inert form, and astonish us by soaring from our body into the empyrean.[48] Cradle and infancy, school and playground, the fear of boys, and dogs, and ferules,[49] the love of little maids and berries, and many another [33]fact that once filled the whole sky, are gone already; friend and relative, profession and party, town and country, nation and world, must also soar and sing.[50]

Of course, he who has put forth his total strength in fit actions has the richest return of wisdom. I will not shut myself out of this globe of action, and transplant an oak into a flower-pot, there to hunger and pine; nor trust the revenue of some single faculty, and exhaust one vein of thought, much like those Savoyards,[51] who, getting their livelihood by carving shepherds, shepherdesses, and smoking Dutchmen, for all Europe, went out one day to the mountain to find stock, and discovered that they had whittled up the last of their pine-trees. Authors we have, in numbers, who have written out their vein, and who, moved by a commendable prudence, sail for Greece or Palestine, follow the trapper into the prairie, or ramble round Algiers, to replenish their merchantable stock.

If it were only for a vocabulary, the scholar would be covetous of action. Life is our dictionary.[52] Years are well spent in country labors; in town; in the insight into trades and manufactures; in frank intercourse with many men and women; in science; in art; to the one end of mastering in all their facts a language by which to illustrate and embody our perceptions. I learn immediately from any speaker how much he has already lived, through the poverty or the splendor of his speech. Life lies behind us as the quarry from whence we get tiles and copestones [34]for the masonry of to-day. This is the way to learn grammar. Colleges and books only copy the language which the field and the work-yard made.

But the final value of action, like that of books, and better than books, is that it is a resource. That great principle of Undulation in nature, that shows itself in the inspiring and expiring of the breath; in desire and satiety; in the ebb and flow of the sea; in day and night; in heat and cold; and, as yet more deeply ingrained in every atom and every fluid, is known to us under the name of Polarity,—these "fits of easy transmission and reflection," as Newton[53] called them, are the law of nature because they are the law of spirit.

The mind now thinks, now acts, and each fit reproduces the other. When the artist has exhausted his materials, when the fancy no longer paints, when thoughts are no longer apprehended and books are a weariness,—he has always the resource *to live.*

Character is higher than intellect. Thinking is the function. Living is the functionary. The stream retreats to its source. A great soul will be strong to live, as well as strong to think. Does he lack organ or medium to impart his truth? He can still fall back on this elemental force of living them. This is a total act. Thinking is a partial act. Let the grandeur of justice shine in his affairs. Let the beauty of affection cheer his lowly roof. Those "far from fame," who dwell and act with him, will feel the force of his constitution in the doings and passages of the day [35]better than it can be measured by any public and designed display. Time shall teach him that the scholar loses no hour which the man lives. Herein he unfolds the sacred germ of his instinct, screened from influence. What is lost in seemliness is gained in strength. Not out of those on whom systems of education have exhausted their culture comes the helpful giant to destroy the old or to build the new, but out of unhandselled[54] savage nature; out of terrible Druids[55] and Berserkers[56] come at last Alfred[57] and Shakespeare. I hear therefore with joy whatever is beginning to be said of the dignity and necessity of labor to every citizen. There is virtue yet in the hoe and the spade,[58] for learned as well as for unlearned hands. And labor is everywhere welcome; always we are invited to work; only be this limitation observed, that a man shall not for the sake of wider activity sacrifice any opinion to the popular judgments and modes of action.

I have now spoken of the education of the scholar by nature, by books, and by action. It remains to say somewhat of his duties.

They are such as become Man Thinking. They may all be comprised in self-trust. The office of the scholar is to cheer, to raise, and to guide men by showing them facts amidst appearances. He plies the slow, unhonored, and unpaid task of observation. Flamsteed[59] and Herschel,[60] in their glazed observatories, may catalogue the stars with the praise of all [36]men, and, the results being splendid and useful, honor is sure. But he, in his private observatory, cataloguing obscure and nebulous[61] stars of the human mind, which as yet no man has thought of as such,—watching days and months sometimes for a few facts; correcting still his old records,—must relinquish display and immediate fame. In the long period of his preparation he must betray often an ignorance and shiftlessness in popular arts, incurring the disdain of the able who shoulder him aside. Long he must stammer in his speech; often forego the living for the dead. Worse yet, he must accept—how often!—poverty and solitude. For the ease and pleasure of treading the old road, accepting the fashions, the education, the religion of society, he takes the cross of making his own, and, of course, the self-accusation, the faint heart, the frequent uncertainty and loss of time, which are the nettles and tangling vines in the way of the self-relying and self-directed; and the state of virtual hostility in which he seems to stand to society, and especially to educated society. For all this loss and scorn, what offset? He is to find consolation in exercising the highest functions of human nature. He is one who raises himself from private considerations and breathes and lives on public and illustrious thoughts. He is the world's eye. He is the world's heart. He is to resist the vulgar prosperity that retrogrades ever to barbarism, by preserving and communicating heroic sentiments, noble biographies, melodious verse, and the conclusions of [37]history. Whatsoever oracles the human heart, in all emergencies, in all solemn hours, has uttered as its commentary on the world of actions,—these he shall receive and impart. And whatsoever new verdict Reason from her inviolable seat pronounces on the passing men and events of to-day,—this he shall hear and promulgate.

These being his functions, it becomes him to feel all confidence in himself, and to defer never to the popular cry. He and he only knows the world. The world of any moment is the merest appearance. Some great decorum, some fetich[62] of a government, some ephemeral trade, or war, or man, is cried up[63] by half mankind and cried down by the other half, as if all depended on this particular up or down. The odds are that the whole question is not worth the poorest thought which the scholar has lost in listening to the controversy. Let him not quit his belief that a popgun is a popgun, though the ancient and honorable[64] of the earth affirm it to be the crack of doom. In silence, in steadiness, in severe abstraction, let him hold by himself; add observation to observation, patient of neglect, patient of reproach, and bide his own time,—happy enough if he can satisfy himself alone that this day he has seen something truly. Success treads on every right step. For the instinct is sure that prompts him to tell his brother what he thinks. He then learns that in going down into the secrets of his own mind he has descended into the secrets of all minds. He learns that he who [38]has mastered any law in his private thoughts is master to that extent of all men whose language he speaks, and of all into whose language his own can be translated. The poet, in utter solitude remembering his spontaneous thoughts and recording them, is found to have recorded that which men in cities vast find true for them also. The orator distrusts at first the fitness of his frank confessions, his want of knowledge of the persons he addresses, until he finds that he is the complement[65] of his hearers;—that they drink his words because he fulfills for them their own nature; the deeper he dives into his privatest, secretest presentiment, to his wonder he finds this is the most acceptable, most public and universally true. The people delight in it; the better part of every man feels—This is my music; this is myself.

In self-trust all the virtues are comprehended. Free should the scholar be,—free and brave. Free even to the definition of freedom, "without any hindrance that does not arise out of his own constitution." Brave; for fear is a thing which a scholar by his very function puts behind him. Fear always springs from ignorance. It is a shame to him if his tranquility, amid dangerous times, arise from the presumption that like children and women his is a protected class; or if he seek a temporary peace by the diversion of his thoughts from politics or vexed questions, hiding his head like an ostrich in the flowering bushes, peeping into microscopes, and turning rhymes, as a boy whistles to keep his courage up. [39]So is the danger a danger still; so is the fear worse. Manlike let him turn and face it. Let him look into its eye and search its nature, inspect its origin,—see the whelping of this lion,—which lies no great way back; he will then find in himself a perfect comprehension of its nature and extent; he will have made his hands meet on the other side, and can henceforth defy it and pass on superior. The world is his who can see through its pretension. What deafness, what stone-blind custom, what overgrown error you behold is there only by sufferance,—by your sufferance. See it to be a lie, and you have already dealt it its mortal blow.

Yes, we are the cowed,—we the trustless. It is a mischievous notion that we are come late into nature; that the world was finished a long time ago. As the world was plastic and fluid in the hands of God, so it is ever to so much of his attributes as we bring to it. To ignorance and sin it is flint. They adapt themselves to it as they may; but in proportion as a man has any thing in him divine, the firmament flows before him and takes his signet[66] and form. Not he is great who can alter matter, but he who can alter my state of mind. They are the kings of the world who give the color of their present thought to all nature and all art, and persuade men, by the cheerful serenity of their carrying the matter, that this thing which they do is the apple which the ages have desired to pluck, now at last ripe, and inviting nations to the harvest. The great man makes the great thing. [40]Wherever Macdonald[67] sits, there is the head of the table. Linnæus[68] makes botany the most alluring of studies, and wins it from the farmer and the herb-woman: Davy,[69] chemistry; and Cuvier,[70] fossils. The day is always his who works in it with serenity and great aims. The unstable estimates of men crowd to him whose mind is filled with a truth, as the heaped waves of the Atlantic follow the moon.[71]

For this self-trust, the reason is deeper than can be fathomed,—darker than can be enlightened. I might not carry with me the feeling of my audience in stating my own belief. But I have already shown the ground of my hope, in adverting to the doctrine that man is one. I believe man has been wronged; he has wronged himself. He has almost lost the light that can lead him back to his prerogatives. Men are become of no account. Men in history, men in the world of to-day, are bugs, are spawn, and are called "the mass" and "the herd." In a century, in a millenium, one or two men;[72] that is to say, one or two approximations to the right state of every man. All the rest behold in the hero or the poet their own green and crude being,—ripened; yes, and are content to be less, so *that* may attain to its full stature. What a testimony, full of grandeur, full of pity, is borne to the demands of his own nature, by the poor clansman, the poor partisan, who rejoices in the glory of his chief! The poor and the low find some amends to their immense moral capacity, for their acquiescence in a political and social inferiority.[73][41]They are content to be brushed like flies from the path of a great person, so that justice shall be done by him to that common nature which it is the dearest desire of all to see enlarged and glorified. They sun themselves in the great man's light, and feel it to be their own element. They cast the dignity of man from their downtrod selves upon the shoulders of a hero, and will perish to add one drop of blood to make that great heart beat, those giant sinews combat and conquer. He lives for us, and we live in him.

Men such as they[74] are very naturally seek money or power; and power because it is as good as money,—the "spoils," so called, "of office." And why not? For they aspire to the highest, and this, in their sleep-walking, they dream is highest. Wake them and they shall quit the false good and leap to the true, and leave governments to clerks and desks. This revolution is to be wrought by the gradual domestication of the idea of Culture. The main enterprise of the world for splendor, for extent, is the upbuilding of a man. Here are the materials strewn along the ground. The private life of one man shall be a more illustrious monarchy, more formidable to its enemy, more sweet and serene in its influence to its friend, than any kingdom in history. For a man, rightly viewed, comprehendeth[75] the particular natures of all men. Each philosopher, each bard, each actor has only done for me, as by a delegate, what one day I can do for myself. The books which once we valued [42]more than the apple of the eye, we have quite exhausted. What is that but saying that we have come up with the point of view which the universal mind took through the eyes of one scribe; we have been that man, and have passed on. First, one, then another, we drain all cisterns, and waxing greater by all these supplies, we crave a better and a more abundant food. The man has never lived that can feed us ever. The human mind cannot be enshrined in a person who shall set a barrier on any one side to this unbounded, unboundable empire. It is one central fire, which, flaming now out of the lips of Etna, lightens the capes of Sicily, and now out of the throat of Vesuvius, illuminates the towers and vineyards of Naples. It is one light which beams out of a thousand stars. It is one soul which animates all men.

But I have dwelt perhaps tediously upon this abstraction of the Scholar. I ought not to delay longer to add what I have to say of nearer reference to the time and to this country.

Historically, there is thought to be a difference in the ideas which predominate over successive epochs, and there are data for marking the genius of the Classic, of the Romantic, and now of the Reflective or Philosophical age.[76] With the views I have intimated of the oneness or the identity of the mind through all individuals, I do not much dwell on these differences. In fact, I believe each individual passes through all three. The boy is a Greek; the youth, [43]romantic; the adult, reflective. I deny not, however, that a revolution in the leading idea may be distinctly enough traced.

Our age is bewailed as the age of Introversion.[77] Must that needs be evil? We, it seems, are critical. We are embarrassed with second thoughts.[78] We cannot enjoy anything for hankering to know whereof the pleasure consists. We are lined with eyes. We see with our feet. The time is infected with Hamlet's unhappiness,—

"Sicklied o'er with the pale cast of thought."[79]

Is it so bad then? Sight is the last thing to be pitied. Would we be blind? Do we fear lest we should outsee nature and God, and drink truth dry? I look upon the discontent of the literary class as a mere announcement of the fact that they find themselves not in the state of mind of their fathers, and regret the coming state as untried; as a boy dreads the water before he has learned that he can swim. If there is any period one would desire to be born in, is it not the age of Revolution; when the old and the new stand side by side and admit of being compared; when the energies of all men are searched by fear and by hope; when the historic glories of the old can be compensated by the rich possibilities of the new era? This time, like all times, is a very good one, if we but know what to do with it.

I read with some joy of the auspicious signs of the coming days, as they glimmer already through [44]poetry and art, through philosophy and science, through church and state.

One of these signs is the fact that the same movement[80] which effected the elevation of what was called the lowest class in the state assumed in literature a very marked and as benign an aspect. Instead of the sublime and beautiful, the near, the low, the common, was explored and poetized. That which had been negligently trodden under foot by those who were harnessing and provisioning themselves for long journeys into far countries, is suddenly found to be richer than all foreign parts. The literature of the poor, the feelings of the child, the philosophy of the street, the meaning of household life, are the topics of the time. It is a great stride. It is a sign—is it not?—of new vigor when the extremities are made active, when currents of warm life run into the hands and the feet. I ask not for the great, the remote, the romantic; what is doing in Italy or Arabia; what is Greek art, or Provençal minstrelsy; I embrace the common, I explore and sit at the feet of the familiar, the low. Give me insight into to-day, and you may have the antique and future worlds. What would we really know the meaning of? The meal in the firkin; the milk in the pan; the ballad in the street; the news of the boat; the glance of the eye; the form and the gait of the body;—show me the ultimate reason of these matters; show me the sublime presence of the highest spiritual cause lurking, as always it does lurk, in these suburbs and extremities [45]of nature; let me see every trifle bristling with the polarity that ranges it instantly on an eternal law;[81] and the shop, the plow, and the ledger referred to the like cause by which light undulates and poets sing;—and the world lies no longer a dull miscellany and lumber-room, but has form and order: there is no trifle, there is no puzzle, but one design unites and animates the farthest pinnacle and the lowest trench.

This idea has inspired the genius of Goldsmith,[82] Burns,[83] Cowper,[84] and, in a newer time, of Goethe,[85] Wordsworth,[86] and Carlyle.[87] This idea they have differently followed and with various success. In contrast with their writing, the style of Pope,[88] of Johnson,[89] of Gibbon,[90] looks cold and pedantic. This writing is blood-warm. Man is surprised to find that things near are not less beautiful and wondrous than things remote. The near explains the far. The drop is a small ocean. A man is related to all nature. This perception of the worth of the vulgar is fruitful in discoveries. Goethe, in this very thing the most modern of the moderns, has shown us, as none ever did, the genius of the ancients.

There is one man of genius who has done much for this philosophy of life, whose literary value has never yet been rightly estimated:—I mean Emanuel Swedenborg.[91] The most imaginative of men, yet writing with the precision of a mathematician, he endeavored to engraft a purely philosophical Ethics on the popular Christianity of his time. Such an attempt of [46]course must have difficulty which no genius could surmount. But he saw and showed the connexion between nature and the affections of the soul. He pierced the emblematic or spiritual character of the visible, audible, tangible world. Especially did his shade-loving muse hover over and interpret the lower parts of nature; he showed the mysterious bond that allies moral evil to the foul material forms, and has given in epical parables a theory of insanity, of beasts, of unclean and fearful things.

Another sign of our times, also marked by an analogous political movement, is the new importance given to the single person. Everything that tends to insulate the individual—to surround him with barriers of natural respect, so that each man shall feel the world is his, and man shall treat with man as a sovereign state with a sovereign state—tends to true union as well as greatness. "I learned," said the melancholy Pestalozzi,[92] "that no man in God's wide earth is either willing or able to help any other man." Help must come from the bosom alone. The scholar is that man who must take up into himself all the ability of the time, all the contributions of the past, all the hopes of the future. He must be an university of knowledges. If there be one lesson more than another that should pierce his ear, it is—The world is nothing, the man is all; in yourself is the law of all nature, and you know not yet how a globule of sap ascends; in yourself slumbers the whole of Reason; it is for you to know all; it is for you to [47]dare all. Mr. President and Gentlemen, this confidence in the unsearched might of man belongs, by all motives, by all prophecy, by all preparation, to the American Scholar. We have listened too long to the courtly muses of Europe. The spirit of the American freeman is already suspected to be timid, imitative, tame. Public and private avarice make the air we breathe thick and fat. The scholar is decent, indolent, complaisant. See already the tragic consequence. The mind of this country, taught to aim at low objects, eats upon itself. There is no work for any one but the decorous and the complaisant. Young men of the fairest promise, who begin life upon our shores, inflated by the mountain winds, shined upon by all the stars of God, find the earth below not in unison with these, but are hindered from action by the disgust which the principles on which business is managed inspire, and turn drudges, or die of disgust, some of them suicides. What is the remedy? They did not yet see, and thousands of young men as hopeful now crowding to the barriers for the career do not yet see, that if the single man plant himself indomitably on his instincts, and there abide, the huge world will come round to him. Patience,—patience; with the shades of all the good and great for company; and for solace the perspective of your own infinite life; and for work the study and the communication of principles, the making those instincts prevalent, the conversion of the world. Is it not the chief disgrace in the world, not to be an [48]unit; not to be reckoned one character; not to yield that peculiar fruit which each man was created to bear, but to be reckoned in the gross, in the hundred, or the thousand, of the party, the section, to which we belong; and our opinion predicted geographically, as the north, or the south? Not so, brothers and friends,—please God, ours shall not be so. We will walk on our own feet; we will work with our own hands; we will speak our own minds. Then shall man be no longer a name for pity, for doubt, and for sensual indulgence. The dread of man and the love of man shall be a wall of defense and a wreath of joy around all. A nation of men will for the first time exist, because each believes himself inspired by the Divine Soul which also inspires all men.

Emerson Translation Activity

Emerson is a heady thinker, filling his paragraphs with aphorisms (memorably sayings) and connections that we often have to translate. He is known as being tough to remember, too! Readers revisiting him often note this feature of his style. As critical readers, we need to analyze, or break down, the material into our own terms. To this end, take on the following translation task of one of his paragraphs. Put it into your own words.

> To the young mind, every thing is individual, stands by itself. By and by, it finds how to join two things, and see in them one nature; then three, then three thousand; and so, tyrannized over by its own unifying instinct, it goes on tying things together, diminishing anomalies, discovering roots running under ground, whereby contrary and remote things cohere, and flower out from one stem. It presently learns, that, since the dawn of history, there has been a constant accumulation and classifying of facts. But what is classification but the perceiving that these objects are not chaotic, and are not foreign, but have a law which is also a law of the human mind? The astronomer discovers that geometry, a pure abstraction of the human mind, is the measure of planetary motion. The chemist finds proportions and intelligible method throughout matter; and science is nothing but the finding of analogy, identity, in the most remote parts. The ambitious soul sits down before each refractory fact; one after another, reduces all strange constitutions, all new powers, to their class and their law, and goes on for ever to animate the last fibre of organization, the outskirts of nature, by insight.

Ralph Waldo Emerson, Self-Reliance

"Self-Reliance" is an essay written by American transcendentalist philosopher and essayist Ralph Waldo Emerson. It contains the most thorough statement of one of Emerson's recurrent themes, the need for each individual to avoid conformity and false consistency, and follow his or her own instincts and ideas. It is the source of one of Emerson's most famous quotations: "A foolish consistency is the hobgoblin of little minds, adored by little statesmen and philosophers and divines." This essay is an analysis into the nature of the "aboriginal self on which a universal reliance may be grounded."

"Ne te quæsiveris extra."[145]

"Man is his own star; and the soul that can
Render an honest and a perfect man,
Commands all light, all influence, all fate;
Nothing to him falls early or too late.
Our acts our angels are, or good or ill,
Our fatal shadows that walk by us still."[146]

Cast the bantling on the rocks,
Suckle him with the she-wolf's teat;
Wintered with the hawk and fox,
Power and speed be hands and feet.[147]

I read the other day some verses written by an eminent painter which were original and not conventional. The soul always hears an admonition in such lines, let the subject be what it may. The sentiment they instill is of more value than any thought they may contain. To believe your own thought, to believe that what is true for you in your private heart is true for all men,—that is genius. [148] Speak your latent conviction, and it shall be the universal sense;[149] for the inmost in due time becomes the outmost,—and our first thought is rendered back to us by the trumpets of the Last Judgment. Familiar as the voice of the mind is to each, the highest merit we ascribe to Moses, Plato,[150] and Milton[151] is, that they set at naught books and traditions, and spoke not what men, but what they thought. A man should learn to detect and watch that gleam of light which flashes across his mind from within, more than the luster of the firmament of bards and sages. Yet he dismisses without notice his thought, because it is his. In every work of genius we recognize our own rejected thoughts:[152] they come back to us with a certain alienated majesty. Great works of art have no more affecting lesson for us than this. They teach us to abide by our spontaneous impression with good-humored inflexibility then most when[153] the whole cry of voices is on the other side. Else, to-morrow a stranger will say with masterly good sense precisely what we have thought and felt all the time, and we shall be forced to take with shame our own opinion from another.

There is a time in every man's education when he arrives at the conviction that envy is ignorance; that imitation is suicide;[154] that he must take himself for better, for worse, as his portion; that though the wide universe is full of good, no kernel of nourishing corn can come to him but through his toil bestowed on that plot of ground which is given to him to till. The power which resides in him is new in nature, and none but he knows what that is which he can do, nor does he know until he has tried. Not for nothing one face, one character, one fact, makes much impression on him, and another none. This sculpture in the memory is not without preëstablished harmony. The eye was placed where one ray should fall, that it might testify of that particular ray. We but half express ourselves,[155] and are ashamed of that divine idea which each of us represents. It may be safely trusted as proportionate and of good issues, so it be faithfully imparted, but God will not have his work made manifest by cowards. A man is relieved and gay when he has put his heart into his work and done his best; but what he has said or done otherwise shall give him no peace. It is a deliverance which does not deliver. In the attempt his genius deserts him; no muse befriends; no invention, no hope.

Trust thyself:[156] every heart vibrates to that iron string. Accept the place the divine providence has found for you, the society of your contemporaries, the connection of events. Great men have always done so, and confided themselves childlike to the genius of their age, betraying their perception that the absolutely trustworthy was seated at their heart, working through their hands, predominating in all their being. And we are now men, and must accept in the highest mind the same transcendent destiny; and not minors and invalids in a protected corner, not cowards fleeing before a revolution, but guides, redeemers, and benefactors, obeying the Almighty effort, and advancing on Chaos[157] and the Dark.

What pretty oracles nature yields us on this text, in the face and behavior of children, babes, and even brutes! That divided and rebel mind, that distrust of a sentiment because our arithmetic has computed the strength and means opposed to our purpose, these[158] have not. Their mind being whole, their eye is as yet unconquered, and when we look in their faces we are disconcerted. Infancy conforms to nobody: all conform to it, so that one babe commonly makes four or five[159] out of the adults who prattle and play to it. So God has armed youth and puberty and manhood no less with its own piquancy and charm, and made it enviable and gracious and its claims not to be put by, if it will stand by itself. Do not think the youth has no force, because he cannot speak to you and me. Hark! in the next room his voice is sufficiently clear and emphatic. It seems he knows how to speak to his contemporaries. Bashful or bold, then, he will know how to make us seniors very unnecessary.

The nonchalance[160] of boys who are sure of a dinner, and would disdain as much as a lord to do or say aught to conciliate one, is the healthy attitude of human nature. A boy is in the parlor what the pit is in the playhouse;[161] independent, irresponsible, looking out from his corner on such people and facts as pass by, he tries and sentences them on their merits, in the swift, summary way of boys, as good, bad, interesting, silly, eloquent, troublesome. He cumbers himself never about consequences about interests; he gives an independent, genuine verdict. You must court him: he does not court you. But the man is, as it were, clapped into jail by his consciousness. As soon as he has once acted or spoken with *éclat*[162] he is a committed person, watched by the sympathy or the hatred of hundreds, whose affections must now enter into his account. There is no Lethe[163] for this. Ah, that he could pass again into his neutrality! Who[164] can thus avoid all pledges, and having observed, observe again from the same unaffected, unbiased, unbribable, unaffrighted innocence, must always be formidable. He would utter opinions on all passing affairs, which being seen to be not private, but necessary, would sink like darts into the ear of men, and put them in fear.

These are the voices which we hear in solitude, but they grow faint and inaudible as we enter into the world. Society everywhere is in conspiracy against the manhood of everyone of its members. Society is a joint-stock company, in which the members agree, for the better securing of his bread to each shareholder, to surrender the liberty and culture of the eater. The virtue in most request is conformity. Self-reliance is its aversion. It loves not realities and creators, but names and customs.

Whoso would be a man must be a nonconformist.[165] He who would gather immortal palms must not be hindered by the name of goodness, but must explore if it be goodness.[166] Nothing is at last sacred but the integrity of your own mind. Absolve you to yourself, and you shall have the suffrage[167] of the world. I remember an answer which when quite young I was prompted to make to a valued adviser, who was wont to importune me with the dear old doctrines of the church. On my saying, What have I to do with the sacredness of traditions, if I live wholly from within? my friend suggested: "But these impulses may be from below, not from above." I replied: "They do not seem to me to be such; but if I am the Devil's child, I will live then from the Devil." No law can be sacred to me but that of my nature. Good and bad are but names very readily transferable to that or this;[168] the only right is what is after my constitution, the only wrong what is against it. A man is to carry himself in the presence of all opposition, as if everything were titular and ephemeral but he. I am ashamed to think how easily we capitulate to badges and names, to large societies and dead institutions. Every decent and well-spoken individual affects and sways me more than is right. I ought to go upright and vital, and speak the rude truth in all ways. If malice and vanity wear the coat of philanthropy, shall that pass? If an angry bigot assumes this bountiful cause of Abolition, and comes to me with his last news from Barbadoes,[169] why should I not say to him: "Go love thy infant; love thy wood-chopper: be good-natured and modest: have that grace; and never varnish your hard, uncharitable ambition with this incredible tenderness for black folk a thousand miles off. Thy love afar is spite at home." Rough and graceless would be such greeting, but truth is handsomer than the affectation of love. Your goodness must have some edge to it,—else it is none. The doctrine of hatred must be preached as the counteraction of the doctrine of love when that pules and whines. I shun father and mother and wife and brother, when my genius calls me. I would write on the lintels of the door-post, *Whim*.[170] I hope it is somewhat better than whim at last, but we cannot spend the day in explanation. Expect me not to show cause why I seek or why I exclude company. Then, again, do not tell me, as a good man did to-day, of my obligation to put all poor men in good situations. Are they *my* poor? I tell thee, thou foolish philanthropist, that I grudge the dollar, the dime, the cent, I give to such men as do not belong to me and to whom I do not belong. There is a class of persons to whom by all spiritual affinity I am bought and sold; for them I will go to prison, if need be; but your miscellaneous popular charities; the education at college of fools; the building of meeting-houses to the vain end to which many now stand; alms to sots; and the thousand-fold Relief Societies;—though I confess with shame I sometimes succumb and give the dollar, it is a wicked dollar which by and by I shall have the manhood to withhold.

Virtues are, in the popular estimate, rather the exception than the rule. There is the man *and* his virtues. Men do what is called a good action, as some piece of courage or charity, much as they would pay a fine in expiation of daily non-appearance on parade. Their works are done as an apology or extenuation of their living in the world,—as invalids and the insane pay a high board. Their virtues are penances. I do not wish to expiate, but to live. My life is for itself and not for a spectacle. I much prefer that it should be of a lower strain, so it be genuine and equal, than that it should be glittering and unsteady. I wish it to be sound and sweet, and not to need diet and bleeding.[171] I ask primary evidence that you are a man, and refuse this appeal from the man to his actions. I know that for myself it makes no difference whether I do or forbear those actions which are reckoned excellent. I cannot consent to pay for a privilege where I have intrinsic right. Few and mean as my gifts may be, I actually am, and do not need for my own assurance or the assurance of my fellows any secondary testimony.

What I must do is all that concerns me, not what the people think. This rule, equally arduous in actual and in intellectual life, may serve for the whole distinction between greatness and meanness. It is the harder, because you will always find those who think they know what is your duty better than you know it. It is easy in the world to live after the world's opinion; it is easy in solitude to live after our own; but the great man is he who in the midst of the crowd keeps with perfect sweetness the independence of solitude.
[172]

The objection to conforming to usages that have become dead to you is, that it scatters your force. It loses your time and blurs the impression of your character. If you maintain a dead church, contribute to a dead Bible-society, vote with a great party either for the government or against it, spread your table like base housekeepers,—under all these screens I have difficulty to detect the precise[173] man you are. And, of course, so much force is withdrawn from your proper life. But do your work, and I shall know you.[174] Do your work, and you shall reinforce yourself. A man must consider what a blindman's-buff is this game of conformity. If I know your sect, I anticipate your argument. I hear a preacher announce for his text and topic the expediency of one of the institutions of his church. Do I not know beforehand that not possibly can he say a new and spontaneous word? Do I not know that, with[175] all this ostentation of examining the grounds of the institution, he will do no such thing? Do I not know that he is pledged to himself not to look but at one side,—the permitted side, not as a man, but as a parish minister? He is a retained attorney, and these airs of the bench[176] are the emptiest affectation. Well, most men have bound their eyes with one or another handkerchief,[177] and attached themselves to some one of these communities of opinion.[178] This conformity makes them not false in a few particulars, authors of a few lies, but false in all particulars. Their every truth is not quite true. Their two is not the real two, their four not the real four; so that every word they say chagrins us, and we know not where to begin to set them right. Meantime nature is not slow to equip us in the prison-uniform of the party to which we adhere. We come to wear one cut of face and figure, and acquire by degrees the gentlest asinine expression. There is a mortifying experience in particular which does not fail to wreak itself also in the general history; I mean "the foolish face of praise," the forced smile which we put on in company where we do not feel at ease in answer to conversation which does not interest us. The muscles, not spontaneously moved, but moved by a low usurping willfulness, grow tight about the outline of the face with the most disagreeable sensation.

For nonconformity the world whips you with its displeasure.[179] And therefore a man must know how to estimate a sour face. The bystanders look askance on him in the public street or in the friend's parlor. If this aversation had its origin in contempt and resistance like his own, he might well go home with a sad countenance; but the sour faces of the multitude, like their sweet faces, have no deep cause, but are put on and off as the wind blows and a newspaper directs.[180] Yet is the discontent of the multitude more formidable than that of the senate and the college. It is easy enough for a firm man who knows the world to brook the rage of the cultivated classes. Their rage is decorous and prudent, for they are timid as being very vulnerable themselves. But when to their feminine rage the indignation of the people is added, when the ignorant and the poor are aroused, when the unintelligent brute force that lies at the bottom of society is made to growl and mow, it needs the habit of magnanimity and religion to treat it godlike as a trifle of no concernment.

The other terror[181] that scares us from self-trust is our consistency;[182] a reverence for our past act or word, because the eyes of others have no other data for computing our orbit[183] than our past acts, and we are loth to disappoint them.

But why should you keep your head over your shoulder? Why drag about this corpse of your memory, lest you contradict somewhat[184] you have stated in this or that public place? Suppose you should contradict yourself; what then? It seems to be a rule of wisdom never to rely on your memory alone, scarcely even in acts of pure memory, but to bring the past for judgment into the thousand-eyed present, and live ever in a new day. In your metaphysics you have denied personality to the Deity; yet when the devout motions of the soul come, yield to them heart and life, though they should clothe God with shape and color. Leave your theory, as Joseph his coat in the hand of the harlot, and flee.[185]

A foolish consistency is the hobgoblin of little minds, adored by little statesmen and philosophers and divines. With consistency a great soul has simply nothing to do. He may as well concern himself with the shadow on the wall. Speak what you think now in hard words, and to-morrow speak what to-morrow thinks in hard words again, though it contradict everything you said to-day.—"Ah, so you shall be sure to be misunderstood."—Is it so bad, then, to be misunderstood? Pythagoras[186] was misunderstood, and Socrates,[187] and Jesus, and Luther,[188] and Copernicus,[189] and Galileo,[190] and Newton,[191] and every pure and wise spirit that ever took flesh. To be great is to be misunderstood.

I suppose no man can violate his nature. All the sallies of his will are rounded in by the law of his being, as the inequalities of Andes[192] and Himmaleh[193] are insignificant in the curve of the sphere. Nor does it matter how you gauge and try him. A character is like an acrostic or Alexandrian stanza;[194]—read it forward, backward, or across, it still spells the same thing. In this pleasing, contrite wood-life which God allows me, let me record day by day my honest thought without prospect or retrospect, and, I cannot doubt, it will be found symmetrical, though I mean it not, and see it not. My book should smell of pines and resound with the hum of insects. The swallow over my window should interweave that thread or straw he carries in his bill into my web also. We pass for what we are. Character teaches above our wills. Men imagine that they communicate their virtue or vice only by overt actions, and do not see that virtue or vice emit a breath every moment.

There will be an agreement in whatever variety of actions, so they be each honest and natural in their hour. For of one will, the actions will be harmonious, however unlike they seem. These varieties are lost sight of at a little distance, at a little height of thought. One tendency unites them all. The voyage of the best ship is a zigzag line of a hundred tacks.[195] See the line from a sufficient distance, and it straightens itself to the average tendency. Your genuine action will explain itself, and will explain your other genuine actions. Your conformity explains nothing. Act singly, and what you have already done singly will justify you now. Greatness appeals to the future. If I can be firm enough to-day to do right, and scorn eyes,[196] I must have done so much right before as to defend me now. Be it how it will, do right now. Always scorn appearances, and you always may. The force of character is cumulative. All the foregone days of virtue work their health into this. What makes the majesty of the heroes of the senate and the field, which so fills the imagination? The consciousness of a train of great days and victories behind. They shed an united light on the advancing actor. He is attended as by a visible escort of angels. That is it which throws thunder into Chatham's[197] voice, and dignity into Washington's port, and America into Adams's[198] eye. Honor is venerable to us because it is no ephemeris. It is always ancient virtue. We worship it to-day because it is not of to-day. We love it and pay it homage, because it is not a trap for our love and homage, but is self-dependent, self-derived, and therefore of an old immaculate pedigree, even if shown in a young person.

I hope in these days we have heard the last of conformity and consistency. Let the words be gazetted and ridiculous henceforward. Instead of the gong for dinner, let us hear a whistle from the Spartan[199] fife. Let us never bow and apologize more. A great man is coming to eat at my house. I do not wish to please him; I wish that he should wish to please me. I will stand here for humanity, and though I would make it kind, I would make it true. Let us affront and reprimand the smooth mediocrity and squalid contentment of the times, and hurl in the face of custom, and trade, and office, the fact which is the upshot of all history, that there is a great responsible Thinker and Actor working wherever a man works; that a true man belongs to no other time or place, but is the center of things. Where he is, there is nature. He measures you, and all men, and all events. Ordinarily, everybody in society reminds us of somewhat else, or of some other person. Character, reality, reminds you of nothing else; it takes place of the whole creation. The man must be so much, that he must make all circumstances indifferent. Every true man is a cause, a country, and an age; requires infinite spaces and numbers and time fully to accomplish his design;—and posterity seem to follow his steps as a train of clients. A man Cæsar[200] is born, and for ages after we have a Roman Empire. Christ is born, and millions of minds so grow and cleave to his genius, that he is confounded with virtue and the possible of man. An institution is the lengthened shadow of one man; as Monachism, of the hermit Antony;[201] the Reformation, of Luther; Quakerism, of Fox;[202] Methodism, of Wesley;[203] Abolition, of Clarkson.[204] Scipio,[205]Milton called "the height of Rome"; and all history resolves itself very easily into the biography of a few stout and earnest persons.

Let a man then know his worth, and keep things under his feet. Let him not peep or steal, or skulk up and down with the air of a charity-boy, a bastard, or an interloper, in the world which exists for him. But the man in the street, finding no worth in himself which corresponds to the force which built a tower or sculptured a marble god, feels poor when he looks on these. To him a palace, a statue, a costly book, have an alien and forbidding air, much like a gay equipage, and seem to say like that, "Who are you, Sir?" Yet they all are his, suitors for his notice, petitioners to his faculties that they will come out and take possession? The picture waits for my verdict: it is not to command me, but I am to settle its claims to praise. That popular fable of the sot who was picked up dead drunk in the street, carried to the duke's house, washed and dressed and laid in the duke's bed, and, on his waking, treated with all obsequious ceremony like the duke, and assured that he had been insane,[206] owes its popularity to the fact that it symbolizes so well the state of man, who is in the world a sort of sot, but now and then wakes up, exercises his reason, and finds himself a true prince.

Our reading is mendicant and sycophantic. In history, our imagination plays us false. Kingdom and lordship, power and estate, are a gaudier vocabulary than private John and Edward in a small house and common day's work; but the things of life are the same to both; the sum total of both is the same. Why all this deference to Alfred,[207] and Scanderbeg,[208] and Gustavus?[209] Suppose they were virtuous; did they wear out virtue? As great a stake depends on your private act to-day, as followed their public and renowned steps. When private men shall act with original views, the luster will be transferred from the actions of kings to those of gentlemen.

The world has been instructed by its kings, who have so magnetized the eyes of nations. It has been taught by this colossal symbol the mutual reverence that is due from man to man. The joyful loyalty with which men have everywhere suffered the king, the noble, or the great proprietor to walk among them by a law of his own, make his own scale of men and things, and reverse theirs, pay for benefits not with money but with honor, and represent the law in his person, was the hieroglyphic[210] by which they obscurely signified their consciousness of their own right and comeliness, the right of every man.

The magnetism which all original action exerts is explained when we inquire the reason of self-trust. Who is the Trustee? What is the aboriginal Self, on which a universal reliance may be grounded? What is the nature and power of that science-baffling star, without parallax,[211] without calculable elements, which shoots a ray of beauty even into trivial and impure actions, if the least mark of independence appear? The inquiry leads us to that source, at once the essence of genius, of virtue, and of life, which we call Spontaneity or Instinct. We denote this primary wisdom as Intuition, whilst all later teachings are tuitions. In that deep force, the last fact behind which analysis cannot go, all things find their common origin. For the sense of being which in calm hours rises, we know not how, in the soul, is not diverse from things, from space, from light, from time, from man, but one with them, and proceeds obviously from the same source whence their life and being also proceed. We first share the life by which things exist, and afterwards see them as appearances in nature, and forget that we have shared their cause. Here is the fountain of action and of thought. Here are the lungs of that inspiration which giveth man wisdom, and which cannot be denied without impiety and atheism. We lie in the lap of immense intelligence, which makes us receivers of its truth and organs of its activity. When we discern justice, when we discern truth, we do nothing of ourselves, but allow a passage to its beams. If we ask whence this comes, if we seek to pry into the soul that causes, all philosophy is at fault. Its presence or its absence is all we can affirm. Every man discriminates between the voluntary acts of his mind, and his involuntary perceptions, and knows that to his involuntary perceptions a perfect faith is due. He may err in the expression of them, but he knows that these things are so, like day and night, not to be disputed. My willful actions and acquisitions are but roving;—the idlest reverie, the faintest native emotion, command my curiosity and respect. Thoughtless people contradict as readily the statement of perceptions as of opinions, or rather much more readily; for, they do not distinguish between perception and notion. They fancy that I choose to see this or that thing. But perception is not whimsical, it is fatal. If I see a trait, my children will see it after me, and in course of time, all mankind,—although it may chance that no one has seen it before me. For my perception of it is as much a fact as the sun.

The relations of the soul to the divine spirit are so pure, that it is profane to seek to interpose helps. It must be that when God speaketh he should communicate, not one thing, but all things; should fill the world with his voice; should scatter forth light, nature, time, souls, from the center of the present thought; and new date and new create the whole. Whenever a mind is simple, and receives a divine wisdom, old things pass away,—means, teachers, texts, temples, fall; it lives now, and absorbs past and future into the present hour. All things are made sacred by relation to it,—one as much as another. All things are dissolved to their center by their cause, and, in the universal miracle, petty and particular miracles disappear. If, therefore, a man claims to know and speak of God, and carries you backward to the phraseology of some old moldered nation in another country, in another world, believe him not. Is the acorn better than the oak which is its fullness and completion? Is the parent better than the child into whom he has cast his ripened being?[212] Whence, then, this worship of the past?[213] The centuries are conspirators against the sanity and authority of the soul. Time and space are but physiological colors which the eye makes, but the soul is light; where it is, is day; where it was, is night; and history is an impertinence and an injury, if it be anything more than a cheerful apologue or parable of my being and becoming.

Man is timid and apologetic; he is no longer upright; he dares not say "I think," "I am," but quotes some saint or sage. He is ashamed before the blade of grass or the blowing rose. These roses under my window make no reference to former roses or to better ones; they are for what they are; they exist with God to-day. There is no time to them. There is simply the rose; it is perfect in every moment of its existence. Before a leaf-bud has burst, its whole life acts; in the full-blown flower there is no more; in the leafless root there is no less. Its nature is satisfied, and it satisfies nature, in all moments alike. But man postpones, or remembers; he does not live in the present, but with a reverted eye laments the past, or, heedless of the riches that surround him, stands on tiptoe to foresee the future. He cannot be happy and strong until he too lives with nature in the present, above time.

This should be plain enough. Yet see what strong intellects dare not yet hear God himself, unless he speak the phraseology of I know not what David, or Jeremiah, or Paul. We shall not always set so great a price on a few texts, on a few lives.[214] We are like children who repeat by rote the sentences of grandames and tutors, and, as they grow older, of the men and talents and characters they chance to see,—painfully recollecting the exact words they spoke; afterwards, when they come into the point of view which those had who uttered those saying, they understand them, and are willing to let the words go; for, at any time, they can use words as good when occasion comes. If we live truly, we shall see truly. It is as easy for the strong man to be strong, as it is for the weak to be weak. When we have new perception, we shall gladly disburden the memory of its hoarded treasures as old rubbish. When a man lives with God, his voice shall be as sweet as the murmur of the brook and the rustle of the corn.

And now at last the highest truth on this subject remains unsaid; probably cannot be said; for all that we say is the far-off remembering of the intuition. That thought, by what I can now nearest approach to say it, is this. When good is near you, when you have life in yourself, it is not by any known or accustomed way; you shall not discern the footprints of any other; you shall not see the face of man; you shall not hear any name;—the way, the thought, the good, shall be wholly strange and new. It shall exclude example and experience. You take the way from man, not to man. All persons that ever existed are its forgotten ministers. Fear and hope are alike beneath it. There is somewhat low even in hope. In the hour of vision, there is nothing that can be called gratitude, nor properly joy. The soul raised over passion beholds identity and eternal causation, perceives the self-existence of Truth and Right, and calms itself with knowing that all things go well. Vast spaces of nature, the Atlantic Ocean, the South Sea,—long intervals of time, years, centuries,—are of no account. This which I think and feel underlay every former state of life and circumstances, as it does underlie my present, and what is called life, and what is called death.

Life only avails, not the having lived. Power ceases in the instant of repose; it resides in the moment of transition from a past to a new state, in the shooting of the gulf, in the darting to an aim. This one fact the world hates, that the soul *becomes*; for that forever degrades the past, turns all riches to poverty, all reputation to shame, confounds the saint with the rogue, shoves Jesus and Judas[215] equally aside. Why, then, do we prate of self-reliance? Inasmuch as the soul is present, there will be power not confident but agent.[216] To talk of reliance is a poor external way of speaking. Speak rather of that which relies, because it works and is. Who has more obedience than I masters me, though he should not raise his finger. Round him I must revolve by the gravitation of spirits. We fancy it rhetoric, when we speak of eminent virtue. We do not yet see that virtue is Height, and that a man or a company of men, plastic and permeable to principles, by the law of nature must overpower and ride all cities, nations, kings, rich men, poets, who are not.

This is the ultimate fact which we so quickly reach on this, as on every topic, the resolution of all into the ever-blessed One. Self-existence is the attribute of the Supreme Cause, and it constitutes the measure of good by the degree in which it enters into all lower forms. All things real are so by so much virtue as they contain. Commerce, husbandry, hunting, whaling, war eloquence, personal weight, are somewhat, and engage my respect as examples of its presence and impure action. I see the same law working in nature for conservation and growth. Power is in nature the essential measure of right. Nature suffers nothing to remain in her kingdoms which cannot help itself. The genesis and maturation of a planet, its poise and orbit, the bended tree recovering itself from the strong wind, the vital resources of every animal and vegetable, are demonstrations of the self-sufficing, and therefore self-relying soul.

Thus all concentrates: let us not rove; let us sit at home with the cause. Let us stun and astonish the intruding rabble of men and books and institutions, by a simple declaration of the divine fact. Bid the invaders take the shoes from off their feet, for God is here within.[217] Let our simplicity judge them, and our docility to our own law demonstrate the poverty of nature and fortune beside our native riches.

But now we are a mob. Man does not stand in awe of man, nor is his genius admonished to stay at home to put itself in communication with the internal ocean, but it goes abroad to beg a cup of water of the urns of other men. We must go alone. I like the silent church before the service begins, better than any preaching. How far off, how cool, how chaste the persons look, begirt each one with a precinct or sanctuary! So let us always sit. Why should we assume the faults of our friend, or wife, or father, or child, because they sit around our hearth, or are said to have the same blood? All men have my blood, and I have all men's.[218] Not for that will I adopt their petulance or folly, even to the extent of being ashamed of it. But your isolation must not be mechanical, but spiritual, that is, must be elevation. At times the whole world seems to be in conspiracy to importune you with emphatic trifles. Friend, client, child, sickness, fear, want, charity, all knock at once at thy closet door, and say, "Come out unto us." But keep thy state; come not into their confusion. The power men possess to annoy me, I give them by a weak curiosity. No man can come near me but through my act. "What we love that we have, but by desire we bereave ourselves of the love."

If we cannot at once rise to the sanctities of obedience and faith, let us at least resist our temptations; let us enter into the state of war, and wake Thor and Woden,[219] courage and constancy, in our Saxon breasts. This is to be done in our smooth times by speaking the truth. Check this lying hospitality and lying affection. Live no longer to the expectation of these deceived and deceiving people with whom we converse. Say to them, O father, O mother, O wife, O brother, O friend, I have lived with you after appearances hitherto. Henceforward I am the truth's. Be it known unto you that henceforward I obey no law less than the eternal law. I will have no covenants but proximities.[220] I shall endeavor to nourish my parents, to support my family, to be the chaste husband of one wife,—but these relations I must fill after a new and unprecedented way. I appeal from your customs. I must be myself. I cannot break myself any longer for you, or you.[221] If you can love me for what I am, we shall be the happier.

If you cannot, I will still seek to deserve that you should. I will not hide my tastes or aversions. I will so trust that what is deep is holy, that I will do strongly before the sun and moon whatever inly rejoices me, and the heart appoints. If you are noble, I will love you; if you are not, I will not hurt you and myself by hypocritical attentions. If you are true, but not in the same truth with me, cleave to your companions; I will seek my own. I do this not selfishly, but humbly and truly. It is alike your interest, and mine, and all men's however long we have dwelt in lies, to live in truth. Does this sound harsh to-day? You will soon love what is dictated by your nature as well as mine, and, if we follow the truth, it will bring us out safe at last.[222] But so may you give these friends pain. Yes, but I cannot sell my liberty and my power, to save their sensibility. Besides, all persons have their moments of reason, when they look out into the region of absolute truth; then will they justify me, and do the same thing.

The populace think that your rejection of popular standards is a rejection of all standard, and mere antinomianism;[223] and the bold sensualist will use the name of philosophy to gild his crimes. But the law of consciousness abides. There are two confessionals, in one or the other of which we must be shriven. You may fulfill your round of duties by clearing yourself in the *direct*, or in the *reflex* way. Consider whether you have satisfied your relations to father, mother, cousin, neighbor, town, cat, and dog; whether any of these can upbraid you. But I may also neglect this reflex standard, and absolve me to myself. I have my own stern claims and perfect circle. It denies the name of duty to many offices that are called duties. But if I can discharge its debts, it enables me to dispense with the popular code. If any one imagines that this law is lax, let him keep its commandment one day.

And truly it demands something godlike in him who has cast off the common motives of humanity, and has ventured to trust himself for a taskmaster. High be his heart, faithful his will, clear his sight, that he may in good earnest be doctrine, society, law, to himself, that a simple purpose may be to him as strong as iron necessity is to others!

If any man consider the present aspects of what is called by distinction *society*, he will see the need of these ethics. The sinew and heart of man seem to be drawn out, and we are become timorous, desponding whimperers. We are afraid of truth, afraid of fortune, afraid of death, and afraid of each other. Our age yields no great and perfect persons. We want men and women who shall renovate life and our social state, but we see that most natures are insolvent, cannot satisfy their own wants, have an ambition out of all proportion to their practical force,[224] and do lean and beg day and night continually. Our housekeeping is mendicant, our arts, our occupations, our marriages, our religion, we have not chosen, but society has chosen for us. We are parlor soldiers. We shun the rugged battle of fate, where strength is born.

If our young men miscarry in their first enterprises, they lose all heart. If the young merchant fails, men say he is *ruined*. If the finest genius studies at one of our colleges, and is not installed in an office within one year afterwards in the cities or suburbs of Boston or New York, it seems to his friends and to himself that he is right in being disheartened, and in complaining the rest of his life. A sturdy lad from New Hampshire or Vermont, who in turn tries all the professions, who *teams it, farms it*,[225]*peddles*, keeps a school, preaches, edits a newspaper, goes to Congress, buys a township, and so forth, in successive years, and always, like a cat, falls on his feet, is worth a hundred of these city dolls. He walks abreast with his days, and feels no shame in not "studying a profession," for he does not postpone his life, but lives already. He has not one chance, but a hundred chances. Let a Stoic[226] open the resources of man, and tell men they are not leaning willows, but can and must detach themselves; that with the exercise of self-trust, new powers shall appear; that a man is the word made flesh,[227] born to shed healing to the nations,[228] that he should be ashamed of our compassion, and that the moment he acts from himself, tossing the laws, the books, idolatries and customs out of the window, we pity him no more, but thank and revere him,—and that teacher shall restore the life of man to splendor, and make his name dear to all history.

It is easy to see that a greater self-reliance must work a revolution in all the offices and relations of men; in their religion; in their education; in their pursuits; their modes of living; their association; in their property; in their speculative views.

1. In what prayers do men allow themselves![229][106] That which they call a holy office is not so much as brave and manly. Prayer looks abroad and asks for some foreign addition to come through some foreign virtue, and loses itself in endless mazes of natural and supernatural, and mediatorial and miraculous. Prayer that craves a particular commodity,—anything less than all good,—is vicious. Prayer is the contemplation of the facts of life from the highest point of view. It is the soliloquy of a beholding and jubilant soul.[230] It is the spirit of God pronouncing his works good. But prayer as a means to effect a private end is

meanness and theft. It supposes dualism and not unity in nature and consciousness. As soon as the man is at one with God, he will not beg. He will then see prayer in all action. The prayer of the farmer kneeling in his field to weed it, the prayer of the rower kneeling with the stroke of his oar, are true prayers heard throughout nature, though for cheap ends. Caratach,[231] in Fletcher's Bonduca, when admonished to inquire the mind of the god Audate, replies,—

"His hidden meaning lies in our endeavors; Our valors are our best gods."

Another sort of false prayers are our regrets. Discontent is the want of self-reliance; it is infirmity of will. Regret calamities, if you can thereby help the sufferer; if not, attend your own work, and already the evil begins to be repaired. Our sympathy is just as base. We come to them who weep foolishly, and sit down and cry for company, instead of imparting to them truth and health in rough electric shocks, putting them once more in communication with their own reason. The secret of fortune is joy in our hands. Welcome evermore to gods and men is the self-helping man. For him all doors are flung wide: him all tongues greet, all honors crown, all eyes follow with desire. Our love goes out to him and embraces him, because he did not need it. We solicitously and apologetically caress and celebrate him, because he held on his way and scorned our disapprobation. The gods love him because men hated him. "To the persevering mortal," said Zoroaster,[232] "the blessed Immortals are swift."

As men's prayers are a disease of the will, so are their creeds a disease of the intellect. They say with those foolish Israelites, "Let not God speak to us, lest we die. Speak thou, speak any man with us, and we will obey."[233] Everywhere I am hindered of meeting God in my brother, because he has shut his own temple doors, and recites fables merely of his brother's, or his brother's brother's God. Every new mind is a new classification. If it prove a mind of uncommon activity and power, a Locke,[234] a Lavoisier,[235] a Hutton,[236] a Betham,[237] a Fourier,[238] it imposes its classification on other men, and lo! a new system. In proportion to the depth of the thought, and so to the number of the objects it touches and brings within reach of the pupil, is his complacency. But chiefly is this apparent in creeds and churches, which are also classifications of some powerful mind acting on the elemental thought of duty, and man's relation to the Highest. Such is Calvinism,[239] Quakerism,[240] Swedenborgism.[241] The pupil takes the same delight in subordinating everything to the new terminology, as a girl who has just learned botany in seeing a new earth and new seasons thereby. It will happen for a time, that the pupil will find his intellectual power has grown by the study of his master's mind. But in all unbalanced minds, the classification is idolized, passes for the end, and not for a speedily exhaustible means, so that the walls of the system blend to their eye in the remote horizon with the walls of the universe; the luminaries of heaven seem to them hung on the arch their master built. They cannot imagine how you aliens have any right to see,—how you can see; "It must be somehow that you stole the light from us." They do not yet perceive that light, unsystematic, indomitable, will break into any cabin, even into theirs. Let them chirp awhile and call it their own. If they are honest and do well, presently their neat new pinfold will be too strait and low, will crack, will lean, will rot and vanish, and the immortal light, all young and joyful, million-orbed, million-colored, will beam over the universe as on the first morning.

2. It is for want of self-culture that the superstition of Traveling, whose idols are Italy, England, Egypt, retains its fascination for all educated Americans. They who made England, Italy, or Greece venerable in the imagination did so by sticking fast where they were, like an axis of the earth. In manly hours, we feel that duty is our place. The soul is no traveler; the wise man stays at home, and when his necessities, his duties, on any occasion call him from his house, or into foreign lands, he is at home still; and shall make men sensible by the expression of his countenance, that he goes the missionary of wisdom and virtue, and visits cities and men like a sovereign, and not like an interloper or a valet.

I have no churlish objection to the circumnavigation of the globe, for the purposes of art, of study, and benevolence, so that the man is first domesticated, or does not go abroad with the hope of finding somewhat greater than he knows. He who travels to be amused, or to get somewhat which he does not carry,[242] travels away from himself, and grows old even in youth among old things. In Thebes,[243] in Palmyra,[244] his will and mind have become old and dilapidated as they. He carries ruins to ruins.

Traveling is a fool's paradise. Our first journeys discover to us the indifference of places. At home I dream that at Naples, at Rome, I can be intoxicated with beauty, and lose my sadness. I pack my trunk, embrace my friends, embark on the sea, and at last wake up in Naples, and there beside me is the stern fact, the sad self, unrelenting, identical, that I fled from.[245] I seek the Vatican,[246] and the palaces. I affect to be intoxicated with sights and suggestions, but I am not intoxicated. My giant goes with me wherever I go.

3. But the rage of traveling is a symptom of a deeper unsoundness affecting the whole intellectual action. The intellect is vagabond, and our system of education fosters restlessness. Our minds travel when our bodies are forced to stay at home. We imitate; and what is imitation but the traveling of the mind? Our houses are built with foreign taste; our shelves are garnished with foreign ornaments; our opinions, our tastes, our faculties, lean, and follow the Past and the Distant. The soul created the arts wherever they have flourished. It was in his own mind that the artist sought his model. It was an application of his own thought to the thing to be done and the conditions to be observed. And why need we copy the Doric[247] or the Gothic[248] model? Beauty, convenience, grandeur of thought, and quaint expression are as near to us as to any, and if the American artist will study with hope and love the precise thing to be done by him considering the climate, the soil, the length of the day, the wants of the people, the habit and form of the government, he will create a house in which all these will find themselves fitted, and taste and sentiment will be satisfied also.

Insist on yourself; never imitate.[249] Your own gift you can present every moment with the cumulative force of a whole life's cultivation; but of the adopted talent of another, you have only an extemporaneous, half possession. That which each can do best, none but his Maker can teach him. No man yet knows what it is, nor can, till that person has exhibited it. Where is the master who could have taught Shakespeare?[250] Where is the master who could have instructed Franklin,[251] or Washington, or Bacon,[252] or Newton?[253] Every great man is a unique. The Scipionism of Scipio[254] is precisely that part he could not borrow. Shakespeare will never be made by the study of Shakespeare. Do that which is assigned to you, and you cannot hope too much or dare too much. There is at this moment for you an utterance brave and grand as that of the colossal chisel of Phidias,[255] or trowel of the Egyptians,[256] or the pen of Moses,[257] or Dante,[258] but different from all these. Not possibly will the soul all rich, all eloquent, with thousand-cloven tongue, deign to repeat itself; but if you can hear what these patriarchs say, surely you can reply to them in the same pitch of voice; for the ear and the tongue are two organs of one nature. Abide in the simple and noble regions of thy life, obey thy heart, and thou shalt reproduce the Foreworld[259] again.

4. As our Religion, our Education, our Art look abroad, so does our spirit of society. All men plume themselves on the improvement of society, and no man improves.

Society never advances. It recedes as fast on one side as it gains on the other. It undergoes continual changes; it is barbarous, it is civilized, it is Christianized, it is rich, it is scientific; but this change is not amelioration. For everything that is given, something is taken. Society acquires new arts, and loses old instincts. What a contrast between the well-clad, reading, writing, thinking American, with a watch, a pencil, and a bill of exchange in his pocket, and the naked New Zealander,[260] whose property is a club, a spear, a mat, and an undivided twentieth of a shed to sleep under! But compare the health of the two men, and you shall see that the white man has lost his aboriginal strength. If the traveler tell us truly, strike the savage with a broad ax, and in a day or two the flesh shall unite and heal as if you struck the blow into soft pitch, and the same blow shall send the white to his grave.

The civilized man has built a coach, but has lost the use of his feet. He is supported on crutches, but lacks so much support of muscle. He has a fine Geneva[261] watch, but he fails of the skill to tell the hour by the sun. A Greenwich nautical almanac[262] he has, and so being sure of the information when he wants it, the man in the street does not know a star in the sky. The solstice[263] he does not observe; the equinox he knows as little; and the whole bright calendar of the year is without a dial in his mind. His notebooks impair his memory; his libraries overload his wit; the insurance office increases the number of accidents; and it may be a question whether machinery does not encumber; whether we have not lost by refinement some energy, by a Christianity entrenched in establishments and forms, some vigor of wild virtue. For every Stoic was a Stoic; but in Christendom where is the Christian?

There is no more deviation in the moral standard than in the standard of height or bulk. No greater men are now than ever were. A singular equality may be observed between great men of the first and of the last ages; nor can all the science, art, religion, and philosophy of the nineteenth century avail to educate greater men than Plutarch's[264] heroes, three or four and twenty centuries ago. Not in time is the race progressive. Phocion,[265]Socrates, Anaxagoras,[266] Diogenes,[267] are great men, but they leave no class. He who is really of their class will not be called by their name, but will be his own man, and, in his turn, the founder of a sect. The arts and inventions of each period are only its costume, and do not invigorate men. The harm of the improved machinery may compensate its good. Hudson[268] and Bering[269] accomplished so much in their fishing boats, as to astonish Parry[270] and Franklin,[271] whose equipment exhausted the resources of science and art. Galileo, with an opera-glass, discovered a more splendid series of celestial phenomena than any one since. Columbus[272] found the New World in an undecked boat. It is curious to see the periodical disuse and perishing of means and machinery, which were introduced with loud laudation a few years or centuries before. The great genius returns to essential man. We reckoned the improvements of the art of war among the triumphs of science, and yet Napoleon[273] conquered Europe by the bivouac, which consisted of falling back on naked valor, and disencumbering it of all aids. The Emperor held it impossible to make a perfect army, says Las Casas,[274] "without abolishing our arms, magazines, commissaries, and carriages, until, in imitation of the Roman custom, the soldier should receive his supply of corn, grind it in his handmill, and bake his bread himself."

Society is a wave. The wave moves onward, but the water of which it is composed does not. The same particle does not rise from the valley to the ridge. Its unity is only phenomenal. The persons who make up a nation to-day, next year die, and their experience with them.

And so the reliance on Property, including the reliance on governments which protect it, is the want of self-reliance. Men have looked away from themselves and at things so long, that they have come to esteem the religious, learned, and civil institutions as guards of property, and they deprecate assaults on these, because they feel them to be assaults on property. They measure their esteem of each other by what each has, and not by what each is. But a cultivated man becomes ashamed of his property, out of new respect for his nature. Especially he hates what he has, if he see that it is accidental,—came to him by inheritance, or gift, or crime; then he feels that it is not having; it does not belong to

him, has no root in him, and merely lies there, because no revolution or no robber takes it away. But that which a man is, does always by necessity acquire, and what the man acquires is living property, which does not wait the beck of rulers, or mobs, or revolutions, or fire, or storm, or bankruptcies, but perpetually renews itself wherever the man breathes. "Thy lot or portion of life," said the Caliph Ali,[275] "is seeking after thee; therefore be at rest from seeking after it." Our dependence on these foreign goods leads us to our slavish respect for numbers. The political parties meet in numerous conventions; the greater the concourse, and with each new uproar of announcement, The delegation from Essex![276] The Democrats from New Hampshire! The Whigs of Maine! the young patriot feels himself stronger than before by a new thousand of eyes and arms. In like manner the reformers summon conventions, and vote and resolve in multitude. Not so, O friends! will the god deign to enter and inhabit you, but by a method precisely the reverse. It is only as a man puts off all foreign support, and stands alone, that I see him to be strong and to prevail. He is weaker by every recruit to his banner. Is not a man better than a town? Ask nothing of men, and in the endless mutation, thou only firm column must presently appear the upholder of all that surrounds thee. He who knows that power is inborn, that he is weak because he has looked for good out of him and elsewhere, and so perceiving, throws himself unhesitatingly on his thought, instantly rights himself, stands in the erect position, commands his limbs, works miracles; just as a man who stands on his feet is stronger than a man who stands on his head.

So use all that is called Fortune.[277] Most men gamble with her, and gain all, and lose all, as her wheel rolls. But do thou leave as unlawful these winnings, and deal with Cause and Effect, the chancelors of God. In the Will work and acquire, and thou hast chained the wheel of Chance, and shalt sit hereafter out of fear from her rotations. A political victory, a rise of rents, the recovery of your sick, or the return of your absent friend, or some other favorable event, raises your spirits, and you think good days are preparing for you. Do not believe it. Nothing can bring you peace but yourself. Nothing can bring you peace but the triumph of principles.

The Second Great Awakening and Transcendentalism

Historians estimate that only about 30–40% of Americans were members of churches or regularly attended church in the late-eighteenth century, but by 1850 the number was closer to 75–80%. Further, whereas at the end of the eighteenth century, the two largest religious denominations in the United States were the Congregationalists (the descendants of the Puritans) and the Episcopalians (the American version of the state-sponsored Anglican Church of the colonial era), by 1850 the Baptists and Methodists had become more numerous with a great dispersion of Protestants into numerous new denominations. This upsurge in religious activity, along with its concomitant shifts in theology and practice, changes to the social organization of religion, and developments in the relationship between religion and politics, has usually been termed the "Second Great Awakening," as a way of referring to the earlier revival in Protestantism in the 1730s and 1740s in the colonies.

The Second Great Awakening rendered the nation more united in terms of a broadly accepted Protestantism even as it led to the multiplication of different sects and denominations. It helped propel numerous reform movements, most notably involving temperance and abolition, even as it attempted to return Christianity to its primitive roots. And it reinforced American beliefs in the individual's priority and agency even as it helped to bring a sense of community to a highly mobile populace. The Second Great Awakening transformed American religion and society in a number of ways and can be traced to a number of interrelated causes. Perhaps the most helpful way to begin understanding it is by emphasizing how different the dominant strains of Protestantism in 1850 were from those of the 1700s. By 1850, most Protestants had come to accept some version of Arminianism, the notion that God offers the possibility of salvation to any and all who accept Christ as their savior and through that acceptance undergo a true change of heart, a spiritual rebirth. This move towards the possibility of universal salvation represented a distinct break from Calvinism that had dominated American Protestantism throughout the colonial era. Calvinist theology holds that humankind, due to Adam's fall, is born sinful (innate depravity), and God will only save a select few (the elect) who have been chosen before time began. The saved can only passively accept a gift which they have not and could not possibly have earned. While the new Protestantism of the Second Great Awakening still emphasized a Gospel of Grace (only God could save the individual's soul) over a Gospel of Works (one could earn his way into heaven through good behavior), it stressed individual volition—the individual's choice to accept God's free gift of grace—in a way Calvinists never had. In doing so, this theological shift simultaneously weakened the idea of innate depravity. While all humans might be prone to sinfulness and only through God's help could they overcome those sinful tendencies, they were not doomed to sinfulness in a way older Calvinist theology sometimes seemed to suggest.

This theological shift both proceeded from and furthered social and political changes. In moving from an idea of the elect to the notion of universal salvation, this transformation followed the democratic emphasis of the American Revolution and its faith in the universal capacity of individuals to decide for themselves on personal and political matters. While much of the intellectual energy behind the American Revolution was grounded in secular philosophy concerning natural rights, American Protestantism had played an important role in the movement towards independence. Much of the revolutionary fervor coming from American Protestantism centered on concerns about the imposition of religious beliefs through the established Anglican Church. While the Constitution's 1st Amendment assured that there would be no nationally established religion, the amendment was taken to apply only to the Federal government, and numerous states, especially in the northeast, maintained an established religion well into the nineteenth century. This meant that all citizens of the state were presumed to be members of the established church and could be taxed to support that church. By the 1830s, however, the Enlightenment's emphasis on individual reason and agency and continuing concerns about the tyranny of established religion from both secular and religious perspectives led to the disestablishment of churches in all the states. While some religious leaders feared that decoupling the church from state support would lead to a decline in faith, it instead led to the flourishing of religion, if in more dispersed form.

In place of being a state-sponsored institution, religious institutions came to take on some of the features of the marketplace, as individuals now could decide on their own with which church to associate. This emphasis on individual choice in the religious as well as the economic and political spheres was fundamental to the emergence of what has been called Jacksonian democracy.

Where the majority of the founding fathers held deep reservations about expanding the franchise to all citizens and tended to believe that a democratic republic (with republic—the public good—emphasized over democracy) could only thrive if the masses deferred to their better educated, wiser betters, by the time Andrew Jackson was elected president in 1828 almost all states had lifted property restrictions on voting rights, thus opening elections to all adult white men. This overturning of long-standing assumptions of deference to an educated elite in the political arena was accompanied by a similar shift in religion. Not only did individuals feel empowered to make spiritual choices on their own, especially in the wake of the disestablishment of religion, but many of them took up the charge to preach. One of the distinct features of the Second Great Awakening, then, was the democratization of the clerisy, as many barely literate men (and occasionally women), including both African Americans and American Indians, became church leaders and, sometimes, licensed ministers.

This emphasis on individual volition and choice paralleled a theological shift that echoed the Enlightenment's emphasis on humankind over the divine and on human agency over supernatural agency. In turn, against Calvinism's very weak notion of free will, the Protestant synthesis that emerged from this period stressed the individual's free choice and, relatedly, suggested that humans had some inborn tendency towards good. While Protestantism continued to foreground God's role in human transformation and salvation, the emerging synthesis emphasized to a much greater extent than earlier ministers and thinkers that the individual could decide for him or herself whether to accept salvation and that more physical, more worldly means could lead to salvation.

Charles Grandison Finney, one of the most important religious leaders during this period, can help to ground these theological innovations and connect them to the political and social changes undergirding them. Like many of the ministers and converts of the Second Great Awakening, Finney grew up in a relatively non-religious home. Self-educated, he was part of an emerging middle-class of professionals (he was originally a lawyer), artisans, and small farmers who would form the core of the Second Great Awakening. He came to adulthood in central and western New York, a region he nicknamed the burned over district to suggest how fervent the revival spirit became there. The Second Great Awakening burned most brightly in similar areas throughout the Midwest, South, and Northeast, areas recently settled, consisting of displaced people seeking social and economic stability and simultaneously looking for a spiritual foundation to counterbalance the relative instability of their lives.

Finney became famous through his itinerant ministry, as he traveled the country conducting revivals. Much of the fervor and energy of the Second Great Awakening came through less formally established ministers who moved from place to place, attempting to bring as many believers to the faith as possible. Finney famously stressed that revivals worked through "the right exercise of the powers of nature," emphasizing the emotional roots of the spiritual transformation of rebirth over God's direct, miraculous intercession. Critics, especially from older established churches and more conservative theological positions, rejected such revival spirit as nothing more than emotionalism, as lacking in the intellectual and spiritual groundwork needed to assure salvation and a long-term commitment to Christ. They further attacked Finney for allowing women to take an active role in revival proceedings, for focusing on individuals by specifying them by name in prayers, and for using colloquial language, among other things. Their critique reiterates some of the most noteworthy features of the Second Great Awakening—its populist spirit, including its opening religious services to the participation of women, and its emotional nature. In particular, the Second Great Awakening has sometimes been seen in terms of the feminization of American religion, as women began to take a much more active role in a variety of Protestant denominations and Protestant theology took on a decidedly more sentimental cast, emphasizing the more maternal, loving vision of Jesus over the strict patriarchal Jehovah. Finally, Finney saw his Christianity as directly related to the social issues of the day, becoming a leader in the temperance movement and in abolitionism. This shift in focus from theology to morality, from discerning the exact, abstract laws of God to feeling God's truth and power internally and acting accordingly, undergirded both the emotional appeal of much anti-slavery activity and other reform movements and the development of domestic sentimentalism as one of the most popular literary forms of the period.

At the same time, Finney's differences from others within the Second Great Awakening suggest the disunity of the movement. While Finney was ordained a Presbyterian minister, he almost immediately broke with its Calvinist doctrine, leading to a convention where New Light Calvinists (such as Lyman Beecher) attempted to reconcile with Finney's new ways. Where Beecher and the New Lights can be included within the Second Great Awakening, they represent a more conservative version of it—

a reaction on the part of the established churches (here Presbyterian and Congregationalists) to revise their methods and theology to fit better with the new nation. Unlike other Calvinists, the New Lights saw religious experience as an essential component to salvation. They tended to embrace the idea of a sudden-rebirth into grace rather than foregrounding the importance of slow preparation for it. In that way, they anticipated and paralleled Finney, but they worried over his methods, seeing them as relying too heavily on worldly means. On the other hand, the fastest growing denominations of the era, the Baptists and Methodists, tended to go further than Finney in breaking with the older more denominations, yet tended to remain less committed to their Christianity becoming a guiding force in social and political reforms. The success of these denominations in the South paralleled their reticence on slavery, even as many Baptists and Methodists began to preaching to African Americans in broad numbers, leading to one of the Second Great Awakening's most long-lasting impacts, the more thorough-going integration of African-American culture into American Protestantism. New faiths and denominations, such as the Church of Christ and the Church of the Latter Day Saints (the Mormons) along with numerous offshoots and short-lived sects and utopian communities, moved even further from the older social and theological structures of American Protestantism.

Because of all these differences, a number of historians have disputed the usefulness of placing these disparate religious developments under the umbrella of the Second Great Awakening, arguing that it incorrectly links together largely disconnected, sometimes contradictory or conflicting developments within American Protestantism over the course of the first half of the nineteenth century. Yet most historians have agreed that although never centralized those changes followed many parallel tracks, emphasizing its overall tendency towards democratization of the ministry, its decentering of religious authority, its foregrounding of emotion, and its theological emphasis on universal salvation and individual rebirth through the active acceptance of Christ as one's savior. That is to say, that we need to understand the Second Great Awakening as a term for viewing a number of often disconnected intellectual, cultural, and social processes as moving towards similar endpoints. It is within this broader framework that we might consider transcendentalism, one of the most important American literary-philosophical movements of the nineteenth century, as part of the Second Great Awakening.

The next subunit of this course will explore the transcendentalists in more depth, but here it is important to place them within this broader context of religious fervor and upheaval. While, as we will see, the movement grew out of a number of philosophical, literary, and political developments and movements in the transatlantic world, in terms of American religion, transcendentalism most directly emerged out of Unitarianism. Unitarianism had represented the liberal development of New England Congregationalism growing out of the Enlightenment and the First Great Awakening. Where more traditional, if innovative, theologians and ministers such as Jonathan Edwards continued to hew to strict Calvinist beliefs in innate depravity and election, drawing on developments within the sensational psychology of John Locke and his followers to defend the use of emotion in the conversion process (thus paving the way for New Light Calvinism), the more liberal wing of Congregationalism tended to move away from the emphasis on humankind's incapacity to affect their own spiritual change due to their inherent sinfulness and to remain skeptical of what they saw as emotional excess. With the formal rejection of the trinity (instead of viewing Jesus as a part of God seeing him as a great spiritual leader), Unitarianism split from Congregationalism in the late-eighteenth century, exemplifying a type of Enlightenment Christianity that emphasized reason, progress, learning, stability, and harmony. While Unitarianism was still seen as heretical by more traditional Congregationalists, it had come to represent the established church in parts of New England by the 1820s, especially in the Boston area. Emerging in the 1830s, transcendentalism, in many ways, reacted against Unitarianism as others within the Second Great Awakening reacted against the more established denominations, rejecting what they saw as its cold rationality and its elitist tendencies in emphasizing doctrine and erudition over feeling. Many of the leading transcendentalists began as Unitarian ministers before abandoning what they saw as the restrictive theology and rituals in favor of less organized philosophical and personal explorations of the relations among the self, nature, and the divine. While the transcendentalists differed from the majority involved in the Second Great Awakening due to their own elite status (many were college-educated), the ways they grounded their focus on experience in their own eclectic learning, and their movement away from even the loosest religious community in favor of the individual's self-culture and away from Christianity to a form of naturalistic spirituality, they paralleled the Second Great Awakening's attention to a kind of ecstatic, life-changing spiritual experience, their emphasis on the inner life and the individual conscience over book-learning, and their tendency to connect spiritual regeneration with moral and social change.

About the Text's Creator

OER books are usually blends of different texts, so I cannot speak to the original Lumen authors' backgrounds.

Here is a little bit of background about myself, though (written in that third person that is always a warning sign for individuals, as *Seinfeld* episodes show us).

Josh Dickinson is an Associate Professor of English at Jefferson Community College in Watertown, NY. He teaches English and Education courses with a focus upon American Literature 1 and 2, Native American Literature, and non-Western Literature. Josh attended SUNY Jefferson, SUNY Potsdam, Syracuse University, and Colgate University.

Josh also supervises Jefferson's EDGE (concurrent enrollment) English offerings at over a dozen local high school and BOCES sites.

He enjoys participating in the National Novel Writing Month contest, having completed ten novels so far each November. His best finish was an eight-day novel.

Josh has officiated high school soccer matches for 27 years and supports pro teams Tottenham Hotspur, FC Barcelona, and Borussia Dortmund.

At the Canadian Museum of History, Ottawa: Go Habs, Go!